Edited and designed by
Time Out Guides Limited
Universal House
251 Tottenham Court Road
London W1T 7AB
Tel + 44 (0)20 7813 3000
Fax + 44 (0)20 7813 6001
Email guides@timeout.com
www.timeout.com

Editorial

Editor Will Tizard
Deputy Editor Ismay Atkins
Copy editing Rhonda Carrier, Christi Daugherty and Jenny Piening
Listings Researchers Daniela Jedličková, Martina Lišková Pavla Kozáková, Radka Slaba
Proofreader Tamsin Shelton
Indexer Marion Moisy

Editorial Director Peter Fiennes
Series Editor Ruth Jarvis
Deputy Series Editor Jonathan Cox
Guides Co-ordinator Anna Norman

Design

Group Art Director John Oakey
Art Director Mandy Martin
Art Editor Scott Moore
Senior Designer Lucy Grant
Designers Benjamin de Lotz, Sarah Edwards
Scanning/Imaging Dan Conway
Ad Make-up Glen Impey
Picture Editor Kerri Littlefield

Deputy Picture Editor Kit Burnet
Picture Librarian Sarah Roberts

Advertising

Group Commercial Director Lesley Gill
Sales Director Mark Phillips
International Sales Co-ordinator Ross Canadé
Advertisement Sales (Prague) ARBOMedia.net Praha
Advertising Assistant Sabrina Ancilleri

Administration

Chairman Tony Elliott
Managing Director Mike Hardwick
Group Financial Director Kevin Ellis
Group Marketing Director Christine Cort
Marketing Manager Mandy Martinez
US Publicity & Marketing Associate Rosella Albanese
Group General Manager Nichola Coulthard
Production Manager Mark Lamond
Production Controller Samantha Furniss
Accountant Sarah Bostock

Features in this guide were written and researched by: Introduction Will Tizard. **History** Jonathan Cox, Paul Lewis (*A five-star fraud, Bad day in Prague 7* Will Tizard). **Prague Today** James Pitkin (*The ultimate absurd theatre* Mark Baker). **Architecture** Jonathan Cox, Ky Krauthamer, Siegfried Mortkowitz, Damon McGee. **Literary Prague** Jenny Smith, Will Tizard (*Robert Eversz: on the Prague hack* Robert Eversz). Prague on Screen, Will Tizard (*Prague-spotting 101* Raymond Johnston). **Accommodation** Ky Krauthamer, Anthony Maes, Dinah Spritzer. **Sightseeing** Carole Cadwalladr, Jonathan Cox, Lacey Eckl, Ky Krauthamer, Will Tizard, Emma Young. **Museums** Mimi Rogers. **Restaurants & Cafés** Will Tizard. **Pubs & Bars** Will Tizard (*Drunk as a Dane* Pavla Kozáková). **Shops & Services** Jennifer Sokolovsky, Jennifer Hamm (*Everybody must get stoned, Different by design* Jennifer Sokolovsky; *Czech glass bounces back, Mind your beets* Jennifer Hamm). **By Season** Will Tizard. **Children** Karin Johnson. **Clubs** Will Tizard (*The Roxy holds out* James Pitkin). **Film** Raymond Johnston. **Galleries** Ky Krauthamer, Mimi Rogers. **Gay & Lesbian** Heather Faulkner, Jean-Jacques Soukoup. **Music: Classical & Opera** Michael Halstead, Will Tizard. **Music: Rock, Roots & Jazz** Will Tizard. **Nightlife** Will Tizard. **Sport & Fitness** František Bouc, Julia Gray, Sam Beckwith. **Theatre & Dance** Theodore Schwinke, Lizzie Lequesne. **Trips Out of Town** Jonathan Cox, Julia Gray, Pavla Kozáková, Dave Rimmer, Anna Sutton, Will Tizard. **Directory** Mark Baker, Daniela Jedličková, Martina Lišková, Will Tizard, Emma Young. **Further Reference** Dave Rimmer, Will Tizard.

The Editor would like to thank: Pavel Baňka; Susan and Eric Benson; Tom, Cathy and Eleanor Bowman; Matt Carr and Nina Valvodová; Markéta Červenková; Selena Cox; Kristof Dabrowsky; Nancy Davis; Robert Eversz; Pani Foerstová and the Galerie Rudolfinum; Hotel Élite for accommodation assistance; Luboš Košťak; Scott MacMillan; Lesley McCave; Jiří Sedlák and Divadlo Archa; Sasha Štěpán; Julie, Barbara and Bill Tizard; Pani Foerstová and the Galerie Rudolfinum; Luboš Košťak; Pavel Obermajer and the adept members of the Blue Moon Quartet; the Statní Opera; Stillking Productions; and especially Martina Lišková. Transport graciously provided by Hertz Czech Republic.

Maps by (john@jsgraphics.co.uk).

Photography by Julie Denesha except: pages 6, 18, 22, 23 Associated Press; pages 8, 9, 10, 13, 15, 16, 17 AKG; page 36 "FROM HELL" ©2001 Twentieth Century Fox All rights reserved"; page 34 Tomáš Třestlík/Stillking Productions; page 216 Statní Opera; pages 239, 243 Getty Images Allsport; page 252 Nathan Benn/Corbis; pages 242, 247, 250, 253, 254, 256, 258, 259, 263, 265, 266, 267, 268 Czech Tourist Authority.

The following pictures were provided by the featured establishments/artists: pages 33, 46, 52, 107, 171, 197, 203, 204, 205, 210, 215, 221, 235, 237.

Contents

Introduction

The celebrated Czech novelist Milan Kundera once wrote that you can immediately detect the presence of a Prague girl in a crowd of people by her hearty laugh. Czechs in general tend to be shy, perhaps even a bit cagey, arguably as the result of endless foreign occupation, yet Kundera's observation is spot on. Prague is the kind of city that enchants the visitor immediately with its ancient architecture, art, music, Bacchanalian nights and its penchant for stimulants and absinthe – in short, the stuff that made 'Bohemian' synonymous with hedonism. Of course, it's also eminently affordable to get to and cheaper still to enjoy.

Falling in love with its people, however, usually takes longer. Like the Czech herbal tipple Becherovka, best drunk ice cold, it is a taste that needs cultivating, but then stays with you for life. People often dismiss the frostiness commonly encountered in Prague's shops, or the fawning manner you run into in high-end restaurants, as the result of 41 years of communism. Yet citizens of other former Eastern bloc nations are notably warmer, more themselves, if no more concerned with Western-style efficiency.

The Czech case is that of a small nation, whose population is steeped in fairytales from childhood. Visitors to Prague will encounter a renaissance on the restaurant and bar scenes, a full calendar of top-notch symphony performances, dozens of dance clubs, a burgeoning cyber culture... all incongruously

set amid palaces and castles. Prague has used its cachet as a filmmaking capital to crank out a regular stream of movies for domestic consumption that feature princesses in idyllic green lands filled with Gothic keeps and populated by gnomes and dragons. With the first signs of warm weather the asphalt in every park is covered in children's chalk sketches of the same scenes. And Prague has more beauty contests per capita than anywhere else in the world.

Perhaps the inner child just has a bit more of a prominent role in Czech society than it does in most. A taxi driver will speak baby talk to a cop when he's pulled over. Grown, married Czech men will want their mother's approval for their choice of holiday destination. And taking responsibility for a wrong order in a restaurant is a skill that's still being mastered in Prague.

Probably the quickest route to Czech appreciation is to guzzle a beer or seven in any of the city's hundreds of pubs, where you'll share a bench with locals who've been going there every night for the last ten years. They'll toast your health with a 'Na zdrávi!' each round and, by the third, you'll have pals for life. An immature, indulgent way to spend time that does little to advance the economy? Or just the best way to finally see the real sparkle in a Bohemian's eye?

Either way, it's a fair bet that you'll treasure the evening even more than your visit to Prague Castle.

ABOUT TIME OUT GUIDES

This is the fifth edition of the *Time Out Prague Guide*, one of the expanding series of Time Out guides produced by the people behind London and New York's definitive listings magazines. It paints a detailed picture of the heart of Europe, as the city is historically known. This edition has been completely updated and all listings checked by a team of Prague-based writers and experts. Some chapters have been rewritten, others have been revised and brought up to date. Many more hotels, restaurants and bars have been added.

THE LIE OF THE LAND

Prague – the capital of the province of Bohemia – is divided into both numbered postal districts and into areas with names. Sometimes these correspond and sometimes they don't, so in our listings we have provided both. After the street name and address, we supply the name of the district and then its basic postal code. The main central areas of Prague are Hradčany, Malá Strana, Staré Město and Nové Město (all of which – bar part of Nové Město – fall into Prague 1) and these are the main divisions we have used in our Sightseeing section and in chapters that are organised by area.

Prague buildings have two street plaques. Ignore the red one, used for administrative purposes; the blue numbers are used used for location and mailing and are the ones given in this book.

ESSENTIAL INFORMATION

For all the practical information you might need for visiting the area – including local transport systems, emergency numbers and useful websites – turn to the Directory chapter at the back of this guide. It starts on page 270.

THE LOWDOWN ON THE LISTINGS

We have tried to make this book as easy to use and practically useful as possible. Addresses, websites, phone numbers, transport information, opening times, admission prices and credit card information are all included. However, owners and managers of establishments can change their arrangements at any time and this is a particularly common practice in Prague. Before you go out of your way, we would strongly advise you to phone ahead to check opening times and other particulars. While every effort has been made to ensure the accuracy of the information contained in this guide, the publishers cannot accept responsibility for any errors it may contain.

PRICES AND PAYMENT

In the listings, we have noted which of the following credit cards are accepted: American Express (AmEx), Diners Club (DC), MasterCard (MC) and Visa (V). It's possible that other cards may also be taken.

For every restaurant we have given the price range for main courses, and set menus where relevant. The prices we've supplied should be treated as guidelines, not gospel. If prices vary wildly from those we've quoted, ask whether there's a good reason. If not, go elsewhere. Then please let us know. It is our aim to give the best and most up-to-date advice, so we want to know if you've been badly treated or overcharged.

TELEPHONE NUMBERS

To phone Prague from outside the Czech Republic, first dial the international code, followed by 42 (the code for the Czech Republic), then 02 (the code for Prague) and finally the local number (four to eight digits). When within the Czech Republic, all telephone numbers now require that the area code is dialled as part of the number if you are calling from another area inside the country. To dial a mobile phone number from outside the Czech Republic, just call the international code, then 42, then the mobile number.

MAPS

At the back of this guide (and within the **Sightseeing** chapter) you'll find a series of maps of Prague and the Czech Republic. Every place listed in this guide that falls within these maps is accompanied by a map reference to aid location. Maps start on page 304.

LET US KNOW WHAT YOU THINK

We hope you enjoy the *Time Out Prague Guide*, and we'd like to know what you think of it. We welcome your tips for places to include in future editions and take notice of your criticism of our choices. There's a reader's reply card at the back of this book – or you can email us on pragueguide@timeout.com.

There is an online version of this guide, as well as weekly events listings for 35 international cities, at **www.timeout.com**

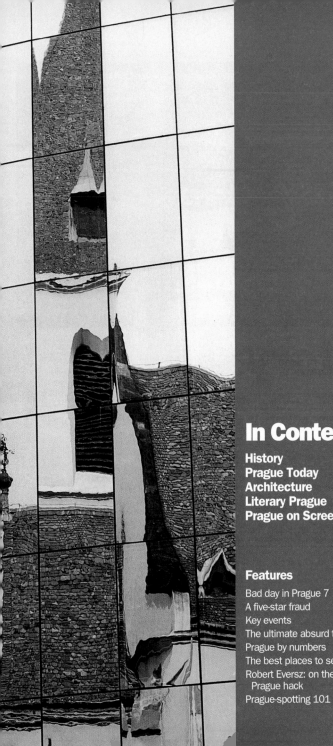

In Context

Springtime for the communists.

History

From Celts to communists, the Czech lands were claimed by most major powers in Europe. Identity crisis, anyone?

In around 400 BC, a Celtic tribe called the Boii occupied the region where the Czech Republic now lies and gave it the name Bohemia. The Boii successfully repelled attacking armies for the best part of 1,000 years, but they were eventually driven out by the Germanic Marcomanni and the Quadi tribes who in turn were wiped out by Attila the Hun in AD 451. Slavic tribes are believed to have moved into the area sometime during the seventh century. They were ruled over by the Avars whose harsh regime provoked a successful Slavic rebellion.

PŘEMYSLID ROOTS

The Czechs had to wait until the eighth century and the founding of the **Přemyslid dynasty** for real independence. The dynasty's origins are shrouded in myths. One relates that, in the absence of a male heir, **Čech** tribe leader Krok was succeeded by his soothsaying daughter Libuše. But the men of the tribe, indignant at being ruled over by a woman, told her to go and find a husband. Libuše went into a trance and sent her white horse over the hills. The

horse, she foretold, would find a ploughman with two spotted oxen and he would become their leader. Her horse quickly located the farmer, whose name was **Přemysl**.

Similarly, Prague is supposed to have been founded following a similar trance-induced vision. This time Libuše declared from the hilltop at Vyšehrad that 'a city whose splendour will reach to the stars' would be created nearby. Everyone then went into the woods again, this time to search for a craftsman making a door sill (*práh*), for, as Libuše said, 'mighty Lords bend before a low door'. When the craftsman was found, the site of the city was determined.

In the ninth century, Charlemagne briefly occupied the region and a Slavic state was created in Moravia under Prince Mojmír. In 860 Mojmír's successor, Rostilav, appealed to the pope for Christian apostles with a knowledge of Slavic to help him put an end to the worship of sun gods. The Byzantine emperor sent two Greek monks, **Cyril** and **Methodius** (designers of the Cyrillic alphabet), but Frankish and

German priests objected and so, following Methodius's death in 885, the Slavonic liturgy they had established was made illegal.

Rostilav's nephew **Svatopluk** (871-94) had sided with the Germans over the liturgical issue, and so with their assistance he ousted his uncle. Svatopluk built an empire that encompassed Moravia, Bohemia and Slovakia. After Svatopluk's death the Magyars grabbed a chunk of Slovakia. They were to hold on to it right up until the early 20th century and their presence there was to disrupt all attempts to unite Slovaks and Czechs.

'In the storm of ages the Czechs were about to drown as a state and a nation'

A SHAKY RISE

Over the next four centuries, Bohemia rode a rollercoaster that alternately descended into chaos and rose to the heights of political supremacy in Central Europe. One of the pinnacles came during the humane rule of **Prince Václav** or **Wenceslas** (921-9). Although Christmas carols still sing his praises, many Czech nobles felt that 'Good King' Wenceslas sold out to the Germans, and neglected Slavic interests. They sided with Wenceslas's brother **Boleslav the Cruel** (935-67), who had Wenceslas murdered in 929 in present-day Olomouc. Boleslav then fought with the Germans for 14 years.

Bohemia was briefly united with Moravia and Prague made a bishopric in 973, completing the process of bringing Christianity to Bohemia. By the end of the 12th century, though, internal bickering over succession had become so bad that, as the historian Palacký put it, 'in the storm of ages the Czechs were about to drown as a state and a nation'.

A peaceful division was negotiated and national prestige reached new heights with **Přemysl Otakar II** (1253-78) grabbing Cheb from the Germans and briefly controlling an empire that stretched from Florence to Poland. But then Otakar challenged Rudolf of Habsburg for the throne of the Holy Roman Empire – and Rudolf won. In 1276 Rudolf invaded Bohemia and Otakar's successor Václav II (1278-1305) was forced to look east and south for conquests in Poland, Hungary, Croatia and Romania. His son Václav III was assassinated in 1306, allegedly by Habsburg agents. Since he left no heir, the Přemyslid dynasty came to an end.

During this period German immigration to the Czech lands flourished and these new arrivals filled top positions in the Church and other trades. German administrators divided Prague into three autonomous areas: Malá Strana, Hradčany and Staré Město. Malá Strana's Jewish community was forced into a ghetto in Staré Město in order to give the Germans more *Lebensraum*.

By the 14th century, Czech and German nobles had begun a conflict that was to underlie much of the country's history. In 1310 **John of Luxembourg**, the 14-year-old son of the Holy Roman Emperor, was elected king of Bohemia. John's interest in Prague was ephemeral; he once attempted to recreate the Knights of the Round Table by inviting all the great knights of Europe to the city, but none of them turned up. John spent most of his time wheeling and dealing in the diplomatic circles of Europe. Back home the nobles' power grew. Prague gained a town hall, became the dominant centre of Bohemia and scored an archbishopric in 1344.

THE GOLDEN AGE OF CHARLES IV

John died in a kamikaze charge against Welsh archers at the Battle of Crécy. His son **Charles IV** was elected Holy Roman emperor in 1346, which made his position as king of Bohemia unassailable. His plans for the development of Prague had the full force of the Empire behind them and ushered in a golden age. Charles (1346-78) brought to Bohemia the stability that his father had failed to achieve. Prague escaped the Black Death that ravaged Europe in 1348 and under Charles emerged as one of Europe's dazzling centres. Through his mother Charles laid claim to Přemyslid lineage and thus became known as the 'Father of his Country' and 'Priest Kaiser'.

Charles brought the 23-year-old Swabian architect **Peter Parler** to Prague to build the **Charles Bridge** (*see p90*) and to work on **St Vitus's Cathedral** (*see p65*), then, in 1348, he established Central Europe's first university. In a far-sighted move, he founded the **Nové Město** (New Town), relieving the Old Town of the stress created by the concentration of artisans' workshops. He also undercut the power of the nobility in 1356 by reorganising the city's electoral system.

Availing himself of his omnipotent position in the Holy Roman Empire, Charles declared the union of Bohemia, Moravia, Silesia and Upper Lusatia indissoluble, and grafted chunks of Germany on to Bohemia. He abandoned claims to Italian territories but also refused to accept papal dictates north of the Alps. He was a devout Christian, and under his rule clergy owned half the land. But at the same time he was intensely conscious of the growing corruption in the Church and often sided with preachers who condemned its excesses.

NOT-SO-GOOD KING WENCESLAS

The seeds of religious indignation may have been sown under Charles, but the bitter fruits were tasted during the reign of his incorrigible son **Wenceslas IV** (1378-1419). A champion of the common man, he would go out shopping dressed in commoners' clothing and, if the shopkeepers cheated him, he would have them executed. Despite (or because of) such displays of temper as roasting a chef who had spoilt his lunch, there was supposedly a virtual absence of crime in Prague during his reign.

Wenceslas and quiet piety never sat easily together. At his christening he was alleged to have urinated into the holy water and he was still unable to control himself at his coronation. He is said to have spent most of his last years in a drunken stupor. The nobles formed a 'League of Lords' hoping to have him imprisoned, but he escaped while in the royal bathhouse, and persuaded a beautiful bath attendant to row him down the Vltava to safety.

Clearly, Wenceslas lacked the moral and intellectual authority to steer Bohemia through the dangerous religious waters ahead. In 1403 the rector of Prague University, **Jan Hus**, took up the campaign against Church corruption. At the university Czech supporters of Hus squabbled with the Germans, who left for Leipzig to found their own university. The Church establishment was quick to launch a counter-offensive. Hus's arguments were deemed heretical and he was persuaded by Wenceslas to leave Prague in 1412, continuing his crusade in the countryside.

In November 1414, Hus was summoned by Wenceslas's brother Sigismund, king of Hungary, to appear before the General Council at Constance. Hus went in good faith carrying a safe conduct pass but on arrival was arrested and ordered to recant. He refused and on his 46th birthday was burnt at the stake.

Hus embodied two vital hopes of the Czech people: reform of the Church and independence from German dominance. It was not, therefore, surprising that he was to become a martyr. His motto 'truth will prevail' and the chalice, which represented lay participation in the Sacrament, became rallying symbols for his followers.

HUSSITES GIVE 'EM HELL

A few weeks after Hus's death, several hundred nobles in Bohemia sent a protest to the Council of Constance, declaring their intention to defend Hus's name and promote his teachings. Under pressure from the Church, Wenceslas IV suppressed the Hussites, but on 30 July 1419 an angry Hussite mob stormed the town hall protesting the detention of religious dissenters. They threw the mayor and his councillors through the window to their deaths.

Jan Hus takes on the Church.

Wenceslas withdrew his decrees and died in an apoplectic fit a few days later. Hussite mobs marked the occasion by rioting and sacking the monasteries. Sigismund elbowed his way on to the Bohemian throne, and moderate Utraquist nobles, the followers of Hus, were keen to find a compromise. But radical preachers such as Jan Želivský furiously denounced Sigismund and Rome, prompting the pope to call for a holy crusade against Bohemia.

Prague was almost under siege but the Hussites were undaunted. Radical Hussites arrived in the city in force and, as a sign of their seriousness, burnt alive nine monks in front of the Royal Garrison.

Rome's call to arms against the heretic nation was taken up all over Europe and the Czechs soon found themselves surrounded. They were united, however, behind a powerful moral cause and their brilliant one-eyed general, **Jan Žižka**. He not only repelled the enemies at Vítkov Hill (in what is now Žižkov in Prague), but, by 1432, he and his 'Warriors of God' (as the Czechs called themselves) were pillaging all the way up to the Baltic coast. Women fought and died equally alongside men.

Most Hussites, known as **Praguers**, were moderate and middle class and their leaders were based at Prague University. The more extreme group, known as **Táborites**, were based on a fortified hillside. They banned all class divisions, shared their property and held religious services only in Czech.

Once the pope realised that the holy war had failed, he reluctantly invited the Czechs to discuss a peace settlement. The Táborites were cynical about the pope's overtures, whereas the Praguers had never wanted to break with Rome and viewed their Hussite allies in Tábor as a little too revolutionary. In 1434, the Prague nobles marched their army down to confront the Táborites and wiped out 13,000 of them at the **Battle of Lipany**, thereby settling the issue of negotiations with Rome.

THE FIRST BOHEMIAN KING
Without a strong king, Prague was descending into national, religious and class anarchy. The Hussite wars had altered the political balance in the land. The Church's power was devastated and the vacuum filled by the nobles who seized Church property and ruled mercilessly over the peasants. A hard-fought power struggle between the new Czech king, **George of Poděbrady** (Jiří z Poděbrad), and the nobles forced the king to look to the Polish **Jagellon** dynasty for a successor. Following George's death in 1471, Vladislav II became the king of Bohemia, to be followed by Ludvík in 1516.

> **'Rudolf II was a dour, melancholic monarch engrossed in alchemy, who ignored everyone except Otakar, his pet lion.'**

Two Jagellon monarchs, ruling in absentia, only worsened conditions. At Ludvík's death, the Estates of Bohemia elected the Habsburg Duke **Ferdinand I** as king of Bohemia. He knew just how precarious his status was as a foreign Catholic monarch. At first he did refrain from persecuting the growing number of Lutherans in the region, but later he sent troops into Prague to suppress Protestant dissidents. He appointed Catholics to key official posts and invited the Jesuit Order to Bohemia to spearhead the Counter-Reformation.

EMPEROR RUDOLF'S PARTY PALACE
In 1583 the Habsburg **Rudolf II** (1576-1611) moved his court from Vienna to Prague and for the first time in 200 years the city became the centre of an empire. But the Empire badly needed a man of action, vision and direction to deal with Turkish invaders raging to the south and the demands of Bohemia's Protestants. What it got was a dour, eccentric monarch engrossed in alchemy, who tended to ignore everyone except Otakar, his pet lion. While Europe headed towards the Thirty Years' War, Prague became a surreal fantasy world.

Yet Rudolfine Prague was a dazzling confluence of art, science and mysticism, host to scores of brilliant or mad creatives. As word of Rudolf's sponsorships spread, the flood began. One recipient was **Tycho Brahe**, the Danish astronomer who first shattered Aristotle's thoeries, had a metal nose and died of an intestinal implosion after overeating. As Turkish armies thrust northwards, however, and an attack on Vienna loomed, a coterie of archdukes concluded that Rudolf had to go. His brother **Matthias** picked up the reins.

LOOK OUT BELOW
Neither Matthias nor his successor, **Ferdinand II**, both strong Counter-Reformation Catholics, did much to win over Protestants. In Prague,

Hussite fighters: inventors of the tank. *See p8.*

on 23 May 1618, an assembly of Protestants marched to the Old Royal Palace. They were met by the emperor's diehard Roman Catholic councillors, Slavata and Martinic. After a fierce struggle, the two councillors and their secretary were thrown out of the window, but they landed in a dung heap and survived.

Prague's most famous defenestration turned out to be the first violent act of the **Thirty Years' War**. When **Frederick of the Palatinate**, son-in-law of James I of England and Scotland, was elected to the Bohemian throne he had little idea what a battlefield really looked like, though the Czechs believed that he would rally the powerful Protestant princes of Europe to defend Bohemia.

By November 1620 the combined forces of the Roman Catholic League, consisting of Spain, Italy, Poland and Bavaria, were massing in support of Ferdinand. Frederick had failed to rally anyone except the Protestants of Transylvania. On 8 November 1620 the two armies faced each other at White Mountain (Bílá Hora) on the outskirts of Prague, but on the second Imperial charge the Protestant infantry fled.

HEADS WILL ROLL

On the first anniversary of the defenestration a large crowd gathered in Prague's Old Town Square to witness the beheading of 27 leading Protestant nobles and scholars. Some of the less privileged had their tongues ripped out, hands chopped off and their heads skewered on the towers of Charles Bridge.

Ferdinand made no bones about his plan for Bohemia when he confided that it he felt it was 'better to have no population than a population of heretics'. In the ensuing years Bohemia lost three-quarters of its native nobility, along with its eminent scholars and any vestige of national independence. The country was ravaged by the war, which reduced its population from three million to 900,000. Three-quarters of the land in Bohemia was seized to pay war expenses. All Protestant clergy and anyone refusing to abandon their faith were driven from the country or executed. In all, 30,000 wealthy Protestant families were exiled. While the depopulated towns and villages filled with German immigrants, the peasants were forced to stay and work the land. Opposition was suppressed and Jesuits swarmed in to 're-educate' them.

Ferdinand moved his court back to Vienna in 1624 and cancelled all significant powers of the Bohemian Diet (Parliament). Czechs were taxed to the hilt and the money used to prettify Vienna and pay war debts. During the Thirty Years' War, Prague was invaded by Saxon Protestants but then retaken by **General Wallenstein** (or Valdštejn), a Bohemian-born convert from Protestantism who rose from obscurity to become leader of the Imperial Catholic armies of Europe. He totted up a spectacular series of victories but was disliked by the emperor's Jesuit advisors who conspired to have him dismissed. Wallenstein, who had been secretly negotiating with the Swedish enemy, then joined the Protestants.

When he entered Bohemia in 1634, the Czech exiles pinned their hopes on a Wallenstein victory. He didn't get far. Later that year a band of Irish mercenaries burst into his Cheb residence, where he was recovering from gout, stabbed him and dragged him down the stairs to his death. The Thirty Years' War, which had begun in Prague Castle, petered out on Charles Bridge in 1648, as Swedish Protestants scuffled with newly Catholicised students and Jews.

OPPRESSIVELY BAROQUE

By the mid 17th century, German had replaced Czech as the official language of government. Czech nobles sent their sons to German schools, Charles University was renamed Charles-Ferdinand University and handed over to the Jesuits, who taught in Latin. The lifeline of Czech heritage now rested entirely with the enslaved and illiterate peasantry.

Paradoxically, this period of oppression produced some of Prague's most stunning baroque palaces and churches. Infused with the glorification of God and Rome, Prague's citizens were seduced. Before the century was out most had reverted to Catholicism.

The 18th century was a dull time for Prague. Empress **Maria Theresa** lost Silesia to the Prussians and woke up to the fact that unless the Empire was efficiently centralised more of the same was going to happen. A new wave of Germanisation in schools and government was soon under way and the small Prague cog

Tycho Brahe: head in the stars. *See p9.*

turned within the grand Viennese machine. The Czechs felt that they could do little but merely survive and wait for better times.

Maria Theresa's successor, the enlightened despot **Joseph II**, had little patience with the Church. He kicked out the Jesuits, closed monasteries, nationalised the education system, freed Jews from the ghetto and vastly expanded the Empire's bureaucracy. Internal tolls were abolished and the industrial revolution was beginning. This was all good news for the Czechs except for one thing: all the reforms were taking place in the German language.

ČESKY, PROSÍM

For the first 75 years of the 18th century, Czech became virtually extinct as a language. But gradually Czechs reasserted themselves with a vigour that recalled the good old Hussite days. It started with the revival of the Czech language, and ended in 1918 with political independence.

By the end of the 18th century a number of suppressed works were published, notably Balbín's *Defence of the Czech Language*; the Bohemian Diet began to whisper in Czech; the Church, seeing rows of empty pews, started to preach in Czech; and Emperor Leopold II even established a chair in Czech Language at Prague University. But Napoleon's conquests made it harder for Czech leaders to claim it was all just a harmless cultural development.

> **'In his will Emperor Francis I had only two words of advice for his successor, Ferdinand V: 'Change nothing!'**

Emperor **Francis I** (1792-1835) was taking no chances with liberal nationalist nonsense. In his will he had only two words of advice for his successor, **Ferdinand V** (1835-48): 'Change nothing!' But the cultural revival continued. Philologist Josef Dobrovský produced his *Detailed Textbook of the Czech Language* in 1809; Jungmann reconstructed a Czech literary language; František Palacký wrote a *History of the Czech Nation*; František Škroup composed the Czech national anthem; Prague's theatres staged patriotic dramas; and Čelakovský had the nation singing Czech verses.

1848: AN EMPIRE SHAKEN

The cultural revival inevitably took a political turn. The Czechs demanded equal rights for their language in government and schools. Then, in 1848, revolution once again swept through Europe. A pan-Slav Congress was held in Prague during which a conservative scholarly group led by Palacký clashed with the radicals. Copycat demonstrations were multiplying throughout the Empire, finally bringing down the previously impregnable Viennese government of Prince Metternich. Shaken, Emperor Ferdinand V bought time by tossing promises in Prague's direction.

In Prague the force of reaction came in the sinister figure of Prince Windischgrätz. He fired on a peaceful gathering in Wenceslas Square, provoking a riot to give himself an excuse for wholesale suppression. The new emperor, **Franz Josef** (1848-1916), came to the throne on 2 December 1848 on a tidal wave of terror. In 1849 he issued the March Constitution declaring that all the Habsburg territories were one entity ruled from the Imperial Parliament in Vienna.

Though weakened by a bashing from Bismarck in 1866, the new Austro-Hungarian structure conciliated rather than acknowledge Czech claims for independence. Chafing under an electoral system in Bohemia that favoured the German population, a group known as the **Young Czechs** attacked the establishment for pursuing a 'policy of crumbs'. Adopting Jan Hus as their hero and supported by Realist Party leader Professor **Tomáš Garrigue Masaryk,** they swept the board in the 1891 elections to the Diet. Masaryk focused attention on the moral traditions of Czech history, pointing to the Hussite and National Revival movements as beacons for the nation.

The Czechs began to forge the political, social and economic infrastructure of a nation. Rapid industrialisation transformed the region, and an efficient rail network criss-crossed Bohemia and Moravia, linking the Czech lands to the European economy. Industrialisation gave rise to working class political movements; Catholic parties also emerged.

Czech arts also flourished. The era produced composers Smetana, Dvořák and Janáček, and painters such as Mucha. Literature blossomed in the writings of such as Mácha, Neruda and Vrchlický. The Czech Academy of Sciences and Arts achieved renown. Only the political expression of nationhood remained frustrated.

WORLD WAR I

The outbreak of World War I ended the stalemate. At first the Czechs assumed that they could win concessions on a federal constitution in return for support for the war. However, the mere mention of a constitution provoked repression from Vienna. It would prove a costly policy for the Empire. The Czechs soon realised that their hopes lay in the downfall of the Empire itself and, along with millions of soldiers from other minority groups, deserted to the other side. Six divisions of Czechs were soon fighting for the Allies, while in Prague an underground society known as the 'Mafia' waged a campaign of agitation against the imperial regime.

Meanwhile, Masaryk and **Edvard Beneš** were trying to drum up Allied support for an independent state. They found, however, that the Habsburgs were often viewed more as misguided conspirators than as evil warmongers. In fact, many diplomats had no wish to see the Austro-Hungarian Empire pulled apart, while most of Europe's crowned heads and nobles were certainly opposed to the destruction of a powerful member of their club.

> ## 'The new Republic of Czechoslovakia suffered little destruction during the war; ethnic rivalry was the biggest strain.'

Even so, the United States took the lead, and granted *de jure* recognition to a provisional Czechoslovak government under Masaryk. On 18 October 1918 the new National Committee agreed upon a republican constitution. But their power was only theoretical; the key to actual power lay in controlling the empire's limited food supplies. Bohemia was the breadbasket of the empire, and Habsburg generals, fearing a revolution if food did not get to the population, gave the nod to the provisional council.

On 28 October a National Committee member, Antonín Švehla, marched into the Corn Institute and announced that the Committee was taking over food production. Later that day the Habsburg government sent a note to American President Woodrow Wilson acquiescing to Czechoslovak independence.

FINALLY, INDEPENDENCE

The new Republic of Czechoslovakia suffered hardly any destruction during the war; it was highly industrialised, with generous reserves of coal and iron ore; and it also had an efficient communications infrastructure along with a well-trained and educated bureaucracy. Its workforce was both literate and politically represented. The national leadership were internationally respected diplomats, and the new nation bloomed into a liberal democracy.

Ethnic rivalry was the biggest strain. The Pittsburgh Agreement, which had promoted the concept of a new state, referred to a hyphenated Czecho-Slovakia in recognition of both regions' different histories. The Slovaks were largely an agricultural people and had been ruled by

Hungarians rather than Habsburgs. Unlike the Czechs, they looked upon the Catholic Church as a symbol of freedom. The Slovaks resented what they felt was a patronising air from Prague, but until the late 1930s only a minority of voters backed the separatist Slovak People's Party.

In Prague, ethnic tensions were characterised more by rivalry than by jealousy. The Jews, who comprised only 2.5 per cent of the population, were primarily concentrated in Prague and formed a significant part of the intelligentsia. That most Jews spoke German also created some Czech resentment.

The Germans, who formed 23 per cent of the population and had their own political parties, presented the biggest obstacle to a united nation. Educated, professional and relatively wealthy, they were spread throughout the Czech lands, although Prague and the Sudeten area near the German border had the greatest concentration. The Czechs were sensitive towards, if perhaps also a little sanctimonious about, minority rights, and so they allowed Germans to run their own schools and universities.

Only a few years earlier, however, the German language had dominated the region and the Germans were not pleased with their minority status. They had lost out in the land reforms, had suffered disproportionately from the 1930s depression, and Sudeten savings kept in Weimar Republic bank accounts had gone up in inflationary smoke.

'A FARAWAY COUNTRY'

These economic and ethnic resentments found a political voice in young gymnastics teacher **Konrad Henlein**, who vaulted to prominence as head of the pro-Hitler Sudeten German Fatherland Front. By 1935 the Sudeten Party was the second largest parliamentary bloc. But the sizeable Czech Communist Party was ordered by Stalin to back the liberal Beneš in the presidential elections to counter the Henlein threat, and Beneš took an easy victory.

In 1938 after intimidating their rivals, the Sudeten Nazis won 91 per cent of the German vote and demanded union with Germany. British Prime Minister Neville Chamberlain, for whom the Sudeten crisis was a 'quarrel in a faraway country between people of whom we know nothing', went to Munich with the French premier to meet both Mussolini and Hitler. All of the parties involved in the crisis (except Czechoslovakia, which wasn't invited) agreed that Germany should take the Sudetenland. In return Hitler guaranteed that he would make no further trouble.

The announcement was met with large demonstrations in Prague. Czechoslovakia had a well-armed, well-trained army but was

Tomáš Masaryk. *See p11*.

in a hopeless position. With Poland and Hungary also eyeing its borders, the country found itself encircled, outnumbered, abandoned by its allies and attempting to defend a region that did not want to be defended. Beneš capitulated. Six months later Hitler broke his promise and took the rest of the country, with Poland snatching Těšín, and Hungary grabbing parts of southern Slovakia. On 14 March 1939, a day before Hitler rode into Prague, the Slovaks declared independence and established a Nazi puppet government. Hitler dubbed the remnants of Czechoslovakia the Reich Protectorate of Bohemia and Moravia.

THE LIGHTS GO OUT

In Czechoslovakia, everybody except for Jews and Gypsies fared better under occupation than did people in most European countries. German was made the official language of government and a National Government of Czechs was set up to follow Reich orders. Hitler had often expressed his hatred of 'Hussite Bolshevism' but he needed Czech industrial resources and skilled manpower for the war. Almost all of Czechoslovakia's military hardware was taken over by Germany during that time.

Many Czechs avoided acts of defiance, sitting out the war and hoping for an Allied victory. Hitler lost no time in demonstrating the ferocity of his revenge on those who did resist. When a student demonstration was organised, nine of its leaders were executed, 1,200 students were sent to concentration camps and all Czech universities were closed.

Reinhard Heydrich, later to chair the infamous Wannsee Conference on the Final Solution, was appointed Reichsprotektor and as part of his duties he specialised in leading rounds of calculated terror targeted primarily against the intelligentsia, while enticing workers and peasants to collaborate.

Beneš fled to London where he joined Jan Masaryk (son of Tomáš) to form a provisional Czechoslovak government in exile. There they were joined by thousands of Czech soldiers and airmen who fought alongside the British forces. Czech intelligence agents passed approximately 20,000 messages on to London, including the details of Germany's ambitious plans for the invasion of the Soviet Union.

Beneš, with the help of British Special Operations Executive (*see p14* **Bad Day in Prague 7**), hatched a plan for the assassination of Heydrich. British-trained Czech parachutists **Jan Kubiš** and **Josef Gabčik** were dropped into Bohemia and, on 27 May 1942, successfully ambushed Heydrich's open-top Mercedes, fatally injuring the hated Reichsprotektor.

German reprisals were swift and terrible. The assassins and their accomplices were hunted down to the crypt of the **Orthodox Cathedral of Sts Cyril and Methodius** (*see p107*). Anyone with any connection to the paratroopers was murdered. The villages of **Lidice** and **Ležáky** were mistakenly picked out for aiding the assassins and razed to the ground; the adult males were murdered, the women were sent to concentration camps (in Ležáky they were shot) and the children were 're-educated', placed with German families or killed. The transportation of Jews to concentration camps was stepped up.

Occasional acts of sabotage continued, but the main resistance took place in the Slovak puppet state where an uprising that began on 30 August 1944 lasted four months. The Czechs' act of defiance came in the last week of the war. In May 1945, 5,000 died during a four-day uprising in Prague.

The US forces that had just liberated Pilsen (Plzeň) to the west were only a few miles from Prague. But Allied leaders at Yalta had agreed other plans. Czechoslovakia was to be liberated by the Soviets, and General Eisenhower ordered his troops to pull back. General Patton was willing to ignore the order and sent a delegation to the leaders of the Prague uprising asking for an official request for the American troops to liberate the capital. The communist leaders refused. Although communist power was not consolidated until 1948, the country had found itself inside the Soviet sphere of influence.

UP IN SMOKE

More than 300,000 Czechoslovaks perished in the war, most of them Jews. The Jewish population of Czechoslovakia was destroyed. Most of them were rounded up and sent to the supposedly 'model' **Theresienstadt** (Terezín; *see p251*) ghetto. Many died there, but the remainder were transported to Auschwitz and other concentration camps. In fact, around 90 per cent of Prague's ancient Jewish community had been murdered.

For at least 1,000 years the community had been walled into a ghetto in Old Town, where life was characterised by pogroms, poverty and mysticism. Between the late 18th century, when they left the ghetto, and the arrival of the Nazis, Jews had dominated much of Prague's cultural life. Now the rich literary culture that had produced Franz Kafka had been wiped out. Indeed, Kafka's family perished in Auschwitz. The only thing that saved some of Prague's synagogues and communal Jewish buildings from destruction was the Germans' morbid intention to use them after the war to house its 'exotic exhibits of an extinct race'.

The Czech government under the Reich Protectorate actively supported the extermination of its Romany citizens and helped to run dozens of concentration camps for Gypsies in Bohemia and Moravia. An estimated 90 per cent of the Czech Romany population died in Nazi concentration camps, mostly in Germany and Poland. Beneš's faith in liberalism had been dented by the way the Western powers had ditched his country. He began to perceive the political future of Czechoslovakia as a bridge between capitalism and communism. His foreign minister Jan Masaryk was less idealistic, stating that 'cows like to stop on a bridge and shit on it'.

Beneš needed a big power protector and believed that if he could win Stalin's trust, he could handle the popular Communist Party of Czechoslovakia while keeping the country independent and democratic. During the war he signed a friendship and mutual assistance treaty with the Soviet Union, and later on he established a coalition government comprising principally communists and socialists. In 1945 Stalin knew that a straightforward takeover of a formerly democratic state was not politically expedient. He needed Beneš as an acceptable front in order to buy time. For all his tightrope diplomacy, Beneš was effectively shuffling his country into Soviet clutches.

THE COMMUNIST TAKEOVER

The Soviets and Czech communists were widely regarded as war heroes and so they won a handsome victory in the 1946 elections.

Bad day in Prague 7

The killing of Reichsprotektor **Reinhard Heydrich** was the most dramatic and controversial resistance act of World War II, and the result of incredible persistence, ingenuity and luck. With Nazi-controlled Czech factories churning out a third of the Reich's armaments, President-in-exile Edvard Beneš, then living in London, was desperate for a resistance to impress the British command. He feared a negotiated settlement with Hitler that might leave Czechoslovakia in German hands. With a resistance coup, he reasoned, the Czechs would surely be accorded a bigger role in future Allied plans.

The operation to kill Heydrich, known as Anthropoid, was hastily assembled in October 1941. The British SOE began training two Czech assassins, Josef Gabčik and Jan Kubiš – two of several thousand young Czech men who fled to Britain during the occupation to fight the Nazis – along with two radio intelligence teams.

Their odds were virtually nil: earlier such teams had been discovered as soon as they landed with their badly forged papers and the addresses of safe houses that turned out to be useless. Some had even turned themselves in to the Nazi Gestapo, who then squeezed them for information on plans for future air drops.

A crackdown by the newly appointed Heydrich had cut off all communications with the home resistance by 29 December 1941, but Gabčik and Kubiš were dropped anyway to fend for themselves. They landed outside Pilsen, but the injured Kubiš only made it to safety because the pair were discovered hiding by a local Czech patriot. (This was a crucial stroke of luck because their false papers were also no good.)

After obtaining shelter with sympathisers, the men made contact with an old labourer at Prague Castle, who provided details of Heydrich's schedule. The Reichsprotektor resided at Panenské Břežany just outside Prague and was most vulnerable on the road between home and Prague Castle. Fortunately, he was also vain and thought himself invincible (he disregarded Hitler's orders to have armoured plating in his cars and almost always travelled in an open Mercedes with no security escort).

On 27 May 1942, Gabčik and Kubiš waited for Heydrich at a sharp corner in the

Klement Gottwald became prime minister of a communist-led coalition. Beneš, still hoping that Stalinist communism could co-exist in a pluralistic democracy, remained president. The communists made political hay while the sun shone. They set up workers' militias in the factories, installed communist loyalists in the police force and infiltrated the army and rival socialist coalition parties.

One of the first acts of the government, approved by the Allies, was to expel more than 2.5 million Germans from Bohemia. It was a popular move and, as Klement Gottwald remarked, 'an extremely sharp weapon with which we can reach to the very roots of the bourgeoisie'. Thousands were executed or given life sentences, and many more were killed in a wave of self-righteous revenge.

In 1947 Czechoslovakia was forced to turn down the American economic aid under the Marshall Plan. Stalin knew that aid came with strings and he was determined to be the only puppetmaster. In February 1948, with elections looming and communist popularity declining, Gottwald sent the workers' militias on to the streets of Prague. The police occupied crucial

party headquarters and offices, and the country was incapacitated by a general strike. Beneš's diplomatic skill was no match for the brutal tactics of Moscow-trained revolutionaries. With the Czech army neutralised by communist infiltration and the Soviet army casting a long shadow over Prague, Beneš capitulated and consented to an all-communist government. Gottwald now became Czechoslovakia's first 'Working Class President'.

Shortly after the coup, **Jan Masaryk** fell to his death from his office window. The communists said it was suicide. But when his body was found, the window above was tightly fastened. The defenestration had a distinctly Czech flavour but the purges that followed had the stamp of Moscow. They were directed against resistance fighters, Spanish Civil War volunteers, Jews (often survivors of concentration camps) and anyone in the party hierarchy who might have posed a threat to Moscow. The most infamous trial was that of **Rudolf Slánský**, a loyal sidekick of Gottwald who had orchestrated his fair share of purges. After being showered with honours, he was arrested just a few days later. In March 1951

Nazis cook up a martyr.

Holešovice district where his car would be forced to slow down. Kubiš, armed with a bomb, was in sentry position and signalled Gabčik when he spotted the car. Gabčik stepped in front of the car to fire, but his gun jammed. Heydrich, not seeing Kubiš, saw a chance to play the hero by shooting down a man who couldn't shoot back and stopped his driver from speeding off. This gave Kubiš the chance to throw the bomb, which detonated

by the rear tyre. Without any armour plating on the vehicle, the shrapnel passed easily through the seat and into Heydrich's body.

The price of his death a few days later was to be a string of brutal Nazi reprisals that have been debated ever since, though no one has ever disputed the moral victory that was scored by wiping out Hitler's right-hand man, the head of the SS and the man most often credited with originating the Final Solution.

Slánský and ten senior communists (mostly Jews) were found guilty of being Trotskyite, Titoist or Zionist traitors in the service of US imperialists. They 'confessed' under torture, and eight were sentenced to death.

PRAGUE SPRING

Gottwald dutifully followed his master, Stalin, to the grave in 1953 and the paranoia that had gripped Prague took a long time to ease. By the 1960s communist student leaders and approved writers on the fringes of the party hierarchy began tentatively to suggest that, just possibly, Gottwald and Stalin might have taken the wrong route to socialism, somehow. Slowly, the drizzle of criticism turned into a shower of anger and awkward questions. Then, on 5 January 1968, an alliance of disaffected Slovak communists and reformists within the party replaced Antonín Novotný in a political move with a reformist Slovak communist named **Alexander Dubček**.

A five-star fraud

Easily the most popular figure on the Charles Bridge – and in the city's countless baroque cathedrals – is **Jan of Nepomuk**. Tourists can be spied day and night beneath his statue on the bridge, depicting him getting tossed into the Vltava in 1393, rubbing the bronze plaque at its base for luck. But beyond the fact that he was a priest in the court of Wenceslas IV, little of what has caught the public's imagination about Nepomuk turns out to be true, including the story of his demise – he was executed for incurring the anti-clerical king's wrath, and not, as the legend goes, for keeping the queen's confession a secret.

Nor does the tale of the miracle said to have accompanied his body's exhumation in 1719 hold water. During the height of the Counter-Reformation following the Battle of White Mountain in 1620, at a time when the Church was trying desperately to win back a Protestant Prague flock, it needed a Czech martyr as galvanising as the iconic Jan Hus, the maverick rector of Charles University who had preached against Church corruption and been burned at the stake as a Bohemian heretic reformer. Nepomuk was, quite literally, made for the part of new Counter-Reformation martyr, which explains the 'miracle': three centuries after his demise, his tongue, which is still memorialised in silver on top of his tomb in St Vitus's Cathedral (*see p65*), was pronounced by the attending priests to be alive and licking (a handy symbol for the story of his saintly silence in refusing to reveal a confession).

Although the Vatican, finally faced with evidence that the Nepomuk tale was really a composite of two other saints' lives, revoked his sainthood in 1963, and although researchers who exhumed poor Jan again in the mid '80s determined that the living

tongue was actually dead brain matter, Nepomuk remains a favourite in Prague's Catholic churches, with his distinct five-star halo. How rubbing his plaque is supposed to translate into good luck is anyone's guess, though. Still, no harm in trying.

For the next eight months, the whole world watched the developments in Prague as Dubček rehabilitated political prisoners and virtually abandoned press censorship. Understandably, Moscow was alarmed and tried to intimidate Dubček by holding massive, full-scale military manoeuvres in Czechoslovakia, but still the reforms continued. On 27 June, 70 leading writers signed the widely published *Two Thousand Word Manifesto* supporting the reformist government. Suppressed literature was published or performed on stage, and Prague was infused with the air of freedom. Dubček called it 'socialism with a human face'.

Soviet leader Leonid Brezhnev, despite 'full and frank' discussions, failed to influence the Czechoslovak leader. On the night of 20 August 1968 nearly half a million Warsaw Pact troops entered the country, took over the castle and abducted Dubček and his closest supporters. The leaders fully expected to be shot, but Brezhnev needed some sort of a front for his policy of repression with a human face.

Meanwhile, on the streets of Prague, crowds of thousands of people confronted the tanks. Free radio stations using army transmitters continued to broadcast, and newspapers went underground and encouraged Czechs to refuse any assistance to the occupiers. Street signs and house numbers were removed, and the previously Stalinist workers' militia found a way to defend a clandestine meeting of the national party conference.

'An era of apathy and widespread demoralisation began, an era of grey, everyday totalitarian consumerism'.

The resistance prevented nothing. Dubček stayed in power for eight more months and watched his collaborators being replaced by pro-Moscow ministers. In April 1969 Dubček, too, was removed in favour of **Gustáv Husák** who was eager to push for more of Moscow's 'normalisation'. Husák purged the party and state machinery, the army and the police, the unions, the media, every company and every other organ of the country that might have a voice in the nation's affairs. Anyone who was not for Husák was assumed to be against him. Within a short time every aspect of daily Czechoslovak life was dictated by Husák's many mediocre yes-men. In fairly short order, without ever firing a shot, Husák was able to subdue the nation back into apathy by permitting a limited influx of consumer goods.

Russian tanks during bloody 1968.

A QUIET MARTYR

On 16 January 1969, a 21-year-old philosophy student called **Jan Palach** stood at the top of Wenceslas Square, poured a can of petrol over himself and set himself alight. He died four days later. A group of his friends had agreed to burn themselves to death one by one until the restrictions were lifted. On his deathbed Palach begged his friends not to go through with it, though some of them did.

Palach's death symbolised, with malicious irony, the extinguishing of the flame of hope. As Václav Havel wrote: 'People withdrew into themselves and stopped taking an interest in public affairs. An era of apathy and widespread demoralisation began, an era of grey, everyday totalitarian consumerism'.

Instead of mass arrests, tortures and show trials, the communists now bound up the nation in an endless tissue of lies and fabrications, and psychologically bludgeoned all critical thought by rewarding people for not asking awkward questions and punishing them for refusing to spy on their neighbours. Punishment could mean spells in prison and severe beatings, but for most it meant losing a good job and being forced into menial work. During this time, Prague had an abormally high percentage of window cleaners with PhDs.

There were some, however, who refused to be bowed. A diverse alternative culture emerged in which underground (*samizdat*) literature was circulated around a small group of dissidents. In December 1976 a group led by Václav Havel issued a statement demanding that leading Czechoslovak authorities should observe human rights obligations, and Charter 77 became a small voice of conscience inside the country, spawning a number of smaller groups trying to defend civil liberties. In 1989 it had 1,500 signatories. But there seemed little hope for real change unless events from outside took a new turn. Then, in the mid 1980s, Mikhail Gorbachev came to power in the Soviet Union and initiated his policy of *perestroika*.

THE VELVET REVOLUTION

The Soviet leader came to Prague in 1988. When his spokesman was asked what he thought the difference was between the Prague Spring and *glasnost*, he replied '20 years'. In the autumn of 1989 the Berlin Wall came down and then the communist regimes of Eastern Europe began to falter. The Czechoslovak government, one of the most hardline regimes in Eastern Europe, seemed firmly entrenched until 17 November. When police violently broke up a demonstration on Národní třída commemorating the 50th anniversary of the closure of Czech universities by the Nazis. A rumour, picked up by Reuters news agency, said that a demonstrator had been killed. Another demonstration was called to protest against police brutality.

> ### 'Given the involvement of the KGB, the Velvet Revolution might have been called the Velvet Putsch.'

On 20 November, 200,000 people gathered in Prague to demand the resignation of the government. The police behaved with restraint and the demonstrations were broadcast on television. The government announced that the man who had allegedly been killed on the 17th was alive, but many were sceptical. Some months after the revolution it emerged that the KGB had probably been behind the rumour as part of their plan to replace the government with something in line with Soviet *glasnost*.

That there had not been a death made little difference ultimately. A committee of opposition groups formed themselves into the **Civic Forum** (Občanské fórum), led by Václav Havel, who addressed the masses in Wenceslas Square. On 24 November some 300,000 people assembled there to see him joined by Dubček. The government had lost control of the media, and millions watched the scenes on television. Students from Prague raced out to factories and farms to galvanise the workers into supporting a general strike for the 27th. Workers' militias had put the communists into power in 1948; it was now crucial that they did not choose to stand by communism in its final hour.

Acting communist Prime Minister Adamec also appealed to the crowds, and further purges within the Communist Party followed. The party then declared that it felt the 1968 Soviet invasion had been wrong after all, promising free elections and a multi-party coalition. It was all too late. A new government of reform communists was proposed, but rejected by Civic Forum. Negotiations continued between the communists and Civic Forum for weeks until 27 December, when a coalition of strongly reformist communists and a majority of non-communists – mainly from Civic Forum – took power with Havel as president. Not a single person died. Havel's co-revolutionary Rita Klimová called it the Velvet Revolution. But in some ways, given the KGB's involvement in the handover of power, it might as well have been called the Velvet Putsch.

THE WILD FREE-MARKET RIDE

For months after the revolution Prague floated in a dream world. The novelty of the playwright-president captured the world's imagination, but the serious issues of economic

The most peaceful of the East bloc revolutions occurred in Prague in 1989.

transformation and the relationship between Czechs and Slovaks loomed as formidable challenges. In the summer of 1992 the right of centre Civic Democratic Party (ODS), led by **Václav Klaus**, a no-nonsense free marketeer, was voted into power. But just as Klaus got down to the business of privatisation and decentralisation, calls for Slovak independence grew to a deafening roar. Nationalist sentiments had grown in Slovakia but remained a fringe issue until the electoral rise of **Vladimír Mečiar**'s Slovak separatist HZDS party.

Slovaks had always resented what they had felt was a benign neglect by Prague, and Havel had never been hugely popular among them. One of his first acts as president was to abandon the arms trade. Unfortunately, his pacifist intentions took the heart out of the Slovak economy. Slovaks complained that economic reforms were going too fast. But Klaus would not compromise, and had a mandate from Czech voters to press on. Mečiar upped his separatist threats until, with Machiavellian manoeuvring, Klaus called Mečiar's bluff and announced that he would back Slovak independence.

The two leaders divided up the assets of the state, and the countries peacefully parted ways on 1 January 1993 without so much as a referendum. Havel was elected president of the new Czech Republic, but Klaus had also outmanoeuvred him, forcing Havel into a predominantly ceremonial role.

Klaus indicated that he had little time for a policy of flushing out communists from responsible positions (known as 'lustration'). Thus communists successfully dodged the spotlight amid a blizzard of accusations and counter-accusations. A significant number of Czechs seemed to have skeletons in their cupboards, and it nearly became impossible to untangle the good from the bad. As dissidents watched helplessly, communists remained in charge of the country's largest factories.

The first four years of the Czech Republic under Klaus's leadership produced massive economic changes, which helped make the Czechs the envy of the East and the pride of the West. Foreign investors and businesses quickly capitalised on the massive opportunities for profit and development. The Czech Republic moved to the head of the queue for accession into the European Union.

THE PARTY'S OVER

Economic differences between the haves and have-nots have increased drastically since 1992. Klaus's Pragocentric policies and the decision to prioritise macroeconomic issues backfired in the 1996 elections, when his ODS

party barely managed to keep power. A year later, with the boom days of foreign investment clearly over and headlines alleging secret ODS campaign funding from interested parties, he shocked the nation by stepping down. Miloš Zeman and his Czech Social Democratic Party gained the most votes but not an absolute majority. Zeman agreed to become prime minister with Klaus and his party in charge of Parliament. This pact of political opposites was called absurd by everyone, including Havel, who was also alarmed by the duo's next move: a proposal to limit the power of smaller parties.

Czech membership in NATO, announced before the start of the bombing campaign against Serbia in 1999, was followed almost immediately by further embarrassment. Zeman announced that he had no intention of providing Czech ground troops for UN patrols in Kosovo. It soon became apparent that leadership from the left deserved no more credibility than had Klaus's government. Cynicism and apathy began to return.

Where once the hot issues were civic questions, now attention is focused on salaries, family and home. Large sectors – pensioners, industrial workers, doctors, labourers, teachers, the service industry – have watched their incomes dwindle. Others, meanwhile, have prospered tremendously since 1989: hundreds of bold, honest entrepreneurs but also scores of sleazy developers, speculators, media barons and sex kings. Crises continue in health care, education and housing and the majority of Czechs now feel somehow passed by.

A yawning chasm has opened up between party-crazed youth, who have no real memory of the grey days, and their parents, who have watched as their hopes for a new and improved society have become increasingly compromised. Among the old, nostalgia for the communist days has never been higher.

As Havel's last term draws to an end, the next major milestone facing the Czech Republic is the projected entry into the European Union in 2004. The standards of transparency, solvency and human rights required by the EU are doing much to accomplish what Havel could not; perhaps it's human nature to respond faster to threats and deadlines than to a moral leader.

Whatever the cause, Prague's transformation to a Western-style capital, replete with fast food culture and consumerist lifestyle, remains counterbalanced by a Czech trait as old as the Slavic myths of Libuše: they tend to take everything with a healthy dose of scepticism. Life's tumultuous transitions come and go, but most Czechs survive by believing there's little point getting agitated over transitory things when the corner pub is beckoning.

Key events

c400 BC Celtic Boii tribe occupies Bohemia.
7th century AD Slavic tribes settle in region.
c700 The Přemyslid dynasty begins.
863 Cyril and Methodius bring writing and Christianity to Great Moravia.
929 'Good King' Wenceslas is killed by his brother and becomes a martyr and the Czech patron saint.
973 Prague is made a bishopric.
1235 Staré Město gets a Royal Charter; Jews forced into the ghetto.
1253 Otakar II becomes king.
1306 Přemyslid dynasty ends with the murder of Václav III.
1346 Charles IV becomes Holy Roman emperor and king of Bohemia; founds Central Europe's first university, in Prague.
1352 Swabian architect Peter Parler begins work on St Vitus's Cathedral.
1357 Foundations laid for Charles Bridge.
1378 King Wenceslas IV crowned.
1389 3,000 Jews killed in pogrom.
1403 Jan Hus, rector of Prague University, begins preaching against Church corruption.
1415 Hus, having been excommunicated and declared a heretic, is burned at the stake.
1419 Hussite mob throws the mayor out of the new town hall window; the Hussite wars begin.
1420s-1430s Hussites repel all attacks.
1434 Moderate Hussites wipe out the radicals and the pope agrees to allow them considerable religious freedom.
1458 Czech noble George of Poděbrady becomes the 'People's king' but is soon excommunicated by the pope.
1471-1526 The Jagellon dynasty rules in Bohemia.
1526 Habsburg rule begins with Ferdinand I.
1556 Ferdinand invites the Jesuits to Prague to counter fierce anti-Catholicism in Bohemia.
1583 Habsburg Emperor Rudolf II moves the court to Prague, where it remains for the next two decades.
1609 Tycho Brahe's work leads to his *Laws of Planetary Motion*; Rudolf concedes some religious rights to Bohemia's Protestants.
1618 Protestants throw two Catholic councillors from a window in the castle, thus starting the Thirty Years' War.
1620 Protestants lose the Battle of White Mountain.
1621 27 Protestant leaders executed in Old Town Square.

1648 The Thirty Years' War ends on Charles Bridge as the citizens of Prague repel the invading Swedes.
1740 Maria Theresa becomes empress.
1743 French attack Prague.
1757 Prussians attack Prague.
1781 Emperor Joseph II abolishes the Jesuits and closes monasteries.
1848 Revolutions in Europe; unsuccessful uprisings in Prague against Austrian troops.
1893 Clearing of the Jewish ghetto begins.
1914 Outbreak of World War I; Habsburgs refuse concessions on federalism and Czech soldiers desert to the Allies.
1918 Czechoslovak Republic founded with Tomáš Masaryk as its first president.
1938 Chamberlain agrees to let Hitler take over the Sudetenland.
1939 Hitler takes all Czechoslovakia.
1942 Czech paratroopers assassinate Reichsprotektor Reinhard Heydrich. Nazis destroy villages Lidice and Ležáky in revenge.
1945 Prague uprising; the Red Army arrives.
1948 The Communist Party assumes power under Klement Gottwald.
1951 The Slánský show trials and mass purges take place.
1968 Reformist communist Dubček becomes first secretary and promotes 'socialism with a human face', but the Prague Spring is crushed by Warsaw Pact troops.
1969 Philosophy student Jan Palach immolates himself in protest.
1977 The underground movement Charter 77 is established to monitor human rights abuses.
1989 Student demos turn into full-scale revolution and the communist regime falls.
1990 Poet, writer and anti-communist activist Václav Havel elected president of Czechoslovakia.
1993 The Slovak Republic and Czech Republic become separate, independent states.
1996 Michael Jackson's statue briefly takes up the spot vacated by Stalin's in Letná Park, as part of his History tour.
1998 The largest demonstrations since the Velvet Revolution sweep the city to celebrate the Czech hockey team winning an Olympic gold.
2000 The largest demonstrations since the Olympics fill Wenceslas Square to demand the ousting of Prime Minister Miloš Zeman and ODS head Václav Klaus.

Prague Today

So long, sleaze – hello, gritty reality

It's no coincidence that the recent Czech film *Anděl Exit* – a cynical account of life among Prague's jilted young generation – takes place almost entirely in the historic, and historically run-down, neighbourhood of Smíchov. Sandwiched between Prague's flashy downtown districts and its decaying outskirts, Smíchov is a perfect metaphor for the state of the city today and the mixed effects that 12 years of capitalism have had upon the capital and its people.

Consider the metro station from which the film takes its title. Originally called Moskevská ('Moscow'), when the communists opened Prague's metro in 1974, the name was changed to 'Angel' after 1989's Velvet Revolution. Despite the change, the entrance to the station remained a dilapidated wreck throughout the 1990s – and despite the overwhelming optimism that reigned as the last Russian troops left the city, the busy intersection outside Anděl station soon became a testament to the worst gifts capitalism had bestowed on the city.

On the corner stood U Holubů, a casino-restaurant-bordello set-up and a meeting point for the international mafia that was quickly making Prague its new European headquarters. Next door to this, Colonel Sanders and Ronald McDonald stand shoulder to shoulder, casting their gaudy glow on the faces of grandmothers passing by, whose meager pensions would never allow them to eat there. Come night-time, prostitutes – often culled from the ranks of the neighbourhood's increasingly desperate Romany inhabitants – populated the corner in droves.

But those were the 1990s, before the Wild East was fully won. In the space of just two years, Anděl became home to three new hypermodern business complexes, complete with shopping malls, corporate offices and multiplex cinemas. The slick, glass-and-steel **Zlatý Anděl** complex now sits atop the old communist metro station. Moneyed managers breeze in and out of designer fashion outlets, high-end electronics stores and Dutch-owned supermarkets. And U Holubů, though it clings to life, looks distinctly quiet these days.

The ultimate absurd theatre

For more than a decade, Czechs have benefited enormously from having an international superstar like Václav Havel as president. It's not what he's done inside the country that stands out, as the Czech president has little real power and Havel hasn't been a particularly effective domestic politician. Rather it's Havel's influence abroad and his moral integrity during the communist period that earned him enormous international respect.

Much of that glow has naturally rubbed off on his country and countrymen. The Czech Republic is widely viewed as the most advanced of Europe's formerly communist countries, and no small part of the credit goes to its larger-than-life dissident playwright president.

But 2003 will see the end of Havel's reign. The Czech constitution allows the president only two five-year terms in office, and Havel's second term is set to expire. The Czechs are scrambling to find someone to fill the void.

It won't be easy. The major political parties are led by common or garden politicians more concerned with getting votes than with admirable but pointless notions like 'Living in Truth' – the title of one of Havel's books. The generation to emerge after communism is still too young to have spawned a great statesman or man or women or letters. And at this stage there are no obvious or widely admired businessmen or religious leaders to step in.

At press time, the leading candidates to succeed Havel were a constitutional lawyer, a respected former university professor and the leader of the main opposition party.

FAST TIMES

The rehabilitation of Anděl is just one of the signs that Prague has returned to her rightful place as a respectable European capital. But at least some of the city's residents are questioning the cost. Monster cinemas like the one at Anděl, playing Hollywood blockbusters, are gradually gobbling up the traditional small neighbourhood theatres where homegrown talents like Václav Havel once showcased their work. Street crime and drug abuse are on the rise as the frenzied pace of economic change leaves more and more ordinary Praguers stranded by the wayside. And the early years of rapid growth left behind some distinctly embarrassing stretch marks.

The first wave of privatisation in the early 1990s, led by Václav Klaus as prime minister, at first made the Czech Republic seem the tiger economy of Central Europe. As time went on, however, it became painfully apparent that behind the scenes, the process was a poorly regulated free-for-all. By inventing ways of skirting the law and greasing a few well-placed palms, a handful of asset strippers – known locally as 'tunnellers' – made off with millions by intentionally bankrupting their companies or even entire industries, leaving employees on the street and shareholders out of luck.

The whole fiasco hit home especially hard in the capital, where the cosmopolitan Klaus draws most of his support, and led to the rise of Miloš Zeman's Social Democratic government in 1998. One of Zeman's principal campaign promises was to round up high-rolling financial criminals in what he dubbed 'Operation Clean Hands'. Not surprisingly, few were ever arrested.

Watching the local industrialist padlock his factory for the last time and drive off in a new Mercedes taught many Czechs a valuable lesson. Corruption – from under-the-table business scams to cronyism – is rampant. The Czech Republic's rating on Transparency International's corruption index gets worse with each passing year.

All have their respective strengths, but none come close to Havel in terms of integrity and international recognition.

In the end, though, these factors will have limited influence as the Czech president is not directly elected by the people, but is chosen by Parliament. Any successful candidate will have to be seen by the major parties as pliant enough to be palatable. Havel's last election in 1998 can be viewed as something of a fluke. He was too big to be denied. But the next president is unlikely to be such a moral maverick, who says and does what he likes.

But maybe that's not so bad. Havel was the right man at the right time. In the aftermath of the Velvet Revolution, the Czechs needed a beacon who could attract foreign attention, investment and trust, and someone with no ties to the communist regime. Those days, arguably, have passed.

Havel – although widely admired – also tended to rankle ordinary Czechs with his rhetoric; the next president is unlikely to occupy so high a pedestal. Maybe the time has come for a littler man, more in tune with his countrymen. Someone who would grow into the office, and with him pull his country along.

Predictably, Praguers – who have always survived by assimilating – have proven adept at navigating capitalism, and not always dishonestly. But for those with minimal education, no language skills, or who are just unfashionably past 40, making ends meet can be a daily struggle, as prices rise much faster in Prague than in the rest of the country.

To be sure, many residents are now far better off than they were under communism. Wages have rocketed, unemployment in the capital remains almost at zero and in recent years the salary gap between imported Western corporate guns and the new generation of savvy Czech managers has significantly narrowed.

A telling moment came when the annual summit of the IMF and World Bank was held here in September 2000. Thousands of anti-globalisation protesters from across Europe showed up to battle police in the streets, and the cops obliged them with billy clubs, tear gas and water cannons. There were a few local anarchists and Bolsheviks in the crowd, but most Praguers

stayed at home and scratched their heads, wondering why in the world their city was being trashed. For Czechs who had lived through communism, the sight of a bunch of privileged Western kids smashing the windows of a McDonald's was a bit hard to swallow.

Though Praguers will be the first to complain about the commercial tack and trash that has infiltrated the city's medieval streets, no one would deny that capitalism has brought with it amazing diversity. Waves of enterprising Eastern immigrants, invasions by numerous Western retailers, and not least the cleverness and quirkiness of local entrepreneurs have all imbued the city with a vibrancy unmatched in its 1,000-year history. From Thai food to tapas bars, Ukrainian avant-garde galleries to Viennese Gilded Age cafés, with the advent of an open market, Prague has finally regained its position as Central Europe's crossroads, while still somehow managing to maintain its own distinctive character. At least for now.

LIFE AFTER HAVEL

Prague is not only the country's economic engine but also its seat of political power. Despite the massive changes that have taken place in corporate offices througout the city, if one takes a peek in the halls of Parliament, it's

Václav Klaus: Havel's successor?

The **Zlatý Anděl** complex struts its capitalist stuff. *See p21.*

amazing how little has changed since a small group of ex-dissidents and former communist officials took the reins in 1990.

By and large, those faces are the same ones voters see staring at them from campaign posters and newspapers today. Václav Klaus, a finger-wagging father figure who was ousted by a party finance scandal in 1997 during his second term as prime minister, still leads the country's most popular political party, the conservative Civic Democrats.

For a bunch of ex-communists, the Social Democrats did surprisingly well at steering the country after taking power in 1998. Sure, the shady deals that were common under Klaus continued, and Prime Minister Miloš Zeman did have a tendency to plant his foot in his mouth – a fault that was only exacerbated by his love for the potent herbal liqueur *Becherovka*. He outraged observers by comparing Palestinian leader Yasser Arafat to Hitler, and by calling Austrians the Third Reich's willing accomplices. But his party's rule was far from the calamity most conservatives predicted.

Of course, the country's most famous political holdout, and the only Czech politician who carries any currency abroad, is President Václav Havel, the dissident playwright whom the Velvet Revolution elevated to the role of philosopher king. Since then, Havel has ceaselessly preached to his people about the moral and civic responsibilities that come with democracy. Havel's many humanitarian pronouncements may get good play in the West, but at home he's gained a reputation as a brooding moraliser too far removed from party politics to engage fully with the everyday problems faced by the Czech people (*see p22* **The ultimate absurd theatre**).

Havel's final term ends in 2003. Whether he leaves as a success or a failure is open to debate. After 13 years of Havel, it's difficult for most Czechs to imagine anybody else in Prague Castle. Nonetheless, Klaus is making a strong bid for the presidency, and seems the most likely heir at this stage.

EU OR BUST

Not surprisingly, Klaus has taken on – as a personal cause – the biggest change looming on the horizon for the country: European Union (EU) membership. Having joined NATO in 1999, the Czech Republic is expected to enter the EU in 2004. For Klaus, it's not so much a question of whether the country should join; he knows full well there is no viable option. Rather, the issue is what conditions the EU will impose on the Czech Republic and other former communist countries. Western members want a limit on free movement of workers, fearing a flood of cheap labour from the East, as well as lower subsidies for farmers and other caveats. Klaus would rather delay membership than enter the EU as a second-class citizen.

Before the country joins the EU, though, it has some mess to clean up at home. Foremost among them is the country's treatment of its Romany minority, who come up against discrimination in almost every facet of life, from education to employment to housing. A growing neo-Nazi movement is responsible for frequent assaults against Roma, which often go ignored by the police. The issue made waves in 2001, when British immigration officials started screening UK-bound passengers at Prague's Ruzyně airport. The reason was to stem a rising tide of Czech asylum seekers in Britain, nearly all of whom were Roma claiming they were in danger at home. Rights workers accused the Brits of racism but the incident was mainly an embarrassment for the Czechs, and focused international attention on the plight of Roma in the Czech Republic.

Prague also made worldwide headlines in January 2001 when reporters at state-run Czech Television went on strike over political influence at the station. After close associates of Klaus were chosen for key positions, rebel reporters occupied the newsroom, beaming their own pirate broadcasts over the airwaves while 250,000 citizens – the largest demonstration since the Velvet Revolution – gathered on Wenceslas Square to protest.

Klaus bore most of the blame, but his fellow politicians didn't seem to learn any lessons from the debacle. Prime Minister Zeman made a series of attacks on the media, vowing to destroy independent newspapers by burying them in lawsuits. He didn't succeed, but his threats earned the country black marks in several human rights reports.

In reality, these issues don't much affect the employees at the new business centres in Smíchov. Salaries are on their way up, the country is on its way into the EU, and come 5pm the young analysts at ING Barings above Anděl station are off to dinner at the new sushi bar down the street. Sure, everyone remembers the '90s – the streets were a little darker, the music was a little louder, and life in Prague was wilder all round. But that was puberty. We're older now, with certain responsibilities that come with being a mature European capital. And besides, who cares if U Holubů closes down anyway?

Prague by numbers

1.2 million: population of Prague

10.3 million: Population of Czech Republic

78,866 sq km: Area of Czech Republic

Ethnic divisions:

Czech **94.4 per cent**
Slovak **3 per cent**
Polish **0.6 per cent**
German **0.5 per cent**
Romany **0.3 per cent**
Hungarian **0.2 per cent**
Other **1 per cent**

Religions

Atheist **39.8 per cent**
Roman Catholic **39.2 per cent**
Protestant **4.6 per cent**
Orthodox **3 per cent**
Other **13.4 per cent**

72: average life expectancy for a Czech male

78: average life expectancy for a Czech female

£8,860 ($12,900): GDP per capita

8.8 per cent: unemployment rate

11,709 Kč: average monthly wage in the Czech Republic

1st: ranking of taxes and insurance among the expenses of an average Czech family

26.8 days: average duration of one sick leave from work

2:1: ratio of people to cars in Prague

628,000: average number of vehicles that pass daily through the centre of Prague

4.3: number of Czechs with mobile phones to every 3.8 with land lines

3000: number of illegal foreign residents of the Czech Republic expelled in 2001

16.2: Percentage of Czechs who indicated they would vote for communists before voting for the Václav Klaus, the Thatcherite leader of ODS

30: approximate number of offices you must obtain an approval stamp from to start a business enterprise in Prague

75: percentage of Roma children removed from mainstream education and sent to schools for the developmentally disabled

26: percentage of all crimes committed in the Czech Republic that occur in Prague

28: percentage of people surveyed by *Reflex* magazine who regularly sneak on to the Prague metro without a ticket

1: approximate number of students eventually admitted to Charles University out of every 400 who apply

50: percentage by which the sale of legal CD recordings fell over the last three years

510 Kč: typical price difference between legal Western CD and a high-quality Czech copy

3: number of organic farms operating in the Czech Republic in 1990

654: number of organic farms operating in the Czech Republic at the beginning of 2002

1st: world ranking of Czechs as consumers of beer per capita

30 billion: annual amount of cigarettes produced by Phillip Morris's factories in the Czech Republic

Architecture

A living 'Best of' in stone and brick, Prague transports visitors through a millennium of engineering and ornament.

If architecture is frozen music, then Prague is an unfinished symphony of staggering proportions. Largely spared the destruction of two world wars, Prague contains a huge diversity of architectural genres melded into a harmonious unit. The solemn chant of the Romanesque happily cohabits with baroque sensuality, deconstructivist sampling and even cubist dissonance.

Take the controversial **'Fred & Ginger Building'** by Frank Gehry and Vladimír Milunič. It's the indirect result of 'collateral damage' from World War II: an errant US bomber, whose crew mistook Prague for Dresden, created a prime vacant lot for it on the New Town bank of the Vltava river. This exuberantly swooping building ingeniously reflected the more staid historic structures around it, yet revived Prague's reputation as a city of visual daring and distinction.

Projects on a huger scale, like Getty Museum creator Richard Meier's proposed 'Prague Manhattan' skyscraper complex, may bring a more homogenised tone to outlying districts. But so far, with one or two exceptions, the historic core of the city remains blessedly free of 'prestigious' glass-and-aluminium boxes.

BEGINNINGS

Though inhabited continuously for tens of thousands of years, the hill-encircled Prague basin did not see a real town until Slav tribes began to build on the banks of the Vltava in the seventh century. Then, in the second half of the ninth century, a stone fortress was built on a rocky outcrop on the left bank, and, in the early tenth century, another castle was constructed on the right bank a little upstream. Around these structures – **Prague Castle** (*see p63*) and Chrasten Castle (now **Vyšehrad**; *see p108*) respectively – the settlements began to develop that eventually grew into the city of Prague.

From the 11th to the 13th centuries, architecture in Prague was characterised by the simple forms, heavy, rounded arches, tunnel and cross vaults and thick columns

Worker heroes remain.

of the Romanesque, as seen in the **Rotunda of St Martin** (second half of the 11th century, Vyšehrad, Prague 2).

The most extensive surviving Romanesque building in the city is **St George's Basilica** in the Castle complex (*see p68*). The marshy right bank of the river, less densely populated than the area around the Castle and more liable to flood, began expanding with the creation of a marketplace (now **Old Town Square**) in 1100 and saw a profusion of Romanesque buildings. By 1170 the two settlements were linked by the Judith Bridge (later replaced by **Charles Bridge**; *see p90*), and the Old Town was established by decree in 1287. Romanesque

structures made perfect foundations for Gothic buildings and many Romanesque basements still exist, such as that in the **House of the Lords of Kunštát and Poděbrady** (*see p90*).

GOTHIC

Gothic architecture, imported from France around 1230, offered greater spatial dynamism through ribbed vaulting, pointed arches and buttressing, enabling taller, wider and more delicate buildings. The **Old-New Synagogue** (*see p94*) is one of the best-preserved medieval synagogues in Europe. Two pillars in the centre of its vaulted hall-nave support six bays of ribbed vaulting reaching heights of up to nine metres (30 feet). Its portal, one of the oldest in Prague, features a beautifully carved decoration in the tympanum. The oldest Gothic complex in Bohemia is **St Agnes's Convent** (*see p95, p112 and p214*), now part of the National Gallery. Prague's Gothic heyday came under Charles IV (1346-78), who summoned German Peter Parler to implement his grand design for a new, fortified city. This New Town, planned to have four geometric sections with a central axis on **Wenceslas Square** (*see p96*), doubled the size of the city. Construction began in 1348, the year Charles University was founded. Parler also built **Charles Bridge** (*see p90*) and added innovative additions to **St Vitus's Cathedral** (*see p65*).

A fascinating hybrid of Gothic and modern is the **Emmaus Monastery** (*see p103*). Its spires and vaults were destroyed in the same World War II air raid that made space for the 'Dancing House'. Luckily, the Gothic frescoes in the cloister survived. For better or worse, new spires made of reinforced concrete shell plates designed by František Černý were added in 1967. Viewed from the riverbank, they seem to have been placed there as a prank.

The best Places to see...

... Romanesque roots
St George's Basilica (*see above*), **Prague Castle** (*see above*), **House of the Lords of Kunštát and Poděbrady** (*see above*).

... Medieval Gothic façades
St Agnes's Convent (*see above*).

... Renaissance sgraffito
Belvedere, Royal Gardens, **Prague Castle** (*see p26 and p28*), **Schwarzenberg Palace** (*see p28*).

... Baroque extravagance
Wallenstein Palace (*see p28*), **Church of St Nicholas** (*see p28*).

... Art nouveau frills
Municipal House (*see p29*), **Grand Hotel Evropa** (*see p29*).

... Communist central planning
Nová Scéna (*see p30*).

... New beauty
The 'Fred & Ginger building' (*see p30*).

Architectural epochs sit side-by-side on Prague's streets.

RENAISSANCE

Under the first Habsburg ruler of Bohemia, Ferdinand I (1526-64), brick – cheaper, easier and more conducive to rapid construction than raw stone – facilitated the Renaissance renovation of Malá Strana after the fire of 1541. The period saw a move towards more human-scale, horizontal spaces – simpler masses and clearer forms, punctuated by columns and arches. The Renaissance arrived in earnest with the construction of Paolo della Stella's extraordinary **Belvedere** (*see p70*) in the **Royal Gardens** by the Castle. In the same gardens is Bonifác Wohlmut's **Ball Game Court** (*see p71*), a marvellous display of 16th-century sgraffito. This technique of scratching through black or brown mortar to create a pattern or picture, is particularly suited to trompe l'oeil effects such as imitation stonework, as seen in the **Schwarzenberg Palace** on Hradčanské náměstí, now home of the Military Museum (*see p116*).

BAROQUE

Prague's first baroque edifice, designed by Giovanni Pieronni, was the titanic **Wallenstein Palace** (*see p78*), which prefigured the dominance of the new style after the Thirty Years' War. Construction after 1648 boomed, fuelled in part by the need to rebuild

much of war-damaged Prague. With Bohemia now securely tucked within the Habsburg empire, the Jesuits set about consolidating the Counter-Reformation with their own building programme. The most significant result was the **Church of the Holy Saviour** in the **Clementinum** (*see p89*), an elegant and austere example of early baroque. The more elaborate and decorative Czech baroque style is best reflected in Prague's baroque magnum opus, the extravagant **Church of St Nicholas** (*see p214*). The Habsburg-friendly gentry also caught the baroque wave, visible in some of the city's finer townhouses. The War of the Austrian Succession and the Seven Years' War brought yet more extensive damage to the city, and yet another rebuilding programme. Niccolo Pacassi restored the south side of the **Castle** for Empress Maria Theresa and gave it the late baroque unity that we see today from Charles Bridge. None of it can touch the opulence of the **Loreto** (*see p74*), much of it due to the father-and-son team of Christoph and Kilian Ignaz Dientzenhofer, of Church of St Nicholas fame.

REVIVALISM

The beginning of revivalist architecture came in 1780, when newly crowned Joseph II issued a decree of religious tolerance and another specifying the precise height, materials and construction methods for new buildings. Antonín Haffenecker built the neo-classical **Estates Theatre** (*see p211 and p234*) for Count Nostitz with new materials, such as cast iron. The manufacturing middle classes, rather than the Church or nobility, now began to call the tune with Prague's first suburb, Karlín, which had a rational grid plan that included blocks of flats with common water facilities alongside factories. Municipal construction responded to newly recognised social needs – schools, houses and hospitals, rather than churches and palaces. The spread of railways and growing engineering expertise gave rise in 1845 to the first train station, **Masarykovo nádraží** (Havlíčkova, Nové Město, Prague 1, map p309 L3), with its airy iron canopy.

On 16 May 1868, 50,000 people walked in procession behind the foundation stone for the **National Theatre** (*see p101, p214 and p234*), designed by Josef Zítek, soon to be an icon of Czech identity. The 'National Theatre Generation' of artists and designers, sadly, saw their collective effort burnt to the ground shortly after the opening. Within two months, though, money was raised through public subscription to rebuild, this time according to the designs of one of Zitek's colleagues, Josef Schulz. He went on to build the **National Museum** (*see p97 and p118*). Neo-Renaissance and neo-baroque were the order of the day: heavy, monumental, civic, grand.

ART NOUVEAU

A rise in banking wealth and a Czech business class demanded a new direction. Decorative style, symbolism and decadence sprouted in art nouveau (called secessionism in the Austro-Hungarian empire). Viennese-trained architect Friedrich Ohmann created the **Hotel Central** (1902, Hybernská 10, Nové Město, Prague 1, map p309 L3), with its glass cornice and floral motifs, reflecting a French-indebted sensibility. At the same time, municipal and residential art nouveau buildings spread, many still visible in neighbourhoods such as Vinohrady and Vršovice. Osvald Polívka built both the heavily ornamented **Prague Insurance Building** (the windows below the cornice spelling out 'Praha') and the **Topič Building** next door (1903-5, Národní třída, Staré Město, Prague 1, map p308 G5). Polívka helped bring about the culmination and possibly the death of art nouveau in the extraordinary **Municipal House** (*see p86, p100 and p213*). The most tenacious art nouveau edifice in Prague is surely the **Grand Hotel Evropa** (*see p52*), which clings to its original purpose. Though its interiors have never really recovered from communist neglect, the gilt in its grand façade gleams brightly in the morning sun on Wenceslas Square.

CUBISM

Perhaps it was the city's architectural diversity and abundance that drew Czech architects to this radical form of expression at a time when

Over-the-top: its all glam and glitz at the **Municipal House**.

The **House of the Black Madonna**.

nearly everyone else was turning to functional logic in construction. Josef Chochol's apartment buildings and family homes below **Vyšehrad** (*see p108*) show the result. The house at Neklanova 30, Prague 2, and the villa at Libušina 3, Prague 2, are almost baroque in their depth and profusion of angular surfaces. The movement's most overlooked achievement is the world's only cubist lamp-post (Jungmannovo náměstí, Nové Město, Prague 1, map p308 J5). But Prague's first plunge into cubist architecture was Josef Gočár's **House of the Black Madonna** (*see p113*), currently housing a collection of Czech cubist paintings and furniture.

CZECH MODERNISM

As aspirations of independence grew, Czech architects began to make their mark on the city. Jan Kotěra, a pupil of Vienna's Otto Wagner, planted the seeds of Czech modern architecture with geometric functionalism. His **Urbánek Publishing House** (1911-12, Jungmannova 30, Nové Město, Prague 1, map p308 J5) used planes of brick to create a pared-down, singular façade. During the First Republic, President Tomáš Garrigue Masaryk asked Slovenian Josip (or Jože) Plečnik to renovate and modernise Prague

Castle. His sensitivity and innovation greatly enhanced the ancient structure, as seen in the classically inspired Columned Hall. Russian constructivism and the influence of Adolf Loos got their turn at the stripped-down, yet extravagant modernist mansion, the **Müller Villa** (1928), now open to the public (Nad Hradním vodojemem 14, Střešovice, Prague 6). The constructivist icon of the Veletržní palác in Holešovice, now housing the **National Gallery Collection of 19th-, 20th & 21st-Century Art** (*see p111*) used reinforced concrete liberally. Its huge atrium is wonderful.

COMMUNISM

On the whole, communism brought with it architectural disaster. The overbearing Stalinist bulk of the **Crowne Plaza Hotel** admittedly holds a grim fascination, but it's readily apparent that it was planned by a team from the Military Design Institute. Further out, Prague was quickly surrounded by gargantuan, shoddy and soulless housing estates (*paneláky*) that are now suburban slums. At the **National Theatre** (*see p214 and p234*) communist design nearly accomplished what fire could not. A 1960s competition to add a new auditorium resulted in the **Nová Scéna**, a two-part monstrosity clad in glass and completed in the 1980s. But the masterpiece of communist design is surely the **Žižkov Tower** (*see p110*), which dominates the entire city and seems set to blast off into space at any moment.

BEYOND THE VELVET REVOLUTION

Since 1989 Prague has been preoccupied with restoration and enrichment. Enormous infrastructure investments and countless complex state and private renovations are taking place. But not all that glitters here is gold. Preservationists rail against the inauthentic colours of the Renaissance and baroque palaces, now a part of the Czech Parliament, forming the northern side of Malostranské náměstí. The most eye-catching new addition to Prague's skyline remains Vladimír Milunic and Frank Gehry's Tančící dům, called in English the 'Dancing House' or **'Fred & Ginger Building'** (corner of Rašínovo nábřeží and Resslova, Nové Město, Prague 2; map p310 G8), a seemingly swaying glass tower held close by a rigid 'masculine' block. The **Myslbek Centre** (*see p161*), a crassly commercial project, destroyed the elegant lines and scale of the Na Příkopě historic promenade. Indeed, commercialism continues to threaten. But Prague has survived wars, floods, fires, Nazis and Bolsheviks with its splendour and soul intact. With luck, these may also withstand globalisation.

Literary Prague

The city of Kafka, Rilke and once banned Václav Havel plays is experiencing a quiet publishing revival.

Tell someone you're starting a magazine in Prague and they'll usually roll their eyes. 'What, again? And in English, I suppose!' The number of expat publications in a city of 1.2 million people, only one per cent of whom are native English speakers, is indeed curious. But with literary credentials dating back to the Czech National Revival of 1848 and Habsburg café culture, it's only natural that Prague should attract droves of writerly sorts.

One penniless mogul at the heart of Prague's literary scene, Howard Sidenberg, of the small imprint Twisted Spoon, contends that the literary scene in Prague is evolving just as it should. 'After the revolution, people in their infinite shallowness wanted and expected a "scene" to appear overnight,' he observes. 'When that didn't happen, there was talk about the "death of the scene" or "end of an era" – equally artificial. And now, after the birth and death of the scene, there actually seem to be a lot of talented people here writing and doing some interesting stuff.'

The Twisted Spoon imprint specialises in introducing such unknown writers, both Czech and Western, to the world. The Twisted Spoon website (www.twistedspoon.com) features a catalogue of wondrous publications from contemporary and classic writers who share only one thing: no conventional, profit-conscious publisher would touch them with a ten-foot pole.

Aside from some titles unknown outside Prague crowding the shelves of the **Globe Bookstore & Coffeehouse** (*see p33, p141 and p165*), the literary scene in Prague is most evident at the city's many literary festivals. Come decent spring weather, it seems there's one every three or four weeks.

ORIGINS

The city's literary appeal has its roots in the Czech National Revival of the mid 19th century. That's when the watershed novel by the writer **Božena Němcová**, *Babička* (*Grandmother*), was published, inaugurating a new era for writing in colloquial Czech. Němcová remains a much-loved figure – her face can be found on the 500 Kč note – and her fairytales are still read to children today.

Jaroslav Hašek also made a major contribution to Czech literary history with *The Good Soldier Švejk*, a rambling novel whose protagonist never misses an opportunity to get an order wrong, a strategy that helps him to make it through World War I intact. Whether his subversion is mischievously purposeful or merely idiotic is never clear, giving rise to a philosophical school of survival under occupation. This near mysticism is quintessentially Czech, and makes Švejk required reading for anyone who wants to penetrate the national character (*see p275*).

Franz Kafka, meanwhile, ranks as Prague's most famous icon and was an avid admirer of Němcová. Of all the writing to emerge from Prague's German-speaking Jewish community, his is by far the best known, although his contemporaries, the poet **Max Brod** and novelists **Paul Leppin** (*Severin's Journey into the Dark*) and **Gustav Meyrink** (*The Golem*), were much more famous at the time. That culture was nearly wiped out by the Holocaust, but two survivors, **Jiří Weil** and **Arnošt Lustig**, wrote devastating accounts of life behind the barbed wire.

The surrealist vein running through much of this work is a survivor from the pre-war First Republic. Its source can be traced to poet **Vítězslav Nezval**, who founded the Czech Surrealists in the 1930s. He was also a member of the Devětsil avant-garde movement, as was Nobel laureate poet **Jaroslav Seifert**.

After the communists seized power in 1948, independent-minded writers were banned, jailed, forced into menial jobs or exiled. Those who continued to write were obliged to publish *samizdat* manuscripts, illicitly distributing individually typewritten pages between themselves. **Václav Havel** was part of that network while penning his satirical and absurdist plays *The Memorandum*, *The Garden Party* and *Audience*, among others, some of which are still sporadically performed.

Other dissident writers worth discovering are **Zdeněk Urbánek** (*On the Sky's Clayey Bottom*), whose short stories offer a fantastic and often absurd view of everyday life under communism, and the scientist-poet **Miroslav Holub**. The novels of **Bohumil Hrabal** (*Closely Observed Trains*, *I Served the King of England*) are masterpieces of Czech literature, and his writing remains popular. Hrabal died in 1997 after a fall from a fifth-floor window while feeding pigeons. Though this was officially ruled an accident, many readers still wonder – a character in one of his books written decades earlier met exactly the same fate.

The new generation of Czech writers is typified by poet and novelist **Jáchym Topol**, whose *City, Sister, Silver* explores a gritty world of free-market sleaze and opportunism. **Lukáš Tomin**'s introspective *Ashtrays*, *The Doll* and *Kye* are open-ended poetic collections, whose sombre mood is true to the perpetually tangled life of a Prague intellectual. Tomin's death in an accident early in his career will diminish 21st-century Czech literature. The vivid prose of **Ewald Murrer**, collected in *The Diary of Mr Pinke* and *Dreams at the End of the Night*, is another instance of a coup by Twisted Spoon (for other new titles of Czech works in translation, *see* **Directory: Further Reference**). Two recent anthologies of strange and experimental modern Prague

Robert Eversz: on the Prague hack

Ten years ago Prague was a fine city for leading the Bohemian life of the expatriate writer, but it was a lousy place in which to actually write. The problem is that the act of committing literature is best done in boredom. Excitement distracts. Prague was a town of epic vices and virtues then. The Soviet bloc had crumbled, and the citizens imprisoned within it were oversexed and impoverished idolaters of all things Western. Nobody had any money – an ideal condition for writers – and there was nothing to buy except cigarettes and alcohol. Anyone owning a nice set of clothes and drinking imported whisky passed for rich. Writers whose fingers ached from clinging to the bottom of the economic ladder in their own countries perched at the top in Prague. Even better, people didn't laugh out loud when you told them you were writing a book.

Very few writers I knew at the time took full advantage of the cheap rents to hole up for a year to write the Great Canadian Novel. Most

of us learned to excel in the time-honoured expatriate arts of smoking, drinking, sleeping around and engaging in intense literary discussions with people who understood every fifth word of what we said, and most importantly for the expatriate writer, we practised the art of not writing. Writers drew on life experience in their work, we all knew. The more serious minded of us considered debauchery legitimate research, and thus fully tax deductible. Writer friends of mine have allowed themselves to be bilked by black market money changers and robbed by whores in hotel rooms that rent by the hour because they thought these were the kinds of experiences all writers should have. I thought I was dying of a brain tumour at the time, and later realised I was merely suffering from a chronic hangover induced by 48 consecutive nights of boozing.

We were leading the dissolute life we had read about in the books of DH Lawrence, Lawrence Durrell and Henry Miller. We all writing from multinational writers are *Daylight in Nightclub Inferno* (Catbird Press, 1997) and *This Side of Reality* (Serpent's Tail, 1996).

JOURNALS

Expat and international publications that present the best and worst of new prose and poetry, usually in instalments on no fixed schedule, are *Optimism*, a Czech and expat monthly, and *Jejune*, a journal of unorthodox new writing from varied tongues.

Trafika and the *Prague Revue* are both annuals that publish Czech and international writing, much of it never before seen in print. *One Eye Open*, a Czech/English magazine of poetry, fiction and essays, focuses on women's issues and writing. All of these publications can usually be found at the **Globe Bookstore & Coffeehouse** (*see p33, p141 and p165*).

FESTIVALS

This rich literary tradition is celebrated in Prague by numerous international writing and literary festivals. In summer, a month doesn't go by without an important writers' gathering. The action starts in April with the **Prague Writers' Festival**, a star-studded series that has brought the likes of Harold Pinter, William Styron and EL Doctorow to town. See its web page (www.pwf.pragonet.cz) for details. July sees the **Prague Summer Seminars**, run by

the University of New Orleans (check details at www.uno.edu/prague). Both hold readings open to the public, sometimes featuring well-known Czech writers with English translation.

READINGS

The Globe Bookstore and Coffeehouse

Pštrossova 6, Nové Město, Prague 1 (2491 7230/ www.globebookstore.cz). Metro Národní třída/ 6, 9, 18, 21, 22, 23 tram. **Open** 10am-midnight Mon-Thur; 10am-1am Fri, Sat; 10am-midnight Sun. **No credit cards. Map** p310 G7.

Hosts an infrequent but wonderful programme of readings. If a well-known writer is in town, it's more than likely that he or she will make an appearance here. The Globe has presented readings by Allen Ginsberg, Robert Creeley, Amy Tan, Ian McEwan and scores of other literary luminaries. *See also p141 and p165.*

Jazz Club Železná

Železná 16, Staré Město, Prague 1 (2423 9697). Metro Můstek/3, 9, 14, 24 tram. **Open** 3pm-midnight daily. **Admission** 70 Kč. **No credit cards. Map** p308 J3.

In One Voice, an irregular slam that attracts a full range of talents, is a good place to sample a mix of unpublished young foreign and Czech writers – admittedly a risky proposition. Performances may consist of live music doing audio battle with the young poets they are accompanying.

believed we could drink and fuck our way to a great novel. Our predecessors had, we thought, so why couldn't we? Regrettably, many great novels were lost when the most talented of us forgot that in order to produce a great novel one first must write it.

Prague has changed since then, and though a new generation of writers has filled the ranks of those departed to anonymity or publication, it is no longer such a fine city in which to lead the life of the expatriate writer. The Czechs have been hustled too often to be much impressed by foreigners, and their English has improved considerably, so it's more difficult to fool them with flashes of false intellect. Making things worse, rents have gone up, beer is pricier, and both men and women have become more discriminating in their choices of bed partners. It seems as if Prague is nearly a normal city now.

Not coincidentally, it has become an incredible place in which to actually write.

Stunts are king at **Stillking**.

Prague on Screen

Any time you see Nazis or musketeers in a new movie, the odds are you're watching Prague – Europe's new Hollywood does big box office.

The economics of shooting a period film in Prague have been touted in every trade journal in print: it has a highly skilled workforce, low labour costs, and a long history of technically advanced filmmaking. Add to that the biggest soundstage outside England, and you barely need to glance at the comparative shooting costs to decide: Prague's a star.

Universal, the maker of *The Bourne Identity*, (whose daily shooting costs worked out to be about $100,000 per day, as opposed to $250,000 if they had shot it in Paris), is one of a long list of recent converts. *From Hell*, *The Affair of the Necklace*, *Hart's War* and *A Knight's Tale* were all shot in or around Prague and the latter was even written with a Czech shooting in mind.

All this has meant big business for some savvy local film production companies. What it has meant for Barrandov, once a state-run enterprise (as were all businesses in these parts, of course) is a massive missed opportunity. The enormous production facility was built by President Havel's uncle during the 1930s. Located just south of the city's Smíchov district, the company was privatised early on but is now owned by a Czech steel company with no background in film.

Leaner, more canny startups, like Stillking and Milk & Honey, let out space at Barrandov and at a newer, equally impressive facility in Letnany outside Prague. These small, agile firms have built a name for themselves as a sort of who's who when you want to shoot in Prague. Unlike the monolithic Barrandov, which has gone through a series of directors and has been too slow to grow its facilities to match demand, companies like Stillking speak the language of Hollywood moguls. They give good meetings, they do lunch, they know who to call when *Plunkett & Macleane* wants to use the Czech Parliament building for a backdrop and explode a truckload of fireworks there besides.

SHINING STAR OF STILLKING

Matthew Stilllman, head of Stillking, came to Prague in 1993 with $500 in his pocket and a typewriter under his arm, according to the company's official bio. Though that rings a bit of Hollywood in itself, there can be no denying the company's success. In addition to being responsible for Prague shoots on most of the films mentioned above, the firm spends just as much time producing commercials for a variety of top agencies throughout the Western world. All told, Stillking brings in about $5 million annually these days and it's grown so fast it now has offices around the globe, including Milan, Krakow and Los Angeles.

Athough many of Stillking's fortunes come from the West Coast, it's Prague's differences from LA that are the major selling point in Tinsel Town. For one thing, although there's a highly skilled and educated workforce in the Czech Republic, labour unions have no real power here. It is the same factor that has made Mexico such an appealing place to shoot in recent years. Prague is also infamous for its dreary weather but even the depressing climate and short summers seem to have been turned to the city's advantage, as they are ideal for period film shoots. The great thing about dream sequences and flashbacks to the 19th century is, 'They're always dank and grey, aren't they?' Stillman posits.

Even so, it's commercial films that pay the rent and the ones shot here, apart from the inevitable war films, tend increasingly to be modern action movies. Prague production companies are well set up for these films by now, of course, so there's no difficulty in finding the staff you need to shoot even complex stunts in downtown Prague.

But more personally rewarding projects are also in the pipeline – and Stillking isn't waiting for Universal to approach him with a few fresh ideas. Instead, he's turned to what may just be Prague's best untapped resource yet: its well-developed community of writers. The company is moving into a new phase, actively developing original scripts with local writers for eventual production by some of the impressive directors and West Coast moguls with whom Stillking has built up a rapport. The projects are closely guarded but rumour has it there just might be a gripping new Golem tale among them, in addition to several thrillers, a few comedies and some nostalgic pieces.

Stillking is also one of the top contenders for the possible purchase of Barrandov, a prospect that has many parties lobbying and lunching furiously. Though it would be a massive undertaking to moderdise and expand the studios, most film insiders in Prague believe that, with proper direction and some well-planned growth to meet demand, it is very likely that Barrandov could still become a major success – a gold mine, in fact.

HOLLYWOOD EAST

As a newly star-studded capital, Prague is taking the movie glitz in its stride. Nobody registers much shock when Bruce Willis shows up at the Italian restaurant Cicala, or when Samuel L Jackson takes up the next seat along at a casino (turns out he's a bit of a sullen gambler, though). When strolling idly through the quaint, cobblestoned streets of the Malá Strana district, you should never be too surprised to suddenly come across troops in WWII Wermacht uniforms marching around carrying swastika banners. On an evening walk in front of Prague Castle on a mild summer night you may well find your quietude rudely interrupted by an encounter with the French Revolution, complete with galloping horses and the sound of flintlocks firing.

When helicopters are looping around overhead all day, it's most like not a military exercise or a police surveillance but an elaborate stunt being shot along the Vltava river. The city has become good at transmuting intelf into other things as needed. With such a long history of foreign occupations, perhaps Prague has become good at being a chameleon.

But quite apart from the city making the perfect backdrop and the question of economics, it's easy to persuade big-time stars to come to Prague for a shoot. In one recent interview with the Czech Radio 1, the Hughes brothers, who made the new Jack the Ripper tale *From Hell*, spoke at length about the frustrations of shooting in Hollywood, or even in America, where too many filmmaking decisions are made by marketing teams and careful investors who are afraid to deviate from a proven formula.

By the interview's end, the respected filmmaking team were ready to announce they were considering giving up on LA life entirely and moving to Prague.

The Czech Republic has come a long way since a testy Tom Cruise (who also had to admit he liked Prague itself) ripped the city's film industry as primitive during interviews about *Mission: Impossible*. Since then a galaxy of other stars has made shooting in the city as fashionable as mudbath treatments in Palm Springs. And a good deal more exotic. As Mark Wolper, exec producer of *The Mists of Avalon*, put it, 'Prague sounds sexy and in and hip.'

It would seem there's just no other city that looks quite so good in a screentest. Prague is ready for its close-up, dear.

Prague-spotting 101

You may not realise it, but you probably know Prague quite well. Anyone's who caught Bille August's 1998 *Les Misérables* has taken in the time-frozen streets just above Prague Castle. That's where Liam Neeson's Jean Valjean was first found sleeping by the kindly priest in the film. Conveniently around the corner, on Hradčanské náměstí, the French Revolution later transpired. The sgraffitoed walls of **Schwartzenberg Palace** (*see p116*) are clearly visible in the background.

Viewers of the Johnny Depp movie, *From Hell*, one of the most technically elaborate films recently shot in Prague, will have a harder time recognising the foggy exteriors. That's because they don't exist. A six-block area was built as a mock-up of Whitechapel for the film, with cobblestones rented from the City of Prague. The **National Museum** (*see p118*) does turn up, standing in as a government chamber building in the film.

Of course the classic and best introduction to Prague is to rent *Amadeus* from the local video store. The **Estates Theatre** (*see p234*), numerous streets in the Malá Strana district and more than one Prague palace act as backdrops for this pre-Velvet Revolution shoot by Czech-born director Miloš Forman.

Steven Soderbergh's *Kafka*, based loosely on the life of the famous writer who lived in Prague, is less well-known, but also makes good use of Prague as a soundstage, one of the first films to do so after the end of communism. Disney's *Swing Kids* followed, which also relied on the city's historical-looking backdrops.

No film has shown the city off better than *Mission: Impossible*, though. This 1996 production featured Tom Cruise running around the Charles Bridge and through the Prague metro system, at one point calling in the Prague river police team, who instantly responded in speedboats. Czech audiences had a good laugh at that scene – local police never do anything fast and the Vtava river is so broken up by weirs that it's not navigable unless you have several hours to wait in locks. Sadly the restaurant featured in the film with the exploding fish tank was pure fantasy – tour guides invariably have to disappoint visitors who want to eat there.

Despite Tom Cruise's well-publicised complaints about shooting troubles in the city while making of *Mission: Impossible*,

Depp in *From Hell*.

the city was on screen again shortly after, this time as London of old for *Plunkett & Macleane*, the stylistic tale of highwaymen starring Robert Carlyle and Liv Tyler. The climax scene occurs in Wallenstein Gardens, which are attached to the Czech Parliament building. Getting permission to shoot there took some work, but the well-connected Prague-based production company StillKing managed it – in part by promising the city a $30,000 refurbishment of Prague's major icon, the Charles Bridge, in return.

Prague turns up again as medieval London in *A Knight's Tale*, another historical piece full of intentional anachronisms, featuring Heath Ledger and Shannyn Sossamon. And the city's mix-and-match architecture, with a few computer-generated additions, was found to be perfect for the fantasy world of *Dungeons & Dragons*, which brought *Kafka* star Jeremy Irons back to town.

Prague-spotting at the movies is bound to become more tricky in the future as reality blends with more sophisticated artificial sets and digital enhancements. The most recent megafilm to shoot in Prague, the extreme sports/espionage drama *XXX*, starring Vin Diesel, relied even more heavily on a vast, newly modernised studio complex opened outside the city, housed in a factory that used to make MiG fighter planes.

Accommodation

Accommodation

Plush rooms and pampering are on the rise, as are improved backpacker crashes, but there's little exciting middle ground.

Prague may be a budget traveller's dream come true with its cheap eats, rock gigs and abundant hostels. But those wanting anything more than the basics will find that the average summer hotel price – more than $90 a night – makes Prague one of the former Eastern bloc's most expensive cities to sleep in. The Czech capital runs over with tourists when the weather is fine and rooms then are at a premium, which keeps prices high. However, thanks to a recent spate of hotel building, competition is especially rigorous in the off-season (October-March), so this is the best time to get a deal on a room.

Though a few traces of the bad old days remain at some of the cheaper pensions, the days of scarce amenities are long gone. In fact, few European capitals can claim a better range of well-appointed lodgings these days, with everything from French soap and Belgian waffles to jacuzzi baths and goose-down duvets.

That's not to say that everything is rosy now, especially if you fall in between the two main categories of visitors to Prague – the down-at-heel and the very well-heeled. Backpackers can choose from dozens of hostels and hundreds of spare rooms, many of which sprout like dandelions every summer only to wither with the autumn. Those at the other end of the spectrum enjoy a wide choice of luxury hotels. But the situation mid-spectrum still needs improvement.

The good news is the growing number of hotels and pensions where, for less than 4,000 Kč, you can get a decent room for two with bath, breakfast and all the German TV you can watch. True, the room may have bright orange curtains, red plastic rotary phones and the smell of antiseptic, but even the cheapies are showing fewer traces of the pre-1989 days.

INFORMATION AND BOOKING

Prague has a diverse profusion of renovated or brand-new hotels, from medieval, family-run inns to giant, corporate-owned multi-star hotels. Many hotels give discounts to groups and for longer stays (normally around ten days or more); rooms are generally 20-40 per cent cheaper off-season, and many deluxe hotels give 10-20 per cent discounts in July and August when business travel dwindles. Smaller places may offer a significant reduction for cash payment,

or a hefty credit card surcharge. Try to establish this, preferably with hard-copy confirmation, before you arrive.

Service at the higher end hotels is comparable to that in any European capital. That is not the case at some of the more moderate hotels, where the staff can give the impression that it is your privilege to stay with them. As is the case at luxury hotels worldwide, you can get hit with ludicrous charges for both local and international phone calls. Watch out also for the taxis that cluster around the hotel entrances: for these hustlers, a taxi meter is a jackpot that always pays out. If the hotel has its own fleet, it's a better option, although charges may still be double those set for regular city taxis. Hotels are also infamous for refusing to call honest taxi services for guests, such as **AAA** or **Profi** (*see* **Directory: Getting Around**), because they're in on the game.

Even with all the new accommodation that has sprouted, rooms in Prague have still not caught up with summer demand. If you come to the city in peak months without reservations, expect to pound the pavement for hours before you find a clean, well-lit place. Even off-peak, it's still wise to book ahead.

All deluxe hotels have English-speaking staff; those at cheaper establishments may struggle, though you can usually make yourself understood. Many hotels can arrange airport pick-ups for a fixed price, which will save you time, money and hassle.

PRICES AND CLASSIFICATION

Hotels are classified below according to their cheapest double room; prices include breakfast, unless stated otherwise. Note that these prices are usually only available off-season and also be aware that some of the more upmarket hotels fix their room rates in euros or US dollars. For ease of use we have converted all prices into Czech crowns, but exchange-rate fluctuations may affect these.

Hotels are listed by area and our price categories work as follows: a **Deluxe** hotel is one in which the cheapest double room costs 8,000 Kč or more per night; an **Expensive** hotel costs 6,000-8,000 Kč; **Moderate** is 3,000-6,000 Kč; **Budget** hotels cost under 3,000 Kč; and **Hostels** are grouped together.

All rooms in the 'Deluxe' and 'Expensive' categories have an en suite bathroom. This also applies to the 'Moderate' category, unless otherwise stated. Facilities in other categories vary – it's always best to check exactly what you'll be getting when you book. Longer-term accommodation is covered at the end of the chapter (*see p57*), and a selection of hotels that are particularly welcoming to gay people is listed in the **Gay & Lesbian** chapter.

Accommodation agencies

Unless otherwise noted, the following agencies will organise private accommodation in flats and can also book hostel beds, pensions and hotels at no extra charge. Think about getting a flat outside the city centre: it can cut the cost of accommodation by around 35 per cent. **Travellers' Hostel** (*see p51*) in Old Town functions as a booking office for a whole network of hostels.

Ave
Hlavní nádraží, Wilsonova 8, Nové Město, Prague 2 (2422 3521/3226/fax 2423 0783/www.avetravel.cz). Metro Hlavní nádraží. **Open** 6am-11pm daily. **Credit** AmEx, DC, MC, V. **Map** p309 M5.

Situated inside the city's main rail station, this is probably Prague's most convenient option for those who are arriving by train or at a late hour and have no place to go.
Branches: Na příkopě 16, Nové Město, Prague 1 (2422 6087); Ruzyně Airport, Prague 6 (2011 4650); Nádraží Holešovice, Prague 7 (6671 0514); Old Town Bridge Tower (Staroměstská Mostecká věž), Křižovnické náměstí, Staré Město, Prague 1 (5753 1591) (summer only); Staroměstské náměstí 2, Staré Město, Prague 1 (2422 3613).

Čedok
Na Příkopě 18, Staré Město, Prague 1 (2419 7111/ fax 2421 6324/www.cedok.cz). Metro Můstek or Náměstí Republiky/3, 5, 8, 9, 14, 24 tram. **Open** 9am-7pm Mon-Fri; 9.30am-2.30pm Sat, Sun. **Credit** AmEx, DC, MC, V. **Map** p306 K4.
The oldest travel agency in the country, Čedok still has the best variety of accommodation for visitors to choose from.

City of Prague Accommodation Service
Haštalská 7, Staré Město, Prague 1 (2481 3022/ fax 2231 6640/www.apartmentforrent.cz). Metro Náměstí Republiky/5, 8, 14 tram. **Open** 10am-1pm, 2-7pm daily. **No credit cards.** **Map** p308 J2.
A reputable firm offering a range of private apartments and rooms.

The best Hotels

For a romantic weekend
Residence Nosticova (*see p46*), **Romantik Hotel U raka** (*see p41*), **U krále Karla** (*see p42*) and **Hotel U páva** (*see p45*).

For straying off the beaten path
Pension Dientzenhofer (*see p46*) and **Hotel 16 U sv. Kateřiny** (*see p53*).

For old-world atmosphere
U Červeného Lva (*see p42*) and **U zlaté studny** (*see p50*).

For deals your travel agent's never heard of
Betlem Club (*see p50*), **Hotel U Klenotníka** (*see p50*), **U krále Jiřího** (*see p50*) and **U Šuterů** (*see p53*).

For hostelling in style
Klub Habitat (*see p54*) and **Travellers' Hostel** (*see p51*).

For fine dining
Four Seasons Hotel Prague (*see p47*), **Radisson SAS** (*see p51*) and **Mövenpick** (*see p54*).

For a luxurious bath
Hotel Adria Prague (*see p52*), **Hotel Paříž Praha** (*see p47*) and **Hotel U Prince** (*see p49*).

For meeting some interesting characters
The Clown & Bard (*see p57*) and **Charles University Dorms** (*see p53*).

For a taste of the pre-Velvet Revolution days
Grand Hotel Evropa (*see p52*).

For getting away from it all
Hostel Boathouse (*see p57*) and **Pension Větrník** (*see p57*).

For Žižkov pubbing
Arcotel Hotel Teatrino (*see p55*), **Hotel Tříska** (*see p56*), **Hotel Sieber** (*see p56*) and **The Clown & Bard** (*see p57*).

For a good workout
Hotel Axa (*see p53*), **Diplomat Hotel Praha** (*see p54*), **Inter-Continental** (*see p47*) and **Marriott** (*see p51*).

E-Travel

Ostrovní 7, Nové Město, Prague 1 (2499 0990/0991/ fax 2499 0999/www.travel.cz). Metro Národní třída/6, 9, 17, 18, 22, 23 tram. **Open** 8am-8pm daily. **Credit** AmEx, DC, MC, V. **Map** p310 G6.

A veteran Prague agency that can book two- to five-star hotels, pensions, apartments and hostels and offers free airport transfer with advance bookings. Also handy for booking rooms in other Czech cities.

Mary's Accommodation Service

Italská 31, Vinohrady, Prague 2 (2225 4007/fax 2225 2215/www.marys.cz). Metro Náměstí Míru/ 11 tram. **Open** 9am-9pm daily. **Credit** AmEx, MC, V. **Map** p311 M7.

A friendly, English-speaking, low- to mid-priced agency that places visitors in pensions, hotels and private apartments throughout the city. The minimum rate is for two people, and all reservations must be guaranteed with a credit card (for which a surcharge is added). Generally, breakfast is not included in the prices.

Prague Accommodations

Petřínská 4, Prague 5 (5151 2502/ www.pragueaccommodations.com).

It makes no sense to visit this new apartment and pension company in person – either book by phone or online before you come. Although the agency has only a handful of properties, they include some of the most centrally located and elegant historic buildings that you could possibly stay in. Prices range from cheap to moderate, depending on how many people stay in one apartment.

RHIA Agency

Školská 1 (at Žitná 17), Nové Město, Prague 2 (2223 0858/3190/fax 2223 2506/www.rhia.cz). Metro IP Pavlova, Můstek or Národní třída/3, 9, 14, 16, 22, 23, 24 tram. **Open** 10am-8pm daily. **Credit** AmEx, MC, V. **Map** p310 J7.

A full-service travel agency offering great alternatives to hostels for just a bit more dosh. Staff can arrange accommodation with safe parking, and you can also change currency here.

Stop City

Vinohradská 24, Vinohrady, Prague 2 (2252 1233/ fax 2252 1252/www.stopcity.com). Metro Muzeum or Náměstí Míru/11 tram. **Open** Apr-Oct 10am-9pm daily. *Nov-Mar* 11am-8pm daily. **Credit** AmEx, MC, V. **Map** p311 M6.

Stop City's helpful, incredibly patient staff will book you into a pension, hotel, private room or apartment starting at less than 500 Kč per person. They don't handle hostel bookings but are willing to make reservations for callers from abroad, provided a credit card number is given via fax.

Hradčany

Some of Prague's most romantic and atmospheric lodgings are nestled around Prague Castle in Hradčany, though budget options are scarce. Hotels round here tend to be small and may lack the gadgetry a business traveller needs. Hiking uphill to your bed on a Castle lane could be a bit of a bother – or it could be the best aid to digesting a heavy old-fashioned Czech dinner and put a romantic finish on your day.

Deluxe

Hotel Savoy

Keplerova 6, Prague 1 (2430 2430/fax 2430 2128/ www.hotel-savoy.cz). Tram 22, 23. **Rooms** 61. **Rates** 7,200-9,900 Kč; doubles from 9,000 Kč; 3,000 Kč extra bed. **Credit** AmEx, DC, MC, V. **Map** p306 A3.

Stepping into the dignified lobby, complete with reading room and fireplace, it may seem hard to imagine this as a haven for prima donna celebs such as Tina Turner and Princess Caroline of Monaco. But this is a peaceful bastion of first-class service with tasteful, modern rooms. Standard rooms are spacious, and the deluxes amount almost to a suite. **Hotel services** *Beauty salon. Disabled: adapted room. Gym. Interpreting services. Jacuzzi. No-smoking rooms.* **Room services** *Dataport. Fax. Room service (24hrs). TV: pay movies/satellite. VCR.*

Expensive

Romantik Hotel U raka

Černínská 10, Prague 1 (2051 1100/fax 3335 8041/ www.romantikhotels.com). Tram 22, 23. **Rooms** 6. **Rates** 6,200-7,200 Kč single; 6,900-7,900 Kč double; 8,900 Kč triple. **Credit** AmEx, MC, V. **Map** p304 A2.

Dating back to 1739, this small, rustic pension is a good choice for couples with time to spare. It's located a short stroll from the Castle and within earshot of the bells of the Loreto. There are just six rooms here – two in the main house and four adjacent cottages – plus a beautiful breakfast room/inn/ café/reading room with brick hearth. Invariably booked out, so reserve well in advance. No children under 12. No bar.
Hotel services *Air-conditioning. Limousine service. Parking. Safe.* **Room services** *Room service (6am-8pm).*

Moderate

Dům U velké boty

Vlašská 30, Prague 1 (5753 2088/fax 5753 3234/ www.volweb.cz/rippl). Metro Malostranská/12, 22 tram. **Rooms** 8. **Rates** (excl breakfast) 1,800 Kč single; 3,000-3,760 Kč double; 4,100 Kč suite; 500 Kč extra bed. **No credit cards. Map** p306 C3.

This charming family-run house is hidden away in the thick of Malá Strana. Attentive service and loads of gorgeous period furniture make this a perfect nest from which to explore romantic Prague. The house dates back to 1470 and has recently had a thorough renovation from walls to furniture trim. It has also

The inn-side dope

One typical overcast day in Prague in the early '90s, Charlotte Ripple (*pictured*) was out shopping for antique furniture to give her newly restored pension just the right aristocratic touch. The owner of **Dům U velké boty** (*see p41*), possibly the most inviting pension in the cobblestone cradle of Malá Strana, was particularly keen on a crystal chandelier that she uncovered in a pile of merchandise at an obscure antique dealer. After examining the glass artefact more closely, the fledgling hotelier received the shock of the decade: the carefully catalogued chandelier had been a fixture in her family home for centuries. It had sparkled at the mansion-turned-pension before the communists seized the property – stealing all of its precious belongings in the process.

For 50 years the state controlled the house because Charlotte Ripple's father had been considered too bourgeois. Then the remarkable home across from the German Embassy was restituted to the Ripple family by the post-communist government, an act of financial reconciliation that has brought tremendous rewards and challenges to families across the Czech Republic.

Luckily for visitors, many entrepreneurs like the Ripples are unable to come up with the millions of crowns required to renovate and maintain a house that dates back to medieval times without turning it into a profit-making venture: a boutique hotel. Better still for guests, the Ripples and other such innkeepers must adhere to strict standards of preservation, so that the authenticity of architecture is not in any way impinged upon by replaced floors, for example, or the creation of a breakfast nook. From marble fixtures and ceiling frescoes to wrought iron banisters and vaulted arcades, the countless historic boutique hotels that are flourishing in Prague, none of which existed prior to the 1989 Velvet Revolution, provide guests with a museum-quality stay.

That's not to say the former East bloc tackiness hasn't overshadowed some efforts to preserve original character. Unlike the Ripples, who painstakingly searched for period furnishings that complemented their home's Renaissance interior, more than a handful of proprietors, eager to make fast cash, maintain historic façades but choose 1970s-style carpets and fixtures. Guests at such places sometimes wonder if they've

been frequented by many European writers, artists and actors. There's no big sign, so look for the 'Ripple' buzzer. Breakfast is an extra 200 Kč.
Hotel services *Fax. Gym. Laundry.*

U Červeného Lva

Nerudova 41, Prague 1 (5753 3832/fax 5753 2746/www.hotelredlion.com). Metro Malostranská/12, 22 tram. **Rooms** 8. **Rates** 3,500-6,300 Kč single; 3,900-6,900 Kč double; 800-1,000 Kč extra bed. **Credit** AmEx, MC, V. **Map** p306 D3.
There are few small hotels on the royal route leading up to the Castle that can boast such authentic 17th-century decor, including colourful hand-painted vaulted ceilings. This reconstructed burgher's house provides guests with a sense of Prague during the Renaissance.
Hotel services *Bar. Parking (off-site). Restaurants (3).* **Room services** *Minibar. Safe. TV: satellite.*

U krále Karla

Úvoz 4, Prague 1 (5753 2869/3594/fax 5753 3591/www.romantichotels.cz). Metro Malostranská/12, 22 tram. **Rooms** 19. **Rates** 4,550-6,100 Kč single; 5,200-6,900 Kč double; 7,000-7,900 Kč suite; 1,100 Kč extra bed. **Credit** AmEx, MC, V. **Map** p304 C3.
The solid oak furnishings, painted vaulted ceilings, stained-glass windows and various baroque trea-

sures lend this hotel the feel of an aristocratic country house. In fact, it was once owned by the Benedictine order. If the daily hike up the hill from the tram seems daunting, try U krále Karla's cousin, Hotel U páva (*see p45*), opposite the Vojanovy Gardens. Major discounts for payment in cash are sometimes available here.
Hotel services *Babysitting. Parking. Solarium.* **Room services** *Room service. Safe.*

Zlatá Hvězda

Nerudova 48, Prague 1 (5753 2867/fax 5753 3624/www.hotelgoldenstar.com). Metro Malostranská/12, 22 tram. **Rooms** 26. **Rates** 3,500-6,300 Kč single; 3,900-6,900 Kč double; 800-1,000 Kč extra bed. **Credit** AmEx, MC, V. **Map** p306 C3.
This fairytale house – standing in the shadow of Prague Castle on the celebrated royal road – attracts the attention of visitors daily, who wonder if it is a tourist attraction. Known in English as the 'golden star', the hotel dates to 1372, when it belonged to the mayor of the Hradčany district. A reconstruction in 2000 preserved the house's original architectural elements, including vaulted ceilings and a spiral staircase. Period furniture makes guests feel they are staying in a museum. Several stunning views. Service is adequate, if a bit frosty.

slipped down a surreal rabbit hole. Such can be the consequences when, unlike the hospitable Ripples, owners don't live on the third floor of their own hotel.

If booking from abroad, the best way to protect yourself from such an aesthetic let-down, assuming the place is not reviewed herein, is to check out the inn's website or ask the staff about decor before reserving.

As for the chandelier, Ripple re-acquired it – for a price – and it is now the proud (and only original) item in Dům U velké boty. With one possible exception: Ripple's husband says that there was another reason they stuck to the original style of the home: 'Get rid of the home's character, get rid of its history, and you get rid of the ghosts.' At Dům U velké boty, hauntings come at no additional charge.

Hotel services *Internet. Laundry. Parking (off-site). Restaurant.* **Room services** *Minibar. Safe. TV: satellite.*

Malá Strana

Second only to Hradčany in views and atmosphere, Malá Strana is filled with evocative little inns and pensions that are much easier to ramble back to after a long day out – it's only a stroll across Charles Bridge from all the entertainments of Old Town. Although the district attracts a steady flow of tourists, many of its backstreets have remained blissfully untouched by modern times. They don't feature many bars or much nightlife, however.

Expensive

Hotel Hoffmeister

Pod Bruskou 7, Prague 1 (5101 7111/fax 5101 7100/www.hoffmeister.cz). Metro Malostranská/12, 18, 22 tram. **Rooms** 38. **Rates** (excl breakfast) 4,500-11,880 Kč single; 6,120-11,880 Kč double; extra bed (only in some rooms) 1,440 Kč. **Credit** AmEx, DC, MC, V. **Map** p307 F1.

This is a good option for those who are more interested in exploring romantic Prague than in networking and closing a deal. It's situated on a busy junction, but the soundproofed windows are effective. The lobby and rooms are filled with original works by artist Adolf Hoffmeister, father of the present owner. Downstairs you'll find a superb wine bar that has a cosy, 1920s speakeasy feel and a well-thought-out selection of Moravian and international vintages. Breakfast costs extra.
Hotel services: *Air-conditioning. Babysitting. Business services. Disabled: adapted room. Limousine service. Parking. Safe. Terrace.* **Room services**: *Dataport. Room service (7am-midnight).*

Rezidence Lundborg

U Lužického semináře 3, Prague 1 (5701 1911/fax 5701 1966/www.lundborg.cz). Metro Malostranská/ 12, 22 tram. **Suites** 13. **Rates** 5,400-28,800 Kč; doubles from 6,000 Kč. **Credit** AmEx, DC, MC, V. **Map** 305 F3.

With a prime view of Charles Bridge, and built on the site of the older Juditin Bridge, this new Scandinavian-owned hotel exudes luxury and charm. A prime example of the executive residence/hotel hybrid, Rezidence Lundborg pampers its guests with 13 suites, each a distinct and tasteful blend of recon-

structed Renaissance decor and modern business amenities. It's a major splashout, but every conceivable need has been anticipated from wine cellar to free internet. The desk will efficiently arrange anything else you can think of asking for.
Hotel services *Air-conditioning. Bar. Internet.*
Room services *Dataport. Fax. Jacuzzi. Kitchenette. Minibar. Safe. Stereo. TV: satellite.*

U Tří pštrosů

Dražického náměstí 12, Prague 1 (5753 2410/ fax 5753 3217/www.utripstrosu.cz). Metro Malostranská/12, 22 tram. **Rooms** 18.
Rates 5,300-5,900 Kč single; 7,300-7,900 Kč double; 12,000-15,000 Kč suite; 1,200 Kč extra bed.
Credit AmEx, DC, MC, V. **Map** p307 E3.
This hotel's location at the foot of Charles Bridge may scare away some who fear the non-stop din of tourists shrieking 'This is just like Disney World!' in 34 different languages, but once you're inside the noise factor is surprisingly minimal. Unfortunately, service has slipped several notches recently, but the 18 rooms are pretty, with original ceiling beams giving a rustic feel. The stairs are steep, so this is not a good choice for the less agile. If you want a view of the bridge, ask for it.
Hotel services *Babysitting. Parking.*
Room services *Internet. Minibar. Room service (7am-midnight). Safe. TV: satellite.*

Moderate

Best Western Kampa Hotel

Všehrdova 16, Prague 1 (5732 0508/0837/fax 5732 0262/www.euroagentur.cz). Metro Malostranská/ 12, 22 tram. **Rooms** 84. **Rates** 3,400-4,900 Kč single; 4,460-5,800 Kč double; 5,700-7,500 Kč triple.
Credit AmEx, DC, MC, V. **Map** p307 E5.
Located on a quiet backstreet in Malá Strana, the Kampa has retained its 17th-century architecture and style through recent renovations. Rooms are elegantly arranged. The vaulted 'Knights Hall' dining room and outdoor garden restaurant offer Czech and international cuisine. Small stylish salons are available for special events.
Hotel services *Laundry. Limousine service. Parking. Restaurant (garden). Safe.*
Room services *Internet. Minibar. TV: satellite.*

The Blue Key

Letenská 14, Prague 1 (5753 4361/fax 5753 4372/ www.bluekey.cz). Metro Malostranská/12, 22 tram.
Rooms 28. **Rates** 2,400-4,200 Kč single; 3,000-5,100 Kč double; 4,950-8,250 Kč suite; 900-1,200 Kč extra bed; under-14s free with 2 adults.
Credit AmEx, MC, V. **Map** p307 E3.
This 14th-century townhouse is the sort of place that ordinary Praguers used to live in before the free market brought with it skyrocketing housing costs. In the refit, rooms were kitted out in restrained Italian furnishings with, yes, a blue colour scheme. Most rooms and suites come with kitchenettes. Ask for a room facing the courtyard rather than one

overlooking busy Letenská. The lower rates apply from January to March.
Hotel services *Internet. No-smoking rooms. Sauna. Whirlpools (2).* **Room services** *Fridge. Safe. TV: satellite.*

Hotel Čertovka

U Lužického semináře 2, Prague 1 (5753 2235/fax 5753 4392/www.certovka.cz). Metro Malostranská/ 12, 22 tram. **Rooms** 21. **Rates** 3,690-3,990 Kč single; 4,920-5,607 Kč double; 1,290 Kč extra bed.
Credit AmEx, MC, V. **Map** p307 F2.
Few hotels in the heart of Malá Strana can match the location, price and romance of this boutique hotel. Opened in 2000, it's named after the little canal that it sits on. Formerly a baroque mansion, it's been transformed by the Richmond Group into an upscale hideaway at reasonable prices. Rooms provide views of Prague Castle and the Charles Bridge tower. The most romantic room, albeit without a bathtub, fronts the canal. Furnishings are tastefully modern with hints of 18th-century poshness. A wrought iron staircase railing and velvet curtains help to carry the aristocratic theme throughout. Another bonus is that the staff are warm and attentive.
Hotel services *Disabled: adapted room.* **Room services** *Dataport. Minibar. Safe. TV: satellite.*

Hotel Pod Věží

Mostecká 2, Prague 1 (5753 2041/2060/fax 5753 2069/www.podvezi.com). Metro Malostranská/12, 22 tram. **Rooms** 12. **Rates** 4,500-5,000 Kč single; 5,500-6,800 Kč double; 7,500-8,900 Kč suite; 1,000 Kč extra bed. **Credit** AmEx, DC, MC, V. **Map** p307 E3.
Enthusiastically styling itself as 'a place of retreat for the visitor, service for the guest who – as we know – is the messenger of joy', this is a good option for tourists who want to be in the thick of Malá Strana. The hotel is a few cobblestones further from Charles Bridge than U Tří pštrosů (*see above*) and offers slightly lower prices, if less ye olde charm. The standard room, called a suite, is really a deluxe double; the two 'double' rooms have twin beds.
Hotel services *Babysitting. Garden. Parking.*
Room services *Internet. Room service (11am-10pm). Safe. TV: satellite. VCR.*

Hotel U páva

U Lužického semináře 32, Prague 1 (5753 3573/ fax 5753 0919/www.romantichotels.cz). Metro Malostranská/12, 22 tram. **Rooms** 27.
Rates 4,300-6,400 Kč single; 4,500-6,900 Kč double; 6,900-7,900 Kč suite; 1,100 Kč extra bed.
Credit AmEx, MC, V. **Map** p307 F3.
The dark oak ceilings and crystal chandeliers don't synthesise as well here as at U krále Karla (also owned by Karel Klubal; *see p42*), where the elegance is seamless, but the ideal location in a serene corner of Malá Strana makes one quite forgiving. Suites 201, 301, 401 and 402 look on to the Castle, but some other rooms are dark and viewless. The adjacent house was converted in 2000 into an annexe with an additional 27 plush rooms.

Baroque chic at **U Červeného Lva**. *See p42.*

Hotel services *Limousine service. Massage. No-smoking rooms. Parking. Restaurant. Sauna.* **Room services** *Internet. Room service (7.30am-10pm).*

Na Kampě 15

Na Kampě 15, Prague 1 (5753 1432/fax 5753 3168/ www.nakampe15.cz). Metro Malostranská/12, 22 tram. **Rooms** 26. **Rates** 3,600-5,400 Kč single; 4,000-5,800 Kč double; 5,400-7,200 Kč apartment; 500-1,000 Kč extra bed. **Credit** AmEx, DC, MC, V. **Map** p307 F4.

This Kampa Island venture affords some fine views of Charles Bridge and Old Town, yet it's situated at a sufficient distance from the bridge to provide its guests with some peace and quiet. The management has done a sensitive restoration job on what used to be a 15th-century tavern that brewed one of the city's pioneering beers. The guest rooms feature exposed beams and garret windows alongside modern furnishings. The cellar restaurant and beer garden out the back offer a reasonably varied menu and a good assortment of Czech and French wines.
Hotel services *Bar. Garden. Restaurant.* **Room services** *Minibar. Safe. TV: satellite.*

Pension Dientzenhofer

Nosticova 2, Prague 1 (5731 1319/fax 5732 0888/ www.dientzenhofer.cz). Metro Malostranská/12, 22 tram. **Rooms** 9. **Rates** 2,750-3,100 Kč single; 3,600-3,950 Kč double; 600 Kč extra bed. **Credit** AmEx, DC, MC, V. **Map** p307 E4.

Tucked away off a busy street, this 16th-century house is the birthplace of one of the greatest baroque architects, Kilian Ignaz Dientzenhofer, whose work fills this quarter of the city. The quiet courtyard and back garden offer a lovely respite in the midst of Malá Strana while rooms are bright and the staff friendly. Book well ahead, though, as it invariably fills up for summer.
Hotel services *Airport/railway station shuttle (for fee). Bar. Internet. Laundry. Parking.* **Room services** *Minibar. Room service (24hrs). TV: satellite.*

Residence Nosticova

Nosticova 1, Prague 1 (5731 2513/fax 5731 2517/ www.nosticova.com). Metro Malostranská/12, 22 tram. **Rooms** 10. **Rates** 4,860-6,360 Kč suite; 7,140-10,920 Kč large suite. **Credit** AmEx, DC, MC, V. **Map** p307 E4.

A classy little nook for those who plan to stay longer, this recently modernised baroque 'residence' is on a quiet lane just off Kampa Island. The suites range from ample to capacious and come with antique furniture, bathrooms big enough to swim in and, best of all, fully equipped kitchenettes. Two have working fireplaces. If you don't feel like cooking your own, continental breakfast is served in the elegant wine bar for an extra charge. No restaurant.
Hotel services *Parking.* **Room services** *Internet (on request). Kitchenettes. Minibar. Safe.*

Budget

U červené sklenice

Na Kampě 10, Prague 1 (5753 3158/fax 5753 2918/ www.hotel-kampa.cz). Metro Malostranská/12, 22, 23 tram. **Rooms** 5. **Rates** 2,900-4,600 Kč single/double; 3,300-5,200 Kč apartment. **Credit** V. **Map** p307 F4.

There's nothing fancy at this tiny baroque house on Kampa Island, but if you're fascinated by parades of Charles Bridge walkers, this is the place to be. Two rooms face the bridge and two face the recently prettied-up Na Kampě Square. The outdoor café is handy, though the restaurant is cramped. Significant discounts from January to April.
Hotel services *Bar. Restaurant.* **Room services** *Minibar. TV: satellite.*

Hostels

Hostel Sokol

Újezd 450, Prague 1 (5700 7397/fax 5700 7340). Metro Malostranská/12, 22 tram. **Beds** 90. **Open** 24hrs daily. **Rates** 270 Kč per person. **No credit cards. Map** p307 E5.

Supremely cheap lodging in an ideal location. Follow a labyrinth of halls through the Sokol sports centre to get to reception. There you'll finally find the reception desk you've found budget travel paradise. Great terrace for beer-sipping with a view. Not far from the Castle and Charles Bridge.
Hostel services *Bedding. Kitchen. Lockers. Terrace.*

Staré Město

You can't do better for pubbing and clubbing than Old Town but you do pay for the convenience in room rates, and at some locations in noise and crowds. Large, modern and central hotels abound in this right bank district. Fine restaurants and galleries are also most highly concentrated here, as is much of Prague's more alternative shopping.

Deluxe

Casa Marcello

Řásnovka 783, Prague 1 (2231 1230/fax 2231 3323/ www.casa-marcello.cz). Metro Náměstí Republiky/5, 8, 14 tram. **Rooms** 32. **Rates** 8,280 Kč single/double; 10,440 Kč junior suite; 11,880 Kč apartment; 1,440 Kč extra bed. **Credit** AmEx, DC, MC, V. **Map** p308 J2.
This rambling hotel wedged into an untrafficked Old Town nook has a picturesque location almost impossible to find without a large map. The owners know how good it is, though, and charge accordingly. Although opened less than a decade ago, the hotel feels older, with clunky furniture and carpets in need of cleaning. There's no lift, and some rooms lack air-conditioning. Better-equipped rooms can be had more cheaply elsewhere, but for atmosphere, look no further.
Hotel services *Bar. Garden. Gym. No-smoking rooms. Restaurant. Sauna.* **Room services** *Dataport. Minibar. TV: satellite.*

Four Seasons Hotel Prague

Veleslavínova 2A, Prague 1 (2142 7000/fax 2142 6000/www.fourseasons.com/prague). Metro Staroměstská/17, 18 tram. **Rooms** 162. **Rates** 8,280-16,920 Kč single; 8,820-17,460 Kč double; 3,600 Kč extra bed (not standard room); 23,400-34,200 Kč apartments. **Credit** AmEx, MC, V. **Map** p308 G3.
Presenting itself as the be-all and end-all of Prague's luxury accommodation, the Four Seasons is nonetheless terribly predictable. The hotel is actually a combination of four buildings from the Gothic, baroque, Renaissance and neo-classical periods, yet inside, there is almost no trace of local colour or historical detail. Sure, rooms have the trademark goose-down duvets and monumentally fluffy pillows, but unless you are lucky enough to have landed quarters with panoramic views of the Charles Bridge and Castle quarter, then you might as well be staying at a Four Seasons in Texas. The restaurant and lobby bar, of course, serve superb drinks and cuisine, and service is first rate.
Hotel services *Babysitting. Disabled: adapted rooms. Gym. Parking. Sauna. Translation service.* **Room services** *CD player. Dataport. Laundry. Minibar. Room service (24hrs). Safe. TV: pay movies/satellite.*

Hotel Paříž Praha

U Obecního domu 1, Prague 1 (2219 5195/ fax 2422 5475/www.hotel-pariz.cz). Metro Náměstí Republiky/5, 8, 14 tram. **Rooms** 95.

Rates 8,000-10,000 Kč single/double; 14,000 Kč executive single/double. **Credit** AmEx, DC, MC, V. **Map** p308 K3.
A century-old, family-run Prague fixture immortalised in a bawdy chapter of Bohumil Hrabal's *I Served the King of England*, this sumptuous art nouveau hotel has gone a long way toward raising quality to match its sky-high prices. The public spaces are as elegant as any in the city, and the replica fittings in the rooms, along with touches such as bathrobes and tiled bathroom floors, are reminders of a more genteel age. But if it's sheer pampering and slavish service you're after, though, a more modern hotel may better fit the bill.
Hotel services *Bar. No-smoking floor. Restaurant.* **Room services** *Dataport. Internet. Minibar.*

Inter-Continental

Náměstí Curieových 43-45, Prague 1 (2488 1111/ fax 2481 1216/www.interconti.com). Metro Staroměstská/17, 18 tram. **Rooms** 372.
Rates 10,500-13,000 Kč double; 1,232 Kč extra room; 12,950-24,500 Kč suite. **Credit** AmEx, DC, MC, V. **Map** p308 H1.
Once you get over the first impression of its brutalist 1970s design, the Inter-Continental will charm the beast in you, from the shoe-shine service to the view from the terrace. All traces of communist design were expunged during a $50-million refurbishment in the 1990s. The conference facilities leave nothing to be desired and the fitness centre is complete, although a curious island in the pool prevents lap swimming (almost impossible in Prague). Service is sometimes more grovelling than effectual. The spacious suites feature a full range of electronic widgets for the professional business traveller. Excellent views on the river side.
Hotel services *Beauty salon. Disabled: adapted room. Gym. No-smoking floors. Putting green. Secretarial services. Swimming pool.* **Room services** *Dataport (some rooms). Fax (some rooms). Internet (some rooms). Room service (24hrs). Voicemail.*

Expensive

Grand Hotel Bohemia

Králodvorská 4, Prague 1 (2480 4111/fax 2232 9545/www.grandhotelbohemia.cz). Metro Náměstí Republiky/5, 8, 14 tram. **Rooms** 78. **Rates** 5,700-6,900 Kč single; 7,950-10,050 Kč double; 14,100 Kč suite; 1,800 Kč extra bed. **Credit** AmEx, DC, MC, V. **Map** p309 K3.
Grand indeed, this gorgeous hotel under Austrian management makes an art deco counterpoint to the neighbouring art nouveau gem, the Municipal House. Even standard rooms are chock-full of amenities, including fax machine, trouser press and satellite TV. Most rooms on the sixth to eighth storeys have fabulous views over the red roofs of Old Town. The Boccaccio Room doubles as a grand ballroom or an extravagant conference room, which can hold up to 140 people.

Hotel services *Bar. Coffeehouse. Disabled: adapted rooms. No-smoking floors. Restaurant.* **Room services** *Air-conditioning. Dataport. Fax. Minibar. Safe. Trouser press. TV: satellite.*

Moderate

Apostolic Residence

Staroměstské náměstí 25, Prague 1 (2163 2206/fax 2163 2204/www.prague-residence.cz). Metro Národní třída/9, 18, 22, 23 tram. **Rooms** 3. **Rates** 4,200 Kč double; 8,000 Kč apartment. **Credit** AmEx, MC, V. **Map** p308 J3.

Amazingly, this enchanting Renaissance-era inn overlooks Old Town Square. With just three rooms (a double and two apartments) and a location like this in the epicentre of Old Town, the Apostolic should be booked well ahead. But bedding down on these antique dark wood beds, in quarters with original ceiling beams, thick cream-coloured walls and engaging service is surely worth planning ahead for. One advantage to the ancient heavy masonry is that it effectively muffles most of the all-night noise from Old Town Square below.

Hotel services *Bar. Internet. Parking (off-site). Restaurant.* **Room services** *Minibar. TV: cable.*

Cloister Inn

Konviktská 14, Prague 1 (2421 1020/fax 2421 0800/www.cloister-inn.cz). Metro Národní třída/6, 9, 18, 22, 23 tram. **Rooms** 73. **Rates** 3,000-3,800 Kč single; 3,400-4,400 Kč double; 500 Kč extra bed. 4,200-5,300 Kč triple. **Credit** AmEx, DC, MC, V. **Map** p308 G5.

Resting behind the cheaper Pension Unitas run by the same people (*see p50*), this three-star hotel has a lot going for it: attentive staff, great location, good prices and a nearby house full of nuns in case you are in need of redemption. The boxy rooms exude an institutional feel, but at this price in Old Town, no one should be grumbling.

Hotel services *Concierge. Internet. Laundry. No-smoking rooms. Parking.* **Room services** *Fax (executive rooms only). Minibar (executive rooms only). Safe.*

Hotel Černá liška

Mikulášská 2, Prague 1 (2423 2250/fax 2423 2249). Metro Staroměstská/17, 18 tram. **Rooms** 12. **Rates** 2,800-4,400 Kč single; 3,850-5,700 Kč double; 4,700-6,900 Kč suite; 950-1,100 Kč extra bed. **Credit** DC, MC, V. **Map** p308 H3.

Though a location right on Old Town Square is not for everyone, the newish Black Fox offers excellent value in the medieval centre of Prague. Wake up to the sound of the Týn church bells (and the rumble of tourist traffic), then stumble out into gallery-hopping, pubbing and clubbing central, without ever needing to risk your trip's budget on one of Prague's infamous crooked taxis. Welcoming staff oversee these dozen neatly furnished rooms with modern baths.

Hotel services *Concierge. Laundry. Restaurant. Safe. Secretarial services.* **Room services** *Minibar. Room service (8-10am). TV: satellite.*

Hotel Černý Slon

Týnská 1, Prague 1 (2232 1521/fax 2231 0351/www.hotelcernyslon.cz). Metro Staroměstská/17, 18 tram. **Rooms** 13. **Rates** 1,700-2,990 Kč single; 3,000-5,250 Kč double; 3,920-6,180 Kč triple. **Credit** AmEx, MC, V. **Map** p308 J3.

With an incredible location in the shadow of the Týn church just off Old Town Square, this cosy 13-room inn is ensconced in a 14th-century building. Genteel service, Gothic stone arches and wooden floors go along with the smallish, but comfortable, clean rooms laid out with basic amenities. Windows look out on the cobbled mews of Old Town, with a constant parade of characters. Fortunately, they are some of the district's quieter lanes, despite being just metres from the hordes in Staroměstské náměstí.

Hotel services *Bar. Parking (off-site). Restaurant.* **Room services** *Minibar. Safe. TV: satellite.*

Hotel Liberty

28 října 11, Prague 1 (2423 9598/fax 2423 7694/www.hotelliberty.cz). Metro Můstek/6, 9, 11 18, 21, 23 tram. **Rooms** 32. **Rates** 4,650 Kč single; 4,950 Kč double; 1,200 Kč extra bed. **Credit** AmEx, MC, V. **Map** p308 J5.

Ultra-modern with jacuzzis and Italian style, the elegant Hotel Liberty opened in the summer of 2002, centrally located with rooms tailored more to spoiled business travellers than tourist looking for signs of Bohemia. Rich red fabrics in the rooms and top-notch Italian design might make you overlook the fact that your splendid decor has little to do with Prague. The three suites have balconies and one has a sensational view of Prague Castle. Some rooms have whirlpool baths and there is an inviting hot tub in the basement gym. Service is superb.

Hotel services *Air-conditioning. Disabled: adapted room. Gym. Parking. Sauna.* **Room services** *Dataport. Internet. Minibar. Safe. TV: satellite.*

Hotel Mejstřík Praha

Jakubská 5, Prague 1 (2480 0055/fax 2480 0056/www.hotelmejstrik.cz). Metro Náměstí Republiky/5, 8, 14 tram. **Rooms** 29. **Rates** 2,200-5,500 Kč single; 3,100-6,200 Kč double; 6,200-8,300 Kč suite; 900-1,200 Kč extra bed. **Credit** AmEx, MC, V. **Map** p309 K3.

A newly renovated former strip club handily located in the heart of Old Town, now returned to the family that founded it in 1924. Individually decorated rooms are a hybrid of ubiquitous modern hotel decor and 1920s style. Art deco elements and wood trim are a nice touch and corner rooms offer great vantages for spying on streetlife and gables.

Hotel services *Bar. Disabled: adapted rooms. Limousine service. No-smoking rooms. Parking (off-site). Restaurant.* **Room services** *Dataport. Minibar. TV: satellite.*

Hotel U Prince

Staroměstské náměstí 29, Prague 1 (2421 3807/3807/www.hoteluprince.cz). Metro Staroměstská/17, 18 tram. **Rooms** 24. **Rates** 3,790-6,990 Kč single; 3,990-7,990 Kč double; 1,200 Kč extra bed. **Credit** AmEx, MC, V. **Map** p308 J3.

An authentic slice of history smack in the centre of Old Town Square. Opened in 2001, the hotel is a reconstruction of a 12th-century building and boasts huge rooms with antiques and individually designed canopy beds and armoires. The marble bathrooms make for splendid decadence and the hotel has several eateries, including a seafood cavern. Its rooftop restaurant offers some of the most scenic dining in the city, but the service is miserable and the cuisine overpriced and mediocre (same goes for the street tables out front). Still, this is one of the most interesting and best-located hotels in the city.

Hotel services *No-smoking room. Parking. Restaurants (3).* **Room services** *Dataport. Minibar. Room service (24hrs). Safe. TV: satellite.*

Pension Metamorphosis

Malá Štupartská 5 (Ungelt Square), Prague 1 (2177 1011/fax 2177 1099/www.metamorphis.cz). Metro Náměstí Republiky/5, 14, 26 tram. **Rooms** 24. **Rates** 3,350-4,450 Kč single; 3,940-5,230 Kč double; 4,420-5,890 Kč suite; 1,050-1,350 Kč extra bed. **Credit** AmEx, DC, MC, V. **Map** p308 J3.

The once-empty square on which this new pension stands has become a tourist mecca, jammed with craft shops, a respectable bookstore and cafés – the largest of which is on the ground floor of the Metamorphosis itself. This supplies a constant low-grade din but the rooms here are tastefully done and far enough above it all to afford a respite. Great value and location with engaging service, though probably not ideal in high season. Whatever happens, you're unlikely to wake up as a beetle.

Hotel services *Bar. Business services. Internet. Laundry. Parking. Restaurants (2).* **Room services** *Air-conditioning. Minibar. TV: satellite.*

U zlaté studny

Karlova 3, Prague 1 (2222 0262/fax 2222 1112/www.uzlatestudny.cz). Metro Staroměstská/17, 18 tram. **Rooms** 6. **Rates** 4,500-4,700 Kč double; 5,100 Kč suite; 700 Kč extra person (under-15s free). **Credit** AmEx, MC, V. **Map** p308 H4.

This 16th-century Renaissance structure stands on the Royal Route connecting Charles Bridge and Old Town Square. The four roomy suites and two doubles are decorated in Louis XIV antique and replica furnishings and boast finely painted vault ceilings. With good service thrown in, it all adds up to the perfect choice for exploring most of historic Prague on foot.

Hotel services *Fax. Internet. Laundry. Restaurant.* **Room services** *Minibar. Safe.*

Budget

Betlem Club

Betlémské náměstí 9, Prague 1 (2222 1574/fax 2222 0580/www.betlemclub.cz). Metro Národní třída/6, 9, 18, 22, 23 tram. **Rooms** 22. **Rates** 2,100-2,700 Kč single; 2,800-3,900 Kč double; 3,000-4,500 Kč suite; 600-1,000 Kč extra bed; free under-5s. **Credit** MC, V. **Map** p308 H4.

A homey hotel on an agreeable square, only a twist and a turn away from Charles Bridge or, in the other direction, Wenceslas Square. Fairly spacious rooms are adorned by a little too much brass, but are nevertheless clean, attractive and well stocked with necessities. At the price, this is one of Old Town's best bargains, and the small single rooms in the attic are priced even lower. With the money you save here, treat yourself to dinner at nearby V Zátiši (*see p127*).

Hotel U Klenotníka

Rytířská 3, Prague 1 (2421 1699/fax 2422 1025/ www.uklenotnika.cz). Metro Můstek/6, 9, 11, 18, 21, 23 tram. **Rooms** 10. **Rates** 2,100-2,500 Kč single; 2,900-3,800 Kč double; 200 Kč-700 Kč extra bed. **Credit** AmEx, DC, MC, V. **Map** p308 J4.

The good news: you are five minutes' walk from Old Town Square in a burgher house from the 11th century. The bad news: the brown carpeting and garish chairs in the small guest rooms date back to the 1970s – and this ain't no 'retro cool' effect. Still, this narrow street is lined with historic façades and each room features a painting by Czech modern artist Boris Jirků. The first floor of the hotel is a cosy restaurant serving traditional Czech fare.

Hotel services *Restaurant.* **Room services** *Dataport. Minibar. TV: satellite.*

Pension Unitas

Bartolomějská 9, Prague 1 (2421 1020/fax 2421 0800/www.cloister-inn.cz/unitas). Metro Národní třída/17, 18 tram. **Rooms** 35. **Rates** 1,100 Kč single; 1,400 Kč double; 1,750 Kč triple; 2,000 Kč quad. **Credit** AmEx, MC, V. **Map** p308 H5.

One floor has standard, comfortable hostel rooms, the basement has communist-era prison cells that once imprisoned playwright/dissident Václav Havel. No worries, they've been prettied up with fluffy linen since then. Fine and clean, a genuine bargain.

Hotel services *Parking.*

U Medvídků

Na Perštýně 7, Prague 1 (2421 1916/fax 2422 0930/www.umedvidku.cz). Metro Národní třída/6, 18, 21, 22, 23 tram. **Rooms** 22. **Rates** 1,500-2,300 Kč single; 2,200-3,400 Kč double; 400-500 Kč extra bed. **Credit** AmEx, MC, V. **Map** p308 H5.

The Little Bears offers comfortable rooms and good service above one of a dying breed of Prague pubs – the sort that still attracts locals in search of great beer and food at reasonable prices (*see p152*). The pension rooms with raftered ceilings could hardly be better located or better priced. They're not luxurious but are comfortable and charming and the staff are welcoming. Remarkably quiet despite being only one block from one of downtown's busiest streets.

Hotel services *Bar. Garden. Restaurant.* **Room services** *Minibar. Room service (24hrs). TV.*

U krále Jiřího

Liliová 10, Prague 1 (2222 0925/2424 8797/fax 2222 1707/www.kinggeorge.cz). Metro Staroměstská or Národní třída/17, 18 tram. **Rooms** 12. **Rates** 1,500-2,000 Kč single; 2,700-3,300 Kč double;

The northerly areas of this district are within walking distance of Old Town and are undergoing an exciting renaissance.

Expensive

K+K Fenix

Ve Smečkách 30, Prague 1 (3309 2222/fax 2221 2141/www.kkhotels.com). Metro Muzeum/3, 9, 14, 23 tram. **Rooms** 130. **Rates** 6,540 Kč single; 7,440 Kč double; 1,080 Kč extra bed. **Credit** AmEx, DC, MC, V. **Map** p311 K6.

The newly built, Austrian-owned K+K is a fresh and efficient business hotel situated off the top of Wenceslas Square. Professional, with standard conference amenities plus a bistro and a small, streamlined fitness centre.

Hotel services *Bar. Conference rooms. Gym. Massage. No-smoking rooms. Parking. Sauna.* **Room services** *Dataport. Room service (7am-10pm). Safe. TV: satellite.*

Marriott

V Celnici 8, Prague 1 (2288 8888/fax 2288 8889/ www.marriotthotels.com). Metro Náměstí Republiky/ 3, 8, 24 tram. **Rooms** 293. **Rates** 7,200 Kč all rooms; 8,700 Kč executive suites. **Credit** AmEx, DC, MC, V. **Map** p309 L3.

The recently built Prague Marriott set out to become the epitome of modern convenience for both business and pleasure in Prague – and largely succeeded. With built-in casino, shopping arcade, fitness centre and its own metro entrance, you could be tempted never to venture outside. That would be a pity, as the hotel is just one block from Old Town.

Hotel services *Babysitting. Bar. Beauty salon. Business services. Disabled: adapted rooms. Gym. Parking. Restaurant. Solarium. Swimming pool.* **Room services** *Air-conditioning. Safe. TV: pay movies/satellite.*

Hotel Palace Praha

Panská 12, Prague 1 (2409 3111/fax 2422 1240/ www.palacehotel.cz). Metro Můstek/3, 9, 14, 24 tram. **Rooms** 124. **Rates** 6,000-8,400 Kč single; 6,600-9,000 Kč double; 1,500-3,000 Kč extra bed. **Credit** AmEx, DC, MC, V. **Map** p309 K5.

Quite possibly the best service in Prague, with enthusiastic staff who insist the hotel should have six stars. Simple but comfortable rooms, two restaurants and a café, each with its own piano player, and a location just close enough – but thankfully not too close – to Wenceslas Square. Some more expensive rooms have fax machines.

Hotel services *Disabled: adapted rooms. Interpreting services. No-smoking floors. Sauna.* **Room services** *Dataport. Internet. Minibar.*

Radisson SAS

Štěpánská 40, Prague 1 (2282 0000/fax 2282 0100/ www.radisson.com/praguecs). Metro Muzeum/3, 9, 14, 23 tram. **Rooms** 211. **Rates** 6,270-8,850 Kč single/double; 10,050 Kč suite, 1,500 Kč extra bed. **Credit** AmEx, DC, MC, V. **Map** p311 K6.

Wooden it be nice: **Travellers' Hostel**'s best room.

3,900-4,500 Kč triple; 2,700-5,900 Kč apartment; 1,000 Kč extra bed. **Credit** AmEx, DC, MC, V. **Map** p308 G4.

This pension above the James Joyce pub (*see p151*) has attic rooms with sloped ceilings and ancient beams. On a picturesque but busy lane, within walking distance of Charles Bridge and Old Town Square.

Hotel services *Bar. Fax. Garden. Safe.* **Room services** *Minibar. TV: satellite.*

Hostels

Travellers' Hostel

Dlouhá 33, Prague 1 (2482 6662/6663/fax 2482 6665/www.travellers.cz). Metro Náměstí Republiky/ 5, 14, 26 tram. **Open** 24hrs daily (all branches). **Rates** (per person) 620 Kč double; 480 Kč triple; 430-450 Kč 4-6-bed rooms; 370 Kč dormitory. **Credit** MC, V. **Map** p309 K2.

This hostel, built over the Roxy club (*see p228*), also functions as a booking office connecting travellers to a whole network of hostels. The two constants are good value and English-speaking backpackers. The Dlouhá street location features a surprisingly romantic double suite complete with beamed ceilings. Make sure to book ahead.

Hostel services *Bar. Fax. Internet. Laundry.* **Branches**: throughout town. Check the phone book for your nearest.

Nové Město

Prague's fast, cheap and clean public transport makes New Town a viable option for business travellers looking for better value and modern facilities without sacrificing easy motorway access or proximity to the centre.

High art at the **Hotel Elite**. *See p53.*

Hotel services *Babysitting. Bar. Business services. Disabled: adapted rooms. Executive lounge. Gym. Parking. No-smoking floors. Solarium. Swimming pool.* Room services *Dataport. TV. VCR (extra charge).*

Moderate

Grand Hotel Evropa

Václavské náměstí 25, Prague 1 (2422 8117/ fax 2422 4544). Metro Můstek/3, 9, 14, 24 tram. Rooms 93 (53 en suite). Rates 2,990 Kč single; 3,990 Kč double; 4,990 Kč triple; 5,200 Kč quad; 5,000 Kč apartment. Credit AmEx, MC, V. Map p309 K5.

A grandiose exemplar of art nouveau on the outside, the Evropa remains a time capsule of communism on the inside. Built in 1889 and given its current cream and gold façade in 1905, it has witnessed a lot from its perch over Wenceslas Square. So have the staff, and the changes seem to have worn them all out thoroughly. Still, the frisson of the bad old days can be a trip if taken with a sense of humour – and it's an unquestionable bargain for its location bang in the centre of things.

Hotel Adria Prague

Václavské náměstí 26, Prague 1 (2108 1111/fax 2108 1200/www.hoteladria.cz). Metro Můstek/3, 9, 14, 24 tram. Rooms 88. Rates 4,800 Kč single; 5,700 Kč double; 6,300-7,200 Kč triple. Credit AmEx, MC, V. Map p309 K5.

A cut above the other hotels on Wenceslas Square, the Adria suits people who want to be in the centre of the action but away from the riff-raff. The contemporary and rather generic guest rooms are nothing special, and it could easily be argued that this four-star hotel property is not quite worth the price. Repeat guests, however, like the hotel's grotto fish restaurant, Triton, which is a bit on the tacky side but serves up memorable meals. Deluxe room amenities and marble bathrooms are also appealing. Hotel services *Disabled: adapted rooms. Parking. Translation service.* Room services *Dataport. Laundry/dry-cleaning. Minibar. Room service. Safe. TV: pay movies/satellite.*

Hotel Ambassador Zlatá Husa

Václavské náměstí 5-7, Prague 1 (2419 3111/fax 2422 6167/www.ambassador.cz). Metro Můstek/3, 9, 14, 24 tram. Rooms 162. Rates 4,320-8,640 Kč single; 5,400-10,080 Kč double; 1,440 Kč extra bed. Credit AmEx, DC, MC, V. Map p309 K5.

A remodelled art nouveau masterpiece, the Ambassador is one of the few hotels in the Wenceslas Square district that at least attempts to have period furniture in the rooms. An alternative to the nearby Grand Hotel Evropa (*see above*) for those with a little more cash. Prices vary wildly depending on how full the hotel is. The spacious rooms are brightened by flowing silk draperies and beige accents. Zlatá Husa means golden goose and refers to the daughter of the hotel's original 19th-century owner, a woman with a big dowry who was nonetheless unable to find a husband.

Constructed in 1930 as the Alcron Hotel, this stylish phantom has awakened after a ten-year dormancy. Its restoration was one of the most extensive in Prague's modern hotel history, involving liberal doses of art deco. Just off Wenceslas Square, it's now New Town's most luxurious business hotel, with first-rate techno gadgets, five phone lines per room, infra-red dataports, heated bathroom tiles and a downstairs jazz bar serving some of city's best cocktails. Hotel services *Bar. Concierge. Disabled: adapted rooms. Dry cleaning. Gym. Laundry. Parking. Restaurant.* Room services *Dataport. Fax. Internet. Minibar. Room service (24hrs). Safe. Trouser press. TV: pay movies.*

Renaissance Prague Hotel

V Celnici 7, Prague 1 (2182 1111/fax 2182 2200/ www.renaissancehotels.com). Metro Náměstí Republiky/3, 5, 14, 24, 26 tram. Rooms 315. Rates (excl breakfast) 6,600 Kč single/double; 7,950 Kč suite. Credit AmEx, DC, MC, V. Map p309 L3.

This most central of Prague's giant luxury hotels offers exemplary service for tourists and business folk, while resisting the trend to raise prices to offset the decline in Czech currency. The Marriott chain owns the Renaissance as well as operating its flagship hotel in Prague across the street (*see p51*), with even shinier brass-and-marble fittings and slightly higher prices. Breakfast costs extra.

Hotel services *Bar. Casino. Disabled: adapted rooms. Meeting rooms (8). Parking. Restaurant.*
Room services *Dataport. Laundry. Minibar.*
Room service (24hrs). Safe. TV: pay movies/satellite.

Hotel Axa

Na Poříčí 40, Prague 1 (2481 2580/fax 2232 2172/ www.vol.cz/AXA). Metro Florenc or Náměstí Republiky/3, 8, 24, 26 tram. Rooms 131.
Rates 2,200-2,900 Kč single; 3,100-3,600 Kč double; 3,700-4,300 Kč triple; 3,800-4,500 Kč suite; 600-700 Kč extra bed; 220 Kč pets. Credit AmEx, DC, MC, V.
Map p309 M2.
Sorely needed renovation work undertaken over the past five years has raised the Depression-era Axa out of the ranks of backpackerdom. The prices remain quite fair, there's a good range of services, and the location isn't bad – halfway between two central metro stations. If you're a light sleeper, make sure to ask for a room at the back of the hotel away from the tram tracks. There is a decent work-out centre, pool and sauna, though these are not run by the hotel and cost extra.
Hotel services *Bar. Beauty salon. Business services. Disabled: adapted rooms. Fax. Gym. Laundry. Restaurant. Safe. Swimming pool.*
Room services *Fridge. TV: satellite.*

Hotel Elite

Ostrovní 32, Prague 1 (2493 2250/www.hotelelite.cz). Metro Národní třída/18, 22, 23 tram. Rates 2,720-5,200 Kč single; 3,040-5,950 Kč double; 4,300-6,500 Kč suite. Credit AmEx, DC, MC, V.
Map p310 H6.
The finest example in a new wave of restored micro-hotels located in Prague's old centre, the Elite claims a 14th-century pedigree. Delicate baroque frescoes adorn some room ceilings, while others are braced with ancient beams, parquet floors and metre-thick walls. The Elite also has the best restaurant-bar of any hostelry in central Prague, the Ultramarin (*see p154*). A labyrinth of halls leads to rooms that no noise could ever penetrate. The genial staff and the location a short hop from Old Town don't hurt either.
Hotel services *Bar. Concierge. Hairdresser. Parking. Restaurant.* Room Services *Dataport. Minibar. Safe. TV: satellite.*
Hotel services *Bar. Laundry. Restaurant. Safe.*

Hotel Opera

Těšnov 13, Prague 1 (2231 5609/fax 2231 1477/ www.hotel-opera.cz). Metro Florenc/3, 26 tram.
Rooms 67. Rates 3,500 Kč single; 4,200 Kč double; 6,600 Kč suite; 1,000Kč extra bed. Credit AmEx, DC, MC, V. Map p309 M1.
This place has always been good value, considering that it's just blocks away from Old Town, but renovation has improved things so that guests no longer need to sacrifice comfort for location. The rooms remain small and simply furnished and the staff are helpful. The neo-Renaissance façade of this 1890s building is a sight in itself.
Hotel services *Bar. Internet. Limousine service. Restaurant.* Room services *TV: satellite.*

Budget

Hotel 16 U sv. Kateřiny

Kateřinská 16, Prague 2 (2492 0636/2491 9676/ fax 2492 0626/www.hotel16.cz). Metro IP Pavlova/ 16, 22, 23 tram. Rooms 14. Rates 2,500 Kč single; 2,700-3,400 Kč double; 3,200-4,600 Kč apartment. Credit MC, V. Map p311 K8.
This small family-run inn is on a quiet street within easy walking distance of the Botanical Gardens, and as such it's not very central. However, it is tranquil, intimate and good value.
Hotel services *Bar.* Room services *Air-conditioning. Minibar. Safe. TV: satellite.*

Jerome House

V Jirchářích 13, Prague 1 (2493 3207/ fax 2493 3212/www.jerome.cz/jerome-house.html). Metro Národní Třída/6, 18, 21, 22, 23 tram.
Rooms 65. Rates 2,100-3,210 Kč single; 2,610-3,900 Kč double; 3,210-4,860 Kč triple. Credit MC, V. Map p310 H6.
A combination travel agency and recently renovated budget hotel. Tucked away on a side street near the National Theatre, it's in a great location for getting around on foot. The house is bright and modern and the staff are helpful, but the rooms themselves are basic dorm-style.
Hotel services *Safe. Terrace.*
Room services *TV: satellite.*

U Šuterů

Palackého 4, Prague 1 (2494 8235/http://usuteru.jsc.cz). Metro Můstek/3, 9, 14, 24 tram. Rates 1,790-2,190 Kč single; 2,390-3,900 Kč double. Credit MC, V. Map p310 J6.
Just two blocks off Wenceslas Square stands this old European-style hotel and pub, with foundations dating back to 1383. Offering outstanding comfort and atmosphere for less than most of the chain hotels, its steep, winding wooden stairs lead up to rooms fitted with antique Bohemian oak furnishings and hardwood floors. At street level, patrons of the lamp-lit pub sit under vaulted ceilings, sipping fine Krusovice beer while dining on venison goulash and dumplings. All this is surrounded by the galleries, shops, clubs and bars of New Town.
Hotel services *Bar. Restaurant.*
Room services *Minibar. TV: satellite .*

Hostels

Charles University Dorms

Voršilská 1, Prague 1 (2493 3825/fax 2493 0361). Metro Národní třída/6, 9, 17, 18, 21, 22, 23 tram.
Open 9am-1pm Mon, Tue, Thur, Fri; 1-4pm Wed. Rates 165-295 Kč per person, double.
No credit cards. Map p310 H6.
One central office takes care of booking approximately 1,000 dorm rooms throughout the city. The rooms are only available from late June to late September but are incredibly good value. Just don't expect too much of them.

Hotel Imperial

Na Poříčí 15, Prague 1 (2331 6012/ www.hotelimperial.cz). Metro Náměstí Republiky/3, 5, 8, 14 tram. **Beds** 280. **Open** 24hrs. **Rates** 750-1,500 Kč single; 1,180-2,360 Kč double; 1,620-3,240 Kč triple. **No credit cards. Map** p309 L2.

Despite the name and the grand dame of a building (Kafka sipped coffee in the attached coffeehouse), the Imperial is really a hostel. The seemingly endless warren of rooms are plain as they come and the baths are shared, but the friendly staff and location do much to compensate.

Hostel services *Bedding. Kitchen access. Lockers. Restaurant.*

Klub Habitat

Na Zderaze 10, Prague 2 (tel/fax 2492 1706/2491 8252). Metro Karlovo náměstí/3, 6, 14, 18, 21, 22, 24 tram. **Rooms** 7. **Rates** 430 Kč per person (incl breakfast). **No credit cards. Map** p310 H7.

Watch for the easily missable sign and the unscrupulous place around the corner that sometimes poses as Klub Habitat. The genuine article is a friendly, owner-run spot in a handy downtown location. It has wood floors, clean shared bathroom, munchies and lemonade at reception. Excellent value and a step up from most hostels. All proceeds go to Czech children's charities. Book well ahead as there are few enough rooms for this place to have full occupancy all year.

Hostel services *Bar. Kitchen.*

Further afield

Žižkov – just east of the centre – is pubbing heaven, a magnet for young bohemians, and home to some truly frightful housing stock. **Holešovice** and **Dejvice** are leafy northern boundaries just across the Vltava from the city centre. **Vyšehrad** and neighbouring **Vinohrady**, south and south-east of the centre, offer classy, up-and-coming residential streets.

Deluxe

Prague Hilton

Pobřežní 1, Karlín, Prague 8 (2484 1111/fax 2484 2378/www.hilton.com). Metro Florenc/8, 24 tram. **Rooms** 788. **Rates** 7,710-9,600 Kč single; 8,040-9,930 Kč double; 11,190-12,450 Kč suite; 23,790 Kč family apartment. **Credit** AmEx, DC, MC, V.

This massive, mirrored cube frames the largest atrium in the Czech Republic. Huge leather armchairs, lots of greenery and gently bubbling fountains spell relaxation and recreation, as do the pool, sauna, salon and indoor tennis courts. Not for those raring to grab a map and tramp through the city sights. That may be why the likes of Richard Nixon, Nelson Mandela and the Clintons chose this hotel's Presidential Suite. There is an abundance of services for both business guests and tourists, but only the executive rooms and suites include breakfast.

Hotel services *Beauty salon. Disabled: adapted rooms. Gym. Interpreting services. Massage. No-smoking floors. Putting green. Sauna. Swimming pool. Whirlpool.* **Room services** *Dataport (business-class rooms only). Minibar. Safe (business-class rooms only). TV: satellite.*

Expensive

Corinthia

Kongresová 1, Vyšehrad, Prague 4 (6119 1111/fax 6121 1673/www.corinthia.com). Metro Vyšehrad/7, 18, 24 tram. **Rooms** 544. **Rates** 6,900-7,500 Kč single/ double; 10,800-15,150 Kč suite. **Credit** DC, MC, V.

This 24-storey hotel is an unmissable if unlovely landmark on the southern skyline. It made headlines in the Czech press in the late '90s when the US government declared it off-limits to Americans because of its owners' alleged ties to Libya. The embargo remains in effect. The new owners have cranked the service up a notch, and the hotel continues to have a loyal following of business travellers. Although a bit out of the centre, it's right next to the metro, a major motorway and the city's biggest conference centre. Rooms are on the small side, but the views over the city are as expansive.

Hotel services *Beauty salon. Bowling. Computer room. Disabled: adapted rooms. Gym. Interpreting services. No-smoking rooms. Squash court. Swimming pool.* **Room services** *Dataport. Fax (some rooms). Minibar. Safe.*

Diplomat Hotel Praha

Evropská 15, Dejvice, Prague 6 (2439 4111/fax 2439 4215/www.diplomat-hotel.cz). Metro Dejvická/ 2, 20, 26 tram. **Rooms** 398. **Rates** 5,400-6,300 Kč single; 6,300-7,200 Kč double; 3,000 Kč extra bed; 9,600-13,200 Kč suite. **Credit** AmEx, DC, MC, V.

A 20-minute drive from the airport, the Diplomat is best suited for business people. Executive rooms go at premium prices, as they recently underwent the refurbishment that the other rooms are crying out for. There's a go-kart track in the basement for those who like to mix pleasure with duty. Use of the fitness centre is included in the room prices. Prague Diplomat offers international plugs for electrical appliances in rooms on executive floors, which is a bit of a first.

Hotel services *Air-conditioning. Beauty salon. Business services. Disabled: adapted rooms. Gym. Interpreting services. Limousine service. No-smoking floors. Parking. Safe.* **Room services** *Dataport (executive rooms only). Minibar. Room service (6am-midnight). Safe (executive rooms only). TV: satellite.*

Mövenpick Hotel

Mozartova 1, Smíchov, Prague 5 (5715 1111/fax 5715 3131/www.movenpick-prague.com). Metro Anděl/4, 7, 9 tram. **Rooms** 434. **Rates** 5,820 Kč single; 6,420 Kč double; 1,140 Kč extra bed. **Credit** AmEx, MC, V.

A big orange block of a building across from the heralded Mozart Museum, the Mövenpick is more than just a place to get decent Swiss ice-cream. Yes, it is

The **Hotel Imperial**: a hostel with built-in swank appeal. *See p54.*

a generic big-chain hotel and it is far from the centre of town, but the property offers two bonuses: a family-friendly atmosphere where children get special attention, and a cable car that takes you up to the executive wing (upper building) where breathtaking views and fine dining attract many a Czech celebrity. Pets welcome.

Hotel services *ATM machine. Disabled: adapted rooms. Fitness centre. Gift shop. Massage. Mobile phone rental. Parking. Restaurants (2). Safe. Sauna. Shuttle bus to Anděl.* **Room services** *Dataport. Laundry/dry-cleaning. Minibar. Room service (24hrs). Safe. TV: satellite/pay movies.*

Moderate

Arcotel Hotel Teatrino

Bořivojova 53, Žižkov, Prague 3 (2142 2211/fax 2142 2222/www.arcotel.at). Metro Jiřího z Poděbrad/ 5, 9, 26 tram. **Rooms** 75. **Rates** 4,400 Kč single; 5,800 Kč double; 2,900 Kč extra bed. **Credit** AmEx, MC, V. **Map** p313 C2.

Once an ornate 19th-century theatre, then a communist cultural centre, the Teatrino is a blend of modern chic, tasteless historical detail and unfortunate room colour schemes. Located in the heart of trendy Žižkov, the hotel is one block from tram services into the centre, which take about ten minutes. Highlights include a stylish restaurant and bar where the theatre once was and framed quotations and art throughout by the likes of Mozart, Kafka and Rilke. Rooms have a pleasant minimalist design, but the candy stripe curtains and polka-dot carpeting do not jibe well with the Teatrino's many art nouveau flourishes.

Hotel services *Parking. Restaurant. Safe. Sauna.* **Room services** *Dataport. Laundry/dry-cleaning. Minibar. Room service. Safe. TV: pay movies/satellite.*

Dorint Don Giovanni

Vinohradská 157A, Žižkov, Prague 3 (6703 1111/ fax 6703 6704/www.dorint.de). Metro Želivského/ 10, 11, 16, 26 tram. **Rooms** 400. **Rates** 4,200-7,600 Kč single/double; 5,600-8,400 Kč suite. **Credit** AmEx, DC, MC, V. **Map** p313 E2.

This relative newcomer to the Prague scene may well represent the best value in this class, especially when it comes to business travellers; guests in a hurry will appreciate the stellar business services. The lobby contains impressive, if sometimes rather scary, original art and sculpture. You shouldn't be put off by the location; the hotel is right at the Želivského metro stop, so the city centre is less than ten minutes away. Adjacent to Franz Kafka's final resting place, this is a hotel offering rock-solid value.

Hotel services *Air-conditioning. Business services. Concierge. Disabled: adapted rooms. Gym. No-smoking floors. Parking. Restaurant.* **Room services** *Dataport. Fridge. Minibar. Room service (24hrs). Safe. TV: satellite.*

Hotel Schwaiger

Schwaigrova 3, Bubeneč, Prague 6 (3332 0271/fax 3332 0272/www.schwaiger.cz). Metro Hradčanská/ 131 bus. **Rooms** 22. **Rates** 3,100-3,500 Kč single; 4,000-4,500 Kč double; 7,500 Kč suite; 600 Kč extra bed. **Credit** AmEx, MC, V. **Map** p312 A2.

Hanuš Schwaiger, one of the 'National Theatre Generation' of painters, once occupied this pale yellow villa. It's now a simple yet comfortable small hotel in the lush diplomatic quarter of Bubeneč, and not as hard to find as the village-like quality of the neighbourhood might make you think. The rooms are furnished for comfort rather than style, although some of them have handsome coffered ceilings. There's a garden restaurant on the premises and just down the road is a gate into Prague's prettiest park, Stromovka.

Hotel services *Bar. Garden. Internet. Parking. Restaurants (2). Sauna.* **Room services** *Dataport. Minibar.*

Hotel Sieber

Slezská 55, Žižkov, Prague 3 (2425 0025/fax 2425 0027/www.johansen.com). Metro Jiřího z Poděbrad/ 11, 16 tram. **Rooms** 20. **Rates** 4,480 Kč single; 4,780 Kč double; 5,480 Kč suite. **Credit** AmEx, DC, MC, V. **Map** p313 C3.

An efficiently run place close to both the raucous pubs of Žižkov and the upmarket shopping of Vinohrady, the Sieber makes up in friendliness what it lacks in luxury amenities. No antique furnishings here, just solid, tasteful comfort and reliable business services. Note that the lift stops a half-flight of stairs from the room levels.

Hotel services *Air-conditioning. No-smoking rooms. Parking.* **Room services** *Dataport. Minibar. TV: satellite.*

Budget

Hotel Anna

Budečská 17, Vinohrady, Prague 2 (2251 3111/ fax 2251 5158/www.hotel.cz/anna). Metro Náměstí Míru/16, 22, 34 tram. **Rooms** 23. **Rates** 2,300 Kč single; 2,900 Kč double; 3,900 Kč triple; 4,200 Kč apartment.* **Credit** AmEx, MC, V. **Map** p313 B3.

Situated on a quiet, tree-lined street in Vinohrady, the Hotel Anna is an exceptional choice, with its stained-glass windows, wrought-iron staircase and tall french windows. It may not be terribly central in terms of location, but the trade-off for clean air is reasonable enough, and it's only a short tram ride or a pleasant walk into town.

Hotel services *Air-conditioning. Fax. Laundry. Parking.* **Room services** *Minibar. TV: satellite.*

Hotel Abri

Jana Masaryka 36, Vinohrady, Prague 2 (2251 5124/ fax 2425 4240). Metro Náměstí Miru/4, 16, 22, 23, 34 tram. **Rooms** 26. **Rates** 2,300-3,100 Kč single; 2,800-3,600 Kč double; 400 Kč extra bed. **Credit** AmEx, MC, V.

Surrounded by leafy streets and tranquillity, the Abri has an off-the-beaten-path location a 20-minute walk from Wenceslas Square that helps to make up for its distinctly nondescript demeanour. By far its most appealing feature is its backyard terrace, which is an ideal spot for summer beer sipping. Rooms have some unattractive furniture and colour schemes dating from the communist era. But the staff are friendly and you are not likely to want for any creature comforts.

Hotel services *Disabled: adapted room. Parking. Restaurant.* **Room services** *TV: satellite.*

Alpin penzion

Velehradská 25, Žižkov, Prague 3 (2272 3970/fax 2272 3551/www.alpin.cz). Metro Jiřího z Poděbrad/ 11 tram. **Rooms** 28. **Rates** 1,170-1,500 Kč single; 1,270-1,600 Kč double; 1,770-2,100 Kč triple. **Credit** MC, V. **Map** p313 C2.

On the pleasant borderline between Vinohrady and Žižkov, this is one of the best deals in town for those who don't mind being far from Old Town Square. And even so, the metro is a five-minute walk, as are lots of trendy restaurants and bars that have sprung up in recent years in this eclectic neighbourhood. A clean-as-a-whistle pension (a few steps up from a hostel), the Alpin has simple furnishings sure to appeal to the bargain-hunting minimalist. Service is warm.

Hotel services *Disabled: adapted room. Parking.*

Hotel City

Belgická 10, Vinohrady, Prague 2 (2252 1606/ fax 2252 2386/www.hotel.city.cz). Metro Náměstí Míru/4, 6, 11, 16, 22, 34 tram. **Rooms** 19. **Rates** 1,160-1,670 Kč single; 1,550-2,320 Kč double; 1,830-2,610 Kč triple; 2,015-2,800 Kč quad. **Credit** AmEx, DC, MC, V. **Map** p311 M9.

In quiet Vinohrady, this pension has upgraded itself to a hotel. It's still borderline, but it's good value for the no-frills traveller, and is reasonably central.

Hotel services *Fax. Safe.* **Room services** *Fridge. Minibar. TV: satellite (extra charge).*

Hotel Tříska

Vinohradská 105, Žižkov, Prague 3 (2272 7313/ fax 2272 3562/www.hotel-triska.cz). Metro Jiřího z Poděbrad/11 tram. **Rooms** 51. **Rates** 1,890 Kč single; 2,310 Kč double; 3,150 Kč triple; 3,990 Kč quad. **No credit cards. Map** p313 C3.

A friendly hotel with clean bright rooms in a funky old building in the centre of Vinohrady. The spare, all-white rooms – the best of which face away from the noisy street – have high ceilings that tend to dwarf the woodwork furnishings.

Hotel services *Parking. Restaurant.* **Room services** *Fridge. TV: satellite.*

Julian

Elišky Peškové 11, Smíchov, Prague 5 (5731 1144/ fax 5731 1149/www.julian.cz). Tram 6, 9, 12. **Rooms** 32. **Rates** 2,220-3,580 Kč single; 2,520-3,880 Kč double; 700-1,000 Kč extra bed. **Credit** AmEx, DC, MC, V.

On the edge of Smíchov, the Julian is slightly off the beaten track, but is just a ten-minute walk or a quick tram ride from Malá Strana. The fireside reading room and reception area is the Julian's jewel. The fourth floor is air-conditioned and all apartments have kitchenettes. Pets are welcome.

Hotel services *Bar. Fax. Gym. Laundry. Parking. Sauna. Solarium. Whirpool.* **Room services** *Safe. TV: satellite.*

Pension Chaloupka

Nad hradním vodojemem 83, Střešovice, Prague 6 (tel/fax 2051 1761/www.web.telecom.cz/ pensionchaloupka). Metro Hradčanská/1, 2, 18 tram. **Rooms** 8. **Rates** 800-900 Kč single; 1,350-1,600 Kč double; 1,800-2,100 Kč triple; 2,200-2,800 Kč apartment. **No credit cards.**

A basic Czech pension, so only a half-step up from dormitory life, but good value all the same. A 15-minute walk from the Castle and on a night tram line.

Hotel services *Bar. Parking. TV.*

Pension Větrník

*U Větrníku 40, Břevnov, Prague 6 (2061 2404/
fax 3536 1406). Metro Hradčanská, then tram 1,
18.* **Rooms** 6 (all en suite). **Rates** 2,000 Kč single/
double; 3,000 Kč apartment; 500 Kč extra bed.
Credit MC.

This pension situated away from the city centre is
definitely a spot for those who favour comfort over
location. The six rooms in this restored 18th-
century windmill overlook a large secluded garden
with high walls, blocking the less pleasant views
beyond. Charming owners and a private tennis
court are further enticements.
Hotel services *Fax. Garden. Laundry. Parking.
Restaurant. Safe.* **Room services** *TV: satellite.*

Pension Vyšehrad

*Krokova 6, Vyšehrad, Prague 2 (4140 8455/
fax 6122 2187/www.pension-vysehrad.cz).
Metro Vyšehrad/8, 24 tram.* **Rooms** 4 (all en suite).
Rates 1,000 Kč single; 1,600 Kč double; 2,100 Kč
triple. **No credit cards.**

This beautiful and tranquil family home on a hillside with a wonderful garden and view has been a
pension for ten years. The family cat has the run of
the house and guests' pets are welcome.
Hotel services *Garden. Parking.*

Hostels

Arena Hostel

*U Výstaviště 1, Holešovice, Prague 7 (870 252).
Metro Holešovice/5 tram.* **Rates** 300 Kč per person.
Credit AmEx, MC, V.

The city's newest hostel offers reasonable bare-
bones accommodation with friendly service and
easy access to the metro and the city centre. A
newly renovated building in the Holesovice district,
just north and across the River Vltava from Old
Town, contains clean dorm rooms and a sociable
crowd of backpackers. Arena is the first dirt-cheap
option to open in this district, which features
Veletržní palác (the National Gallery's main modern art venue, *see p111*), lovely Stromovka park
and the hip Mecca club (*see p226*).
Hotel services *Bar. Internet. Laundry.*

The Clown & Bard

*Bořivojova 102, Žižkov, Prague 3 (2271 6453/
9436/www.clownandbard.com). Metro Jiřího
z Poděbrad/5, 9, 11, 26 tram.* **Beds** 90.
Rates 250 Kč single bed in dorm; 450 Kč per person
double room; 350-400 Kč per person in 4-6-person
apartments (with kitchen and private bath).
No credit cards. Map p313 B2.

This hostel and coffee bar is a great place for backpackers and locals alike, surrounded by numerous
pubs and restaurants in arty, working-class Žižkov.
The ground-floor pub (*see p157*) features live music
several nights a week and attracts an eclectic mixture of guests, expats and hip Czechs. No lockout
and no reservations. Breakfast available.
Hostel services *Bar. Fax. Laundry.*

Hostel Boathouse

*Lodnická 1, Modřany, Prague 4 (tel/fax 4177 0051/
www.aa.cz/boathouse). Tram 3, 17, 52.* **Beds** 56.
Open 24hrs daily. **Rates** 270-350 Kč per person.
No credit cards.

Seasonal regulars engage in first-name banter with
the friendly staff at this hostel set amid Vltava riverbank meadows. It's a good 20-minute tram ride
south of Old Town but lines run 24 hours from the
Černý kůň stop ten minutes' walk away. Bikes are
available for rent, and there's even a driving range.
Booking at least a week ahead is recommended in
summer, but management will try to find a place for
anyone who turns up. A basic breakfast and dinner
are served (70 Kč and 100 Kč respectively).
Hostel services *Internet. Laundry. Parking.*

Longer stays

If, like so many who come to Prague for a week,
you decide to stay on indefinitely, be prepared
for the joys of the Czech residential maze. If
you've finally met the list of requirements for
a residence permit (*see* **Directory: Resources
A-Z**), you're ready to take on hardcore
competition for apartment space. In Prague,
where families fight over who'll get granny's
flat decades before her death, it's not too
surprising that the average Czech landlord isn't
overly concerned with foreigners' demands for
luxuries. Generally, you'll look at a dozen dives
before finding the right flat.

Free-market landlord–tenant rights are still
evolving and many apartments in Prague are
still state-owned. This can mean renting a black
market apartment from the Czech family who
is legally the tenant. Though this may be the
cheapest option, your host will be very leery of
putting anything on paper and your rights will
be non-existent should they move a nephew
in with you. You're best off finding a privately
owned flat and signing a legally binding lease.

Word of mouth is an effective way to flathunt
in the expat community. Subscribe to a bulletin
board such as prahabulletinboard@yahoo.com
or put up notices at **Radost FX** (*see p227*)
or the **Globe Bookstore & Coffeehouse**
(*see p141*). **Capital Management**
(capital_m@hotmail.com) and **Happy House
Rentals** (www.happyhouserentals.com) are
recommended flat hunters. A good estate agent
such as **Agentura Kirke** can help to take
much of the pain out of the process as well.

Agentura Kirke

*Moskevská 25, Vršovice, Prague 10 (7172 0399).
Metro Náměstí Míru/4, 22 tram.* **Open** 8.30am-5pm
Mon-Fri. **No credit cards.**
Run by British expat Nicholas Kirke, this respected
estate agency offers long- and short-term rentals on
flats (minimum lease two years).

Sightseeing

Introduction

A living art and architecture museum that cries out for strolling –
a perfect backdrop for the adventure movie that travel should be.

Sightseeing

Prague's old centre takes you on a visual trip through every period over the last millennium, all of it fortunately contained within an easily manageable area, much of it traffic-free and pedestrianised. Within blocks of each other you'll encounter palaces, galleries, cellar pubs and mysterious passageways, and then emerge into the formal gardens of some count or other in a scene straight out of *Amadeus*.

A bend of the Vltava river makes an arc through the heart of the city, gracing it with nine dramatic bridges, all scaled perfectly for a stroll from one side of Prague to the other. The river eventually runs north to the Baltic after curling around Letná, the high country on the left bank that first provided a strategic vantage to Stone Age peoples. The neighbouring hill of **Hradčany** gave the first Czech princes, the Přemyslids, their castle foundations, which still exist today under the Prague Castle complex. This is the ideal place for a heart-stopping first overview of the town below.

Between Hradčany and the Vltava river, the **Malá Strana** district is a delightfully jumbled tapestry of its former histories: a craftsman's quarter during the medieval period, prize real estate granted to nobles for supporting the crown during the late Renaissance, and a hotbed of poets bristling against foreign domination in coffeehouse cabals during the 19th century. Cottages, fabulous palaces and smoky cafés from each era respectively are side by side today on its narrow, twisting streets.

On the right bank, the river is also responsible for the unique underworld of flat **Staré Město**, the Old Town, with its subterranean drinking holes, cinemas, music halls and galleries. These countless vaulted, stone-walled spaces were once at street level, but constant medieval flooding of the Vltava prompted city fathers to raise the streets one storey to the level at which they lie today. Which means that ordinary-looking doorways to pubs and clubs often lead to vast underground labyrinths held up by stone arches.

The city's layers are a good part of the reason why people come here for a week and end up staying for years. It would seem that no matter how deep you dig, you're constantly making new discoveries. People who have lived here for years still stop in amazement when a new

passage between favourite streets is reopened to the public. Many of these walkways through building courtyards haven't seen the light of day for 50 years or more but now host designer shops and smart bars. Prague is rediscovering itself, as it excavates itself from its grey pre-Velvet Revolution days – a thrilling event to witness as you wander through town.

Bordering Old Town to the south and east is **Nové Město**, the New Town, the first area of the city to be laid out with broad modern streets, thoughtfully planned by Charles IV in 1348. This is where the city's commerce gets done, as it has been for centuries, also where the uniquely Czech form of political dissent known as defenestration was perfected. All of Europe was plunged into chaos as a result of the tossing out the window of city mugwumps from the **New Town Hall** (*see p103*). Much of **Nové Město** is of limited interest to the visitor, but Wenceslas Square is very much the heart of modern Prague and the adjoining Na příkopě street is now the place to witness improbably beautiful young Czechs shopping for lifestyle essentials in a wave of consumerism that would warm hearts on Wall Street. The area south of the National Theatre, known to locals as **SONA** (*see p100* **Some call it SONA**), is also in full bloom as a fashionable quarter of expat hedonism.

To the east of the city centre lies the rough and tumble district of **Žižkov**. This area of crumbling tenements proudly boasts the highest number of pubs per capita in the world – an obvious draw for the boho expats who are doing their best to make this traditionally working class district their own. It's also the place to catch phenomenal regional music acts, indie artists trying to create conceptual breakthroughs and meet up with irascible Prague characters, both young and old. The hippest clubs outside Staré Město are in this quarter, usually with badly lit entrances that look like you must be in the wrong place. *See also chapter* **Nightlife**.

For getting to the right place, the **Prague Card**, a combination public transport and museum entry pass, is good value at 560 Kč for adults and 460 Kč for students. Available at American Express (Václavské náměstí 56, Nové Město, Prague 1; 2421 9992) and at the Museum

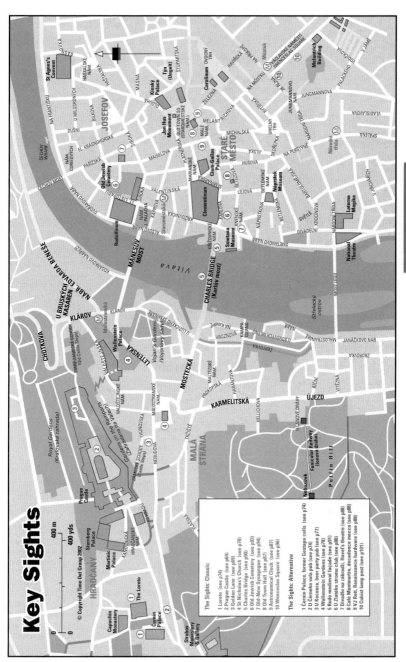

Key Sights

© Copyright Time Out Group 2002

The Sights: Classic

1 Loreto (see p74)
2 Prague Castle (see p64)
3 Golden Lane (see p69)
4 St Nicholas's Church (see p78)
5 Charles Bridge (see p80)
6 Old Jewish Cemetery (see p83)
7 Old-New Synagogue (see p94)
8 Old Town Hall (see p87)
9 Astronomical Clock (see p87)
10 Wenceslas Square (see p95)

The Sights: Alternative

1 Černín Palace, former Gestapo cells (see p74)
2 U Černého vola pub (see p74)
3 U Kocoura, beer party pub (see p77)
4 Wallenstein Gardens (see p78)
5 Rude medieval façade (see p91)
6 U Zlatého stromu club (see p88)
7 Divadlo na zábradlí, Havel's theatre (see p88)
8 Café Montmartre, decadence mecca (see p88)
9 Rott, Renaissance hardware (see p88)
10 Cubist lamp post (see p101)

Introduction

Sightseeing

Charles Bridge: best enjoyed at dawn. *See p90.*

and Holešovice metro stations, it's valid for three days' metro, tram or bus travel throughout the city. It also admits pass-holders to a host of the city's greatest museums, including Prague Castle, the National Gallery, the National Museum, the Dvořák Museum and the Museum of Decorative Arts (*for all, see chapter* **Museums**).

For a city whose fortunes have changed as often as the power balance of Central Europe, all of Prague has remained remarkably intact as essentiall one great museum. Everything from socialist realist monstrosities to the relics of Prague's first tenth-century rotundas surround you, and most cost nothing to see.

But for intrepid visitors who prefer to immerse themselves in a more in-depth guided experience, the folks at **City Walks** (0608 200 912) host a half-day daily walking tour of the centre of town, with a beer and food break, that departs (weather permitting) from the St Wenceslas equestrian statue on Wenceslas Square. As no advance booking is required, just turn up at the statue at 9.45am any day of the week with 450 Kč per person (300 Kč concessions). Look for the person holding up the City Walks poster. The following tour companies also provide informative central walking tours:

Pragotur

Old Town Hall, Staroměstské náměstí, Staré Mesto, Prague 1 (2448 2562/fax 2448 2380/www.prague-info.cz). Metro Staroměstská/17, 18 tram.
Open 9am-6.30pm Mon-Fri; 9am-3.30pm Sat, Sun.
Rates 2,700-4,000 Kč for 2-10 people. **No credit cards. Map** p308 H3.
Four-hour walking tours of Old Town and Prague Castle. Tours are informative, if pricey, and are geared mainly to groups. Fax to book ahead or arrange tours in person at the office, located at the rear of the Prague Information Service bureau (*see* **Directory: Resources A-Z**) in Old Town Hall.

Bohemia Travel Service

Narodní trída 38, Nové Mesto, Prague 1 (2482 6262). Metro Můstek/3, 9, 14, 24 tram.
Open 8am-8pm daily. **Rates** 600 Kč/hr guided walk (per guide); 690 Kč guided tour with river cruise (per person); 990 Kč river cruise with dinner (per person). **Credit** AmEx, MC, V. **Map** p308 J5.
Informative guided tours of Prague and most of the starring towns and castles of the republic. Well-versed leaders are friendly, if slightly pedantic, and are fond of keeping up a brisk pace. One boon here is free hotel pick-up and return. Also, tours of Jewish Prague, Prague by night and cruises add appeal. Discounts of 10% are offered if you arrange the tour in person at the Bohemia Travel Service office.

Hradčany

A magnificent collection of palaces, battlements and spires, the Castle complex rises high above Prague, forming the centrepiece of the city's skyline.

Prague Castle: Czechdom on guard.

Maps p306 & p307

The roots of the Czech nation have a tangible manifestation in **Prague Castle**, at the centre of the Hradčany district. The dizzying heights of its Gothic spires and the flying buttresses of St Vitus's Cathedral can't help but affect you no matter how often you've seen them before. The coronation of Charles IV and the Nazis' march through the gates are just two moments in Hradčany's 1,000-year history that are likely to give you goose bumps. Nowhere else in Prague resonates with as much national identity and symbolism, increased by the pride Czechs take in having the Castle finally returned to them in 1989. Locals and foreigners alike, if they want to escape the hordes that come here by day, will be seen rambling through late at night or on drizzly days when the ghosts of Hradčany are apparently most strongly felt.

The rest of Hradčany comprises the surrounding streets, which stretch north and west from the Castle across the hilltop. It's quiet, enchanting and less heavily touristed than the Castle itself. The Castle grounds demand lengthy strolling but there are a fair number of options for refuelling in the near vicinity and a handful of terrace restaurants visible below. Otherwise, there are richer pickings down the hill in Malá Strana.

Prague Castle

Founded some time around 870 by Přemysl princes, the impressive, if somewhat sombre collection of buildings that make up the Castle – including a grand palace, three churches and a monastery – has been variously extended, torn down and rebuilt over the centuries. The final touches, including the present shape of St Vitus's Cathedral, were not added until the early 20th century, thus the Castle calls to mind some kind of enormous festival of architectural styles stretching all the way back to the Romanesque.

The grandiose façade enclosing the complex is the result of the Empress Maria Theresa's desire to bring some coherence to the jumble of mismatched parts that the Castle had become by the mid 18th century. But the outcome of Nicolo Pacassi's monotonous design concept is uninspiring – 'an imposing mass of building in the factory style of architecture', as one 19th-century commentator put it. After Maria Theresa's son, Joseph II, attempted to turn the Castle into a barracks, it was largely deserted by the Habsburgs. Václav Havel chose not to live here, although his presidential office was installed in the Castle. He did his best to enliven the palace, opening it to the public and hiring the costume designer from the film *Amadeus* to remodel the guards' uniforms (*see p73* **Designer history**).

You really can't get away without spending at least half a day up here. Unfortunately, every visitor to Prague knows this. The result is a notable lack of any real city life, and an awful lot of chattering tour groups and whirring video cameras. To avoid the worst of the crush, come as early or as late in the day as you can.

The first & second courtyards

The grandest entrance to the Castle complex, through the Hradčanské náměstí gates, is now overseen from a discreet distance by an approving Tomáš Garrigue Masaryk, the first president of free Czechoslovakia, whose bronze likeness was added during the cultural festival Praha 2000. The gateway has been dominated since 1768 by Ignatz Platzer's monumental sculptures of battling Titans. They create an impressive, if not exactly welcoming, entrance. The changing of the guard takes place in this courtyard, a Havel-inspired attempt to add some ceremonial pzazz to the Castle. Though the change is carried out hourly every day between 5am and 10pm, the big crowd-pulling ceremony, complete with band, takes place at noon. The two tapering flagpoles are the work of Slovene architect Josip Plečnik, who was hired by President Masaryk during the 1920s to create a more uniform look for the seat of the First Republic.

To reach the second courtyard go through the Matthias Gate (Matyášova brána), a baroque portal dating from 1614, topped by a double-headed German Imperial Eagle that pleased Hitler when he came to stay in 1939. A monumental stairway is visible from inside the passage (on the lefthand side) which leads up to the magnificent gold and white **Spanish Hall** (Španělský sál). It's open to the public only during occasional concerts but they are worth watching for. Built in the 17th century for court ceremonies, the decor was redone in the 19th century when the trompe l'oeil murals were covered with white stucco, and huge mirrors and gilded chandeliers were brought in to transform the space into a suitably glitzy venue for the coronation of Emperor Franz Joseph I.

Franz Joseph, however, failed to show up and it was not until the 1950s that the hall was given a new use – it was here that the Politburo came to discuss the success of their latest five-year plan, protected from assassins by a reinforced steel door. Behind the austere grey walls of the second courtyard lies a warren of opulent state rooms whose heyday dates from the time of Rudolf II. The state rooms of the airy second courtyard, which are rarely open to the public, housed Rudolf's magnificent art collection and such curiosities as a unicorn's horn and three nails from Noah's ark. The bulk of the collection was carried off in 1648 by Swedish soldiers, although some remnants are housed in the **Prague Castle Picture Gallery** (*see p113*) on the north side of the courtyard near the **Powder Bridge** (U Prašného mostu) entrance. A 17th-century baroque fountain, and the Chapel of the Holy Rood, dominate the yard. The houses a box office for Castle tours and concert tickets and rents out audio guides.

Prague Castle

Hradčanské náměstí, Prague 1 (info in English & Czech 2437 3368/www.hrad.cz). *Metro Malostranská/12, 22, 23 tram.* **Open** *May-Oct* 9am-5pm daily. *Nov-Mar* 9am-4pm daily. **Admission** 220 Kč; 120 Kč concessions; 300 Kč guided tours for up to 5 people. Tickets valid for 3 days. **No credit cards. Map** p306 C2.

Charge! The castle makes great war booty.

There's no charge to enter the grounds of the Castle, but you'll need a ticket to see the main attractions. An audio guide (available in English) costs extra and is available from the information centre in the second courtyard. One ticket covers entrance to the Old Royal Palace, the Basilica of St George, the Golden Lane, the Powder Tower and the choir, crypt and tower of St Vitus's Cathedral. Entrance to the art collection of **St George's Convent** (*see p112*) and the **Toy Museum** (*see p118*) costs extra.

It's a stiff walk up to the Castle from Malá Strana's Malostranská metro station. The least strenuous approach is to take the 22 tram up the hill and get off at the Pražský hrad stop. There are a handful of adequate cafés within the Castle complex.

St Vitus's Cathedral

The third courtyard – the oldest and most important site in the Castle – is entirely dominated by the looming towers, pinnacles and buttresses of **St Vitus's Cathedral** (Katedrála sv. Víta). Entry is free to the nave and chapels, but a ticket's required for the rest of the cathedral. Although St Vitus was only completed in 1929, exactly 1,000 years after the murdered St Wenceslas was laid to rest on the site, it's no doubt the magnificent building is the spiritual centre of Bohemia. This has always been a sacred place: in pagan times Svatovít, the Slavic god of fertility, was

worshipped on this site, a clue as to why he cathedral was dedicated to his near namesake St Vitus (svatý Vít in Czech) – a Sicilian peasant who became a Roman legionnaire before he was thrown to the lions. Right up until the 18th century young women and anxious farmers would bring offerings of wine, cakes and cocks. The cathedral's Gothic structure owes its creation to Charles IV's lifelong love affair with Prague. In 1344 he managed to secure an archbishopric for the city, and work began on the construction of a cathedral under the instructions of French architect Matthew of Arras. Inconveniently, Matthew dropped dead eight years into the project, so the Swabian Peter Parler was called in to take up the challenge. He was responsible for the 'Sondergotik' or German late Gothic design. It remained unfinished until late 19th-century nationalists completed the work according to Parler's original plans. The skill with which the later work was carried out makes it difficult to tell where the Gothic ends and the neo-Gothic begins, but a close look at the nave and the twin towers and rose window of the west end will reveal the tell-tale lighter-coloured newer stone.

From outside, as from anywhere in the town below, the **Great Tower** is easily the most dominant feature. The Gothic and Renaissance structure is topped with a baroque dome. This

Sightseeing

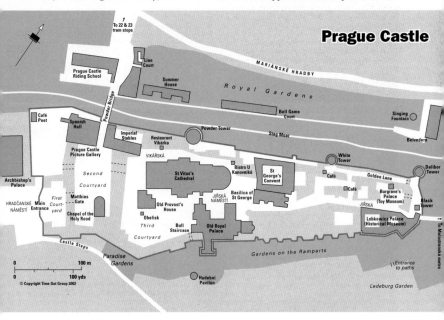

Prague Castle

St Vitus's Cathedral: Gothic heights and a constant play of light. *See p65.*

houses **Sigismund**, unquestionably the largest bell in Bohemia, weighing in at a hefty 15,120 kilgrams (33,333 pounds). Getting Sigismund into the tower was no mean feat: according to legend it took a rope woven from the hair of the city's noblest virgins to haul it into position. Below the tower is the **Gothic Golden Portal** (Zlatá brána), visible from the courtyard south of the cathedral. It's decorated with a mosaic of multicoloured Venetian glass depicting the Last Judgement. A Getty-funded project has restored its original lustre after years of refurbishment. On either side of the centre arch are sculptures of Charles IV and his wife Elizabeth of Pomerania, whose talents allegedly included being able to bend a sword with her bare hands.

Inside, the enormous nave is flooded with multicoloured light from the gallery of stained-glass windows created at the beginning of this century. All 21 of them, during a period of nationalist fervour, were sponsored by finance institutions including (third on the right) an insurance company whose motto – 'those who sow in sorrow shall reap in joy' – is subtly incorporated into the biblical allegory. The most famous is the third window on the left, in the Archbishop's Chapel, created by Alfons Mucha. It depicts the struggle of Christian Slavonic tribes; appropriately enough, the art work was paid for by Banka Slavia.

On the right is the **Chapel of St Wenceslas** (Svatováclavská kaple), on the site of the original tenth-century rotunda where 'Good King' Wenceslas was buried. Built in 1345, the chapel has 1,345 polished amethysts, agates and jaspers incorporated into its design, and contains some of the saint's personal paraphernalia, including armour, chain shirt and helmet. Alas, it is closed to the public – too many sweaty bodies were causing the gilded plaster to disintegrate – but a glint of its treasure trove glory can be glimpsed over the railings.

Occasionally, on state anniversaries, the skull of the saint is put on display, covered with a cobweb-fine veil. A door in the corner leads to the chamber that contains the crown jewels (*see p68* **Stashing the crown**). A papal bull of 1346 officially protects the jewels, while legend has it that fate prescribes an early death for anyone who uses them improperly. The door to the chamber is locked with seven keys, after the seven seals of Revelations.

The most extraordinary baroque addition to the cathedral was the silver tombstone of St John of Nepomuk, the priest who was flung from Charles Bridge in 1393 as a result of King Wenceslas IV's anti-clericalism (*see p16*; **A five-star fraud**). The tomb, designed by Fischer von Erlach the Younger in 1733-6, is a

Stashing the crown

Unless you're being sworn in as president, you're unlikely to see the crown jewels while visiting Prague Castle. As national symbols go, the priceless crown, sceptre and orb are particularly elusive. Since the creation of the crown in 1345 it's been stored in a chamber whose only entrance is at the south-west corner of the **Chapel of St Wenceslas** (*see p67*), whose door is locked with seven locks. The keys to the locks are distributed among seven VIPs in the Czech Republic and needless to say it's a fairly exclusive club: the president, the prime minister, the head of the Chamber of Deputies, the president of the Senate, the mayor of Prague, the archbishop of Prague and the deacon of St Vitus's Cathedral.

Unfortunately, these folks don't often mingle with the masses, so the crown jewels were only placed on public display eight times in the 20th century. The last time they were trotted out, for the swearing in of President Václav Havel in 1993, it rained cats and dogs on people who queued

for hours. Alas, it would seem that a glimpse of the crown jewels is only for the dedicated and true of heart.

Any unauthorised person who touches the crown gets instant excommunication by the terms of a deal worked out by Charles IV and the pope. And it's said that Hitler's man in Prague, Reichsprotektor Reinhard Heydrich, slipped on the crown for a laugh once. He was dead within days, assassinated by Czech patriots.

But in truth, there may be another reason why the crown jewels are so seldom seen: historically, they haven't really spent that much time here. For nearly two centuries, from 1436, the jewels lived at **Karlštejn**, King Charles's summer castle (*see p253*); during the Thirty Years War they were kept in various hiding spots around Prague; and for another century and a half after the war they were held at the Habsburg imperial treasury in Vienna.

When the jewels do come out, it's fair to say they make an impression. They're often accompanied by the decapitated skull of St

---

flamboyant affair (the entry ticket is now required to get a proper look at it). Two tons of silver were used for the pedestal, statue of the saint and fluttering cherubs holding up a red velvet canopy. The phrase 'baroque excess' scarcely does it justice. Close by is the entrance to the crypt. Below lie the remains of various Czech monarchs, including not only George of Poděbrady but Rudolf II. Easily the most eye-catching tomb is Charles IV's modern, streamlined metal affair that was designed by Kamil Roškot (1934-5).

The third courtyard

After the cathedral, the second most noticeable monument in the third courtyard is the fairly incongruous 17-metre (50-foot) high granite obelisk, a memorial to the dead of World War I erected by Plečnik in 1928.

Close to the Golden Portal is the entrance to the **Old Royal Palace** (Starý královský palác, ticket required), which contains three levels of royal apartments. Six centuries of kings called the palace home and systematically built over new parts over the old. In what is now the basement you can see the dingy 12th-century Romanesque remains of Prince Soběslav's residence. The palace contains a worthwhile highlight, the **Vladislav Hall**. Designed by

Benedict Ried at the turn of the 16th century, its exquisitely vaulted ceiling was the last flowering of the Gothic, while the large, square windows are the first expressions of the Renaissance in Bohemia. It is here that the National Assembly elects its new president. The specially designed **Rider's Steps** allowed knights to enter the hall without dismounting. Higher up again (in the Louis Wing) is the **Bohemian Chancellery** and the window through which the victims of the defenestration of 1618 were ejected.

Just east of the cathedral is Jiřské náměstí, named after **St George's Basilica** (Bazilika sv. Jiří). If you stand far enough back from the

Castle courtyards: a neo-classic make-over.

Vikářská lane, on the north side of the cathedral, is where Picasso and Eluard came to drink in the Vikářská tavern (closed for renovations at press time). It gives access to the 15th-century Mihulka or **Powder Tower** (Prašná věž). Here Rudolf II employed his many alchemists, who were engaged in attempts to distil the Elixir of Life and transmute base metals into gold. The tower now hosts exhibits about alchemy, bell- and cannon-forging and Renaissance life in the Castle.

Elsewhere on the Castle grounds

Going down the hill from St George's, signposts direct you to the most visited street in Prague, **Golden Lane** (Zlatá ulička, ticket required). The tiny multicoloured cottages that cling to the Castle's northern walls were thrown up by the poor in the 16th century out of whatever waste materials they could find. Some allege that the name is a reference to the alchemists of King Rudolf's time, who supposedly were quartered here. Others contend that it alludes to a time when soldiers billeted in a nearby tower used the lane as a public urinal. In fact, the name probably dates from the 17th century, when the city's goldsmiths worked here. Houses used to line both sides of the street, with barely enough space to pass between them, until a hygiene-conscious Joseph II had some of them demolished in the 18th century. Although the houses look separate, a corridor runs the length of their attics and used to be occupied by the sharpshooters of the Castle Guard. The house at No.22 was owned by Kafka's sister Otla, and he stayed here for a while in 1917, reputedly drawing the inspiration from the streets for his

Wenceslas. The crown itself is in coronet form, made of gold plate and divided into four sections adorned with sculpted lillies, contains a large cameo made up of 19 sapphires, 44 spinels, 30 emeralds, 22 pearls and an economy-sized ruby. The whole shebang weighs in at 2.475 kilogrammes (5.46 pounds), which may explain why it's not worn much. Alas, no historical records seem to indicate what hat size it is, but it does come with some lovely accessories. The fabulously jewelled sceptre and orb, which were crafted later, also come accessorised with the sword of St Wenceslas, a fashionable ermine mantle and a coronation cross.

You might just get away with a virtual peek at the crown jewels (with abundant statistics) at the website of Prague Castle (www.hrad.cz) without putting yourself at too much risk. The only real danger there is putting yourself through the purple prose that fills the webpages.

basilica's crumbling red and cream baroque façade, you'll notice the two distinctive Romanesque towers jutting out behind. The Italian craftsmen who constructed them in 1142 built a fatter male tower (Adam, on the right) standing guard over a more slender female one (Eve, on the left). The basilica, founded by Prince Vratislav in 921, has burned down and been rebuilt over the centuries. Its first major remodelling took place 50 years after it was first erected when a Benedictine convent was founded next door. A major renovation in the early 20th century swept out most of the baroque elements and led to the uncovering of the original arcades, remnants of 13th-century frescoes and the bodies of a saint (Ludmila, who was strangled by assassins hired by Prince Wenceslas's mother Drahomíra) and a saint-maker (the notorious Boleslav the Cruel, who martyred his brother Wenceslas by having him stabbed to death). The basilica's rediscovered simplicity and clean lines seem far closer to godliness than the mammon-fuelled baroque pomposity of most Prague churches.

On the left of the main entrance is an opening built to give access for the Benedictine nuns from **St George's Convent** next door (now housing part of the National Gallery's vast collections; *see p112*) and to keep to a minimum their contact with the outside world.

Golden Lane: Kafka's 'hood.

Heavy breathing on the Castle Steps.

President Novotný decided that his genitals were not an edifying sight for the masses and ordered them to be removed. Happily the boy and his equipment have since been reunited.

The lane passes under the **Black Tower** (Černá věž) and ends at the **Old Castle Steps** (Staré zámecké schody), which lead to Malá Strana, as do the **Castle Steps** on Thunovská. Before descending, pause at the top for a view over the red tiled roofs, spires and domes of the 'Lesser Quarter'. An even better view can be had from the **Paradise Gardens** on the ramparts below the Castle walls (enter from the Bull Staircase, or from outside the Castle, to the right of the first courtyard). This is where the victims of the second and most famous defenestration fell to earth. They were fortunate that it was a favoured spot for emptying chamber pots, as the dung heap surely saved the lives of the defenestrated Catholic counsellors. The site is now marked by an obelisk, signifying ground consecrated by the victorious Habsburgs after putting down the upstart Czech Protestants.

The gardens laid out in 1562 were redesigned in the 1920s by Josip Plečnik. The spiralling Bull Staircase leading up to the Castle's third courtyard and the huge granite bowl are his work. Their restoration is finally complete, and you can now make the descent to Malá Strana via the terraced slopes of five beautiful Renaissance gardens, open, like most gardens in Prague only from April to October. The pride of the restoration is the lovely **Ledebour Gardens**, featuring fountains, ornate stone stair switchbacks and palace yards, and empties you out on to the middle of Valdštejnská. Fit hikers might consider ascending to the Castle this way as well, though there's an entrance fee of 60 Kč whichever way you go.

novel *The Castle*. If he rewrote it today, he'd call it *The Souvenir Shop*. Atmospheric at night, by day the lane is a logjam of shuffling tourists.

At the eastern end some steps take you under the last house and out to the **Dalibor Tower** (Daliborka), named after its most famous inmate, who amused himself by playing the violin while awaiting execution. According to legend (and Smetana's opera *Dalibor*), he attracted crowds of onlookers who turned up at his execution to weep en masse. Continuing down the hill takes you past another **Lobkowicz Palace** (Lobkovický palác), one of several in the town. This one, finished in 1658, houses the Historical Museum. Opposite is Burgrave House, now home of the **Toy Museum** (*see p118*). The statue of a naked boy in the courtyard fell victim to Marxist-Leninist ideology when

The Royal Garden & the Belvedere

When crossing over the **Powder Bridge** (U Prašného mostu) from the Castle's second courtyard, you reach the **Royal Garden** (Královská zahrada), on the outer side of the Stag Moat. It was laid out for Emperor Ferdinand I in the 1530s and once included a maze and a menagerie, but was devastated by Swedish soldiers in the 17th century.

At the eastern end of the gardens is the **Belvedere** saved from French fire in the 18th century by a canny head gardener's payment of 30 pineapples. The stunning Renaissance structure was built by Paola della Stella between 1538 and 1564 (though work was interrupted by a fire at the Castle in 1541). The strangely shaped green copper roof is

Heads up: Hradčany spikes the horizon.

supported by delicate arcades and columns.
The Belvedere was the first royal structure
in Prague to be dedicated to pleasure-seeking
rather than power-mongering – it was
commissioned by Ferdinand I as a gift for his
wife Anne – a loveshack one remove away from
the skulduggery of life in the Castle. But the
long-suffering Anne never got to see 'the most
beautiful piece of Renaissance architecture
north of the Alps' (as the city's gushing tourist
brochures invariably call it). She drew her
last breath after producing the 15th heir to the
throne. The royal couple are immortalised in
the reliefs adorning the façade. The Belvedere
went on to become the site of all sorts of goings-
on: mad King Rudolf installed his astronomers
here and the communists later bricked up the
windows of the upper level to prevent assassins
from getting too close to the president. People

come here today to see occasional art shows
(*see also p28*). In front of the palace is the so-
called **Singing Fountain**, created in bronze
by Bohemian craftsmen in the 1560s. It used to
hum as water splashed into its basin, but sings
no longer since an extensive reconstruction.

On the southern side of the garden
overlooking the Stag Moat is another lovely
Renaissance structure, completed by Bonifác
Wohlmut in 1563 to house the king's **Ball
Game Court** (Míčovna). The elaborate black
and white sgraffito has to be renewed every 20
years. The last time this was done some
decidedly anachronistic elements were added
to the allegorical frieze depicting Science, the
Virtues and the Elements: look carefully at the
lovely ladies on the top of the building and
you'll see that the woman seated next to Justice
(tenth from the right) is holding a hammer and

Amsterdam · Barcelona · Berlin · Boston · Brussels · Budapest
Buenos Aires · Chicago · Copenhagen · Dublin · Edinburgh · Florence
Havana · Hong Kong · Istanbul · Las Vegas · Lisbon · London
Los Angeles · Madrid · Miami · Milan · Moscow · Naples
New Orleans · New York · Paris · Prague · Rome · San Francisco
South of France · Sydney · Tokyo · Venice · Vienna · Washington, DC

The **Time Out City Guides** spectrum

Available from all good bookshops and at www.timeout.com/shop

www.timeout.com   www.penguin.com

sickle. On the same side of the garden, by the entrance, is the quaint, mustard-coloured **Dientzenhofer Summer House**, the presidential residence between 1948 and 1989. During this period, large sections of the Castle were closed to the public and huge underground shelters were excavated to connect the exalted president's residence with the remainder of the complex. No sooner were the shelters completed than it was seen that the subterranean passages might help to conceal counter-revolutionary saboteurs, and so the exit shafts were blocked off with enormous concrete slabs.

Hradčany

Hradčany owes its grand scale and pristine condition to a devastating fire in 1541, which destroyed the medieval district, and the frenzied period of Counter-Reformation building following the Protestant defeat at the Battle of White Mountain in 1620. Little has changed here in the last two centuries.

The area's focal point is **Hradčanské náměstí**, one of the grandest squares in the city, lined with imposing palaces built by the Catholic aristocracy, anxious to be close to the

Designer history

The noon changing of the guard at Prague Castle is a stirring sight with the semblance of an age-old ritual. And that's just what the 1990 administration ordered: the semblance. For the ceremony is a piece of confected theatre produced by master dramatist Václav Havel.

Havel once remarked that he did not believe democracy could be founded in a nation with 'grubby-looking troops'. With that in mind, he commissioned Theodor Pištěk, the Academy Award-winning costume designer for Miloš Forman's films *Amadeus* and *Valmont*, to design new outfits for the guards. Out went the ill-fitting, Soviet-style green uniforms and in their place appeared stately navy blue tunics and tri-colour shoulder braiding, adorned with epaulettes, collars and belt buckles emblazoned with insignia of Czech legionnaires from World War I. New caps were conceived with the help of a US Naval attaché who happened to be in town (creating an impression that will be oddly familiar to anyone who's ever lived near an American naval base).

Duty assignments were changed from keeping Castle visitors at bay to standing benignly at attention before the entry gates, looking picturesque for tourist cameras, and putting up with the taunts of children trying to make them laugh. The newly outfitted troops were an unqualified success.

But there was still something missing. Enter Michal Prokop, Czech pop star extraordinaire, formerly of the Prague 1960s sensation Framus Five. A convincing fanfare for an elaborate changing of the guard ceremony was composed without much difficulty, but where to put the brass band? The first courtyard is awfully small, even without a crowd of onlookers. So the musicians play

their sousaphones and trumpets out of a Castle window, standing on tables for acoustical reasons. And for the choreography, the head of the Castle Guard took a video camera to Buckingham Palace to record suitably ceremonial-looking steps.

Designer history? Perhaps, but then there's little in the historical record for Czechs to work with. A history of Bohemia and Moravia didn't even exist in Czech until the cultural revival of the 19th century. If the Castle Guard is guilty of theatre, they surely aren't any more so than the architects who knocked down medieval chapels to put a neo-Gothic front on to the unfinished St Vitus's Cathedral a century ago.

And sentry parades are surely more innocent than the *Rukopis královédvorský*, a historical account of ancient Czech victories 'discovered' by Václav Hanka in 1817, later pronounced a complete fraud by President Masaryk.

Besides, if the first non-violent revolution in the history of these lands isn't worthy of a little ceremony and spectacle, then what is? Now if the director could just get the guards to stop smirking on duty...

Guards: Look right!

Habsburg court. It was nonetheless cut off from the Castle and its temperamental inhabitants by a complicated system of fortifications, and moats, which remained until Empress Maria Theresa had a grand spring clean in the mid 18th century. Along with the moat went the tiny Church of the Virgin Mary of Einsedel, which used to stand next to the Castle ramp. Lovely as this was said to have been, it's hard to believe that it was lovelier than the superb panorama of Malá Strana, the Strahov Gardens and Petřín Hill that the demolition opened up.

On the north side of the square, next to the Castle, is the domineering 16th-century **Archbishop's Palace** (Arcibiskupský palác), tarted up with a frothy rococo façade in 1763-4. Next door, slotted between the palace and a lane of former canons' houses, stands the **Sternberg Palace** (Šternberský palác), which houses part of the National Gallery's collection of European art (*see p112*). Opposite stands the heavily restored **Schwarzenberg Palace** (Schwarzenberský palác), one of the most imposing Renaissance buildings in Prague. It was built between 1545 and 1563, the outside exquisitely decorated with 'envelope' sgraffito. It now contains the **Military Museum** (*see p116*), which has a comprehensive collection of killing instruments – perhaps an appropriate exhibit for the country that gave the world the words 'pistol' and 'Semtex'.

Further up Loretánská is the respected pub **U Černého vola** (*see p146*), a Renaissance building with a crumbling mural on the façade. As a result of some direct action in 1991, it's one of the few places left in Hradčany where the locals can afford to drink. The regulars foiled several attempts at privatisation by forming a co-operative to run it in conjunction with the Friends of Beer, now downgraded from a political party to a civic association. You don't have to feel guilty about the amount you drink here – all profits from the sale of beer go to a nearby school for the blind.

The pub overlooks Loretánské náměstí, a split-level square on the site of a pagan cemetery. Half of it is taken up by a car park for the Ministry of Foreign Affairs in the monolithic **Černín Palace** (Černínský palác) – an enormous and unprepossessing structure; its long and imposing grey façade, articulated by an unbroken line of 30 pillars, is telling. Commissioned in 1669 by Humprecht Johann Černín, the Imperial ambassador to Venice, the construction of the palace financially ruined his family. As a result, the first people to move in were hundreds of 17th-century squatters. Gestapo interrogations were later conducted here during the Nazi occupation. Its curse surfaced again in 1948, when Foreign

Minister Jan Masaryk, the last major political obstacle to Klement Gottwald's communist coup, fell from an upstairs window a few days after the takeover and was found dead on the pavement below. No one really believed the official verdict of suicide but no evidence of who was responsible has ever come to light.

Somewhat dwarfed by the Černín Palace is the **Loreto** (*see below*), a baroque testimony to the Catholic miracle culture that swept the Czech lands after the Thirty Years War. The façade (1721) is a swirling mass of stuccoed cherubs, topped with a bell tower. Every hour the 27 bells ring out the cacophonous melody 'We Greet You a Thousand Times'.

The streets behind the Loreto are some of the prettiest and quietest in Hradčany. The quarter was built in the 16th century for the Castle staff; its tiny cottages are now the most prized real estate in the city. Going down Kapucínská, you pass the Domeček or 'Little House' at No.10, once home to the notorious Fifth Department – the counter-intelligence unit of the Defence Ministry. At No.5 on the nearby Černínská is **Gambra**, a funky gallery specialising in surrealist art. Its owner, the world-renowned animator Jan Švankmajer, lives in the attached house. At the foot of the hill is **Nový Svět** ('New World'), a street of brightly coloured cottages restored in the 18th and 19th centuries – all that remains of Hradčany's medieval slums. Most of the rest were destroyed in the great fire of 1541. Tycho Brahe, the Danish alchemist known for his missing nose and breakthroughs in accurate observations of orbits, lived at No.1, called 'The Golden Griffin'.

Back up from Loretánské náměstí is Hradčany's last major square, **Pohořelec**. The passage at No.8 leads to the peaceful surroundings of the **Strahov Monastery** (*see p75*). The monastery contains some magnificent libraries and religious art.

The Loreto

Loretánské náměstí 7, Prague 1 (2051 6740).
Tram 22. **Open** 9am-12.15pm, 1-4.30pm Tue-Sun. **Admission** 80 Kč; 60 Kč concessions. **No credit cards. Map** p306 B3.
The Loreto is probably the most outlandish piece of baroque fantasy in Prague. Its attractions include a sculpture of the bearded St Wilgefortis, the skeletons of another two female saints, an ecclesiastical extravagance, and the highest concentration of cherubs to be found anywhere in the city. It was built as part of a calculated plan to reconvert the masses to Catholicism after the Thirty Years War.

At its heart is a small chapel, the Santa Casa, whose history is so improbable that it quickly gained cult status. The story goes that the original Santa Casa was the home of Mary in Nazareth until

Czech myth and might...   ... in the struggle for domination.

it was miraculously flown over to Loreto in Italy by angels, spawning a copycat cult all over Europe (there are 50 in Bohemia alone). This one, from 1626-31, boasts two beams and a brick from the 'original', as well as a crevice left on the wall by a divine thunderbolt that struck an unfortunate blasphemer. The red colour scheme makes it look less like a virgin's boudoir and more like a place to hold a black mass.

The shrine was a particular hit with wealthy ladies who donated the money for baroque maestri Christoph and Kilian Ignaz Dientzenhofer to construct the outer courtyards and the Church of the Nativity (1716-23) at the back. They also sponsored the carving of St Wilgefortis (in the corner chapel to the right of the main entrance), the patron saint of unhappily married women, who grew a beard as a radical tactic to get out of marrying a heathen, and that of St Agatha the Unfortunate, who can be seen carrying her severed breasts on a meat platter (in the Church of the Nativity). The famous diamond monstrance, designed in 1699 by Fischer von Erlach and sporting 6,222 stones, is in the treasury.

Strahov Monastery

Strahovské nádvoří 1, Prague 1 (2051 7451). Tram 8, 22/143, 149, 217 bus. **Open** 9am-12.30pm, 1-5pm Tue-Sun. **Admission** 50 Kč; 30 Kč concessions. **No credit cards. Map** p306 A4.

The Premonstratensian monks set up house here in 1140, and soon after embarked upon their austere programme of celibacy and silent contemplation. The complex still has an air of seclusion and a fragrant orchard stretching down the hill to Malá Strana. Since 1990, several cowled monks have

returned to reclaim the buildings nationalised by the communists in 1948. They can sometimes be seen from Úvoz street walking laps around green fields and meditating and services are once again being held in the Church of Our Lady, which retained its 12th-century basilica ground plan after remodelling in the early 17th century.

The highlights of the complex are surely the superb libraries, which appear on posters in universities all over the world. Within the frescoed Theological and Philosophical Halls alone are 130,000 volumes. There are a further 700,000 volumes in storage and together they form the most important collection in Bohemia. Visitors cannot, unfortunately, stroll around the libraries. They are, however, generously allowed to gawp through the doors. The comprehensive acquisition of books didn't begin until the late 16th century. When Joseph II effected a clampdown on religious institutions in 1782, the Premonstratensians managed to outwit him by masquerading as an educational foundation, and their collection was swelled by the libraries of less shrewd monasteries. Indeed, the monks' taste ranged far beyond the standard ecclesiastical tracts, including such highlights as the oldest extant copy of *The Calendar of Minutae or Selected Times for Bloodletting*. Nor did they merely confine themselves to books: the 200-year-old curiosity cabinets house a collection of deep-sea monsters that any land-locked country would be proud to possess.

In another part of the monastery complex, the Strahov Gallery exhibits a small part of the monks' considerable collection of religious art.

Malá Strana

An island park, riverside dining, jazz bars and backstreets that parliamentarians keep to themselves. Nothing lesser about the 'Lesser Quarter'.

Map p307

Prague's Malá Strana district is a maze of quiet lanes that lie between the Vltava River and Prague Castle, skirting the hill that makes up Hradčany. Historically the home of nobles in favour with the king, it's full of palaces, embassies and fantastically ornate churches; best of all, the once private formal gardens are now open to strollers. This little leftbank area has always been home to Prague's boho poets, artists and musicians, as well, something you'll pick up on as you hear string serenades emanating from conservatories on your way to a coffee joint or a tiny jazz cellar.

Malá Strana was founded by the Přemyslid Otakar II in 1287, when he invited merchants from Germany to set up shop on the land beneath the Castle walls. Very little remains of this Gothic town today – the present-day appearance of the quarter dates to the 17th century. The area was transformed into a sparkling baroque district by the wealthy Catholic aristocracy, who won huge parcels of land in the property redistribution that followed the Thirty Years' War. When the fashionable followed the court to Vienna in the 17th century, the poor took back the area. It has been the home of poets, drunks and mystics ever since, living cheek by jowl with the ambassadors and diplomats who also inhabit what is one of Prague's two diplomatic quarters – the British, American, German, Irish, Italian and French embassies, among many others, are situated in Malá Strana.

Today the character here is changing rapidly, as accountancy firms, bankers and wine bars set up shop. It's still remarkable, though, just how few businesses there are in what is one of the most central Prague districts. Malostranské náměstí now throbs with life deep into the night, but this is mostly down to overt tourism marketing, and its many bars, restaurants and music venues. Apart from stores selling souvenirs and cut glass, there is very little shopping in the area.

Thus the district has been lucky enough to preserve its ancient look and the back streets of Malá Strana are a favourite locale for an endless stream of film crews shooting period pieces in the city. Local residents are unfazed by the attention, however, and carry on as ever.

Malostranské náměstí & around

The short, main drag between Charles Bridge and Malostranské náměstí is **Mostecká**. It's a continuation of the Royal Route – the path taken by the Bohemian kings to their coronation – and is lined with elegant baroque dwellings. One at No.15 is the **Kaunitz Palace** (Kaunicův palác), built in 1773 for Jan Adam Kaunitz, an advisor to Empress Maria Theresa, who sycophantically had the exterior painted her favourite colours – yellow and white. It's now the embassy of the former Yugoslavia. Just off Mostecká are the **Blue Light** jazz pub (see p147) and **U Patrona** restaurant (see p122), both oases of quality in a stretch that is over-dominated by naff souvenir shops. At the heart of the quarter is wide open **Malostranské náměstí**, a lively square edged

Malá Strana: not so bad from Charles Bridge.

by large baroque palaces and Renaissance gabled townhouses perched on top of Gothic arcades. At press time the 100-year-old **Malostranská kavárna** was undergoing major renovations but was poised to be a major addition to Prague's reviving café culture. The historic space that helped shape many of the beloved **Jan Neruda's** *Prague Tales* (*see p81* **Lights, camera, Jan Neruda**) has been taken over by Nils Jebens, an accomplished restaurateur, so expectations are high. Bang in the middle of the square, dividing it in two, is the girth of **Church of St Nicholas** (*see p78*), a monumental late baroque affair, whose dome and adjoining bell tower dominate the skyline of Prague's left bank. Built between 1703 and 1755, it's the largest and most ornate of the city's many Jesuit-founded churches. During its construction, the Society of Jesus waged a pitched battle against local residents loath to let go of the two streets, two churches and various other structures that had to be demolished to make room for the church.

The grim block next door at No.25 is yet another Jesuit construction, built as a college for its priests and now housing harassed-looking maths students. More appealing is the **Lichtenstein Palace** (Lichtenštejnský palác; *see p214*) opposite, finished in 1791. The Lichtensteins used to be major landowners in Bohemia and the Alpine principality has been battling to regain the palace, which was confiscated in 1918. The palace is currently used as a venue for classical concerts. Also in the square, located in the former town hall at No.21, is the club **Malostranská beseda** (*see p217*), home to music of a more raucous bent. Opposite the south side of St Nicholas is a parade of pubs and restaurants. The American backpacker hangout **Jo's Bar** (*see p147*) and the seafood restaurant **Circle Line** (*see p123*) are all on this stretch. The tables outside this last, in the south-west corner of the square, are a grand spot for summer dining.

Nerudova heads up from the north-west corner of the square towards the Castle, and is a fine place to begin deciphering the ornate signs that decorate many Prague houses: the Three Fiddles at No.12, for example, or the Devil at No.4. This practice of distinguishing houses continued up until 1770, when that relentless modernist Joseph II spoiled all the fun by introducing numbered addresses. The street, which is crowded with restaurants, cafés, and shops aimed at the ceaseless flow of tourists to and from the Castle, is, as you might expet, named the poet and novelist Jan Neruda. He lived at No.47, the Two Suns (U dvou slunců). The house was turned into a pub and during the communist period was a favourite

hangout of the Plastic People of the Universe, the underground rock band who were later instrumental in the founding of Charter 77, the petition carried out in December 1976 against restrictions of the regime. The place is now a joyless tourist trap. Also to be ignored is the turquoise drinking establishment at No.13 where Václav Havel, in an uncharacteristic lapse of taste, took Yeltsin for a mug of beer. A better bet is **U Kocoura** at No.2. It's owned by the Friends of Beer, formerly a political party, now a civic association. Although its manifesto is a bit vague, the staff's ability to pull a good, cheap pint is beyond question. The more recent **Bazaar Mediterranée** (*see p123*) at No.40 offers enviable terrace views for lunch and ridiculous striptease and dragshow entertainments with dinner.

The alley next door leads up to the British Embassy at Thunovská 14, which a diplomatic wag christened 'Czechers'. Leading up from here are the **New Castle Steps** (Nové zámecké schody), one of the most peaceful (and least strenuous) routes up to the Castle, and a star location in the film *Amadeus*.

There are still more embassies back on the Nerudova, the Italians occupying the **Thun-Hohenstein Palace** (Thun-Hohenštejnský palác) at No.20, built by Giovanni Santini-Aichel in 1726 and distinguished by the contorted eagles holding up the portal, the heraldic emblem of the Kolowrats for whom the palace was built. The Italians were trumped for a while by the Romanians, however, who used to inhabit the even more glorious **Morzin Palace** (Morzinský palác) opposite at No.5. Also the work of Santini-Aichel (1714), the façade sports two hefty Moors, a pun on the family's name, who hold up the window ledge. Their toes have been rubbed shiny by passers-by who believe that touching them will bring luck.

Nerudova also leads up to Prague Castle, and with the added incentive of a fine respite from the crowds and a good midway break, provided by **U zavešeného kafe** (*see p148*), a mellow pub around the corner from the top of this street.Walking back down Nerudova, if you continue straight down the tram tracks instead of veering off on to Malostranské náměstí, you'll see on your left the **Church of St Thomas** (*see p78*). Its rich baroque façade is easy to miss, tucked into the narrow side street of Tomášská. Based on a Gothic ground plan, the church was rebuilt in the baroque style by Kilián Ignaz Dientzenhofer for the Augustinian monks. The symbol of the order – a flaming heart – can be seen all over the church and adjoining cloisters (now an old people's home) and it makes a distinct

Sightseeing

St Nicholas's Church: 'splendour' seems somehow inadequate.

impression as seen held tightly in the hand of St Boniface, a fully dressed skeleton who occupies a glass case in the nave.

On the corner of Josefská and Letenská is the **Church of St Joseph** (sv. Josef), a tiny baroque gem set back from the road and designed by Jean-Baptiste Mathey. Since 1989 it has been returned to the much-diminished Order of English Virgins, who were also one-time owners of the nearby **Vojan's Gardens**, one of the most tranquil spots in the city.

Running parallel to U lužického semináře is **Cihelná**, a street named after the former brick factory now being renovated into studios. The street provides an opening on to the river and an almost perfect view of the Vltava and Charles Bridge beyond. Back on Letenská, towards Malostranská metro station, is a door in a wall leading into the best-kept formal gardens in the city. The early 17th-century **Wallenstein Gardens** belonged, along with the adjoining **Wallenstein Palace**, to General Albrecht von Wallenstein (Valdštejn), commander of the Catholic armies in the Thirty Years' War and a formidable property speculator. The palace (which now contains the Czech Parliament) is simply enormous. Designed by the Milanese architect Andrea Spezza between 1624 and 1630, it once had a permanent staff of 700 servants and 1,000 horses. A little-noticed entrance to the palace gardens, just to the right of the Malostranská metro station exit, provides a wonderful way of cutting through the district and leaving tourists behind.

Much of the area of Malá Strana between Malostranská metro station and the square is these days sprouting cosy little bars and cafés, one of the best being **Palffy Palác** (*see p122*).

Another, just uphill from Parliament, and a new favourite of its members, is **U zlaté studně** (*see p122*), up the tiny street of the same name.

Church of St Nicholas

Malostranské náměstí, Prague 1 (2419 0991). Metro Malostranská/12, 22 tram. **Open** noon-4pm Mon; 10am-4pm Tue-Sun. **Admission** free. **Map** p307 D3.
The immense dome and belltower of St Nicholas, which dominate Malá Strana, are monuments to the money and effort that the Catholic Church sank into the Counter-Reformation. The rich façade by Christoph Dientzenhofer, completed around 1710, conceals an interior and dome by his son Kilián Ignaz dedicated to high baroque at its most flamboyantly camp – bathroom-suite pinks and greens, swooping golden cherubs, swirling gowns and dramatic gestures; there's even a figure coyly proffering a pair of handcuffs.

Commissioned by the Jesuits, it took three generations of architects, several financial crises and the demolition of much of the neighbourhood between presentation of the first plans in 1653 to final completion in 1755. Inside, a trompe l'oeil extravaganza created by the Austrian Johann Lukas Kracker covers the ceiling, seamlessly blending with the actual structure of the church below. Frescoes portray the life and times of St Nicholas, best known as the Bishop of Myra and the bearer of gifts to small children, but also the patron saint of municipal administration. Maybe this is why St Nicholas's was restored by the communists in the 1950s when the rest of Prague's baroque churches were left to crumble. The church tower also happened to make a favourite spy roost for teams of secret police.

Church of St Thomas

Kostel sv. Tomáše
Josefská 8, Prague 1 (5753 0556). Metro Malostranská/12, 22 tram. **Open** 10.30am-1pm daily. **Admission** free. **Map** p307 E3.

The **Church of St Nicholas** tower, former secret police roost. *See p78.*

Saska ulička: where flowers go to die. *See p81.*

It's worth craning your neck to get a good look at the curvy pink façade of St Thomas's. The lopsided structure is the legacy of an earlier Gothic church built for the Order of Augustinian hermits. After the structure was damaged by fire in 1723, Kilián Ignaz Dientzenhofer was employed to give it the baroque touch. The newly rich burghers of Malá Strana provided enough cash for the frescoes to be completed at breakneck speed (they took just two years) and for Rubens to paint the altarpiece *The Martyrdom of St Thomas*. They even bought the bodies of two saints. The original altarpiece is now part of the National Gallery's collection on show in the Šternberg Palace (*see p112*) and has been replaced by a copy, but the skeletons of the saints dressed in period costume are still on display. Next door are 17th-century cloisters, where the monks dabbled in alchemy before realising that transforming hops into beer was easier and more lucrative than trying to make gold out of lead. A door on Letenská leads to their former brewery, now a tourist-infested restaurant.

Kampa Island

The approach to Malá Strana from Staré Město via Charles Bridge affords one of the best photo opportunities in the city: the twin towers of the bridge, framing an almost perfect view of the Church of St Nicholas and the Castle behind. Before continuing, however, take the flight of steps on the left, leading down to Na Kampě, the principal square of **Kampa Island**. Until 1770, it was known simply as Ostrov or 'island', which understandably led to confusion with the other islands of the Vltava – especially since Kampa's southern end looks as if it's attached to land. A little fork of the Vltava, the burbling Čertovka, translated as Little Devil, runs briefly

underground at the south end but resurfaces to slice Kampa from the mainland. It went by the altogether unromantic name of the 'Ditch' until it was cleaned up and rechristened in the 19th century. The communists proposed filling the Čertovka to create a major road but were thwarted by a sudden outbreak of good sense, and this singular place, with its medieval water wheels, has survived.

Kampa is an oasis of calm on even the most crowded August day. At the south end is one of the loveliest parks in the city. This was created in the 19th century when an egalitarian decision was made to join the gardens of three private palaces and throw them open to the public. Washerwomen once rinsed shirts on the banks – note the **Chapel to St John of the Laundry** near the southern end. Today it's taken up by snoozing office workers and bongo-beating hippies. The river and bridge views are as romantic as they come, while the chestnut trees make shady spots for reading and recharging. In spring the park is filled with pink blossom. **Kampa Park** the restaurant (*see p123*), one of Prague's classier and pricier places to eat, is at the north end of the island where the Čertovka runs back into the river by Charles Bridge, and offers the finest waterfront view of any dining establishment in town.

Between Kampa & Petřín Hill

Across the tiny bridge on Hroznová that leads to tranquil Velkopřevorské náměstí is the elegant **Buquoy Palace** (Buquoyský palác), a pink stucco creation dating from 1719, which now houses the French Embassy. Opposite is the John Lennon Wall. During the 1980s this became a place of pilgrimage for the city's hippies, who dedicated it to their idol and scrawled messages of love, peace and rock 'n' roll across it. The secret police, spotting a dangerous subversive plot to undermine the state, lost no time in painting over the graffiti, only to have John's smiling face reappear a few days later. This continued until 1989 when the wall was returned to the Knights of Malta as part of a huge restitution package. The Knights proved even more uptight than the secret police and were ready to whitewash the graffiti when an unlikely Beatles fan, in the form of the French Ambassador, came to the rescue. Claiming to enjoy the strains of *Give Peace a Chance* wafting through his office window, he sparked a diplomatic incident but saved the wall. In the summer of 1998 the Knights had a change of heart, the graffiti and crumbling remains of Lennon's face were removed, the wall was replastered and the Beatle's portrait repainted by artist František Flasar. The John Lennon Peace Club is encouraging modest graffiti – preferably in the form of little flowers.

Just around the corner is the quiet and lovely **Maltézské náměstí**. The Knights of Malta lived here for centuries until the communists dissolved the order. The Knights regained great swathes of property under the restitution laws. Opposite the church, is the excellent little café **Cukrkávalimonáda** (*see p123*) and round the corner on **Saska ulička** are the prettiest flower shops and boutiques for club clothes in town. Prokopská street is home to **U Maltézských rytířů** restaurant (*see p122*) occupies a Gothic cellar that was once a hospice operated by the Knights. The baroque building on the corner of the square was once known as the Museum of Musical Instruments. It has suffered more than its fair share of misfortune: its priceless Flemish tapestries were given to Von Ribbentrop, Hitler's foreign affairs adviser, and its Stradivarius violins were stolen in 1990; now the museum is closed for good.

Although the museum is gone, the sound of students practising at the nearby conservatory provides a soundtrack for wandering around the area. The highlight of the square is the strange **Church of Our Lady Beneath the Chain** (Panny Marie pod řetězem), the oldest Gothic

Sightseeing

Lights, camera, Jan Neruda

For most Czechs, the streets of Malá Strana conjure up images of the characters and scenes that inhabited in the stories they read at school. By far the most favoured of those scenes were penned by the 19th-century writer Jan Neruda. A fascinating character in himself (the modern-day poet Pablo Neruda adopted the Czech surname of his idol), Neruda's tales and verses were an important part of the Czech National Revival movement, which took place from the mid to late 19th century.

Essential Czech foibles and passions are often revealed in Neruda's classic *Prague Tales*, first published as *Povídky malostranské* in 1878. In one typical tale, 'A Beggar Brought to Ruin', a sense of Czech soulfulness runs throughout. The local constable, Mr Kedlický, is ostensibly an officer of the Habsburg rulers. But, being Czech, he 'had a kind heart' and a tendency to look the other way when smallish laws were skirted.

The beggar of the story's title, Mr Vojtíšek, for example, is tolerated, even watched out for as the story opens, by the constable and the district as a whole. Only one miserly German, Mr Herzl, would begrudge him a

decent donation, offering him only a pinch of tobacco on Sundays.

Mr Vojtíšek isn't a terribly industrious or patriotic sort — he could clearly work if he chose to – but he tells a colourful story and always has a joke at hand, which makes him as important a member of society as anyone. And someone worth sponsoring.

'He would cover the entire district in the course of a week. Everyone let him in; indeed, as soon as a housewife heard his gentle voice outside her door, she would take him a half-kreuzer. Half a kreuzer was worth quite a bit in those days.'

Though 'strong as an ox' and nearly 80, Mr Vojtíšek has one fatal flaw. He does not take care with the feelings of an old beggarwoman he encounters on the steps of the St Nicholas Church. He brushes her affections off rudely and soon after rumours begin to circulate that he has a secret fortune he's been concealing.

Soon all of Mr Vojtíšek's donors turn a cold shoulder and the kindly officer Kedlický finds him frozen solid one February day. It would seem that, of all the Czech strengths, generosity is the greatest prize. And envy the most terrible weakness to invoke.

Best approach: **Charles Bridge** brings the world to Malá Strana.

parts of which were built by a military-religious order to guard the Judith Bridge that spanned the Vltava close to where Charles Bridge stands today (bits of the original bridge are visible in the lobby of the **Rezidence Lundborg** (*see p43*). Two heavy towers still stand be the entry – only they now contain some of the most prized apartments in Prague. The Hussite wars barred the construction of the church and it was never completely finished. In place of a nave is an ivy-covered courtyard that leads up to a baroque addition (dating from 1640-50) built in the apse of the original structure.

At the foot of Petřín Hill runs Újezd, which becomes Karmelitská as it runs north before leading into Malostranské náměstí. There are peculiar diversions along the way. The first is at the intersection of Újezd and Vítězná (the border between Malá Strana and Smíchov), where you'll find the popular **Bohemia Bagel** (*see p123*) spilling rock music and American college kids on to the street. There they mix with Death Metal fans from **Újezd** (*see p229*) next door. Just to the north is the **Michna Palace** (Michnův palác), a fine baroque mansion built in 1640-50. It was intended to rival the Wallenstein Palace, which was itself built to compete with the Castle. With these gargantuan ambitions, Francesco Caratti took Versailles as his model in designing the garden wing of Michna. Today the gardens contain little but tennis courts.

Just north up Karmelitská, at No.9, is the **Church of Our Lady Victorious** (*see below*), the first baroque church in Prague (1611-13). It belongs to the Barefooted Carmelites, an order that returned to the city in 1993 and has taken charge of the church's most celebrated exhibit: the doll-like, miracle-working **Bambino di Praga**. Porcelain likenesses of the wonderbaby fill shop windows for blocks around and pilgrims from around the world file into the church. Heading left up the hill from Karmelitská is Tržiště, on the corner of which stands **U Malého Glena** (*see p148*), a convivial jazz pub owned by American Glen Spicker. A little further up is the hip **St Nicholas Café** cellar bar (*see p148*) and opposite it is the cosy little **Gitanes** (*see p121*), ideal for a traditional romantic dinner. The 17th-century **Schönborn Palace** (Schönbornský palác), now the American Embassy, is at Tržiště 15. It was built by Giovanni Santini-Aichel, who, despite his Mediterranean-sounding name, was a third generation Praguer and one of the descendants of Italian craftsmen who formed an expat community on Vlašská just up the hill.

From here, Tržiště becomes a tiny lane that winds up the hill, giving access to some of the loveliest hidden alleys in Malá Strana. Developers have been busy converting most of the flats here into investment property but No.22 is a great survivor, **Baráčnická rychta** (*see p147*). It's one of the most traditional – and certainly the most insalubrious – drinking establishments of the Little Quarter.

Vlašská runs on up the hill from Tržiště and contains the **Lobkowicz Palace** (Lobkovický palác) at No.19. This is one of four Lobkowicz Palaces in Prague and its design (1703-69) is based on Bernini's unrealised plans for the Louvre. In 1989 the gardens sheltered thousands of East Germans, who ignored the *verboten* signs and scaled the high walls, setting up camp in here until they were granted permission to leave for the West. The Lobkowicz family were major landowners in Bohemia until the nationalisation of property in 1948.

Vlašská ambles on upwards, fading out as it passes a hospital and chapel founded in the 17th century by the area's Italian community, and eventually leading back on to Petřín Hill.

Church of Our Lady Victorious

Kostel Panny Marie Vítězné
Karmelitská 9, Prague 1 (5753 3646). Tram 12, 22. **Open** 8.30am-6pm Mon-Sat; 9am-7pm Sun. **Map** p307 D4.

The early baroque church is entirely eclipsed by its diminutive but revered occupant: Il Bambino di Praga (Pražské Jezulátko). This 400-year-old wax effigy of the baby Jesus draws pilgrims, letters and lots of cash from grateful and/or desperate believers the world over. The list of miracles that the Infant of Prague is supposed to have performed is long and impressive and over 100 stone plaques expressing gratitude attest to the efficacy of his powers. The effigy, brought from Spain to Prague in the 17th century, was placed under the care of the Carmelite nuns just in time to protect them from the plague. It was later granted official miracle status by the Catholic Church.

A wardrobe of over 60 outfits befits this dazzling reputation: the baby Jesus is always magnificently turned out, and his clothes have been changed by the Order of English Virgins at sunrise on selected days for 200 years. While he is said to be anatomically correct, the nuns' blushes are spared by a specially designed wax undershirt. At the back of the church is a shamelessly commercial gift shop where tour groups jostle for miraculous souvenirs.

Petřín Hill

Rising up in the west of Malá Strana is **Petřín Hill** (Petřínské sady), the highest, greenest and most peaceful of Prague's seven hills. This area is the largest expanse of greenery in central Prague – a favourite spot for tobogganing children in winter and canoodling couples in

Sightseeing

summertime. 'Petřín' comes from the Latin word for rock, a reference to the hill's past role as the source for much of the city's Gothic and Romanesque building material. The southern edge of the hill is traversed by the so-called **Hunger Wall** (Hladová zeď), an eight-metre (23-foot) high stone fortification that was commissioned by Charles IV in 1362 in order to provide some work for the poor of the city.

The lazy (and most fun) way up to the top of the hill is to catch the funicular from Újezd (running roughly every ten minutes from 9.15am until 8.45pm, stopping halfway up by the touristy Nebozizek restaurant). At the top is a fine collection of architectural absurdities. Ascend the 299 steps of **Petřín Tower** (*see below*), a fifth-scale copy of the Eiffel Tower, for spectacular views over the city. The tower was erected in 1891 for the Jubilee Exhibition, as was the neighbouring mock-Gothic castle that houses the **Mirror Maze** (*see below*), a fairground-style hall of wacky reflectors. There's a café at the base of the tower, and a basic refreshment hut nearby. The third and least-frequented of the Petřín attractions is **Štefánik Observatory** (*see below*) at the top of the funicular.

While kids get the most out of the hilltop attractions, Petřín's meandering paths are the attraction for grown-ups. You wind through the trees for hours, seeking the statue of Karel Hynek Mácha, unofficial patron saint of lovers. The shadowy bowers are a favourite of his disciples. **Strahov Monastery** (*see p75*) and the 22 tram stop are a gentle stroll downhill.

Saints alive: what, baroque again?

Exhibition. Its fiercest opponent was Adolf Hitler, who looked out of his room in the Castle and immediately ordered 'that metal contraption' to be removed. Somehow it survived. It's fairly tatty these days, but the stiff climb to the top is made worthwhile by phenomenal views of the city. The view of St Vitus's Cathedral includes the complete building, not just the usual vista of a set of spires poking over the top of the rest of the Castle. Just try not to think about the way the tower sways in the wind.

Mirror Maze

Zrcadlové bludiště

Petřín Hill, Prague 1 (5731 5212). Tram 12, 22, then funicular railway. **Open** *Apr-Oct* 10am-6.30pm daily. *Nov-Mar* 10am-4.30pm daily. **Admission** 30 Kč; 20 Kč children. **No credit cards.** **Map** p306 C5.

Housed in a cast-iron mock-Gothic castle complete with drawbridge and crenellations is a hall of distorting mirrors that still causes remarkable hilarity among kids and their parents. Alongside is a wax diorama of one of the proudest historical moments for the citizens of Prague: the defence of Charles Bridge during the Swedish attack of 1648.

Petřín Tower

Rozhledna

Petřín Hill, Prague 1 (5732 0112). Tram 12, 22, then funicular railway. **Open** *Apr-Oct* 10am-7pm daily. *Nov-Mar* 10am-4.30pm Sat, Sun; closed in poor weather. **Admission** 25 Kč; 10 Kč students; 5 Kč children. **Map** p306 B5.

While Parisians were still hotly debating the aesthetic value of their newly erected Eiffel Tower, the Czechs decided they liked it so much that they constructed their own version out of recycled railway tracks in a lightning 31 days for the 1891 Jubilee

Štefánik Observatory

Hvězdárna

Petřín Hill, Prague 1 (5732 0540). Tram 12, 22, then funicular railway. **Open** *Mar* 7-9pm Tue-Fri; 10am-noon, 2-6pm, 7-9pm Sat, Sun. *Apr-Aug* 2-7pm, 9-11pm Tue-Fri; 10am-noon, 2-7pm, 9-11pm Sat, Sun. *Sept* 11am-6pm, 8-10pm Tue-Fri; 10am-noon, 2am-6pm, 8-10pm Sat, Sun. *Oct* 7-9pm Tue-Fri; 10am-noon, 2-6pm, 7-9pm Sat, Sun. *Nov-Feb* 6-8pm Tue-Fri; 10am-noon, 2-8pm Sat, Sun. **Admission** 30 Kč; 20 Kč concessions; free under-6s. **No credit cards.** **Map** p306 C5.

Prague is justly proud of its historical astronomical connections. Both the haughty Dane Tycho Brahe and his protégé Johannes Kepler resided in the city. The duo feature in the observatory's stellar displays (which contain some English). Telescopes offer glimpses of sunspots and planets during the day and panoramas of the stars and the moon on clear nights.

Staré Město

Old Town Square, the royal coronation route, the Old Jewish Cemetery, expat sleaze, smart bars and cafés, rustic pubs. Prague's heart is tragically beautiful.

Maps p308-309

Shadowy Gothic lanes that have witnessed many a real-life horror story make up the web of a medieval town that is the heart of Prague. But the grim, blackened stone façades and arches that have lined the district since the tenth century have also witnessed the making of many a fortune. Now the home of fashion designers and expensive international law firms, Old Town Square is where merchants always traded while the city's rulers plotted and intrigued up on the hill across the river.

The Powder Gate to the Old Town Square

The **Powder Gate** (*see p85*), a Gothic gateway dating from 1475 at the eastern end of Celetná, marks the boundary between the Old and New Towns and is also the start of the so-called Královská Cesta, or Royal Route – the traditional coronation path taken by the Bohemian kings and now a popular tourist track. The first stretch runs west down Celetná, a pleasant pedestrianised promenade lined with freshly restored baroque and Renaissance buildings. A more recent addition is the **House of the Black Madonna** (U Černé matky boží), at No.34, the first cubist building in the city (built in 1913; *see also p30*), and now, appropriately enough, housing an exhibition of Czech cubist art, furniture and architecture (*see p113*). The Madonna herself, a treasured artefact that adorned the outside corner, has been moved indoors for safekeeping and a copy has replaced it.

On the other side of Celetná, an alley leads in to Templová, where you'll be immersed in a part of town where ancient façades are jumbled with fresh new pastel paint jobs, and meticulous restoration has revitalised long-dormant lanes. Round here is the hub of expat nightlife, where backpackers, tourists and foreign residents disappear into a warren of bars, clubs and restaurants, most of which, for some reason, have French names: **La Provence** (*see p128*), **Chateau** (*see p149*) and the **Marquis de Sade** (*see p151*) are all within a block of each other, and the **Radegast Pub** (*see p151*). Late at night, the strip outside **Chateau** (which has the longest

hours of all these places) is filled with youths of all nationalities, vomiting on the street, groping in corners, conducting minor drug deals, annoying the neighbours and squabbling with Chateau's Neanderthal bouncers.

Opposite is the **Church of St James** (*see p85*) on Malá Štupartská – a typical baroque reworking of an older Gothic church. Arguably the city's best English-language bookshop, **Big Ben Bookshop** (*see p164*), is just across the street. From here you can find a sharp contrast to the sleaze of the popular bars in this neighbourhood and stroll through the crisply restored, café- and restaurant-lined square of Týn, better known by its German name of Ungelt. This square now houses upscale businesses such as **Brasserie Le Patio** (*see p137 and p176*), the laddy sport bar **Legends** (*see p151*) and the **Ebel Coffee House** (*see p133*). Continuing through the square to the west will take you past the **Church of Our Lady before Týn** (*see p87*), Staré Město's parish church since the 12th century, and on to Old Town Square. The Týn church is a scary structure, looming ominously over the square and somehow redolent of a Monty Python animation – you almost expect the building to uproot itself and set off squelching tour groups across the city.

Church of St James

Sv. Jakuba
Malá Štupartská (2482 8816). Metro Náměstí Republiky/5, 14, 26 tram. **Open** 9.30am-12.30pm, 2.30-4pm Mon-Sat; 2-3.45pm Sun. **Map** p308 J3.
St James's boasts a grand total of 21 altars, some fine frescoes and a desiccated human forearm hanging next to the door. This belonged to a jewel thief who broke into the church in the 15th century and tried to make off with some gems from the statue of the Virgin. The Madonna grabbed him by the arm and kept him captive until the offending limb had to be cut off. However, its appearance – it looks like a piece of dried-up salami – could be explained by the fact that the church's most prominent worshippers were members of the Butchers' Guild.

Powder Gate

Prašná brána
U prašné brány, Prague 1 (no phone). Metro Náměstí Republiky/5, 14, 26 tram. **Open** *Apr-Oct* 10am-6pm daily. **Admission** 20 Kč; 10 Kč under-6s. **Map** p309 K3.

Drink under the nose of an emperor at **U Radnice**. *See p88.*

The Powder Gate, or Tower, is a piece of late 15th-century flotsam, a lonely relic of the fortifications that used to ring the whole town. The bridge that incongruously connects it to the art nouveau masterpiece of the **Municipal House** (*see p29, p134 and p213*) used to give access to the royal palace that stood on the same site during the 10th century. By the mid 14th century Charles IV had founded the New Town, and the city's boundaries had changed. The Powder Gate remained mouldering until it finally gained a purpose, and a name, when it became a store for gunpowder in 1575. This unfortunately made it a legitimate target for invading Prussian troops and it was severely damaged during the siege of 1757. It was once again left to crumble until the neo-Gothic master Josef Mocker provided it with a new roof and redecorated the sides in the 1870s. Today you can ascend a precipitous staircase to the top.

The Old Town Square

For centuries the beautiful **Old Town Square** (Staroměstské náměstí), edged by an astonishing jumble of baroque and medieval structures, has been the natural place for people visiting Prague to gravitate to. This was the medieval town's main market place and has always been at the centre of the action: criminals were executed here; martyrs were burnt at the stake; and, in 1948, huge crowds greeted the announcement of the communist takeover. Most of the houses are much older

than they look, with Romanesque cellars and Gothic chambers hiding behind the pastel-coloured baroque and Renaissance façades. If the effect seems somewhat toy-town today, especially in comparison to the crumbling structures in many of the surrounding streets, it should come as no surprise to learn that it was the communists who spent an unprecedented $10 million smartening up the formerly grimy square for the 40th anniversary of the Czechoslovak Socialist Republic.

The west side is lined with stalls selling kitschy crafts and untempting souvenirs. The grassy area behind them was thoughtfully provided by the Nazis, who destroyed much of the **Old Town Hall** on 8 May 1945 when the rest of Europe was holding street parties and celebrating the end of World War II. The town lost most of its archives, though it gained a fine vista of the lovely **Church of St Nicholas** (sv. Mikuláš). Built in 1735 by Kilián Ignaz Dientzenhofer, this is an inside-out church: the exterior, with its white stucco and undulating façade, is even more ornate than the interior. An added attraction in winter is provided by the heated seats, installed to prevent your bottom freezing during organ concerts.

The **Old Town Hall** (*see p87*) was begun in 1338, after the councillors had spent several fruitless decades trying to persuade the king to allow them to construct a suitable chamber for their affairs. John of Luxembourg finally relented, but with the bizarre proviso that all work was to be financed from the duty on wine. He obviously underestimated the high-living inhabitants of the Old Town, because within the year they had enough money to purchase the house adjoining the present tower.

You can go and look at what remains of the Old Town Hall after the Nazis' handiwork, although trying to decipher the extraordinary components of the **Astronomical Clock** (*see below*) is more rewarding. It was constructed in the 15th century, sometime before the new-fangled notion that Prague revolves around the sun and not vice versa. Undismayed, the citizens kept their clock with its gold sunburst swinging happily around the globe. One of Prague's most famous tourist rituals is waiting for the clock to strike the hour while souvenir sellers buzz around.

The brief appearance of figures of the apostles over the clock is remarkably short and laughably unspectacular. Far more entertaining is watching the embarrassed faces of the crowds as they exchange 'is that it?' looks with one another before shuffling away.

Perhaps the finest of the houses that make up what is left of the Old Town Hall is the **Minute House** (U minuty), the beautiful black and white sgraffitoed house on the corner, which dates from 1611. Franz Kafka lived here as a boy; opposite the Astronomical Clock is the **Café Milena** (*see p132*), named after Milena Jesenská, the radical journalist who is best remembered for being Kafka's girlfriend. The area teems with other Kafka sites. The writer was born in a house at U Radnice 5, lived for a while at Oppelt's House on the corner of Přaížská and the square (this is the house where *Metamorphosis* takes place), went to primary school on nearby Masná and later attended the strict German Gymnasium on the third floor of the Golz-Kinský Palace. This frothy stuccoed affair in the north-east corner of the square once contained Kafka's father's fancy goods shop; it's now the **Franz Kafka Bookshop** (Knihkupectví Franze Kafky). Adjoining the palace is the **House of the Stone Bell** (*see p201*), the baroque cladding of which was removed in the 1980s to reveal a 14th-century Gothic façade.

The focal point of the square is the powerful Jan Hus Monument dedicated to the reformist cleric, designed by Ladislav Šaloun and unveiled in 1915 (and received as a passé artistic flop). Here tourists and school groups pause to rest their feet, chat, consult their guidebooks and sing along with buskers. On the orders of the pope, Hus was burnt at the stake in 1415 for his revolutionary thinking, although the Catholic Church, some 500 years after the fact, has finally formally apologised. Hus's fans may

at last feel vindicated as they point to the quote on the side of his monument that reads 'Pravda vítězí' ('Truth will prevail'). Those words were also used by President Gottwald in the 'Glorious February' of 1948, accurately as it finally turned out in 1989.

Church of Our Lady before Týn

Kostel Matky boží ped Týnem
*Staroměstské náměstí 14, Prague 1 (2232 2801).
Metro Náměstí Republiky or Staroměstská/
17, 18 tram.* **Open** *Services* 5.30pm Mon-Fri; 1pm Sat; 11.30am, 9pm Sun (opens 30mins before services).* **Map** p308 J3.

The twin towers of Týn topped by what look like witches' hats are one of the landmarks of the Old Town. The church nave is much lighter and more inviting than its foreboding exterior would lead you to believe. The church dates from the same period as St Vitus's Cathedral (late 14th century), but whereas St Vitus's was constructed to show the power of King Charles IV, Týn was a church for the people. As such it became a centre of the reforming Hussites in the 15th century, before being commandeered by the Jesuits in the 17th. They commissioned the baroque interior, which blends uncomfortably with the original Gothic structure. At the end of the southern aisle is the tombstone of Tycho Brahe, Rudolf II's personal astronomer, famous for his false nose-piece and his fine line in gnomic utterances. If you look closely at the red marble slab, you'll see the former, while the lines above provide evidence of the latter, translating as 'Better to be than to seem to be'. Lit up at night, the Týn looks like some kind of monstrous spacecraft. If you're lucky, you may see bats swooping around the steeples at dusk, completing the fairytale Gothic image.

Old Town Hall & Astronomical Clock

Staroměstská radnice/Orloj
Staroměstské náměstí, Prague 1 (2448 2909). Metro Staroměstská/17, 18 tram. **Open** 9am-4.30pm daily. **Admission** 40 Kč; tower an additional 30 Kč. **Map** p308 H3.

The Old Town Hall, established in 1338, was cobbled together over the centuries out of several adjoining houses, but only around half of the original remains standing today. The present Gothic and Renaissance portions have been carefully restored since the Nazis blew up a large chunk of it in the last days of World War II. The Old Town coat of arms, adopted by the whole city after 1784, adorns the front of the Old Council Hall, and the clock tower, built in 1364, has a viewing platform that is definitely worth the climb. The 12th-century dungeon in the basement became the headquarters of the Resistance during the Prague Uprising in 1944 when reinforcements and supplies were spirited away from the Nazis all over the Old Town via the connecting underground passages. Four scorched beams in the basement, which is newly opened to

Sightseeing

the public, remain as a testament to the Resistance members who fell there. On the side of the clock tower is a plaque, marked by crossed machine guns, giving thanks to the Soviet soldiers who liberated the city in 1945. There's also a plaque honouring Dukla, a pass in Slovakia where the worst battle of the Czechoslovak liberation took place, resulting in the death of 84,000 Red Army soldiers.

The Astronomical Clock has been ticking, tocking and pulling in the crowds since 1490. Every hour on the hour between 8am and 8pm crowds gather to watch wooden statuettes of saints emerge from behind trap doors while below a lurid lesson in medieval morality is enacted by Greed, Vanity, Death and the Turk. The clock shows the movement of the sun and moon through the 12 signs of the zodiac as well as giving the time in three different formats: Central European Time, Old Czech Time (in which the 24-hour day is reckoned around the setting of the sun) and, for some reason, Babylonian Time. A particularly resilient Prague legend concerns the fate of the clockmaker, Master Hanuš, who was blinded by the vainglorious burghers of the town to prevent him from repeating his horological triumph elsewhere. In retaliation Hanuš thrust his hands inside the clock and simultaneously ended both his life and (for a short time at least) that of his masterpiece. Below the clock face is a calendar painted by Josef Mánes in 1865, depicting saints' days, the astrological signs and the labours of the months.

Old Town Square to Charles Bridge

The simplest and most direct route from the Old Town Square to Charles Bridge is along Karlova, although twisting and curling as it does, the lane would not be particularly obvious were it not for the inevitable crowds proceeding along it. This is the continuation of the Royal Route and becomes an unrelenting bottleneck in the summertime when tour groups and souvenir hawkers jostle for supremacy on the narrow way.

Before heading down Karlova, fuel up at **U Radnice** (*see also p132*), a traditional cellar restaurant. To reach Karlova, walk past the Old Town Hall into Malé náměstí (Little Square). In the centre is a plague column enclosed by an ornate Renaissance grille and overlooked by the neo-Renaissance **Rott House**, built in 1890 and entirely decorated with murals of flowers and peasants by Mikoláš Aleš. For many years it operated as Prague's biggest hardware shop but now it hosts mainly luxury food and wines, with all the rope and nails relegated to a small shop around the corner on Linhartská. **Friday's American Bar**, a newer addition to the square, attracts weekending punters with impressive burgers and a total absence of Czechness. Jeweller

Mappin & Webb sits on the corner, evidence of the rapid upmarket trajectory of this area. (On the other side of the square, a block down Celetná, Pařížská is crowded with designer outlets.)

The twists and turns of Karlova lead past a procession of souvenir shops and retailers of Bohemian glass. At the third twist it winds past the massive, groaning giants that struggle to hold up the portal of the **Clam-Gallas Palace** (Clam-Gallasův palác) on Husova. Designed by Fischer von Erlach and completed in 1719, the palace now houses the city's archives.

An alternative route to Charles Bridge that's amazingly free of tourists is to take Řetězová just a block south of Karlova. This walk, down a narrow lane full of funky smells, takes you past No. 7, **Café Montmartre** (*see p132*), a historic scene of hedonism that's now been revived as a mellow sipping space with embroidered parlour sofas. It was here during the glory days of the inter-war First Republic that opium, absinthe and jazz mixed into a potent cocktail that at one point led to black masses and orgies. Or so the owners say, at any rate. A block further west on Anenské náměstí you'll find quiet little **Divadlo Na zábradlí** (Theatre on the Balustrade; *see p235*), the theatre where a set builder named Václav Havel first tried his hand at absurdist playwrighting and soon landed himself in jail.

Back on Karlova, the vast bulk of the **Clementinum** (*see p89*) makes up the right-hand side of Karlova's last stretch. After the Castle, it's the largest complex of buildings in Prague. The Jesuits, storm troopers of the Counter-Reformation, set up home here on the site and carried on the tradition of book-burning and brow-beating. Like much of the Old Town, Karlova is best viewed at night when most of the tour groups are safely back at their hotels. And if you get peckish along the way there are two all-night eateries: **U zlatého stromu** (*see p230*) at Karlova 6, where there's a non-stop restaurant in a bizarre complex that also includes a hotel, disco and softcore strip show, and **Pizzeria Roma Due** (*see p131*) at Liliová 18. Further up Liliová is the **James Joyce** (*see p151*), Prague's principal Irish pub, and the **U krále Jiřího** (*see p152*), which serves radically cheaper beer in a smoke-filled cellar next door. Yet another cellar in the same courtyard offers respectable blues, the Blues Sklep.

At the foot of Karlova, tourists have trouble crossing the road past the continuous stream of trams and cars that race through **Křižovnické náměstí** (Knights of the Cross Square). The eponymous Knights, an elderly bunch of neo-medieval crusaders, have come out of retirement and reclaimed the **Church of St Francis** (sv. František). Designed by Jean-

The **Astronomical Clock** tells time in Babylonian. *See p87.*

Baptiste Mathey in the late 17th century, the church, which has a massive red dome and has been described as looking as if it has been 'gouged out of so much Dutch cheese', is unusual for Prague, not least because its altar is facing the wrong way. The gallery next door houses a job-lot of religious bric-a-brac that the Knights extricated from various museums, and a subterranean chapel decorated with stalactites made out of dust and eggshells, an 18th-century fad that enjoyed unwarranted popularity in Prague. Concert and café schemes sometimes fill the space these days.

On the eastern side of the square is the **Church of St Saviour** (sv. Salvátor), which marks the border of the Clementinum. Opposite, guarding the entrance to Charles Bridge, is the **Old Town Bridge Tower** (*see p91*), a Gothic gate topped with a pointed, tiled hat. Climb the tower for a bird's-eye view of Prague's domes and spires, the wayward line of Charles Bridge and the over-the-top **Mlýnec** (*see p131*), the naff **Klub Lávka** (*see p227*) and the newest major edition to Prague clubbing, **Karlovy Lázně** (*see p225*), all below on the river and beyond.

Clementinum

Klementinum
Mariánské náměstí 4, Prague 1 (2166 6311). Metro Staroměstská/17, 18 tram. **Open** *Library* 9am-7pm Mon-Fri; 8am-7pm Sat. Chapel of Mirrors for concerts only. **Map** p308 G3/4.

In the 12th and 13th centuries this enormous complex of buildings was the Prague headquarters of the Inquisition, and when the Jesuits moved in during the 16th century, kicking out the Dominicans who had set up home there in the meantime, they carried on the tradition of fear, intimidation and forcible baptising of the city's Jews. They replaced the medieval Church of St Clement with a much grander design of their own (rebuilt in 1711-15 and now used by the Greek Catholic Church) and gradually constructed the building of today, which is arranged around five courtyards, demolishing several streets and 30 houses on the way. Their grandest work was the Church of St Saviour (sv. Salvátor), whose opulent but grimy façade faces the Staré Město end of Charles Bridge and was designed to reawaken the joys of Catholicism in the largely Protestant populace. It was built between 1578 and 1653 by the Jesuits and was the most important Jesuit church in Bohemia. The Jesuits' main tool was education and their library is a masterpiece. It was finished in 1727, and has a magnificent trompe l'oeil ceiling split into three parts, showing the three levels of knowledge, with the Dome of Wisdom occupying the central space. However, the ceiling started crumbling and to prevent the whole structure from collapsing the Chapel of Mirrors was built next door in 1725 to bolster the walls. The interior, decorated with fake pink marble and the original mirrors, is lovely. Mozart used to play here and it is still used for chamber concerts today, which is the only way you can get in to see it. At the centre of the complex is the Astronomical Tower, where Kepler, who lived on nearby Karlova, came to stargaze. It was used

Havelský Market: another happy customer. *See p91.*

until the 1920s for calculating high noon: when the sun crossed a line on the wall behind a small aperture at the top, the Castle would be signalled and a cannon fired.

House of the Lords of Kunštát & Poděbrady

Dům páný z Kunštátu a Poděbrad
Řetězová 3, Prague 1 (2421 2299 ext 22). Metro Staroměstská/17, 18 tram. **Open** *May-Sept* 10am-6pm Tue-Sun. **No credit cards. Admission** 20 Kč. **Map** p308 H4.

This house is one of the few accessible examples of Romanesque architecture in Prague. It was begun in 1250, originally built as a walled-in farmstead, but like its neighbours in the Old Town was partially buried in the flood-protection scheme of the late 13th century, which reduced the vaulted ground floor to a cellar. By the mid 15th century it was quite palatial, a suitably grand dwelling for George of Poděbrady, who set out from here for his election as king. The upper storeys were later greatly altered. Now it houses a modern art display and an interesting little exhibition in honour of George of Poděbrady, whose well-meaning scheme for international co-operation is hailed as a forerunner of the League of Nations.

Charles Bridge

Charles Bridge (Karlův most) is the most popular place in the city to come and get your portrait painted, take photos of the Castle, have your pocket picked or pick up a backpacker.

The range of entertainment is always dodgy and diverse, from blind folk-singers through assorted dubious portrait painters to the man who plays Beethoven concertos on finger bowls.

The stone bridge was built in 1357 (replacing the earlier Judith Bridge that collapsed in a flood in 1342) and has survived over 600 years of turbulent city life, although a large and embarrassing chunk of it tumbled into the Vltava in 1890. The **Old Town Bridge Tower** (*see p91*) was added in 1373. The statues lining the bridge didn't arrive until the 17th century, when Bohemia's leading sculptors, including Josef Brokof and Matthias Braun, were commissioned to create figures to inspire the masses as they went about their daily business. The strategy proved more effective than an earlier Catholic decoration – the severed heads of Protestant nobles. More mundane statues were added in the 19th century.

The third statue on the right from the Old Town end is a crucifixion bearing a mysterious Hebrew inscription in gold. This was added in 1696 by a Jew found guilty of blaspheming in front of the statue, according to local lore; his punishment was to pay for the inscription 'Holy, Holy, Holy, Holy Lord' to be added. A plaque has recently been added by the Jewish community, telling the full story.

St John of Nepomuk – perhaps the most famous figure (*see p16* **A five-star fraud**) – is eighth on the right as you walk towards Malá

Strana and recognisable by his doleful expression and the cartoon-like gold stars fluttering around his head. According to popular belief, John was flung off the bridge after refusing to reveal the secrets of the queen's confession, but he was actually just in the wrong place at the wrong time during one of Wenceslas IV's anti-clerical rages. A bronze bas-relief below the statue depicts the scene and people stop and rub it for luck. The statue – placed here in 1683 – is the bridge's earliest. It was cast in bronze and has survived better than the sandstone statues, which have been badly damaged by the elements and have mostly been replaced by copies.

Further towards Malá Strana, fourth from the end on the left, is the Cistercian nun St Luitgard, made by Matthias Braun in 1710, and shown in the middle of her vision of Christ. The statue is considered by many, including Prince Charles, to be the finest statue on the bridge; he pledged the money to save her from the elements, which were threatening to wipe the look of wonder off her face. On the same side, second from the Malá Strana end, is the largest and most complex grouping on the bridge. It commemorates the founders of the Trinitarian Order, which built its rep by ransoming captured Christians: Saints John of Matha and Felix of Valois (accompanied by his pet stag) plus a rogue St Ivan, included for no obvious reason. Below them stand a lethargic figure of a Turk and his snarling dog framing three imprisoned true believers.

If you've fallen for the city, seek out the gold cross located halfway across the bridge, touch it, make a wish – and hey presto, it's guaranteed that you'll return. The best time to come is at night when the Castle is floodlit in various pastel shades and appears to hover overhead.

Old Town Bridge Tower

Staroměstská mostecká věž
Křížovnické náměstí, Staré Město, Prague 1 (no phone). Metro Staroměstská/17, 18 tram. **Open** Apr-Oct 10am-7pm daily. Nov-Mar 10am-5pm daily. **Admission** 30 Kč; 20 Kč concessions. **No credit cards. Map** p308 G4.
Built in 1373, along the shadow line of St Vitus's Cathedral, the Old Town Bridge Tower was badly damaged in 1648 by marauding Swedes, but Peter Parler's sculptural decoration on the eastern side survives. There's a boring exhibit on the tower's history inside, but the real reason it's worth venturing in is to take in the splendid view. Most visitors miss the medieval groping of the figures on the tower's outer corners – just visible before you go under the tower, coming from the Old Town direction. Each depicts a buxom lass, clearly getting felt up by a gentleman friend.

Southern Staré Město

Canny German merchants were the first to develop the area south of the Old Town Square. They built a church dedicated to St Havel (more commonly known as St Gall) when Charles IV generously donated some spare parts of the saint from his burgeoning relic collection. The onion domes of the existing **Church of St Havel** (on Havelská) were added later in 1722 by the Shod Carmelites (the Barefooted Carmelites settled on the other side of the river). The opposite end of Havelská is lined with slightly bowed baroque houses precariously balanced on Gothic arcades. The merchants have at last returned, and the street now contains Prague's best market (see p163). As well as handmade wooden toys, there are abundant piles of fruit and vegetables.

Between here and Celetná, on Ovocný trh, is one of Prague's finest neo-classical buildings: the **Estates Theatre** (see p214 and p234), dubbed 'The Mozart Theatre'. Unlike Vienna, Prague loved Mozart and Mozart loved Prague. During the composer's lifetime, the theatre staged a succession of his greatest operas, including the première of Don Giovanni, conducted by Wolfgang Amadeus himself. The building was paid for by Count Nostitz, after whom it was named when it opened in 1783 – aimed at promoting productions of works in German. But by the late 19th century most productions were being performed in Czech, and the name was changed to the Tyl Theatre, after the dramatist JK Tyl. His song 'Where Is My Home?' was played here for the first time and later adopted as the Czech national anthem.

The massive oriel window overlooking the theatre belongs to the **Carolinum**, the university founded by Charles IV. Charles never made a move without consulting the stars, and ascertained that Aries was an auspicious sign for the first university in Central Europe, which was founded on 7 April 1348. It came to grief at the hands of another Aries, Adolf Hitler, when it was badly damaged in World War II.

Opposite the Estates Theatre is the **former Soviet House of Science and Culture**. Boutiques have taken over most of the complex but there's a permanent exhibition of gaudy Russian paintings and some Russian books and CDs on sale. Just around the corner on Michalská is the ominous shape of tourist attractions to come: **St Michael's Mystery** (see below).

St Michael's Mystery

Michalská 27-9, Staré Město, Prague 1 (2421 3253). Metro Staroměstská/6, 9, 18, 22 tram. **Open** 10am-8pm daily. **Admission** 355 Kč. **Credit** MC, V. **Map** p308 H4.

A massive cash infusion has transformed St Michael's Church from ruined baroque cathedral into the supremely kitsch St Michael's Mystery. Billed as a 'Kafka-esque' tour through Prague history, it assails visitors with 14 Disney-style scenes and audio in English, German and Czech, featuring talking file drawers, polystyrene figures from the Old Town clock tower, a souped-up special effects elevator and old newsreel footage. If all that fails to seduce visitors inside, there's still the culinary marvels of fries and coffee at the adjoining, subtly dubbed restaurant, 'Mike's'.

Around Betlémské náměstí

Once the poorest quarter of the Old Town and a notorious area of cut-throats and prostitutes (their present-day sisters can be seen lining Perlova and Na Perštýně a few blocks away), this was the natural breeding ground for the radical politics of the late 14th century. On the north side of Bethlehem Square are the swooping twin gables of the aesthetically plain **Bethlehem Chapel** (see below), a reconstructed version of the 1391 building where Jan Hus and other independent-minded Czech preachers passed on their vision of the true church to the Prague citizenry. Across the courtyard is the **Galerie Jaroslav Fragnera**, with the **Klub Architektů** (see p127) offering passable cheap eats in the vaulted basement and, in the summer, also at tables outside. The square's other refreshment station is the 'Keltic Bar' Boji, a pricey new sports drinking hole capitalising on the name of the earliest known tribe of Bohemians, believed to be Celts. The next-door gallery, **Galerie Jiřího a Běly Kolářových** (see p203), owned by the Czech legend of collage, Jiří Kolář, testifies to continuing advances in Old Town's art scene.

On the other side of the square is the **Náprstek Museum** (see p118). After making his fortune by inebriating the masses, Vojta Náprstek installed a collection of ethnological knick-knacks in the family brewery. A 19th-century do-gooder, he didn't just spend his time hunting down shrunken heads, but also founded the first women's club in the country. The room, untouched for 100 years, can still be seen, although the peep hole he drilled through from his office perhaps draws into question the purity of his motives.

One of the three Romanesque rotundas in the city, the **Church of the Holy Rood** (Rotunda sv. Kříže), is on nearby Konviktská. The tiny, charming building, dating from the early 12th century, was built entirely in the round so that the devil had no corner to hide in. Today it's dwarfed by the surrounding tenement buildings. If you don't manage to get a look inside, try the **Hostinec U rotundy**. Covered with lovely sgraffito, it's as authentic a pub as you'll find in the Old Town, with cheap beer and a contingent of locals who'll try to stare you out when you walk in.

On Husova, to the north-east, is the **Church of St Giles** (sv. Jiljí), a massive Gothic structure that looks like a fortress from the outside. It was built by the Dominicans in 1340-70, an order that has recently come back to reclaim its heritage and inhabit the monastery next door. Nearby is **U Zlatého tygra** (see p152), favourite watering hole of **Bohumil Hrabal** (see p32), the author and Nobel Prize nominee who spent half his life inside a pub and the other half writing about what goes on inside pubs. The irascible octagenarian died in 1997. If the snarling old-timers within make you feel unwelcome, go instead to the **House of the Lords of Kunštát and Poděbrady** on Řetězová. In the basement are the atmospheric remains of a Romanesque palace, and temporary exhibitions from the puppet faculty of Charles University, spookily spotlit against the crumbling vaults and pillars.

Parallel to Konviktská is the unnaturally quiet Bartolomějská. Czechs still avoid its environs – a legacy of the role it played in communist times. Police departments line the street and most dissidents of note did time in the StB (Secret Police) cells in the former convent. The building, now containing the **Pension Unitas** (see p50), has been restored to the Sisters of Mercy and you can stay the night in the cell where President Havel was once locked up to ponder the error of his ways. The river is only a few dozen yards away and from here you have a perfect view across it to Kampa, with the Castle high up on the hill. Turning right will take you past Novotného lávka, a cluster of buildings jutting into the river centred around a 19th-century water tower and a small cluster of bars, and back to Charles Bridge. Turn left to reach the National Theatre and the beginning of the New Town.

Bethlehem Chapel

Betlémská kaple

Betlémské náměstí, Staré Město, Prague 1 (2424 8595). Metro Národní třída/6, 9, 18, 22 tram. **Open** Apr-Oct 9am-6pm daily. Nov-Mar 9am-4.30pm daily. **Admission** 30 Kč; 20 Kč concessions. **Map** p308 H4.

The Bethlehem Chapel, a huge, plain, barn-like structure dating from 1391, was where the proto-Protestant Jan Hus delivered sermons in the Czech language accusing the papacy of being, among other things, an institution of Satan. It is perhaps not surprising that he was burnt at the stake in 1415. His last request before being thrown to the

Old Jewish Cemetery.

flames was for 'history to be kind to the Bethlehem Chapel'. In response, the fanatical Jesuits bought up the site and promptly turned it into a woodshed. In the 18th century, German merchants moved in and built two houses within the walls. Hus's wish was finally fulfilled under the communists. They chose to look on him as a working class revolutionary thwarted by the forces of imperialism and spared no expense in the extensive restoration of the chapel. Three of the original walls remain and still show the remnants of the scriptures that were painted on them to enable people to follow the service. A team of friendly ladies are happy to answer any queries. Upstairs is a small exhibition, captioned in spectacularly broken English, that chronologically runs through the development of Hussitism and the history of the chapel.

Josefov

The main street of Josefov is Pařížská, an elegant, tree-lined avenue of designer shops, flash restaurants, expensive cocktail bars and international airline offices, which leads from the Old Town Square down to the

Inter-Continental (*see p47*) and the river. Here you'll find swish places like **Barock** (*see p131*) and **Bugsy's** (*see p149*). This is all, however, in sharp contrast to the rest of what was once Prague's Jewish quarter.

The spiritual heart of Josefov is the **Old-New Synagogue** (*see p94*), which stands on a wedge of land between Maiselova and Paižská. Built around 1270, this is the oldest synagogue in Europe. Legend has it that the foundation stones were flown over by angels from the Holy Temple in Jerusalem under the condition (*al tnay* in Hebrew) that they should be returned on Judgement Day, hence the name Alt-Neu in German or Old-New in English.

Next door is the former **Jewish Town Hall** (Maiselova 18), dating from the 1560s, with a rococo façade in various delicate pinks, and a Hebraic clock whose hands turn anti-clockwise. The money to build the Town Hall and neighbouring **High Synagogue** was provided by Mordecai Maisel, a contemporary of Rabbi Löw's and a man of inordinate wealth and discriminating taste. The Town Hall has been the centre of the Jewish community ever since. The High Synagogue, built at the same time as the Town Hall and attached to it, was returned to the community early in 1994 and is now, once again, a working synagogue serving the Jewish community (not open to sightseers).

Further down Maiselova you'll find the **Maisel Synagogue**. This, with the Pinkas, Klausen and Spanish synagogues, and the Old Jewish Cemetery and Ceremonial Hall, comprise the extraordinary **Jewish Museum** (*see p113*), also funded by the wealthy 16th-century money-lending mayor. Sadly, the current building is a reconstruction of the original (apparently the most splendid synagogue of them all), which burnt down in the great fire of 1689 when all 316 houses of the ghetto and 11 synagogues were destroyed. The present structure, sandwiched between tenement blocks, dates from 1892 to 1905, and houses a permanent exhibition of Jewish history from its origins in Bohemia through to the 19th century.

On U starého hřbitova is the **Old Jewish Cemetery** (*see p114*), a small, unruly patch of ground that contains the remains of thousands upon thousands of bodies. Forbidden to enlarge their burial ground, the Jews had to bury bodies on top of each other in an estimated 12 layers, so that today crazy mounds of earth are jammed with lopsided stone tablets.

To the left of the entrance is the **Klausen Synagogue** (*see p114*), built in 1694 by the same craftsmen responsible for many of Prague's baroque churches. Inside, the pink marble Holy Ark could almost pass for a

Sightseeing

Catholic altar were it not for the gold inscriptions in Hebrew. Here you'll find displayed various religious artefacts and prints as well as explanations of Jewish customs and traditions. Facing the synagogue is the **Former Ceremonial Hall** (*see p114*), designed in the style of a Romanesque castle at the beginning of this century, which hosts an exhibition of funeral ceremony and ornament.

On the other side of the cemetery is the **Pinkas Synagogue** (*see p116*), built as the private house of the powerful Horowitz family in 1607-25. The building is now primarily given over to a memorial to the more than 80,000 Jewish men, women and children who died in Nazi concentration camps according to German transport lists. A communist-era 'refurbishment' once obscured the names recorded on the Pinkas walls, but every one was painstakingly repainted in a two-year project started in April 1997. Josefov's final synagogue, the **Spanish Synagogue** (*see p116*), was built just outside the boundaries of the ghetto in 1868, on Dušní. It was constructed for the growing number of Reform Jews, and its façade is of a rich Moorish design. Since being returned to the community

it has been meticulously restored and is now a working synagogue again, featuring a permanent exhibition on Jewish history in the Czech lands up to the beginning of World War II.

Old-New Synagogue

Staronová synagoga
Červená 2, Prague 1 (no phone). Metro Staroměstská/17, 18 tram. **Open** *Apr-June* 9am-6pm Mon-Thur, Sun; 9am-5pm Fri. *Nov-Mar* 9am-4pm Mon-Thur, Sun; 9am-2pm Fri. **Admission** 200 Kč; 140 Kč concessions; free under-6s. **No credit cards**. **Map** p308 H2.

The Old-New Synagogue is a rather forlorn piece of medievalism. The oldest survivor of the ghetto and the spiritual centre of the Jewish community for over 600 years, it has now been returned to the community and is still used for services. The austere exterior walls give no clues to its peculiar Gothic interior. An extra rib was added to the usual vaulting pattern to avoid the symbolism of the cross. Instead the decor and structure revolve around the number 12, after the 12 tribes of Israel: there are 12 windows, 12 bunches of sculpted grapes, and clusters of 12 vine leaves decorate the pillar bases. The interior was left untouched for 500 years as a reminder of the blood spilled here dur-

The last square you'll ever see

If any place in Prague has bad karma, it's Old Town Square. There's no question that it's the historic heart of the city, and a worthy focal point.

It's just that if you spend much time here, you begin to notice the traces of a fair amount of spilled blood. Dominating the square is the statue of Jan Hus, looking gaunt and otherworldly as he rises above his followers in a towering bronze sculpture. **Hus** (*see p8*), who personifies Czech martyrdom, was a Catholic priest and rector of Charles University burnt at the stake for refusing to recant his criticism of Church corruption. Though his death did not occur in Prague, it set off the conflict that eventually became the Thirty Years' War, sending much of Europe to slaughter.

One of the later fallouts in the continuing struggle for a distinctly Czech ideology was the execution of 27 Bohemian Protestants by the Habsburg forces after their victory at the Battle of Bílá Hora in what is now Prague 6. Crosses on the pavement in front of the Old Town tower mark the points where the mayors, estates and religious leaders were beheaded in a day-long public ceremony. Ironically, one of those executed,

Dr Jesenius, is credited with having performed the first public autopsy, in the interest of Renaissance-era enlightenment, on this very square.

The Nazis were fond of holding rallies on Old Town Square, of course, and found the **Church of Our Lady before Týn** (*see p87*) an ideal place from which to drape swastika banners. Aside from approximately 80,000 Czechs who died in concentration camps during the war, the Nazis added to the death toll on Old Town Square itself during the Prague Uprising of 5-9 May 1945. Wherever you see a plaque featuring an upturned hand – they can be seen on walls all over Old Town and the city centre – it means that a resister was shot nearby.

On the opposite side of the square from the Old Town Hall plaque commemorating the martyred Czech Protestants is the Kinský Palace. On the balcony of this elegant building **Klement Gottwald** (*see p15*), the first self-proclaimed 'Working Class President', announced he was taking over the reigns of power in 1948. Gottwald's Stalinesque regime executed nearly as many intellectuals, dissidents and unfortunate bourgeois as the Nazis would have.

Sightseeing

ing the pogrom of 1389, when the men, women and children who sought sanctuary in the synagogue were slaughtered by Christians. The 19th-century neo-Gothic crusaders, however, couldn't resist the temptation to 'restore' the original look and slapped a fresh coat of paint over the top.

Oak seats line the walls facing the *bema*, or platform, protected by a Gothic grille, from which the Torah has been read aloud every day for more than 700 years, with the exception of the Nazi occupation. The tall seat marked by a gold star belonged to Rabbi Löw, the most famous inhabitant of the ghetto. The rabbi lived to the age of 97, and a sculpture by Ladislav Šaloun to the right of the New Town Hall in Mariánské náměstí depicts the manner of his death. Unable to approach the scholar, who was always absorbed in study of the scriptures, Death hid in a rose that was offered to Löw by his innocent granddaughter. The rabbi's grave can be found in the Old Jewish Cemetery, recognisable by the quantity of pebbles and wishes on scraps of paper that are placed upon the tomb to this day.

Despite its wealth of historical and religious significance, there's not much to see once you're inside the Old-New synagogue and precious little explanation is provided.

Precious Legacy Tours

Maiselova 16, Staré Město, Prague 1 (2232 1954). Metro Staroměstská/17, 18 tram. **Open** 9am-6pm Mon-Fri, Sun. **Credit** AmEx, MC, V. **Map** p308 H3.
This Jewish travel agency purveys tickets for the various Jewish Museum sights, the Old-New Synagogue, tours of Prague and trips to Terezín (*see p251*), a small town that was used in 1941 as a holding camp for Jews destined for concentration camps. The English-speaking staff at Precious Legacy Tours are also able to book boat tours, meals in kosher restaurants and accommodation.

Northern Staré Město

The site along the banks of the Vltava wasn't incorporated into the new design of Josefov, and the grandiose buildings have their backs turned upon the old ghetto. Going down Kaprova towards the river will bring you to Náměstí Jana Palacha, named in memory of Jan Palach, the first of the students who set themselves on fire in 1969 in protest at the Soviet invasion (the second, Jan Zajíc, didn't get a square named after him, but he is remembered on the memorial on Wenceslas Square). Dominating the square is the breathtakingly beautiful **Rudolfinum** (*see p213*), or 'House of Arts', which houses the Dvořák hall and the Suk hall. It was built between 1876 and 1884 (and named after Rudolf II) in neo-classical style and entirely funded by the Czech Savings Bank to display its 'patriotic, provincial feelings'. You can see the bank's corporate logo, the bee of thrift, in the paws of

the two sphinxes with remarkably ample breasts who guard the riverfront entrance. In 1918 the concert hall became home to the parliament of the new Republic.

When Chamberlain returned to England from meeting Hitler in 1938 disclaiming responsibility for the 'quarrel in a faraway country between people of whom we know nothing', it was here that 250,000 of these people came to take an oath and pledge themselves to the defence of the Republic. The Nazis, having little use for a parliament building, turned it back into a concert hall and called it 'the German House of Arts'. Legend has it that a statue of the Jewish composer Mendelssohn was ordered to be removed for obvious reasons, but the workmen, not knowing what Mendelssohn looked like, took their lessons in racial science to heart and removed the figure with the biggest nose – which turned out to be Richard Wagner. Opposite, with its back to the Old Jewish Cemetery, is the magnificent **Museum of Decorative Arts** (*see p115*).

Few visitors make it over to the streets of semi-derelict art nouveau tenement houses in northern Staré Město, but they are well worth inspection, even without the attraction of **St Agnes's Convent** (Klášter sv. Anežky České; *see p112*), the oldest example of Gothic architecture in the city. Its founder St Agnes died a full 700 years before the Pope deigned to make her a saint. Popular opinion held that miracles would accompany her canonisation, and sure enough within five days of the Vatican's announcement the Velvet Revolution was under way. St Agnes's Convent now hosts the National Gallery's 16th-century art collection, recently transferred from St George's Convent (*see p112*).

Nearby is Dlouhá or 'Long Street', which contained no fewer than 13 breweries in the 14th century when beer champion Charles IV forbade the export of hops. These days its main attraction is the **Roxy** at No.33 (*see p228*). It's a thoroughly crumbling cinema that was once the headquarters of the Communist Youth Association and is now the city's most atmospheric club (*see p230* **The Roxy holds out**). Next door is the serene **Dahab** (*see p135*) tea house, which moved out of the club itself to make way for, after seven years, the installation of the Roxy's first proper bar. In the pleasantly quiet streets between Dlouhá and the river lie several more convivial bars and cafés including the French-style **Chez Marcel** (*see p127*), the impossibly Irish **Molly Malone's** (*see p151*), the crowded and fashionable **Alcohol Bar** (*see p148*), the neo-Bohemian **Blatouch** (*see p132*) and the all-American **Žiznivý pes** (*see p152*).

Nové Město

The Nové Město district shows off the face of New Capitalism in Prague, with wide avenues, Wenceslas Square, fashionable shoppers and gritty streetlife.

Maps p309, p310 & p311

When the king of Bohemia's Golden Age, Charles IV, decided Prague needed a modern town, Nové Město, or New Town, just fitted the bill. Founded in 1348 as a hygienic, wide open and fire proof district, this part of Prague still features broad green squares that have by now attracted big international auditing firms, ad agencies and high-tech retail. Fortunately for visitors to the district, they are counterbalanced by some of the finest of the new breed of Czech and expat food and drink ventures around (*see p100* **Some call it SONA**).

Old and New Towns meet along the line of Národní třída, Na příkopě and Revoluční. Nové Město, bounded to the east by traffic-pounded Wilsonova, wraps around Old Town and Josefov, stretching from the river in the north down to Vyšehrad in the south.

Wenceslas Square

Wenceslas Square (Václavské náměstí), once known as the Horse Market, is the hub of city life. You'll find yourself passing through it several times a day. More of a broad boulevard than a square, it was laid out over 600 years ago under Charles IV, and has always been a good place to check out the changing fortunes of the city. Last century, Nazis, communists, anti-communists and a naked Allen Ginsberg have all paraded its length.

The May Day parades have these days been replaced by a sleazy collection of drug dealers, pickpockets and crooked cab drivers. You'll be assailed by the smell of frying sausages and, if you're a businessman, by any number of strip club promoters. The shops, which used to have dull names like House of Fashion or House of

Wenceslas Square: horse market no more.

Food, have been privatised, glamorised and outfitted with McDonald's counters. All the designer names and discount chains of the Western world have now come here to stay.

The bottom end of the square is a pedestrianised area, invariably thronging with tour parties, backpackers and Euro-teens heading for one of the cheesy discos that invariably open here just for the summer, their lights pulsing out over the square. The kiosks here are the best place to buy foreign newspapers and magazines.

A tour of the square

Almost every architectural style of the last 150 years is represented somewhere on the square. Starting at the lower end by the newsstands, the revolutionary **Baťa** building (Ludvík Kysela, 1927-9) at No.6, with its massive expanses of plate glass, was an important functionalist structure. Pioneering cubist architect Emil Králíček, together with Matěj Blecha, built the Asiatic-inspired **Adam Pharmacy** at No.8, giving it a cubist interior. Jan Kotěra's first building in Prague, **Peterka House**, stands a few doors up at No.12, signalling art nouveau's first moves towards more geometric forms. Unashamedly retro, the **Wiehl House** (1896) on the corner of Vodičkova was built by Antonín Wiehl in neo-Renaissance style and decorated with elaborate sgraffito. Beyond are the arcades of the Lucerna complex and Blecha's **Supich Building** (1913-16) at Nos. 38-40, complete with likeably bizarre Assyrian-style masks adorning its façade. The second-floor balcony of the **Melantrich Building** (No.30) became the unlikely venue for one of the most astounding events of the Velvet Revolution: on 24 November 1989, in front of a crowd of over 300,000 people, Václav Havel and Alexander Dubček stepped forward here and embraced, signifying the end of 21 years of 'normalisation'. Within weeks the entire cabinet had resigned.

Up at the top end, crowning the whole of the square, is Josef Schulz's impressive neo-Renaissance **National Museum** (1885-90; see p118), a swaggering, monumental 19th-century block, cut off from the rest of the square by a dual carriageway. Across the road is the ugly 1970s building that housed the Federal Assembly until the Czech-Slovak split in 1993. The building has now become the base for **Radio Free Europe**, which, after playing its part in the toppling of totalitarianism, moved in to take advantage of the cheap rent. At press time, however, Czechs were getting increasingly anxious about the possibility of a terrorist attack on the building as a result of RFE's

Night of the living night tram. *See p101.*

broadcasts to hostile Muslim fundamentalist states. There was talk that the station may have finally worn out its welcome and could be moving to a more welcoming nation – or at least to the suburbs.

Also at the top end of the square are two of Prague's most symbolic sites – one ancient in inspiration, one modern. The former is Josef Václav Myslbek's huge equestrian **statue of St Wenceslas** (Václav). Although some form of monument to the Czech patron saint has stood here since the late 17th century, Myslbek's serene prince wasn't unveiled until 1912. The surrounding saints Agnes, Adalbert, Procopius and, of course, Ludmila, Wenceslas's grandmother, were added during the 1920s. Wenceslas is now parodied in an inverted polystyrene version just inside the **Lucerna** shopping passage down the street, courtesy of political artist David Černý. Just down from the statue is the **memorial to the victims of communism**, commemorating the sacrifice of Jan Palach who burned himself alive on 16 January 1969 protesting the Soviet invasion.

On the north side, past the Soviet-style Jalta Hotel, is the square's best-known building, the glittering art nouveau **Grand Hotel Evropa** (see p52) at Nos.25-7, built by Alois Dryák and Bedřich Bendelmayer (1903-6). Past the **Krone/Julius Meinl** department store (see p160), at the bottom of the square is Antonín Pfeiffer's 'Babylonian'-inspired **Koruna Palace** (1912-14), fashionable once because of archaeological digs in Mesopotamia.

Sightseeing

Be there, be (Wenceslas) square

Stick around Wenceslas Square long enough and you're bound to see authority put to the test. More than 250,000 people rang out communism here with jangling keys in November 1989. Their choice of location was appropriate: the square is well-versed in uprisings and revolution.

A generation earlier it witnessed throngs of student protestors who would not be so successful. In August 1968, hordes turned out to cheer on Alexander Dubček's 'Socialism with a Human Face', a brave but doomed attempt at a compromise between central planning and totalitarianism. On that occasion, the students were answered by an invasion of Warsaw Pact tanks.

During WWII Wenceslas Square also saw mass demonstrations, once in spontaneous protest and once in a staged display of obedience to fascism.

The earlier of these demos took place in 1938 when Czechs took to the square to denounce the Munich Treaty, in which England, France and Italy offered up a chunk of Czechoslovakia to Nazi Germany. The second rally, the ones most Czechs would clearly rather forget, took place after the Nazis had overrun the capital. A Czech Television documentary aired in the mid 1990s showed the square filled with people raising their arms in unison in a fascist salute to the Reichsprotektorat of Böhmen and Mähren. In the days following the broadcast,

the station was deluged by sacks of mail containing angry letters from viewers.

Easier to swallow is the memory of the thousands who filled Wenceslas Square a generation earlier to weep for joy as TG Masaryk, the country's first president, stood on a balcony in the square and announced the formation of the Czechoslovak Republic on October 28, 1918, following the defeat of the Austrian-Hungarian Empire in WWI.

Nearly as many turned out 70 years earlier for the 'národní obrození' or National Awakening of 1848, which shook the Habsburg Empire to its foundations. Had that uprising not foundered on nationalist splits between Czech and German Praguers, true independence might have arrived in the Czech lands much earlier than it did.

In early 2000, a protest movement known as Díky a odejděte ('Thank you, now get out') once more packed Wenceslas Square with demonstrators calling for the resignation of Prime Minister Miloš Zeman and the head of the leading ODS Party, Václav Klaus. Both have lost a lot of points in the polls since their Velvet Revolution glory days, after corruption scandals within ODS and Zeman's remarkable knack for offending his constituents and the electorate with crass behaviour.

But it would seem demos on Wenceslas Square are not always terribly effective. At press time both of these figures were still hanging on to considerable power.

Wenceslas Square: beyond the hype.

Northern Nové Město

The pedestrianised Na příkopě runs from Wenceslas Square to Náměstí Republiky along the line of what was once a moat. It has been quaintly dubbed 'Prague's Wall Street' because of its concentration of banks, and the financial institutions range from the neo-Renaissance Živnostenská banka at No.20 to the lushly art deco Komerční banka at No.28. With the opening of the **Juice Bar** (*see p134*) and a Carli Gry branch, it seems clear which way the tone of the street is going. Slovanský dům (*see p161*), the former home of both the Gestapo and Communist Party offices, is now home to Prague's swankiest mall and multiplex cinema, a sushi place, and the patio restaurant **Kogo Pizzeria & Caffeteria** (*see p129*). **Čedok** (*see* **Directory: Resources A-Z**), the national tourist office, is at No.18, good for leaflets, events tickets and train and bus tickets.

Dominating Náměstí Republiky is the luscious art nouveau **Municipal House** (*see p134 and p213*), which stands on the border of the Old and New Towns. Built between 1905 and 1911, and lavishly restored in the mid 1990s, this combination of colour and curves was where Czechoslovakia was signed into existence in 1918. Attached to the Municipal House is the blackened Gothic **Powder Gate** (*see p85*), predating it by half a millennium.

Facing the Municipal House is the neo-classical former customs house, U Hybernů (The Hibernians), now modernised for trade shows and exhibitions. Running east from Náměstí Republiky is Hybernská, named after the Irish monks who settled here in the 16th century after falling foul of Elizabeth I. Their contribution to city life was to introduce the potato, an event from which Czech cuisine has never recovered. The street itself is unremarkable save for the baroque Lidový dům at No.7, a building that used to house the Lenin Museum, then later the **American Center for Culture and Commerce**. At No.4 the Café Arco, meeting place of the self-styled 'Arconauts' who included Franz Kafka and Max Brod, has recently reopened after years but, alas, as a cold and soulless modern café. Across the road in the Masaryk railway station – Prague's first, built in 1845 – is the late-night buffet **Bistro Flip** (*see p229*), serving fried cheese until 11pm every night to the cream of the city's unsavouries. Right next to it, for the more discriminating street urchin, a Dunkin Donuts has now opened. Typical of the district's transformation is the monolithic **Marriott** (*see p51*) across the street, with the city's most elaborate fitness centre in its basement. For a last blast of what

accommodation used to look like in Prague, the **Hotel Imperial** (*see p54*) just up the street offers hundreds of cheap, dorm-like rooms, while the café itself, **Café Imperial** (*see p141*) is an incredibly ornate taste of the 1920s.

The largely anonymous streets south of here contain one of Prague's newest art museums, the **Mucha Museum** (*see p115*), on Panská, and the main post office, on Jindřišská. It's an extraordinary covered courtyard with newly modernised booths, but bustling with all the shuffling paperwork of a huge bureaucracy.

Two buildings make it worth braving the streaming traffic of the Wilsonova expressway, bounding Nové Město in the east. One is the **State Opera** (*see p214*), built by the Viennese architects Fellner and Helmer in 1888, something of a last gasp assertion of identity by Prague's German community in the midst of the great Czech National Revival. More interesting, though, is the city's main station, Hlavní nádraží, also known as **Wilsonovo nádraží** (*see* **Directory: Getting Around**). Smelly, crumbling, inhabited by lowlifes and one of Prague's main gay cruises, the station might seem an unlikely place to seek out the pleasures of Prague's bourgeois age. That it had been dedicated first to Emperor Franz Joseph and then American President Woodrow Wilson gave the communists two very good reasons to plant a high-speed bypass outside its front door and create a modern extension beneath. The upper levels, which were left to rot in obscurity until the Fantova kavárna opened there in the mid 1990s, are an atmospheric remnant of a bygone age. The café contains some of the best art nouveau murals anywhere in Prague, with languorous women serving as a backdrop to the rent boys who now congregate beneath them. The cavernous lower levels are tacky, dirty, bustly and a must for fans of communist architecture.

Just north of Náměstí Republiky is the **Kotva** department store (*see p160*). This was once one of the shopping showpieces of the Eastern bloc, and 75,000 people a day would come from as far away as Bulgaria to snap up its fine selection of acrylic sweaters, orange plastic cruets and official portraits of Gustav Husák. It has now been overhauled and the communist idea of fashion replaced by the German one. There's another classic communist-era department store, Bílá labuť, not far away on busy Na Poříčí; its glass-curtain wall is a classic functionalist feature. Almost opposite is a rare example of the rondo-cubist style: Pavel Janák's Banka Legií from the early 1920s. On the other side of the Wilsonova flyover is the beleaguered neo-Renaissance block containing the **Museum of the City of Prague** (*see p116*).

Sightseeing

National Theatre: cultural shrine. *See p101.*

Further north, on the embankment nábřeží Ludvíka Svobody, is a monolithic place with a dome that glows at night, the Ministry of Transport, built in the 1920s and for a spell the HQ of the Central Committee of the Communist Party. It was here that on 21 August 1968 tanks arrived to escort Alexander Dubček to be flown off to the Kremlin for 'fraternal discussions'.

Municipal House

Obecní dům

Náměstí Republiky 5, Prague 1 (2200 2100). Metro Náměstí Republiky/5, 14, 26 tram. **Map** p309 K3.

All the leading artists of the day were involved in the creation of the Municipal House or Obecní dům (1905-11), a masterpiece of stained glass, coloured mosaics, tiled murals and gold trimmings. Erected during the death throes of the Austro-Hungarian Empire, the building became a symbol of the aspirations of the new republic, representing a stylistic and structural break with the *ancien régime*. It was here that the proud and newly independent state of Czechoslovakia was officially signed into existence in 1918, and a plaque on the side pays a tribute to a country that no longer exists.

Prague Symphony Orchestra (*see p210*) concerts are held in the Smetana Hall, and other magnificent rooms include, the Lord Mayor's Salon, covered with Alfons Mucha murals of Czech heroes. The façade and exquisite **Kavárna Obecní Dům** (*see p134*) are by Osvald Polívka; the monumental mosaic 'Homage to Prague' above the main entrance, featuring languid ladies in an altogether un-urban setting, is by Karel Spillar. It is offset by Ladislav Šaloun's sculptural composition, 'The Humiliation and Resurrection of the Nation'. The café, restaurant, basement bars and gallery are all open to the public, and a guided tour provides access to the other splendid corners. *See also p213.*

Some call it SONA

The dozen-block area South of Národní třída inevitably had to be labelled with something, and SONA seemed as good as anything at capturing the almost San Franciscan flavour of the buzzy international community.

Within minutes of each other are **The Globe Bookstore and Coffeehouse** (*see p141*) and the 'semi-industrial' **Ř Bar** (*see p154*), both of which organise literary evenings, and the classic Czech student hangout **Velryba** (*see p142*), with its backroom photography gallery down the spiral metal stairs. In the immediate area are half a dozen other bars, cafés and lifestyle outfitters of the hip, new plugged-in Prague.

This pocket of Nové Město has become emblematic of a new breed of Praguer: one who savours the derelict environs of post-communist decay but likes to see it infused with house music, high bandwidth information sharing and the aroma of powerhouse latte. SONA has been celebrated by international design magazines as the place to be in Prague and the Globe has become the spot to

listen out for the first rumblings of new creative collectives, theatre groups, writers' festivals and weekend raves.

The new identity of SONA began to emerge shortly before the Globe moved here from the outlying Holešovice district in 2000, followed by two other expat magnets, the low-key foodie heavens of **Angel Café**, **Gargoyle's Restaurant** and the **Red Room** bar, all on the corner of Křemencova and Opatovická.

As is inevitable in the fits and starts of post-Velvet Revolution, free-market Prague, such places tend to live a precarious existence and all three had just closed their doors at press time, though they were regular hangouts of local entrepreneurs, designers, artists, film people and hacks.

Such folks, when living in Prague, learn to keep their radar finely tuned to changes and to savour a good drinking hole while they can. The city's landlords can be arbitrary, lease contracts are often impossible to enforce and the 'buzz' tends in any case to be something temperamental and fleeting.

Southern Nové Město

Just south of the Old Town end of Wenceslas Square is Jungmannovo náměstí, site of the world's only **cubist lamp post** (*see p30*). Tucked away in an obscure corner, Emil Králíček's bizarre and somewhat forlorn-looking creation, much derided when it was completed in 1913, has become something of a Prague cultural icon. It stands in front of the towering **Church of Our Lady of the Snows** (*see p103*), a would-be St Vitus's Cathedral. A path from here leads to an unexpected oasis, the **Franciscan Gardens** (Františkánská zahrada), a haven of clipped-hedge calm in the middle of the city.

From Jungmannovo náměstí, Národní třída (National Avenue) divides the Old and New towns, meeting the river at the *most Legií* (Legionnaires' Bridge). Národní was the playground of generations of Czechs in the last century and the battleground of another generation this century. Standing proudly on the banks of the Vltava, topped by a crown of gold and with sculptures of bucking stallions lining the balustrade, the **National Theatre** (*see also p234*) is a product and symbol of the fervour of 19th-century Czech nationalism. It took 20 years to persuade the general public to

cough up the money to begin construction, and from 1868 to 1881 to build it. Then, just days before the curtain was to go up on the first performance, it was gutted by fire. An emotive appeal, launched immediately by the leading lights of the city's cultural institutions, raised enough money to start all over again in just six weeks. In 1883 the building finally opened with a gala performance of *Libuše*, an opera about the mythical origins of the Czech nation written especially for the occasion by Smetana. A big bronze memorial halfway down on the south side (by No.20) pays tribute to the events of 17 November 1989, where the violent police suppression of a student demo sparked the beginning of the Velvet Revolution.

The department store on the corner of Spálená is a barometer of the changes since then. It used to be called Máj after the most sacred date in the communist calendar, 1 May. Now it's owned by **Tesco** (*see p160*). Gather here after clubbing to catch a **night tram**. These conveyors of colourful characters all converge on Spálená, the street out front.

By the memorial at No.20 is **Reduta** (*see p221*), the venerable jazz club where Bill Clinton tested his saxophone skills before a global audience. The next-door **Brasserie Le Patio** (*see p137*) is a much better bet for

Sightseeing

But one rumour from a good source had it that the Angel Café space was already being considered for takeover by a cutting-edge expat mogul who edits a slick little magazine and is looking to create a whole new groove for drinking and chilling. How the venture will fare in the challenging waters of Prague's SONA is yet to be seen. Never easy to be cool, alas.

Red Room: another one bites the dust.

The riverfront façades of Nové Město soak up the afternoon rays.

atmosphere and also has excellent small jazz combos. Further down at No.7, through an exquisite wrought-iron entrance, is Viola, once a literary hangout that sports one of the several framed Václav Havel signatures to be found in various drinking holes around town. Next door, with a fine view across the river to the Castle, is the redoubtable **Slavia** (*see p135*), once the centre of Prague's café life and, after a long closure, happily reopened and hoping to regain a little of its past glory.

The embankment running south contains a fine if not terribly remarkable collection of art nouveau apartment houses. At No.78 stands the block containing Václav Havel's flat. In a deliberate break with tradition, Havel declined to move into the swanky presidential quarters at the Castle and stayed on in his own down-at-heel tenement across the river. Now the

gesture has been made, admired and written about, he has purchased an altogether more upmarket residence in Prague 6. Not that he can necessarily be blamed, however, since the plot next door at the old place was for some time a building site while a controversial Frank Gehry construction was going up: the so-called **'Fred & Ginger Building'**, the form of which supposedly resembles that pair of twirling Hollywood stars (*see p30*).

The climax of this art nouveau promenade is **Palackého náměstí**, which is dominated by a huge Stanislav Sucharda sculpture of 19th-century historian František Palacký, who took 46 years to write a history of the Czech people. The solemn Palacký sits on an giant pedestal, oblivious to the beauties and demons flying around him. Behind him rise the two modern spires of the altogether more ancient **Emmaus**

Monastery or Monastery of the Slavs (klášter Na Slovanech), which was founded by Charles IV, the towers destroyed after the baroque versions were destroyed by a stray World War II bomb.

The island closest to the embankment, at the bottom of Národní třída, is **Slovanský Island**. In the days before slacking became an art form, Berlioz came here and was appalled at the 'idlers, wasters and ne'er-do-wells' who congregated on the island. With a recommendation like that it's hard to resist the outdoor café here or a few lazy hours in one of the rowing boats for hire. There's also a fine statue of Božena Němcová, as seen on the front of the 500 Kč note. She was the Czech version of George Sand, a celebrated novelist whose private life scandalised polite society. At the southern tip is the art gallery **Výstavní síň Mánes** (see p206), a 1930s functionalist building oddly attached to a medieval water tower. The intelligentsia used to gather here between the wars, while in 1989 Civic Forum churned out posters and leaflets from here. The island is also home to the newly restored cultural centre **Žofín** – a large yellow building dating from the 1880s that has long been associated with the Czech cultural psyche, and hosted tea dances and concerts until just before World War II. Today it hosts conventions and classical concerts and features one of the loveliest beer gardens in Bohemia at the back (but avoid its restaurant side unless desperate).

Church of Our Lady of the Snows

Kostel Panny Marie Sněžné
Jungmannovo náměstí, Prague 1 (2224 6243). Metro Můstek/3, 9, 14, 24 tram. **Open** 9am-5pm daily. **Map** p308 J5.
Charles IV founded the church to mark his coronation in 1347, intending it to stretch more than 100m (330ft), but, after the 33m (110ft) high chancel was completed in 1397, funds dried up. What remains is a voluptuous, vertiginous affair that sweeps the eyes upwards, scaling the towering and typically over-the-top black and gold baroque altarpiece. Despite this oppressive presence, the church is a wonderfully light, tranquil space, with an interesting marbling effect on the walls. The church was erected 1,000 years after the Virgin Mary appeared to 4th-century Pope Liberius in a dream, telling him to build a church where the snow fell in August. He knocked off Santa Maria Maggiore in Rome.

Around Karlovo náměstí

There are some lovely backstreets to explore in what's now known as the SONA area (see p100 **Some call it SONA**), between Národní třída and Karlovo náměstí, as well as some major thoroughfares. Jungmannova contains the incredibly well-stocked **Bontonland Megastore** (see p179) music shop, always

strong on local bands, while Pštrossova is the address for an icon, **The Globe Bookstore & Coffeehouse** (see p141 and p165), always at the heart of the expat literary scene, and the new **Ř Bar** (see p154). The best-known fixture in this area is, alas, the **U Fleků** (see p154) pub, at Křemencova 11, the world's oldest operating brew pub and the place to go if you want to offload some cash and meet many Germans bellowing drinking songs (the beer tastes wonderful, though). Its entrance is marked by a picturesque old clock, hung like a tavern sign. At Spálená 82 is the **Diamant House**, designed by Emil Králíček in 1912, which takes its name from the broken-up prisms that constitute the façade. The ground floor is now a Škoda car showroom and the neon strip lights that decorate it are a dubious aesthetic addition. A nice touch of the more pleasing old-fashioned design school is the cubist arch that shelters a piece of baroque statuary and bridges the gap, literally and historically, between this building and the more traditional 18th-century Church of the Holy Trinity next door.

Karlovo náměstí is an enormous expanse that used to be a cattle market and the site of Charles IV's relic fair. Once a year he would wheel out his collection of sacred saints' skulls, toenails and underwear, the townsfolk dutifully gawped, cripples would throw down their crutches and the blind would miraculously regain their sight. These days you're most likely to come across the square in a night tram, minor miracles in their own right. Its other attractions include the 14th-century **New Town Hall** (Novoměstská radnice). It was from here that several Catholic councillors were pitched out from an upstairs window in 1419 – and the word 'defenestration' entered the language of realpolitik.

On the eastern side of the square is the splendidly restored **Jesuit Church of St Ignatius** (sv. Ignác), a typically lush early baroque affair in cream, pink and orange stucco, emblazoned all over its façade with gold leaf trimmings. No.24, now the pastel accented **Amiveo** nightclub and eatery (see p224), was once a restaurant used for training waiters employed by the secret police. The James Bonds of the catering world learnt how to plant bugs in dissidents' soup and dish up the sauce to their eager employers. In the south-west corner is the **Faust House** (Faustův dům), an ornate 17th-century building that has more than a few legends attached to it. Edward Kelly, the earless English alchemist, lived here, as apparently did the Prince of Darkness, who carried off a penniless student and secured the house a place in Prague's mythic heritage.

Halfway across the square on Resslova is the baroque **Cathedral of Sts Cyril and Methodius** (*see p104*), scene of one of the most dramatic and poignant events of World War II – the last stand of the assassins of Reichsprotektor Reinhard Heydrich (*see p14* **Bad day in Prague 7**).

Going in the opposite direction up the hill is Ječná, where Dvořák died at No.14; but rather than staring at the plaque on the wall, go to the **Dvořák Museum** (*see p117*) on nearby Ke Karlovu, where you can catch a chamber recital. It's quartered in a gorgeous summer house designed by Dientzenhofer – the Villa Amerika – these days surrounded by incongruous modern bits of concrete.

At the far end of the street is a museum of a very different sort – the **Police Museum** (*see p118*). Brek, the stuffed wonder dog responsible for thwarting the defection of several hundred dissidents, has been given a decent burial, but there are still plenty of gruesome exhibits here to delight the morbid.

If it all gets too much, you can seek sanctuary in the unusual church next door, which is dedicated to Charlemagne, Charles IV's hero and role model. The octagonal nave of Na Karlově was only completed in the 16th century and for years the superstitious local townsfolk refused to enter it for fear that it would collapse around their ears. The ornate, gilt frescoed walls inside were restored after the building was partially destroyed in the Prussian siege of 1757, but bullets can still be seen embedded in them. From the garden there are extensive views across the Nusle Valley to Vyšehrad on the other side. A few blocks to the west on Vyšehradská is the **Church of St John on the Rock** (sv. Jan Na skalce), a fine Dientzenhofer structure built in the 1730s, perched at the top of an impressive double stairway. A little further to the south from that are the delightful but little-visited Botanical Gardens, where the hothouses have recently been rebuilt and the tranquil terraces retain a strong attraction for pram-wielding mothers, couples and old folk on benches.

Orthodox Cathedral of Sts Cyril & Methodius

Kostel sv. Cyrila a Metoděje
Resslova 9, Prague 2 (2492 0686). Metro Karlovo náměstí/4, 7, 9, 12, 14, 16, 18, 22, 24 tram. **Open** 10am-4pm Tue-Sun. **Admission** 30 Kč adults; 10 Kč concessions. **Map** p310 H8.
This baroque church, built in the 1730s, was taken over and restored by the Czech Orthodox Church in the 1930s. A plaque and memorial outside, together with numerous bullet holes, still attract tributes and flowers today, and are clues to what happened inside during World War II. On 29 December 1941 two

Czech paratroopers trained in England were flown into Bohemia, together with five colleagues, to carry out, among other resistance acts, the assassination of Reinhard Heydrich, Reichsprotektor of Bohemia and Moravia and the man who chaired the infamous 1942 Wannsee Conference on the Final Solution. Josef Gabčík, Jan Kubiš and their co-conspirators were given sanctuary in the crypt here after the event, until they were betrayed to the Germans. In the early hours of 18 June, 350 members of the SS and Gestapo surrounded the church and spent the night bombarding it with bullets and grenades. The men, who managed to survive until dawn, used their final bullets to shoot themselves.

The incident did not end there. Recriminations were swift, brutal and arbitrary. Hundreds of people, many of them Jews, were rounded up in Prague and shot immediately, while five entire villages and most of their inhabitants were liquidated, the most famous being Lidice. The events brought about a turning point. Britain repudiated the Munich Agreement and Anthony Eden declared that Lidice had 'stirred the conscience of the civilised world'. The story of the assassination and its aftermath is movingly told (in English) in the crypt of the church (entrance on Na Zderaze) where the Czech paratroopers made their last stand.

Nové Město: past under glass.

Sightseeing

Further Afield

Rambling parks, monastries, entombed communists, a cheesy funfair, modern
art treasures and neighbourhood caffs. Who said the suburbs are boondocks?

Holešovice, Letná & Troja

Maps p312-313

The somewhat blighted look of Holešovice is
your first clue that you've found out-of-centre
neighbourhood life – though with Prague's
small layout, Old Town is still in view from
some parts of the district. The ostensibly
unremarkable 19th-century suburb has a lot
more going for it than grimy tenement blocks
(alongside increasingly spruced-up ones) and
factories, and one of Prague's two international
train stations. Indeed, this district to the north
of Old Town over the Vltava also contains two
of Prague's finest green spaces and has become
one of Prague's hippest areas.

Down towards the river on Kostelní is the
National Technical Museum (*see p118*),
a constructivist building dating from 1938-41,
whose dull name belies a fascinating collection
of Czechnology that instantly wows kids. Five
minutes' walk east is Holešovice's main drag,
Dukelských hrdinů. Here stands a sleek
constructivist building, the enormous, modern
Veletržní palác, built in the mid 1920s to
house the trade fairs that had long outgrown
Výstaviště (*see p106*). It was gutted by fire
in 1974 but has been splendidly restored; the
stunning white-painted atrium rises up seven
storeys and is lined with sweeping guard rails,
giving it the feel of a massive ocean liner. Pop
in to peak at the atrium even if you don't want
to look around the new **National Gallery
Collection of 19th-, 20th- and 21st-
Century Art** (*see p111*) within. **The Globe
Bookstore & Coffeehouse**, the expat
institution once around here, has now moved
to New Town (*see p33, p141 and p165*).

A couple of minutes' walk to the north is
Výstaviště, an unusual wrought-iron pavilion
built to house the Jubilee Exhibition of 1891 and
considered the first expression of art nouveau
in the city. Here, in the **Lapidárium**, you'll find
an intriguing collection of reject monuments that
once stood around the city. From the top of
the Ferris wheel in the nearby Lunapark there
are fine views over the woody environs of
Stromovka, a vast park laid out by Rudolf II
in the 16th century, as a place where he could
commune with nature. His favoured companion
here was English alchemist John Dee, who got

the job when he claimed to understand both the
language of the birds and the one Adam and Eve
spoke in Eden. Today the leafy park makes a
wonderful spot for a stroll or picnic. Just south of
Stromovka lie two of the city's hotbeds of expat
late-night lifestyling: **Fraktal** (*see p155*), the
half-finished bar where you'll find performance
artists and affable international drunks sitting
around tattered tables in beat up chairs, and **La
Bodega Flamenca** (*see p155*), the Czech-owned
expat cellar haven of sangria sipping – one of the
city's best after-hours refuelling options. Around
the corner, **Wakata** (*see p228*) also stays up
all night with grimy, smoky, breakbeats kind
of space. (For more cleaned-up clubbing, with
proper elbow room and a stylish long bar, try
the Holešovice dance haven known as **Mecca**
(*see p226*) on the eastern side of the district.)

For a breath of fresh air, take the half-hour
walk back to the Old Town via the sedate
embassy-land of Bubeneč, just to the west
of these bars and clubs, and ramble on past
the Sparta Stadium and through **Letná Park**
(Letenské sady). This was where the biggest
demonstration of 1989 took place, attended
by nearly a million people. On the edge of the
park, with a fine view overlooking the town, is
the plinth, which now houses just an innocent,
if giant, metronome in the place where the
massive statue of Stalin once stood.

Alternatively, a 20-minute walk north of
Stromovka (or bus 112 from Nádraži Holešovice
metro) brings you to **Troja Chateau** (*see
below*). Commissioned by Count Šternberg in
the 1700s and built by a French architect and
Italian craftsmen, it contains some stunning
trompe l'oeil frescoes. Count Šternberg's horses
inhabited a vast, sumptuous stable block with
marble floors and decorated with frescoes of
their noble forebears. The inmates of **Prague
Zoo** (*see p189*) across the road can only curse
their historical mistiming, for, despite having
found a new patron in Coca-Cola, their living
conditions are altogether less salubrious.

Troja Chateau

Trojský zámek
*U trojského zámku 1, Holešovice, Prague 7 (688
5146). Metro Nádraži Holešovice/112 bus.*
Open *Apr-Sept* 10am-6pm Tue-Sun. *Oct-Mar*
10am-5pm Sat, Sun. **Admission** 80 Kč adults;
40 Kč concessions. **No credit cards.**

After winning huge tracts of land in the property lottery that followed the Thirty Years War, Count Šternberg embarked upon creating a house worthy of his ego. A Czech nobleman, he was anxious to prove his loyalty to the Habsburg emperor and literally moved mountains to do so. The hillside had to be dug out to align the villa with the royal hunting park of Stromovka and the distant spires of the cathedral. The result is a paean to the Habsburgs, modelled on a classical Italian villa and surrounded by formal gardens in the French style. On the massive external staircase, gods hurl the rebellious giants into a dank grotto. In the Grand Hall the virtuous Habsburgs enjoy a well-earned victory over the infidel Turks. This, a fascinating though slightly ludicrous example of illusory painting, is Troja's main attraction. To see it you have to don huge red slippers to protect the marble floors. An insensitive restoration programme has essentially destroyed the villa's atmosphere, and the installation of a small collection of 19th-century Czech painting has done little to redeem it.

Výstaviště

Prague 7 (2010 3111). Metro Nádraží Holešovice/ 5, 12, 17 tram. **Open** 2-9pm Tue-Fri; 10am-9pm Sat, Sun. **Admission** free Tue-Fri; 20 Kč Sat, Sun; free under-6s. **Map** p312 D1.

Built out of curvaceous expanses of wrought iron to house the Jubilee Exhibition of 1891, Výstaviště signalled the birth of the new architectural form in Prague. During the 1940s it became the site of various communist congresses, but today it is principally used to house car and computer expos. It's worth dodging past the salesmen to see the interior.

The industrial feeling of the wrought-iron structure is offset by vivid stained glass and exquisite floral decorations. The best view of the exterior is from the back, where a monumental modern fountain gushes kitschily at night in time to popular classics, accompanied by a light show. The grounds are filled with architectural oddities such as the Lapidárium, an open-air cinema and the delightfully dilapidated funfair, Lunapark, which pulls in crowds of Czech families at the weekends and teens any time.

Dejvice & further west

Some of the most exclusive residences in the city are located in Prague 6, the suburbs that lie beyond the Castle. This neighbourhood is filled with embassies and the former residences of court and republic retainers of all stripes. You'd never guess this, though, from the rather desolate hub of the area, Vítězné náměstí, where a statue of Lenin used to stand.

Playing a different tune

If there's anywhere you're least likely to run into Britney Spears in Prague it's Žižkov. The bands and artists in this district of grimy pubs and mean dogs would likely eat her for breakfast.

It's not that Žižkov bands are entirely against pop music. It's just that they tend to like it a little rougher. The biggest draws at Žižkov's cultural heart – the **Akropolis** (*see p217*) – are acts that provoke, go nuts, or both: the Berlin *klezmer* sounds of Di Grine Kuzine or the Romany lounge music of Ida Kellerova and Romano Rat. Howling hip hop and French rap are also big sellers.

Žižkov tends to be the district where nude performance artists live, where crusty DJs spin out breakbeat records made in their tenement living rooms, where you need to keep your antennae up on the way home from the pub – no small achievement after the requisite 12 beers – lest some blotto football hooligans or skinheads decide you look like you're not from around here.

In short, it's the kind of place where the B Movie Heroes (pictured) do quite well. Forged from a group of Czech fringe rock players in

1994, the core of this band was originally known as Krucipusk and was fond of playing huge concerts in disused factories. In 1998 when they joined forces with the British singer-songwriter Rebecca Eastwood of the local band Freak Parade, they knew they were on to something. Her rough, postmodern sleaze style added a dimension to the band that gave them that indefinable oomph.

Žižkov's Akropolis.

Leading north from the square is the wide Jugoslávských partyzánů (Avenue of Yugoslav Partisans), at the end of which you'll find the **Crowne Plaza Hotel**, formerly known as Hotel International. This monumental piece of 1950s socialist realism is one of the last remaining bastions of Marxist-Leninist decor in the city. The façade over the main entrance features Russian war heroes being greeting by grateful Czech peasants. Just a bit out of place now, juxtaposed as they are with the bars inside the lobby, which have now been taken over by yuppies and foreign business folk who look like they use the hotel's new fitness centre. Very much a sign of the times.

On the hill above the hotel are the **Baba Villas**, a colony of constructivist houses built after, and inspired by the huge success of, the 1927 Exhibition of Modern Living in Stuttgart. Under the guidance of Pavel Janák, all 33 of the houses were individually commissioned to provide simple but radically designed living spaces for ordinary families. However, they were quickly snapped up by leading figures of the Czech avant-garde, and many of them are still decorated with original fixtures and fittings. None, alas, is open to the public, but they are still a must-see for any fan of modern architecture. Take bus 131 to U Matěje and walk up Matějská to reach the estate.

On the western fringe of the city, just off Patočkova, is the **Břevnov Monastery**, inhabited by Benedictine monks since 993 and modelled on 'God's perfect workshop'. The monks celebrated their millennium with an enormous spring clean, sweeping out traces of the Ministry of the Interior, which for the last 40 years had used the **Basilica of St Margaret** (sv. Markéta) as a warehouse for its files on suspicious foreigners. This Romanesque church was remodelled by the Dientzenhofer father-and-son act in the early 18th century, and is one of their most successful commissions, with a single high nave and unfussy interior.

Close by, near the terminus of tram 22, a small stone pyramid marks the site of *Bílá Hora*, or White Mountain, the decisive first battle of the Thirty Years War, fought in 1620. In the park is the **Hvězda Hunting Lodge** (Letohrádek Hvězda), an extraordinary product of the Renaissance, its angular walls and roof arranged in the pattern of a six-pointed star (*hvězda* in Czech). It was built in the 1550s for Archduke Ferdinand of Tyrol who was obsessed with numerology, and

Sightseeing

Now made up of Rebecca, Paza, Petr, Shoopy and Tomáš, the group has released two singles, a video and now their première CD, which gets airplay on Czech and international radio. They put in a good deal of road time on the festival circuit in Bohemia, belting out songs about power-mad American presidents, angst, transcendence and Žižkov itself. Their posters depict them standing before urban bonfires and high school muscle cars. Perhaps 'subtle' would not be the first word to come to mind. But certainly Žižkov. Very Žižkov.

The band has become symbolic of what this working class Prague district can produce: attitude, noise, in-your-face style and a taste for going over the top. Such a band is well in tune with the history of this hinterland of respectable Prague, where rough-and-ready types have always held sway.

The hero of the most beloved Czech novel of the 20th century was such a type: Good Soldier Svejk. And if he had a chance to catch the acts heard around the 'hood today, he'd realise that unlike the rest of Boom Town Prague, Žižkov has remained the same.

is conceived as an intellectual conundrum. It contains a terrifically dull museum on printing presses and typography.

North of here, off Evropská, is the extensive and wonderfully wild **Divoká Šárka** (*see p242, p244 and p251*), a fine place to stroll, swim or cycle away from the city crowds and fumes. There's a nude sunbathing area in summer.

Smíchov & Barrandov

Smíchov has undergone some changes since Mozart stayed here. Rapid industrialisation rather spoilt the ambience of the aristocracy's summer houses and the area has since been taken over by factories (including the Staropramen Brewery) and factory workers. More recently, it has exploded with sleek new malls, multiplexes and office complexes (*see p161*). A few remnants of proletarian glories are still commemorated in the massive socialist realist murals in Anděl metro station. You can get an idea of what Smíchov was once like at **Bertramka**, the house with lilac gardens that belonged to František and Josefina Dušek, now a museum to their most famous house guest, **Wolfgang Amadeus Mozart** (*see p213*).

South of Smíchov is Barrandov, the Czech version of Hollywood. On the cliffs below there are even white Hollywood-style letters that spell out Barrande, although this is actually in homage to the 19th-century geologist after whom the quarter takes its name. Enormous studios were built here in the 1930s and the site has been the centre of the Czech film industry ever since.

Vyšehrad

Vyšehrad, the rocky outcrop south of Nové Město, is where all the best Prague myths were born. Here Libuše, the mythic mother of Prague, fell into a trance and sent her horse out into the countryside to find her a suitable spouse, the ploughman called Přemysl, after whom the early Bohemian kings take their name. The non-legend version has it that, a castle was founded here in the first half of the tenth century, enjoying a period of importance when King Vratislav II (1061-92) built a royal palace on the rock. Within half a century, though, the Přemyslid rulers had moved back to Prague Castle and Vyšehrad's short-lived period of political pre-eminence was over.

The easiest way to reach Vyšehrad is to take the metro to the Vyšehrad stop, under the enormous road bridge spanning the Nusle Valley. Built in the 1970s, the bridge was hailed as a monument to socialism, a description hastily dropped when chunks of concrete began falling

on passing pedestrians, and it became the most popular spot for suicides in the city. Walk away from the towering **Corinthia** (*see p54*) and past the unappealing, monolithic **Congress Centre** (*see p216*), completed in 1980 as the supreme architectural expression of the 'normalisation' years, then through the baroque gateway into the park. The information centre to the right can provide maps of the area.

One of the first sights you will pass is the over-restored **Rotunda of St Martin**. Dating from the second half of the 11th century, it is the oldest complete Romanesque building in Prague and now hosts evening mass.

There's been a church on the same site at Vyšehrad since the 14th century, but it was apparently irrevocably damaged when Lucifer, angered by an insubordinate cleric, threw three large rocks through the roof. The granite slabs (known as the Devil Pillars) can be found close to the Old Deanery, but the holes are gone and Joseph Mocker's neo-Gothic Church of Sts Peter and Paul (sv. Petr a Pavel) dates from the beginning of the 20th century. Restoration has brought out the best of the splendid polychrome interior, decked out with art nouveau-style saints and decorative motifs.

Next door is the **Vyšehrad Cemetery**, conceived by the 19th-century National Revival movement and last resting place of the cream of the country's arts worthies, including the composers Dvořák and Smetana, writers Karel Šapek and Jan Neruda and painter Mikoláš Aleš. The *slavín* (pantheon) was designed by Antonín Wiehl and jointly commemorates further artistic big cheeses such as painter Alfons Mucha and sculptor Josef Václav Myslbek. Surrounded by Italianate arcades, the cemetery contains an abundance of fine memorials, many of them displaying art nouveau influences. Though it covers just a small area, it's very much a sacred intellectual ground in Czech history.

On the south side of the church are four monumental sculptural groups by Myslbek depicting mythological heroes from Czech history; the couple nearest to the church are the legendary founders of Prague – Pemysl and Libuše. The park extends to the cliff edge overlooking the Vltava, from where there are fine views across the water to the Castle.

If you continue down the hill from Vyšehrad along Přemyslova, you'll find one of Prague's most outstanding pieces of cubist architecture, a corner apartment block designed by Josef Chochol at Neklanova 30 (1911-13). Some way south is a railway bridge popularly known as 'the Bridge of Intelligence', because it was built by members of the intellectual elite who ended up working as labourers after losing their jobs during the purges of the 1950s.

Vinohrady & Žižkov

Map p313

Vinohrady came into existence in what the communist guidebooks called the period of Bourgeois Capitalism, and it's an area of magnificent, if crumbling, *fin de siècle* tenements. The heart of the neighbourhood is Náměstí Míru, with the twin spires of the neo-Gothic **Church of St Ludmila** (sv. Ludmila) and the opulent Vinohrady Theatre. The **Radost FX** café, gallery and nightclub complex (*see p140 and p227*), still one of Prague's premier clubs, is nearby on Bělehradská. The **Medúza** café (*see p144*) on quiet Belgická is one of the city's cosiest, if threadbare, winter hideout spots, and, just over on the border of Prague 10, **Café Atelier** (*see p145*) on Na Kovárně is one of the trendiest venues in town. The area south of Náměstí Míru has become a centre of Prague's gay scene, with bars, clubs and pensions.

The main artery of Vinohrady, however, is Vinohradská, a little further north. Formerly called Stalinova třída, it saw some of the 1968's fiercest street battles against Warsaw Pact troops. Art nouveau apartment blocks line Vinohradská, looking out on to the **Church of the Sacred Heart** (Nejsvětější Srdce Páně), one of the most inspiring pieces of modern architecture in the city, dominated by its huge glass clock. It was built in 1928-32 by Josip Plečnik, the pioneering Slovenian architect.

Fans of ecclesiastical modernism might also enjoy Pavel Janák's 1930s **Hussite Church** (Husův sbor) on the corner of U vodárny and Dykova, as well as Josef Gočár's functionalist **Church of St Wenceslas** (sv. Václav) on náměstí Svatopluka Čecha.

Near Plečnik's church is the scary **Žižkov Tower** (*see p110*), which was completed in 1989. A couple of nearby venues worthy of note are **Hapu** (*see p157*), a contender for top living-room cocktail bar, and **U Sadu** (*see p158*), cheap and Czech, with well-located outside seating in the summer.

Down the hill to the north and east is Žižkov, a district notorious for its insalubrious pubs and whorehouses and for its large Romany population. Žižkov, always a working class district, not surprisingly became a popular interment place for post-war presidents. The massive **National Memorial** (*see p110*) on top of Vítkov Hill is a mausoleum with the largest equestrian statue in the world, a 16.5-ton effigy of Hussite hero **Jan Žižka**. The corpses were ejected from the mausoleum in 1990; now it's an eerie place that occasionally hosts raves.

Further east on Vinohradská are two cemeteries. The first, **Olšany Cemetery** (*see p110*), is the largest in Prague – a huge city of the dead. Since 1989 the cemetery has begun to suffer from graffiti and grave-robbing. The cemetery extends from the Flora metro station to Jana Želivského, and includes a Garden of Rest, where the Red Army soldiers who died liberating Prague are buried.

Next door is the Jewish Cemetery (Židovské hřbitovy), not to be confused with the Old Jewish Cemetery (*see p114*) in Old Town. Here fans of Franz Kafka come to pay respects at his simple grave (follow the sign at the entrance by Zelivského metro station; it's approximately 200 metres (660 foot) down the row by the southern cemetery wall). Though founded in 1890, only a fraction has been used since World War II. Neglect is evident everywhere.

Public art on **Žižkov Tower**. See p110.

National Memorial

Národní památník

U památníku, Prague 3 (627 8452). Metro Florenc/133, 168, 207 bus. **Map** p313 B1.

One of the city's best-known and least liked landmarks is this hulking mass of concrete. Looming above Žižkov, the immense, constructivist block and equally enormous equestrian statue high up on Vítkov Hill can be seen from around the city. It was built in 1925 by Jan Zázvorka as a dignified setting for the remains of the legionnaires who fought against the Austro-Hungarian Empire in World War I. In 1953 the communist regime turned it into a mausoleum for Heroes of the Working Class. The mummified remains of Klement Gottwald, first communist president, were kept here, tended by scientists who unsuccessfully tried to preserve his body for display, Lenin-style, before the project was abandoned and the decaying body fobbed off on Gottwald's family in 1990.

No one is quite sure what to do with either the memorial or the mausoleum. Opening times are unpredictable, but it doesn't really matter as most of what you might want to see can be seen from the outside. In front stands the massive equestrian statue of one-eyed General Žižka, scourge of 14th-century Catholics and the darling of the communists who subsequently adopted him in an effort to establish genuine Bohemian credentials.

Olšany Cemetery

Olšanské hřbitovy

Vinohradská/Jana Želivského, Prague 3. Metro Flora or Želivského. **Open** dawn-dusk daily. **Map** p313 D2.

The overgrown yet beautiful Olšany Cemetery is the last resting place of two unlikely bed fellows: the first communist president, Klement Gottwald, who died after catching a cold at Stalin's funeral, and the most famous anti-communist martyr, Jan Palach, the student who set fire to himself in Wenceslas Square in 1969. In death their fates have been strangely linked, as neither of their mortal remains have been allowed to rest in peace. Palach was originally buried here in 1969, but his grave became such a focus of dissent that the authorities disinterred his body and reburied it deep in the Bohemian countryside. In 1990 he was dug up and brought back to Olšany. His grave is just to the right of the main entrance. Gottwald is harder to locate, hidden away in Section 5 and sharing a mass grave with various other discredited party members. In 1990 his mummified remains were ejected from the National Memorial (*see above*) and returned to the family.

Žižkov Tower

Mahlerovy sady, Prague 3 (6700 5778). Metro Jiřího z Poděbrad/5, 9, 26 tram. **Open** *Tower* 10am-11pm daily. *Café* 11am-11.30pm daily. **Admission** 60 Kč; 30 Kč concessions; free under-10s. **Map** p313 C2.

The huge, thrusting, three-pillared television tower in Žižkov has been dubbed the *Pražský pták* or 'Prague Prick' by local fans. Seemingly modelled on a Soyuz rocket ready for blast-off, or maybe something out of *Thunderbirds*, it has been more of a hit with space-crazy visitors than with the locals. The tower also has a guest appearance in the movie *Blade II*. It was planned under the communists (who tore up part of the adjacent Jewish Cemetery to make room for it), completed early in 1989, and no sooner started operating in 1990 than it came under attack from nearby residents who claimed it was guilty of, among other things, jamming foreign radio waves and giving their children cancer. You can take a lift up to the eighth-floor viewing platform, or have a drink in the fifth-floor café, but in many ways standing at the base and looking up the 216m (709ft) of grey polished steel is even more scary. Views from the platform and the café are splendid, except at night, when they're obscured by reflections off the glass. More than 20 TV channels broadcast from behind the white plastic shielding that defends against the elements. Transmitters lower down deal with radio stations and emergency services. The tower is now the subject of public art, with several large black babies crawling on its exterior. The intriguing, rather disturbing *Miminky* are the work of Czech bad boy artist and satyrist David Černý (*see also p199*).

Jižní Město & Háje

To the south and east of the city centre lies the wilderness of Prague 4. Though parts are very old and beautiful, the postcode has come to mean only one thing for Praguers: *paneláky*.

Panelák is the Czech word for a tower block made from prefabricated concrete panels. These blocks sprouted throughout the 1960s and '70s as a cheap solution to the postwar housing crisis. Jižní Město, or Southern Town, has the greatest concentration, housing 100,000 people, and now inspires Czech rap music polemics by its more youthful residents, who fancy themselves akin to homeboys in South LA 'hoods. There have been recent efforts to individualise the buildings with pastel exteriors but this has only made the district look like an nightmarish toy town.

Háje, the last metro stop on the red Line C, is another good place to see the best of the worst. Before 1989, Háje used to be known as Kosmonautů, a nod in the direction of the USSR, and a rather humorous sculpture of two cosmonauts is outside the metro station. **Galaxie** (*see p195*), Central Europe's first multiplex cinema and perhaps the only place in the world that sells pork-flavoured popcorn, is nearby, as is the popular swimming spot of **Hostivař Reservoir** (*see p244*). Just beyond this bold new free market venture is the odd combination of the **Stodola Czech Country Bar**, where the waitresses wear complete cowgirl kit, and the adjoining mega-bordello **Lotos** (*see p231*), where they don't.

Museums

Small though Prague may be, its museums cover everything from mastodons to police identikits in halls that are often wonders in themselves.

Prague's museums reflect its location on the crossroads of Europe, where every successive wave of people and cultures seems to have left behind it a variety of remains. The city hosts an amazingly varied and odd range of collections, many revealing the tantalising tastes of eras and fashions long since abandoned. Revolution and restitution have, of course, taken their toll, and some great collections still remain homeless – or can only be spied as moving targets.

Still, Prague has witnessed the inauguration of several new museums recently, including the wonderful **Kampa Museum** (*see p113*) on the picturesque island of the same name. Located in an ancient mill complex, the museum is the new permanent home of the stellar Mládek collection of Czech and Central European art. And the revamped **Museum of Decorative Arts** (*see p115*) and the **Jewish Museum** (*see p113*), one of the city's most visited sites, never fail to impress.

Be advised that some places posing as museums are unabashed tourist traps, like the **Sex Machine Museum** and the **Museum of Torture Instruments**, both located in the heart of Prague's Old Town. Don't say you weren't warned.

National Gallery

The dust is starting to settle after a whirlwind of musical chairs at several **National Gallery** venues. And another changeover is on the horizon, with the National Gallery taking over the operation of the cubist building **House of the Black Madonna** (*see p113*), which has been the **Czech Museum of Fine Arts**' (*see p201*) showcase for cubist art and design. The National Gallery will install its own exposition of all things cubist, and is also reviving the cubist café in the museum's basement. The venue is due to reopen towards the end of 2002. The fragmented National Gallery comprises five relatively small permanent collections: a modern art centre and a handful of exhibition spaces across the city including the **Prague Castle Riding School** (see *p113*), **Wallenstein Riding School** (see *p202*) and **Kinský Palace** (see *p201*). The unwieldy conglomeration is coming into some kind of

order after a decade of shoddy leadership and shrinking finances – though not everyone agrees with its new direction.

The outspoken conceptual artist Milan Knížák, formerly of the Fluxus movement, was appointed head of the gallery in 1999. He has already streamlined the staff, set up a fund to compensate owners of works confiscated by Nazis and communists, and reorganised three of the National Gallery's largest branches. The 19th-century Czech art from **St Agnes's Convent** (*see p112*) was moved to the **National Gallery Collection of 19th-, 20th- and 21st-Century Art**, (*see below*) while art formerly in **St George's Convent** (*see p112*) has a suitably Gothic new home at St Agnes's.

National Gallery Collection of 19th-, 20th- & 21st-Century Art

Sbírka moderního a současného umění
Veletržní palác, Dukelských hrdinů 47, Holešovice, Prague 7 (2430 1122/www.ngprague.cz). Metro Vltavská/5, 12, 17 tram. **Open** 10am-6pm Tue-Sun. **Admission** *1 floor* 100 Kč; 50 Kč concessions. *2 floors* 150 Kč; 20 Kč concessions. *3 floors* 200 Kč; 100 Kč concessions. *Temporary exhibitions* 50 Kč; 20 Kč concessions; free under-10s. **No credit cards**. **Map** p312 D2.

Public response to the country's newly reconceived modern art display has been mixed. Gone is its linear historical progression of movements and styles, in favour of highlighting the major personalities of Czech art, though often at the expense of putting them in proper context. The fourth floor contains the museum's 19th-century collection. Highlights include paintings by Karel Purkyně, informed by close observation and a thorough knowledge of Old Master techniques, and the mystical strain of 19th-century Czech art represented by symbolists Max Švabinský and František Bílek.

On the third floor is Czech art from 1900 to 1930 plus the gallery's impressive holdings of French art, put together during Parisian spending sprees by former gallery director Vincenc Kramář. The groundbreaking abstract artist František Kupka is the major figure on this floor, where you'll also find the Czech cubists, surrealists and social art from the 1920s.

The second floor covers art from 1930 to the present, including surrealist works by Toyen and Jindřich Štýrský, an amusing display of Stalin-era socialist realism and existentialist Art Informel from around the same period. The display ends rather abruptly with works by some of the 1980s generation,

The jewel of the Jewish Museum: the **Spanish Synagogue**. *See p115.*

who were active as unofficial artists before 1989. There is also the 'Laboratory of Contemporary Trends', a selection of works by younger Czech artists that changes every six months.

St Agnes's Convent

Klášter sv. Anežky české
U milosrdných 17, Staré Město, Prague 1 (2481 0628). Metro Náměstí Republiky/5, 8, 14 tram. **Open** 10am-6pm Tue-Sun. **Admission** 100 Kč; 150 Kč family; free under-10s. **No credit cards**. **Map** p308 J1.

In the recent National Gallery reshuffle, this gallery received the art from **St George's Convent** (*see below*) up to the 16th century. During the reign of Charles IV (1346-78), Prague was at the forefront of European artistic development. The bronze statue of St George and the Dragon, for example, is so Renaissance in spirit that scholars still argue over its date. One of the outstanding artists of the end of the 14th century was the Master of Třeboň. Here you can see his altarpiece featuring the Resurrection of Christ and his Madonna of Roudnice, an example of the 'Beautiful Style' that prevailed until the outbreak of the Hussite wars. Gothic remained popular in Bohemia right up to the 16th century, as seen in the extraordinary wood carving by the monogrammist IP, depicting the skeletal, half-decomposed figure of Death brushed aside by the Risen Christ.

St George's Convent

Klášter sv. Jiří
Jiřské náměstí 33, Hradčany, Prague 1 (5732 0536). Metro Malostranská and up the Old Castle steps/ 22, 23 tram. **Open** 10am-6pm Tue-Sun. **Admission** 100 Kč; 50 Kč concessions; 150 Kč family; free under-10s. **No credit cards**. **Map** p307 D2.

Works here include a handful of paintings that survive from the collections of Rudolf II (1576-1611). They include masterpieces by the Antwerp mannerist Bartholomaeus Spranger, whose sophisticated colours, elegant eroticism and obscure themes typify the style.

The baroque selection starts with Karel Škréta, a down-to-earth painter in contrast to the feverishly religious work of Michael Leopold Willmann and Jan Kryštof Liška. The tendency in baroque painting and sculpture to borrow from each other can be seen in the paintings of Petr Brandl, the most acclaimed Czech artist of the early 18th century. His work is displayed near that of the two great sculptors of the time, Mathias Bernard Braun and Ferdinand Maxmilián Brokof.

Sternberg Palace

Šternberský palác
Hradčanské náměstí 15, Hradčany, Prague 1 (2051 4636). Metro Malostranská/22, 23 tram. **Open** 10am-6pm Tue-Sun. **Admission** 100 Kč; 50 Kč concessions; 150 Kč family; free under-10s. **No credit cards**. **Map** p306 C2.

Enlightened aristocrats trying to rouse Prague from provincial stupor founded the Sternberg Gallery here in the 1790s. The palace now houses the National Gallery's 'European Old Masters'. Not a large or well-balanced collection, especially since some of its most famous works were returned to their pre-war owners, but some outstanding paintings remain, including a brilliant Frans Hals portrait and Dürer's *Feast of the Rosary*. The gallery finished renovations early in 2002, making space for more paintings from the repositories, and restoring ceiling frescoes and mouldings that had long been covered up.

Zbraslav Château

Zámek Zbraslav
Bartoňova 2, Zbraslav, Prague 5 (5792 1638). Metro Smíchovské nádraží/129, 241, 243, 255, 360 bus to Zbraslavské náměstí. **Open** 10am-6pm Tue-Sun. **Admission** 80 Kč; 40 Kč concessions; 120 Kč family. **No credit cards**.

This baroque pile at the southern tip of Prague houses the National Gallery's surprisingly good collection of Asian art. The Chinese and Japanese holdings are particularly fine. There's also a smattering of

Indian, South-east Asian and Islamic pieces, plus a handful of Tibetan thangka scrolls crawling with fire demons and battling monks. A 20-30 minute bus ride from the metro.

Other collections

Bílek Villa

Bílkova vila
Mickiewiczowa 1, Hradčany, Prague 1 (2432 2021).
Metro Hradčanská/18, 22 tram. **Open** *May-Oct*
10am-6pm Tue-Sun. *Oct-May* 10am-5pm Sat, Sun.
Admission 50 Kč; 20 Kč concessions.
No credit cards. Map p312 A3.
This must be the only building in the world designed to look like a wheatfield. Built in 1911-12 by mystic sculptor František Bílek as his studio and home, it still contains much of his work. Bílek went to Paris to study as a painter, but discovered that he was partially colour-blind. He then turned to sculpture and illustration. The wheatfield, representing spiritual fertility and the harvest of creative work, was one of his many motifs. The results range from the sublime to the repellent. If the grouping of Hobbit-like wooden figures out front takes your fancy, you should have a look inside.

House of the Black Madonna

Dům U černé Matky Boží
Celetná 34, Staré Město, Prague 1 (2421 1732).
Metro Náměstí Republiky/5, 8, 14 tram.
Open 10am-6pm Tue-Sun. **Admission** 100 Kč; 50
Kč concessions. **No credit cards. Map** p309 K3.
Closed at press time for renovations, this fantastic building is scheduled to reopen in December 2002 with a new conception aimed at creating a totally cubist environment. Part of this new image will be a revival of the original cubist café in the building's basement. Worth a visit for the building alone, this is perhaps the finest example of Prague cubist architecture (*see p30*). It was used from 1994 to 2001 by the Czech Museum of Fine Arts (*see p201*) for a permanent exhibition of Czech cubism from 1911-19; that operation was recently transferred to the National Gallery.

House at the Golden Ring

Dům U Zlatého prstenu
Týnská 6, Staré Město, Prague 1 (2482 7022).
Metro Náměstí Republiky/5, 8, 14 tram. **Open** 10am-6pm Tue-Sun. **Admission** 60 Kč; 30 Kč concessions;
120 Kč family; free under-6s. **No credit cards.**
Map p308 J3.
Run by the Prague City Gallery, this showpiece space, housed in a beautiful Renaissance building just off Old Town Square, proves that the National Gallery isn't the only institution willing to invest in the presentation of Czech modern art. The collection comprises a broad spectrum of 20th-century Czech works, organised intriguingly by themes rather than by artist or period. There's a fine basement exhibition space for temporary installations, though the gallery itself has limited space.

Kampa Museum

Muzeum Kampa
U Sovových mlýnů 2, Kampa, Prague 1 (5728 6147).
Tram 6, 9, 22. **Open** 10am-5pm Tue-Sun.
Admission 40-120 Kč; 40 Kč concessions.
No credit cards. Map p307 F4.
This new museum in a completely overhauled mill, one of the city's oldest, makes a suitably stunning home for the first-rate collection of Czech and Central European art amassed by Czech émigré Jan Mládek and his widow, Meda Mládek (*see p116* **An oasis for Central European art**). She bought works by Kupka directly from his atelier in Paris, and the couple has particularly strong Czech art from the 1960s.

Prague Castle Picture Gallery

Obrazárna Pražského hradu
Prague Castle (2nd courtyard), Hradčany, Prague 1 (2437 3531/www.hrad.cz). Metro Malostranská and up the Old Castle Steps/22, 23 tram. **Open** 10am-6pm daily. **Admission** 100 Kč; 50 Kč concessions;
150 Kč family; free under-6s. **No credit cards.**
Map p306 C2.
Home of Giuseppe Archimboldo's infamous mannerist work *Vertumnus*, which cast Rudolf II as a Roman harvest god, this remnant of the eccentric emperor's private collection also includes works by Rubens, Titian, Veronese and lesser-known masters. Though there's no hope of ever piecing together the original collection, which has been scattered to the winds, the Castle has recently bought back on the open market a handful of works from the original cache.

Jewish Museum

The Jewish Museum was founded in 1906 to preserve the historical monuments of the former Jewish ghetto. By a gruesome irony, Hitler was responsible for today's comprehensive collections, though the story that he wanted a 'museum of an extinct race' is sometimes debated. Another suggestion is that Prague's German overlords allowed museum workers to catalogue and store the property of the 153 Czech Jewish communities, the better to plunder them. The loot remained here after the war because there was nobody to whom it could be returned.

The museum, comprising five different buildings and the Old Jewish Cemetery, is one of Prague's busiest – and most costly – tourist draws. You have to buy a ticket for all six components of the museum. You can buy a separate ticket for only the **Old-New Synagogue** (*see p94*), not officially part of the Jewish Museum.

Tickets are sold at the **Klausen** (*see p114*), **Maisel** (*see p114*), **Pinkas** (*see p115*) and **Spanish Synagogues** (*see p115*). English-language tours are conducted from Sunday to Friday from the Maisel Synagogue (call the Jewish Museum beforehand for details and reservations; *see p114*).

Sightseeing

The thrilling **National Musuem**: no napping, now. *See p118.*

Former Ceremonial Hall
Obřadni síň
U starého hřbitova 3A, Josefov, Prague 1 (2231 7191). **Map** p308 H2.
The Romanesque turrets and arches of this building at the exit of the cemetery make it appear as old as the gravestones. In fact, it was built in 1906 for the Prague Burial Society, which used the building for only 20 years. It currently houses part of an exhibition on Jewish customs and traditions, focusing on illness and death.

Jewish Museum
Židovské Muzeum
Josefov, Prague 1 (2481 9456/www.jewishmuseum.cz). Metro Staroměstská/17, 18 tram. **Open** *Apr-Oct* 9am-6pm Mon-Fri, Sun. *Nov-Mar* 9am-4.30pm Mon-Fri, Sun. Closed Jewish holidays. **Admission** 300 Kč; 200 Kč concessions; under-6s free. *Old-New Synagogue* 200 Kč; 150 Kč concessions. **No credit cards**.
Map p308 H2/3.
The central address for the Jewish Museum complex; buy tickets here for its other locations.

Klausen Synagogue
Klausová synagóga
U starého hřbitova 3A, Josefov, Prague 1 (no phone). **Map** p308 H2.
The original was destroyed in the great ghetto fire of 1689, along with 318 houses and ten other synagogues. The existing synagogue, hastily constructed on the same site in 1694, has much in common with Prague's baroque churches, as it was built by the same craftsmen. Its permanent exhibition explores religion in the lives of the ghetto's former inhabitants.

The best view of the synagogue is from the Old Jewish Cemetery, where the simple façade rises behind the ancient gravestones, topped by two tablets of the Decalogue with a golden inscription.

Maisel Synagogue
Maiselova synagóga
Maiselova 10, Josefov, Prague 1 (no phone). **Map** p308 H3.

Mordecai Maisel (1528-1601), mayor of the Jewish ghetto during the reign of Rudolf II, was one of the richest men in 16th-century Europe. Legend traces his wealth to a lucky intervention by goblins, but more realistic historians suggest that Rudolf II granted Maisel a lucrative trading monopoly. The original building on this site, funded by Maisel, was apparently the most splendid of all the quarter's synagogues, until it burned down along with most of the others in 1689. The present structure, sandwiched between tenement blocks, has a core dating to the 1690s; the rest was redone between 1892 and 1905. The Maisal Synagogue now houses an exhibition on the Jewish history of Bohemia and Moravia from the 10th to the 18th century.

Old Jewish Cemetery
Starý židovský hřbitov
Široká 3, Josefov, Prague 1 (no phone).
Map p308 H2.
The Old Jewish Cemetery, where all of Prague's Jews were buried until the late 1600s, is one of the eeriest remnants of the city's once thriving Jewish community.

The 12,000 tombstones crammed into this tiny, tree-shaded patch of ground are a forceful reminder of the lack of space accorded to the ghetto, which remained walled until the late 1700s. Forbidden to enlarge the burial ground, the Jews was forced to bury the dead on top of one another. An estimated 100,000 bodies were piled up to 12 layers deep. Above them, lopsided stone tablets were crammed on to mounds of earth.

Burials began here in the early 15th century, although earlier gravestones were brought in from a cemetery nearby. Decorative reliefs on the headstones indicate the name of the deceased or their occupation: a pair of scissors, for example, indicates a tailor. The black headstones are the oldest, carved from 15th-century sandstone; the white ones, of marble, date from the 16th and 17th centuries. One thing, though: the constant flow of toursits through gravestones seems somehow incongruous.

Pinkas Synagogue

Pinkasova synagóga
Široká 3, Josefov, Prague 1 (2232 6660).
Map p308 H2/3.
The story goes that a Rabbi Pinkas founded this synagogue in 1479 after falling out with the elders at the Old-New Synagogue. The building was enlarged in 1535, and a Renaissance façade added in 1625. In the 1950s the names of more than 80,000 men, women and children of Bohemia and Moravia who died in the Holocaust were inscribed on the synagogue's walls as a memorial. In 1967, after the Six Day War, the Czechoslovak government expelled the Israeli ambassador and closed the synagogue for 'restoration'. In the ensuing 22 years the writing became indecipherable.

Not until after 1989 could the museum begin restoring the names, a job completed in 1994. The Pinkas also houses a powerful exhibition of drawings by children interned in Terezín (*see p251*), the last stop en route to the death camps in the east.

Spanish Synagogue

Španělská synagóga
Vězeňská 1, Josefov, Prague 1 (2481 9464).
Map p308 J2.
The Old Synagogue or Altschul, older still than the Old-New Synagogue, stood on this site as an island amid Christian territory, to which Jews could cross from the main ghetto only at certain times. It became a Reform synagogue in 1837, then the prospering congregation rebuilt it in 1868 in the then-fashionable Moorish style. After painstaking reconstruction the long-decrepit building reopened in 1998. Its lovely domed interior again glows with hypnotic floral designs traced in green, red and faux gold leaf, lit by stained-glass windows. It now houses the second part of the exhibition on the Jewish history of Bohemia and Moravia continued from the Maisel Synagogue and in its upper-floor prayer hall an exhibition of synagogue silver. It occasionally hosts concerts; tickets are available in the lobby.

Decorative Arts

Mucha Museum

Muchovo muzeum
Kaunický palác, Panská 7, Nové Město, Prague 1 (2145 1333/www.mucha.cz). Metro Můstek/3, 9, 14, 24 tram. **Open** 10am-6pm daily. **Admission** 120 Kč; 60 Kč concessions. **No credit cards. Map** p309 K4.
Opened in 1998, this museum is dedicated to perhaps the most famous of all Czech visual artists, Alfons Mucha (1860-1939). Known for commercial work such as mass-produced decorative panels and posters for Sarah Bernhardt's theatre performances, Mucha exercised his greatest influence through his *Encyclopaedia for Craftsmen* (1902), a catalogue of art nouveau decorative elements, forms and designs. Mucha created a stained-glass window for St Vitus's Cathedral (*see p65*) and the Slavonic Epic, a series of gigantic narrative oil paintings now residing in Moravský Krumlov castle, south-west of Brno. The museum also displays paintings, drawings, sketches, notebooks and a video on his life.

Museum of Decorative Arts

Uměleckoprůmyslové muzeum
ulice 17. listopadu 2, Staré Město, Prague 1 (5109 3111). Metro Staroměstská/17, 18 tram. **Open** 10am-6pm Tue-Sun. **Admission** 80 Kč; 40 Kč concessions; free under-10s. **No credit cards. Map** p308 G2.

Sightseeing

Museum of Communism: Big Brother welcomes you to his junk shop. *See p116.*

Built between 1897 and 1900, this neo-Renaissance museum is a work of art in itself, with richly decorated halls, stained- and etched-glass windows, and intricately painted plaster mouldings. The exhibits were recently completely overhauled to group objects according to material, and to bring the hitherto unseen 20th-century collection out of the storeroom.

The permanent, pre-20th century, collections comprise lavishly crafted pieces including exquisite furniture, tapestries, pottery, clocks, books, a beautifully preserved collection of clothing, and fine displays of ceramics and glass.

History

Military Museum
Schwarzenberg Palace, Hradčanské náměstí 2, Hradčany, Prague 1 (2020 2020). Metro Malostranská then tram 22, 23. **Open** May-Oct 10am-6pm Tues-Sun. **Admission** 80-120 Kč. **No credit cards.**

A scraffitoed Renaissance building that's quite an attraction in itself, this newly renovated palace of the once-powerful Schwarzenberg family contains an impressive array of medieval armour, weaponry and displays of might and strategy. The Military Museum is bristling with cudgels and javelins and a full complement of arms dating from 13th-century battles with Mongols up to those used in WWI. The toy soldiers on in the gift shop make souvenir points with kids. The displays seem a bit cluttered, probably inevitable in such a confined space. Still, they convey a good sense of the gore of Bohemia's many battles.

Museum of the City of Prague
Muzeum hlavního města Prahy
Na Poříčí 52, Nové Město, Prague 1 (2481 6772). Metro Florenc/3, 8, 24 tram. **Open** 9am-6pm Tue-Sun. **Admission** 30 Kč; 15 Kč concessions; 45 Kč family; under-10s free. Free to all 1st Thur of mth. **No credit cards. Map** p309 M2.

Antonín Langweil spent 11 years of the early 19th century building an incredibly precise room-sized paper model of Prague, which is now this museum's prize exhibit. It is the only complete depiction of what the city looked like before the Jewish ghetto was ripped down. The displays follow the city's development from pre-history through to the 17th century, with some English labels provided in the rooms devoted to medieval and later events. The upstairs galleries host temporary exhibitions and the original of the Josef Mánes painting reproduced below the Old Town Hall's astronomical clock.

Museum of Communism
Muzeum komunismu
Na příkopě 10, New Town, Prague 1 (2421 2966/ www.muzeumkomunismu.cz). Metro Můstek/3, 9, 14, 24 tram. **Open** 9am-8pm daily. **Admission** 150 Kč; 140 Kč concessions. **No credit cards. Map** p308 J4.

An oasis for Central European art

Situated on the quiet and picturesque Kampa Island, with no automobile traffic and graceful old buildings that seem to rise straight out of the Vltava River, is the stunning new **Kampa Museum** (*see p113*). Situated in a former mill, the museum houses the world-class art collection of Jan and Meda Mládek.

Jan Mládek was a Czech émigré who died in 1989, just as his native country was tasting its first breaths of freedom. An economist who studied with John Keynes, he later became one of the first governors of the International Monetary Fund.

His wife, Meda, studied art history in Paris, where she acquired the couple's first work of art by František Kupka, the metaphysical Czech artist whose colourful geometric paintings were among the pioneering examples of pure abstraction. That painting started what became a lifelong passion for the Mládeks, culminating in a collection of more than 200 paintings and drawings by Kupka, plus more than a thousand pieces of artwork by other Czech, Central and Eastern European artists.

Meda Mládek made it one of her missions to present these under-appreciated artists to the rest of the world. Before settling on Kampa, Meda searched for a permanent venue for the collection in Prague for five years, and ran up against nothing but resistance from local bureaucrats in the process. But finally Mládeks found the sprawling mill where the collection finally landed. The 14th-century Sovovy mlýny, one of Prague's oldest mills, had lain empty in an advanced state of decay for decades. After the city of Prague won possession of the site from the Czech state, it awarded it to Mládek for her ambitious project. Another five years went into planning and renovation, with nearly all of the construction materials having to be transported to the site by barge, since lorries aren't allowed on the island. Kampa Museum finally opened to the public with its first temporary exhibition in September 2001, and the permanent display of works in the Mládek collection went on view in summer 2002. In addition to beautifully appointed exhibition halls there is also a library, study

Opened in 2001 as the first of its kind in the country, the museum, whose co-founder is an American restaurateur, puts the communist era in historical perspective through its ample archive photographs with explanatory texts, as well as hundreds of artefacts. It has mock-ups of a schoolroom from the period, with Czechoslovak and Soviet flags hanging side by side and a Russian lesson on the blackboard, plus an interrogation room like those used by the secret police. Irony of ironies, it is directly above a McDonald's and shares a floor in the building with a casino.

Music & musicians

Dvořák Museum

Muzeum Antonína Dvořáka
Villa Amerika, Ke Karlovu 20, Nové Město, Prague 2 (2491 8013). Metro IP Pavlova/4, 6, 11, 16, 22, 23, 34 tram. **Open** 10am-5pm Tue-Sun. **Admission** 40 Kč; 20 Kč concessions. **No credit cards.**
Map p311 K8.
This small red and ochre villa was built by Kilian Ignaz Dientzenhofer in 1720 for Count Jan Václav Michna, then became a cattle market during the 19th century. It now houses the Dvořák Society's well-organised tribute to the most famous Czech composer. Memorabilia and photographs make up the ground-floor display. Upstairs are further exhibits and a recital hall, decorated with frescoes by Jan Ferdinand Schor. Concerts held here are the

best way to appreciate the building's past as a retreat for the composer. Outdoor recitals in warm weather are particularly evocative. Dvořák himself ironically spent very little time here as his career was mainly established in the grand concert halls of Western Europe.

Mozart Museum

Bertramka
Mozartova 169, Smíchov, Prague 5 (5731 8461/7465/www.bertramka.cz). Metro Anděl/4, 7, 9, 10 tram. **Open** *Apr-Oct* 9.30am-6pm daily. *Nov-Mar* 9.30am-5pm daily. **Admission** 90 Kč; 50 Kč concessions; free under-6s. **No credit cards.**
In a grimy but quickly gentrifying neighbourhood choked with traffic, the Villa Bertramka – restored to its 18th-century glory – is a welcome refuge in its walled park. To find it, look for the garish Mövenpick Hotel (*see p54*) next door. Mozart stayed here several times as a guest of the villa's owners, composer František Dušek and his wife, Josefina. And it was here, in 1787, that he composed the overture to *Don Giovanni*, the night before its première in the Nostitz Theatre, now called the Estates Theatre (*see p234*). Tranquillity is the villa's greatest asset – mid morning or late afternoon, it is possible to linger over cappuccino in the courtyard café and remain relatively undisturbed by tour groups. There are also occasional evening recitals on the terrace.

centre, a repository for works not currently on display, a restaurant and café.

The newly refurbished spaces are a curious mix of artists' loft, patrician manor and swinging '60s pad. In the attic-like top floor, rough-hewn ceiling beams with exposed bolts and industrial-grey concrete floors cohabitate with antique furniture, chrome-and-Lucite tables and white leather cushions. A glass-enclosed tower containing a central staircase is crowned by a glass sculpture. In the mill's former engine room is a sculpture hall with the works gently illuminated by large skylights. The walls, in shades of ochre and yellow, radiate with golden sunlight glinting off the river's surface.

A roof patio also offers lovely views of the enclosed courtyard below and the sounds of water rushing over a weir on the Vltava. The museum's heady mix of art, architecture and ambience makes it an oasis Kupka would have appreciated: the visionary painter once asserted that 'colour affects the senses like music.'

Natural history & ethnography

Náprstek Museum

Náprstkovo muzeum

Betlémské náměstí 1, Staré Město, Prague 1 (2222 1417/www.aconet.cz/npm). Metro Můstek or Národní třída/6, 9, 17, 18, 22, 23 tram. **Open** 9am-5.30pm Tue-Sun. **Admission** 40 Kč; 20 Kč concessions; free under-6s. Free to all 1st Fri of the mth. **No credit cards. Map** p308 G4/5.

The 19th-century nationalist Vojta Náprstek had two passions: modern technology and primitive cultures. While the gadgets he collected are now in the National Technical Museum (*see below*), the ethnographic oddities he acquired from Czech travellers are here in an extension to his house. The displays concentrating on native peoples of the Americas, Australasia and the Pacific Islands are interesting and exemplarily arranged. Temporary exhibitions favour travelogues of exotic cultures by Czech photographers.

National Museum

Národní muzeum

Václavské náměstí 68, Nové Město, Prague 1 (2449 7111/www.nm.cz). Metro Muzeum/11 tram. **Open** *May-Sept* 10am-6pm daily. *Oct-Apr* 9am-5pm daily. Closed 1st Tue of mth. **Admission** 80 Kč; 40 Kč concessions; free under-6s. Free to all 1st Mon of mth. **No credit cards. Map** p311 L6/7.

The city's grandest museum is also its biggest disappointment. The vast edifice dominates the top of Wenceslas Square, its neo-Renaissance flamboyance promising an intriguing interior. Instead it is filled with rooms of dusty fossils and stuffed animals. The 10,000 specimens of rocks on display (one of the largest collections in Europe) might impress.

However, a revival may be under way if the museum's unlikely new twentysomething director has his way. One of his first goals is to put on temporary exhibitions with popular appeal to pull in the crowds. Exhibitions on East European *samizdat*, underground literature and Czech football are planned.

The architecture and interior decorations are the most appealing features. Designed by Josef Schulz and finished in 1890, it was a proud symbol of the Czech National Revival. Today the exterior is as well known for its many scars from shelling when Warsaw Pact tanks invaded Prague in 1968.

Miscellaneous

Miniatures Museum

Muzeum miniatur

Strahovské nádvoří 11 (grounds of Strahov Monastery), Hradčany, Prague 1 (3335 2371). Metro Malostranská/22, 23 tram. **Open** 9am-5pm daily. **Admission** 40 Kč; 30 Kč students; 20 Kč children and seniors. **No credit cards. Map** p306 A4.

With the aid of magnifying glasses and microscopes, you'll be able to see truly tiny works of art – portraiture on a poppy seed, a caravan of camels painted on a grain of millet, a prayer written out on a human hair, a book less than 1sq mm in area, minuscule copies of masterpieces by the likes of Rembrandt and Botticelli. Everything here is the work of Anatolij Koněnek.

National Technical Museum

Národní technické muzeum

Kostelní 42, Holešovice, Prague 7 (2039 9111/ www.ntm.cz). Metro Hradčanská or Vltavská/ 8, 25, 26 tram. **Open** 9am-5pm Tue-Sun. **Admission** 70 Kč; 30 Kč concessions; 150 Kč family. **No credit cards. Map** p312 C3.

Don't let the mundane name put you off: this is a fascinating collection, enjoyable for both kids and adults. The museum, one of few in Prague to use interactive displays, traces the development of technology and science in Czechoslovakia, which, until the communist era, was one of the most innovative and industrially advanced of European nations. The Transport Hall contains steam trains, vintage motorcycles, racing cars and biplanes, while the claustrophobic mine in the basement has sinister coal-cutting implements displayed in tunnels. Guided tours of the mine are available in English. There's also an extensive photography and cinematography section, and a collection of rare astronomical instruments.

Police Museum

Muzeum policie ČR

Ke Karlovu 1, Nové Město, Prague 2 (2492 3619/ www.mvcr.cz/policie/muzeum.htm). Metro IP Pavlova/6, 11 tram. **Open** 10am-5pm Tue-Sun. **Admission** 20 Kč; 10 Kč concessions; 40 Kč family. **No credit cards. Map** p311 K10.

A former convent attached to the Karlov Church is the incongruous home of Prague's surprisingly interesting Police Museum. In the section on crime detection techniques you can take your own fingerprints or try to reconstruct events at a creepy scene-of-the-crime mock-up. Kids love it, though parents are warned that some of the photographs are quite graphic. The final room contains an arsenal of home-made weaponry that would please James Bond: sword sticks, hand-made pistols, pen guns, even a converted lighter. Labelling is almost entirely in Czech.

Toy Museum

Muzeum hraček

Jiřská 4, Hradčany, Prague 1 (2437 2294). Metro Malostranská/12, 18, 22, 23 tram. **Open** 9.30am-5.30pm daily. **Admission** 50 Kč; 20-30 Kč concessions; 60 Kč family; under-5s free. **No credit cards. Map** p307 E1.

Part of Czech émigré Ivan Steiger's large collection is displayed on the two floors of this museum in the Castle grounds. Brief explanatory texts accompany cases of toys, from wooden folk toys to an incredibly elaborate train set made of pure tin. Kitsch fans will love the little robots and the enormous collection of Barbie and friends clad in vintage costumes throughout the decades. Good for a rainy day.

Eat, Drink, Shop

Restaurants & Cafés

A new era in Prague dining is under way, serving up fusion and world cuisine alongside classic Bohemian fare.

Dining out in Prague, once considered a hazardous sport, has finally come of age. Central European cuisine, with the exception of fresh game, has always had a reputation as more solid and sensible than exciting. *Vepřo-knedlo-zelo*, the Czech classic platter of pork, dumplings and sauerkraut, is still the top offering in half the restaurants in Prague, invariably accompanied by frothy, full-bodied beer. But the new places standing alongside the old guard eateries now feature genuinely cosmopolitan menus. And (at least half the time) the cuisine's pulled off with panache.

After the Velvet Revolution, fashionable meant anything outside the usual spectrum of pub food or its counterpart: the stiff, elitist dining rooms favouring green pepper steak and flagrantly overpriced wine. These days name designers have taken over the decor, replacing boring white linen and crystal with sunlit rooms of teak, iron and rice paper. **Brasserie Le Patio** (*see p137*), just such a place, adds exotic Asian delicacies to the formula, while customers at **Opera Garden** (*Zahrada v opeře, see p140*) are willing to wind through military barricades to sample plum mascarpone in a minimalist Zen space (it shares a building with Radio Free Europe, which has beefed up security since the World Trade Center attacks).

Another new wave has swept over hotel cuisine. Some of Prague's top high-end eateries are now to be found at places like **Allegro**, the Four Seasons' smash hit restaurant (*see p125*), where Milanese chef Vito Mollica works his magic. And the **Alcron** (*see p139*), the Czech Republic's first seafood-only restaurant in the lobby of the Radisson SAS, is where rival chefs go to seethe in envy. But in a city like Prague a vibrant expat community dedicated to the bohemian lifestyle will ensure there are plenty of affordable options as well. From giddy jazz brunches to bagel shops, and Cajun cooking to California cuisine, there are rich and reasonable offerings to be had all over the old heart of town.

Meanwhile, what's known as the Refrigerator effect has really begun to thaw. This pheno-menon, the impact of closed borders and a homogenous Slavic population, until recently made chop suey look worldly. These days diners can stop off for authentic Indian, Thai or Afghan food on the way to the **Roxy** club (*see p228*). **Rasoi** (*see p128*), **Orange Moon** (*see p125*) and **Ariana** (*see p125*) are all just a block away, as is **Dahab** (*see p135*), the highest form of a different Prague phenomenon – the **čajovna** or tearoom. This harem-like place comes fully equipped with Persian pillow seating, jangly belly dancing shows, steamed couscous and mint tea.

It would still be a tad optimistic to expect a city with a population of 1.2 million people, even 12 years into the free market, to be on a par with Paris, London or even Berlin for variety and quality. But price-wise, Prague easily beats them all and it's good to bear in mind that dining here, like most things, should be considered an adventure. Sometimes just getting your waiter's attention is one. Though service has advanced aeons since all food servers were state employees, rude waiters with suspect maths are still encountered at times, as are annoyingly short opening hours. Eating after 10pm is difficult, with the exception of a few savvy night-owl spots.

As for vegetarian cuisine, this meat-loving culture still offers limited choices. One gourmet restaurant that's sensitive to non-carnivores is **Le Bistrot de Marlène** (*see p138*), while **Radost FX Café** (*see p140*) is an up-all-night option. **Lotos** (*see p131*) offers a healthy veggie menu as does the buffet-style **Country Life** (*see p131*). Otherwise it may come down to *smažený sýr*, the fried cheese served at most pubs – mind they don't slip ham (*šunka*) in.

CAFÉS

Café culture in Prague offers everything from imperial elegance to American experiments. The *kavárna* in Prague has long been at the centre of intellectual life and, with secret police now gone, some classics have rebounded. Jam doughnuts fly at the legendary **Café Imperial** (*see p141*) while the cosy **Café Montmartre** (*see p132*) has bounced back from the bon vivant days when it hosted black masses during the 1930s. The **Slavia** (*see p135*), where dissidents like Václav Havel and Jiří Kolář once planned and plotted, has been slightly too cleaned up, alas. Meanwhile, expat caffeine addicts often get their fix at **Ebel Coffee House** (*see p133*), **Café Break** (*see p141*) and **The Globe Bookstore & Coffeehouse** (*see p141*).

TIPPING AND ETIQUETTE

Tables are often shared with other patrons who, like you, should ask *'Je tu volno?'* ('Is it free?') and may also wish each other *'dobrou chuť'* before tucking in. Prague dines with a relaxed dress code and reservations are necessary at only the fanciest spots in town.

Waiters record your tab on a slip of paper, which translates at leaving time into a bill. Pay the staff member with the folding wallet in their waistband, not your waiter (the phrase *'Zaplatím, prosím'* means 'May I pay, please?'). A small cover charge and extra charges for milk, bread and the ubiquitous and frightful accordion music are standard, as is tipping by rounding the bill up to the nearest 10 Kč.

While you should have little trouble making a phone reservation in English at swankier establishments, just about everywhere else it might be easier to book in person.

Hradčany

Czech

U Ševce Matouše

Loretánské náměstí 4, Prague 1 (2051 4536). Tram 22. **Open** 11am-11pm daily. **Main courses** 100-200 Kč. **Credit** AmEx, MC, V. **Map** p306 A3.
Fish and chips and generous slabs of steak in a dozen or so guises are served up in this former shoemaker's workshop (where it was once possible to get your boots repaired while lunching). Reasonable prices given the prime location.

Tearooms

Malý Buddha

Úvoz 46, Prague 1 (2051 3894). Tram 8, 22. **Open** 2-10.30pm Tue-Sun. **No credit cards. Map** p306 A3.
The 'Little Buddha' is a teahouse with a difference: great vegetarian spring rolls and noodle dishes go hand in hand with the dozens of teas brewed by the laid-back owner, who's always on hand. Mellow doesn't half describe it. No smoking.

Malá Strana

Continental

David

Tržiště 21, Prague 1 (5753 3109/www.btcguide.cz/david). Metro Malostranská/12, 22 tram. **Open** 11.30am-11pm daily. **Main courses** 360-700 Kč. **Credit** AmEx, MC, V. **Map** p307 D3.
Frequented by touring rock stars, this family-run, discreet little dining room knows how to pamper, oldclub style. The waiters seem more like butlers as they whisk roast boar and port to your table. The strong suit is definitive Bohemian classics like roast duck with red and white sauerkraut or rabbit fillet with spinach leaves and herb sauce. Booking essential.

Gitanes

Tržiště 7, Prague 1(5753 0163). Metro Malostranská. **Open** 11am-11pm daily. **Main courses** 150-290 Kč. **Credit** DC, MC, V. **Map** p307 D3.
Stuffed peppers, home-made bread, traditional Yugoslavian milk fat spreads, hearty red wines and homey service, all in a hideaway covered with ging-

The best Restaurants in town

For authentic Bohemian cuisine
U Sádlů (*see p125*) and U radnice (*see p125*).

For an authentic rude Czech waiter encounter
Novoměstský Pivovar (*see p140*) and Café Louvre (*see p141*).

For soul-soothing Balkan food
Gitanes (*see above*); Modrá řeka (*see p144*).

For generous Euro cuisine at backpacker prices
Bar Bar (*see p122*), Klub Architektů (*see p127*) and Café Imperial (*see p141*).

For 'interesting' floorshows and cannelloni
Bazaar Mediterranée (*see p123*) and La Provence (*see p128*).

For an affordable, romantic, baroque palace dinner
Palffy Palác (*see p122*).

For fine Vltava riverfront dining
Allegro (*see p125*) and Kampa Park (*see p123*).

For a top-flight cuisine splashout
Amici Miei (*see p129*) and U Zlaté studně (*see p122*).

For a top-flight cuisine splashout in view of heavily armed guards
Opera Garden (*Zahrada v opeře, see p140*).

For late-night dining
Radost FX Café (*see p140*) and Pizzeria Roma Due (*see p131*).

Eat, Drink, Shop

Paint the town red at glossy **Kampa Park**. *See p123.*

ham and doilies. It's like coming home to your Balkan granny's house, only with much cooler music – emanating from speakers hidden in the birdcages. Don't miss the private table available for curtained off dalliances and the charming and restful winter garden at the rear.

Palffy Palác

Valdštejnská 14, Prague 1 (5753 0522/ www.czechreality.cz/palffy). Metro Malostranská/ 12, 18, 22 tram. **Open** 11am-midnight daily. **Main courses** 130-270 Kč. **Credit** AmEx, MC, V. **Map** p307 E2.

This place is a breathtaking, if a bit threadbare, baroque palace with fine service, brunch menu and a tiny, fantastic terrace above a sweet garden. Cuisine nearly measures up to the decor but the aubergine lasagne is gone after a few bites; duck stuffed with dried plums is more substantial. The crepes and salads are generous and delicate affairs. All in all, excellent value for money.

Czech

U Maltézských rytířů

Prokopská 10, Prague 1 (5753 3666). Tram 12, 22. **Open** 11am-11pm daily. **Main courses** 260-540 Kč. **Credit** AmEx, MC, V. **Map** p307 E4.

A candlelit, Gothic cellar once an inn for the eponymous Knights of Malta, this place is justly proud of its venison châteaubriand. Mrs Černíková, whose family runs the place, does a nightly narration on the history of the house, then harasses you to eat the incredible strudel. Booking essential.

U Patrona

Dražického náměstí 4, Prague 1 (5753 0725/ www.uhi.cz/upatrona/index.html). Metro Malostranská/12, 22 tram. **Open** *Nov-Apr* 6-11.30pm Mon-Sat. *May-Oct* noon-11.30pm Mon-Sat. **Main courses** 260-540 Kč. **Credit** AmEx, MC, V. **Map** p307 E3.

A quaint parlour room dominated by a Jazz Age mural and a season-fresh menu. Three streetside tables look out at the Charles Bridge, and arty sauce arrangements on large white plates make for a pretty chicken saltimbocca. The menu can be described as Czech nouvelle cuisine with lighter versions of traditional Bohemian game to suit traditional tastes.

U Zlaté studně

U Zlaté studně 166, Prague 1(5753 3322/ www.zlatastudna.cz). Metro Malostranská/12, 22, 23 tram. **Main courses** 400-600 Kč. **Credit** AmEx, DC, MC, V. **Map** p307 E2.

In mild weather, stopping here is the perfect reward for tramping about Prague Castle – you can walk right in here from the Castle gardens. Spectacular views, sharp service and a menu that starts off with decadent choices including duck livers marinated in armagnac. Czech classics of duck, beef, pork and dumplings follow. Not to be mistaken for the Old Town hotel of the same name.

French

Bar Bar

Všehrdova 17, Prague 1 (5731 2246). Tram 12, 22. **Open** noon-2am daily. **Main courses** 80-140 Kč. **No credit cards**. **Map** p307 E5.

Pleasant and unpretentious but crowded local cellar bar and restaurant on a picturesque Malá Strana backstreet. The open sandwiches, salads and grill dishes will pass but the savoury crepes are the real highlight. English-style dessert pancakes with lemon and sugar are priced at a pittance. Waiters are cool and reasonably flexible about substitutions.

U malířů
Maltézské náměstí 11, Prague 1 (5753 0000). Tram 12, 22. **Open** 11.30am-10.30pm daily. **Main courses** 500-1,000 Kč. **Credit** AmEx, MC, V. **Map** p307 E4.

Prague's most expensive restaurant by far lurks within a quaint 16th-century house with original painted ceilings. Authentic, quality French cuisine and a clientele that dines to impress. The seasonal menu runs from snails or paté served with Sauternes to sea bass, lobster, lamb and squab. An excellent cheeseboard and wine list – although the price of a bottle will double the cost of an already overly expensive meal. Service on the stiff side.

Italian

Bazaar Mediterranée
Nerudova 40, Prague 1 (5753 5050/ www.restaurantbazaar.cz). Tram 12, 22. **Open** noon-midnight daily. **Main courses** 250-500 Kč. **Credit** AmEx, MC, V. **Map** p307 D3.

This surreal labyrinth of cellars and terraces presents overdone pasta as if it were the pride of the kitchen. Unfortunately, it is. The cellar bar trots out oddball nightly entertainment ranging from drag shows to striptease acts, as does its kitschy sister establishment, **Banana Bar**. Well, at least you get impressive terrace views.

Seafood

Circle Line
Malostranské náměstí 12, Prague 1 (5753 0021). Metro Malostranská, 22 tram. **Open** noon-11pm Mon-Fri; 11am-11pm Sat, Sun. **Main courses** 330-670 Kč. **Credit** AmEx, MC, V. **Map** p307 D3.

Fresh seafood in the elegant, arched cellar of the Hartigovský Palace or at street tables in summer. It lays on the luxury trappings a bit thick, but otherwise this place is hard to fault. Outstanding service, artful seasonal salads and main courses like roast turbot in creamy crab sauce prepared French-style. Vegetarians are well provided for and the wine list is excellent if you can afford to splash out.

Kampa Park
Na Kampě 8B, Prague 1 (5753 2685/ www.kampapark.com). Metro Malostranská/12, 22 tram. **Open** 11.30am-1am daily; kitchen closes at 11pm. **Main courses** 300-650 Kč. **Credit** AmEx, DC, MC, V. **Map** p307 F4.

Kampa Park's location is arguably the finest in Prague – in the shadow of Charles Bridge with a beautiful riverside terrace. Al fresco dining on oysters or Thai tuna steak in summer complements a slick bar-room scene inside, favoured by the business crowd. Tasteful wood and glass accents, punchy Scandinavian sauces, and notably sharp service.

Pubs

Na Kampě 15
Na Kampě 15, Prague 1 (5753 1430/ www.nakampe15.cz). Metro Malostranská/12, 22 tram. **Open** noon-midnight daily. **Main courses** 90-200 Kč. **Credit** AmEx, DC, MC, V. **Map** p307 F4.

Forget about the pricey restaurant at this address and swing around the corner to the pub of the same name – goulash and dumplings, fried mushrooms and well-tapped beer all go for loose change. The scattering of outdoor tables on the edge of Kampa Park are among the perks.

U Sedmi Švábů
Jánský vršek 14, Prague 1 (5753 1455/ www.viacarolina.cz). Metro Malostranská/12, 22, 23 tram. **Open** 11am-5pm, 7pm-11pm daily. **Main courses** 150-350 Kč. **Credit** AmEx, MC, V. **Map** p306 C3.

A *krčma*, or Czech medieval tavern, the Seven Swabians is a trippy, if borderline tacky experience, with occasional live troubadour music, traditional sweet honey liqueur and salty platters of pork knuckle. Only in Prague.

Cafés

Bohemia Bagel
Újezd 16, Prague 1 (5731 0694/ www.bohemiabagel.cz). Tram 6, 9, 12, 22. **Open** 7am-midnight Mon-Fri; 8am-midnight Sat, Sun. **No credit cards**. **Map** p307 E5.

Glen Spicker of U Malého Glena fame created this place – the republic's first true bagel café – five years ago and it seems like it's been packed ever since. Free refills, another breakthrough idea in Prague, help wash down the fresh muffins, breakfast bagels and bagel sandwiches. There's also usually something of interest – courses, places to rent, exhibitions – on the bulletin board.
Branch: Masná 2, Staré Město, Prague 1 (2481 2560).

Cukrkávalimonáda
Lázeňská 7, Prague 1 (5753 0628). Metro Malostranská/12, 22 tram. **Open** 9am-7pm Mon-Fri; 10am-7pm Sat, Sun. **No credit cards**. **Map** p307 E4.

This is a hip café just a block off the main tourist drag leading off the Charles Bridge. Look out on to a quiet corner of Maltézské náměstí while sipping a Californian Chardonnay or tucking into one of the daily specials of chicken roulades with heaps of mashed potatoes. Expect tall, foamy lattes, a sort of casually alert service, designer benches, hanging greenery and slick magazines for leafing through.

Staré Město & Josefov

American

Red Hot & Blues

Jakubská 12, Staré Město, Prague 1 (2231 4639).
Metro Náměstí Republiky/5, 14, 26 tram. **Open** 9am-
11pm daily. **Main courses** 120-230 Kč. **Credit**
AmEx, MC, V. **Map** p309 K3.

Expat institution with requisite blues player on a
stool, Cajun chicken recipes and American-style
brunch served on the patio. Reliable and relaxed, but
avoid the overpriced drink specials.

Asian

Ariana

Rámová 6, Staré Město, Prague 1 (2232 3438/
ariana.dreamworx.cz). Metro Náměstí Republiky/5,
8, 14 tram. **Open** 11am-11pm daily. **Main courses**
280-360 Kč. **Credit** AmEx, DC, MC, V. **Map** p308 J2.

This cosy little Afghan restaurant on a short backstreet is well worth tracking down. Excellent, tender, spiced lamb, but also a sumptuous vegetarian
chalou of spinach leaves, aubergine and basmati rice.
Features traditional straightback chairs, woven rugs
and familial service.

Arsenal

Valentinská 11, Staré Město, Prague 1 (2481 4099).
Metro Staroměstská/17, 18 tram. **Open** 10am-
midnight daily. **Main courses** 300-600 Kč.
Credit AmEx, DC, MC, V. **Map** p308 H3.

Pricy designer Thai and Japanese *teppan* fare, but
some of the fieriest in Old Town and a consistent
favourite among expats. The furnishings and cruet
sets, and works by glass artist Bořek Šipek compete
unashamedly with the cuisine but, in the end, it all
makes for a memorable night.

Orange Moon

Rámová 5, Staré Město, Prague 1 (2232 5119/
www.orangemoon.cz). Metro Náměstí Republiky/
5, 8, 14 tram. **Open** 11.30am-11.30pm daily.
Main courses 180-350 Kč. **Credit** AmEx, MC, V.
Map p308 J2.

Thai, Burmese and Indian in a warm, well-lit cellar
space. Eager servers bring on the curries and Czech
beer. The entrance is easy to miss, but the voices of
customers regaling will lead you down the right
stairs. The bar section's a popular hangout.

Restaurance po Sečuánsku

Národní třída 25, Staré Město, Prague 1 (2108
5331). **Open** 10am-11pm daily. **Main courses** 59-
220 Kč. **No credit cards. Map** p308 G5.

A clean, bright little spot for Chinese fast food, but
with an vast list of *rychlé*, or quick, items for 59 Kč.
Kung pao, sweet and sour chicken and fried rice all
come in these light sizes (although they all can be
scaled up for bigger appetites). The entrance is
inside the Palác Metro shopping passage.

Sushi Sandwich

Divadelní 24, Staré Město, Prague 1 (2222 1117/
www.sushisandwich.cz). Metro Staroměstská/
Národní třída. **Open** 11am-7pm Mon-Fri. **Main**
courses 80-200 Kč. **No credit cards. Map** p308 G5

A peaceful Zen temple of a sushi place, with lunch
specials of big maki triangles, miso soup, green tea
and fresh-baked sweet beancakes. Take out or eat
in among the blond and black wood, you'll get a gracious smile either way.

Czech

U Bakaláře

Celetná 13, Staré Město, Prague 1 (2481 7369).
Metro Náměstí Republiky/5, 8, 14 tram. **Open** 9am-
7pm daily. **Main courses** 40-70 Kč. **No credit**
cards. Map p308 J3.

This convenient Old Town lunch buffet is a stalwart
example of that pre-revolutionary classic, the workers' cafeteria. It's also a good standby for the likes
of toasted sandwiches, pancakes and soup.
Communal seating, friendly-ish service and far too
much salt in everything.

U modré kachničky

Michalská 16, Staré Město, Prague 1 (2421 3418/
www.umodrekachnicky.cz). Metro Staroměstská/17,
18 tram. **Open** 11.30am-11.30pm daily. **Main**
courses 500-800 Kč. **Credit** AmEx, DC, MC, V.
Map p308 H4.

On an obscure side street of Old Town, this little
room with its heavy wooden decor offers fine interpretations of dishes such as the duck roasted with
pears and the boar steak with mushrooms. It also
offers an array of excellent Moravian wines. The
Malá Strana branch has long been a favourite with
parliamentarians and visiting Hollywood actors.
Branch: Nebovidská 6, Malá Strana, Prague 1
(5732 0308).

U Sádlů

Klimentská 2, Staré Město, Prague 1 (2481 3874/
www.usadlu.cz). Metro Náměstí Republiky/5, 14, 26
tram. **Open** 11am-1am daily. **Main courses** 120-230
Kč. **Credit** MC, V. **Map** p309 K2.

This medieval kitsch – but efficient, tasty and
affordable medieval kitsch – and it can be a good
laugh on a Friday night. Hoist a mead and lay on the
pepper steak or boar – if you can work out the illuminated menu. Nice armour in the bar.
Branch: Balbínova 22, Vinohrady, Prague 2
(2225 2411).

Continental

Allegro

Veleslavínova 2A, Staré Město, Prague 1 (2142
6880/www.fourseasons.com/prague/dining/dining.ht
ml). Metro Staroměstská/17, 18 tram. **Open**
Restaurant 6.30am-midnight daily. *Bar* until 1am.
Terrace until 9pm. **Main courses** 500-1,200 Kč.
Credit AmEx, DC, MC, V. **Map** p310 G3.

Eat, Drink, Shop

Excellent food in airy surroundings at **Pravda**. *See p131.*

Chef Vito Mollica has been Prague's star of kitchen feats since the Four Seasons opened at this prime location across the Vltava from Prague Castle. From the grilled prawns and snails wrapped in Italian bacon to the exquisite Italian cheeses drizzled in 13-year-old *balsamico*, it's a splurge to savour.

Bellevue

Smetanovo nábřeží 18, Staré Město, Prague 1 (2222 1438/www.praguefinedining.cz). Metro Národní třída/17, 18 tram. **Open** noon-3pm, 5.30-11pm Mon-Sat; 11am-3pm (jazz brunch), 7-11pm Sun. **Main courses** 490-790 Kč. **Credit** AmEx, MC, V. **Map** p308 G5.

Duck in apricot sauce sautéed with chanterelle mushrooms, and the veal tenderloin topped with fresh truffles are winners and the service is generally head and shoulders above the competition. Gob-smacking views of Prague Castle from the streetside tables. Booking is essential.

Klub Architektů

Betlémské náměstí 5A, Staré Město, Prague 1 (2440 1214). Metro Národní třída/6, 9, 18, 22, 23 tram. **Meals served** 11.30am-midnight daily. **Main courses** 70-140 Kč. **Credit** AmEx, DC, MC, V. **Map** p308 H5.

In the dim designer cellar of an architecture and design gallery, this place is better at style than fine cuisine. But the summer patio offers quiet respite, rare in Old Town, with low prices and decent vegetarian dishes. Cheapish Pilsner Urquell on tap.

Metamorphis

Malá Štupartská 5, Staré Město, Prague 1 (2482 7058/www.metamorphis.cz). Metro Náměstí Republiky/5, 14, 26 tram. **Open** 9am-1am daily. **Main courses** 280-420 Kč. **Credit** AmEx, DC, MC, V. **Map** p308 J3.

Sedate and capable, this family-run pasta café and pension has just one disadvantage: it's directly on a main tourist route to Old Town Square. The cellar restaurant within is enhanced by live jazz at night.

Století

Karolíny Světlé 21, Staré Město, Prague 1 (2222 0008/www.stoleti.cz). Metro Národní třída. **Open** noon-midnight daily. **Main courses** 300-450 Kč. **Credit** AmEx, MC, V. **Map** p308 G5.

A blue cheese, pear and almond salad named after Valentino is a typical starting point at this refreshingly adept Old Town eatery. Better-than-average veggie polenta and tender steaks go along with the old world decor and swift service in this classic baroque-era building.

V Zátiší

Liliová 1, Betlémské náměstí, Staré Město, Prague 1 (2222 1155/www.praguefinedining.cz). Metro Národní třída/6, 9, 18, 22, 23 tram. **Open** noon-3pm, 5.30-11pm daily. **Main courses** 400-600 Kč. **Credit** AmEx, MC, V. **Map** p308 G4.

On a narrow cobbled lane, and owned by the management of Mlýnec and Bellevue (*see p131*), this is one of the city's most elegant dining rooms. Quail

and fresh thyme start your mouth watering, but the house special – rabbit roasted with garlic – is the pinnacle. Formal, sometimes slow service. Don't miss out on the cardamom crème brûlée.

Zlatá ulička

Masná 9, Staré Město, Prague 1 (232 0884). Metro Náměstí Republiky/5, 8, 14, tram. **Open** 11am-midnight daily. **Main courses** 80-170 Kč. **No credit cards. Map** p308 J2.

A tiny place with excellent beef- and veal-based dishes defying the usual Czech bland-is-better attitude. The veal stew with mashed potatoes is a knockout, as is the *palačinka* (sweet pancake), big enough for two. The kitsch decoration scheme is based on Prague Castle's eponymous Golden Lane. **Branch**: Petrská 21, Nové Město, Prague 1 (2231 7015).

French

Alizée Restaurant

Široká 4, Josefov, Prague 1 (2481 9668). Metro Staroměstská. **Open** *Bistro* 9am-midnight daily. *Restaurant* 11.30am-2.30pm, 7-10.30pm. **Main courses** 450-650 Kč. **Credit** AmEx, DC, MC, V. **Map** p308 G3.

Warm, soft tones create a gracious space opposite the Old Jewish Cemetery, where the Michelin star-decorated chef serves up reasonably priced bistro cuisine like *salade campagnarde* and lasagne with *herbes de Provence*. Or, on the more formal restaurant side, you can sup on swordfish ragoût or Asian lamb with acacia honey. The gliding, enchanting waiters don't hurt either.

Chez Marcel

Haštalská 12, Staré Město, Prague 1 (2231 5676). Metro Náměstí Republiky/5, 8, 14 tram. **Open** 8am-1am daily. **Main courses** 200-350 Kč. **No credit cards. Map** p308 J2.

This is a thoroughly French brasserie with all of the requisite brass accents, copies of *Le Monde* and views on to Old Town's most lovely cobbled square that you might hope for. They also make the deepest quiche in town which goes well with the big baskets of crispy fries, dappled with Dijon mustard. By night this is a favourite rendezvous for clubbers and by day it offers high chairs (rare in Prague restaurants) and a non-smoking section. **Branches**: Brasserie le Moliére, Americká 20, Vinohrady, Prague 2 (2251 3340); Jules Verne, Rybná 29, Staré Město, Prague 1 (2481 9767).

Francouzká restaurace

Municipal House, Náměstí Republiky 5, Staré Město, Prague 1 (2200 2770/www.obecnidum.cz). Metro Náměstí Republiky/5, 8, 14 tram. **Open** noon-4pm, 6-11pm daily. **Main courses** 250-500 Kč. **Credit** AmEx, MC, V. **Map** p309 K3.

The aesthetics rarely get any better than they do in this place. The city's preeminent shrine to art nouveau (and one of its top concert halls) has been painstakingly renovated, including this space, which acts as its dining room. Service is laid on thick rather than well, as in many an upmarket Prague restaurant, but the rabbit in mustard sauce and the French cheese plate are both treats.

La Provence

Štupartská 9, Staré Město, Prague 1 (2232 4801/ reservations 5753 5050/www.laprovence.cz). Metro Náměstí Republiky/5, 8, 14 tram. **Open** noon-midnight daily. **Open** *Bar* 8pm-2am daily. *Café* 11am-2am daily. **Main courses** 130-270 Kč. **Credit** AmEx, MC, V. **Map** p308 J3.

Billed as a 'restaurant, bistro and tapas bar' and sharing its premises with the ultra cheesy Banana Bar (*see p148*), this place suffers from more than just an identity crisis. The restaurant, with its rustic decor, offers good service, some decent wines and a nice cassoulet, but you have to elbow through a dense beefcake and hair-product mob to get there.

Le Café Colonial

Široká 6, Josefov, Prague 1 (2481 8322). Metro Staroměstská/17, 18 tram. **Open** 10am-midnight daily. **Main courses** 300-550 Kč. **Credit** AmEx, MC, V. **Map** p308 H3.

The airy café section has teak accents, and serves miniature quiches, roasted duck and delightful salads. More formal dining comes on the other side while a veranda has designer furniture in Matisse tones. Resolutely French.

Trocadero

Betlémská 9, Staré Město, Prague 1 (2222 0716/ www.trocadero.cz). Metro Národní třída. **Open** 11am-1am daily. **Main courses** 260-540 Kč. **Credit** AmEx, MC, V. **Map** p308 G5.

Designer French cuisine in Prague has made major leaps forward with Trocadero, while affordability has unusually stayed just about where it should. Czech-French owner Vlad Strnad brings select wines from small French vintners to this classy wine bar and dining room. Saint-Emilion grand cru is priced better nowhere in Prague, and that's a good thing since it goes so well with the remarkable bacon-wrapped venison, marinated in thyme. The interior is by President Havel's personal decorator, Bořek Šípek. A pétanque ground and boutique adjoins.

Kosher

Jeruzalém Kosher Restaurant

Břehová 5, Josefov, Prague 1 (2481 2001/ www.jerusalem1.cz). Metro Staroměstská/17, 18 tram. **Open** 8am-11pm daily. **Main courses** 120-230 Kč. **No credit cards. Map** p308 H2.

Fast, informal and professional, this diner is also exactly where you need it when your feet swell from touring Josefov synagogues. The decor is nondescript, but the engaging right-to-left menu with some sections in Hebrew delights. Dishes on offer include smoky mushroom pancakes, an array of imported kosher wines and a generous chocolate pudding that's unrivalled in Prague.

Au Gourmand: sweet indeed. *See p133.*

King Solomon

Široká 8, Josefov, Prague 1 (2481 8752/ www.kosher.cz). Metro Staroměstská/17, 18 tram. **Open** 11am-11pm Mon-Thur, Sun; 11am-90mins before sundown Fri; open by request on Sat with reservation. **Main courses** 200-500 Kč. **Credit** AmEx, MC, V. **Map** p308 H3.

Just a block from the Jewish Museum, this is an incongruous but solid addition to Prague's new wave of upscale kosher restaurants. The atrium in the back, the long and authoritative Israeli wine list and austere sandstone and iron decor all clash with homey comfort food offered in generous servings. The menu includes the likes of gefilte fish, chicken soup and carp with prunes.

Indian

Rasoi Restaurant/Bombay Café

Dlouhá 13, Staré Město, Prague 1 (232 4040/3349/www.rasoi.cz). Metro Náměstí Republiky or Staroměstská/5, 8, 14 tram. **Open** *Restaurant* 11.30am-11pm daily. *Bar* 5pm-4am daily. **Main courses** 280-480 Kč. **Credit** AmEx, DC, MC, V. **Map** p308 J2.

Big on tandoori and pan-cooked regional specialities from the subcontinent. The twee cellar dining room gives no hint of what awaits: an outstanding hotbed of curries, dhal and an impressive vindaloo. The Bombay Café at street level gives way to strange Latin dance shows but mixes a killer Martini.

Italian

Amici Miei

Vězeňská 5, Staré Město, Prague 1(2481 6688/ www.amicimiei.cz). Metro Můstek. **Open** 10am-4pm, 6-11pm Mon-Sat. **Main courses** 350-550 Kč. **Credit** AmEx, MC, V. **Map** p308 J2.
Outstanding cuisine in a slightly overlit hall discreetly curtained off from the street. Main courses run from expertly done scampi in garlic to tender *scaloppini al limone.* Service can be warm rather than effectual, but there is an exceptional wine list.

Don Giovanni

Karolíny Světlé 34, Staré Město, Prague 1 (2222 2060/dongiovanni.cz). Metro Staroměstská/17, 18 tram. **Open** 11am-11pm daily. **Main courses** 200-500 Kč. **Credit** AmEx, DC, MC, V. **Map** p308 G5.
Grand but understated surroundings host some of the finest Italian dining in Prague at this restaurant. Owner Avelino Sorgato oversees the home-made fettucine, and pappardelle with boar and porcini mushrooms, and the Parma ham is the real stuff. Sample from one of over 30 grappas or stick to the noteworthy, if expensive Italian wine list.

Kogo Pizzeria & Caffeteria

Havelská 27, Staré Město, Prague 1 (2421 4543/ www.kogo-prague.cz). Metro Můstek/6, 9, 18, 22 tram. **Open** *Restaurant* 11am-11pm daily. *Café* 8am-11pm Mon-Fri; 9am-11pm Sat, Sun. **Main courses** 150-300 Kč. **Credit** AmEx, MC, V. **Map** p308 J4.
With a growing empire of restaurants, this Old Town venue is still the most popular. Here one side serves quick pizza and pasta while the other has linen-covered tables for a relaxed meal. An espresso or mushroom pizza is served faster than any place around and the new location in the Slovanský dům mall is perfect for pre-movie dining and courtyard views. It stocks a good selection of Chiantis too.
Branch: Na Příkopě 22, Nové Město, Prague 1 (2145 1259).

Maestro

Křížovnická 10, Staré Město, Prague 1 (2232 0294). Metro Staroměstská/17, 18 tram. **Open** 11am-midnight daily. **Main courses** 130-270 Kč. **Credit** AmEx, DC, MC, V. **Map** p308 G3.
It may not be authentic Italian, but the pizzas can hold their own against any in Old Town and service is several notches above the Prague average. The chicken cacciatore is inspiring, as is the baroque trompe-l'oeil decor.

Modrá Zahrada

Národní třída 37, Staré Město, Prague 1 (2423 9055). Metro Národní třída/6, 9, 17, 18, 22, 23 tram. **Open** 11am-1am daily. (Meals served until midnight.) **Main courses** 120-280 Kč. **Credit** AmEx, DC, MC, V. **Map** p308 H2.
At street level a blue, futuristic mod bar with vanity tables in the window for exhibitionists. One level up (stairs hidden at the back) the regulars gather from all around for cheap, pleasant pizzas – a far safer bet than the fairly dodgy salads, nearly all of which contain some kind of meat. It's a relaxing place, and a bargain given the location. Service can be somewhat dizzy, though.
Branch: Pařížská 14, Josefov, Prague 1 (232 7171); Vinohradská 29, Vinohrady, Prague 2 (2225 3829).

Ostroff

Střelecký ostrov 336, Staré Město, Prague 1 (2491 9235/www.ostroff.cz). Tram 6, 9, 17, 18, 22. **Open** noon-2pm, 7-11pm Mon-Fri; 7-11pm Sat; 11am-3pm, 7-11pm Sun; *Terrace* 2-11pm Apr-Oct. **Main courses** 310-680 Kč. **Credit** AmEx, MC, V. **Map** p307 F5.
This place offers a perfect idyll, a classy bar perch and a decadent splurge, all rolled up into one. Located on a Vltava island, the bar here can't be beat for sleek style and visuals, while the menu consists of competent Sicilian and Tuscan fare. But the real draw here is the perfect location. It's just a short walk across Most Legii (Legionnaire's Bridge) to this eaterie on Střelecký ostrov (Shooter's Island), and so

Top five · Sunday brunches

Bohemia Bagel
A fast, kid-friendly location for light brunching on bagels with toppings galore, muffins and American-style bottomless filtered coffee. *See p123.*

Red Hot & Blues
Heaps of Tex-Mex and Cajun, plus killer coffees on the patio. *See p125.*

Radost FX Café
An old fave that's hit-or-miss on quality but always packed with clubbing survivors. *See p140.*

Palffy Palác
You'll find nothing but classy, formally informal pampering, at this place on which both locals and expats rely for help as they're reviving from the night before. *See p122.*

Bellevue
This venue has renowned and expensive jazz brunches – it's the city's pioneer of haute cuisine. *See p127.*

See also chapter **Accommodation** *for top Marriott, Hilton and Mövenpick hotel brunches.*

it offers commanding Old Town views, that are best enjoyed from the rooftop terrace on sunny days. Excellent brunch on Sundays.

Pizzeria Roma Due
Liliová 18, Staré Město, Prague 1 (0606 287 943 mobile). Metro Staroměstská/17, 18 tram. **Open** 24 hrs daily. **Main courses** 70-150 Kč. **No credit cards. Map** p308 G4.
Pizza that merits mention only because it's cheap, warm and available right around the clock. It's also usefully within stumbling distance of many trendy nightspots including the Roxy and Chateau.
Branch: Jagellonská 19, Žižkov, Prague 3 (0606 225 930 mobile).

Seafood

Reykjavík
Karlova 20, Staré Město, Prague 1 (2222 1218/ www.reykjavik.cz). Metro Staroměstská/17, 18 tram. **Open** 11am-midnight daily. **Main courses** 250-500 Kč. **Credit** AmEx, DC, MC, V. **Map** p308 G4.
Smack-bang on the main tourist route to Charles Bridge, this comfortably elegant restaurant nevertheless boasts fresh seafood in abundance at reasonable prices. The Icelandic owner flies in fish and lobster and the local crowds lap it up. Soups, starters, burgers and chicken are not quite as strong. There's a street terrace in summer, but the upstairs loft offers the quietest seating.

Rybí trh
Týnský dvůr 5, Staré Město, Prague 1 (2489 5447/ www.flambee.cz). Metro Náměstí Republiky/5, 8, 14 tram. **Open** 11am-midnight daily. **Main courses** 200-500 Kč. **Credit** AmEx, DC, MC, V. **Map** p308 J3.
This is a posh new seafood emporium in a sleek, cavernous space in the touristy Ungelt Square, where the chefs will boil or grill a pike-perch, carp or eel, then present it with turmeric rice. In summer, grab a table in the courtyard but avoid the shellfish, as is usually the rule in Prague.

Vegetarian

Country Life
Melantrichova 15, Staré Město, Prague 1 (2421 3366). Metro Národní třída/6, 9, 18, 22, 23 tram. **Open** 9am-8.30pm Mon-Thur; 9am-3pm Fri; 11am-8.30pm Sun. **Main courses** 50-100 Kč. **No credit cards. Map** p308 H4.
Though this place has expanded from a shop with salad bar into a full-blown cafeteria with seating and beautiful Old Town street views, Country Life has managed to continue as a low-key, dirt-cheap source of organically grown vegetarian fare. It specialises in massive DIY salads, fresh carrot juice, delectable lentil soup, crunchy wholegrain breads, along with slightly disquieting mashed potato casseroles. By all means avoid the lunchtime crush.
Branch: Jungmannova 1, Nové Město, Prague 1 (5704 4419).

Lotos
Platnéřská 13, Staré Město, Prague 1 (2232 2390). Metro Staroměstská/17, 18 tram. **Open** noon-10pm daily. **Main courses** 130-270 Kč. **Credit** AmEx, DC, MC, V. **Map** p308 G3.
Though a few of the tofu-based creations, served amid pastel bunting and ambient classical music, have met with lukewarm responses, the banana ragoût is a more imaginative winner. The small shop at the front sells a limited range of organic fare.

World

Barock
Pařížská 24, Josefov, Prague 1 (232 9221). Metro Staroměstská/17, 18 tram. **Open** 8.30am-1am Mon-Wed; 8.30am-2am Fri; 10am-2am Sat; 10am-1am Sun. (Meals served until 10.45pm.) **Main courses** 250-500 Kč. **Credit** AmEx, DC, MC, V. **Map** p308 H2.
Glam dining was never more overt. Gleaming steel bar, floor-to-ceiling windows, and a credible sushi platter with suitably aesthetic *nigiri*. A reasonably priced breakfast menu of croissants, sandwiches and powerhouse lattes attracts a contemplative morning crowd to the street tables.

Mlýnec
Novotného lávka 9, Staré Město, Prague 1 (2108 2208/www.praguefinedining.cz). Metro Staroměstská/17, 18 tram. **Open** noon-3pm, 5-11pm daily. **Main courses** 400-800 Kč. **Credit** AmEx, MC, V. **Map** p308 G4.
The newest venture of Prague's star restaurateur Sanjiv Suri goes for the theatrical with a mixture of traditional folk elements (including your server's costume) and global fusion cuisine. Tuna steak in ginger and berry sauce is a typically novel treat, as is the view from this Vltava weir location. Handy for pre-clubbing as it's surrounded by no fewer than six neighbouring dancefloors.

Pravda
Pařížská 17, Josefov, Prague 1 (2232 6203). Metro Staroměstská/17, 18 tram. **Open** noon-1am daily. (Meals served until 11.45pm.) **Main courses** 330-670 Kč. **Credit** AmEx, DC, MC, V. **Map** p308 H2.
Owner Tommy Sjoo, who was instrumental in bringing fine dining to post-1989 Prague, presides over an airy multi-level establishment on fashionable Pařížská where chicken in Senegal peanut sauce vies against Vietnamese *nem* spring rolls and borscht, all done credibly. Cool and graceful service from waitstaff in long black aprons.

Pubs

Pivnice u Pivrnce
Maiselova 3, Josefov, Prague 1 (2322 9404). Metro Náměstí Republiky/5, 8, 14 tram. **Open** 11am-midnight daily. **Main courses** 120-230 Kč. **Credit** MC, V. **Map** p308 H3.
Traditional Czech cooking and above-average presentation in the Jewish Quarter. *Svíčková* (beef in

Eat, Drink, Shop

The revolution's over at **Slavia**. *See p135.*

lemon cream sauce), duck with sauerkraut and walls covered with crude cartoons, guaranteed to offend. Radegast here is well tapped and nicely priced.

U Radnice

U radnice 2, Staré Město, Prague 1 (2422 8136). Metro Staroměstská/17, 18 tram. **Open** 11am-11pm daily. **Main courses** 50-100 Kč. **Credit** AmEx, DC, MC, V. **Map** p308 H3.
One of the last places around Old Town Square with traditional food served at prices meant for locals. Tasty Czech specialities like goulash or beef in cream sauce go for a pittance. Dark panelling and communal tables create a comfortable pub atmosphere.

Cafés

Au Gourmand

Dlouhá 10, Staré Město, Prague 1 (232 9060). Metro Staroměstská/17, 18 tram. **Open** 8.30am-7pm Mon-Fri; 9.30am-6pm Sat, Sun. **No credit cards.** **Map** p308 J3.
The richest little French bakery in town, with savoury baguette sandwiches and quiches on one side, luscious pear tarts and Black Forest cakes on the other. Sit down at a wrought iron table in the middle, surrounded by unique, turn-of-the-19th-century tile interiors, and you can watch half of Prague slip in for a bite of sin.

Bakeshop Praha

Kozí 1, Staré Město, Prague 1 (2231 6823). Metro Staroměstská/17, 18 tram. **Open** 7am-7pm daily. **No credit cards.** **Map** p308 J2.
San Franciscan Anne Feeley launched this expat mainstay three years ago and hasn't looked back since. Zesty quiches, traditional nut breads, muffins and peanut butter cookies have every Westerner in town ducking in. Take-out sandwiches and salads are perfect for sunny weather.

Blatouch

Vězeňská 4, Staré Město, Prague 1 (232 8643). Metro Staroměstská/17, 18 tram. **Open** 11am-midnight Mon-Thur; 11am-2am Fri; 1pm-2am Sat; 1pm-midnight Sun. **No credit cards.** **Map** p308 J2.
Two sisters run this gentle, reasonably priced café, a long-time favourite among new bohemians, clean-cut Czech students and intellectuals. Jazz and soul waft through the narrow, high-ceilinged space and up the metal stairwell to a loft space softened by carpets and armchairs. The wooden floors and bookcase add to the civilised atmosphere. Salads and melted cheese amalgams are available but can't be recommended.

Blinis Bar

Maiselova 16, Josefov, Prague 1 (2481 2463). Metro Staroměstská. **Open** 10am-11pm daily. **Credit** AmEx, DC, MC, V. **Map** p308 H3.
Appealing traditional pancakes are served up on truly jarring red, white and blue surfaces (the colour scheme being in honour of the Russian Federation). The pancakes come topped with wine-marinated mushrooms, red cabbage or jam and nestled against portions of sour cream.

Café Indigo

Platnéřská 11, Staré Město, Prague 1 (no phone). Metro Staroměstská/17, 18 tram. **Open** 9am-midnight Mon-Fri; noon-midnight Sat, Sun. **Main courses** 150-350 Kč. **No credit cards.** **Map** p308 G3.
Post-industrial, yet comfortable art café with huge streetside windows and a limited menu of toasts, soups, dubious omelettes, and nachos. It's a favourite with students from nearby Charles University, which means a lot of smoke, cheap wine and a consistently upbeat and easygoing vibe. Small children's corner in the back.

Café Milena

Staroměstské náměstí 22, Staré Město, Prague 1 (2163 2602). Metro Staroměstská/17, 18 tram. **Open** 10am-8pm daily. **Credit** DC, MC, V. **Map** p308 J3.
Milena Jesenská was one of Kafka's lovers but it's doubtful if the couple would have ever met at this saccharine-sweet dessert spot in the centre of Prague's tourist area. Waiters in grey waistcoats serve pancakes and ice-cream in the main room opposite the Astronomical Clock, while the Franz Kafka Society maintains an office upstairs.

Café Montmartre

Řetězová 7, Staré Město, Prague 1 (2222 1244).
Metro Staroměstská/17, 18 tram. **Open** 9am-11pm
daily. **No credit cards**. **Map** p308 H4.
Czech literati like Gustav Meyrink, Jaroslav Hašek
and Franz Werfel all tippled here before it became a
Jazz Age hotspot. Pilsner Urquell and Velvet are on
tap, but wine is better suited to the crowd of creative
miscreants that gather around the threadbare set-
tees and battered tables for late-night talks. You'd
best go to dinner first, as apple strudel is just about
the only thing to eat here.

Cream & Dream

Husova 12, Staré Město, Prague 1 (2421 1035).
Metro Staroměstská. **Open** 11am-midnight Mon-Fri;
10am-midnight Sat, Sun. **No credit cards**.
Map p308 H4
No, it's not another of Prague's many sex clubs, just
a nice clean ice-cream shop. But admittedly one with
sinful waffle cones stuffed with *frutti di bosco*,
caramel or orange *zmrzlina*. If you can make it past
the gleaming freezer, however, a microbar awaits in
the back, serving pastis, though it's a precious, modern space that doesn't encourage lingering

DaMúza

Řetězová 10, Staré Město, Prague 1 (2222 1749/
www.damuza.cz). *Metro Staroměstská/17, 18 tram.*
Open 11am-12.30am daily. **Credit** AmEx, DC, MC,
V. **Map** p308 H4.
Just across from the **Café Montmartre** (*see p132*),
this is the official café of the Academy of Dramatic
Arts, whose Czech acronym is contained in the
name. Six kinds of beer are on tap, as are fairly

substantial steaks – an unusual option for a Prague
café. Schedules on the tables list the irregular theatre pieces and concerts performed in the cellar. Nice
glass-roofed garden.

Ebel Coffee House

Týn 2, Staré Město, Prague 1 (2489 5788). *Metro*
Náměstí Republiky/5, 8, 14 tram. **Open** 9am-10pm
daily. **Credit** AmEx, DC, MC, V. **Map** p308 J3.
The Ebel touches the heights of the art of coffee
brewing. Journalist and designer Malgorzata Ebel
serves Prague's finest bean blends any way you
like them, whether in the form of macchiato or
mélange, espresso or cappuccino. More than 30
prime arabica coffees from her neighbouring shop,
Vzpomínky na Afriku, are available to go into your
cup. Passable quiches, bagels and brownies are
served as well, on tables in Prague's most fashionable Old Town courtyard.

Érra Café

Konviktská 11, Staré Město, Prague 1 (2222 0568/
www.sweb.cz/erra.cafe). *Metro Národní třída/*
6, 9, 18, 22, 23 tram. **Open** 10am-midnight Mon-
Fri; 11am-midnight Sat, Sun. **No credit cards**.
Map p308 G5.
It's as if a copy of Czech *Elle* exploded in an Old
Town cellar – even the menu poses in here: salads
of smoked duck and artfully arranged spinach
leaves are a favourite lunch item, as are the garlic-
sesame chicken baguettes and rich banana milk-
shakes. The service is great by Prague standards,
but the chairs are slightly less comfortable. Gay-
friendly scene by night, when the permanent house
music soundtrack seems more appropriate.

Get jiggy wit' it, at **Dahab**. *See p135*.

Eat, Drink, Shop

Franz Kafka Café

Široká 12, Josefov, Prague 1 (2231 8945). Metro Staroměstská/17, 18 tram. **Open** *10am-10pm daily.* **No credit cards. Map** p308 H2/3.

Surprisingly untacky, this old-world coffeehouse features dark, deep wooden booths, old engravings of the Jewish Quarter (it's just around the corner from the Jewish Cemetery) and, naturally, lots of Kafka portraits. Decent coffee and tables on the street make it convenient when touring Josefov.

Juice Bar

Na Příkopě 3-5, Prague 1 (no phone). Metro Můstek/3, 9, 14, 24 tram. **Open** *10am-10pm daily.* **Fresh juices** 80-140 Kč. **No credit cards. Map** p308 J4.

Prague's only source of freshly squeezed juices, smoothies and other California-style delights. The entrance to this sleek second-storey bar, just north of the bottom of Wenceslas Square above the Clock House fashion shop, is surprisingly tricky to locate. Great views of street life.

Káva Káva Káva

Národní třída 37, Staré Město, Prague 1 (2422 8862/www.kava-coffee.cz). Metro Národní třída/6, 9, 18, 22 tram. **Open** *7am-9pm Mon-Fri; 9am-9pm Sat, Sun.* **Credit** AmEx, MC, V. **Map** p308 H5.

Prague's first full-blown coffee emporium is a kinder, gentler kind of Starbucks, with a quiet courtyard and a dozen varieties of bean on offer. It also sells decent bagels and carrot cake.

Kavárna Obecní dům

Náměstí Republiky 5, Staré Město, Prague 1 (2200 2763/www.vysehrad2000.cz). Metro Náměstí Republiky/5, 14, 26 tram. **Open** *7.30am-11pm daily.* **Credit** AmEx, MC, V. **Map** p309 K3.

The magnificently restored Municipal House has a concert space, galleries and a decent French restaurant, but this café really takes the biscuit. Replete with elaborate secessionist brass chandeliers, balconies, a pianist and always a few grand dames, there's no more memorable venue for an espresso.

Lights, camera, Zdeněk Pohlreich

'It's not my job to make friends,'says Le Patio's sous-chef Zdeněk Pohlreich. Not a problem. Prague's great white hope of home-grown restaurateurship, **Brasserie Le Patio** (*see p137*), did not recruit this Czech-born master chef for his lovability.

It had more to do with what he had previously created in the **Alcron** (*see p139*), the minuscule dining room of the Radisson SAS. The first seafood-only restaurant in Prague, which served up the likes of tender Kamchatka crab alongside the soft-shelled, San Francisco-style blue variety, quickly became a culinary celebrity in its own right within the Czech Republic.

The expense of sourcing fresh seafood to landlocked Bohemia – to say nothing of training staff and adapting a kitchen set up for the meat-heavy diets of Central Europe – was not slight. 'I doubt they are making any money,' Pohlreich says. 'But what they do at Alcron is so special that it brings in a lot of guests.'

Le Patio was a successful decor shop that had branched into a successful café at Národní třída 22 and decided to take on a new serious restaurant venture in 2001. Monika Vostřáková was put in charge and faced with a considerable challenge. Le Patio had been a hit as a shop from day one with every piece of furniture created by a local craftsperson, all of which could be bought at the cafe. But the food was essentially limited to desserts. To break into the big restaurant league, they would need some new blood –

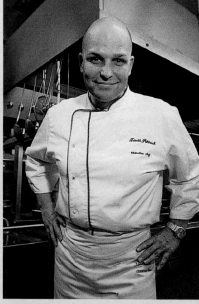

and more than a little muscle. The Prague restaurant world is notorious for its lack of polish but Le Patio was shooting for international standards. Vostřáková, herself a former Czech diplomat to Vietnam and a

Slavia

Smetanovo nábřeží 2, Prague 1 (2421 8493). Metro Národní třída/6, 9, 17, 18, 22 tram. **Open** 9am-11pm daily. **Credit** AmEx, DC, MC, V. **Map** p308 G5.
The mother of all Prague cafés, where Karel Tiege, Jiři Kolář and a struggling Václav Havel once tippled and plotted the overthrow of communism, the Slavia would hardly be recognised by its former customers today. The art deco fixtures and crisp service were overdue but are not the stuff of Jaroslav Seifert's classic poem 'Café Slavia'. Still, it does offer stunning Castle views, a decent salmon toast and a fine Old Town respite just opposite the National Theatre.

Týnská literární kavárna

Týnská 6, Staré Město, Prague 1 (2482 6023). Metro Staroměstská/17, 18 tram. **Open** 10am-11pm daily. **No credit cards. Map** p308 J3.
This place is a jumble of art students, smoke and bad coffee that all leads on to a lovely hidden courtyard secreted behind Prague's newest gallery of modern art, the House of the Gold Ring. With its arty location and hipper-than-thou attitude, it is the place to hang with Charles University students.

Tearooms

Dahab

Dahab 33, Staré Město, Prague 1 (2482 7375/ www.dahab.cz). Metro Náměstí Republiky/5, 8, 14 tram. **Open** 1pm-1am daily. **Credit** AmEx, MC, V. **Map** p309 K2.
Prague's newest tearoom is nothing less than a harem tent strewn with pillows and teak, providing a perfect candlelit counterpoint to the crazed goings-on at the Roxy next door. Pistachio cookies, cous-cous, Turkish coffees and occasional belly dancing. Otherwise, thoroughly calming. At the Boršov branch, pull the ringer to get in.
Branch: Boršov 2, Staré Město, Prague 1 (2222 1430/ www.dahab.cz).

Nové Město

American

Jáma

V jámě 7, Prague 1 (2422 2383/www.praguepivo. com). Metro Můstek/3, 9, 14, 24 tram. **Open** 11am-1am daily. (Meals served until 11.40pm.) **Main courses** *Dinner* 180-260 Kč. *Lunch & brunch* 100-200 Kč. **Credit** AmEx, MC, V. **Map** p311 K6.
American-owned and outfitted, with a prime patio space out back and a bank of internet terminals by the door, Jáma still has the loud college vibe that made its name. Czech scenesters are here by day (the kids' playground is great for brunching) and young business types by night. Lunch specials and happy-hour deals are a big draw, as is the Czech-Mex menu and well-poured Gambrinus. The video-rental counter also does brisk business.

Asian

Millhouse Sushi

Slovanský dům, Na Příkopě 22, Staré Město, Prague 1 (2145 1771). Metro Mĕstek or Náměstí Republiky. **Open** 11am-11pm daily. **Main courses** 400-800 Kč. **Credit** AmEx, DC, MC, V. **Map** p309 K4.
The trendiest sushi bar in town, ensconced in a gleaming fashion mall that once housed Communist Party offices and the Gestapo before that. This is a good option before catching a movie in the adjoining state-of-the-art multiplex.
Branch: Sokolovská 84-6, Karlín, Prague 8 (2283 2583).

Thanh Long

Ostrovní 23, Staré Město, Prague 1 (2493 3537/ www.thanhlong.cz). Metro Národní třída/6, 9, 18, 22, 23 tram. **Open** 11.30am-3pm, 5-11.30pm daily. **Main courses** 100-200 Kč. **Credit** AmEx, DC, MC, V. **Map** p310 H6.

passionate Asian food junkie, thought Pohlreich was well enough travelled to pull it off. It only added to his attraction that he was a formidable bulldog.

Pohlreich had decided to break out of communist Czechoslovakia 13 years before to pursue his dream of becoming a master chef. He and his wife had just escaped across the border in 1989 when the communist regime fell. Finding it impossible to get asylum status in Western Europe, they went to Australia to look for a job, making an entry-level start with a French restaurant called La Guillotine in Adelaide. Thus began a steep learning curve in world cuisine and Western service standards.

By 2002 Pohlreich was back home and had opened two award-winning kitchens in Prague. Looking for a new challenge, he bought into Le Patio's ambitious restaurant venture at V celnici where he promptly fired half the waiters and a third of the kitchen staff. The menu suffered similarly radical revision. Out went the frozen tapas that passed for exotic food and in came grilled tuna steak with courgette and candied garlic, and fish quenelles with sauce Nantua.

Surveying the lush environs of his new empire, a kind of updated palace out of *The King and I*, he nods with approval and says, 'When I see this place, I think of something a little more... sexy.'

Distinguished mainly by its central location and blissfully over-the-top trappings, such as the revolving 'Lazy Susan' tables, pagoda lanterns and the huge moving-light painting in the back. Cuisine blanded down to suit Czech tastes.

Continental

Brasserie Le Patio
V Celnici 4, Prague 1 (9632 5466). Metro Náměstí Republiky/5, 8, 14 tram. **Open** 9am-midnight Mon-Fri; 10am-midnight Sat, Sun. **Main courses** 600-700 Kč. **Credit** AmEx, MC, V. **Map** p309 L3.
An entire train car and pounds of gold leaf make up the interior, but the terrace tables fill up first in summer. Chef Zdeněk Pohlreich oversees an ambitious menu of Mediterranean and Asian cuisine and fusion interpretations of classic Czech fare. Servers are sharp and fleet of foot. The Národní třída branch features hot jazz torch singers at weekends. **Branch:** Národní třída 22, Nové Město, Prague 1 (2493 4402).

Červená Tabulka
Lodecká 4, Prague 1 (2481 0401/ www.originalart.cz). Metro Náměstí Republiky. **Open** 11.30am-midnight daily. **Main courses** 400-700 Kč. **Credit** AmEx, MC, V. **Map** p309 L2.
Bold, whimsical decor and menus make the Red Tablet an Old Town star. Turkey livers baked pink with lavender and pistachio sauce are cheerily served up alongside quail in a courgette nest and honey carrots. Decadent desserts and a rare kid's menu make it a weekend family favourite.

Chaoz
Masarykovo nábřeží 26, Prague 1 (2493 3657). Metro Národní třída/6, 9, 17 18, 22, 23 tram. **Open** 11am-11pm daily. **Main courses** 130-270 Kč. **Credit** AmEx, MC, V. **Map** p310 G6.
Hidden under an extraordinary art nouveau entryway on the New Town embankment is this beloved neighbourhood secret. The generous Waldorf salad and Bohemian roast duck are standouts, while the salmon in pastry with wild rice does very well solo.

Dynamo
Pštrossova 220-29, Prague 1 (2493 2020/ www.mraveniste.cz). Metro Národní třída/6, 9, 18, 22, 23 tram. **Open** 11.30am-midnight daily. **Main courses** 170-330 Kč. **Credit** AmEx, MC, V. **Map** p310 G6.
This sleek designer diner typifies the food and drink renaissance sweeping through the SONA area (south of the National Theatre). The steaks and pasta cuisine doesn't quite keep up with the stream-lined decor, but the collection of single-malt Scotches makes the bar a connoisseur's favourite.

Modrá Terasa
Na Můstku 9, Wenceslas Square, Prague 1 (2422 6288/www.modraterasa.wz.cz). Metro Můstek. **Open** 11am-11pm daily. **Credit** AmEx, MC, V. **Map** p308 H5.

The best view, bar none, of Wenceslas Square, an attraction that admittedly outshines the New Zealand lamb and pepper steaks. Still, for an eagle's perch on the deck in sunny weather, it's surely a kick. Accessed via lift next to the westernmost Můstek metro entrance.

Czech

Černý kůň
Lucerna Passage, Vodičkova 36, Prague 1 (2421 2559/www.lucerna.cz). Metro Můstek/3, 9, 14, 24 tram. **Open** 11am-midnight daily. **Main courses** 350-550 Kč. **Credit** AmEx, MC, V. **Map** p309 K5.
The Black Horse is an eatery with a colourful history located in a cellar just off Wenceslas Square – jazz legends like Josephine Baker used to dine here in the glory days of the interwar First Republic. Now President Havel's wife, Dáša, has restored some of its glory, adding Czech and Slovak classics like *haluška* and *brynza*, a kind of Slavic gnocchi with sauerkraut and bacon. Fish tanks with sea horses and old timber do for decor.

Demínka
corner of Škrétova & Angelická, Prague 2 (0603 185 699 mobile). Metro IP Pavlova/4, 6, 11, 16, 22, 23, 34 tram. **Open** 11am-11pm daily. **Main courses** 250-380 Kč. **No credit cards.** Map p311 L7.
This historic First Republic restaurant for the elite has reopened after years of closed doors. Its new face is that of a slick, modern eatery for the stylish – though with essentially the same classic Czech grub that's always been synonymous with Demínka. Think *svíčkova* (beef in cream sauce), or duck with potato dumplings. All dishes are proferred on white plate arrangements, and its usually served up by a bevy of would-be models.

Fast food

Gyrossino
Spálená 43, Prague 1 (2491 5894). Metro Národní třída/6, 9, 18, 22, 23 tram. **Open** 24 hrs daily. **Main courses** 50-80 Kč. **No credit cards.** Map p310 H6.
Actually two places, side by side, separated by a building entryway. The left half is a bakery, the right serves up roast chicken, falafel, kebabs and just-edible mini-pizzas.

U Rozvařilů
Na Poříčí 26, Prague 1 (2481 1736). Metro Náměstí Republiky/5, 8, 14 tram. **Open** 7.30am-7.30pm Mon-Fri; 7.30am-7pm Sat; 10am-5pm Sun. **Main courses** 40-75 Kč. **No credit cards.** Map p309 L2.
A chrome-covered, mirrored version of that old pre-revolutionary classic, the workers' cafeteria. The cast of characters, from servers in worn white aprons to harassed-looking customers in white socks and sandals, all remain. So do the incredibly cheap soups, *guláš*, dumplings and *chlebíčky* (open-faced mayonnaise and meat sandwiches).

Eat, Drink, Shop

Brassierie Le Patio: home of Prague's most ambitious chef.
See p137.

French

La Perle de Prague

*corner of Rašínovo nábřeží & Resslova, Prague 2
(2198 4160/www.laperle.cz). Metro Karlovo
náměstí/17 tram.* **Open** noon-2pm, 7-10.30pm Tue-
Sat; 7-10.30pm Mon. **Main courses** 470-730 Kč.
Credit AmEx, DC, MC, V. **Map** p310 G8.

This eyrie atop Frank Gehry's 'Fred and Ginger'
building (*see chapter* **Architecture**) was once king
of the hill. For some time after it opened, the chance
to eat atop the dancing building was enough to bring
the diners in. But things have slipped. Bold plans to
fly in a new international chef each month have been
scrapped, and patrons are drifting away. Even the
views are a bit disappointing – especially as you
have to peer out of smallish recessed windows.

Le Bistrot de Marlène

*Plavecká 4, Prague 2 (2492 1853/www.
bistrotdemarlene.cz). Metro Karlovo náměstí/3,
7, 16, 17 tram.* **Open** noon-2.30pm, 7-10.30pm
Mon-Fri; 7-10.30pm Sat. **Main courses** 500-1000 Kč.
Credit AmEx, MC, V. **Map** p310 G10.

The chalkboard menus out front in French and Czech
belie enchanting, market-fresh meals of fine traditional Franche-Comté cuisine in a newly done, overly sleek and modern room with red accents. The
seasonal pheasant, venison and boar are the only
things not imported and the expertly done mushroom
flan in parsley sauce, filets mignons and salades
niçoises have become a cause célèbre among Prague
patrons. Attentive, vegetarian-friendly service.

Universal

*V Jirchářích, Prague 1 (2493 4416). Metro Národní
trída/6, 9, 17, 18, 22, 23 tram.* **Open** 11.30-1am
Mon-Sat; 12.30pm-1am Sun. **Main courses** 250-350
Kč. **No credit cards**. **Map** p310 G6.

A cosy red and cream interior and old-fashioned
French advertisements cue you that Universal's a
unique find in Prague. The servers here know their
stuff, and tip you to the daily specials (cod in white
sauce, tender flank steak and rolled veggie lasagne
are all typical), which come with delectable sides of
fresh spinach or roasted gratin potatoes. The vegetarian-friendly menu is clearly created by chefs who
exercise a French passion for tasty greens. In addition, the coffee here is supercharged and goes down
well with a massive lemon tarte.

Greek

Řecká Taverna

*Revoluční 16, Prague 1 (2231 7762). Metro Náměstí
Republiky/5, 8, 14 tram.* **Open** 10am-midnight Mon-
Fri; 11am-midnight Sat, Sun. **Main courses** 180-250
Kč. **No credit cards**. **Map** p309 K2.

Affordable, authentic Greek delights are found in
this cheerfully tacky tavern that somehow managed
to drift far off the normal course to Prague's Old
Town and landed a block from the hip Roxy club. An
array of the usual Greek favourites lead the way
here – stuffed vine leaves in tzatziki, spinach pie and
saganaki cheese stand alongside savoury souvlaki
and kebabs. Ouzo, retsina and cold frappé coffee are
on hand to wash it all down.

Italian

Cicala

Žitná 43, Prague 1 (2221 0375). Metro IP Pavlova/ 4, 6, 16, 22, 23 tram. **Open** 11.30am-10.30pm daily. **Main courses** 200-400 Kč. **No credit cards.** **Map** p311 J7.

Get the tip on which fresh Italian wonder the proprietor has had driven in this week: it might be calamari or it might be figs; either way, it will be presented like a work of art. This subterranean two-room eaterie on an otherwise unappealing street is well worth seeking out as a bastion of home cooking and a mainstay of Prague's Italian community.

Il Ritrovo

Lublaňská 11, Prague 2 (2426 1475/ www.ilritrovo.cz). Metro IP Pavlova/4, 6, 11, 22, 23 tram. **Open** noon-3pm, 6-11pm Mon-Fri; reservation only Sat. **Main courses** 130-270 Kč. **Credit** MC, V. **Map** p311 L8.

This restaurant features 30 varieties of pasta, several of which are home-made. Florentine proprietor Antonio Salvatore's most secret Tuscan sauces are only offered when you ask for them (eavesdrop on his visiting friends as they order to catch the hot tip for the day), but following the menu is by no means limiting. Try the antipasti bar, four-cheese linguine and ravioli in cream and sage and, if you fancy it, brandy. Just beware the gramophone collection of sentimental Italian ballads.

Pizza Coloseum

Vodičkova 32, Prague 1 (2421 4914/www. pizzacoloseum.cz). Metro Můstek/3, 9, 14, 24 tram. **Open** 11.30am-11.30pm Mon-Sat; noon-11.30pm Sun. **Main courses** 100-200 Kč. **Credit** AmEx, MC, V. **Map** p310 J6.

Popular cellar joint just off Wenceslas Square that's a cut above the usual Prague pizzeria. Excellent bruschetta, flame-baked pizza and big, saucy pastas complement well-stocked wine racks, an oil-heavy antipasti bar and a familiar range of dependable steak and fish dishes.
Branches: Ovocní trh 8, Staré Město, Prague 1 (2423 8355); Nádražní 25, Smíchov, Prague 5 (5732 2622).

Middle Eastern

Casablanca

Na příkopě 10, Prague 1 (2421 0519). Metro Můstek/3, 9, 14, 24 tram. **Open** 11am-midnight daily. **Main courses** 250-500 Kč. **Credit** AmEx, MC, V. **Map** p308 J4.

French-Moroccan tagines, harissa soups and home-made sweetmeats exude sincerity, but this is decidedly a place of high production values. And it's priced like one. For an evening of all-out indulgence amid satin pillows, houkahs and the odd belly dancer, however, it's hard to outdo.

Seafood

Alcron

Štěpánská 40, Prague 1 (2282 0038). Metro Můstek/3, 9, 14, 24 tram. **Open** 5.30-10.30pm Mon-Sat. **Main courses** 600-1,200 Kč. **Credit** AmEx, DC, MC, V. **Map** p311 K6.

This historic hotel dining room is a symphony in miniature. With just seven tables, it is nonetheless a serious seafood star in this deeply landlocked Czech country. Chef Jiří Štift is a master of the pike-perch and the savoury sauce, while the decor out-shines even that of the swanky SAS Radisson Hotel. The hotel was known as the Alcron during the

Bold cuisine in posh environs at **Červená Tabulka**. *See p137.*

Prague's first vegetarian restaurant still has the latest opening hours around with all-night pastas, couscous and meatless Mexican food. The closet-sized kitchen turns out food of variable quality and the restaurant, though the place to meet up for clubbers (*see p227*), is jammed so full of ornamental furnishings that your knees get bashed. Nevertheless, it remains as popular as ever and every movie star in town makes an obligatory visit to the groovy backroom lounge.

U Govindy Vegetarian Club
Soukenická 27, Prague 1 (2481 6631). Metro Náměstí Republiky/5, 8, 14, 26 tram. **Open** 11am-5.30pm Mon-Sat. **Main courses** 75 Kč set meal. **No credit cards. Map** p309 L2.

Cheap although not so cheerful, this Indian restaurant offers an affordable, basic self-service vegetarian Indian meal for a mere 75 Kč. The simple fare can be embellished with extras, such as pakora vegetables on a skewer, for another 30 Kč or so. At these prices you wouldn't expect much charm, and, frankly, you don't get any. But the good news is that virtually all of the ingredients served here are grown on the Krishnas' organic farm outside Prague. Or, is that actually good news?
Branch: Na Hrázi 5, Palmovka, Prague 8 (8482 3805).

World

Opera Garden
Zahrada v opeře
Legerova 75, Prague 1 (2423 9685/www. zahradavopere.cz). Metro Muzeum/11 tram. **Open** 11am-1am daily. **Main courses** 165-440 Kč. **Credit** AmEx, DC, MC, V. **Map** p311 L6.

The Opera Garden restaurant, as it translates into English, inadvertently came under siege when the Czech government set up a security phalanx to safeguard the adjoining Radio Free Europe offices. But no one has yet minded walking under gun barrels for the intricate, sumptuous feasts at this Czech and international dining room. Tuna steak in filo is a delight, while some of the dessert platters are almost too beautiful to eat. Fabulously airy minimalist decor and unsurpassed cuisine served by gliding waiters.

A garden indeed at **Opera Garden**.

interwar First Republic, but the name now applies only to the tiny dining room which sits off to one side of the larger main restaurant here, La Rotonde, so ask to make sure you're in the right place.

Vegetarian

Radost FX Café
Bělehradská 120, Prague 2 (2425 4776/ www.radostfx.cz). Metro IP Pavlova/4, 6, 11, 16, 22, 34 tram. **Open** *Restaurant* 11am-4am Mon-Sat; 10.30am-4am Sun. *Club* 10pm-4am Mon-Sat. **Main courses** 150-300 Kč. **No credit cards. Map** p311 L8.

Pubs

Novoměstský Pivovar
Vodičkova 20, Prague 1 (2223 2448/www. npivovar.cz). Metro Můstek/3, 9, 14, 24 tram. **Open** 8am-11.30pm Mon-Fri; 11.30am-11.30pm Sat; noon-10pm Sun. **Main courses** 120-230 Kč. **Credit** AmEx, MC, V. **Map** p310 J6.

This is one of surprisingly few brew pubs in Prague. The vast underground warren of rooms is fascinating to explore and, perhaps unsurprisingly, a good glass of beer is served here. On the other hand, in the rush, the bills can occasionally get confused, so it's worth taking the time to check your total.

Cafés

Café Break

Štěpánská 32, Prague 1 (2223 1065). Metro Můstek/3, 9, 14, 24 tram. **Open** 8am-11pm Mon-Fri; 9.30am-7pm Sat. **No credit cards. Map** p311 K6.
This café is bright, lively and a lifeline for expats around Wenceslas Square. The owner camps out here all day, ensuring that everybody feels welcome, a practice that is absolutely all too rare in Prague. Window seats offer a prime spot for people-ogling, while your formally polite waiter brings on fresh oysters, French table wine by the glass, or a meal-sized salad or ciabatta sandwich – and that's just lunch. More substantial plates of lasagne and steaks are served in the evening.

Café Imperial

Na Poříčí 15, Prague 1 (2231 6012/www. hotelimperial.cz). Metro Náměstí Republiky/5, 8, 14, 26 tram. **Open** 9am-11pm Mon-Thur, Sun; 9am-12pm Fri-Sat. **Main courses** 150-180 Kč. **Credit** AmEx, MC, V. **Map** p309 L2.
Once the very picture of decadence during Czechoslovakia's First Republic, the former Café Imperial has yet to really finish being renovated. But that hasn't stopped people from filling tables where they sit to take in the incredible floor-to-ceiling art nouveau sculpted porcelain tiles. Order the Saturnin's Bowl of *koblihy* (jam doughnuts) if you'd like to spend 1,943 Kč for the privilege of throwing them at anyone you like. It's good to know that the attached hostel (*see p54*) is also a major bargain.

Café Louvre

Národní třída 20, Prague 1 (2493 0949). Metro Národní třída/6, 9, 18, 22 tram. **Open** 8am-11.30pm daily. **Credit** AmEx, DC, MC, V. **Map** p308 H5.
A long, lofty café that somehow manages to get away with a garish cream and turquoise colour combination, perhaps because it leads to a fine backroom pool hall. Solid weekend breakfasts.

French Institute Café

Štěpánská 35, Prague 1 (2140 1011/www.ifp.cz). Metro Můstek/3, 9, 14, 24 tram. **Open** 8.30am-7pm Mon-Fri. **No credit cards. Map** p311 K6.
A crucial source of croissants, philosophy and good, strong espresso before the opening of Chez Marcel and Le Café Colonial (*for both see p127*). The French Institute carries on as a Gallic nerve centre with an unapologetically Francophile art gallery downstairs and free cinema adjoining. Elegant, prime posing space with an open courtyard and a fair chance of starting an intellectual romance.

The Globe Bookstore & Coffeehouse

Pštrossova 6, Prague 1 (2491 6264/www. globebookstore.cz). Metro Národní třída/6, 9, 18, 22, 23 tram. **Open** 10am-midnight Mon-Thur, Sun; 10am-1am Fri, Sat. **No credit cards. Map** p310 G7.
The city's original expat bookstore café has been pegged from the outset as the literary heart of post-

Decadence rules at **Café Imperial**.

Eat, Drink, Shop

Getting busy at **Kavárna v sedmém nebi**. See p143.

revolutionary Prague, blamed for encouraging all the wannabe Hemingways. The Globe carries its burden graciously, offering a cosy reading room and comfortable café surroundings to scribblers of both novellas and postcards. Passable pasta salads and such do for food, easily surpassed by the tall lattes and enormous brownies. But books are at the heart of things: Gore Vidal is signing one Sunday, a struggling poet is reading the next. The internet terminals and bulletin board are vital lifelines for expat life.

U Svatého Vojtěcha

Vojtěšská 14, Prague 1 (2493 3087). Metro Národní třída/6, 9, 17, 18, 22 tram. **Open** 8am-11pm Mon-Fri; 10am-10pm Sat; 10am-8pm Sun. *July, Aug* 10am-11pm daily. **No credit cards**. **Map** p310 G7.
Just behind the National Theatre and largely untainted by the presence of non-Czechs, this quiet, unassuming café is frequented by local actors and intellectual types who sit by the large window, have a leisurely smoke and leaf through the morning papers looking pensive. No food to speak of.

Tearooms

Velryba

Opatovická 24, Prague 1 (2491 2391). Metro Národní třída/6, 9, 18, 22, 23 tram. **Open** 11am-

noon Mon-Thur, Sat, Sun; 11am-2pm Fri.
No credit cards. **Map** p310 H6.
A firmly established young Czech hipster hangout, the Whale combines clamorous front-room dining on pastas and chicken steaks with backroom chess and a cellar gallery specialising in fringe art and photography. Curiously, the bar only serves bottled Gambrinus. The lack of air once prompted a no-smoking policy that lasted about a week before the nicotine-crazed clientele won the day. Avoid the healthy sounding tofu karbanátky – it isn't anything of the sort.

Dobrá čajovna

Václavské náměstí 14, Prague 1 (2423 1480/ www.cajovna.com/www.tea.cz). Metro Můstek/3, 9, 14, 24 tram. **Open** 10am-11pm Mon-Sat; 1.30-11pm Sun. **No credit cards**. **Map** p308 J5.
The romanticised Asian fantasy setting was an early Prague *čaj hit* (tea house), with its dozens of Darjeelings, Assams, Algerian mint leaves and unpronounceable Chinese varieties. Ring the brass bell that comes with your menu to summon a serene, sandalled waiter.

Further afield

Dejvice

Café Orange

Puškinovo náměstí 13, Prague 6 (0603 894 499 mobile). Metro Hradčanská. **Open** 10am-11pm Mon-Fri. **No credit cards**.
Prague's most overlooked café sometimes hosts jazz trios on Friday nights, making it even better for a secret rendezvous than it already was. The first daytime venue in Prague 6 with fresh OJ, lattes, mozzarella ciabattas and street tables, it's on a quiet square that's hard to find. Worth it, though, if a bit too quiet some of the time.

Ristorante da Emanuel

Charles de Gaulla 4, Prague 6 (2431 2934). Metro Dejvice/25 tram. **Open** noon-11pm daily. **Main courses** 250-450 Kč. **Credit** AmEx, MC, V.
With new menu additions like swordfish carpaccio and *pappardelle al cinghiale* (mildly spiced ground boar), this little neighborhood pasta joint always requires reservations these days. Expatriate Italians commute across Prague to eat at the tiny tables in an atmosphere of doting servers, terrible seaport decor and Charlie Chaplin signs to the loo.

Holešovice

La Creperie

Janovského 4, Prague 7 (2087 8040/www. lacreperie.cz). Metro Vltavská/1, 8, 14, 25 tram. **Open** 9am-11pm Mon-Sat; 9am-10pm Sun. **No credit cards**. **Map** p312 D2.
This French-owned niche serves generous sized crepes, both sweet and savoury, for a pittance.

Eat, Drink, Shop

Seating here is in a comfortable but closet-sized basement, so it's probably not ideal for office parties. Above average wine list, and fresh croissants.

Puccelini

Tusarova 52, Prague 7 (8387 1134). Metro Vltavská/1, 3, 14, 25 tram. **Open** 11am-11pm Mon-Fri; noon-11pm Sat, Sun. **Main courses** 450-550 Kč. **Credit** AmEx, DC, MC, V. **Map** p312 E2.

A major Italian bistro contender in this otherwise bleak semi-industrial Prague district. Adorned throughout with music scores and lamps hidden inside trumpets, Puccelini's wood-fired pizzas are dappled with excellent, punchy sauce. But starters like baked stuffed aubergine and mozzarella, potato and thyme soup are just as impressive. There is a fairly good winelist here and the house tiramisu is a creamy, generous wonder.

Karlín

Orso Bruno

Za Poříčskou bránou 16, Prague 8 (2231 0178). Metro Florenc/8, 24 tram. **Open** 11am-3pm, 6-11pm Mon-Sat. **Main courses** 130-270 Kč. **Credit** MC, V.

This is an authentic, family-run Italian pasta spot where subtle sauces dominate along with a daft and inexplicable decor of teddy bear motifs. Ignore the fuzzy bears and note instead that the great value and endearing service here make it worth veering out of Old Town to the blighted next-door district.

Smíchov

Café Savoy

Zborovská 68, Prague 5 (5732 9860/www.cafesavoy.cz). Tram 6, 9, 12, 22. **Open** 8am-midnight daily. **Main courses** 300-600 Kč. **Credit** AmEx, MC, V.

This is a bright, high-ceilinged 19th-century café that's had a modern makeover. It offers an excellent menu of fresh mussels, courtesy of its new owner, the seafood importer across the street. Classy service and a fashionable crowd.

Kavárna v sedmém nebi

Zborovská 68, Prague 5 (5731 8110). Tram 6, 9, 12, 22. **Open** 10am-1am Mon-Fri; 2pm-1am Sat, Sun. **No credit cards.**

Take a perch in the loft to spy on those in the comfy junkshop chairs below, or slip into the back room for a quiet read and a cup of green tea. This mecca for the local film community is half work of sculpture, half living room. The menu is limited to coffee and tea along with *babovka*, or Czech Bundt cake, toasted sandwiches and potato crisps.

What's on the menu

Czech menus generally list two categories of dishes: *minutky*, cooked to order (which may take ages), and *hotová jídla*, ready-to-serve fare. The usual accompaniments are rice, potatoes or fried béchamel dough (*krokety*), all of which are ordered separately. When dining in pubs, the closest thing to fresh veg is often *obloha*, a garnish of pickles, or a tomato on a single leaf of cabbage. Tasty appetisers are Prague ham with horseradish, or rich soups (*polévka*), while a dessert staple is *palačinky*, filled pancakes.

Meals (*jídla*)
snídaně breakfast; **oběd** lunch; **večeře** dinner.

Preparation (*příprava*)
bez masa or **bezmasá jídla** without meat; **čerstvé** fresh; **domácí** home-made; **dušené** steamed; **grilované** grilled; **míchaný** mixed; **na roštu** roasted; **pečené** baked; **plněné** stuffed; **smažené** fried; **špíz** grilled on a skewer; **uzené** smoked; **vařené** boiled.

Basics (*základní*)
chléb bread; **cukr** sugar; **drůbež** poultry; **karbanátek** patty of unspecified content; **máslo** butter; **maso** meat; **ocet** vinegar;

olej oil; **omáčka** sauce; **ovoce** fruit; **pepř** pepper; **rohlík** roll; **ryby** fish; **smetana** cream; **sůl** salt; **sýr** cheese; **vejce** eggs; **zelenina** vegetables.

Drinks (*nápoje*)
čaj tea; **káva** coffee; **mléko** milk; **pivo** beer; **pomerančový džus** orange juice; **sodovka** soda; **víno** wine; **voda** water.

Appetisers (*předkrmy*)
boršč Russian beetroot soup (borscht); **chlebíček** open-faced mayo and meat sandwich; **hovězí vývar** beef broth;

The Sushi Bar

*Zborovská 49, Prague 5 (0603 244882 mobile/
www.sushi.cz). Tram 6, 9, 12, 22.* **Open** noon-10pm
daily. **Main courses** 300-600 Kč. **Credit** DC, MC, V.
This is a minimalist maki bar with maximal prices.
The *nigiri* is served in small, beautiful portions on
small, beautiful, enamel plates. Focus on the fine
view of the old Savoy across the street rather than
on your mounting bill.

Vinohrady

Barracuda

*Krymská 2, Prague 2 (7174 0599). Metro Náměstí
Míru/4, 22 tram.* **Open** *Upstairs* 11.30am-11.30pm
Mon-Fri; 5-11.30pm Sat, Sun. *Downstairs* 5-11.30pm
Mon-Fri. **Main courses** 130-270 Kč. **Credit** AmEx,
DC, MC, V.
Judging by the inevitable dinner-hour rush here,
Prague has voted this little cellar in desert hues its
best Mexican restaurant. No complimentary tortilla
chips, but the sizzling fajitas and overstuffed tacos.

Grosseto Pizzeria

*Francouzká 2, Vinohrady, Prague 2 (2425 2778/
www.grosseto.cz). Metro Náměstí Míru/4, 16, 22, 23
tram.* **Open** 11.30am-11pm daily. **Main courses**
100-200 Kč. **No credit cards. Map** p313 A3.

With two booming locations, Grosseto does flame-
cooked pizzas, most notably the four-cheese version
– beware imitations elsewhere using anything called
eidam or *hermelín* (generic Czech cheeses). The mine-
strone is hearty, too, and the carpaccio in tomato
sauce is perfect for sopping up with the complimentary fresh hot peasant bread.
Branch: Jugoslávských partyzánů 8, Dejvice,
Prague 6 (3334 2694).

Medúza

*Belgická 17, Prague 2 (2251 5107). Metro Náměstí
Míru/4, 22, 34 tram.* **Open** 10am-1am daily.
No credit cards. Map p311 M9.
Relaxed and friendly women-run café with good coffee and a limited menu of snacks and sandwiches.
Comfortable old furniture, antique mirrors and faded
photos on the walls, complemented by classical
music or old Czech chansons playing in the background, make this a great place to chill.

Modrá řeka

*Mánesova 13, Prague 2 (2225 1601). Metro
Muzeum/11 tram.* **Open** 11am-11pm Mon-Fri;
5-11pm Sat; 3-11pm Sun. **Main courses** 130-270 Kč.
No credit cards. Map p313 A2.
Muhamed Londrc and his wife run this Vinohrady
hideaway, where they welcome customers like prodi-
gal children and proceed to stuff them senseless with

► **What's on the menu
(continued)**

jazyk tongue; **kaviár** caviar; **paštika** pâté;
polévka soup; **uzený losos** smoked salmon.

Meat (*maso*)

biftek beefsteak; **hovězí** beef; **játra** liver;
jehně lamb; **jelení** venison; **kanec** boar;
klobása sausage; **králík** rabbit; **ledvinky**
kidneys; **párek** sausage; **slanina** bacon;
srnčí roebuck; **šunka** ham; **telecí** veal;
vepřové pork; **zvěřina** game.

Poultry & fish (*drůbež a ryby*)

bažant pheasant; **husa** goose; **kachna** duck;
kapr carp; **křepelka** quail; **krocan** turkey; **kuře**
chicken; **losos** salmon; **pstruh** trout; **úhoř** eel.

Main meals (*hlavní jídla*)

guláš goulash; **sekaná** meat loaf; **řízek**
schnitzel; **smažený sýr** fried cheese; **svíčková**
beef in cream sauce; **vepřová játra na cibulce**
pig's liver stewed with onion; **vepřové koleno**
pork knee; **vepřový řízek** fried breaded pork.

Side dishes (*přílohy*)

brambor potato; **bramborák** potato pancake;
bramborová kaše mashed potatoes; **hranolky**
chips; **kaše** mashed potatoes; **knedlíky**
dumplings; **krokety** potato or béchamel dough

croquettes; **obloha** small lettuce and tomato
salad; **rýže** rice; **salát** salad; **šopský salát**
cucumber, tomato and curd salad; **tatarská
omáčka** tartar sauce; **zelí** cabbage.

Cheese (*sýr*)

balkán a saltier feta; **eidam** hard white
cheese; **hermelín** soft, similar to bland brie;
Madeland Swiss cheese; **niva** blue cheese;
pivný sýr beer-flavoured semi-soft cheese;
primátor Swiss cheese; **tavený sýr** packaged
cheese spread; **tvaroh** soft curd cheese.

Vegetables (*zelenina*)

česnek garlic; **chřest** asparagus; **cibule**
onion(s); **čočka** lentils; **fazole** beans;
feferonky chilli peppers; **hrášek** peas;
kukuřice corn; **květák** cauliflower; **mrkev**
carrot; **okurka** cucumber; **petržel** parsley;

home-made *somun* bread, *čevabčiči* (finger sausages) served in piles of ten and *Šarena dolma* (lamb-stuffed grape leaves with peppers and onions).

Vršovice

Akropolis

Kubelíkova 27, Žižkov, Prague 3 (9633 0913). Metro Jiřího z Poděbrad/11 tram. **Open** 4pm-2am Mon-Sat; 4pm-midnight Sun. **No credit cards. Map** p313 B2.

As much a culture hub as restaurant, the Akropolis dining room was designed by surrealist artists. Fortunately, the cuisine is less surreal, with mild versions of chicken satays and such to take in before or after a show in the adjoining concert hall. Service is laid-back to say the least.

Café Atelier

Na Kovárně 8, Prague 10 (7172 1866). Trams 4, 22, 23. **Open** 11.45am-midnight Mon-Sat. **Main courses** 350-550 Kč. **No credit cards.**

Outstanding French and continental cuisine in a modern, elegant brick and whitewash space that's always packed. A mouth-watering tomato *mille-feuille* and rabbit with Dijon mustard are two top vote-getters, plus there is a top-notch wine list. The chocolate mousse is pure sin.

Včelín

Kodaňská 5, Prague 10 (7174 2541). Tram 4, 22, 23. **Open** 11am-midnight Mon-Fri; 11.30am-1am Sat; 11.30am-11pm Sun. **Main courses** 250-400Kč. **Credit** MC, V.

The Beehive is a well-named gathering spot for up-and-coming Prague creative types, but without the attitude that ruins most such places. The quick, amiable waitstaff hustle from table to table bearing any of three great Czech beers on tap – Kozel, Radegast and Pilsner Urquell. The house special, gnocchi in spinach sauce, is the hit of this little room, which is done up with graphic design magazine covers.

Žižkov

Mailsi

Lipanská 1, Prague 3 (2271 7783). Tram 5, 9, 26. **Open** noon-3pm, 6pm-midnight daily. **Main courses** 250-350 Kč. **Credit** AmEx, DC, MC, V. **Map** p313 C2.

There's not much atmosphere here, just lots of good, solid Pakistani food, which goes down well in Žižkov, one of Prague's few truly ethnically mixed districts. The Kebabs, dahl and other traditional dishes are all expertly prepared and spiced and served up with fast and friendly gusto.

Eat, Drink, Shop

---

rajčata tomatoes; **salát** lettuce; **špenát** spinach; **žampiony** mushrooms; **zelí** cabbage.

Fruit (*ovoce*)

ananas pineapple; **banány** banana; **borůvky** blueberries; **broskev** peach; **hrozny** grapes; **hruška** pear; **jablko** apple; **jahody** strawberries; **jeřabina** rowanberries; **mandle** almonds; **meruňka** apricot; **ořechy** nuts; **pomeranč** orange; **rozinky** raisins; **švestky** plums; **třešně** cherries.

Desserts (*moučník*)

buchty traditional curd-filled cakes; **čokoláda** chocolate; **dort** layered cake; **koláč** cake with various fillings; **ovocné knedlíky** fruit dumplings; **palačinka** crepe; **pohár** ice-cream sundae; **šlehačka** whipped cream; **zákusek** cake; **závin** strudel; **žemlovka** bread pudding with apples and cinnamon; **zmrzlina** ice-cream.

Useful phrases

May I see the menu? **Mohu vidět jídelní lístek?**
Do you have...? **Máte...?**

I am a vegetarian **Jsem vegetarián/ vegetariánka** (m/f)
How is it prepared? **Jak je to připravené?**
Did you say 'beer cheese'? **Říkal jste 'pivní sýr'?**
Wow, that smells! **Páni, to smrdí!**
Can I have it without...? **Mohu mít bez...?**
No ketchup on my pizza, please **Nechci kečup na pizzu, prosím.**
I didn't order this **Neobjednal jsem si to**
How much longer will it be? **Jak dlouho to ještě bude?**
I've got the Sahara desert here [*use when your waiter's in hiding*] **Tady je Sahara**
The bill, please **Účet, prosím**
I can't eat this and I won't pay for it! [*use with extreme caution*] **Nedá se to jíst a nezaplatím to**
Takeaway/to go **S sebou**
A beer, please **Pivo, prosím**
Two beers, please **Dvě piva, prosím**
Same again, please **Ještě jednou, prosím**
What'll you have? **Co si dáte?**
Not for me, thanks **Pro mě ne, děkuji**
No ice, thanks **Bez ledu, děkuji**
He's really smashed **Je totálně namazaný**

Pubs & Bars

Cocktails for two, please – *pivo, prosím* is only half the story.

With its 500-year history as a nation of brewmasters, you might not expect the Czech Republic to feature many decent cocktail bars – which shows just how misleading reputations can be. The magic words *pivo, prosím* (beer, please) won't get you very far in some of Prague's new bars. In one three-block area of Old Town there are three cocktail bars – **Bugsy's** (*see p149*), **Tretter's Cocktail Bar** (*see p151*) and **Alcohol Bar** (*see p148*) – that stand up against any a major Western European capital has to offer. While the crowds here vary wildly, all feature bar staff who shake, rattle and roll all night while never letting you see them sweat. Even in the traditional working class district of Žižkov (famed for having more pubs per capita than any other place on earth), classic American dry Martini glasses can now be heard clinking. Just head for **Hapu** (*see p157*), a Czech-owned and -run living room of a bar. It's not much to look at, it's true, but just ask for a Continental or a frozen Margarita and watch the bar staff light up. Then kiss tomorrow goodbye.

These recent developments on the bar scene dovetail nicely with the more established beer drinking tradition. There's still no place better for pub crawling in terms of both affordability and quality than Prague. You can savour the workhorses of *pivo* – Pilsner Urquell, Radegast, Staropramen and Gambrinus – just about anywhere. Then head for the speciality bars for less well-known Czech beer delights: **Zoo Bar** (*see p153*) for Herold, **Letenský zámeček**

(*see p155*) for Bernard, **U Černého vola** (*see below*) for Kozel, and so on. Pubs now run the gamut from clean, well-lit brewery-owned places like **Kolkovna** (*see p151*) to the timeless neighbourhood beerhalls like the **Radegast Pub** (*see p151*). Often they feature hearty Bohemian fare like smoked meat platters and/or intriguing pub food such as the magnificently smelly *pivní sýr* (beer cheese). With a few exceptions noted below, though, there's still nothing much to eat when you're out after 10pm.

All that's left to do at the end of an evening's drinking in Prague is to make sure you catch the right night tram. After that you're home and dry – so to speak.

Hradčany

U Černého vola
Loretánské náměstí 1, Prague 1 (2051 3481).
Tram 22. **Open** 10am-10pm daily. **No credit cards. Map** p306 B3.
One of the best pubs in Prague. The murals make it look like it's been here forever, but in fact the Black Ox was built after World War II. Its superb location, right above the Castle, made it a prime target for redevelopment in the post-1989 building frenzy, but the rugged regulars, in co-operation with the former Beer Party, bought it to ensure that local bearded artisans would have at least one place where they could afford to drink. The Kozel beer is perfection and, although the snacks are pretty basic, they do their job of lining the stomach for long sessions.

The best Pubs & bars

For taking a break from beer
La Tonnelle (*see p156*) and La Bodega Flamenca (*see p155*).

For the vintage beerhall experience
U medvídků (*see p152*), U Buldoka (*see p156*), U Holanů (*see p157*), U Sadu (*see p158*) and U Sudu (*see p155*).

For 'scoping out the action'
Chateau (*see p149*) and Solidní nejistota (*see p154*).

For buying rounds for struggling artists
Akropolis (*see p157*) and U vystřelenýho oka (*see p158*).

For buying rounds for struggling expats
Fraktal (*see p155*), Jáma (*see p153*) and Ř Bar (*see p154*).

For a blast from the past, Prague style
Bar Práce (*see p156*).

Eat, Drink, Shop

St Nicholas Café: a stellar cellar. *See p148.*

Malá Strana

Baráčnická rychta

Tržiště 23, Prague 1 (5753 2461). Metro Malostranská/12, 22, 23 tram. **Open** noon-midnight Mon-Sat; noon-9pm Sun. **No credit cards.** **Map** p307 D3.

Czech pub-goers complain frequently that the tourist trade has all but killed the indigenous pub culture – immortalised in Jan Neruda's *Prague Tales* – that thrived in Malá Strana from the 19th century onwards. This place is one of the few authentic remnants. Just off Nerudova, Baráčnická rychta eludes the mob behind a series of archways. Beyond these, it's split into two: a small beerhall frequented by hardcore *pivo* drinkers, both of the student and middle-aged variety, and a downstairs music hall that these days features live gigs by local rock hopefuls increasingly often. Obvious tourists may catch the occasional scowl in here, but in general this is a friendly place.

Blue Light

Josefská 1, Prague 1 (5753 3126). Metro Malostranská/12, 22, 23 tram. **Open** 6pm-3am daily. **No credit cards.** **Map** p307 E3.

Cosy bar featuring occasional live jazz music, jazzy sounds on the stereo, and jazz posters all over the dilapidated walls. By day Blue Light is a convivial spot to sit with a friend, especially when there's room at the bar. At night it gets more rowdy and conversation becomes nigh impossible but the vibe is certainly infectious. The bar stocks a good selection of malt whiskies.

Café El Centro

Maltézské námesti 9, Prague 1 (5753 3343/www.elcentro.czrb.cz). Metro Malostranská/ 12, 18, 22, 23 tram. **Open** noon-midnight daily. **Credit** AmEx, MC, V. **Map** p305 E4.

Easily overlooked Malá Strana bar just a block off the main square that specialises in mambo soundtracks and tropical cocktails. Efforts to expand into a full restaurant specialising in paella aren't winning over the Daiquiri lovers, but the postage-stamp patio at the rear is a boon.

Jo's Bar

Malostranské námestí 7, Prague 1 (0602 971 478/www.josbarprague.com). Metro Malostranská/ 12, 22, 23 tram. **Open** 11am-2am daily. **Credit** MC, V. **Map** p307 E3.

This street-level bar is an adjunct to the rollicking downstairs Jo's Bar & Garáž (*see p225*). It was once renowned for being every backpacker's first stop in Prague and the original source of nachos in the Czech Republic, but founder Glen Emery has since moved on and Jo's is under new ownership. It's still a good place to meet fellow travellers, but it lacks soul these days – as well as the once rare Mexican food menu and foxy servers.

Petřínské Terasy

Seminářská zahrada 13, Prague 1 (9000 0457). Metro Malostranská/12, 18, 22, 23 tram. **Open** 11am-11pm daily. **No credit cards.** **Map** p306 C4.

One of two tourist traps on Petřín Hill, the Petřín Terraces offer exquisite views of Prague Castle and the city, unfortnately alongside expensive Krušovice and indifferent service.

Double clown, please

The panák or 'little clown' – as shots are known – is a serious business in the Czech drinking world. If you'll take a shot with someone, and match them one for one all night, you're to be trusted and will have a lifelong friend. That is, should they remember who you are the next day.

Becherovka, a ubiquitous sweetish yellow herbal liqueur from Karlovy Vary, is drunk straight or cut with tonic, in which case it's known as *beton* – 'concrete'. **Fernet**, a bitter liqueur similar to Hungary's Unicum, goes better with beer. This, too, can be lightened with tonic water to create a *Bavorské pivo* or 'Bavarian beer' – which, of course, has no beer in it and is unknown in Bavaria. The cheapest ticket to oblivion, and thus favoured by local drunks, is **Tuzemský Rum**, made from beets. With sugar, hot water and a slice of lemon it actually makes a good warming grog in winter. **Borovička** is a juniper brandy, more Slovak than Czech and not unlike Dutch Jenever, while **Slivovice** (plum brandy), if not home-made, is smooth and goes down a treat.

Absinthe, at a staggering 170 proof, has long been banned in most countries. It's a wormwood distillate, but contains a slightly smaller (and allegedly less brain-damaging) percentage of wood alcohol than the version that once pickled the best minds of Paris. It's a translucent green liquid that tastes much like alcoholic shampoo.

The proper ritual is to soak a spoonful of sugar with absinthe then set the sugar alight in the spoon to caramelise it. When the fire goes out, dump the spoonful back into the glass and stir. Then hang on to your socks.

St Nicholas Café

Tržiště 10, Prague 1 (5753 0204). Metro Malostranská/12, 22, 23 tram. **Open** 1pm-1am daily. **Credit** MC, V. **Map** p307 D3.

An atmospheric vaulted cellar decked out with steamer trunk tables, painted arches and Pilsner Urquell on tap. A mellow but lively crowd gathers in the nooks for late evening conversation about nothing in particular. Also good for giving the brew a rest and taking up a glass of Havana Club rum.

U Malého Glena

Karmelitská 23, Malá Strana, Prague 1 (5753 1717/ www.malyglen.cz). Metro Malostranská/12, 22 tram. **Open** 10am-2am daily. **No credit cards**. **Map** p307 D4.

From looking at the rowdy pub at street level you'd never guess that the downstairs bar is one of Prague's top jazz holes. Tall Staropramen mugs are swung with gusto by expats and Czechs, the servers are as sexy as they get and there are large tables and benches, perfect if you're in a big group. Always an easygoing, affable vibe, but less noisy in the afternoons.

U zavěšenýho kafe

Úvoz 6, Prague 1 (5753 2868). Metro Malostranská/ 12, 22, 23 tram. **Open** 11am-midnight daily. **No credit cards**. **Map** p306 C3.

The Hanging Coffee Cup is a mellow, thoroughly Czech spot with plank flooring, traditional grub (onion soup and duck with sauerkraut) and a long association with local artists and intellectuals. The name comes from an old tradition of paying for a cup of coffee for someone who may arrive later without funds – in which case the coffee, or *kafe*, is considered to be 'hanging' for them.

ZanziBar

Lázeňská 6, Prague 1 (no phone). Metro Malostranská/12, 22, 57 tram. **Open** noon-3am Mon-Sat; 5pm-3am Sun. **No credit cards**. **Map** p307 E3.

If you've just spent half your salary on Italian boots and a Joe Camel expedition jacket, you won't find a better place to show them off – nor more competition. Crowds of revellers orbit around the drink specials lists, grooving to James Brown tracks, and nobody seems to mind paying the steepest prices in town for clumsily mixed drinks. Or maybe everyone's much too cool to care.

Staré Město

Alcohol Bar

Dušní 6, Prague 1 (2481 1744). Metro Staroměstská/17, 18 tram. **Open** 7pm-3am daily. **Credit** AmEx, MC, V. **Map** p308 J3.

The Alcohol Bar – not surprisingly – has a wall of single malt whiskies, with 16-year-old distillations from what looks like every other town in Scotland and Ireland, plus rums and tequilas from respected distillers all over the Caribbean and Mexico. A New York-style sophistication pervades, the barmen are true gents, and the DJs play great house.

Banana Bar

Štupartská 9, Prague 1 (2232 4801/ www.laprovence.cz). Metro Náměstí Republiky/ 5, 8, 14, tram. **Open** Bar/restaurant 11am-2am daily. **Credit** AmEx, MC, V. **Map** p308 J3.

This establishment is in fact home to a bar, café and restaurant. The Banana Bar is a standard-bearer of cheesiness, something that's no small achievement in a new market economy where flashiness often passes for substance. The patrons are mainly Czech yuppies won over by La Provence's multiple identities. The attached café features overpriced standard grub while the downstairs restaurant goes for a mass-produced French country inn ethos. This place is avoidable but it is good for a laugh as you crawl through the many other Old Town options in the vicinity.

Blatnička

Michalská 6, Prague 1 (2422 5836). Metro Můstek/ 6, 9, 18, 22, 23 tram. **Open** 11am-11pm daily. **Credit** MC, V. **Map** p308 H4.

Hidden just off Karlova and away from the tourist hordes, this wine cellar masquerades as a tiny, smoke-filled bar that at first glance appears most unwelcoming. To the back and down the stairs, though, there's a snug little restaurant serving unimaginative Czech food to soak up the drinkable Moravian wines straight from the barrel and served up in half- and one-litre jugs.

Bugsy's

Pařížská 10, Prague 1 (entrance on Kostečná) (232 9943/www.bugsysbar.cz). Metro Staroměstská/ 17, 18 tram. **Open** 7pm-2am daily. **Credit** AmEx, MC, V. **Map** p308 H3.

Living up to its swish Pařížská location, Bugsy's offers a book-length drinks list including 200 cocktails and a bar staff good enough to mix them properly. Prices prohibit all but flush tycoons and wealthy ne'er-do-wells, but it's still packed most evenings. The bar is fun to perch at but the tables are less inviting.

Café Konvikt

Bartolomějská 11, Prague 1 (2423 2427). Metro Národní třída/6, 9, 18, 22, 23 tram. **Open** 9am-1am Mon-Fri; noon-1am Sat, Sun. **No credit cards.** **Map** p308 G5/H5.

Popular, well-lit Old Town spot at which to catch Prague's new generation of penniless creatives with a taste for poor wine. Small, edible sweets are served but it's really just about drink, talk and smoke here – all done in earnest.

Chateau

Jakubská 2, Prague 1 (2231 6328). Metro Náměstí Republiky/5, 14, 26 tram. **Open** noon-3am Mon-Thur; noon-4am Fri; 4pm-4am Sat; 4pm-2am Sun. **No credit cards.** **Map** p308 J3.

Prague's main hangout for young Americans on the make has much in common with hell. It's unbearably hot, crowded, loud and red. It's also the most popular bar in town, which makes for a convincing argument against democracy.

Duende

Karoliny Světlé 30, Prague 1 (2222 1255/ www.duende.cz). Metro Národní třída/6, 9, 17, 18, 22, 23 tram. **Open** 11am-1am daily. **No credit cards.** **Map** p308 G5.

Accordion music emanates from the sound system and fringed lampshades splash diffused light across the crowd of regulars. Duende has become a living room for low-budget Prague intellectuals, who usually ignore the specials menu and just order coffee. The free Sunday movies in English are always a bit of a laugh and the walnut liqueur (*ořechovka*) is a rare old Czech treat.

Duende: laid-back, low-cost and high-brow.

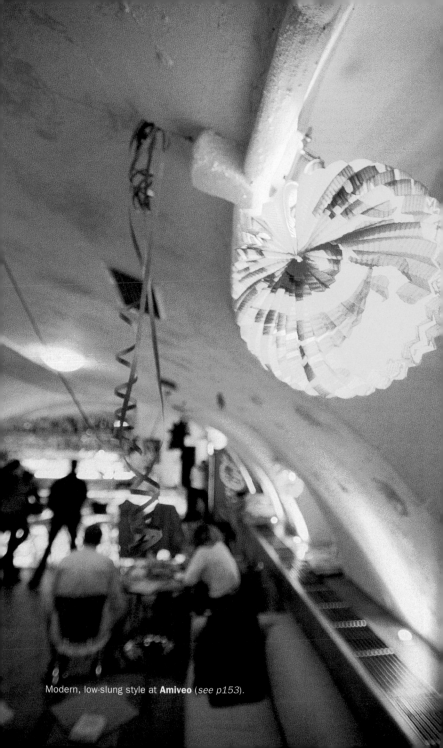
Modern, low-slung style at **Amiveo** (*see p153*).

Escape

*Dušní 8, Prague 1 (2481 8498). Metro
Staroměstská/5, 18, 14 tram.* **Open** 7pm-2am daily.
No credit cards. Map p308 J2.
The main competition for Alcohol Bar (*see p148*) next
door is several steps behind but endeavours to bring
off a plush atmosphere, still relatively rare in Prague.
The clubby soundtrack goes with the gin and tonics.
A good option when nearby bars are overflowing.

James Joyce

*Liliová 10, Prague 1 (2424 8793/www.jamesjoyce.cz).
Metro Staroměstská/17, 18 tram.* **Open** 10.30am-
12.30am daily. **Credit** AmEx, MC, V. **Map** p308 G4.
The Hooray Henry hangout of the expat crowd. Few
Czechs can afford the prices, and that is partly the
purpose of this expat oasis. Arrogance aside, it must
be said that the braying hearties who come here do
know how to have a piss-up. Irish stews and fry-ups
are well done amid an interior imported from a 19th-
century Belfast church.

Kolkovna

*V kolkovně 8, Prague 1 (2481 9701).
Metro Staroměstská/17, 18 tram.* **Open** *Music bar*
1pm-2am daily. *Pub* 11am-midnight daily.
Credit AmEx, MC, V. **Map** p308 J2.
Owned by the brewery Pilsner Urquell, this beautiful bar is a re-creation of the kind of place Prague
was famous for before WWII. Art nouveau interior,
excellent beers on tap and a menu of trad pub food
like dumplings stuffed with *uzeniny*, or smoked
meat. Kolkovna is always packed so it's fortunate
that there's a cellar level that turns into a dance club
at around 10pm (*see p227*).

Kozička

*Kozí 1, Prague 1 (2481 8308/www.kozicka.cz).
Metro Náměstí Republiky/5, 8, 14 tram.* **Open** noon-
4am Mon-Fri; 6pm-4am Sat, Sun. **Credit** MC, V.
Map p308 J2.
A popular, unpretentious local scene in the heart of
the Old Town – hard to beat if only for that reason –
with homely nooks throughout, mighty steaks served
until 11pm and Krušovice on tap.

La Casa Blů

*Kozí 15, Prague 1 (2481 8270/
www.lacasablu.8k.com). Metro Staroměstská/17, 18
tram.* **Open** 11am-1am daily. **No credit cards.
Map** p308 J2.
Decorative rugs draped over hard-back chairs,
Mexican street signs and tequila specials are a somewhat unsuccessful attempt to recreate Latin culture
in Prague. It's a pleasant break from beer hall rowdi-
ness, though, with a new Mexican menu, and is generally packed. Try the buzzer even if the door is locked
– people routinely wheedle their way in past closing.

Legends

*Týn 1, Prague 1 (in the Ungelt Courtyard) (2489
5404/www.legends.cz). Metro Staroměstská/17, 18
tram.* **Open** 11am-1am Mon-Wed, Sun; 11am-3am
Thur; 11am-4am Fri, Sat. **Credit** MC, V. **Map** p308 J3.

A 'music and sports café' catering to the expat business crowd, and an aspiring pick-up joint. The place
begins to fill up from 3pm on weekdays, and the 70
Kč cocktail specials attract so many miscreants that
before long there isn't room to move. A small,
mediocre menu is on offer.

Marquis de Sade

*Templová 8, Prague 1 (no phone). Metro Náměstí
Republiky/5, 14, 26 tram.* **Open** 11am-2am daily.
No credit cards. Map p309 K3.
An expat institution, but one of the more pleasantly sleazy ones. Peeling red vinyl seating runs
around the perimeter of the bar, which manages to
be dim even in broad daylight. Prime seating is on
the balcony, the perfect place to spot a drunken
patron doing something indiscreet. The bar's nothing to write home about and the house brew,
Lobkowicz, is not one of Prague's finest. Yet there's
an undeniably comfortable, broken-in (if not completely dilapidated) feeling throughout. There's
occasional live blues or jazz on the stage – that is,
as long as it continues holding up. The kind of place
you might run into someone you least expect.

Molly Malone's

*U Obecního dvora 4, Prague 1 (2481 8851/
www.mollymalones.cz). Metro Náměstí Republiky/
5, 14, 26 tram.* **Open** 11am-1am Mon-Thur, Sun;
11am-2am Fri, Sat. **Credit** AmEx, V. **Map** p308 J2.
The archetype of Irish pubs everywhere, complete
with roaring log fire, mismatched chairs and tables
constructed out of old beds and sewing machines,
incessant Pogues in the background, 'traditional
Irish food' and lots of backpackers and rowdy
English businessmen. Much as you want to hate it,
the place does have a certain charm. The bar is great
for propping up, the Guinness is excellent, the food
is decent, and in winter there's a warm and welcoming atmosphere. In summer, you risk an irate
neighbour from this quiet corner of the Old Town
throwing water on you if you stand outside after
9pm, but that's all part of the fun.

Radegast Pub

*Templová 2, Prague 1 (232 8069). Metro Náměstí
Republiky/5, 14, 26 tram.* **Open** 11am-midnight
daily. **Credit** AmEx, MC, V. **Map** p309 K3.
One of the last typical Czech pubs in this hub of
expat drinking, its main attractions are the excellent beer and pub food – you could easily pay an
extra 200 Kč in a swanky restaurant and not find a
better goulash. The clientele at Radegast Pub is a
mixture of Czechs, expats and backpackers who
can't believe they've found such a cheap place to eat
and drink right in the centre of Prague. Semi-
enclosed tables give an air of privacy, but the service can be iffy – orders have been known to get lost
in the smoke.

Tretter's Cocktail Bar

*V kolkovně 3, Prague 1 (2481 1165/www.tretters.cz).
Metro Staroměstská/17, 18 tram.* **Open** 7pm-3am
daily. **Credit** AmEx, MC, V. **Map** p308 J2.

Eat, Drink, Shop

A smart and lively scene, with beautiful, but competent bar staff, an incredible selection of cocktails, and a grand old tile bar for gathering at. The staff have garnered several bartending and mixing awards at international competitions, so don't hold back. Mike Tretter's specials, especially anything with blue curaçao and maracuja ice-cream, are recommended. Classy 1930s interiors and a flush local crowd to match.

U krále Jiřího

Liliová 10, Prague 1 (2424 8797). Metro Staroměstská/17, 18 tram. **Open** 5pm-1am. **No credit cards. Map** p308 G4.

This narrow cellar pub is an insider's trump card with cheap Gambrinus 10-degree on tap right in the heart of the Old Town. Frequented mainly by old-time locals, itinerant buskers and long-term expats, U krále Jiřího is a funky, bare-bones drinking hideout for loud debates about the meaning of Velvet Underground lyrics.

U medvídků

Na Perštýně 7, Prague 1 (24211916/ www.umedvidku.cz). Metro Národní třída/6, 9, 18, 22, 23 tram. **Open** 11am-11pm Mon-Sat; 11.30am-10pm Sun. **Credit** AmEx, MC, V. **Map** p308 H5.

With some five centuries as a beerhall behind it, the Little Bears brushed off communism as a passing fad. The only regime that counts here is the one that dictates drinking fine, cheap Budvar – and the half-litre mugs just keep on coming until you tell the waiter to stop. Don't be sidetracked by the modern bar to the left of the entrance; the real thing is on the right. The menu is a step up from pub grub, with mains such as pork in plum sauce and filets in dark beer sauce. Feel free to dine in the haywagon if it's not occupied by the accordion band.

U Vejvodů

Jilská 4, Staré Město, Prague 1 (2421 9999). Metro Můstek/3, 9, 14, 24 tram. **Open** 10am-midnight Sun-Thur; 10am-2am Fri, Sat. **No credit cards. Map** p308 H4/5.

A vast beerhall that caters to big tour groups – stick to the smaller front room to avoid them – but does offer quick service and old-style wood interiors, accented by the obligatory huge copper beer vat lids. For a ye olde pub feel, fine brews and traditional pub fare such as smoked meats, duck and dumplings, this one's hard to beat.

U Zlatého tygra

Husova 17, Prague 1 (2222 1111). Metro Staroměstská/17, 18 tram. **Open** 3-11pm daily. **No credit cards. Map** p308 H4.

Once the second home of Prague's favourite writer, the famously crotchety Bohumil Hrabal (*see chapter* **Literary Prague**), this bar has lost virtually all its appeal since its famous patron fell to his death from a hospital window in 1997. Tourists still besiege the place, which may explain why the Pilsner Urquell is no bargain, but the remaining regulars are none too happy about all this and are likely to blow unfiltered cigarette smoke your way.

Žíznivý pes

Elišky Krásnohorské 5, Prague 1 (2231 0039). Metro Staroměstská/17, 18 tram. **Open** 11am-2am Mon-Fri; noon-2am Sat, Sun. **No credit cards. Map** p308 H2.

The Thirsty Dog is a shrine to the golden days of expat slacking, when its original location was still open and Nick Cave sat and wrote a song about the place. Nowadays it's burgers, Murphy's Stout and Lobkowicz with jubilantly cavorting Yanks and a handful of Czechs. Summer breezes waft through the Psí Bouda (Dog Kennel) patio out back.

The best Beer gardens

For watching twilight hit Old Town
Letenský zámeček (*see p155*).

For spotting local derelicts
U Kotvy (*see p154*).

For sunny streetlife watching
U Holanů (*see p157*).

For meeting local anarchists
U vystřeleného oka (*see p158*).

For replenishment when hiking up Petřín Hill
Petřínské Terasy (*see p147*).

For expat-spotting
Jáma (*see p153*).

For heavy spending
U Fleků (*see p154*).

Zoo Bar

Jilská 18, Prague 1 (0602 190 089). Metro Staroměstská/17, 18 tram. **Open** 5pm-2am Mon-Fri, Sun; 5pm-5am Sat. **No credit cards. Map** p308 H4.
The most anarchic live music space in Old Town, this musty Gothic cellar is invariably peopled by expats and weekenders. Local rock and blues bands play on Saturday nights, which usually leads to an all-night jam as the musicians' friends begin arriving at 1am or so – but the well-oiled crowd often fails to notice. Delectable Herold Beer, not often found in mainstream Czech pubs and bars, is on tap here. Conversation works best in the cave-like front room, accessed via steep wooden stairs leading down from the street.

Nové Město

Amiveo

Karlovo náměstí 24, Prague 2 (2223 2382). Metro Karlovo náměstí/3, 6, 14, 18, 22, 24 tram. **Open** 11.30am-1am Mon-Thur; 11.30am-3am Fri; 5pm-3am Sat. **Credit** AmEx, MC. **Map** p310 J7.
With some stylish backlit interiors and low, pastel sofas, Amiveo comes equipped with a post-modern atmosphere and a full platter of Greek specialities as bar food to boot. When critical mass is reached, this place knows how to party in style, but on a slow night, when too few people have decided to tramp out to Karlovo náměstí, it can be thoroughly dead. Service seems to ebb and flow with the crowds as well. It's also a dance club (*see p224*), so odds of a good night out increase in the wee hours at weekends.

Café Archa

Na Poříčí 26, Prague 1 (2171 6117). Metro Náměstí Republiky or Florenc/3, 24 tram. **Open** 9am-10.30pm Mon-Fri; 10am-10pm Sat; 1-10pm Sun. **No credit cards. Map** p309 M2.
This glass fish tank, with long dangling lamps as bait, has hooked a young, laid-back clientele with cheap drinks, pristine surfaces, and posters and photos from the theatre and rock worlds. You can stare out at the passers-by as you drink, though they're more likely to be staring in at you.

Jágr's Sports Bar

Václavské náměstí 56, Prague 1 (2403 2481). Metro Můstek/3, 9, 14, 24 tram. **Open** 11am-midnight daily. **Credit** AmEx, MC, V. **Map** p311 K6.
A comically over-the-top basement shrine to Jaromir Jágr, the Czech ice-hockey star of the medal-winning Olympic team and later the Pittsburgh Penguins. There are wall-to-wall video screens on which to watch major sports events and matches from back home, including the Premiership on Sky. Expensive.

Jáma

V jámě 7, Prague 1 (2422 2383/ www.praguepivo.com). Metro Můstek/3, 9, 14, 24 tram. **Open** 11am-1am daily. **Credit** AmEx, MC, V. **Map** p311 K6.

Drunk as a Dane

Czechs have a vast vocabulary for conditions related to drinking – tellingly, far more than they do for their general health. When you've really had enough, '*Mam vopice*', or 'I have a monkey', best sums it up. If someone's already nabbed that line, there's always '*Zpitý pod čáru*', to be drunk 'under the line', '*vožralej*' or '*zlitej jak dán*', to be drunk as a Dane. This often happens after drinking 'like a mushroom' or '*nasávat jak houba*'. Do so quickly enough and you'll find yourself 'throwing a sabre'or '*hodit šavli*'. That's vomiting to the less imaginative.

Hopefully, before that stage one can at least enjoy having a head 'like a searching balloon', '*mít hlavu jako pátrací balón*.' Do try to maintain some composure, however, lest you 'swear like a cobblestone layer' or '*nadávat jako dlaždič*'. This is perhaps more forgivable when on a boys' night out, or *pánská jízda*, or at a hen party, *dámská jízda*, both of which, curiously, translate literally as a 'ride'.

You should be careful not to 'stick the axe in' or '*zaseknout sekeru hluboko*' lest you run up a big tab. Better to call it quits while you can still 'slither like a snail' or '*plazit se jako šnek.*' Just don't be surprised the following morning when your mind is found 'to be outside' or '*být mimo*,' that is, useless.

Worse still, you could find you 'have your brain swept up' or '*mít v hlavě jako vymeteno*' or, if you're really overdone it, '*mít hlavu jako střep*', 'have a head like a piece of broken glass.' *Au*.

Loud and collegiate year-round, this long bar serving Mexican food is the choice of the local business crowd. The Arizonans who run it also sponsor the literary quarterly *Prague Revue*, but you'd never guess it from the noisy, beery atmosphere, the extensive menu of cocktails (often on special), faux cacti, video counter or bank of internet terminals. Service is above average and a beer garden in the back offers a break from the noise within.

Jazz Café č. 14

Opatovická 14, Prague 1 (2492 0039). Metro Národní třída/6, 9, 18, 22, 23 tram. **Open** 10am-11pm Mon-Fri; 12am-11pm Sat, Sun. **No credit cards. Map** p310 H6.
A crowd of local writers and arty types clearly considers this a cosy, if smoky winter hideaway, with its mismatched furniture, congenial service and jazz

Eat, Drink, Shop

See and be seen at **Solidní nejistota**.

soundtrack. Oddly enough, there's never live music. Very basic snacks do for victuals – *babovka*, or 'grandmother's cake', is about it – but the *svařák*, or mulled wine, is perfect and there are cold-pressed olive oils, groovy loose teas and locally made honey for sale.

Ř Bar

Křemencova 10, Prague 1 (0604 365 950).
Metro Národní třída/6, 9, 17, 18, 22, 23 tram.
Open noon-2pm Mon-Thur, Sun; noon-4am Fri, Sat.
No credit cards. **Map** p310 H7.
This single room in Prague's new ghetto of cool, the SONA area, is a favourite with local scribblers, and was established by two of the editors of *Think*, a legendary expat party magazine. Hip DJ action, open-mic nights and karaoke are slated as new attractions in this arty, semi-industrial space.

Solidní nejistota

Pštrossova 21, Prague 1 (2493 3086). Metro
Národní třída/6, 9, 17, 18, 22, 23 tram. **Open** noon-6am Mon-Fri; 6pm-6am Sat, Sun. **No credit cards**.
Map p310 G7.
A shrine to posing and pick-ups, Solid Uncertainty comes equipped with the now standard blood-red interior and grill bar. Occasional live rock shows draw in the crowds.

U Fleků

Křemencova 11, Prague 1 (2491
5118/9169/www.ufleku.cz). Metro Národní třída/
3, 6, 14, 18, 24 tram. **Open** 9am-11pm daily.
Credit AmEx, DC, MC, V. **Map** p310 H7.
Prague's most famous pub, instantly identifiable by the buslo⸻ ⸻. Germans who turn up here, has been

brewing fine 13-degree dark beer on the premises for centuries. Though basic Bohemian meat and two veg is also available, you are automatically assumed to be here for the beer. Never accept the over-priced Becherovka when it's suggested by your smiling waiter. The picturesque courtyard is shaded by cherry trees, enclosed by a graffitied wall and leaded windows. Both inside and out, the long tables are invariably filled with hearty Germans swinging glasses to oom-pah music. Hardly the city's hippest venue, but the memorable beer is most definitely worth sampling.

U Kotvy

Spálená 11, Prague 1 (2493 0129). Metro Národní
třída/6, 9, 18, 22, 23 tram. **Open** 9am-10.30pm Mon-Fri; 10am-10.30pm Sat, Sun. **No credit cards**.
Map p310 H6.
In winter, this smoky little hole-in-the-wall is inhabited by assorted intriguing mutants. In summer, the large garden hidden at the back offers a leafy afternoon and evening haven. Slow service, passable food, and beware of the toilets.

Ultramarin

Ultramarin, Ostrovní 32, Prague 2 (2493 2249/
www.ultramarin.cz). Metro Národní třída. **Open** 11am-4am daily. **Credit** AmEx, MC, V. **Map** p310 H6.
One of the city's best stabs at a lifestyle bar, Ultramarin is a quiet sort of hit. With atmospheric retro jazz on the sound system, Santa Fe chicken salad on the menu and blond wood and mottled wall paint throughout, it's about the best option going for late-night refuelling and chilling. At street level Prague's bright young things sip terrible local wine and excellent imported coffee for hours at a time

while downstairs the tiny Ultramarin dance club attracts hip young Czechs till 4am (*see p229*). And, a Prague precedent, friendly waiting staff are actually promised on a placard at the entrance.

U Sudu

Vodičkova 10, Prague 1 (2223 2207). Metro Karlovo náměstí/3, 9, 14, 24 tram. **Open** noon-midnight Mon-Fri; 2pm-midnight Sat, Sun. **No credit cards.** **Map** p310 J6.

Originally a small, dark wine bar on the ground floor, U Sudu has expanded into three Gothic cellars and what seems to be somebody's spare room next door. The cellars have been claimed by students, while upstairs sees everyone from artists to business types to little old ladies. The wine is nothing to write home about, except when the *burčák* (a half-fermented, traditional Czech wine punch) arrives in September.

Further afield

Holešovice

Fraktal

Šmeralova 1, Prague 7 (0606 542 376). Metro Vltavská/1, 8, 25, 26 tram. **Open** 11am-midnight daily. **No credit cards.** **Map** p312 C2.

The newest out-of-centre bar scene phenomenon to emerge in Prague is this cosy little drinking hole with occasional live music and/or book launches. A typical event was the recent party for the release of rocker Phil Shoenfeld's *Junkie Love*, for which Shoenfeld turned in a great music set. The friendly owners have settled on a trashy convivial place

where anything goes. Like most Czech bars, it's still mostly beer that's served, but a few cocktails are worth noting: Mojitos and tequila gold with orange and cinnamon are a treat.

La Bodega Flamenca

Šmeralova 5, Prague 7 (3337 4075). Metro Vltavská/1, 8, 25, 26 tram. **Open** 5pm-5am daily. **No credit cards.** **Map** p312 C2.

The easily missed entrance to this cellar tapas bar, two doors north of Fraktal (*see above*) conceals a perpetual sangria party. Owner Ilona oversees the bar, serving up tapas such as marinated olives, *patatas fritas*, garlic mushrooms and fresh bread in little ceramic plates. Bench-style seats line the walls and fill up fast and, in true Spanish style, things only really start hotting up after 1am. Be forewarned that spontaneous salsa dancing tends to break out just inside the door.

Letenský zámeček

Letenské sady 341, Prague 7 (in Letná Park) (3337 5604/www.letenskyzamecek.cz). Metro Hradčanská/ 1, 8, 25, 26 tram. **Open** *Beer garden* 11am-11pm daily. *Restaurants* 11.30am-3pm, 6-11pm daily. **Credit** AmEx, DC, V. **Map** p312 C3.

This leafy enclave on the hill above the Vltava is arguably the city's finest summer beer garden. A local crowd gathers under the chestnut trees for cheap Kozel beer in plastic cups late into the evening, every evening. The adjoining Brasserie Ullman and Restaurant Belcredi have gone upscale with modern designer interiors, a dressy crowd, and excellent Bernard beer on tap. But the action is at the battered picnic tables with great views of the Old Town across the river. Lots of in-line skaters and dogs.

Quaffing with pedigree

Brewing in the Czech lands dates back to the Middle Ages and the official consumption figure is around 161 litres per person a year. That works out to a bottle of beer a day for every man, woman and child in the country.

Bohemian Žatec hops, barley, malt, yeast and water are the only things allowed in Czech beer – no additives, no preservatives. Nevertheless, it's still cheaper than water is in Western countries and is the one commodity whose price has still not changed much since the end of communism.

It was in the Czech town of Plzeň that modern beer was born in the mid 19th century – bottom-fermented, amber-coloured and hoppy, with a slightly sweet aftertaste. To this day, 'Pilsener' is commonly used to describe any type of light lager.

More than 80 breweries operate in this small country but the big boys are **Pilsner Breweries** (makers of Pilsner Urquell and Gambrinus), **Staropramen** (Prague's largest brewer, owned by UK brewer Bass), **Budvar** (makers of Czech Budweiser), **Radegast** and **Velké Popovice**.

The neighbourhood pub (*pivnice* or *hospoda*) itself is rarely spick and span but is invariably the best source of beer as the staff know how to store and tap it properly. You might get a choice between 10- and 12-degree beers, the former a little lighter and less alcoholic. The alcohol levels vary from brand to brand, but they tend to range from about 3.5 per cent to a little more than five per cent. In more traditional pubs, the waiter will continue bringing rounds until you wave him away.

Most people prefer Czech beer light and bitter (*světle*), though some favour the dark, sweetish version (*tmavé*). To compromise, ask for *řezané*, a half-and-half mix.

Bar Práce
Kamenická 9, Prague 7 (2057 1232). Metro Vltavská/1, 5, 8, 25, 26 tram. **Open** 4pm-5am daily. **No credit cards. Map** p312 C3.

High communist kitsch is the house speciality at Bar Práce, where the walls are lined with portraits of party stooges and a great bust of Lenin overlooks beer drinkers from the end of the bar. The booths that line the walls are appropriately uncomfortable, the beer is pretty cheap and there's a *herna* next to the Lenin bust – the ubiquitous beeping, blinking gambling machine that no worker's joint could do without. Just one inauthentic thing: service is fast and friendly and the hours are incredibly convenient.

Smíchov

U Buldoka
Preslova 1, Prague 5 (5731 9154). Metro Andel/ 6, 9 tram. **Open** 11am-midnight Mon-Thur; 11am-1am Fri; noon-midnight Sat; noon-11pm Sun. **No credit cards.**

At the Bulldog is one of those Prague rarities, a classic cheap Czech pub with well-tapped Staropramen beer and excellent traditional grub but also an inter-

national sensibility, quick service and a cool dance club below decks (*see p228*). All-day specials of *halušky* (Slovak gnocchi with bacon) and *guláš* soup go with the light and dark beer, plus a nice collection of Czech herbal liqueurs are at the bar. Big-screen sport coverage is there for those who want it, but it never drowns out conversation.

Vinohrady

První Prag Country Saloon Amerika
Korunní 101, Prague 2 (2425 6131). Metro Náměstí Míru/16 tram. **Open** 11am-11pm Mon; 11am-midnight Tue-Fri; 5pm-midnight Sat; 6-11pm Sun. **No credit cards. Map** p313 B3.

Live country and western bands fiddle nightly while would-be cowboys and their gals crowd into the hardwood seating, tuck into steaks and admire the animal skins on the walls. The hardcore (but incredibly friendly) crowd here risked jail under the old regime for collecting bits of Americana.

La Tonnelle
Anny Letenské 18, Prague 2 (2225 3690). Metro Náměstí Míru/4, 6, 11, 16, 22, 34 tram. **Open** 11.30am-midnight Mon-Sat. **No credit cards. Map** p313 A3.

Très French bar and vinotheque with some of the best value burgundies and chardonnays in town, plus delightful light bar grub, in an easily overlooked hideaway. La Tonnelle is leading a wine comeback in the district originally named for the vineyards that stood here.

U Holanů

Londýnská 10, Prague 2 (2251 1001).
Metro Náměstí Míru/4, 6, 11, 16, 22, 34 tram.
Open 10am-11pm Mon-Fri; 11am-11pm Sat, Sun.
No credit cards. **Map** p313 L7/8.
The Vinohrady district's most popular outdoor terrace pub for locals serves Gambrinus and Pilsner Urquell at local prices and the usual Czech meat and sauce staples to go with them. Note that it's *bez- obsluhy* (without service) outside: you order indoors, then carry your order out to tables on the leafy, quiet street.

Žižkov

Akropolis

Kubelíkova 27, Prague 3 (9633 0911). Metro Jiřího z Poděbrad/11 tram. **Open** 11.30am-2am daily.
No credit cards. **Map** p313 B2.
The Akropolis, a longtime Žižkov institution of drinking, indie music concerts and networking for arty types, has four separate pubs on site, each with its own crowd and vibe – it can easily suffice for a whole night. The street-level Akropolis restaurant (*see p145*) serves cheap and decent food with the Lobkowicz beer; the Kaaba Café is a small, well-lit place to meet up and get a caffeine fix; the Divadelní Bar is a hot, intense vortex of DJ action

and surreal wood carvings; the Malá Scena, on the other hand, is a red-washed chill-out space with a post-industrial look and battered tables and chairs for getting settled into corners.

The Clown & Bard

Bořivojova 102, Prague 3 (2271 6453/
www.clownandbard.com). Metro Jiřího z Poděbrad/
5, 9, 26 tram. **Open** 9am-midnight daily.
No credit cards. **Map** p313 B2.
About as entertaining as hostel bars get, and that can be quite entertaining if you come on a night when one of the undiscovered bands that regularly play here is actually any good. Otherwise, it's strictly backpacking, backgammon, cheap brews and comparing notes on the sights. *See also p57.*

Hapu

Orlická 8, Prague 3 (no phone). Metro Flora/
11, 16, 26, 51, 58 tram. **Open** 6pm-2am Mon-Sat.
No credit cards. **Map** p313 C2/3.
This homey Žižkov drinking hole was opened by a couple who imagined their ideal bar, then created it for their friends. Fresh mint leaves adorn the tasty rum Mojito; rum, cream, chocolate and yet more mint goes into the house special, *horká novinka*, or 'hot news'. Shooters range from 30-60 Kč, while classic long drinks abound. Dry Martini lovers are catered to particularly well.

Le Clan

Balbínova 23, Prague 3 (0606 264 677 mobile).
Metro Muzeum/11 tram. **Open** 8pm-3am Mon-Fri,
Sun; 8pm-4am Sat. **No credit cards**. **Map** p313 2A.
A dim hideaway of little, plush red sofas, cocktails, house music and the occasional go-go dancing

Chewing the cud at scruffy, convivial **Fraktal**. *See p155.*

Communist-chic at **Bar Práce**. *See p156*.

evening, Le Clan excels at that slightly tawdry, exclusive feel, and it's become something of a mecca for local Francophile clubbers. The appealing bordello decor here makes it a great place for trysting.

Park Café

Riegrovy sady, Prague 3 (2271 7247). Metro Museum/11 tram. **Open** 11am-midnight daily. **No credit cards. Map** p313 B2.
Park Café is the biggest outdoor venue in the east end of central Prague, attracting people from three adjoining neighbourhoods, who are drawn by battered benches, the pleasant shade of chestnut trees and cheap Krušovice beer by the half-litre. Kids of all ages enjoy putting around the minigolf course, dogs run yapping between the tables, bands take to the stage on weekends and there are grassy hills all around for more private moments – a unique advantage of a pub built right into a park.

Potrefena husa

Vinohradská 104, Prague 3 (6731 0360). Metro Jiřího z Poděbrad/11 tram. **Open** 11.30am-1am daily. **Credit** AmEx, MC, V. **Map** p313 E2.
The Wounded Goose, with a better menu than a lot of Prague restaurants, is the new-generation, stylish, almost-too-clean pub of the 21st century. Part of a national chain, it's nearly always packed with young professionals sipping well-tapped Velvet beer and noshing chicken wings and ribs while taking in cable TV sports coverage. Czech pub food classics like the *bramborák*, or potato-thyme pancake, are excellent too.

U Houdků

Bořivojova 110, Prague 3 (2271 1239). Metro Jiřího z Poděbrad/11 tram. **Open** 10am-11pm Mon-Fri; 11am-11pm Sat, Sun. **No credit cards. Map** p313 B2/C2.
U Houdků is a classic neighbourhood Žižkov pub with a blast of South Bohemia thrown in for good measure: Eggenberg and Budvar, both hearty

brews from the Český Krumlov area, are served both light and dark, alongside mounds of typical Czech pub grub for pocket change. The picnic tables at the back under the chestnut trees attract every student and worker drinking in this increasingly trendifying area.

U Sadu

Škroupovo náměstí 5, Prague 3 (627 4967). Metro Jiřího z Poděbrad/11 tram. **Open** 10am-2am daily. **No credit cards. Map** p313 B2.
This classic old-style Czech pub restaurant in the heart of the old-style Žižkov district is popular with students. In a working-class quarter with crumbling apartment blocks and hundreds of earthy pubs, U Sadu can hold its own with any of them. The chilli goulash, schnitzels and fried cheese are a marvellously unhealthy treat, the Pilsner and Gambrinus are well-tapped and the service is thoroughly gruff. It doesn't get any more authentic than this. The kitchen is open pretty late, too, for Prague.

U vystřeleného oka

U božích bojovníků 3, Prague 3 (627 8714). Metro Florenc, then 135 or 207 bus. **Open** 4.30pm-1am Mon-Sat. **No credit cards. Map** p313 C1.
The Shot-Out Eye sits beneath the ominous giant statue of General Jan Žižka, the renowned warrior whose battle injury inspired the gory name. Žižkov has more pubs than any other area of Prague, but this is undoubtedly the best of the lot, and the only one that's genuinely welcoming to foreigners. A three-level outdoor beer garden serves bargain-basement Měšťan, while the taps indoors flow non-stop to a soundtrack of local anarcho-rockers *Psí Vojáci* on the stereo, and a backdrop of grotesquely weird paintings by Martin Velíšek. Upstairs is a quiet, Indian-style tearoom that seems rather out of place amid the beer-fuelled chaos, but it is inviting nonetheless.

Shops & Services

Whether you're mining for amber in a *bazar* or splashing out on Czech designer togs, Prague shopping is still an adventure in new capitalism.

Long gone are the days that once inspired a television commercial suggesting that you could trade a pair of Western jeans for a car in Prague. But the city's shopping culture still hasn't quite caught up with the West's after more than a decade in the free market. Inconvenient opening hours and rude service still linger on in some places, remnants from the days when all sales assistants were civil servants working for state-owned enterprises. Refunds are almost unheard of, while returns are grudgingly accepted as long as you agree to accept other merchandise in lieu of cash. Generic chain clothing stores and liquidation shops peddling cheap, leftover fashions are still more common than private boutiques, while prices are often more reflective of Western standards than Czech wages.

The good news is that things have improved greatly in the last two years. Credit cards are taken at far more places and shopping can be a genuine pleasure if you know what to look for. Besides which, wandering around searching for treasures is one of the best ways to get to know the city. Along with an antique print or an amber ring, you will discover Prague's charm from the ground up. In districts now full of cafés, restaurants and pubs you'll find plenty of places to take a break from the rigours of shopping and take stock of the day's haul.

Czech glass and crystal, along with garnet and amber jewellery, remain justly famous after centuries of skilled craftsmanship. If you can't find a decanter or pendant you like in the myriad shops in and around Wenceslas Square, you just aren't looking. Antiques and second-hand shops also proliferate and simply browsing through their wares can be as fun as taking something home. Designer clothes shops are less common but worth seeking out for truly original fashions and high quality (*see p170* **Different by design**).

There are a few useful words to know: shop clerks will ask '*Máte přání*' (Do you have a wish?) when you walk into a shop and may ask '*Ještě něco?*' (Anything else?) or '*Všechno?*' (Is that all?) when they ring up your purchase. Ask '*Kolik to stojí?*' to find out what something costs.

A little strategic planning will help you to get the most out of Prague's main shopping districts. The following may help in working out a basic itinerary.

SHOPPING AREAS

By and large, the shops in **Hradčany** and around Prague Castle carry only camera film, jester hats and postcards, although there are plenty of tourist-oriented speciality shops – with tourist-oriented prices – all along Nerudova street. For a more rewarding experience, you'll need to head down the hill to the tiny, winding streets of **Malá Strana**. Boutiques just south of the Charles Bridge on Saská ulička offer fashions for the Bohemian at heart, while antiques shops within a few blocks of Malostranské náměstí, and also along Nerudova, are rich in old world atmosphere – if still too well trafficked to offer many bargains. Although obviously catering to the tourist trade, vendor stands on the Charles Bridge sometimes offer some surprising finds, including affordable photographic prints of Prague and unique jewellery.

Staré Město is where you'll find the busiest fashion boutiques (check Jakubská and Jilská for the best Czech boutiques, Na Příkopě for the bigger commercial ones). Otherwise, it's a good area for antiquarian books and art (on Liliová) and second-hand clothes, especially around Karoliny Světlé.

Serious shopping gets done in **Nové Město**, whether it's for filling the freezer or for a new wardrobe. Developers have built up most of New Town's shops all along Na Příkopě (the border between this district and neighbouring Staré Město), which means mass-produced fashions as a rule, but there are some surprises. The mysteries of the Havel family's pre-war enterprise, the Lucerna shopping passage on Wenceslas Square (Václavské náměstí), are ever intriguing, and smaller boutiques offer personal service and are more likely to offer bargains on the sales rack. There's also the popular **Tesco** department store (*see p160*) on Spálená for one-stop shopping and the vast **Bontonland** music megastore (*see p179*) on Václavské náměstí. Bookshops in this area set the standard, and the **Globe Bookstore & Coffeehouse** (*see p165*) is the literary epicentre.

Further afield, in **Žižkov**, buying barrelled wine in shops all along Vinohradská is an adventure; while **Smíchov** is becoming a destination in itself with a burst of new development, including the **Nový Smíchov Centre** mega-mall (*see p161*).

Everybody must get stoned

The Czech lands have long been famous for burgundy-red Bohemian garnets; they were favourites of Emperor Rudolf II, the height of fashion for Russian tsarinas in the 19th century, and ubiquitous during the Victorian era. The stones' fiery beauty has given rise to legends that tout their ability to light up and protect their bearers in darkness (Noah is said to have used a garnet lantern to navigate the ark at night).

One of the oldest specialised gem-cutting schools in Europe operates in Turnov, in North Bohemia, and the Czech Republic is still known for the quality of its garnets – the Turnov firm Art Cooperative Granát, for example, is internationally renowned. The Amber Way, an ancient trading route, also crossed through Bohemia and deposits of the mineral are still found there, although much

of the amber in Czech jewellery now comes from the Baltics. Shops with extensive selections of both stones in a good range of styles and prices still light up the night throughout the city, especially on Wenceslas and Old Town squares. Many offer one-of-a-kind settings and a taste of the mystic.

Vily
Karlova 23, Staré Město, Prague 1 (2322 7687). Metro Staroměstská/17, 18 tram. **Open** 10am-10pm daily. **Credit** AmEx, MC, V. **Map** p308 H4.
Vily, with four stores in Prague's major shopping districts, offers a dazzling display of garnets, amber (in yellow, brown and green) and other gems – and you can have them just about any way you want them. Earrings, rings, pendants, necklaces, bracelets and more come in silver, white gold or gold settings.

One-stop shopping

Department stores

Kotva
Náměstí Republiky 8, Staré Město, Prague 1 (2480 1111). Metro Náměstí Republiky/5, 8, 14 tram. **Open** *Department store* 9am-8pm Mon-Fri; 9am-6pm Sat; 10am-6pm Sun. *Supermarket* 7am-8pm Mon-Fri; 9am-6pm Sat; 10am-7pm Sun. **Credit** AmEx, MC, V. **Map** p309 K3.
This place is generally quite ugly but also well stocked. Work your way up past glossy cosmetics stalls, a pharmacy, stationery, bed linen, fashion, sports gear, car accessories and end up at the fairly naff furniture and lighting section. Good for gourmet chocolate and French wines. Kids love the ramp escalator that takes the shopping carts from one level to the next.

Krone/Julius Meinl
Václavské náměstí 21, Nové Město, Prague 1 (2423 0477). Metro Můstek/3, 9, 14, 24 tram. **Open** *Department store* 9am-8pm Mon-Fri; 9am-7pm Sat; 10am-6pm Sun. *Supermarket* 8am-9pm Mon-Fri; 9am-8pm Sat; 10am-8pm Sun. **Credit** MC, V. **Map** p309 K5.
With a wide array of options to choose from, nonetheless, the best thing here is the handy basement supermarket, from which you can stagger directly into the metro with your carrier bags.

Tesco
Národní třída 26, Nové Město, Prague 1 (2422 7971/9). Metro Můstek or Národní třída/6, 9, 18, 21, 22, 23 tram. **Open** *Department store* 8am-9pm

Mon-Fri; 9am-8pm Sat; 10am-8pm Sun. *Supermarket* 7am-10pm Mon-Fri; 8am-8pm Sat; 9am-8pm Sun. **Credit** AmEx, MC, V. **Map** p308 H5.
This is what became of Máj, the pride of communist Czechoslovakia's retail industry. Soon after the revolution it was sold to American chain K-mart, which revamped the shop and sold it to Tesco in 1996. It now has a nice mix of Czech and Western products, a popular supermarket with a good bakery, as well as aisle after aisle of American peanut butter, tinned salsa and British biscuits.

Malls

Prague's first malls were forced to employ marketing teams to explain the concept to Czechs. They also sold cheap potatoes in the basement in order to bring in the crowds. Czech teens have since grasped that the basic idea is that they should spend Saturdays here, and few young things would consider buying their designer gear from anywhere else. The city's latest ventures are **Slovanský dům** and the **Nový Smíchov Centre**.

Černá růže
Na příkopě 12, Nové Město, Prague 1 (2101 4111). Metro Můstek/3, 9, 14, 24 tram. **Open** 9am-8pm Mon-Fri; 9am-7pm Sat; 11am-7pm Sun. **Credit** AmEx, MC, V. **Map** p309 K4.
An easily overlooked entrance next to McDonald's leads from a main pedestrian drag into this three-level complex full of fashion boutiques, such as Pierre Cardin, as well as the odd shoe store, a few designer furniture outlets and some wine shops. The Bonjour Bar patio café provides relief.

Most of the jewellery is fairly traditional, but the amber rings definitely present funkier (and relatively cheap) options.
Branches: Pařížská 14, Prague 1 (2481 9430); Václavské náměstí 13, Prague 1 (2422 7476); Karlova 16, Prague 1 (2422 7687)

Czech Garnet

Pařížská 1, Staré Město, Prague 1 (no phone). Metro Staroměstská/17, 18 tram.
Open 10am-10pm daily. **Credit** AmEx, MC, V. **Map** p308 H3.
If you are looking for an amber or garnet bracelet, this is the place for you, with a wonderful selection in all colours and styles, most in silver. It also features several unique, modern designs that showcase large pieces of amber for those who dare to be bold.

Dětský dům

Na Příkopě 15, Staré Město, Prague 1 (7214 2401). Metro Můstek/3, 9, 14, 24 tram. **Open** 9am-8pm Mon-Sat; 10am-8pm Sun. **Credit** AmEx, MC, V. **Map** p309 K4.
Once a communist centre for kids' clothing, the Children's House has reopened with a thoroughly capitalist 21st-century attitude. Instead of aisles of matching gray jumpers, it's now packed with shops such as Bim Bam Bum, stocking Ralph Lauren for tykes, the mall also features occasional puppet shows and the odd fashion shop for mum.

Kenvelo Centre

Václavské náměstí 11, Nové Město, Prague 1 (2447 3064/www.kenvelo.cz). Metro Můstek/3, 9, 14, 24 tram. **Open** 9am-9pm Mon-Sat; 10am-9pm Sun. **Credit** AmEx, MC, V. **Map** p308 J5.
The Kenvelo chain – specialising in cheap leather jackets, jumpers and stretchy separates for women, most of which have a Kenvelo label prominently affixed – occupies this modern mall off Wenceslas Square. After a recent makeover, the mall now features shiny glass and chrome walkways, a US-style 'food court' and an Argentine cellar steakhouse that serves every part of the cow including the udder.
Branches: Palác Koruna, Václavské náměstí 1, Nové Město, Prague 1 (2421 5904); Erpet, Staroměstské náměstí 25-6, Staré Město, Prague 1 (2163 2226); Centrum Černý Most, Chlumecká 765-6, Černý Most, Prague 9 (8191 8128).

Myslbek Centre

Na příkopě 19-21, Nové Město, Prague 1 (2423 9550). Metro Můstek/3, 9, 14, 24 tram.
Open 8.30am-8.30pm Mon-Sat; 9.30am-8.30pm Sun. **Credit** AmEx, MC, V. **Map** p309 K4.

While wondering around here, you could be forgiven for thinking you were back in Britain. Calvin Klein Jeans, Marks & Spencer, Next, Tie Rack, Mothercare, Kookai and Vision Express fill the swankiest and certainly most crowded mall in town. For a lesson in insensitive modern architecture, see how the back of the mall fails to relate to the surrounding Ovocný Square outside. Some shops open and close at different times.

Nový Smíchov Centre

Plzeňská & Radlická, Smíchov, Prague 5 (5728 4111). Metro Anděl/4, 6, 7, 9, 10, 14 tram.
Open 7am-midnight daily. **Credit** AmEx, MC, V.
A complex so large it's referred to as a city. The seven-storey, 145,000sq m complex will open in phases throughout 2002. It will ultimately house dozens of retails shops, a handful of hotels, apartments and two multiplex cinemas.

Slovanský Dům

Na příkopě 22, Nové Město, Prague 1 (2145 1400/ info 2421 1295/www.slovanskydum.cz). Metro Můstek/3, 9, 14, 24 tram. **Open** 10am-8pm daily. **Map** p309 K4.
The newest addition to the strip of malls that lines this major downtown drag. It houses fashion shops like Mexx and beauty boutiques such as Clinique. Decent Italian and sushi restaurants can be found, but the major draw is the multiplex cinema.

Prague is an antiques bonanza. *See p163.*

Eat, Drink, Shop

Markets

If you're looking for one of those fabled flea markets jam-packed with 1950s-era biker jackets and old vinyl, try some of the *bazars* listed under **Antiques**. In general, Prague outdoor markets are mostly fruit 'n' veg affairs, although Christmas and Easter markets spring up seasonally along the main tourist routes. If you catch one of the Christmas markets in Old Town Square, Václavské náměstí or Náměstí Republiky, warm yourself with a nice glass of steaming mulled wine – *svařené víno* or *svařák*.

Havelský Market

Havelská, Nové Město, Prague 1 (no phone).
Metro Můstek or Národní třída/6, 9, 18, 22 tram.
Open 7.30am-6pm Mon-Fri; 8.30am-6pm Sat, Sun.
No credit cards. Map p308 J4.
Officially known as Staré Město Market, but universally referred to by its location, this is probably Prague's best market for greens and a taste of daily Bohemian life. Fresh fruit and vegetables are crammed alongside wooden toys, puppets, tourist trinkets and bad art. Good for gifts, and flowers are a tremendous bargain. Best in the morning before the trinket hawkers take over three-quarters of the stalls. Havelská has recently become a prime pickpocket hunting ground – watch your purse.

Market at the Fountain

Spálená 30, Nové Město, Prague 1 (no phone). Metro Národní třída/6, 9, 18, 22 tram. **Open** 7.30am-7pm daily. **No credit cards. Map** p308 H5.
Excellent fruit and vegetable market just outside Tesco – usually cheaper too.

Antiques

There are many antiques shops in Prague, but there are also numerous junk shops, selling everything from old irons and typewriters to prints by Alfons Mucha. Word to the wise: if an antiques shop is on a main tourist route, you can be fairly sure that the prices are aimed at foreigners. For cheaper and more unusual items, seek out a *bazar*, a better class of junk shop. Some are listed here, but more can be found in the *Zlaté stránky* (Yellow Pages) – look for the cross-index in English at the back.

Antique

Kaprova 12, Staré Město, Prague 1 (232 9003).
Metro Staroměstská/17, 18 tram. **Open** 10am-7pm,
Mon-Sat; 10am-6pm Sun. **Credit** AmEx, DC, MC, V.
Map p308 G3.
Expensive but rewarding. Check out the antique art deco watches – stylish and affordable.

Antique Ahasver

Prokopská 3, Malá Strana, Prague 1 (9004 1660).
Metro Malostranská/12, 18, 22, 23 tram. **Open**
11am-6pm Tue-Sun. **Credit** MC, V. **Map** p307 E4.

Antique formal gowns, traditional folk clothing, mother-of-pearl hairpins, beaded purses, brooches and trays of charming oddments. The English-speaking sales assistant is always ready to supply a story and help you decide.

Antique Anderle

Václavské náměstí 17, Nové Město, Prague 1 (2400 9166/www.antiqueanderle.cz). Metro Můstek/3, 9, 14, 24 tram. **Open** 10am-7pm Mon-Sat; 10am-6pm Sun. **Credit** AmEx, DC, MC, V. **Map** p308 J5.
Very expensive shop with the city's best selection of above-par art and Russian icons (with export certificates). For serious collectors only.

Art Deco

Michalská 21, Staré Město, Prague 1 (2422 3076).
Metro Staroměstská or Národní třída/6, 9, 17, 18, 22, 23 tram. **Open** 2-7pm Mon-Fri. **Credit** AmEx, MC, V. **Map** p308 H4.
The remains of a golden era when Prague was the fashion centre of Eastern Europe. Vintage 1920s-50s clothes, beaded hats and costume jewellery at fair prices. See the women's magazines for an interesting look at pre-war fashion.

Bric a Brac

Týnská 7, Staré Město, Prague 1 (2232 6484).
Metro Staroměstská or Náměstí Republiky/5, 8, 14, 17, 18 tram. **Open** 11am-7pm daily. **Credit** AmEx, MC, V. **Map** p308 J3.
A quaint, eclectic mix of antique knick-knacks including everything from tobacco tins to vintage perfume bottles. Bric a Brac also owns a tiny shop around the corner that is stocked with every kind of timepiece imaginable.

Jan Huněk Starožitnosti

Pařížská 1, Staré Město, Prague 1 (2232 5122).
Metro Staroměstská/17, 18 tram. **Open** 10am-6pm daily. **Credit** AmEx, DC, MC, V. **Map** p308 H3.
Exquisite and expensive Czech glass from the 18th century to the 1930s. For dedicated collectors only.

Military Antique Army Shop

Křemencova 7, Nové Město, Prague 1 (2493 0952/0603 210381 mobile). Metro Národní třída/ 6, 9, 18, 21, 22, 23 tram. **Open** 11am-5pm Mon-Fri.
Credit AmEx, MC, V. **Map** p310 H6/7.
Just about everything you'd need to re-enact the Normandy landings. WWII flyers' headgear, goggles, bayonets, swords, badges and lots of those ever-so-handy ammo boxes.

Modernista

Konviktská 5, Staré Město, Prague 1 (2222 0113/www.modernista.cz). **Open** 2-7pm Mon-Fri; 10am-6pm Sat. **Credit** AmEx, MC, V. **Map** p308 G5.
Specialist collectors of Czech 'cubo-expressionism', functionalism and other exquisite modernist pieces, this new shop features restored desk chairs and armoires from the early to mid-20th century. More (or less) portable acquisitions run from gleaming chrome lamps to huge prints of communist propaganda and vintage kiosk ads.

Eat, Drink, Shop

Bookshops & newsagents

English-language books in Prague are often reasonably priced by Western standards, if outrageously priced by local standards. If you're on a budget and not too picky, try one of the *antikvariáty* listed below. You might just find the book you didn't realise you always wanted, and, even if not, browsing can be fun in its own right. Most bookshops listed here can order in new books, but there's often a wait of between three and five weeks.

Academia

Václavské náměstí 34, Nové Město, Prague 1 (2422 3511/3513/www.academia.cz). Metro Můstek/3, 9, 14, 24 tram. **Open** 9am-8pm Mon-Fri; 10am-7pm Sat, Sun. **Credit** DC, MC, V. **Map** p309 K5.

This friendly two-storey bookshop is handily located in the wonderfully restored Wiehl building on Wenceslas Square. Stock is predominantly Czech, but Academia also carries a wealth of English-language history, art and language texts, plus coffee-table books and culture magazines and journals with some English content. Well-lit café upstairs.

Anagram Bookshop

Týn 4, Staré Město, Prague 1 (2489 5737/ www.anagram.cz). Metro Náměstí Republiky/5, 8, 14 tram. **Open** 10am-8pm Mon-Sat; 10am-6pm Sun. **Credit** DC, MC, V. **Map** p308 J3.

This outlet has, in addition to a wide selection of topical books on Prague and Central Europe, a great second-hand English-language rack, with an emphasis on health, fitness, philosophy, self-help and alternative medicine. Everything that's generally hard to find in Prague.

Big Ben Bookshop

Malá Štupartská 5, Staré Město, Prague 1 (2482 6565/www.bigbenbookshop.com). Metro Náměstí Republiky/5, 8, 14 tram. **Open** 9am-6.30pm Mon-Fri; 10am-5pm Sat, Sun. **Credit** AmEx, MC, V. **Map** p308 J3.

If you've used up all your reading material, this welcoming establishment has the standard books on Prague, several shelves of bestsellers, lots of English-language newspapers and magazines, plus the best children's books in English around. The staff will gladly order in books for you and know their stock and writers better than most.

Czech glass bounces back

For a while, glassmaking in Bohemia looked to be resting on its laurels.

Noted for its clarity and toughness, Czech glass was used (and can still be seen) in windows of royal palaces throughout Europe. But the crystal and glass displayed in Prague shop windows today is not nearly what it used to be. Depleted natural resources and the decades of communist control diminished the quality of product and producers, making a distant memory of the Renaissance glory days when Czech crystal eclipsed Venetian glass.

But a handful of artisans and craftsmen are getting back to their roots – and also restoring some of the quality established in the 13th-century in monastery workshops. Among the most recent entrants to the scene is Artěl (*see below*), a nexus of modern design and historical glass-blowing. When American designer and entrepreneur Karen Feldman moved to Prague in 1994, she discovered the city's rich crystal tradition and started collecting flutes, decanters and highballs of the kind lost during communism. Feldman began designing her own glass in 1997, reviving traditional glassmaking techniques and standards.

Artěl was originally the name adopted by a co-operative of Czech artisans working in the early 1900s and is now used by Feldman,

who has opened shops in New York and London. Though Artěl maintains offices in Prague, a small retail outlet (by appointment only) opened here in spring 2002 – and it is already buzzing.

More traditional, and justly famous, is Moser glass and crystal, made in Karlovy Vary since 1857. The masterworks of Moser are only sold in licensed shops and there are just two in Prague.

Though some argue the quality of Czech glass will never be what it once was, it is arguably tough to find a richer variety of glass and crystal in any other city. The streets of Prague are filled with glass and crystal shops, so it pays to discriminate.

Artěl

Vinohradska 164, Vinohrady, Prague 3 (7173 2161/www.artelglass.com). **Open** 9am-5pm Mon-Fri (by appointment only). **Credit** AmEx, DC, MC, V. **Map** p313 D3.

Mainly an export business, Artěl features flutes and tableware with crafty touches no one's seen in Prague for decades.

Erpet

Staroměstské náměstí 27, Staré Město, Prague 1 (2422 9755/ 2421 5257/www.erpet.cz). Metro

The Globe Bookstore & Coffeehouse

Pštrossova 6, Nové Město, Prague 2 (2491 6264).
Metro Národní třída/6, 9, 18, 21, 22, 23 tram.
Open 10am-midnight daily. **Credit** AmEx, MC, V.
Map p310 G7.

One of the most famous bookstores in the world, this expat literary heart is in a multi-level, hardwired space in New Town. Fine second-hand paperbacks still line the walls, and it now has free internet terminals, a sleek balcony and extra legroom. The list of international authors doing readings is star-studded and the food is, well, well-intentioned (*see p141*).

Knihkupectví Jan Kanzelsberger

Václavské náměstí 42, Nové Město, Prague 1 (2421 7335). Metro Můstek/3, 9, 14, 24 tram. **Open** 8am-7pm Mon-Sat; 9am-7pm Sun. **Credit** AmEx, MC, V. **Map** p309 K5.

Very central, with coffee-table books on Prague, a reasonably good selection of Czech fiction in translation and an odd assortment of guidebooks.
Branches: Václavské náměstí 4, Nové Město, Prague 1 (2421 9214); Centrum Zlatý Anděl, Plzeňská 344, Smíchov, Prague 5 (5732 1470).

Knihkupectví U Černé Matky Boží

Celetná 34, Nové Město, Prague 1 (2422 2349).
Metro Náměstí Republiky/5, 8, 14 tram.
Open 8am-7pm Mon-Fri; 9am-6pm Sat; 10am-6pm Sun. **Credit** AmEx, MC, V. **Map** p309 K3.

It's worth tracking down this arty bookshop just to gaze at the building's wonderful cubist exterior. The bookshop itself is good for gift-hunting, with hundreds of maps, art prints, T-shirts, translated Czech novels, coffee-table books and calendars.

Trafika Můstek

Václavské náměstí, Nové Město, Prague 1 (no phone).
Metro Můstek/3, 9, 14, 24 tram. **Open** 8am-10pm daily. **No credit cards. Map** p308 J5.

Two green magazine stands at the bottom of Wenceslas Square stocking everything from Forbes to *Film Threat*. If you can't find a Western period ical here, you can't find it in Prague.

Old books & prints

Prague's second-hand bookshops are known as *antikvariáty*. For a one-of-a-kind Prague souvenir, you couldn't do better than an old

Staroměstská/17, 18 tram. **Open** 10am-8pm daily. **Credit** AmEx, DC, MC, V. **Map** p308 J3.
Not a whole lot of bargains here but an extremely wide and varied selection.

Moser

Na příkopě 12, Staré Město, Prague 1 (2421 1293/www.moser-glass.com). Metro Můstek/3, 9, 14, 24 tram. **Open** 9am-8pm Mon-Fri; 10am-6pm Sat. **Credit** AmEx, DC, MC, V. **Map** p309 K4.

Very expensive but said to be the only Czech crystal worth seeking out. Like most Czech crystal, it's made from a lead-free formula that's safer for storing brandies and will allow it to last for generations.
Branch: Malé náměstí 11, Prague 1 (2161 1520).

communist coffee-table book or a dirt-cheap print by an unknown Czech artist. *Antikvariáty* are also the best places in town to find second-hand novels in English.

Antikvariát Galerie Můstek

Národní 40, Nové Město, Prague 1 (2494 9587). Metro Národní třída/6, 9, 18, 21, 22, 23 tram. **Open** 10am-7pm Mon-Fri; noon-4pm Sat; 2-6pm Sun. **Credit** AmEx, MC, V. **Map** p308 H5/J5.
A discriminating *antikvariát* with fine antiquarian books (19th-century natural history especially) and a reliable stock of major works on Czech art.

Antikvariát Kant

Opatovická 26, Nové Město, Prague 1 (2493 4219/ www.antik-kant.com). Metro Národní třída/6, 9, 18, 21, 22, 23 tram. **Open** 10am-6pm Mon-Fri; 10am-3pm Sat. **Credit** AmEx, MC, V. **Map** p310 G6/H6.
An eclectic mix of prints and dust-encrusted books. There's an impressive selection of second-hand titles in English, from *Jaws* to Germaine Greer.

Antikvariát Pařížská

Pařížská 8, Staré Město, Prague 1 (232 1442). Metro Staroměstská/17, 18 tram. **Open** 10am-7pm Mon-Fri; 10am-6pm Sat, Sun. **Credit** AmEx, DC, MC, V. **Map** p308 H3.
This place is filled with gorgeous prints and maps exclusively from the 16th to 19th centuries.

Makovský & Gregor

Kaprova 9, Staré Město, Prague 1 (2421 6346). Metro Staroměstská/17, 18 tram. **Open** 9am-7pm Mon-Fri; 10am-6pm Sat, Sun. **No credit cards**. **Map** p308 H3.
Dusty, crowded and dimly lit, this shop is everything a good *antikvariát* should be. Stuffed with old books, prints, engravings and coffee-table picture books dating back to the 1950s. It has second-hand novels in English for as little as 30 Kč.

Computers

Apple Macintosh was slow to enter the Czech market and the choice of computers on offer today is still limited. You'll be able to find PC outlets on just about every street corner, and the list of suppliers in the *Zlaté stránky* (*Yellow Pages*) goes on forever.
    Pray that your computer doesn't malfunction in Prague. In case it does, we list a few places where you might be able to get it fixed.

GATC

Rytířská 10, Staré Město, Prague 1 (2421 1544/ www.gatc.com). Metro Můstek/3, 9, 14, 24 tram. **Open** 9am-4pm Mon-Fri. **No credit cards**. **Map** p308 J4.
With helpful, English-speaking staff, this is an authorised repair centre for both IBM and Compaq computers. Repairs usually take less than a week.
Branch: Pod Kavalirkou 18, Košíře, Prague 5 (5721 1450).

HSH Computer

Václavské náměstí 66, Nové Město, Prague 1 (2221 0288/www.hsh.cz). Metro Muzeum/11 tram. **Open** 10am-1pm, 2-7pm Mon-Fri. **Credit** MC, V. **Map** p311 K6.
This shop just off Wenceslas Square specialises in sales and repair of new and used laptops and is an authorised Toshiba dealer. Computer accessories such as batteries, adaptors and portable CD-Rom drives are also available.
Service centre: Gorazdova 5, Nové Město, Prague 2 (9000 2388).
Branch: Department store Kotva, Náměstí Republiky 8, Staré Město, Prague 1 (2480 1111).

MacSource/CompuSource

Bělehradská 68, Vinohrady, Prague 2 (2251 5455/ www.compusource.cz). Metro IP Pavlova/6, 11 tram. **Open** 10am-6pm Mon-Fri. **Credit** AmEx, MC, V. **Map** p311 L8.
Probably the largest and best Macintosh outlet in Prague. But even here, simple repairs can take half a day and shipment of replacement components can sometimes take up to one month. The service is reasonable, but few of the consultants speak English. For an extra fee, MacSource consultants will come to your office or home.

Cosmetics & perfumes

In addition to the places listed below, most of the department stores above have big-name cosmetic booths on their ground floors.

Body Basics

Pavilon, Vinohradská 50, Vinohrady, Prague 2 (2209 7105). Metro Náměstí Míru/11 tram. **Open** 9.30am-9pm Mon-Sat; noon-8pm Sun. **Credit** AmEx, DC, MC, V. **Map** p313 A3.
This Body Shop lookalike has affordable, pleasant-smelling cosmetics that are guaranteed not to have been tested on animals.
Branches: Celetná 17, Staré Město, Prague 1 (2481 2899); Marriott, V Celnici 10, Nové Město, Prague 1 (2288 1855); Koruna Palace, Václavské náměstí 1, Nové Město, Prague 1 (2447 3072); Myslbek Centre, Na příkopě 19-21, Staré Město, Prague 1 (2423 6800); Ruzyně Airport, Ruzyně, Prague 6 (2011 3595); Nákupní centrum, Plzeňská 8, Smíchov, Prague 5 (5732 2947).

Botanicus

Týn 3, Staré Město, Prague 1 (2489 5446/ www.botanicus.cz). Metro Náměstí Republiky/5, 8, 14 tram. **Open** 10am-8pm daily. **Credit** AmEx, MC, V. **Map** p308 J3.
An all-Czech, earthy version of the Body Shop. Tons of soaps, shampoos, body lotions and creams infused with herbs and other natural ingredients, all lovingly wrapped in brown paper.
Branches: Lucerna, Štěpánská 61, Nové Město, Prague 1 (2422 1927); Michalská 2, Staré Město, Prague 1 (2421 2977); Mostecká 4, Malá Strana, Prague 1 (5753 3328).

Eat, Drink, Shop

Caffeine and browsing at **The Globe Bookstore & Coffeehouse**. *See p165.*

Dry-cleaners & launderettes

There are plenty of places to do laundry in Prague. Many are conveniently located, and all the launderettes in the city charge roughly the same for washing and drying, so your choice chiefly depends on location.

CleanTouch

Na Rybníčku 1329, Vinohrady, Prague 2 (9636 8500). Metro IP Pavlova/4, 6, 10, 16, 22, 23 tram. **Open** 8am-8pm Mon-Fri; 8am-1pm Sat. **No credit cards. Map** p311 K7.

CleanTouch offers dry-cleaning at reasonable prices with a quick turnaround. Surprisingly enough, staff are friendly and efficient.

Branches: Dlouhá 20, Staré Město, Prague 1 (2481 9257); Supermarket Delvita, Jeremiášova 7A, Stodůlky, Prague 5 (5162 6371).

Prague Laundromat

Korunní 14, Vinohrady, Prague 2 (2251 0180/ www.volny.cz/laundromat). Metro Náměstí Míru/ 4, 10,16, 22, 23 tram. **Open** 8am-8pm daily. **No credit cards. Map** p313 A3.

The self-proclaimed 'first internet-laundromat in Europe' will do everything your laundry needs except get it dirty in the first place. They leave that part to you. On offer are self- and service washes and dry cleaning, plus internet access, in spotless surroundings. Grab a coffee or a beer at the café and chill in the small but welcoming lounge area, or check your email (at a premium price by Prague standards) while your laundry spins in one of the gleaming, top-of-the-line washers.

Electronics

Electrocity

Václavské náměstí 58, Nové Město, Prague 1 (961 58 132). Metro Muzeum/11 tram. **Open** 9am-9pm daily. **Credit** AmEx, DC, MC, V. **Map** p311 L6.

The Electrocity chain has made a splash at the top of Wenceslas Square with a bright, modern shop carrying everything from computers to sleek household appliances. Looking for a hairdryer? Chances are you'll be able to find the one you want in the colour you want at this electronics emporium.

Branches: Nový Smíchov (100m from Anděl metro station on Plzeňská), Smíchov, Prague 5 (5708 9907); Na Poříčí 50, Nové Město, Prague 1 (232 0413); Centrum Černý Most, Chlumecká 6, Černý Most, Prague 9 (8109 1120).

Fashion

Budget

Catwalk

Husova 8, Staré Město, Prague 1 (no phone). Metro Národní třída/6, 9, 18, 21, 22, 23 tram. **Open** 11am-7pm Mon-Fri; 11am-5pm Sat; noon-6pm Sun. **No credit cards. Map** p308 H4.

This is one of the city's original trendy second-hand shops, whose buyers obviously have discriminating taste. The shop may be tiny, but it's filled to maximum advantage with stylish pieces ranging from leather trench coats to linen shirts. The careful selection means prices are a bit higher than at some other second-hand shops.

Mýrnyx Týrnyx

Saská ulička, Malá Strana, Prague 1 (0603 460 351 mobile/www.myrnyxtyrnyx.com). Metro Malostranská/12, 18, 22, 23 tram. **Open** noon-7pm daily. **No credit cards. Map** p307 E3.

Prague's hippest second-hand fashion store doesn't waste any of its closet-sized space on boring togs. Day-Glo 1960s vinyl hangs alongside feather boas and Homburg hats. Owner Mia Květná buys pieces from indie Czech designers. She also runs an 'alternative models agency' out of the shop that does casting for commercials shooting in Prague. Prices reflect the creativity but you can always haggle – or swap something of your own.

Šatna

Konviktská 13, Staré Město, Prague 1 (no phone). Metro Národní třída/6, 9, 18, 21, 22, 23 tram. **Open** 11am-7pm Mon-Fri; 11am-6pm Sat. **No credit cards. Map** p308 G/H5.

A friendly neighbourhood second-hand shop run by a North American proprietor with taste – this shop actually wouldn't feel out of place in Chicago or Berkeley. Both men's and women's clothes are stocked and all at very reasonable prices. The selection of jeans is extensive and be sure to check out the leather jackets and coats.

Senior Bazar

Senovážné náměstí 18, Nové Město, Prague 1 (2423 5068). Metro Náměstí Republiky/3, 5, 9, 14, 24, 26 tram. **Open** 9am-5pm Mon-Fri. **No credit cards. Map** p309 L4.

A Prague institution and one of the best second-hand clothes shops in the city. Senior Bazar gets its stock straight from Prague's most stylish citizens – the octogenarians. Pick up a handmade 1950s summer dress or leather coat for peanuts. But get there early, as the *Elle* and *Cosmo* girls who work nearby do a clean sweep during their lunch breaks.
Branch: Karolíny Světlé 18, Staré Město, Prague 1 (2222 1067).

Children

Match Kids Wear

Jungmannova 18, Nové Město, Prague 1 (2494 8731). Metro Můstek/3, 9, 14, 24 tram. **Open** 9am-6pm Mon-Fri; 9am-noon Sat. **Credit** DC, MC, V. **Map** p308 J5.

For the kind of kid who won't be seen without his skateboard logos and designer labels. Obligatory fashions moderately priced.

Costume & formal dress hire

Every school and workplace holds its own *ples*, or ball, sometime between November and April – there are, in fact, annual balls for hunters, miners and Moravians. Getting to attend one of these balls is an excellent way to get a peak at Prague life. If you are invited to a ball, but have somehow managed to leave your tux, evening

gown or Napoleon costume at home, try some of the following. Be sure to make your arrangements several days in advance and take your passport as proof of identity.

Barrandov Studio, Fundus

Křiženeckého náměstí 322, Barrandov, Prague 5 (6707 2210). Metro Smíchovské nádraží, then 246, 247, 248 bus. **Open** 7am-3pm Mon-Fri. **No credit cards.**

Prague's main film studio rents everything you can imagine – from bear costumes to Prussian military uniforms – from its extensive wardrobe of over 240,000 costumes and accessories, including 9,000 wigs. None of this comes cheap. There's a 600-1,000 Kč fee for a one- to seven-day hire, plus you will need another 3,000-9,000 Kč for a deposit.

Designer

Nostalgie

Jakubská 8, Staré Město, Prague 1 (232 8030). Metro Náměstí Republiky/5, 14, 26 tram. **Open** 10.30am-6.30pm Mon-Sat. **Credit** AmEx, MC, V. **Map** p309 K3.

Flowing linen clothes in neutral shades designed by Marie Fleischmannová. Classy and conservative in the good sense, with truly lovely long winter coats. Alterations for a nominal fee.
Branch: Husova 8, Staré Město, Prague 1 (2423 9622).

Piano

Betlémské náměstí 6, Nové Město, Prague 2 (2222 0210). Metro Národní třída/6, 9, 18, 21, 22, 23 tram. **Open** 11am-7pm Mon-Fri; 11am-6pm Sat, Sun. **Credit** AmEx, MC, V. **Map** p308 G/H4/5.

Pamper yourself at this high-end shop that features a small but striking collection of Czech designerwear. The beautiful handbags line the shelves like works of art and the staff are friendly and welcoming. But be warned, it will cost you.

Sireal

Veletržní 18, Holešovice, Prague 7 (2080 5941). Metro Vltavská/3, 5, 8, 12, 14, 17 tram. **Open** 11am-7pm Mon-Fri. **Credit** AmEx, DC, MC, V. **Map** p312 D2.

Original designs including Gothic dresses with long flowing sleeves and laced bodices, elegant coats in unusual, tactile fabrics and '20s-style eveningwear. A delightful attention to detail that extends to whimsical buttons and other surprising touches makes this a shop for those who believe fashion should be fun.

Jewellery & accessories

Galerie Módy Heleny Fejkové

Lucerna Passage, Štěpánská 61, Nové Město, Prague 1 (2421 1514/ www.helenafejkova.cz). Metro Můstek/3, 9, 14, 24 tram. **Open** 10am-7pm Mon-Fri; 10am-3pm Sat. **Credit** AmEx, DC, MC, V. **Map** p311 K6.

Different by design

Prague was the fashion capital of Eastern Europe in the brief, shining period between the two world wars. The communist regime, on the other hand, wasn't exactly known for its cutting-edge couture. The fashion-conscious had to either make their own clothes or have the newest looks sent over from friends and family in the West. Fashion in Prague is still playing catch-up and tends to be a year or two behind the European style centres. Plus, Czechs are just more likely to spend their hard-earned crowns on mass-produced basics rather than splurge on one-of-a-kind clothes. But although the local fashion scene is small and scattered, it is steadily expanding as more designers set up business and residents earn more money with which to buy their creations.

Fashion shows at nightclubs are regular occurrences, as are design competitions, and many designers come here from other places to do photo shoots, attracted by the lower costs and abundance of modelling talent. Some of the more risk-taking designers work only on custom commissions or on commercial projects, so while you may be able to see outrageous stuff on the runways, the Czech-designed clothes on offer in boutiques tend to be much more mainstream. There is a variety of looks and styles, though, and the unique details along with the loving

workmanship make them worth a look. Not to mention the refreshingly intimate experience of having the shop's owner help you on with a coat or the chance to actually watch a designer at work as you browse.

For more Prague designer fashion, see also **Nostalgie** (*p169*), **Modes Robes** (*p171*), **Galerie Módy Heleny Fejkové** (*p169*) and **Sireal** (*p169*).

Fashion Galerie No.14

Opatovická 14, Nové Město, Prague 1 (261 367). Metro Národní třída/6, 9, 17, 18, 22, 23 tram. **Open** noon-7pm daily. **Credit** AmEx, MC, V. **Map** p310 H6.

Irena Jarošová's Nikkita line features feminine, delicate designs in tactile fabrics, including chiffon, cut velvet and silk. Although the focus is on exquisite dresses, there is also some casualwear and clubwear. Each piece is an original, and the prices reflect it. There is also handmade beaded jewellery by Inkognito and cute, smart kids' clothes by Bim Bam Bum pack the small shop, giving shoppers a great variety of original Czech pieces to choose from.

Tatiana

Platýz, Národní třída 37, Nové Město, Prague 1 (2421 1635). Metro Národní třída/6, 9, 17, 18, 22, 23 tram. **Open** 10am-7pm daily. **Credit** AmEx, MC, V. **Map** p308 H5.

Look past the racks of uninspiring clothes and you'll find a great designer jewellery section at the back. Getting to the shop is tricky, though. Once you're in Lucerna Passage, look upward to locate it, then head up the cinema staircase. Turn right on the landing and you're there. There's also a nice, quiet coffee shop from which you can gaze down upon the shoppers in the arcade below.

Galerie Vlasta

Staroměstské náměstí 5, Staré Město, Prague 1 (2231 8119). Metro Staroměstská/17, 18 tram. **Open** 10am-6pm Mon-Fri; 10am-1pm Sat. **Credit** DC, MC, V. **Map** p308 H-J3.

The pieces of jewellery designed by Valerie Wasserbauerová are more works of art than mere adornment. And this shop feels more like a gallery, with pieces displayed on the walls, as well as on stands and gleaming shelves. Gold and silver woven wire pieces range from dangling, geometric earrings to Egyptianesque collars. Picking something up here will cost you a pretty penny, but browsing is an experience in itself. And it's free.

Lingerie

Chez Parisienne

Pařížská 8, Staré Město, Prague 1 (2481 7786). Metro Staroměstská/17, 18 tram. **Open** 10am-7pm Mon-Fri; 10am-6pm Sat. **Credit** AmEx, DC, MC, V. **Map** p308 H3.

High-quality boxers, lingerie, T-shirts and pyjamas at sky-high prices just off Old Town Square. Nice selection of comfortable, casual dressing gowns.

Dessous-Dessous

Králodvorská 7, Staré Město, Prague 1 (2481 1779). Metro Náměstí Republiky/5, 8, 14 tram. **Open** 10am-7pm Mon-Fri; 10am-6pm Sat. **Credit** AmEx, MC, V. **Map** p309 K3.

It would be incredibly easy to spend a fortune here on the vast selection of super-sexy lingerie, including all the big names, or even on a pair of designer tights. Great selection of colourful bras and knickers from boy-cut lacy ones to G-strings, as well as pyjamas and chemises. The shop is roomy and bright and the staff are helpful.

This shop offers elegant clothes for the fashionable career woman who is hoping to steer clear of staid workday wear. The suits and separates feature unique details like leather trim or subtle but stylishly patterned fabrics, and the coats are classy. Prices here, as at most designer shops, are steep, but occasional sales offer some relief. Staff are friendly and helpful and the store is roomy, making for a pleasant shopping experience. Not at all intimidating.

Branch: Dušní 1, Staré Město, Prague 1 (2481 3723).

Devátá vlna

Saská ulička, Malá Strana, Prague 1 (2491 7773). Metro Malostranská/12, 18, 22, 23 tram. **Open** 10am-7pm daily. **Credit** AmEx, MC, V. **Map** p307 E3.

Devátá vlna, or 'Ninth Wave', was founded in 1994 by three Czech twentysomething women and is the only Czech design firm focusing largely on street and clubwear for the young and hip. The welcoming, bright little space offers everything you might need to wear when you're out on the town. Tucked away amid the moderately priced jeans, T-shirts and breezy little sundresses are fun surprises such as faux-fur trousers and disco-queen gold lamé dresses. The Devátá vlna workshop will also do custom orders.

Skiny

V Jámě 2, Nové Město, Prague 1 (2421 2535). Metro Můstek/3, 9, 14, 24 tram. **Open** 10am-7pm Mon-Fri; 10am-4pm Sat. **Credit** AmEx, DC, MC, V. **Map** p311 K6.

This boutique is especially good for sporty cotton lingerie and other bodywear for both women and men. Along its well-stocked shelves it also offers impressive quality and a wide range of colours and surprisingly practical layers.

Mid-range

Madeo Boutique

Vodičkova 28, Nové Město, Prague 1 (no phone). Metro Můstek/3, 9, 14, 24 tram. **Open** 10am-7pm Mon-Fri; 10am-3pm Sat. **Credit** AmEx, MC, V. **Map** p310 J6/p307 K5.

This well-stocked boutique features primarily classy casualwear with boutique service and a constantly updated collection. While prices vary depending upon what you're buying, bargains are to be found in the sales, especially on fun clubwear.

Modes Robes

Benediktská 5, Staré Město, Prague 1 (2482 6016/ www.cabbage.cz/modes-robes). Metro Náměstí Republiky/5, 8, 14 tram. **Open** 10am-7pm Mon-Fri; 10am-4pm Sat. **Credit** MC, V. **Map** p309 K2.

Run by a collective of seven local designers, with classy, not-too-outrageous-to-wear skirts, shirts and suits, mostly for women. This is everything a fringe fashion shop should be, with industrial cable twisted into postmodern clothes racks and walls used as canvases for artwork.

Vivienne Butique

Jungmannova 18, Nové Město, Prague 1 (0606 613 309 mobile). Metro Můstek/3, 9, 14, 24 tram. **Open** 10am-6pm Mon-Fri; 10am-2pm Sat. **No credit cards**. **Map** p308 J5.

This little shop offers unique, eye-catching fashions that run the gamut from tailored suits to transparent shirts that shouldn't go anywhere near the office unless you work in a disco. Once you have the basics, this is the place to come for a little pzazz.

Branch: Královodvorská 5, Staré Město, Prague 1 (2494 6023).

Shoes

While clothes shopping in Prague can be a frustrating experience, finding a pair of shoes is another matter. The streets seem to be lined with shoe shops and the selection is good. Shops stocked with Italian imports are very popular, but there are also plenty of Czech and other European chains that offer more reasonable prices and just as many styles. You should be able to find a pair that suits you perfectly in this city where knee-high leather boots are de rigueur.

The ART
Štěpánská 33, Nové Město, Prague 1 (2223 0598).
Metro Můstek/3, 9, 14, 24 tram. **Open** 9.30am-7pm Mon-Fri; 9.30am-5pm Sat. **Credit** AmEx, MC, V. **Map** p311 K6.
This shop has rows and rows of Doc Martens and other big, clunky shoes next to platform boots and mile-high heels, for those who want to put their heaviest, funkiest foot forward.
Branch: Národní 36, Nové Město, Prague 1 (2494 8828).

Baťa
Václavské náměstí 6, Nové Město, Prague 1 (2421 8133). Metro Můstek/3, 9, 14, 24 tram.
Open 9am-9pm Mon-Fri; 9am-8pm Sat; 10am-8pm Sun. **Credit** AmEx, DC, MC, V. **Map** p308 J5.
The Baťa family, whose shoe-making operation was one of the world's first multinational companies, saw trouble coming in 1938, so the owners wisely fled the country and re-established their headquarters in Canada. Whatever was left of the parent company after the war was nationalised ten years later. Now back in the driving seat, the Baťa family has refurbished its original 1928 modernist store on Wenceslas Square, and stocks some of the best-quality bargain footwear in Prague. It's kind of heart-warming in a way, actually.
Branches: Jindřišská 20, Nové Město, Prague 1 (2224 7349); Moskevská 27, Vršovice, Prague 10 (717 2860).

Humanic
Národní třída 34, Nové Město, Prague 1 (2492 0560). Metro Můstek or Národní třída/3, 6, 9, 14, 18, 22, 23, 24 tram. **Open** 9am-8pm Mon-Fri; 9am-7pm Sat; 10am-6pm Sun. **Credit** MC, V. **Map** p308 H5.
This busy shop specialises in cheap and cheerful fashion shoes. It's especially popular among trendy teenagers on tight budgets.

Vagabond
Pasáž Myslbek, Na příkopě 21, Staré Město, Prague 1 (2423 2234). Metro Můstek/3, 9, 14, 24 tram.
Open 10am-8pm Mon-Fri; 10am-7pm Sat; 11am-6pm Sun. **Credit** AmEx, DC, JCB, MC, V. **Map** p309 K4.
This is one of the city's best options for cool shoes and summer sandals that won't break the bank. Every new style is represented, and every imaginable colour is accounted for.

Shoe repairs

There are shoe repair shops in **Baťa** (*see above*) as well as **Tesco** and **Kotva** supermarkets (*see p160*). Failing that, check the *Zlaté stránky* (Yellow Pages) under *obuv-opravy*.

Jan Ondrášek
Navrátilova 12, Nové Město, Prague 1 (2223 1960). Metro Národní třída/3, 9, 14, 24 tram. **Open** 8am-6pm Mon-Thur; 8am-5pm Fri. **No credit cards**. **Map** p310 J7.
All the services you need to make your favourite pair of shoes last a little longer.

Florists

There's no shortage of flower shops in Prague, but most are more or less the same. Your local corner *květinářství* is likely to be as good as the centrally located places listed below. When sending flowers out of the country, plan ahead, as most florists require four or five days' notice.

Bohemia Flowers
Opletalova 22, Nové Město, Prague 1 (2272 2000/www.flowers.cz). Metro Muzeum/3, 9, 14, 24 tram. **Open** 8am-8pm Mon-Fri; 10am-1.30pm Sat. **Credit** AmEx, MC, V. **Map** p309 L5.
An expat-run venture that delivers tasteful, speedy, custom arrangements across town or anywhere else via Interflora. Choose from simple sprigs to wedding bouquets, viewing your selection online at the helpful website. The real-life shop is handily located just north of Wenceslas Square.

Květinářství U červeného Iva
Saská ulička, Malá Strana, Prague 1 (0604 855 286 mobile). Metro Malostranská/12, 22, 23 tram. **Open** 9am-7pm Mon-Fri; 10am-7pm Sat; 11am-7pm Sun. **Credit** AmEx, MC, V. **Map** p307 E3.
The Red Lion is situated in a picturesque little spot on a backstreet around the corner from the Charles Bridge. It sells fresh-cut flowers, charming ceramic pots and tasteful arrangements.

Food & drink

Food shopping in Prague has improved beyond all recognition in recent years and Western-style supermarkets are increasingly common outside the city centre. Still, while you may have to pay a bit more, most everyday shopping can still be done in the local *potraviny* or grocery store (*see p174* **Mind your beets**) and at the *ovoce-zelenina* (greengrocer). It's a good idea to know that supermarket shoppers are expected to have a basket or trolley with them at all times: those failing to observe this rule will be told off. If you want a sturdy plastic bag you will have to pay at least 2 Kč for it, so ask for a *tašku* before the cashier totals your bill.

Specialist

Bakeshop Praha
V Kolkovně 2, Staré Město, Prague 1 (2231 6823).
Metro Staroměstská/17, 18 tram. **Open** 7am-7pm
daily. **No credit cards. Map** p308 J2.
Leading a revolution on the Prague baking scene is
Anne Feeley's little shop selling an array of quiche,
brioche, walnut-raisin bread and sweet peanut butter cookies. Workers from all over Old Town duck
in here at lunchtime. Most take away but there's
always a pot of coffee brewing.

Čaj lepších časů
Národní třída 20, Nové Město, Prague 1 (no
phone). Metro Národní třída/6, 9, 18, 22 tram.
Open 9.30am-7pm Mon-Fri; 10am-7pm Sat;
noon-7pm Sun. **No credit cards. Map** p308 H5.
Join in the Prague tea craze at Čaj lepších časů.
Fresh teas from Sri Lanka are on offer, plus the
shop's own brand of teabags.

Čínská restaurace Hong Kong
Letenské náměstí 5, Holešovice, Prague 7
(3337 6209). Metro Můstek/3, 9, 14, 24 tram.
Open 11am-3pm; 6-11pm daily. **Credit** AmEx, MC,
V. **Map** p312 C2.
Adjoining this favourite, if out-of-the-way, neighbourhood Chinese restaurant is a shop well stocked
with glass noodles, chilli oils, ginger, soy sauces and
a nice range of green and black teas.

Country Life
Melantrichova 15, Staré Město, Prague 1 (2421
3366). Metro Můstek/3, 9, 14, 24 tram. **Open**
8.30am-7pm Mon-Thur; 8.30am-4pm Fri; 11am-6pm
Sun. **No credit cards. Map** p308 H4.
A fully stocked health-food shop with cold-pressed
oils, baked goods, corn meal and tofu. The buffet
restaurant (*see p131*) has been serving soy burgers
for years. The carrot soup here is a cheap treat, and
the DIY salads are hard to beat. The owners have
also opened an excellent soap and essence shop
just across the courtyard.
Branch: Jungmannova 1, Nové Město, Prague 1
(5704 4419).

Dobrá čajovna
Václavské náměstí 14, Nové Město, Prague 1 (2423
1480/www.cajovna.com). Metro Můstek/3, 9, 14,
24 tram. **Open** 10am-11pm Mon-Sat; 2-11pm Sun.
No credit cards. Map p308 J5.
More of a shrine than a tea shop, this place sells a
daunting array of oriental teas that can be sampled
in the dark, womb-like café. It also stocks everything
you might need for a tea ceremony, such as tiny
ceramic teapots and cups, joss sticks and Japanese
tea strainers (*see also p142*).

Fruits de France
Jindřišská 9, Nové Město, Prague 1 (2422 0304/
www.fdf.cz). Metro Můstek/3, 9, 14, 24 tram.
Open 9.30am-6.30pm Mon-Fri; 9.30am-1pm Sat.
No credit cards. Map p309 K5.

Opened by an astute Frenchwoman in 1991 when
Prague was still a gastronomic desert, today this
remains a mouth-watering oasis of fruit, vegetables,
olives, cheese, chocolate, oil and wine. Deliveries
from France arrive weekly. Such luxury does not
come cheap, however. Two stand-up-and-eat tables
at the rear of the shop allow for the service of quick
deli snacks with wine.
Branch: Bělehradská 94, Vinohrady, Prague 2
(2251 1261).

Jarmark lahůdky
Vodičkova 30, Nové Město, Prague 1 (2416 2619).
Metro Můstek/3, 9, 14, 24 tram. **Open** 8am-8pm
Mon-Fri; 10am-4pm Sat. **No credit cards.**
Map p309 K5.
A cracking little Italian deli off Wenceslas Square
with amaretto cakes, great jugs of cheapish chianti
and a fine sausage selection.

La Bretagne
Široká 22, Staré Město, Prague 1 (2481 9672).
Metro Staroměstská/17, 18 tram. **Open** 9.30am-
7.30pm daily. **No credit cards. Map** p308 H2/3.
An impressive range of fresh fish from squid to
shark is always on ice at this friendly, family-run
fishmonger's. Pick up your French chablis at the
same time for a classy night in.

Le Delice Belges
Pavilon, Vinohradská 50, Vinohrady, Prague 2 (786
8063). Metro Náměstí Míru/11 tram. **Open** 9.30am-
9pm Mon-Sat; noon-6pm Sun. **No credit cards.**
Map p313 A3.
Handmade chocolate shipped in each week from
Belgium. The Becherovka chocolates, made spe-
cially for the Czech market, have proved a big hit.
Gift boxes and delivery possible.

Potraviny U Cedru
Československé armády 18, Dejvice, Prague 6 (3334
2119). Metro Dejvická/20, 25 tram. **Open** 7am-11pm
daily. **No credit cards.**
Any grocery keeping these hours is a godsend in
Prague, but one that stocks basmati rice, houmous,
vine leaves and an assortment of other Lebanese
delights? Definitely worth the trek to Dejvice. If you
don't fancy cooking, go to the owners' restaurant, U
Cedru, a favourite Middle Eastern eatery.

Prodejna U Salvatora
Náprstkova 2, Staré Město, Prague 1 (2222 1161).
Metro Národní třída/17, 18 tram. **Open** 10am-6pm
Mon-Fri. **No credit cards. Map** p308 G4.
This sweet little shop in Old Town has more than 120
kinds of spices in paper packets or little glass jars.

Sea Food Fulcrum
Zborovská 49, Smíchov, Prague 5 (5732 0109).
Tram 6, 9, 12, 22. **Open** 10am-8pm Mon-Sat.
Credit DC, MC, V.
Every Wednesday and Saturday a shipment of more
than 35 types of fresh fish and seafood arrives from
Belgium, France and Spain. Salmon and lobsters and
also *escargot* at the cheapest rates in town.

Eat, Drink, Shop

Teuscher

Malá Štupartská 5, Staré Město, Prague 1 (2482 8050). Metro Náměstí Republiky/5, 8, 14 tram. **Open** *Jan-Feb* 10.30am-7.30pm daily. *Mar-Dec* 10am-8pm Mon-Fri; 10am-7pm Sat, Sun. **Credit** AmEx, MC, V. **Map** p308 J3.

A handier source for a quality gifts would be hard to find, and is in fact, unknown in this town. Extraordinary Swiss chocolates from truffles and pralines to beautiful handmade creations.

Vzpomínky na Afriku

Rybná & Jakubská, Staré Město, Prague 1 (0603 544 492 mobile/www.ebelcoffee.cz). Metro Náměstí Republiky/5, 14, 26 tram. **Open** 10am-7pm daily. **Credit** AmEx, DC, MC, V. **Map** p309 K3.

The smell of dark, roasted arabica coffee beans hits you as soon as you step through the doors of this caffeinated shop. If you can't make up your mind between the 30 or so types of beans on offer from all over the world, you can always sit at the table and try a cup. Staff will grind the beans to any grade that you request. Note that credit cards are accepted only on purchases over 500 Kč.

Supermarkets

In addition to the places listed below, there are centrally located supermarkets in the **Kotva** and **Tesco** department stores (*see p160*).

Carrefour

Radlická 1, Smíchov, Prague 5 (5728 4111). Metro Anděl/4, 6, 7, 9, 10, 14 tram. **Open** 7am-midnight daily. **Credit** AmEx, DC, MC, V.

This Paris-based chain, well on its way to taking over the world, is well stocked with a jaw-dropping selection of bread, cheese, meat, fish and produce. It's one of the largest supermarkets in town; you can easily spend an afternoon gliding through the aisles.

Delvita

Sokolovská 14, Karlín, Prague 8 (2232 7015/ 2232 7661). Metro Florenc/8, 24 tram. **Open** 7am-8pm Mon-Fri; 7am-7pm Sat; 9am-7pm Sun. **Credit** AmEx, MC, V.

This well-stocked Belgian chain has good vegetables, meat and wine, but poor bread and very little seafood. There are branches all over town.

Eat, Drink, Shop

Mind your beets

In virtually every sector, Prague is increasingly on a par with the Western European nations it hopes to sit down with soon at the European Union table. Czechs should pray, however, that the membership committee in Brussels never tries grocery shopping at a Prague *potraviny*.

Can't-be-bothered shop assistants, a truly mediocre selection and inconvenient opening hours are the hallmarks of this local shopping institution found on nearly every street corner.

When entering, get off to the right start with a kind, but not too friendly, *dobrý den*. Pick up a basket, even if you're just buying cigarettes, or risk the wrath of the checkout ladies. The prevailing theory is that people with baskets can't shoplift. Though, just to be sure, bored clerks will sometimes take to following you down the aisles, albeit usually at a discreet distance of a yard or two.

As you check out the curious selection, try to keep your cool. The shop may well be out of eggs but will often stock 35 different kinds of yoghurt and 50 brands of alcohol, including a popular new Slovak innovation – canned rum and cola. You can always try asking if there's a bigger selection in the back, but you'll most likely elicit a heavy sigh and a shrug of the shoulders. It also helps to have *potraviny* vocabulary down, as it's a 50-50 shot that you'll get any help, even if the shop assistants do speak some English.

If you forgot the merlot when you were at Carrefour, and were hoping to find one in your *potraviny*'s sea of spirits, forget it. You'll just have to settle for some Czech table wine like Frankovka (if they're out, vinegar will substitute nicely), or if you're lucky, you may just find a drinkable Hungarian Egri Bikaver. But don't expect to find canned tomatoes.

If the cashier's as gruff as a traffic warden, try not to take it personally. The *potraviny* has a long, proud history of customer abuse. It's not unheard of to be yelled at by the shopkeeper for putting the carefully arranged stacks of cans of beets out of order.

But, alas, for those who got some sort of thrill from the anger and misery of these trademark Czech shops, all bad things must come to an end, and there are signs that things are beginning to change even for this last bastion of the pre-Velvet Revolution days. In recent years, the country has seen an invasion of hypermarkets, which are changing shopping habits dramatically. It's forced many a *potraviny*, safe from competition for years, to modernise begrudgingly. A bit. Some closed their doors rather than resort to cheerful service but others, catching on to the new wave, have gone all out with shelves full of exotic items. Even pasta and pre-packaged TV dinners have been sighted.

Krone/Julius Meinl

Václavské náměstí 1, Nové Město, Prague 1 (2421 6331). Metro Můstek/3, 9, 14, 24 tram. **Open** 8am-9pm Mon-Sat; noon-8pm Sun. **Credit** AmEx, MC, V. **Map** p309 K5.

An Austrian-owned supermarket with a good selection of produce, a decent delicatessen and reasonably helpful service. It's also central and open late.
Branch: Václavské náměstí 59, Nové Město, Prague 1 (7265 1563); Pavilon, Vinohradská 50, Vinohrady, Prague 2 (2425 1283).

Food delivery

Délicatesse

Kostelní 6, Holešovice, Prague 7 (2057 1775/ 0601 295 128 mobile/www.delicatesse.cz). Metro Vltavská/1, 3, 14, 25 tram. **Open** 9am-9pm Mon-Fri. **No credit cards. Map** p312 C3/D3.

A French bakery with an assortment of fresh-baked hot and cold sandwiches, quiches and salads, all available for delivery. You can order from anywhere in Prague. Minimum order 200 Kč plus cheap delivery rates of 60-80 Kč per order.

Pizza Go Home

Sokolská 31, Nové Město, Prague 2 (8387 0000/ www.pizzagohome.cz). Metro IP Pavlova/4, 6, 11, 16, 22, 23, 34 tram. **Open** 24 hrs daily. **No credit cards. Map** p311 K7/8.

The pizza won't win any international taste tests, but it will quell the worst fit of 3am hunger pangs. With outlets citywide, Pizza Go Home is never far off. Delivery costs from 20 Kč to 170 Kč depending on the district. A 32cm (13in) pizza costs from 100 Kč to 180 Kč, depending on toppings.
Branches: Argentinská 1, Holešovice, Prague 7 (8387 0000); Ve Lhotce 814, Krč, Prague 4 (8387 0000); Mukařovského 1985, Stodůlky, Prague 5 (8387 0000); Trousilova 4, Kobylisy, Prague 8 (8387 0000).

Wine

Blatnička

Michalská 6, Staré Město, Prague 1 (2423 3612). Metro Národní třída/6, 9, 18, 22 tram. **Open** 10am-6pm Mon-Fri. **No credit cards. Map** p308 H4.

One of dozens of places around town to pick up cheap Moravian plonk or to sample any of a dozen on the spot. '*Sudová vína*' signs indicate that the shop will fill your plastic bottle with, erm, fresh local wine for next to nothing.

Cellarius

Lucerna Passage, Štěpánská 61, Nové Město, Prague 1 (2421 0979/www.cellarius.cz). Metro Můstek/3, 9, 14, 24 tram. **Open** 9.30am-9pm Mon-Sat; 3-8pm Sun. **Credit** AmEx, MC, V. **Map** p311 K6.

This was one of the first Prague shops to organise and collect Moravian wines. It is also an excellent place to pick up some interesting vintages rarely available in the city. It carries a few international wines along with the local stuff.

Dionýsos

Vinařického 6, Vinohrady, Prague 2 (2492 2237). Metro Karlovo náměstí/7, 18, 24 tram. **Open** 10am-6pm Mon-Fri. **Credit** AmEx, MC, V. **Map** p310 H10.

A classy wine merchant patronised by Prague's elite, Dionýsos has a respectable range of foreign wines but specialises in top-quality local varieties, including older vintages. The staff know and love their wines and will guide you along the shelves.

Vinotéka u Svatého Štěpána

Štěpánská 7, Nové Město, Prague 2 (2190 1160). Metro Muzeum/3, 9, 14, 24 tram. **Open** 10am-7pm Mon-Fri. **Credit** AmEx, MC, V. **Map** p311 K6.

Who says Czechs only drink beer? The affordable international selection includes wines from France, Italy, Spain, Austria, Hungary and Chile, as well as prime vineyard areas of South Moravia. Champagnes and malt whiskies also in abundance.

Gifts

Most expats have a nervous breakdown looking for gifts around Christmas time, so don't worry if you're having difficulty locating that special something. The trick is to avoid the tourist tat and go for the less obvious choices – it's just a question of knowing where to look. Czech CDs, both pop and classical, are always a good buy at approximately half the price of CDs back home, and most of the bookshops listed in this chapter stock beautiful calendars and Czech novels translated into English (*see p164*). For booze lovers, you can always try sending them a bottle of Becherovka – that sweet, herby spirit famed as a 'medicine' – will prove an eye-opener. Whatever you do, don't get bullied into buying one of those silly chicken toys flogged around Old Town Square. They're nothing more than half a loo roll on a string and usually fall apart in the first ten minutes. Try one of the stores on our list of toy shops, instead (*see p181*).

Candles Gallery

Újezd 31, Malá Strana, Prague 1 (0603 140 118 mobile/www.candle-gallery.com). Metro Malostranská/12, 18, 22, 23 tram. **Open** 10am-7pm daily. **No credit cards. Map** p307 E5.

The creations of these wax sculptors adorn *les plus chic* restaurants in Prague. If your luggage is large enough, you can take home a lovely 1.2m (4-ft), four-wick, cornflower-blue wax candle or a large sphere covered in Grecian architectural ornamentation.
Branch: Karlova 23, Staré Město, Prague 1 (9632 5464).

Charita Florentinum

Ječná 2, Nové Město, Prague 2 (2492 0448). Metro Karlovo náměstí/4, 6, 16, 22, 34 tram. **Open** 8am-6pm Mon-Fri; 9am-1pm Sat. **No credit cards. Map** p310 J8.

Where Czech priests purchase their robes, incense burners and other gear. Incredibly cheap candles.

Eat, Drink, Shop

Papírový Svět

Václavské náměstí 38, Nové Město, Prague 1 (2422 8462/www.papirovysvet.cz). Metro Můstek/3, 9, 14, 24 tram. **Open** 10am-8pm Mon-Fri; 10am-6pm Sat. **Credit** AmEx, DC, MC, V. **Map** p311 K6.

Cardboard never looked better. All the boxes, bags and wrappings sold in Paper World are handmade from recycled paper and range in price from 50 Kč to 200 Kč. Also in stock are paper-product presents, such as the hand-made chess set made entirely out of cardboard that sells for 12,000 Kč.

Včelařské potřeby

Křemencova 8, Nové Město, Prague 2 (2491 7597/www.beekeeping.cz). Metro Karlovo náměstí/4, 6, 16, 22, 34 tram. **Open** 9am-5pm Mon, Wed; 9am-6pm Tue; 9am-7pm Thur; 9am-2pm Fri. **No credit cards. Map** p310 H6/7.

The creative gift! The Beekeeper's Store has everything you need to start your own hives business: gloves, headgear and manuals (in Czech). For the more casual bee fancier, there's bee shampoo, wine and dozens of fresh honey varieties.

Hair & beauty

Those after the simplest of cuts should be able to get a decent trim in any *kadeřnictví* (hairdresser's) or *holičství* (barbershop) for around 100 Kč. But just because you're in the former Eastern bloc doesn't mean you have to go without the kind of cut you'd expect to walk out of a top Western salon with. Though rates at chic salons can be pricey for locals, anyone who is thinking in terms of Western currency can find a good bargain.

James & Monika

Malá Štupartská 9, Staré Město, Prague 1 (2482 7373/www.jameshair.cz). Metro Náměstí Republiky/5, 8, 14 tram. **Open** 8am-8pm Tue-Fri; 9am-5pm Sat. **No credit cards. Map** p308 J3.

This international stylist and his crew have star status on the Prague fashion scene. Dream cuts and makeovers are all in a day's work and the customer raves have spread throughout town. A cut costs between 550 Kč and 1,150 Kč depending on the level of experience of your hairdresser. Most of the staff stylists speak English.

The Salon

Dušní 6, Staré Město, Prague 1 (2481 7575). Metro Staroměstská/17, 18 tram. **Open** 9am-9pm Mon-Fri; 11am-6pm Sat. **No credit cards. Map** p308 J3.

Devotees of Libor Šula's salon agree that the Italian-born Czech delivers on his promise of 'an international salon without any Czech attitude'. He is personally booked months in advance but you can usually get an appointment to see one of his well-trained English-speaking staff with a week or two's notice. Cuts for women start at 490 Kč and can go up to 1,500 Kč if you want highlights or colour. Cuts for men are usually under 300 Kč.

Šarm

Jungmannova 1, Nové Město, Prague 1 (2422 4814). Metro Můstek/6, 9, 18, 22 tram. **Open** 7am-9pm Mon-Fri. **No credit cards. Map** p308 J5.

A little more upscale than your average *kadeřnictví*, Šarm is still incredibly reasonable. More than 17 locations, a few listed below.
Branches: Dlouhá 1, Staré Město, Prague 1 (2231 0133); Revoluční 25, Staré Město, Prague 1 (2482 6264).

Thai World

Týnská 9, Staré Město, Prague 1 (3338 2428/www.thaiworld.cz). **Open** 11am-8pm daily. **Massage** 590 Kč/hr; 295 Kč/30mins. **No credit cards. Map** p308 J3.

The staff at this relaxation haven in Old Town are certified at the Wat Po medical school in Bangkok and offer traditional Thai massage (which focuses on pressure points in the body), reflexology, Swedish oil massage or combinations. Amazing how good an hour or two of being stretched, pounded, prodded and rubbed can make you feel.

Household

Bauhaus

Budějovická 1A, Pankrác, Prague 4 (4173 2014/www.bauhaus.cz). Metro Pankrác. **Open** 8am-8pm Mon-Sat; 9am-7pm Sun. **Credit** AmEx, MC, V.

This major DIY store in the southern part of Prague has all the tools, lumber and pipe you'd ever need.
Branch: Ústecká 822, Chabry, Prague 8 (8400 1811).

Galerie bydlení

Truhlářská 20, Nové Město, Prague 1 (2231 2383). Metro Náměstí Republiky/5, 14, 26 tram. **Open** 9am-6pm Mon-Thur; 9am-5pm Fri. **Credit** AmEx, MC, V. **Map** p309 L2.

Wacky, surreal, fun furniture design. Well on the way to kitsch, though.

IKEA

Skandinávská 1, Zličín, Prague 5 (5161 0110). Metro Zličín. **Open** 10am-8pm daily. **Credit** MC, V.

When Swedish furniture giant IKEA first opened its megastore in the city in 1996, more than 100,000 people – 8% of the population of Prague – visited it in the first four days. IKEA is a byword for style and western modernisation in Prague and it has yet to meet with a serious competitor to challenge it for quality and value for money. Riding the metro out this way on a Saturday and watching the hordes of excited shoppers on their way home with their IKEA bags is entertainment in itself.

Le Patio

Národní 22, Nové Město, Prague 1 (2493 4853). Metro Národní třída/6, 9, 17, 18, 22, 23 tram. **Open** 10am-7pm Mon-Sat; 11am-7pm Sun. **Credit** AmEx, DC, MC, V. **Map** p308 H5.

This place is a crafty marriage of local ironworking, woodcarving and stone-cutti.ng skills with romantic international designs. Wrought iron constructions

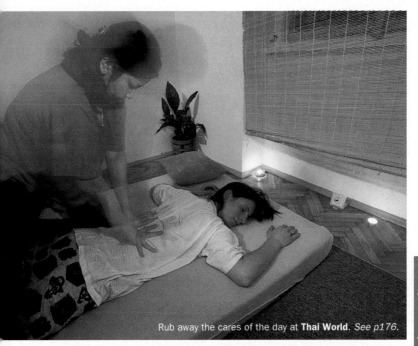

Rub away the cares of the day at **Thai World**. *See p176.*

from candleholders to bird cages are set off by the odd bunch of delicate and colourful paper flowers or by a unique sculptural wooden bowl.
Branches: Pařížská 20, Staré Město, Prague 1 (2232 0260); Ungelt 640, Staré Město, Prague 1 (2489 5773); V Celnici 4, Nové Město, Prague 1 (9632 5464).

Potten & Pannen
Václavské náměstí 57, Nové Město, Prague 1 (2421 4936/www.pottenpannen.cz). Metro Muzeum/ 3, 9, 14, 24 tram. **Open** 10am-7pm Mon-Sat. **Credit** AmEx, DC, MC, V. **Map** p309 K6.
The last word in cookware – grinders, choppers, graters and squeezers, shining pots and pans. Sells Calphalm aluminium saucepans from the US and Emile Henry oven-to-tableware, plus improbable Rosenthal Studio Haus kitchen tools. It also stocks much-coveted Illy coffee products.
Branch: Vodičkova 2, Nové Město, Prague 1 (2223 1697).

Key cutting & locksmiths

The best places to have keys cut are the major supermarkets in town – here you're more likely to find English speakers and you're less likely to be ripped off. Try either **Tesco** (*see p160*) or at the bottom of the escalators at the entrance to the **Kotva** supermarket (*see p160*). For a 24-hour locksmith, try the following.

KEY Non-Stop
Vazovova 3, Kamýk, Prague 12 (401 6616). Bus 117, 165. **Open** 24hrs daily. **No credit cards**.
Lock picking, cheap cutting and copying.

Music

Records, tapes & CDs

234
Bělehradská 120, Nové Město, Prague 2 (2425 2741). Metro IP Pavlova/6, 11 tram. **Open** 9.30am-7.30pm Mon-Fri; 11am-4pm Sat; 1-5pm Sun. **Credit** AmEx, DC, MC, V. **Map** p311 L8.
This small, CD shop specialises in techno, house and hip hop. Owned by a member of the 1970s Czech band *Garáž*, it's an excellent place to find old Czech dissident rock. English-speaking staff.

Bazar
Karoliny Světlé 12, Staré Město, Prague 1 (2423 3467). Metro Národní třída/6, 9, 18, 21, 22, 23 tram. **Open** 10am-1pm, 1.30-7pm Mon-Fri. **Credit** MC, V. **Map** p308 G5.
This aptly named shop has loads of cheap second-hand CDs with a fair range of jazz and classical options, many for only 150 Kč. The place to pick up Czech folk music or Karel Gott records without having to agonise over the price.

Big-hair rock lives on at **Music shop antikvariát**. See p179

Bontonland Megastore

Palác Koruna, Václavské náměstí 1, Nové Město,
Prague 1 (2422 6236/www.bontonland.cz). Metro
Můstek/3, 9, 14, 24 tram. **Open** 9am-8pm daily.
Credit AmEx, MC, V. **Map** p310 J6.

This was one of the first Western-style music mega-
stores in Eastern Europe when it opened in 1996, and
it was a welcome addition for local music lovers. Its
well-stocked shelves hold masses of stereo equipment, videos, CD-Roms, books, vinyl posters, T-
shirts, an instore DJ, listening posts and a café – as
well as CDs and cassettes of every genre. There's
rock and pop aplenty, but stocks of world music and
techno are limited. Good jazz section.

Bontonland

Jungmannova 20, Nové Město, Prague 1 (2494
8718). Metro Národní třída or Můstek/3, 9, 14,
24 tram. **Open** 9am-7pm daily. **Credit** AmEx, DC,
MC, V. **Map** p308 J6.

The former state recording company, now privatised
and owned by Bonton, still has its own shop. To see
what's in stock, flick through the files on the counter.
Knowledgeable staff and an excellent selection of
cheap Czech classical recordings.

Disko Duck

Karlova 12, Staré Město, Prague 1 (2421 3405/
www.diskoduck.cz). Metro Staromestska. **Open** noon-
7pm daily. **No credit cards. Map** p308 G4.

A major mecca for Prague DJs, Disko Duck stocks
Old Town's largest selection of vinyl dance music. It's
all sorted by genre, of course, and there are four
turntables available for checking out the material
before you buy. New stuff is constantly arriving, so
whether it's Goa or drum 'n' bass that's required to
do the job, this place will most likely have the latest.
The shop is easy to miss though, hidden away as it
is in an old shopping arcade that was once a crumbling apartment building.

Maximum Underground

Jilská 22, Staré Město, Prague 1 (2254 1333).
Metro Můstek, Národní třída or Staroměstská/3, 9,
18, 22 tram. **Open** 11am-7pm Mon-Sat; 1-7pm Sun.
No credit cards. Map p308 H4.

Within a sort of alternative shopping mall that
includes clothing stores, tattooing and piercing par-
lours, this friendly shop stocks mainly CDs, with
some cassettes and vinyl. There's a good selection
of techno, ambient and hardcore, and the shop assistants seem to know their stuff.

Music shop-antikvariát

Národní třída 25, Nové Město, Prague 1 (2108
5268). Metro Národní Třída/6, 9, 18, 22 tram.
Open 10.30am-7pm Mon-Sat. **Credit** AmEx, JCB,
MC, V. **Map** p308 H5.

A collectors' paradise, with hundreds of used CDs
and LPs from the 1920s onwards. The selection
includes jazz, blues, country, folk, Czech pop/rock,
classical and a pricey stack of rarities and bootlegs.
Branch: Mostecká 4, Malá Strana, Prague 1
(no phone).

Pohodlí

Benediktská 7, Staré Město, Prague 1 (2482
7028). Metro Náměstí Republiky/5, 14, 26 tram.
Open 9.30am-7pm Mon-Fri; 10am-4pm Sat.
No credit cards. Map p309 K2.

This tiny, family-run ethnic music store carries
everything from Zimbabwean marimba music to
Nusrat Fateh Ali Khan, plus a fair selection of
Moravian folk music and Czech alternative music.
The Polish owner is quite happy to let you listen to
your chosen CD before purchasing. If you're lucky,
you might even be offered a cup of tea.

Musical instruments

Hudební nástroje – Jakub Lis

Náprstkova 10, Staré Město, Prague 1 (2222
1110/www.nastroje-hudebni.cz). Metro Můstek or
Staroměstská/17, 18 tram. **Open** 10am-6pm Mon-
Fri; 10am-4pm Sat. **Credit** DC, MC, V. **Map** p308 G4.

This is a small, cheery shop with a good selection of
second-hand electric and acoustic guitars, violins,
cellos and accordions, plus Indian and African
drums and instruments. All this along with the usual
musicians' paraphernalia – strings, rosin and reeds.
Just think of the money you'll make busking in
Wenceslas Square. Pay for itself in no time.

Praha Music Centre

Soukenická 20, Nové Město, Prague 1 (2231 3972/
www.pmc.cz). Metro Náměstí Republiky/5, 14, 26
tram. **Open** 9am-5pm Mon-Fri. **Credit** MC, V.
Map p309 L2.

Caters admirably to plugged-in musicians. Has the
standard equipment but is especially good for pick-
ups, pedals and second-hand amps.
Branches: Revoluční 14, Staré Město, Prague 1
(2231 1693); Klimentská 34, Staré Město, Prague 1
(2231 5396).

U zlatého kohouta

Michalská 3, Staré Město, Prague 1 (2421
2874). Metro Můstek/3, 9, 14, 24 tram. **Open**
10am-noon, 1-6pm Mon-Fri. **Credit** AmEx, DC,
MC, V. **Map** p308 H4.

Restorers of and dealers in fine old Bohemian string
instruments, from violins to double basses, famed
for the sound quality produced by resonant pine.
How craftsmen of this high calibre survived the
shoddy standards everyone else adopted in the
decades before 1989 (and still seem to have trouble
shaking) is a mystery.

Opticians

It is a nice fact of life that eyeglass frames
and lenses can be incredibly cheap in Prague,
making it possible to get a basic pair of glasses
for around 1,500 Kč. Be aware, though, that
the vast majority of opticians do not use
shatterproof glass. The stores listed here
are more upmarket than the average opticians
and stock high-quality lenses.

Eat, Drink, Shop

AM Optik Studio

Jungmannova 19, Nové Město, Prague 1 (2494 8451).
Metro Národní třída/3, 9, 14, 24 tram. **Open** 8am-
6pm Mon-Fri. **Credit** AmEx, MC, V. **Map** p310 J6.
A reasonably fashionable choice, though without
much help for non-Czech speakers.

Eiffel Optic

Na příkopě 25, Nové Město, Prague 1 (2423 4966).
Metro Můstek/3, 9, 14, 24 tram. **Open** 8am-8pm
Mon-Fri; 9am-8pm Sat; 9.30am-6.30pm Sun.
Credit AmEx, DC, MC, V. **Map** p309 K4.
This shop has a strong reputation for reliable,
speedy service with a smile, and a small but better-
than-average range of frames. Pairs of glasses are
available for as little as 2,000 Kč, and there are
coloured contact lenses if you need a quick and
handy disguise. Free eye tests. Note that the staff
have difficulty with English.
Branches: Ječná 6, Nové Město, Prague 2
(2492 1487); Celetná 38, Staré Město, Prague 1
(2161 3301); Vodičkova 17, Nové Město, Prague 1
(9623 9020); Bělehradská 102, Nové Město, Prague 2
(2252 2272); Centrum Černý Most, Černý Most,
Prague 9 (8191 6946).

GrandOptical

Myslbek Centre, Na příkopě 19-21, Staré Město,
Prague 1 (2423 8371). Metro Můstek/3, 9, 14, 24
tram. **Open** 9am-7pm Mon-Sat; 10am-6pm Sun.
Credit AmEx, MC, V. **Map** p309 K4.
Owned and run by British chain Vision Express,
GrandOptical is well known for fast, precision lens
crafting. Helpful English-speaking staff, but all of
this comes at a premium.

Photocopying

Copy General

Senovážné náměstí 26, Nové Město, Prague 1 (2423
0020/www.copygeneral.cz). Metro Náměstí Republiky/
3, 5, 9, 14, 24, 26 tram. **Open** 24hrs daily. **Credit**
MC, V. **Map** p309 L4.
This is the place to come if you suddenly need a
colour photocopy at four in the morning. Or if you
need binding, black and white digital printing, full-
colour digital printing, pick-up and delivery services
or print-outs from ZIP, CD or JAZ discs. Some assistants speak reasonable English.
Branches: Vinohradská 13, Vinohrady, Prague 2
(2225 3011); Milady Horákové 4, Holešovice, Prague 7
(3337 0013); Na Bělidle 40, Smíchov, Prague 5
(5731 6653).

Photography

Camera shops & repairs

AZ Foto

Senovážná 8, Nové Město, Prague 1 (2421 3443/
www.azfoto.cz). Metro Náměstí Republiky/3, 5, 9, 14,
24, 26 tram. **Open** 8.30am-6pm Mon-Fri; 9am-noon
Sat. **Credit** MC, V. **Map** p309 K4.

This helpful shop offers a variety of both new and
second-hand cameras and various accessories.
Particularly strong on second-hand lenses.

Fototechnika a video

Vodičkova 36, Nové Město, Prague 1 (2423 2246/
www.fotoskoda.cz). Metro Můstek/3, 9, 14, 24 tram.
Open 8.30am-8pm Mon-Fri; 9am-6pm Sat.
Credit AmEx, DC, MC, V. **Map** p308 J6.
One-stop shopping for the professional photographer. You'll find a wider range of film here than in
any other store in the city, plus tripods, lights,
enlargers, and both second-hand and new cameras.
Prices tend to be a little bit higher than at smaller
shops. At the back of the shop you can pick up an
old Soviet or East German camera for around 500
Kč, or a black and white developer for under 4,000
Kč. This section is always crowded with the
cognoscenti, so you'll need to assert yourself if you
want to get served. Note that credit cards aren't
accepted for second-hand merchandise.

Jan Pazdera obchod a opravna

Lucerna Passage, Vodičkova 30, Nové Město, Prague
1 (2421 6197). Metro Můstek/3, 9, 14, 24 tram.
Open 10am-6pm Mon-Fri; 9am-1pm Sat. **No credit**
cards. Map p309 K5.
This shop features used cameras, movie cameras,
enlargers, filters, microscopes, telescopes, tripods
and just about every other photographic accessory
you can imagine. This excellent shop also stocks
plenty of affordable second-hand cameras from the
former communist bloc, which are currently quite
fashionable among photographers in the West. The
staff also carry out simple camera repairs.

Photo developing

Photo shops are rife all over the tourist areas, so
finding a place to get your pictures developed
is never a problem. Don't go just anywhere
though, because, with the exceptions below,
however, old chemicals and inattention can
be common. Try also **Tesco** (*see p160*).

Česká tisková kancelář (ČTK)

Opletalova 5-7, Nové Město, Prague 1 (2209
8353/8237). Metro Muzeum/3, 9, 14, 24 tram.
Open 8am-7pm Mon-Fri; 9am-1pm Sat. **Credit**
MC, V. **Map** p311 K6.
One of the only places to get black and white photos developed 'quickly' – meaning a week, or three
days if you fork out a 50% 'rush' fee. This is a professional developing place in the same building as
the country's leading news agency – though even
here printing quality can be uneven. It's pricey and
very professional, so maybe this isn't really a place
to bring mere holiday snaps.

Fotoplus

Na příkopě 17, Nové Město, Prague 1 (2421 3121).
Metro Náměstí Republiky/5, 14, 26 tram. **Open** 9am-
7.30pm Mon-Fri; 9am-7pm Sat; 10am-7pm Sun.
Credit AmEx, MC, V. **Map** p309 K4.

Quality, one-hour developing and able to handle black and white printing, but not developing. A little English spoken. This place also has a quite nice selection of photo albums.

Stationery & art materials

The ubiquitous *papírnictví* shops sell just about everything from envelopes to toilet paper. If you can't find what you want in one, try **Kotva** (*see p160*) or one of those listed below.

Altamira

Jilská 2, Staré Město, Prague 1 (2421 9950). Metro Národní třída/6, 9, 18, 21, 22, 23 tram. **Open** 9am-7pm Mon-Fri; 9am-4pm Sat. **No credit cards**. **Map** p308 H4.

This is truly a specialist art shop, and so it is just crammed with stretchers, easels, canvases, paints, chalks and brushes. Everything you need to access the Picasso within. Or whoever's in there. Maybe you can get in touch with your inner Jackson Pollock. Filled to the brim with brushes, there's not room for much else here.
Branch: Skořepka 2, Nové Město, Prague 1 (2422 0923).

Loco Plus

Palackého 10, Nové Město, Prague 1 (2494 7732). Metro Národní třída or Můstek/3, 9, 14, 24 tram. **Open** 8.30am-6.30pm Mon-Thur; 8.30am-6pm Fri; 9am-noon Sat. **No credit cards**. **Map** p310 J6.

This art shop offers masses and masses of good, cheap, local stationery and no overpriced imports. Worth a visit when you've suddenly realised that you've got dozens and dozens of letters to write.

McPaper & Co

Dukelských hrdinů 39, Holešovice, Prague 7 (3338 0002). Metro Vltavská/1, 3, 5, 8, 14, 25, 26 tram. **Open** 8.30am-6.30pm Mon-Fri. **No credit cards**. **Map** p312 D2.

Glossy German Berlitz products, including sketch pads, wrapping paper, jiffy bags and tableware.

Toys

An invasion of Barbie dolls and Polly Pockets has hit Prague, sadly, but traditional Czech toys are nonetheless managing to hold their own, at least among visitors. There is no shortage of places to buy – puppets, puzzles and pull-alongs. Prague's department stores have large toy sections to please all but the pickiest kid.

Ivre

Jakubská 3, Staré Město, Prague 1 (232 6644). Metro Náměstí Republiky/5, 14, 26 tram. **Open** 10am-6pm daily. **Credit** MC, V. **Map** p309 K3.

This adorable shop features soft toys hand-sewn in the shape of moons, suns, puppets and pillows by the artist Renáta Löfelmannová.
Branch: U Radnice 22, Staré Město, Prague 1 (2423 6865).

Find traditional Czech puppets at the **Havelský market**. *See p163*.

Eat, Drink, Shop

Every weird film you've ever wanted is at **Virus Video**.

McToy

Jakubská 8, Staré Město, Prague 1 (no phone). Metro Náměstí Republiky/5, 14, 26 tram. **Open** 10am-6.30pm Mon-Sat. **Credit** MC, V. **Map** p309 K3.
This interestingly named shop is neither Scottish nor related to the McDonald's hamburger chain. Instead, it specialises in toy animals. The miniature collection, which includes Smurfs, is particularly impressive. There's a handy, if small, play area for the adorable little tykes in the back.

MPM

Myslíkova 19, Nové Město, Prague 1 (2493 0257/ www.mpm.cz). Metro Karlovo náměstí/3, 6, 14, 17, 18, 22, 24 tram. **Open** 9am-6pm Mon-Fri; 9am-1pm Sat. **Credit** MC, V. **Map** p310 H7.
This is a modeller's paradise with hundreds of kits: including every make of aircraft, tank and ship, plus battalions of toy soldiers.

Sparky's Dům hraček

Havířská 2, Staré Město, Prague 1 (2423 9309/ www.sparkys.cz). Metro Můstek/3, 9, 14, 24 tram. **Open** 10am-7pm Mon-Sat; 10am-6pm Sun. **Credit** AmEx, MC, V. **Map** p308 J4.
If you need to tire your brood quickly with sensory overload, Sparky's House of Toys is the place to go. There are quite literally thousands of playthings here, from building blocks to plush toys that help tots identify their body parts. It's all top of the line, so you won't get off cheaply, but there's little risk of not finding a child's dream acquisition here. All toys meet EU safety directives. A useful hint: the shop is near the bottom of Wenceslas Square, so a visit here may usefully serve as a bribe to get the kids to move quietly through the galleries and museums of neighbouring Old Town.

Video rental

The following stock DVDs and videos in PAL and NTSC format. Other rental outlets include **Jáma** and **Video to Go**.

Video Express

Žitná 41, Prague 2 (2221 1425/www. videoexpress.cz). Metro Muzeum/11 tram. **Open** 11am-11pm daily. **No credit cards. Map** p311 K7.
Half bar, half video shop, the ultra-hip collection includes the newest flicks on video to reach Prague, with a good mix of commercial hits and indie gems like the brilliant *Amores Perros.*
Branch: Prokopská 3, Nové Město, Prague 1 (5753 5139).

Video Gourmet

Jakubská 12, Staré Město, Prague 1 (2232 3364). Metro Náměstí Republiky/5, 8, 14 tram. **Open** 11am-11pm daily. **Credit** AmEx, MC, V. **Map** p309 K3.
Part of the **Red Hot & Blues** restaurant in Old Town (*see p125*), this place stocks consistently cool videos, plus fresh takeaway food like Cajun chicken, curries and carrot cake. Rental videos available in both NTSC and PAL formats.

Virus Video

Dlouhá 33, Prague 1 (0607 508 933 mobile). Metro Staroměstská/17, 18 tram. **Open** 1pm-midnight daily. **No credit cards. Map** p309 K2.
Just inside the lobby of the **Roxy** club (*see p228*) is this tiny counter with the best selection of fringe movies in Prague, from Roger Corman schlock to the complete works of the Czech surrealist animator Jan Švankmajer. From Mangas to Cold War documentaries, this is the place to find what you want.

Arts & Entertainment

By Season

Whether kicking up your heels at a winter ball or dancing around a bonfire on Witches' Night, Prague's a shape-shifting wonder as the seasons roll past.

Prague's elusive summer sun is best spotted in Malá Strana parks.

Like any good fairytale setting, Prague is adept at scene changes. By winter, which seems eternal when you're in it, the city's a sleepy, grog-guzzling, grey and melancholy place, though unquestionably beautiful with it. In Christmas markets, carp are bashed into submission for supper and fireworks light up New Year's Eve (*Silvestr*). As spring arrives, people seem to blossom along with the flowers and chestnut trees, and emerge like moles into the sunlight. Beer gardens fill up even when the crowd is shivering at dusk. Off come the layers, as Stromovka Park fills with runners training for the **Prague International Marathon** (*see p185*). Soon after, the **Prague Spring Festival** (*see p185*) heralds the warm weather as it has for half a century.

With the hot days of June and July, locals (including the staff of most cultural institutions, which go dark until September) tend to clear out to avoid the flood of tourists and head for the country. If you can get an invitation, you may get to experience the joy of the *chata* (cottage), and blueberry picking.

The city does bear its own sweet fruit during the summer months, though, with music fests and the Tanec Praha modern dance recitals. In autumn, symphonies, operas and balls return to town, and with them **Prague Autumn** (*see p186*) – and not a little of the suspiciously mild drink known as **Burčák** (*see p186*). And, of course, with the tourists finally gone, Praguers get their beautiful city back to themselves – just as it begins to fill with ice and smog. Miserable though winter undeniably is, it has its rewards: the glorious spires that tower above Old Town are an incomparable sight in the snow.

Spring

Matejská pouť

Výstaviště, Holešovice, Prague 7 (2010 3204). Metro Vltavská/5, 14, 25 tram. **Admission** 30-50 Kč. **Date** Feb-Mar.
The St Matthew's Fair marks the arrival of warm weather with cheesy rides for the kids at a run-down funfair at Prague's exhibition grounds, Výstaviště. Dodgem cars at 10 Kč a pop and the Ferris wheel bring out the juvenile in all.

Prague Jazz Festival

Various venues (AghaRTA 2221 1275/
www.agharta.cz). **Date** Mar-Oct. **Admission** varies
according to venue. **Map** p309 K7.

The AghaRTA club (*see p220*) that organises this
event works hard to keep the flame of Prague's
strong jazz tradition alive. The festival is small and
sporadic, carrying on intermittently throughout the
spring, summer and autumn. It can bring out excellent performances by top international acts both at
the Lucerna Music Bar (*see p218*) and at various outdoor locations around town.

Easter

Date Mar/Apr.

Men rush around the country beating women on the
backside with willow sticks. Women respond by
dousing the men with cold water but also by giving
them painted eggs. Then everyone does a lot of shots
of alcohol. This ancient fertility rite is rarely seen in
Prague these days, but painted eggs and willow
sticks are on sale all over the city.

Witches' Night

Pálení čarodějnic

Date 30 Apr.

Like Hallowe'en and Bonfire Night rolled into one,
Witches' Night marks the death of winter and the
birth of spring. Bonfires are lit to purge the winter
spirits, an effigy of a hag is burnt (a relic of historical witch hunts) and the more daring observers of
the custom leap over the flames. Most fires are in the
countryside but there's occasionally a pyre in the
capital, sometimes on Petřín Hill in Malá Strana.

Labour Day

Date 1 May.

There is no longer any danger of being run over by
a tank in Wenceslas Square, but May Day is still a
good excuse for a demonstration. The communists,
in an attempt to keep the faith alive, usually have a
small rally in Letná Park and encourage pensioners
to moan about the rigours of the free market.
Prague's anarchists sometimes hold an uncharac-
teristically orderly parade.

May Day

Petřín Hill, Malá Strana, Prague 1. Metro
Malostranská/6, 9, 12, 22, 23 tram. **Date** 1 May.
Map p306 C5.

Czech lovers with their sap rising make a pilgrimage to the statue of Karel Hynek Mácha on Petřín
Hill to place flowers and engage in a spot of neck-
ing. Mácha, a 19th-century Romantic poet, gave rise
to many myths, several bastards and the epic poem
Máj (May). It's actually a melancholy tale of unre-
quited love but nobody lets that spoil their fun.

VE Day

Date 8 May.

The Day of Liberation from Fascism is actually 9
May, the date on which the Red Army reached
Prague in 1945. In their eagerness to be good Euro-
citizens, the Czech government moved the celebra-

tion to 8 May, in line with the rest of the continent.
Flowers and wreaths are laid on Soviet monuments
such as Náměstí Kinských in Smíchov where a
Soviet tank used to stand.

Prague International Marathon

Throughout the city (info 2491 9209/www.pim.cz).
Date May. **Cost** 300-600 Kč.

The biggest race of the year, attracting star runners
from around the world, has a city-wide street party
afterward where more than just mineral water is
tossed back by runners and a few thousand less
healthy types. Those not up to the full 28km (18mile)
race could have a shot at the 10km (6mile) race.

Prague Writers' Festival

Various venues (info 2493 1053/
www.pwf.pragonet.cz). **Date** May.

Czech literary stars get together to read extracts and
hob-nob with famous foreign writers imported specially for the occasion. This is your chance to
observe Ivan Klíma's improbable hairdo and the
quirks of other local literary lions.

Mezi ploty

Ústavní 91, near Bohnice Psychiatric Hospital,
Prague 8 (info 7273 0623/www.meziploty.cz).
Bus 200 from Metro Nádraží Holešovice.
Date last weekend in May. **Admission** 200 Kč/day;
370 Kč/weekend.

This unique festival brings together professional,
amateur, and mentally or physically disadvantaged
artists, dancers and musicians.

Prague Spring Festival

Hellichova 18, Malá Strana, Prague 1 (5731 1921/
5731 0414/www.festival.cz). *Metro Malostranská/*
12, 22, 23 tram. **Admission** varies according to
venue. **Date** mid May-early June. **Map** p307 D4.

The biggest and best of Prague's music festivals
begins on the anniversary of Smetana's death with
a performance of his tone poem *Má Vlast* (My
Homeland). The festival is very popular, so book in
advance if possible. The festival office opens one
month before the first concert, so tickets can't be
booked before this time.

Summer

Respect

Various venues (2271 0050/0603 461 592/
www.respectmusic.cz). **Date** May-June.
Admission varies according to venue.

The world and ethnic music high point of the year
features Balkan folk and Gypsy music, plus local
players such as Alom, the Prague masters of traditional Roma music. The organiser is Prague's main
underground and ethnic music label, Rachot.
Concerts are usually at the Akropolis (*see p145*).

Tanec Praha

Various venues (info 2481 7886/www.tanecpha.cz).
Metro Florenc/8, 24 tram. **Date** June.
Admission varies according to venue.

Really ugly things abound during **Masopust**, Prague's Mardi Gras. *See p188.*

'Dance Prague' is an international gala of modern dance that has become one of the more successful performance festivals in Prague. International participants perform in major theatres and sometimes conduct workshops and symposia.

Autumn

Burčák arrives

Date late Sept-early Oct.

Burčák – a cloudy, half-fermented, early-season wine – arrives in Prague sometime in the autumn. It is a speciality of Moravia, where it would appear that the locals haven't got the patience to wait for their alcohol to finish fermenting. Served straight from the barrel into special jugs. Burčák looks like murky wheat beer, tastes like cherryade and will sneak up on you if you don't treat it with respect.

Prague Autumn

Various venues (info 627 8740/ www.pragueautumn.cz). **Date** mid Sept-early Oct. **Admission** varies according to venue.

The next best thing to Prague Spring, this festival annually attracts world-renowned talents to play in the city's many excellent concert venues, including the splendid Rudolfinu.

Festival of Best Amateur & Professional Puppet Theatre Plays

Various venues (info 4140 9293). **Date** Oct. **Admission** varies according to venue.

This is an unusual festival that celebrates Bohemia's long tradition of puppet-making. Puppets are big in the Czech Republic – some of the country's most innovative artists continue to use them, and a faculty at the university is devoted to the craft.

Anniversary of the Creation of Czechoslovakia

Date 28 Oct.

Public holiday. The country no longer exists but that's no reason to cancel a public holiday – so the people still get a day off. Republicans spend the day in mourning, while various political factions hold demonstrations on Wenceslas Square.

All Souls' Day

Date 2 Nov.

Best time of year to visit any one of the city's cemeteries. Whole families turn out to light candles, lay wreaths and say prayers for the dead. The best place to go is the enormous Olšany Cemetery.

Anniversary of the Velvet Revolution

Národní třída & Václavské náměstí, Nové Město, Prague 1. Metro Národní třída or Můstek/ 3, 6, 9, 14, 18, 22, 23, 24 tram. Date 17 Nov. Map p308 H5.

To commemorate the demonstration that began the Velvet Revolution, flowers are laid and candles lit in Wenceslas Square near the equine statue and on the memorial on Národní třída near No.20.

Winter

St Nicholas's Eve

Around Charles Bridge & Staroměstské náměstí. Staré Město, Prague 1. Metro Staroměstská/ 17, 18 tram. Date 5 Dec. Map p306 H3.

Grown men spend the evening wearing frocks, drinking large amounts of beer and terrorising small children. They wander the streets in threesomes, dressed as St Nicholas, an angel and a devil, symbolising confession, reward and punishment. Rather than a red cloak, St Nicholas usually sports a long white vestment, with a white mitre and staff. The angel hands out sweets to children who have been good, while the devil is on hand to dispense rough justice to those who haven't.

Lights, camera, balls!

Old Austro-Hungarian Empire traditions die hard, as anyone who's ever dealt with bureaucracy in Prague can tell you. But one that fared surprisingly well under communism, considering its blatantly bourgeois ethic, is the winter ball.

Formal foxtrotting in palace ballrooms seems to have shaken off 41 years of proletarian revolution without a scratch. Czech teens by the hundreds are forced to take ballroom dancing lessons and can be spotted in ill-fitting tuxes and princess-pink ballgowns on any weekend winter night at the Lucerna passage. They'll be on their way to a blowout ball in the cavernous Great Hall under the stairs. This prime rock concert venue is filled on many nights with strains of Strauss and dozens of kids doing that quintessentially Czech step, the *valčík*.

No wedding is complete without a round (or five) of waltzing and the average Czech, normally unassuming, can shift into a frenetic Charleston or Lindy Hop at the drop of a hat.

But they're motivated by more than the chance to get close to members of the opposite sex: sides of beef, pheasant, and boars are raffled off at the annual Hunt Ball. The Fireman's Ball, aside from being the inspiration for a Miloš Forman film, is another stellar event on the winter calendar in Prague.

Every city district features an opulent *Národní dům*, or National House, where it's wall-to-wall balls come winter. To catch

Ball season: mind your toes.

Czechs of all ages in their element, cruise on down to any of these palatial venues and there's bound to be a poster for the next hot ball. One sure location for finding a ball of some sort is the ever busy National House in Vinohrady (*see below*).

Národní dům Vinohrady

Náměstí míru, Vinohrady, Prague 2 (2159 6221). Metro Náměstí míru/4, 16, 22, 23, 34 tram. Open 9am-6pm Mon-Fri. Admission 400-1,800 Kč. No credit cards. Map p313 3A.

The busiest of the grand ballrooms in Prague with plush winter dances in great abundance. Not all are open to the public, so check for posters ahead of time.

Christmas

Vánoce
In the week leading up to the holiday, the streets
sport huge tubs of water filled with carp, the traditional Czech Christmas dish. People buy them live
and store them in the bathtub – otherwise, like most
bottom-feeders, they taste of mud. The more squea-
mish get someone else to kill and gut the fish. The
feasting and exchange of gifts happens on the
evening of 24 December, when – apart from midnight masses, the finest of which is at St Vitus's
Cathedral – pretty much everything closes down.
Things don't start opening up again until the 27th.

New Year's Eve

Silvestr
*Václavské náměstí & Staroměstské náměstí, Prague
1. Metro Můstek/3, 9, 14, 24 tram or Metro
Staroměstská/17, 18 tram.* **Map** p309 K5.
At Silvestr the streets are packed with a ragtag
crowd of Euro-revellers, with much of the fun cen-
tered on Wenceslas Square and Old Town Square.
Fireworks are let off everywhere and flung around
with frankly dangerous abandon, then champagne
bottles are smashed.

Anniversary of Jan Palach's death

*Olšanské hřbitovy, Žižkov, Prague 3, & Václavské
náměstí, Nové Město, Prague 1. Metro Flora or
Muzeum/10, 11, 16, 26 tram.* **Date** 16 Jan.
Map p311 D2/L6.
Jan Palach set fire to himself on 16 January 1969 in
Wenceslas Square as a protest against the Soviet
invasion. His grave is adorned with candles and
flowers all year round. Many people visit Olšany
Cemetery or the memorial to the victims of commu-
nism near the St Wenceslas statue to lay a few more.

Masopust

*Akropolis, Kubelíkova 27, Žižkov, Prague 3
(9633 0913/www.palacakropolis.cz). Metro Jiřího z
Poděbrad/11 tram.* **Date** mid Feb (7th Sun before
Easter). **Map** p313 B2.
Traditionally, groups of 12 carolers accompanied by
people in masks parade about, in this whimsical cel-
ebration of what the rest of the world knows as
Shrove Tuesday, the eve of Ash Wednesday (the
original tradition seen in the Czech lands has the holiday on Sunday). According to custom, everyone
who meets this procession should be invited to the
evening feast, a great opportunity to stuff yourself
with a freshly slaughtered pig, and chase it with
rivers of beer. More manageable might be the version of the Masopust street party centred around
Prague's Žižkov district, where a slate of activities
revolve around the Akroplis club.

Out of town

Karlovy Vary International Film Festival

*Hotel Thermal, IP Pavlova 11, Karlovy Vary (2423
5412/www.iffkv.cz).* **Date** July. **Admission** varies.

Prague fests: rite on.

This genteel spa town hosts the Czech version of
Cannes. While hardly in the same league, the festival shows an interesting mix of foreign and home-
grown features. *See p198.*

Barum Rally

*Start/finish line: Interhotel Moskva, Práce
náměstí 2512, Zlín (info 067 320 04 mobile/
www.rallysport.cz/barum).* **Date** Sept.
Admission free.
This is a classic road race dating back decades that
still attracts drivers from across Europe. In 2002 for
the first time Barum Rally made it among the first
10 European races with coefficient 20. Moravian
roads, generally pretty quiet, roar to life as amateur
and pro drivers compete for the big *pohár*, the winner's cup. Autoklub Barum Zlín sponsors the event
and an entry form in English can be downloaded
from its website.

Velká Pardubice Steeplechase

*Pražská 607, Pardubice (040 6335 300/
www.pardubice-racecourse.cz).* **Date** 2nd weekend in
Oct. **Admission** 200-2,000 Kč. **No credit cards.**
The star steeplechase event in the annual calendar
is also a controversial one: horses and riders are
often injured on the difficult course. Celebrity horse
people pour in from all over Europe, putting box
seats at a premium. A full price list appears on the
organisers' website, along with instructions for
ordering an advance ticket.

Children

Prague is straight out of bedtime stories – low-tech, safe and enchanting.

Prague's race for free-market, Western-style living has not much affected people's old-fashioned ideas about – and deep affection for – children, but neither has it produced many high-tech interactive facilities for them. Yet the Czech Republic's own old-world charm and quirks are every bit as interesting and exciting for kids as for wonder-eyed adults.

Though galleries and museums may not always rank highly on a child's list of places to go, some museums in Prague aim to capture the interest of tots, or, at the very least, the inner child. In among the plethora of adult-oriented cultural activities are performances, both musical and theatrical, geared specifically to children. Old Town Square and Charles Bridge often feature enchanting street performances or temporary stages with free acts.

Part of Prague's charm is that half an hour by car or train is the serenity of field and forest. Family excursions into the country can be made with relative ease (*see* **Directory: Getting Around**), and the countryside offers another magical world of bona fide castles and all of their trappings. A still easier option is a trip to one of the parks and playgrounds – of increasing quality – dotted around the city.

With a little imagination, Prague yields plenty of activities and attractions to keep families occupied and offers enough child-oriented services to make staying here with children convenient.

Sightseeing & activities

Some attractions, such as the **Astronomical Clock** (*see p87*) and climbable towers such as **Petřín Tower** (*see p84*), **Old Town Bridge Tower** (*see p91*) and the **Powder Gate** (*see p85*) are as suited to children as to adults.

Sights

Zrcadlové Bludiště
Petřín Hill, Malá Strana, Prague 1 (no phone).
Metro Malostranská/12, 22, 23 tram. **Open** *Apr-Oct* 10am-5pm Sat, Sun. **Admission** 30 Kč; 20 Kč children. **No credit cards. Map** p307 C5.
The Mirror Maze is an old-fashioned leftover from funfair days that somehow got stranded on top of this hill. It's a guaranteed laugh for the kids, but you'll probably catch yourself grinning as well. It's

somewhat of a hike from the centre of things but definitely worth the effort.

Historic tram 91
9612 4900. **Open** *Apr-Nov* hourly noon-6pm Sat, Sun & hols. **Fare** 25 Kč; 10 Kč children. **No credit cards.**
A great sightseeing jaunt for tired feet, this quaint, wood-framed tram travels a loop from Výstaviště, trundling along the banks of Malá Strana, across the Legionnaires' Bridge to the National Theatre, up through Wenceslas Square and then back to Výstaviště via Náměstí Republiky. The antique vehicle can be joined at any stop along the route.

Museums

National Technical Museum
Národní technické muzeum
Kostelní 42, Holešovice, Prague 7 (2039 9111/ www.ntm.cz). Metro Hradčanská or Vltavská/ *1, 8, 25, 26 tram.* **Open** 9am-5pm Tue-Sun. **Admission** 70 Kč; 30 Kč children; 150 Kč family. **No credit cards. Map** p312 C3.
This multi-level museum is a sure hit with kids, especially those interested in planes, trains and automobiles. It's full of original vehicles, some of which can be climbed on or around to afford a good look at the interiors. A popular coal mine replica tour tunnels through the basement, and English-speaking tours can be arranged in advance. The museum itself is located right next to Letná Park, so if the weather allows you can add a picnic or a walk through the park to your day's excursion.

Prague Zoo
Zoologická zahrada v Praze
U Trojského zámku 3, Troja, Prague 7 (9611 2230/ www.zoopraha.cz). Metro Nádraží Holešovice, then *112 bus.* **Open** *Apr-Sept* 9am-6pm daily. *Oct-Apr* 9am-5pm daily. **Admission** 60 Kč; 30 Kč children; free under-3s. **No credit cards.**
Built in 1931, Prague's zoo had become increasingly dilapidated and depressingly out of date by 1989. Thankfully, renovation has created more humane and 'natural' spaces for the animals. The renovation of pavilions as well as new additions are making the zoo more and more aesthetically pleasing and interesting for visitors and animals alike. The lovely sloping grounds are a fine place to stroll, and the chair lift provides stunning views. A visit to the zoo can be easily combined with a walk through Stromovka Park.

Getting playful at **Bohemia Bagel**. *See p191.*

National Museum

Národní Muzeum
*Václavské náměstí 68, Prague 1 (244 97 111, 244
97 212/www.nm.cz). Metro Muzeum/11 tram.* **Open**
May-Sept 10am-6pm daily. *Oct-Apr* 9am-5pm daily.
Closed 1st Tue of the month. **Admission** 80 Kč; 40
Kč children; free under-6s; 90 Kč family. Free to all
1st Mon of month. **No credit cards. Map** p311 L6.
Though many of the displays in this natural history museum are dusty and not always showcased to
allow optimum viewing pleasure, children seem to
be fascinated by the stuffed animal exhibits. There
are also dry rock, fossil and skeleton collections. One
part of the museum features temporary exhibitions.

Toy Museum

Muzeum hraček
*Jiřská ul 4-6, Pražský Hrad, Prague 1 (2437 2294).
Metro Malostranská/12, 18, 22, 23 tram.*
Open 9.30am-5.30pm daily. **Admission** 50 Kč;
20 Kč children; 60 Kč family. **No credit cards.**
Map p307 E1.
An interesting collection of antique and collectable
toys dating from ancient Greece to the present day.
There isn't much to play with, though in one room
kid-level push-buttons activate elaborate displays of
moving teddy bears.

Wax Museum Prague

*Melantrichova 5, Prague 1 (2493 0443/
www.waxmuseumprague.cz). Metro Můstek/3, 9, 14,
24 tram.* **Open** 9am-8pm daily. **Admission** 150 Kč;
60 Kč children; 250 Kč family. **No credit cards.**
Map p308 H4.
More than 60 life-size figures of international celebri-
ties, figures from the pantheon of Czech history and
20th-century political leaders. A short special-effects
film follows your trip through history. Stop in the
souvenir shop on your way out.

Wax Museum

Muzeum Voskových Figurín
*Mostecká 18, Prague 1 (5753 5735). Metro Můstek/
3, 9, 14, 24 tram.* **Open** 9am-8pm daily.
Admission 110 Kč; 50 Kč children; 220 Kč family.
No credit cards. Map p307 E3.
Yet more celebs and sports gods in aspic. A pre-
dictable fave with kids.

Boating

A boat trip is a convenient and entertaining
way to see central Prague. Rowing boats or
paddleboats can be rented for 80-120 Kč per
hour at Novotného lávka (just south of the Staré
Město end of Charles Bridge), Slovanský Island
(near the National Theatre), and on the Malá
Strana side of the river between Charles Bridge
and Mánes Bridge.

EVD

*under Čechův Bridge, next to Hotel Inter-Continental,
Prague 1 (2481 0032/www.evd.cz). Metro
Staroměstská/17, 18 tram.* **Open** *Office* 9am-10pm
daily. **Tickets** 200-1,290 Kč; 100-1,290 Kč 3-11s; free
under-3s. **Credit** MC, V. **Map** p308 H1.
An original and relaxing way to see the sights from
a perspective not offered by the city streets. The city
sightseeing cruise lasts about an hour, but EVD also
offers longer cruises travelling up the river into the
Czech countryside. Some of the boats have on-board
restaurants, so you can wine and dine along the way.

Entertainment & sport

For up-to-date information about children's
shows and events, you should check out the
listings magazine *Kultura v Praze* (Culture in

Prague), which is available in English at bookshops and newsstands on Wenceslas Square, or *The Prague Post*.

Although there's a fair amount of children's programming on Czech television, including live-action fairytales and animated shorts, the language barrier may prove a problem unless you happen upon one of the frequent *Tom & Jerry* broadcasts. However, a children's show called *Večerníček* airs every evening at 7pm on ČT 1. The cartoons featured often don't involve any spoken language and make for a perfect bedtime story. Satellite television provides further options, including Cartoon Network.

Another option is to let children loose in the **Dětský dům** (*see p161*). This recently modernised shopping mall caters specifically to kids, tempting them with toy and game shops plus occasional puppet shows in the basement, usually at the weekend. The merry-go-round is always a hit and there's a café nearby. **Sparky's Dům hraček** (*see p182*), a multi-level toy store, can be found just around the corner, on Havířská.

The **National Theatre** (*see p234*) and **State Opera** (*see p214*) stage matinées during the summer, for which families can book box seats for reasonable prices. Rarely in English, these are best suited to older children, though these theatres do occasionally stage musical or theatre performances for children. Check *The Prague Post* for listings.

Year-round swimming options include the pools and jacuzzis at the **Inter-Continental** and the **Marriott** (*see p47 and p51*). Both are clean and well kept, and can offer a nice change from beaten cobblestone paths for children and parents alike. In summer, visit the *koupaliště* (swimming pool area) at the rambling **Divoká Šárka**.

Divoká Šárka Koupaliště

Evropská, Nebušice, Prague 6 (no phone). Tram 20, 26 to the western terminus, then 5-minute walk north and west through the rocky valley. **Open** *May-Sept* 9am-7pm daily. **Admission** 25 Kč; 10 Kč children. **No credit cards.**
A lovely outdoor swimming area, quiet and shaded, with two pools fed by spring water guaranteed to refresh and revive. The smaller one is for paddling, the larger one is shallow enough for young children to stand in. Swings and a slide are to hand, making this an ideal spot for a family picnic, and the park itself offers kilometres of paths winding through beautiful forests and glens.

Laser Game

Národní 25, Staré Město, Prague 1 (2422 1188). Metro Národní třída/6, 9, 17, 18, 21, 22, 23 tram. **Open** 10am-midnight Mon-Sat; 11am-11pm Sun. **Admission** 120 Kč per 15mins. **Map** p308 G5.

If family tensions are running high, work them out with cyberblast pulse guns. Children transform into Terminators in this dark basement labyrinth, shooting laser guns at sensor lights on their adversaries' belts to score a kill and trying to dodge shots at their own sensor belt. An amusement arcade with diversions such as pinball and air hockey awaits in the upper level (10 Kč per token, two tokens per game).

Diplomat Hotel Praha

Evropská 15, Dejvice, Prague 6, (2439 4297/} www.diplomat-hotel.cz). Metro Dejvická/2, 20, 26 tram. **Open** 6pm-1am Tue-Fri; 4pm-2am Sat; 4pm-midnight Sun. **Rates** 200 Kč/8mins.
Credit AmEx, DC, MC, V.
In the basement of this respectable hotel is a miniature go-kart track where kids can roar around a serpentine course while you wait it out in the bar. The track is safe, well supervised and noisy as hell.

Puppet theatre

Puppet theatre has a rich history in Bohemia, and there are two child-oriented puppet theatres in Prague, the **Spejbl & Hurvínek Theatre** and the **National Marionette Theatre** (for both, *see p237*). They usually feature performances in Czech, though **Opera Mozart** (*see p215*) stages delightful performances or foreigners on a regular basis during the tourist season. Another option is the non-verbal multimedia performances at the **Magic Lantern Theatre** (*see p236*), also aimed at foreigners. You'll see puppeteers in tourist areas such as Charles Bridge too. High-quality puppet productions also tour the Czech Republic. Current listings are run in *The Prague Post*.

Eating out

Prague has a multicultural array of restaurants, and while some are perfect for Mum and Dad's romantic night out, many are appropriate or even intended for families with kids. The Old Town branch of **Bohemia Bagel** (*see p123*) has a kids' play corner with a climber and ball pool, offers quick, healthy, child-friendly food, and has computers with access to the net. For a sweet treat or to cool down on a hot day, visit **Cream & Dream** (*see p133*), where you can get delectable homemade flavours such as white chocolate or tiramisu as well as the old standards to go in cones or cups, or packed into larger containers to take home with you for later.

Practicalities

Tracking down what the dream child or the cranky demon needs is no longer a problem in consumerist Prague.

Arts & Entertainment

Baby requirements

Disposable nappies and baby food are widely available, both at centrally located department stores such as **Carrefour**, **Kotva** and **Tesco** (*for all see p160*) and at specialised stores, including the following.

Chicco

Ondříčkova 20, Žižkov, Prague 3 (627 6338). Metro Jiřího z Poděbrad/5, 9, 11, 26 tram. **Open** 9am-6pm Mon-Fri; 8am-noon Sat. **Credit** AmEx, MC, V. **Map** p313 C2.
Designer togs for designer tots at designer prices. Great quality, though.

Au Pays du Mimis

Československé Armády 21, Prague 6 (3332 6325). Metro Dejvická/20, 25, 26 tram. **Open** 9am-6pm Mon-Fri; 9am-noon Sat. **Credit** DC, MC, V.
Beautiful baby and toddler clothing from, as the name suggests, France.
Branch: Nový Smíchov Shopping Centre, Smíchov, Prague 5 (5732 6314).

Mothercare

Myslbek Pasáž, Na Příkopě 19-21, Prague 1 (2224 0008). Metro Můstek/3, 9, 14, 24 tram. **Open** 9.30am-7pm Mon-Fri; 9am-6pm Sat; 11am-6pm Sun. **Credit** AmEx, MC, V. **Map** p309 K4.
Everything for babies from cribs and cradles to bottles and clothes, plus clothing for young children.

Childminding

The large hotels usually have a babysitting service. Otherwise, try the following, whose prices tend to be 50-150 Kč an hour.

Agentura Korálek

Info 0603 513 546 mobile/www.volny.cz/ag.koralek. **No credit cards**.
Call Korálek direct to book a babysitter, or look over the 200-plus candidates in the company database on its website.

Babysitting Praha

Info 0602 885 074/www.mujweb.cz/www/malickedeti. **No credit cards**.
Call anytime 7pm-7am for quick-response, reasonably-priced babysitting.

Markéta Tomková

Information 0608 082 868 mobile/ www.pendulus.cz/hlidani. **No credit cards**.
Childminding in English or French.

Au Pair Agency of Prague

Vlašská 591-3, Prague 1 (0603 889 016 mobile/ 5753 0118/www.au-pairprague.cz). Metro Malostranská/12, 22, 23 tram. **Open** 9am-5pm Mon-Thur; 9am-1pm Fri. **No credit cards**. **Map** p306 B4/C3.
This agency is a generally reliable provider of multilingual family help.

Divoká Šárka: good for zooming and swimming. *See p191.*

Health

Prague's water, though not especially appealing, supposedly conforms to international standards of cleanliness and safety. It is chlorinated but not fluoridated and its nitrate level is not considered safe for the developing respiratory systems of children and infants. Children up to 12 should get fluoride supplements. Bottled water is cheap and available everywhere – red caps usually indicate carbonated varieties.

Atmospheric pollution is also a problem. On some winter days the radio even warns parents to keep children indoors. If you are planning to live in Prague, you should look for accommodation on the outskirts or on the hills of Prague 5 and Prague 6.

Tick-borne encephalitis and the somewhat less serious (but still requiring prompt treatment with antibiotics) Lyme disease is endemic throughout Eastern Europe. If you intend to travel around the Czech countryside, it's advisable to get a vaccination before leaving home. If you're residing in Prague, **Na Homolce Hospital** (*see p278*) and the **American Medical Center** (*see below*) can provide the three-injection course of the vaccine. If ticks are found, they must be removed intact. Smother them in soap or Vaseline, then use tweezers to twist them off counter-clockwise and disinfect the area thoroughly. If the tick is removed within 24 hours, the chances of disease transmission are very low. Occasionally, the bite causes a red bull's-eye-like mark, which may be a sign of infection or Lyme disease. If in doubt, see a doctor or go to a clinic as soon as possible. Make sure to check for ticks after outdoor jaunts, especially those through tall grasses or in the forest, as this is where ticks are most likely to live.

American Medical Centre

Americké Kulturní středisko, Janovského 48, Holešovice, Prague 7 (2080 7756/ www.amcenters.com). Metro Vltavská/1, 8, 17 tram. **Open** 24hrs daily. **Rates** 1,750-3,500 Kč per consultation (non-members); 3,500-13,125 Kč annual family membership. **Credit** AmEx, MC, V. **Map** p312 D2.

The AMC has a US board certified family physician, offers neonatal, post-natal and paediatric care, as well as adult medical care and has a vaccination/immunisation centre. There is direct insurance billing for members. The AMC also offers family dental services, including orthodontics and emergency services.

Canadian Medical Centre

Veleslavínská 1, Veleslavín, Prague 6, (3536 0133/emergency paediatrics 0602 335 670 mobile/emergency adults 0603 212 320 mobile/ www.cmc.praha.cz). Metro Dejvická, then 20, 25, 26 tram. **Open** 8.30am-5pm Mon-Fri; 9am-noon Sat. **Credit** AmEx, MC, V.

Located in a picturesque setting, the Canadian Medical Centre has English-speaking staff experienced in serving the Prague expat parent community. Both adult as well as paediatric care. German and French are also spoken.

Národní Polyclinic

Národní třída 9, Nové Město, Prague 1 (2207 5120/emergencies 0606 461 628 mobile/ www.poliklinika.narodni.cz). Metro Národní třída/ 6, 9, 17, 18, 21, 22, 23 tram. **Open** 8.30am-5pm Mon-Fri; by appointment only Sat, Sun. **Credit** AmEx, MC, V. **Map** p310 H5.

The Národní Polyclinic has the dual benefits of helpful and highly professional English-speaking staff and a central location in Nové Město that makes it easy to access.

Transport

In Prague children who are up to six years old travel free on public transport, while those aged between six and 15 are allowed to travel for half price. Tickets can be purchased at the majority of news-stands, or you can get them from the yellow machines found in the metro stations. If you're staying for a longer period of time, you should consider getting a weekly pass (*see* **Directory: Getting Around**) to save money.

When it comes to taking a pram on to a public bus or tram, you'll need to signal to the driver as the vehicle pulls up. Push the button above the back door (not the emergency one) to indicate to the driver that you'll require a little extra time getting off to avoid getting your pram stuck in closing doors. Most of the time he will wait long enough for you to lift the pram inside and out. People with prams must enter and exit by the rear door.

Prague's an old-fashioned fairy tale world with kids as stars.

Arts & Entertainment

Film

Czech filmmaking has deep roots but the real gems have never been exported. Catch them in Prague, now with bucket seats and fluffy popcorn.

Few things in Prague have undergone as much of a sea change as the cinema scene – both in terms of what can be seen and what's being produced. As for filmmaking (*see chapter* **Prague on Screen**), Prague has become a place where Hollywood comes to save money – and it always wants to save money. It's not unusual to see production vans taking up entire city blocks as streets and monuments are used for location shooting.

Czech-made films are more low-key and fairly low budget. A few recent films, such as Jan Svěrák's Oscar-winning *Kolja*, his more recent *Dark Blue World* (*Tmavomodrý svět*) and Jan Hřebejk's Oscar-nominated *Divided We Fall* (*Musíme si pomáhat*), have found international audiences to a degree – though it may take a trip to a well-stocked video shop to find copies.

The Czech First Republic caught on fast to filmmaking, as it had to photography generations earlier. The first international splash made by Bohemain filmmakers was in 1932, when *Ecstasy* (*Extáze*) featured cinema's first widely seen nude bathing scene, courtesy of a young Hedy Lamarr. Between then and the 1960s, successive regimes kept a tight lid on film production, though a few stray science-fiction films reached foreign screens, including Karel Zeman's 1958 *The Fabulous World of Jules Verne* (*Vynález zkázy*).

A brief thaw occurred between 1963 and 1968, when Czech New Wave filmmakers such as Miloš Forman, Ivan Passer and Jiří Menzel made some stunning, introspective works that stand alongside the best of European cinema. The coming of Soviet tanks in 1968 put a damper on creative filmmaking for the next 30 years, until the new 'Velvet Generation' was able to get cinema back afloat after the fall of communism (*see p196* **After the fall – the new New Wave**).

BUMS ON SEATS

A wave of multiplex construction hit the city in 2000, and there is almost no end in sight. Once word of advance tickets, bucket seats, popcorn and giant sodas leaked out, local filmgoers abandoned the boxy, uncomfortable, monaural Soviet-era *kinos* to see their favourite imported action fare on giant screens. But screens aren't all that have become larger. Ticket prices can

fluctuate considerably, but at press time they ranged from 140 to 160 Kč in central multiplexes such as **Ster Century Slovanský dům** and **Ster Century Nový Smíchov** (for both, *see p196*); older cinemas in the centre of town charged between 100 and 120 Kč; and outlying older cinemas, including the blessed **Aero** (*see p196*), charged from 60 to 90 Kč a ticket.

The single-screen theatres that didn't sink under right away have upgraded their sound systems and seats, and some have even opened cocktail bars and allow you to take drinks into the cinema. Many smaller cinemas have also tried to be more inventive with their programming by mixing in art movies and second-run hits with new releases.

The most old-fashioned cinema in central Prague is currently **Oko** (*see p195*), but if you want a real pre-revolutionary filmgoing experience, **Ponrepo** (*see p197*) makes you fill out an application for an ID card before you can buy a ticket.

Commercial Hollywood fare makes up the bulk of programming everywhere except at the art cinemas. There is generally a sign at the box office explaining what version the film is in. *Dabing* films are dubbed into Czech, but usually only children's films get this treatment. By and large, films are screened *s českými titulky*, or simply *č t* (with original soundtrack and Czech subtitles). Important Czech films are sometimes screened with English subtitles; look for *s anglickými titulky*.

Tickets have assigned seat numbers and you can usually pick your spot from a computer screen at the box office. Unless you want some latecomer to argue that you're in their place, be sure to find the row (*řada*) and seat (*sedadlo*) that are printed on the ticket. Schedules can be found in the *Prague Post*. Large posters plastered on kiosks and at tram stops also have schedules. Most cinemas have schedules online. Look out, too, for the *Prague Pill*, a free English-language source of movie reviews and listings.

Some nightclubs and cafés show videos or DVDs of feature films, with **Rock Café** (*see p227*) and **Roxy** (*see p228*) having the most consistent schedules. Be warned: sometimes they show the dubbed versions.

Film

Oko
Františka Křížka 15, Holešovice, Prague 7 (3337 5675). Metro Vltavská/5, 12, 17 tram. **No credit cards. Map** p312 D3.
One of the few places that has managed to retain that pre-revolutionary flavour, Oko features second-run films and occasional arthouse hits. It still holds on to its uncomfortable folding wooden chairs and cross-looking ticket seller hidden in a glass booth.

Perštýn
Na Perštýně 6, Nové Město, Prague 1 (2166 8432). Metro Národní třída/6, 9, 17, 18, 22, 23 tram. **No credit cards. Map** p308 H5.
Moveable tables and chairs make for a relaxed atmosphere in which to see recent, usually slightly arty, films. The café offers beverages and a few packaged snacks.

Praha
Václavské náměstí 17, Nové Město, Prague 1 (2224 5881/www.broadway.cz). Metro Můstek/3, 9, 14, 24 tram. **No credit cards. Map** p309 K5.
This duplex, which serves as the headquarters for the Broadway chain, now has digital sound but the hard seats could use an upgrade too. You can take drinks from the bar into the theatre.

64 U Hradeb
Mostecká 21, Malá Strana, Prague 1 (5753 1158). Metro Malostranská/12, 22 tram. **No credit cards. Map** p307 E3.
Hidden down an alley next to a McDonald's is this large and comfortable theatre. The decor isn't stunning, but roomy seats and good sound do much to compensate. Near the Charles Bridge, this is one of the better places to catch a new film.

Multiplexes

Galaxie Multiplex
Arkalycká 877, Háje, Prague 4 (reservations 6791 0616/schedule 6914 1414/www.cinemacity.cz). Metro Háje. **No credit cards.**
The name is the same but everything else is new. When Prague's first multiplex became a dinosaur, the owners built a bigger and better one right next to it, and shut the first one down. The new one is light years better than its predecessor, which had oddly shaped shoebox halls and small screens.

Ládví
Burešova 4, Kobylisy, Prague 8 (8658 7027). Tram 10, 17, 24. **No credit cards.**
Situated in the middle of a large housing project, this neighbourhood theatre has been expanded into a six-hall multiplex. It offers some discounts on certain big titles, but isn't as splashy as its internationally run competitors – though it does feature a killer sound system.

Multikino Modřany Broadway
Sofijské náměstí 2, Modřany, Prague 4 (4440 2256/ www.broadway.cz). Tram 3, 17, 21. **No credit cards.**

Blaník: get there while it lasts.

Commercial cinemas

Atlas
Sokolovská 1, Karlín, Prague 8 (232 6033/ www.broadway.cz). Metro Florenc/8, 24 tram. **No credit cards.**
The main hall shows new 35mm films. The small hall is one of the first dedicated DVD projection cinemas in Europe, showing classic films from *Casablanca* up to last year's hits. You don't need a ticket to drink at the full-service cocktail bar.

Blaník
Václavské náměstí 56, Nové Město, Prague 1 (2403 2172). Metro Muzeum/11 tram. **No credit cards. Map** p311 L6.
A good location, at the top of Wenceslas Square, has helped this old-fashioned but fairly plain movie palace to stay open, although there is talk of turning it into a live theatre featuring Black Light shows (*see also p236*).

Kotva
Náměstí Republiky 8, Staré Město, Prague 1 (2481 1482/www.broadway.cz). Metro Náměstí Republiky/ 5, 8, 14 tram. **No credit cards. Map** p309 K3.
Medium-sized modern cinema next to a department store usually offering fairly recent films. Occasional salsa dancing in the café.

Lucerna
Vodičkova 36, Nové Město, Prague 1 (2421 6972). Metro Můstek/3, 9, 14, 24 tram. **No credit cards. Map** p311 K6.
In the Lucerna Passage off Wenceslas Square, an art nouveau masterpiece that, while admittedly a little worse for wear, remains one of the city's last true movie palaces. Come early so you can clock its delightfully tatty decor while the lights are still up, or hang out in the lobby bar. With a picture window overlooking the 1920s-era shopping arcade and occasionally featuring music from a live pianist, the latter is a prime spot for people-watching.

Arts & Entertainment

After the fall – the new New Wave

A new brood of filmmakers has taken over the spotlight from the Czech New Wave directors of the '60s. They call themselves the Velvet Generation – not unconvincingly, they argue that New Czech New Wave would sound a tad clunky.

The head of the class is Jan Svěrák, whose sentimental end-of-the-Cold-War tale *Kolja* won the Oscar for Best Foreign Film in 1997. His follow-up, *Dark Blue World* (*Tmavomodrý svět*), is the most expensive Czech film ever made, although much of the money came from foreign investors. It tells the tale of Czech fighter pilots who joined the RAF in World War II, only to face imprisonment at home afterwards. Svěrák's 1991 *Elementary School* (*Obecná škola*), which earned an Oscar nomination, also looked back to the 1940s.

His film school colleague Jan Hřebejk has also found inspiration in exploring the dark but recent past. *Cosy Dens* (*Pelíšky*), a look

at the turbulent year of 1968, was seen by more than a million people in 1999, which is no small accomplishment in a country of ten million. Like Svěrák, he also chose World War II as the setting for his most recent flick. *Divided We Fall* (*Musíme si pomáhat*) follows the story of a Jewish escapee from a concentration camp and the family that tries to hide him.

Among films that deal with contemporary themes, *Loners* (*Samotáři*) has been the most popular and brings together two Velvet Generation filmmakers, David Ondříček, who produced and directed, and Petr Zelenka, who wrote the script. The interlocking stories in *Loners* concern a handful of young Praguers struggling with relationships and not a few quirks and obsessions. It's similar in many ways to *Magnolia* or *Short Cuts*, only with a low-budget Central European neuroticism. Zelenka dealt with obsessions before in *The Buttoners* (*Knoflíkáři*), a 1997 surreal comedy

A stone's throw from the now-shuttered functionalist Modřany theatre, this modern four-hall multiplex offers an internet café and fresh pizza to go with the selection of films, which ranges from offbeat premières to slightly stale blockbusters.

Ster Century Nový Smíchov

Plzeňská 8, Smíchov, Prague 5 (5718 1212/ www.stercentury.cz). Metro Anděl/6, 9, 12 tram. **No credit cards**.
The newest of Prague's central multiplexes lays a temporary claim to having the largest screen (at 187sq m), the greatest number of seats (2,726) and the most advanced sound system.

Ster Century Park Hostivař

Švehlova 32, Hostivař, Prague 10 (5718 1212/ www.stercentury.cz). Tram 22, 26. **No credit cards**. Located in a new shopping mall, this modern multiplex has a slightly less adventurous programme than its central cousins. Tickets are a little cheaper and it is also less likely to be sold out.

Ster Century Slovanský dům

Na Příkopě 22, Nové Město, Prague 1 (5718 1212/ www.stercentury.cz). Metro Náměstí Republiky/5, 8, 14 tram. **No credit cards. Map p309 K4**.
With ten screens, stadium seats and a central location, this has quickly become the place to go, even if it is the priciest. Occasionally, this multiplex shows recent Czech films with English subtitles, or subtitled versions of films that play elsewhere dubbed. It also hosts the annual Febiofest (*see p198*) in late January, but mostly shows Hollywood blockbusters.

Village Cinemas Zábavné centrum Černý Most

Chlumecká 8, Černý Most, Prague 9 (6679 0999/ www.villagecinemas.cz). Metro Černý Most. **Credit** AmEx, DC, MC, V.
This comfortable multiplex is fairly out of the way at the far end of a metro line. It sometimes gets new films a week ahead of its competitors, and often holds onto a title after everyone else has stopped showing it.

Arthouse cinemas

Aero
Biskupcova 31, Žižkov, Prague 3 (7177 1349/ www.kinoaero.cz). Metro Zelivského/1, 9, 16 tram. **No credit cards**.
The place to see retrospective films, this ageing movie palace now has state of the art projection and sound. Foreign films often have English subtitles (with Czech translations broadcast to headsets) and filmmakers such as Terry Gilliam sometimes come to discuss their work. The lobby bar, with its old theatre seats and posters, is a place to hang out in even if you don't see a film. Tickets can be booked in advance online.

British Council
Národní třída 10, Staré Město, Prague 1 (2199 1111/www.britishcouncil.cz). Metro Náměstí Republiky/5, 8, 14 tram. **No credit cards**. **Map p308 H5**.
Much less active than it used to be, the Council still shows classic British films on 16mm every second and fourth Wednesday of the month. Free admission.

Anděl Exit: can Czech indies migrate?

and not much to do between the times that a few stray voters wander in.

First love was the theme for Saša Gedeon's first feature, *Indian Summer* (*Indiánské léto*), which has been compared to the classics of the Czech New Wave. His follow-up film, *Return of the Idiot* (*Návrat idiota*), was loosely inspired by Dostoyevsky's novel.

Vladimír Michálek, one of the older members of the Velvet Generation, has proven to be one of the most versatile. His *Forgotten Light* (*Zapomenuté světlo*) takes us into the waning days of communism, when a priest struggles to hold together a small congregation. *Angel Exit* (*Anděl exit*) was shot on digital video and examines the lives of contemporary down-and-outers living near a seedy metro station. His latest, *Bábi léto* – which, confusingly, also translates into *Indian Summer* – gives a cast of elderly Czech actors a chance to shine as characters trying to make the best of their idle time.

he wrote and directed about time surfing, the bomb and people with incredible anal talents.

Local politics form the basis of Alice Nellis's debut picture *Eeny Meeny* (*Enebene*), a tragicomedy set in a small town on election day. Much of the action takes place among ballot box watchers who have little in common

Evald

Národní třída 28, Staré Město, Prague 1 (2110 5225/www.cinemart.cz). Metro Národní třída/ 6, 9, 18, 22 tram. **No credit cards. Map** p308 H5. Relatively small venue usually showing European art films, independent American films and Czech films with English subtitles. Advance booking recommended for new films. A pub restaurant is hidden away down the hall from the cloakroom.

French Institute

Štěpánská 35, Nové Město, Prague 1 (2140 1011/ www.ifp.cz). Metro Můstek/3, 9, 14, 24 tram. **No credit cards. Map** p311 K6.
The best-kept secret in town is that brand-new French films, and some classics, are shown with Czech and sometimes English subtitles for a rock-bottom admission price of 30 Kč in a basement screening room that rivals any cinema for projection quality.

MAT Studio

Karlovo náměstí 19, Staré Město, Prague 1 (2491 5765/www.mat.cz). Metro Karlovo náměstí/3, 4, 6, 14, 16, 18, 22, 24 tram. **No credit cards. Map** p310 H7.
Since installing digital sound, this small screening room has been mixing retrospective screenings of big-budget action fare with art films, Czech films subtitled in English and rare programming from the Czech TV vaults. It's a small place and often sells out so buy tickets in advance. If turned away, you can always wait for the next screening surrounded by cinemaphiles and old Czech movie props and posters in the bar.

Ponrepo

Bio Konvikt Theatre, Bartolomějská 13, Staré Město, Prague 1 (no phone). Metro Národní třída/6, 9, 18, 22 tram. **Annual membership** 150 Kč adults; tickets 30 Kč. **No credit cards. Map** p308 H5.
Screening venue for the Czech Film Archive, though management makes it truly hard to see the films. You need a membership card with a photo, filling out the form takes at least five minutes, and if there is a queue, you're likely to miss the start of the film. The programme includes Czech and Slovak films, plus works by important world filmmakers from Eisenstein to John Ford. Make sure the film doesn't have a live Czech translation announced directly into the hall (denoted by *s překl*).

Festivals & special events

The events listed below are pretty permanent; keep your eyes open, though, for occasional embassy-sponsored events such as the Days of Iranian Film or selections of recent German or Italian films. Most of these offer English-subtitled versions when possible. The **Archa Theatre** (*see p234*) occasionally has interesting mini-festivals and multimedia screenings, including silent films with ambient live accompaniment. Summer outdoor cinemas (*Letní kino*) are less popular than they used to be – the one at Střelecký Island seems to be the most consistent. Look out for posters during the summer months.

Arts & Entertainment

Days of European Film

2421 5558/www.eurofilmfest.cz. **Date** early Mar.
This (roughly) ten-day festival takes over the Lucerna and 64 U Hradeb (for both, *see p195*) to screen co-productions and award-winning European films in their original language – usually with English subtitles. This is often the only chance to catch these films locally. Filmmakers sometimes come to introduce their films and answer questions. The festival is organised by a number of European cultural centres.

FAMU Student Film Festival

www.archatheatre.cz. **Date** Nov.
Discover the juvenilia of tomorrow's big Czech directors at this weekend festival, usually screened at the Archa Theatre (*see p234*).

Febiofest

2421 4815/www.febiofest.cz. **Date** late Jan.
The multiplex at Slovanský dům has become home base for this eclectic festival that shows new and retrospective films from all over the world. Other venues show international art films, documentaries and cult stuff. Beware that some theatres pipe annoying live translations into the hall (denoted by *překl. do sálu*), while others have more discreet translations to headphones (denoted by *překl. do sluch*).

Karlovy Vary International Film Festival

Info: Film Service Festival Karlovy Vary, Panská 1, Staré Město, Prague 1 (2423 5412/www.iffkv.cz).
Date early July.
Centred at the Hotel Thermal but occupying practically every available space in this small spa resort, this is the only film festival in the Czech Republic accredited by the FIAPF, the group that sanctions the Cannes, Berlin and Venice festivals. Gregory Peck, Lauren Bacall and Ben Kingsley have all put in appearances here. The organisation improves every year, but many big films still sell out quickly. Some people come just for the seemingly endless array of distributor-sponsored parties.

One World Human Rights Film Festival

www.oneworld.cz. **Date** late Apr.
Feature and documentary films focusing on refugees, recent conflicts, basic freedoms and related topics. Venues include the MAT Studio and Evald (for both, *see p197*). Most films are shown from videotape with the unfortunate effect that Czech subtitles added for the festival sometimes totally obscure the original English ones underneath.

Project 100

www.artfilm.cz. **Date** Jan-Feb.
Film scholars pick ten films from around the world each year to be included in this travelling retrospective that runs in Prague in January and February at Aero, MAT and other theatres, before touring the country. Films range from recent works to '50s gems, and include some English-language selections.

Films on video

Several shops and two major restaurants hire out imported videotapes, and this is often the only way to see English-language versions of less commercial films and foreign films with English subtitles.

Jáma

V Jámě 7, Staré Město, Prague 1 (0606 406 741 mobile/www.praguepivo.com). Metro Můstek/3, 9, 14, 24 tram. **Open** noon-11pm daily. **Membership** 100 Kč. **Rental** 70-80 Kč. **No credit cards.**
Map p311 K6.
Popular expat bar stocking hundreds of English-language films and TV shows in PAL format. VCR but not TV rental. Deposit of 1,000 Kč required.

Video Express

Žitná 41, Staré Město, Prague 1 (2221 1425/ www.videoexpress.cz). Metro IP Pavlova/4, 6, 11, 22, 23 tram. **Open** 11am-2am daily. **Membership** 400 Kč. **Rental** 50-80 Kč. **No credit cards.**
Map p311 K7.
The only place in Prague to offer a tape-delivery service. Selection includes 3,000 English-language and English-subtitled tapes in NTSC and PAL format.
Branch: Prokopská 3, Malá Strana, Prague 1 (5753 5139/www.videoexpress.cz).

Video Gourmet

Jakubská 12, Staré Město, Prague 1 (232 3364).
Metro Náměstí Republiky/5, 8, 14 tram. **Open** 11am-11pm daily. **Membership** free. **Rental** 50-75 Kč. **No credit cards. Map** p309 K3.
Along with a big selection of videos and DVDs, wine and take-out meals are available for easy one-stop dinner-and-a-movie shopping. If you want to eat out instead, the video store is in the same building as Red Hot & Blues (*see p125*), a popular expat restaurant.

Video to Go

Vítězné náměstí 10, Dejvice, Prague 6 (2431 8981/ www.videotogo.cz). Metro Dejvická/20, 25, 26 tram.
Open 10am-10pm daily. **Membership** 500 Kč.
Rental 100-190 Kč. **No credit cards.**
Prague's largest selection of English-language tapes – though much of it old and uninspiring – can be found at this store's two locations, both of which have 24-hour tape drop boxes. Also hires out TVs, multisystem VCRs and DVD players.
Branch: Čelakovského sady 12, Nové Město, Prague 2 (2423 5098).

Virus Video

Dlouhá 33, Staré Město, Prague 1(0607 508 933 mobile). Metro Náměstí Republiky/5, 8, 14 tram.
Open 1pm-midnight daily. **Membership** 500 Kč.
Rental 80-100 Kč. **No credit cards. Map** p309 K2.
Hires out a wide variety of films, including some classic Czech films with English subtitles and all sorts of horror, sci-fi, action and cult movies. Some are in NTSC format, but most are in PAL. A screening room can be rented for an additional 80 Kč per person.

Galleries

Long-neglected Czech artists are finally getting their due, while the new wave takes up positions in fresh indie art spaces.

A rehabilitation of sorts is sweeping through the Czech art world, finally bringing to light many worthy artists who were long out of official favour. Some of the country's leading art institutions have joined the trend, such as the progressive **Galerie Rudolfinum** (*see p201*). Recent shows there have included the life works of surrealist Mikuláš Medek and massive-scale landscape photography by Pavel Baňka, a new force on the scene who interprets images through primitive techniques (*see p204* **Lights, camera, Pavel Baňka**).

Medias are mixing in fresh new ways as well, the vanguard led by places such as **Galerie NoD** (*see p203*) and **Galerie Jelení** (*see p202*), who both cybercast art 'happenings' and seek out fringe artists for residencies. All of which is adding needed new blood to a scene that's traditionally been hindered by the small size of Prague and the creative roadblocks of a stodgy National Gallery bureaucracy and traditional conservatories with drastic funding problems. Fortunately underground art grew strong under communism and young artists learned not to wait for an official welcome from the large institutions with the greatest exhibitions spaces. And while most Czech artists were cut off by closed borders from the creative centres of Western Europe, a few Czech cultural refugees from before 1989 developed important ties to the scenes in Paris, London, Lisbon and Berlin, which has now led to wonderful cross-pollinisations at places like the **Galerie Jiří Švestka** (*see p202*). Here you might come across Micheal Biberstein's huge, Chinese landscape-influenced canvases or the latest absurdist plastic models of **David Černý**, the Czech bad boy whose public art has ruffled conservative Prague feathers for years. His most recent coup was a parody of the St Wenceslas statue on Wenceslas Square, inverted and hanging in the Lucerna shopping passage.

You'll also find fresh art in bars and bookstores. The city is scattered with small, offbeat spaces, such as **Café Velryba** (*see p142*). Prague's place on the international circuit makes it a great city in which to catch travelling exhibitions by noteworthy foreign artists while some choice homegrown projects include a permanent home on Kampa island for the interesting Jan and Meda Mládek collection of modern Czech and Central European art (*see p116* **An oasis for Central European art**).

The new boldness harkens back to the great days of the inter-war First Republic, when Czech artists marched at the head of the parade. Indeed, the roots of today's Czech art lie deeper in the national psyche than the communist era. Over the centuries, Czech artists have continually returned to muted colours, spiritual yearnings and a sense of irony. Forty years of insularity did not blunt the sensibility that gave rise to visionary medieval court painters, erotic mannerist allegory, cubist architecture and the art nouveau splendour of Alfons Mucha.

WHO'S WHO

Even under communism, artists such as Adriena Šimotová, Karel Malich and Aleš Veselý were able to produce original and provocative work, especially those of the first post-war generation including Vladimír Kokolia. Since 1989 František Skála has emerged as the surrealist sculptor who did the **Akropolis** (*see p145*) interiors. Martin Mainer is a celebrated abstract artist while Petr Nikl is remarkable for fanciful sculptural objects and original theatre performances. A second wave includes modernist Jiří Příhoda, Kateřina Vincourová, with her ghostly sexual and consumer icons, Veronika Bromová and Štěpánka Šimlová working in digital art.

This chapter covers the principal public exhibition spaces for temporary shows and the more interesting private and commercial galleries. For permanent art collections, *see chapter* **Museums**.

INFORMATION

For information on exhibitions, consult the *Prague Post, Culture in Prague* (*Kultura v Praze*) – a listings booklet available from newsstands, in English at some central locations – or *Atelier*, a Czech fortnightly broadsheet with an English summary and listings of all exhibitions in the country. *Umělec* (*Artist*) magazine features reviews of recent shows and articles on the contemporary Czech scene, and is now available in separate English and Czech editions in some galleries and selected central newsstands.

Arts & Entertainment

Most galleries and museums in Prague are closed on Mondays, and some private spaces take a holiday in August, but it's always best before setting out to check that the one you want to visit hasn't closed temporarily for 'technical reasons'.

Exhibition spaces

Exhibition spaces come and go in Prague, but the main organising bodies are the National Gallery, Prague Castle and the City of Prague. Once tiny, their shows are increasingly large in scale, although they are sometimes curated without much cohesion.

In addition, in recent years, Prague has suddenly discovered the concept of the blockbuster multi-venue exhibition.

Czech Museum of Fine Arts

Husova 19-21, Staré Město, Prague 1 (2222 0218/ www.cmvu.cz). Metro Staroměstská/17, 18 tram. **Open** 10am-6pm Tue-Sun. **Admission** 40 Kč; 20 Kč concessions; free under-14s. **No credit cards.** **Map** p308 H4.

Housed in a block of renovated Renaissance townhouses, this museum exhibits mainly 20th-century Czech art, with the occasional exhibition by a foreign artist, and especially goes in for sweeping themes such as people, nature or technology. Experimental art is often shown in the atmospheric Romanesque cellar which is perfect for that purpose.

Galerie Rudolfinum

Alšovo nábřeží 12, Staré Město, Prague 1 (2489 3305/www.galerierudolfinum.cz). Metro Staroměstská/17, 18 tram. **Open** 10am-6pm Tue-Sun. **Admission** 70-100 Kč; 35-50 Kč concessions; free under-15s, ISIC, ITIC card holders, art students. **No credit cards.** **Map** p308 G2.

Despite problems with a dwindling budget, this gallery remains one of the city's best venues for catching exhibitions of Czech and international contemporary art. The only space in the city with a European *Kunsthalle* model, its changing exhibitions lean toward themes of identity and mindscapes. A steady stream of touring shows (Cindy Sherman, for one) are booked in the grand, naturally lit rooms of the 19th-century Rudolfinum concert building (*see p213*). The Rasart series combines music and theatre with art, creatin.

House at the Stone Bell

Dům U Kamenného zvonu
Staroměstské náměstí 13, Staré Mesto, Prague 1 (2482 7526/www.citygalleryprague.cz). Metro Staroměstská/17, 18 tram. **Open** 10am-6pm Tue-Sun. **Admission** 80 Kč; 40 Kč concessions. **No credit cards.** **Map** p308 J3.

David Černý's parodic art. *See p199.*

Operated by the Prague City Gallery, this Gothic sandstone building on the east side of Old Town Square features a gorgeous baroque courtyard and three floors of exhibition rooms, some of which have their original vaulting still in place. It favours retrospectives of Czech artists such as Toyen, Emila Medková and Zdeněk Rykr, and is also the traditional venue for the Zvon biennial of young Czech and Central European artists.

Kinský Palace

Staroměstské náměstí 12, Staré Město, Prague 1 (2481 0758/www.ngprague.cz). Metro Staroměstská/ 17, 18 tram. **Open** 10am-6pm Tue-Sun. **Admission** 100 Kč; 50 Kč concessions; 150 Kč family; free under-10s. **No credit cards.** **Map** p308 J3.

The National Gallery's recently renovated Kinský Palace opened with a bang in 2000 with the polemical 'End of the World?' show. The palace is home to the National Gallery's extensive collection of drawings and graphics, but unfortunately, these works are viewable by the public only during temporary exhibitions, for some reason.

Municipal House Exhibition Hall

Náměstí Republiky 5, Staré Město, Prague 1 (2200 2101/www.obecni-dum.cz). Metro Náměstí Republiky/5, 8, 14 tram. **Open** 10am-6pm daily. **Admission** for single exhibitions 80 Kč; 40 Kč concessions. **Credit** AmEx, MC, V. **Map** p309 K3.

A stunning exhibition space producing shows on themes including historic art glass and architectural greats like Jan Kotěra. Best are the shows that harmonise with the space itself – art nouveau fits well in these rooms as the Municipal House is an art nouveau masterpiece. A ticket to an art show or concert is the only way to see the gorgeous upper floors.

Municipal Library

Mariánské náměstí 1 (entrance on Valentinská), Staré Město, Prague 1 (2231 1724/www.citygallery prague.cz). Metro Staroměstská/17, 18 tram. **Open** 9am-6pm Tue-Sun. **Admission** 80 Kč; 40 Kč concessions. **No credit cards.** **Map** p308 H3.

Closed at press time for renovations, but set to reopen in October 2002, this modern art space dates back to 1945, when its extensive layout of large, well-lit rooms first hosted important exhibitions. The high standards have returned for the most part, with newly refurbished rooms and imaginative installation work, all run by the Prague City Gallery. Typical shows are along engaging themes such as '1960s action art' or a retrospective of modernist photographer Jaromír Funke.

Old Town Hall

Staroměstské náměstí, Staré Město, Prague 1 (2448 2751). Metro Staroměstská/17, 18 tram. **Open** *Apr-Oct* 10am-6pm Tue-Sun. *Nov-Mar* 9am-5pm Tue-Sun. **Admission** 40 Kč; 20 Kč concessions. **No credit cards.** **Map** p308 H3.

There are two separate spaces for exhibitions within the Old Town Hall. The one entered from the ground floor presents a mixed bag of larger shows, while the more adventurous space on the second floor, operated by the Prague City Gallery, usually displays work by young artists like Krištof Kintera and Štepánka Šimlová.

Wallenstein Riding School

Valdštejnská jízdárna

Valdštejnská at Klárov, Malá Strana, Prague 1 (5707 3136). Metro Malostranská/12, 18, 22, 23 tram. **Open** 10am-6pm Tue-Sun. **Admission** 90 Kč; 45 Kč concessions. **No c. edit cards. Map** p307 D2.

Part of the Wallenstein Palace complex, this space has established itself as host to some of Prague's most thought-provoking exhibitions. These range from explorations of social issues to overviews of Czech artists from symbolist Max Švabinský to the *Tvrdohlaví* (Stubborn Ones) art group. Art walks, in which an English-speaking docent guides visitors, are another new addition to the programme here.

Commercial galleries

Prague has a still-developing commercial scene, best viewed at a smattering of galleries around town. A number of these spaces have very high standards. Among these, outstanding galleries such as **Galerie Jiří Švestka** show tantalising artworks, as do contemporary breeding grounds **Galerie Behémót** and **Galerie MXM**. Artists to watch out for include Adriena Šimotová, Petr Nikl, Václav Stratil and Krištof Kintera.

Galerie Bayer & Bayer

Řetězová 7 (Montmartre), Staré Město, Prague 1 (2222 0029/www.galerie-bayer.cz). Metro Staroměstská/17, 18 tram. **Open** noon-6pm Tue-Sat. **Admission** free. **Credit** AmEx, MC, V. **Map** p308 H4.

These two lovely rooms upstairs in the Montmartre building, with their decorative, painted beamed ceilings, are the new home for gallery owner Karolina Bayerová. She represents a small stable of artists and also shows other, mainly middle generation, Czech artists.

Branch: Haštalská 4, Staré Město, Prague 1 (2222 0029).

Galerie Behémót

Elišky Krásnohorské 6, Staré Město, Prague 1 (2231 7829/www.behemot.cz). Metro Staroměstská/17, 18 tram. **Open** 11am-6pm Tue-Sat. **Admission** free. **Credit** AmEx, MC, V. **Map** p308 H2.

Gallery owner Karel Babíček believes that display conditions are nearly as important as the original creative act and thus favours installations, often with the artists creating their works directly on the gallery walls. The resulting exhibitions are some of the most dynamic in Prague. The artists are mostly of the generation that came of age before 1989, such as Martin Mainer, Václav Stratil, Vladimír Kokolia and Otto Placht, but younger artists are also represented by the gallery. More portable work in an upstairs showroom can be viewed upon request.

Galerie Display

Bubenská 3, Holešovice, Prague 7 (0604 722 562 mobile/www.display.cz). Metro Vltavská/1, 3, 8, 14, 25 tram. **Open** 3-6pm Wed-Sun. **Admission** free. **No credit cards.**

This graffiti-covered storefront gallery is an energetic new player on the scene. In addition to a risk-taking exhibition programme it also holds film screenings and discussion evenings with artists.

Galerie Gambit

Mikulandská 6, Nové Město, Prague 1 (2491 0508). Metro Národní třída/6, 9, 18, 21, 22, 23 tram. **Open** noon-6pm Tue-Sat. **Admission** free. **No credit cards. Map** p308 H5.

This tiny gallery just off Národní třída has recently beefed up its exhibition programme in order to concentrate on small shows of new works by well-known names on the Czech scene like Michael Rittstein, Petr Kvičala and Karel Nepraš. It also sometimes exhibits foreign artists.

Gandy Gallery

Školská 7, Nové Město, Prague 1 (9623 3066/www.gandy-gallery.com). Metro Karlovo náměstí/3, 9, 14, 24 tram. **Open** 1.30-6.30pm Tue-Fri; 10am-noon Sat. **Admission** free. **No credit cards. Map** p310 J6.

Owned by Frenchwoman Nadine Gandy, the gallery deals in known Western artists, especially French ones. Also hosts minor exhibitions by not-so-minor names such as Lydia Lunch and Nan Goldin. This is a good place to see work by Václav Stratil.

Galerie Hollar

Smetanovo nábřeží 6, Staré Město, Prague 1 (2423 5243). Metro Národní třída/17, 18 tram. **Open** 10am-1pm, 2-6pm Tue-Sun. **Admission** 10 Kč; 5 Kč concessions. **No credit cards. Map** p308 G5.

The gallery of the Union of Czech Graphic Artists, on the ground floor of Charles University's Faculty of Sociology. The building faces the river so traffic noise competes with the monthly exhibitions, which are normally Czech or Slovak artists. There are large racks of prints to browse through or buy.

Galerie Jelení

Jelení 9, Hradčany, Prague 1 (2437 3178/www.fcca.cz). Metro Malostranská/22, 23 tram. **Open** 10am-5.30pm Mon-Fri. **Admission** free. **No credit cards.**

This space operated by the Centre for Contemporary Art puts on some of the most experimental shows in the city, including student exhibitions. The attached café holds occasional jazz nights.

Galerie Jiří Švestka

Jungmannova 30, Nové Město, Prague 1 (9624 5025/www.jirisvestka.com). Metro Národní třída/6, 9, 18, 21, 22, 23 tram. **Open** noon-6pm Tue-Fri; 11am-6pm Sat. **Admission** free. **No credit cards. Map** p310 J6.

Returned émigré Jiří Švestka has been operating a gallery in the former Mozarteum concert hall since 1995, specialising in bold, internationally recognised

Artists get moving at the **Galerie Jiří Švestka**. *See p202.*

modern Czech art. He represents such names as Stanislav Kolíbal, Jan Kotik from the senior generation and Kateřina Vincourová among the younger artists. The gallery also exhibits international names like Donald Flavin and Dan Graham.

Galerie Jiřího a Běly Kolářových

Betlémské náměstí 8, Staré Město, Prague 1 (2222 0689). Metro Národní třída/6, 9, 17, 18, 21, 22, 23 tram. **Open** 10am-6pm daily. **Admission** free. **No credit cards. Map** p308 H5.

The world knows Jiří Kolář as the master of collage, autocollage, anticollage, rolage, assemblage – he and his wife, Běla, do them all. Czechs also revere him as an influential poet of the 1950s. View or buy a montage or collage of your own, such as a shovel collaged with tiny scraps of paper. This is art that will stick with you. In addition to the Kolář duo, the gallery holds temporary shows with an emphasis on Kolář's cohorts from the inter-war era.

Galerie Kritiků

Jungmannova 31, Nové Město, Prague 1 (2449 4205/www.galeriekritiku.cz). Metro Národní třída/ 6, 9, 18, 21, 22, 23 tram. **Open** 10am-6pm Tue-Sun. **Admission** 25 Kč; 15 Kč concessions. **No credit cards. Map** p308 J5.

This elegant new space in the Adria Palace with its grand pyramid skylight has quickly proved itself to be a class act, particularly in its strong shows of mainly contemporary Czech art. It's also well located for a tour of galleries all around the street of Národní třída, which runs along the Old Town border from here to the Vltava River.

Galerie MXM

Nosticova 6, Malá Strana, Prague 1 (5731 1198/www.galeriemxm.cz) Metro Malostranská/ 12, 22, 23 tram. **Open** noon-6pm Tue-Sun. **Admission** free. **Credit** AmEx. **Map** p307 E4.

Conceived in 1990 to represent Czech artists, this small vaulted space in the heart of Malá Strana is the oldest private gallery in Prague and remains one of the most influential in the country. Though it's a small and unprepossessing space, exhibitions here are consistently good, and recent shows have featured works by Jiří David, Karel Malich and Petr Nikl. Ring bell for entry.

Galerie NoD

Dlouhá 33, Staré Město, Prague 1 (2482 6330/ www.roxy.cz). Metro Náměstí Republiky/5, 8, 14 tram. **Open** 1pm-1am Mon-Sat. **Admission** free. **No credit cards. Map** p309 K2.

Sharing premises with the Roxy club (*see p228*) is this newish space for shows of experimental work by young and otherwise obscure artists. A particular speciality is the eclectic thematic group show, mixing established and up-and-coming artists. Funding from the attached dance club supports and cultivates indie artists, new media and fringe culture cells, all of whom tend to rotate around the surreal-industrial internet bar adjoining the gallery.

Galerie Tvrdohlaví
Vodičkova 36, Nové Město, Prague 1 (9623 6491/ www.tvrdohlavi.cz). Metro Můstek/3, 9, 14, 24 tram. **Open** 10am-10pm daily. **Admission** free. **No credit cards. Map** p311 K6.

Through the foyer of the Lucerna cinema, this gallery is the showcase for works by members of the still-impressive *Tvrdohlaví* (Stubborn Ones) art group, which was rattling the local art establishment before the revolution. Now the members rank among the country's blue-chip artists. Changing exhibitions tend to feature one or more of the group's members, which include well-known names like Petr Nikl, Jiří David and Michal Gabriel. A nook in the back of the gallery shows work by 'guest artists'.

Czech Fund for Art Foundation

The following galleries have exhibitions sponsored by this organisation (Nadace Český fond umění). The shows are always of contemporary artists. The quality of the work varies enormously, but entry tends to be cheap or free and the venues are usually worth a visit. Direct purchases from the artists can usually be arranged through the galleries.

Galerie Václava Špály
Národní třída 30, Nové Město, Prague 1 (2494 6738/www.nadacecfu.com). Metro Národní třída/ 6, 9, 18, 21, 22, 23 tram. **Open** 10am-1pm, 2-6pm Tue-Fri; 1-6pm Sat, Sun. **Admission** 20 Kč; 10 Kč students. **No credit cards. Map** p308 H5.

This gallery has been going for more than 40 years in its present incarnation. It comprises two floors of exhibition space, plus a basement for conceptual art and installations. Of the foundation's venues, this one keeps to the most consistently high standards. Winners of the Chalupecký Award for artists under 35 are traditionally granted a solo show here.

Lights, camera, Pavel Baňka

'My images are about my feelings,' says the latest artist to make waves in the remarkable Czech tradition of photographical art. Following on from Sudek, Drtikol and Funke, Pavel Baňka's enormous black and white images – often inspired by Pacific seascapes and Bohemian fields – deliberately use primitive antique cameras, hand-held

shots, vignetting and multiple exposures. The idea, he says, is to break free from the constraints of literal, technically perfect landscape images that are so prevalent today. His powerful, almost Zen-like photos, recently seen at Prague's most progressive art venue, the **Galerie Rudolfinum** (*see p201*), show his instincts are good ones.

Nová síň

Voršilská 3, Nové Město, Prague 1 (2493 0255/
www.nadacecfu.com). Metro Národní třída/6, 9,
18, 21, 22, 23 tram. **Open** 11am-6pm tram.
Admission free. **No credit cards. Map** p310 H6.
At this single bright, clean room – the proverbial
white cube – in a nondescript building near Národní
třída, the quality of exhibitions has sunk in recent
years, with artists renting out the space and often
curating their own shows. This is not really a serious player these days, but the hope is that the venue
will bounce back to its prior position as a respectable
location for contemporary art.

Výstavní síň Mánes

Masarykovo nábřeží 250, Nové Město, Prague 1
(2493 0754/www.nadacecfu.com). Metro Karlovo
náměstí/17, 21 tram. **Open** 10am-6pm Tue-Sun.
Admission 30 Kč; 15 Kč concessions; children free.
No credit cards. Map p310 G7.
The largest and most prominent of the foundation's
galleries is also a beautiful, if run down, piece of functionalist architecture built by Otakar Novotný in
1930. This riverside gallery usually hosts anything
from international travelling shows to exhibitions of
contemporary Czech artists like Vladimír Kokolia
and Lukáš Rittstein. With proper management,
which has been in flux lately, the gallery could again
become the vibrant centre it was in the past. Be sure
to look up at the cubist ceiling frescoes on the
lower ground floor.

Mikuláš Medek's surrealism at
Galerie Rudolfinum. *See p201.*

Photography galleries

In photography, the long and well-established
Czech tradition is still carried on today by
practitioners such as Jindřich Štreit, Pavel
Baňka and, among the younger generation,
Markéta Othová and the duo of Martin Polák
and Lukáš Jasanský. Overall, the **Czech
Photography Centre** and **Prague House
of Photography** regularly show the best
works from the local scene.

Czech Photography Centre

Náplavní 1, Nové Město, Prague 2 (2492 2726).
Metro Karlovo náměstí/17, 21 tram. **Open** 11am-
7pm daily. **Admission** free. **No credit cards.**
Map p310 G7.
A fairly small but well-lit gallery run by Jiří
Jaskmanický offers consistently compelling shows
by such diverse talents as Miroslav Hák, Jaroslav
Rössler, František Drtikol and the Czech pictorialists.

Josef Sudek Gallery

Úvoz 24, Hradčany, Prague 1 (5753 1489). Metro
Malostranská/22, 23 tram. **Open** 11am-5pm Wed-
Sun. **Admission** 10 Kč; 5 Kč students. **No credit
cards. Map** p306 B3.
The father of modern Czech photography almost
seems to be hanging about the corners in this, his
flat from 1959 to 1976. It once housed a collection of
Sudek's own photographs but now presents a fine

programme of changing exhibitions organised by
the Museum of Decorative Arts, including work by
Sudek contemporaries such as Jindřich Štyrský.

Josef Sudek House of Photography

Komorní galerie Domu fotografie Josefa Sudka
Maiselova 2, Josefov, Prague 1 (2481 9098).
Metro Staroměstská/17, 18 tram. **Open** 10am-7pm
Tue-Sun. **Admission** 20 Kč; 10 Kč concessions.
Credit DC, MC, V. **Map** 308 H3.
The second of three photography galleries in town
bearing Sudek's name (the third is located in his
former atelier on Újezd 30), this space just off Old
Town Square leans toward documentary work with
a dependable programme of fresh young talent.

Prague House of Photography

Pražský dům fotografie
Haštalská 1, Staré Město, Prague 1 (2481 0779/
www.php-gallery.cz). Metro Náměstí Republiky/5, 8,
14 tram. **Open** 11am-6pm daily. **Admission** 30 Kč;
15 Kč concessions. **No credit cards. Map** p308 J2.
The peripatetic PHP seems to have settled in an Old
Town courtyard. It's well on the way to recreating
its early 1990s glory days, when it publicised both
classic and contemporary Czech photography
through its first-rate shows and workshops. Recent
exhibitions of works by Dagmar Hochová and Eva
Fuková prove this is already happening.

Arts & Entertainment

Gay & Lesbian

Prague gays aren't big on 'out and proud', preferring to mingle quietly. And, as ever, 'love for sale' is the motto at many venues.

Being queer in Prague is no big deal – really. Though numerous official organs have policies that appear frightfully intolerant, the reality is that Prague is one of the most mellow cities for gays this side of Amsterdam. Just don't expect a US-style rainbow flag waving, sashaying and boot stomping queer culture. For a population that for decades was forced to parade their allegiance to the state, pomp is something they'd rather forget than reclaim. Unlike America's famous Stonewall Riots, which sparked a nation-wide revolution in gay consciousness in the late 1960s, Prague's gay revolution is happening without much ado.

Homosexuality was declassified as a disease in the 1960s, and illegal (considered dissident behaviour) until after the Velvet Revolution in 1989 (*see p18*). The age of consent is now a peach-fuzzy 15 years across the board. EU membership (projected for 2003) will mean opening the closet door wider – but so far Parliament has shown a reluctance to do more than take a peek. The much-debated registered partnership bill has yet to make it past the homophobic right-wingers and is often being argued against by notorious closet cases.

Gay clubs in Prague are many, although many are mixed. There is only one lesbian establishment, the cosy **A-Club** (*see p207*) located in Žižkov. While there is a plethora of local and international magazines available for men, women for now are more or less struck out of print. And there is just a small handful of lesbigay organisations.

Cafés and small bars, such as the homely **Érra Café** in Old Town (*see p209*) and the hopelessly 1980s **Club Stella** in Žižkov (*see p208*) are the places for socialising and mingling. You will find 'straight' dance clubs such as **Mecca** (*see p226*), the **Roxy** (*see p228*), **Radoxt FX** (*see p227*) and **Akropolis** (*see p217*) to be very accommodating and gay-friendly, especially if you are in to excellent DJs and live music.

Unless you are here for sex, you may find the varying presence of prostitutes at gay clubs to be anything from curious to irritating to downright horrible. Western sex tourists already know Prague well for its easy access to young bodies, available in droves to service them. Whatever your preference or activity,

though, safe sex is very likely to be your own responsibility. Be prepared, and bring protection with you.

You can start planning your trip early by checking out www.planetout.com or www.gayguide.net. Both offer a selection of accommodation, listings and safety information. Be aware that the scene is in constant flux – make your reservations through the proprietor of the accommodation you seek. Once you arrive, you can find recent listings of events in *Amigo* (available at most newsagents in the city).

Boat cruises, drag shows, gay festivals and candlelight vigils are organised throughout the year. *Amigo*, the A-Club bulletin, and GI (*see below*) are the best sources.

Associations

GI (Gay Initiative of the Czech Republic)
Senovážné náměstí 2, 110 00 Prague 1 (242 2381/ 0601 213 840 mobile/www.gay.iniciativa.cz). **Map** p307 L4.
Formerly known as SOHO (the Association of Organisations of Gay Citizens in the Czech Republic), GI carries on much the same activities as its forebear, with Jiří Hromada continuing as president of the organisation. *Amigo* and the A-Club bulletin list GI activies, and the A-Club (*see p207*) also acts as an umbrella for the ever-nebulous lesbian organisation scene.

Project Šance
Ve Smečkách 28, Nové Město, 110 00, Prague 1 (2221 1797). Metro Můstek/3, 9, 14, 24 tram. **Open** 8am-5pm Mon-Fri. **Map** p309 K7.
This small, dingy drop-in centre is a lifeline for most female and male prostitutes ('butterflies') and is in constant need of funding. Posters advertising safe sex awareness for 'butterflies' are posted inside Hlavní nádraži. Donations go towards sex education, AIDS and STD testing, and community outreach programmes.

Logos
Fara CCE, U Školské zahrady 1, Prague 8 (8468 0145/www.ecn.cz/private/logos). Tram 5, 14. **Open** *Office* 2-5pm 1st Sun of mth. *Services* 9.30am Sun.
The Christian gay association is not limited to Catholic interests, though it is hosted by a former nun. Meetings are every Sunday from 2pm for three

Arts & Entertainment

Lesbian bars like **A-Club** are rare in boy-heavy Prague.

or four hours. These meetings are generally informal and relaxed – with more focus on support and community than religion itself. Interesting.

AIDS

The Czech Republic claims to have a low AIDS and HIV infection rate. According to the Czech Ministry of Health, by May 2001 there were a total of 514 HIV-infected people registered in the country. Of these 151 had developed AIDS and 90 fatalities were reported. Still, this is no Shangri-la. AIDS and other STDs are out there, and some health officials estimate the actual infection rate to be up to four times the number reported by the ministry. You can purchase condoms in supermarkets, pharmacies and some clubs. The safest brand is Durex, though Soho and Primeros are trustworthy.

ČSAP (Česká Společnost AIDS Pomoc)/Lighthouse (Dům Světla)
*Malého 3, Prague 8 (2481 0702/http://
web.telecom.cz/AIDS-pomoc). Metro Florenc/8, 24
tram.* **Open** *Volunteers available* 9am-4pm Mon-Fri.
ČSAP is the Czech organisation for AIDS prevention and for the support of people with HIV or AIDS. In addition to a 24-hour hotline, it runs the House of Light, which is a hospice for HIV-infected individuals who would otherwise have nowhere to go. Donations are very welcome.

Accommodation

Arco Guesthouse
*Voroněžská 24, Vršovice, Prague 10 (7174 0734/
fax 7174 0734/www.arco-guesthouse.cz). Metro
Náměstí Míru/4, 16, 22, 23 tram.* **Rates** 950-

1,400 Kč double; 1,700-1,900 Kč apartments (incl breakfast). **No credit cards**.
This is a comfortable, relaxed collection of apartments with a friendly attached restaurant and bar. Reservations are required.

Ron's Rainbow Guest House
*Bulharská 4, Vršovice, Prague 10 (7172 5664/0604
876 694 mobile). Metro Flora/6, 7, 22, 24, 34 tram.*
Open 9am-9pm daily. **Rates** 2,300-2,600 Kč per room. **Credit** MC, V.
The Rainbow comprises four comfortable apartments in residential Prague bordering Žižkov – one with a whirlpool. Ron is always at your service. Reservations required.

Bars & clubs

Don't let the iron-barred doorways deter you; some clubs try to suss out merrymakers from troublemakers. Just buzz the bell, look friendly, and collect your drink card. Remember to pay off your drink card at the bar and present it to the doorperson as you leave – otherwise, some clubs will charge you 1,000 Kč or more for 'losing' the card. And it's best not to argue.

A-Club
*Milíčova 25, Prague 3 (2278 1623/
www.webpark.cz/a-club). Metro Jiřího z Poděbrad/
5, 9, 26, 55, 58 tram.* **Open** 7pm-3am daily (closing times vary). **Admission** 25-50 Kč Fri, Sat. **No credit cards**. **Map** p311 C1.
The only lesbian bar in town is women only on Fridays, but otherwise is open to all persuasions. A kitschy but comfortable cellar establishment, it's the place to hear Cher, Slovak techno pop and a little Nirvana. The dancefloor is small, the walls are damp, but the art is total girl power and so is the spirit of the clientele. The space doubles as a club-

The hip queers always find their way to **Érra Café**. *See p209.*

house for a variety of lesbian interest groups, including artists, poets and musicians. The yearly **Aprilfest** (*see p209*) is organised from here, as are the less cerebral lesbian party boat tours in June. Note that closing times may vary.

Club Stella
Lužická 10, Vinohrady, Prague 2 (2425 7869/ www.stellaclub.webpark.cz). Metro Náměstí Míru/ 4, 22, 23, 34, 57 tram. **Open** 8pm-5am daily. **Admission** free. **No credit cards. Map** p313 B3.
Cosy, with a newly remodelled chrome-and-vinyl front lounge that places you smack-bang in Dirk Diggler's living room. A fun, friendly spot for pre- and post-party activity.

Drake's
Zborovská 50, Smíchov, Prague 5 (no phone). Metro Anděl/6, 9, 12, 22, 57, 58 tram. **Open** 24hrs daily. **Admission** 500 Kč. **No credit cards.**
A Prague sex industry veteran. The high admission price, valid for 24 hours, makes this a venue for tourists rather than locals. It features 20 booths with videos in a downstairs equipped with glory holes. Daily strip shows at 9pm and 11pm. Escort service.

Escape to Paradise
V Jámě 8, Nové Město, Prague 1 (0606 538 111 mobile/www.escapetoparadise.cz). Metro Můstek/3, 9, 14, 24 tram. **Open** *Restaurant* 8pm-2am daily. *Disco* 9.30pm-3am daily. **Admission** 50 Kč Fri, Sat. **No credit cards. Map** p310 J6.
This place comes complete with *Miami Vice* neons, go-go boys, exotic dancers and escorts.

Fajn Bar
Dittrichova 5, Nové Město,Prague 2 (2491 7409). Metro Karlovo náměstí/3, 7, 10, 14, 16, 17 tram. **Open** 1pm-1am Mon-Fri; 2pm-1am Sun. **Admission** free. **No credit cards. Map** p310 G8.
This is a throwback to the Prague of the 1970s, both musically and in terms of its mostly not-so-young-anymore clientele.

Friends
Náprstkova 1, Staré Město, Prague 1 (2163 5408/ www.friends-prague.cz). Metro Národní třída/ 6, 9, 18, 21, 22, 23, 51, 54, 57, 58 tram. **Open** 4pm-3am daily. **Admission** free. **No credit cards. Map** p308 G4.
This popular mixed cellar bar is the place to drink a beer and chat while pondering the next move – be it the opera or the disco.

Piano Bar
Milešovská 10, Žižkov, Prague 3 (2272 7496/ www.sweb.cz/pianobar). Metro Jiřího z Poděbrad/ 11, 51 tram. **Open** 5pm-5am daily. **Admission** free. **No credit cards. Map** p313 C2.
A low-key place with cheapish cold cuts and a piano no one ever seems to play. It's wall-to-wall with patrons all week and there's normally no overtly naughty activities.

Projdejna & Kafírna U českého pána
Kozí 13, Staré Město, Prague 1 (no phone). Metro Staroměstská/17, 18 tram. **Open** 11am-10pm Mon-Fri; 2-10pm Sat, Sun. **Admission** free. **No credit cards. Map** p308 J1/2.
Lace curtains add an atmosphere of discretion to this central bar that caters to middle-aged and intro-verted Czech gay males. In general, this place is good for a cup of tea and a glimpse at gay male life outside the thunderdome.

U Střelce
Karoliny Světle 12, Staré Město, Prague 1 (2423 8278). Metro Národní třída/6, 9, 18, 21, 22, 23, 51, 54, 57, 58 tram. **Open** 9.30pm-5am Wed-Fri, Sat. **Admission** 100 Kč. **No credit cards. Map** 308 G5.
This cellar club is the best place in town to see *travesti*, or drag shows. The clientele here are generally mixed – and often mostly straight on drag nights – If you want to have a table, you'll need to make a reservation on the answering machine.

Arts & Entertainment

Dance clubs

Quite frankly, **Radost FX**, **Roxy** and **Mecca** (*see chapter* **Nightlife**) will satisfy any dance fiend, queer or straight, in a blissfully tolerant and friendly environment. There is one true queer dance hall though, **Gejzír**, and it is not entirely dedicated to the boogie.

Gejzír

Vinohradská 40, Prague 2 (2251 6036/ www.gejzir.cz). Metro Náměstí Míru/11 tram. **Open** 6pm-5am Thur; 9pm-5am Fri, Sat. **Admission** free Thur; 100 Kč Fri; 150 Kč Sat. **No credit cards. Map** p311 M6.
This place is fun, if only because it's the only big queer dance club in the city. One can overlook the video room and darkroom and get down to good DJ mixes. Rentboys cruise here but stick to the corridors and the special, men-only rooms. Be careful on the stairs leading to the darkroom.

Cruising

A large metronome now stands atop Letná plain, replacing the once domineering statue of Joseph Stalin. This metronome is a beacon to all male cruisers, out and closeted, who seek a little twilight action amid the hilly trails adjacent to Prague Castle. The city's main train station (Hlavní nádraží) is a meeting point for male prostitutes ('butterflies') and their mostly German clients. Be careful, though: the Fantova Café upstairs is a no-cruising zone.

Women, on the other hand, will either have to break a sweat or brush up on their philosophy to pick up a little local action. Lesbians here are divided by brawn and brain. Check out the *A-Club* bulletin for sporting events. The philosophical faculty and the unlikely theological faculty of Charles University are good for girl-watching – you will undoubtedly recognise several faces from the clubs.

Restaurants & cafés

Érra Café

Konviktská 11, Staré Město, Prague 1 (no phone/ www.sweb.cz/erra.cafe). Metro Národní třída/6, 9, 18, 21, 23 tram. **Open** 10am-midnight Mon-Fri; 11am-midnight Sat, Sun. **Main courses** 250-350 Kč. **No credit cards. Map** p308 G5.
The warm red walls and subdued lighting here offer the perfect atmosphere for nursing a hangover or getting to know someone a little better. This mixed café is popular amongst the hipper queer and queer-friendly crowd. Downstairs is a bit drab, but a great space to throw a party.

U Brouka (Pytlíka)

Drtinova 20, Smíchov, Prague 5 (0602 37 52 49 mobile). Metro Anděl/6, 9, 12 tram. **Open** 11am-

10pm Mon-Sat; 4-10pm Sun. **Main courses** 300-400 Kč. **No credit cards.**
Prague's latest mixed pub. Food is the usual Czech fare and cocktails are offered. Weekend table reservations are recommended.

Petřínské Terasy

Seminářská zahrada 13, Petřín Hill, Prague 1 (9000 0457/www.petrinsketerasy.cz). Metro Malostranská/12, 22 tram. **Open** 11am-11pm daily. **Main courses** 300-400 Kč. **Credit** AmEx, DC, MC, V.
A bar and restaurant on Petřín Hill offers up a view of Prague Castle when seated outside on the terrace.

Saunas

Sauna Babylonia

Martinská 6, Staré Město, Prague 1 (2423 2304/ www.amigo.cz/babylonia). Metro Můstek/3, 9, 14, 25 tram. **Open** 2pm-3am daily. **Admission** 80-120 Kč. **No credit cards. Map** p308 H5.
The most popular gay sauna in Prague with an active crowd of regulars.

Sauna David

Sokolovská 44, Karlín, Prague 8 (2231 7869/ www.gaysauna.cz). Metro Florenc/8, 24 tram. **Open** noon-midnight daily. **Admission** 80-120 Kč. **No credit cards.**
Prague's first gay sauna is cosy and intimate.

Sauna Marco

Lublaňská 17, Nove Město, Prague 2 (2426 2833). Metro IP Pavlova/4, 6, 11, 16, 22, 23 tram. **Open** 2pm-3am daily. **Admission** 80-120 Kč. **No credit cards. Map** p311 L8.
This is a small but popular sauna that's conveniently centrally located.

Shops

Amigo Shop & Gay Info

Příčná 7, Nove Město, Prague 1(2223 3250/ www.amigo.cz). **Open** 1-7pm Tue-Sat. **Credit** MC, V. **Map** p310 J7.
Pick up copies of *Amigo* and other publications, plus sex aids and the latest information on the scene.

City Fox

Příběnická 12, Žižkov, Prague 3 (6278 542). **Open** 11am-6pm Mon-Sat. **Credit** AmEx, DC, MC, V. **Map** p313 A1.
Offers many Czech-produced videos.

Special events

Aprilfest

Venue varies (info from **A-Club**, *see p207/http://lama-web.cz/aprilfest).* **Date** Apr.
The premiere lesbian festival, which is organised through the A-Club (*see p207*). A welcoming forum for new artists, musicians and speakers. Now in its eighth year, the festival is drawing an increasingly international crowd.

Music: Classical & Opera

Fresh opera, wall-to-wall orchestras and an incredible chamber music history make for virtuoso nights out, even when it's not Prague Spring time.

It's difficult to think of Prague without a string soundtrack coming to mind. You expect Mozartean characters to step from every baroque doorway in Old Town, and when a film crew is shooting, they often do. And every visitor experiences that magic Prague moment when, just as you find yourself lost in the Malá Strana district, a cello solo comes floating out of the window of an apartment.

With three full-time opera theatres, four major orchestras and countless smaller ensembles, Prague does offer an incredible range of classical options. Traditional Czech fare performed by top-quality musicians generally fills out the programmes, though the **Prague Spring Festival** (*see p185 and 215*) goes for avant-garde music as well. The classical high point of the year by far, the event attracts the likes of Kurt Masur and the New York Philharmonic, alongside the best of a considerable array of Czech talents. The **Czech Philharmonic** is a perennial star of the city. Its recordings grow more impressive each year, and lure guest conductors of world renown.

The no less capable **Prague Symphony Orchestra** has a wider repertoire, which embraces 20th-century and non-European music, as well as a strong commitment to Russian symphonic works – **Maxim Shostakovich**, the composer's son, is an annual guest conductor.

Prague's third major ensemble, the **Radio Prague Symphony Orchestra,** lacks the notoriety of the Prague Symphony Orchestra and the Czech Orchestra but generally produces more than creditable performances of contemporary works. The **Prague Chamber Philharmonic**, founded and conducted by Prague Symphony Orchestra conductor **Jiří Bělohlávek**, is an excellent ensemble of younger players and has risen to fame with a mix of the classics and the little known.

Czech conductors such as Bělohlávek and **Libor Pešek** have established themselves on the international circuit, as have divas **Eva Urbanová**, **Dagmar Pecková** and **Magdalena Kožená**. All are likely to come home for the Prague Spring Festival.

If you're hitting the city outside the festival's May-June dates, you've still got the autumn and winter seasons in which to catch the above orchestras at the same stunning venues used during the festival – the **Municipal House**, **Rudolfinum** (*for both, see p213*) and **National Theatre** (*see p214*) are treats in themselves. This last, where Smetana scored the Czech national awakening with his opera *Libuše*, composed for the opening of the theatre in 1881, is a cultural cornerstone of the republic.

Don't be taken in by summer concert packages, though: every major symphony, orchestra and opera company shuts down at the end of June and goes on a two-month holiday just when audience potential is at its greatest. One excellent company that is willing to perform in the summer is the small troupe that stages open-air opera in the **Lichtenstein Palace** (*see p214*). Its shows often sell out. Otherwise, it's strictly chamber recitals – though very good ones, as a rule – that are left for summer visitors.

Prague Symphony Orchestra. *See p215.*

The breathtaking **Rudolfinum**: music to your ears. *See p213.*

Prague opera, a particularly fractious world, has recently had new life breathed into it by the the innovative staging, lighting and repertoire of the **State Opera** (*see p214*). Still, the rivalry between this company and the National Theatre can result in two different productions of the same opera on the same night, a strange extravagance in a city where state funding has decreased dramatically. But business sense is coming into the equation more and more. The **Estates Theatre** (*see p214*) now hires itself out during the summer hiatus to the **Opera Mozart** (*see p215*) company, which fills the house with commercial productions of *Don Giovanni*.

Many small Prague ensembles, meanwhile, have become so good at making profits that they've inundated the city with cliché renditions of *A Little Night Music* and *The Four Seasons*, performed in every vacant church or palace in town – usually at prices above those charged for major concerts by any of the principal orchestras.

Works by Czech musical giants **Bedřich Smetana** and **Antonín Dvořák** are both regularly heard in the performance halls of Prague, particularly their celebrations of Bohemian folk traditions. The bolder, more modern **Leoš Janáček** and **Bohuslav Martinů** aren't so well represented, although Janáček's operas are given increasingly frequent airings at the National Theatre. **Josef Suk,** Dvořák's son-in-law and a late Romantic, is another talented Czech composer,

though he's only really known in the West for the *Asrael* symphony. His heir, a violin virtuoso also named Josef, often performs and records in Prague. **Zděnek Fibich,** a contemporary of Smetana and Dvořák, is another discovery, whose lyrical piano pieces have been released extensively on the Czech classical label Supraphon. Several contemporary composers, such as **Petr Eben,** are also finding their voice, though performances of their work are more commercially risky and therefore infrequent.

Other little-known Czech composers were well established long before the première of *Don Giovanni* in Prague in 1787 (the one landmark in Czech musical history that everyone seems to know). **Zelenka, Mysliveček, Benda, Černohorský** and **Brixi** are just a handful of those who have been slighted by history. Ongoing research continues to uncover material from archives.

Tickets & information

As **Ticketpro** doesn't book for the biggest classical venues and most agencies that do hike prices dramatically for foreigners, it's best to buy directly from the venue's box office if you're already in Prague. Touts buy up all the remaining seats for popular shows so don't worry if something is 'sold out' – just wait around the entrance until the last minute when the touts have to sell or lose their investment.

Prices for concerts vary and some (in the smaller churches) are free, but the cost is usually between 250 Kč and 600 Kč.

Information can be haphazard, but **Bohemia Ticket International** has an online calendar prepared months in advance and is willing to take your telephone order and credit card payment from abroad. Prague has a tradition of subscription evenings, so you may find certain glittering occasions difficult to get into.

Ticket agencies

Bohemia Ticket International

Malé náměstí 13, Staré Město, Prague 1 (2422 7832/fax 2161 2126/www.ticketsbti.cz). Metro Můstek or Náměstí Republiky/17, 18 tram. **Open** 9am-5pm Mon-Fri; 9am-noon Sat, Sun. **No credit cards. Map** p309 K4.

Best non-travel agency for buying tickets in advance from abroad for opera and concerts at the National Theatre, Estates Theatre and State Opera, plus other orchestral and chamber events.

Branch: Na příkopě 16, Nové Město, Prague 1 (2421 5031).

Čedok

Na příkopě 18, Nové Město, Prague 1 (2419 7411/7203/www.cedok.cz). Metro Můstek or Náměstí Republiky/5, 8, 14 tram. **Open** 9am-7pm Mon-Fri; 10am-2pm Sat; 10am-noon Sun. **Credit** AmEx, MC, V. **Map** p309 K4.

Tickets for various events, with some concerts.

Branches: Václavské náměstí 53, Nové Město, Prague 1 (2196 5243); Rytířská 16, Staré Město, Prague 1 (2422 4461).

Ticketpro

Old Town Hall, Staré Město, Prague 1 (2448 2018/www.ticketpro.cz). Metro Staroměstská/17, 18 tram. **Open** 8am-6pm daily. **Credit** AmEx, MC, V. **Map** p308 H3.

Advance booking for major concerts and various smaller events. The automated toll-free number works for all branches – mostly found at Prague Information Service offices and hotels.

Branch: Štěpánská 61 (Lucerna Passage), Nové Město, Prague 1 (2481 8080); Rytířská 31, Staré Město, Prague 1 (2161 0162); Salvátorská 10, Staré Město, Prague 1 (2481 4020/8401 1150).

Principal concert halls

Municipal House

Obecní dům
Náměstí Republiky 5, Nové Město, Prague 1 (2200 2336/2100). Metro Náměstí Republiky/5, 14 tram. **Open** Box office 10am-6pm Mon-Fri. **Tickets** 200-1,100 Kč. **Credit** AmEx, MC, V. **Map** p309 K3.

A stunning example of Czech art nouveau, the Municipal House is built around the Smetana Hall, home to the Prague Symphony Orchestra. The orchestra launches the Prague Spring Festival here

every year, as it has done for over half a century. Listen to Smetana variations on folk tunes while gazing at the ceiling mosaics of old Czech myths for an authentic Bohemian national cultural experience. *See also p134.*

Rudolfinum

Alšovo nábřeží 12, Staré Město, Prague 1 (2489 3352/www.rudolfinum.cz). Metro Staroměstská/17, 18 tram. **Open** Box office mid Aug-mid July 10am-6pm Mon-Fri. **Tickets** 200-1,100 Kč. **Credit** AmEx, MC, V. **Map** p308 G2.

One of the most beautiful concert venues in Europe, built in the neo-classical style at the end of the 19th century, the Rudolfinum has two halls: the Dvořák Hall for orchestral works and major recitals, and the Suk Hall for chamber, instrumental and solo vocal music. Opinions are divided about the acoustics of the Dvořák Hall, but the grandeur of the building's interior – plus the high standard of musicianship on offer – makes an evening here eminently worthwhile. *See also p201.*

Other venues

Venues for chamber music and instrumental recitals are legion. Practically every church and palace offers concerts. Programming is mainly from the baroque and classical repertoire, with the emphasis on Czech music. Performances are usually of a high quality.

Basilica of St James

Bazilika sv. Jakuba
Malá Štupartská 6, Staré Město, Prague 1 (2482 8816). Metro Náměstí Republiky/5, 14, 26 tram. **Open** Box office 1hr before concert. *Concerts* Easter-late Oct. **Tickets** 200-400 Kč. **No credit cards. Map** p308 J3.

A prime example of Czech baroque architecture, complete with resounding organ acoustics and an over-the-top façade of the Fall above the entrance. In addition to large-scale sacred choral works, music for Sunday mass (usually 10am) is impressive.

Bertramka

Mozartova 169, Smíchov, Prague 5 (5731 8461/www.bertramka.cz). Metro Anděl/4, 7, 9 tram. **Open** 9.30am-5pm daily. **Tickets** 110-350 Kč. **No credit cards.**

The house where Mozart stayed when in Prague is now a museum devoted to him (*see p117*) that puts on regular concerts. Nearly all include at least one work by the Austrian who has been all but adopted into the Czech musical pantheon.

Chapel of Mirrors

Zrcadlová kaple
Klementinum, Mariánské náměstí, Staré Město, Prague 1 (2166 3111/3212). Metro Staroměstská/17, 18 tram. **Open** Box office 2hrs before the concert. *Concerts* usually start 5pm & 8pm. **Tickets** 200-500 Kč. **No credit cards. Map** p308 G4.

A pink marble chapel in the vast Clementinum complex, featuring all manner of Romantic, baroque and original chamber recitals. Seemingly an age away from the tourist hordes outside.

Church of St Nicholas

Chrám sv. Mikuláše
Malostranské náměstí, Malá Strana, Prague 1 (2419 0991). Metro Malostranská/12, 22 tram. **Open** *Concerts* Apr-Sept 6pm Tue-Sun; Oct-mid Nov 5pm Tue-Sun; Apr-mid Nov also 9pm Mon, Fri-Sun. **Tickets** 250-450 Kč. **No credit cards.**
Map p307 D3.
This is one of Prague's most celebrated churches, with a stunning baroque interior. Irregular choral concerts and organ recitals are just as grand as the setting *(see also p28 and p78).*

Church of St Nicholas

Kostel sv. Mikuláše
Staroměstské náměstí, Staré Město, Prague 1 (no phone). Metro Staroměstská/17, 18 tram. **Open** 9am-6pm daily. *Concerts* 8pm. **Tickets** 200-400 Kč. **No credit cards. Map** p308 H3.
St Nicholas's hosts regular organ, instrumental and vocal recitals, with an emphasis on baroque music. A somewhat plain setting, having been looted once or twice too often.

Church of St Simon & St Jude

Kostel sv. Šimona a Judy
Dušní & U Milosrdných, Staré Město, Prague 1 (232 1352). Metro Staroměstská/17 tram. **Open** *Box office* 1hr before concert. *Concerts* 7.30pm. **Tickets** 200-450 Kč. **No credit cards. Map** p308 H2.
Renovated with cunning trompe l'oeil work, this deconsecrated church is now a full-time venue for chamber music. The Prague Symphony Orchestra, which also promotes selected ensembles, is responsible for the programming.

Lichtenstein Palace

Lichtenštejnský palác
Malostranské náměstí 13, Malá Strana, Prague 1 (5753 4205). Metro Malostranská/12, 22 tram. **Open** 11am-7pm daily. *Concerts* 7.30pm. **Tickets** *Concerts* 30-80 Kč. *Open-air opera* 600-1,100 Kč. **Credit** MC, V. **Map** p307 E3.
The Lichtenstein Palace is the home of the Czech Academy of Music. Regular concerts are given in the Gallery and in the Martinů Hall, although the real star is the summer open-air series of popular operas that take place in the courtyard.

Lobkowicz Palace

Lobkovický palác
Jiřská 3, Hradčany, Prague 1 (5753 4578). Metro Malostranská/22 tram. **Open** 9am-4.30pm Tue-Sun. **Tickets** 200-600 Kč. **No credit cards. Map** p307 D2.
Concerts of baroque and Romantic chamber works are held in the imposing banquet hall of the Lobkowicz Palace, which has frescoes by Fabián Harovník. *See also p70.*

St Agnes's Convent

Klášter sv. Anežky české
U milosrdných 17, Staré Město, Prague 1 (2187 9270). Metro Staroměstská or Náměstí Republiky/5, 14, 26 tram. **Open** 10am-6pm Tue-Sun. **Tickets** 250-550 Kč. **No credit cards. Map** p308 J1.
The acoustics here are not without their critics, but the convent has a Gothic atmosphere and high-quality chamber music – usually from the classical, Romantic and 20th-century repertoire, with an emphasis on Smetana, Dvořák and Janáček. *See also p112.*

Opera

Estates Theatre

Stavovské divadlo
Ovocný trh 1, Staré Město, Prague 1 (info 2422 8503/box office 2421 5001). Metro Můstek/3, 9, 14, 24 tram. **Open** *Box office* mid Aug-mid July 10am-6pm Mon-Fri; 10am-12.30pm, 3-6pm Sat, Sun. **Tickets** 690-1,950 Kč. **Credit** MC, V. **Map** p308 J4.
A shrine for Mozart lovers, this is where *Don Giovanni* and *La Clemenza di Tito* were first performed. The theatre was built by Count Nostitz in 1784; its beautiful dark-blue and gold auditorium was almost over-renovated after the Velvet Revolution. The theatre began as the Prague home of Italian opera but in 1807 became the German opera, with Carl Maria von Weber as its musical director (1813-17). Today much of the programming is given over to theatre but there is still regular opera here – including, of course, *Don Giovanni. See also p91 and p234.*

National Theatre

Národní divadlo
Národní 2, Nové Město, Prague 1 (2491 3437/2493 3782/www.narodni-divadlo.cz). Metro Národní třída/6, 9, 17, 18, 22 tram. **Open** *Box office* Sept-June 10am-6pm Mon-Fri; 10am-12.30pm, 3-6pm Sat, Sun. **Tickets** 60-750 Kč. **Credit** MC, V. **Map** p310 G6.
Smetana was a guiding light behind the establishment of the National Theatre, a symbol of Czech nationalism that finally opened in 1883 with a performance of his opera *Libuše*. In keeping with tradition, the theatre concentrates on Czech opera, the core of the repertoire being works by Smetana and Dvořák (including lesser-known works such as Dvořák's *The Devil and Kate* and Smetana's *The Kiss*), together with some Janáček. Operas by non-Czech composers and some impressive ballets are also performed – generally three major new productions a year. *See also p101 and p234.*

State Opera

Státní Opera
Wilsonova 4, Nové Město, Prague 2 (9611 7111/box office 2422 7266/www.opera.cz). Metro Muzeum/11 tram. **Open** *Box office* mid Aug-mid July 10am-5.30pm Mon-Fri; 10am-noon, 1-5.30pm Sat, Sun. **Tickets** 200-900 Kč. **No credit cards. Map** p311 L6.
The State Opera (then the German Theatre) opened in 1887. Music directors and regular conductors included Seidl, Mahler, Zemlinský, Klemperer and

The **State Opera** boldly goes where other operas fear to tread.

Szell, and the theatre was regarded as one of the finest German opera houses outside Germany until World War II. After the war it changed its name to the Smetana Theatre and became the second house of the National Theatre. Today it's a separate organisation and presents consistently bold contemporary opera alongside standards from the Italian, German, French and Russian repertoires.

Festivals

The major event in the calendar is the **Prague Spring Festival** (www.festival.cz), which runs from May to June. Since the Velvet Revolution it has a much stronger international flavour and ranks with the Edinburgh Festival or the Proms in its ability to attract first-class international performers. Traditionally, the festival opens with Smetana's patriotic cycle of symphonic poems, *Má Vlast* (*My Country*), and concludes with Beethoven's Ninth. Many of the major events sell out quickly. It's best to obtain tickets from the **Prague Spring Festival Office** rather than from agencies, which add a hefty mark-up. The office opens one month before the festival and there are two price ranges – one for tickets sold in Prague and one for those booked from abroad. If possible, get a Czech friend to buy them for you or wait until you get here.

Opera Mozart is Prague's best-promoted collection of tourist-oriented classical events. It's main draw is the **Mozart Open**, which

takes over the Estates Theatre during the summer for a big-budget Mozart opera performed by foreigners (tickets cost a withering 690-1,950 Kč).

Several summer festivals are held out of town, in popular spots such as **Karlovy Vary** (*see p248*), **Mariánské Lázně** and **Český Krumlov** (*see p259*). Litomyšl and Hukvaldy, the respective birthplaces of Smetana and Janáček, celebrate their music with summer galas. For more information contact PIS, the **Prague Information Service** (*see p289*).

Prague Spring Festival
Office: Hellichova 18, Malá Strana, Prague 1 (5731 0414/ www.festival.cz). Metro Malostranská/12, 22 tram. **Open** mid Mar-May 10am-5pm Mon-Fri. **Credit** AmEx, MC, V. **Map** p307 D4.
Buy your tickets here in person and save a fortune in agents' mark-ups. The office is only open in the month before the festival.

Opera Mozart
Žatecká 1, Staré Město, Prague 1 (2232 2536/ www.mozart.cz). Metro Staroměstská/17, 18 tram. **Open** 10am-6pm daily (concert days 10am-8pm). **Credit** MC, V. **Map** p308 H3.
Tickets for the Mozart Open and Best of Mozart events, and also for the National Marionette Theatre's year-round puppet productions of Don Giovanni (see p237) and the Magic Theatre of the Baroque World. Foreigner-friendly performances make these ideal shows for kids. Performances are at the Theatre on the Balustrade (Divadlo Na zábradlí; *see p235*).

Music: Rock, Roots & Jazz

Intimate venues, world-class jazz, a regional roots revival and a proud history of underground rockin' make up the Prague scene. Strap yourself in.

Prague's a popular destination on any major band's European tour, but particularly for fringe bands you've never heard of. And the city's lack of sonically perfect major halls means you'll catch these bands up close and personal at places like the **Archa Theatre** (*see p234*), the threadbare **Lucerna Music Bar** (*see p218*) or the **Rock Café** (*see p219*). Better still, ticket prices are aimed at the Czech market, meaning catching an act like Manu Chao won't break the bank.

On the dance scene things are less ideal for live music lovers. In the city centre, it's still a chancy business dropping into music clubs, and, with the exception of the new **N11** (*see p219*), you'll be hard-pressed to find a band playing accessible, danceable stuff. DJs rule the scene these days, with live music left mainly to festivals, cover bands and jazz and blues clubs.

Fortunately, there are dozens of festivals each year, the best of them, like **Respect** (http://respect.inway.cz; *see p185*), offering up rocking Roma sounds, klezmer and world music. And a few fine venues, like the **Akropolis** (*see p217*) and the bunker-like **Klub 007** (*see p217*), still frequently book musicians, focusing on regional underground acts.

When taking in Czech rock, it's best to remember the long history of oppression endured by bands like Plastic People of the Universe, who helped spark the Velvet Revolution. Their descendants today – bands like Už jsme doma and Psí vojáci – are used to life on the margins and aren't overly concerned with filling halls or selling albums. Yet they can produce introspective, moody sounds punctuated with squawks of pain that make a night out something to savour.

In summer there's a massive rave scene in the countryside surrounding Prague, where you'll meet Glastonbury survivors by the hundreds. The most epic of these marathon love parties are promoted by Radio 1 DJ Josef Sedloň's busy Lighthouse agency (www.lighthous.cz). In winter they also book dance music fests into disused tram factories, a memorable experience.

Czech jazz has never brought in huge crowds, though it's had a stellar reputation for such a small country ever since the early days, and produced such stars as George Mraz and Jan Hammer. And the **Prague Jazz Festival** (www.agharta.cz; *see p185*) brings world-class talents such as Hiram Bullock or Maceo Parker to the **Lucerna Music Bar** (*see p218*) from spring to autumn.

To see what's coming up, check flyers at **Bohemia Bagel** (*see p123*), or pick up *The Prague Pill* or *The Prague Post* (www.praguepost.cz).

Tickets & information

Tickets should be booked in advance for big-name concerts. For the smaller, funkier ones you'll need to buy directly from the venue.

Ticketpro

Old Town Hall, Staroměstské náměstí, Staré Město, Prague 1 (2448 2018/www.ticketpro.cz). Metro Staroměstská/17, 18 tram. **Open** 8am-6pm daily. **Credit** AmEx, MC, V. **Map** p308 H3.
Advance booking for major commercial concerts and numerous smaller events. The automated toll-free number above works for all branches (when it works at all – it doesn't with old Czech analogue phones), which can be found at Prague Information Service offices and hotels citywide.
Branches: Štěpánská 61 (Lucerna Passage), Nové Město, Prague 1 (2481 8080); Rytířská 31, Staré Město, Prague 1 (2161 0162); Salvátorská 10, Staré Město, Prague 1 (2481 4020).

Venues

Enormous gigs

Prague's largest venue is **Stadium Strahov**, graced in the past by President Havel's mates, the Rolling Stones, as well as Pink Floyd and Billy Idol. Shows are far more frequent at **Výstaviště** (good enough for Bowie), though the sound quality at both is appalling.

Klub 007: worth the hike.

Congress Centre

Kongresové centrum

*5 května 65, Vyšehrad, Prague 4 (6117 1111/
www.kcp.cz). Metro Vyšehrad/18, 24 trams.*
Open *Box office* 9am-6pm Mon-Fri.

The former Palace of Culture has changed its name
in an effort to leave behind its past as a Communist
Party convention facility. It has also installed better
sound and lights, but concerts here still tend to feel
institutional – in the main hall, overstuffed seats
allow no room for dancing.

Stadium Strahov

*Diskařská 100, Břevnov, Prague 6 (3301 4111).
Tram 22 to Újezd, then cable car or 132, 143, 149,
176 bus.* **Map** p306 A5.

Prague's largest stadium can take a staggering
200,000 people. Special bus services for big gigs.

Výstaviště Sportovní hala

*U Výstaviště, Holešovice, Prague 7 (6672 7411).
Metro Nádraží Holešovice/5, 12, 17 tram.*
Map p312 D1.

Officially known as the Sport Hall, this barn has all
the acoustics you'd expect from such. The only indoor
spot in Prague that can accommodate thousands.

Small to middling gigs

Akropolis

*Kubelíkova 27, Žižkov, Prague 3 (9633 0911/
www.palacakropolis.cz). Metro Jiřího z Poděbrad/
5, 9, 11, 26, 55, 58 tram.* **Open** *Concerts* 7.30pm.
Admission 90-650 Kč. **No credit cards.**
Map p313 B2.

This club's United Colours of Akropolis and Jazz
Meets World series promote a rich array of world
beats, dub, roots and avant-garde acts, from
Algerian nomad music to French trip hop. The
downstairs *divadelní* (theatre) bar offers nightly DJs
and MCs free of charge, while the Malá Scena features bongo jams and red-lit sofas. The main basement stage, a tatty former cinema, has lights and
sound as good as any in Prague, but groups you
won't find anywhere else. At street level is a pub
with just passable curries and other quick grub. *See
also p145 and p157.*

Klub 007

*Vaníčkova 5, Koleje ČVUT dorm 7, Strahov, Prague
6 (5721 1439). Metro Dejvická, then bus 143, 149,
217.* **Open** 7.30pm-1am daily. *Concerts* 9.30pm.
Admission 40-100 Kč. **No credit cards.**

Lights, camera, Doc M

Social critic, publisher, neurologist and keyboard player in a basement rock band. It's an unlikely professional combo but Martin Stránsky, the man behind the monthly journal *New Presence*, the biggest thorn in the side of the Czech status quo, is indeed busy presenting slides of nerve degeneration when he's not jamming with guitar man Spyder downstairs at the **N11** club (*see p219*). (Although on nights when he dons his rainbow-coloured toque, assuming the identity of his alter ego Doc M, Martin Stránsky would proabably not want to be pegged for all of the above roles.)

Stránsky's grandfather launched *New Presence* in order to provide a social forum during the days of the First Republic, when Czechoslovakia finally got its first taste of real independence. Back then it was only in Czech, unlike the current bilingual version, and there were no failing health programmes to criticise either. But the outspoken publication and the family behind it still managed to be extremely unpopular with the Nazis and post-war Communist regimes, so the publishing house at Národní 11 was banned and the Stránsky family was impelled to live in exile.

Growing up in the New York area, Stránsky worked in restaurants and clubs while finishing medical school, never dreaming he'd one day launch a club back in the family home in Prague. But when the Velvet Revolution arrived in 1989, he saw the chance to return.

Along with reviving the journal his father and grandfather had established, he returned with an idea that would appeal to any rock-loving physician: Prague's first no-drugs dance club. 'You'll never hear heavy techno or rap here,' he explains. 'People don't do ecstasy to sexy soul.' Smoking grass and popping pills is nearly as common in most Prague clubs as dancing. Though it's illegal, with severe penalties, there's close to zero police presence in the clubs.

Stránsky's not worried about alienating a large share of the clubbing crowd, though, banking instead on the appeal of a safe, clean, friendly club with well-mixed drinks and a respectable restaurant – with no-smoking rooms, of course.

As for the music line-up, it's live dance rock, blues, and, indeed, sexy soul. The dance space is small, but standard for Prague, surrounded by a catwalk where spectators can gather to check each other out. Blue and pink neon lights guide your way into N11 and menu pages from the elegant restaurant that stood here during the 1920s are framed upon the walls.

So far, it's been a quiet hit, filled nightly with a clean-living, fun-loving crowd and barely an advert in the press. But should any incompetent Parliamentarians care to boogie here, they should be aware of the entrance policy: Journalists and health professionals get 10 per cent discount on admission. Politicians pay a surcharge of 50 per cent.

If you can find this place (in the concrete basement of a dorm), you'll never believe this place could be a must on any interational ska tour of Central Europe. But that it is, as you'll discover when the bands start up. As authentic a youth vibe as you'll find in Prague, just mind the bass player doesn't knock your beer over during riffs as you're practically in each others' lap.

Lucerna Music Bar

Vodičkova 36, Nové Město, Prague 1 (2421 7108/ www.musicbar.cz). Metro Můstek/3, 9, 14, 24, 52, 53, 55, 56 tram. **Open** *Concerts* 9pm. **Admission** concerts 80-300 Kč. **No credit cards. Map** p309 K5.
In the faded 1920s Lucerna Passage off Wenceslas Square, this bar and concert space attracts big-time jazz masters such as Wynton Marsalis but also books such local 'Louie Louie' bands as Brutus, who can't hit a straight note. Wood-panelled balconies and white tablecloths remain from its pre-war days of Josephine Baker shows.

Lucerna Great Hall

Vodičkova 36, Nové Město, Prague 1 (2422 5440/ www.lucpra.com). Metro Můstek/3, 9, 14, 24, 52, 53, 55, 56 tram. **Open** *Concerts* start 7-8pm. **Admission** 200-900 Kč. **Credit** AmEx, MC, V. **Map** p309 K5.
Run independently from the Lucerna Music Bar (*see above*), this vast underground performance hall hosts big-time acts from Lou Reed to The Cardigans. Its art nouveau ballrooms, balconies, grand marble stairs and wooden floors add an unusual, palatial feel to rock shows. Acoustics are lousy but, though it feels big and echoey, you're always reasonably close to the band. There are no regular box office hours to speak of.

Malostranská beseda

Malostranské náměstí 21, Malá Strana, Prague 1 (5753 2092). Metro Malostranská0/12, 22, 57 tram. **Open** 5pm-1am daily. *Concerts* 9.30pm. **Admission** 80 Kč. **No credit cards. Map** p307 E3.

covers all bases. The garden pub at Meloun offers traditional Czech schnitzels and the like.

N11

Národní třída 11, Nové Město, Prague 1 (2207 5705/www.n11.cz). Metro Národní třída/6, 9, 18, 22, 51, 54, 57, 58 tram. **Open** 4pm-2am daily. **Admission** 80-150 Kč. **No credit cards.** **Map** p308 H5.

The city's best popular music venue is the immaculately restored headquarters of the *New Presence*, a monthly opinion journal with roots dating back to the inter-war First Republic. Rock guitar king Spyder trades off with blues acts like Stan the Man to keep the crowd on its feet. The attached restaurant and bar are friendly and capable (*see p218* **Lights, Camera, Dr M**).

Rock Café

Národní třída 20, Nové Město, Prague 1 (2491 4416/www.rockcafe.cz). Metro Národní třída/ 6, 9, 18, 22, 51, 54, 57, 58 tram. **Open** 10pm-2.30am Mon-Fri; 7pm-2.30am Sat, Sun. **Admission** 80-300 Kč. **No credit cards.** **Map** p308 H5.

Once a post-revolution rock pioneer, these days more of a backpacker hangout. Features daily rock documentaries and Czech 'revival' bands. Not much in the way of atmosphere.

Roxy

Dlouhá 33, Staré Město, Prague 1 (2482 6296). Metro Náměstí Republiky or Staroměstská/5, 14, 17, 18, 26, 51, 53, 54 tram. **Open** from 9pm daily. **Admission** *DJs* 80-250 Kč. *Live acts* 150-350 Kč. **No credit cards.** **Map** p308 J3.

Although dominated by electronic dance tracks, the Roxy does still host occasional live acts, generally to accompany the digital stuff but occasionally standing alone. When it does, it's someone impressive, such as Mad Professor or a crazed local act like Ohm Square. The space itself is a wonder of a crumbling former movie house that attracts (and sponsors) artists of all genres so long as they're weird (*see p231* **The Roxy holds out**).

Vagon

Národní třída 25, Nové Město, Prague 1 (2108 5599/www.vagon.cz). Metro Národní třída/6, 9, 17, 18, 22, 23 tram. **Open** 6pm-2am Mon-Sat; 6pm-1am Sun. *Concerts* 9pm. **Admission** 60 Kč. **No credit cards.** **Map** p308 H5.

A smoky little cellar with live, young, unrecorded rock, jam nights and reggae, both live and on the sound system. Just a student bar but one with a love for chilled-out, dreadlocked hanging out. Don't miss the entrance, hidden as it is in a shopping passage.

Surprisingly classy rock and roots bands grace this faded glory, plus the occasional retro jazz act. Bottled beer is the only drawback to an otherwise welcoming, well-worn bar and adjacent dance room. Battered wood surfaces and windows overlooking Malá Strana's main square add appeal. Malostranská beseda also has a well-stocked jazz and alternative CD shop.

Meloun

Michálská 12, Staré Město, Prague 1 (2423 0126/ www.meloun.cz). Metro Můstek/3, 9, 14, 24, 51, 52, 53, 54, 55, 56, 57, 58 tram. **Open** 11am-3am daily. *Concerts* 9pm. **Admission** 80-100 Kč. **No credit cards.** **Map** p308 H4.

Highly uneven programming at this Staré Město watering hole means it could be a good blues night or it could be album tracks better left in the pre-1989 community hall of a small Bohemian village. With occasional film screenings as well, this cellar pub

Jazz & blues

Prague's jazz history stretches back to the 1930s, when Jaroslav Ježek led an adored big band while colleague RA Dvorský established a standard of excellence that survived Nazi and communist oppression. Karel Velebný, of the renowned Studio 5 group, continued that tradition post-war, while Czech-Canadian novelist Josef Škvorecký chronicled the eternal struggle of Czech sax men in book after book.

These days, the jazz scene occupies a lower echelon of the club world, but a corps of talented players works the city circuit – to such an extent that you'll find the same dozen top players in any venue you choose. A handful have managed to release original works on CD through the **AghaRTA** (*see p220*) label and club. 'Creative isolation' is a favoured phrase among those who perpetually jam at **U staré paní** (*see p221*), but they seem unable to get far beyond the borders.

Blues is a relative newcomer to Prague but has quickly acquired a dedicated contemporary following **U staré paní**. Concerts by the likes of BB King invariably fill the city's biggest halls. Among local 12-bar practitioners watch out for guitarman Spyder and Luboš Andršt, both of whom play frequent gigs around town.

AghaRTA
Krakovská 5, Nové Město, Prague 1 (2221 1275/ www.agharta.cz). Metro Muzeum or IP Pavlova/ 4, 6, 16, 22, 34 tram. **Open** *Club* 7pm-midnight daily. *Concerts* start 9pm. *Jazz shop* 5pm-midnight Mon-Fri; 7pm-midnight Sat, Sun. **Admission** 100 Kč. **No credit cards. Map** p311 K6.
Named after Miles Davis's most controversial LP, this club off Wenceslas Square is one of Prague's best spots for modern jazz and blues. A fairly even mix of Czechs and foreigners mingle in the relatively small but comfortable space – perfect for sitting back and enjoying solo performances from artists such as guitarman Roman Pokorny. As at many Prague jazz clubs, there's a CD shop selling local recordings for 150-400 Kč. Look for releases on the club's own ARTA label.

Caroica
Václavské náměstí 4, Nové Město, Prague 1 (9632 5314). Metro Můstek/3, 9, 14, 24 tram. **Open** noon-2am daily. **Admission** 30-100 Kč. **No credit cards. Map** p308 J5.
Deep under Wenceslas Square and hidden away in what looks like an imperial bedroom, Caroica was formerly one of the city's best jazz holes. The baroque red and gold setting has remained but new management has joined the salsa craze and considerably downgraded the once excellent cuisine. Still, an experience to say the least.

Jazz Club Železná
Železná 16, Staré Město, Prague 1 (2423 9697/ www.jazzclub.cz). Metro Můstek/3, 9, 14, 24 tram. **Open** 3pm-12.30am daily. **Admission** 100-150 Kč. **Credit** MC, V. **Map** p308 J3.
The music at Jazz Club Železná is finally catching up with its prime location off Old Town Square. This is a fun, stone-walled cellar, with low prices and an excellent CD shop. Theme nights such as 'Ethno' spice it up and fill the space with conga beats and reggae, while Latino nights spice up the traditional midweek jazz programme. This is one of the best places to catch younger players on the rise.

Czech rock 101

The Czech indie rock scene, though not the easiest to penetrate, is worth the effort. For a good, up-to-date sampling of what's out there, the formerly pirate **Radio 1** is a good source (listen in online at www.radio1.cz). DJs Koogie and Kaja, who are themselves icons on the music scene in Prague, have excellent shows introducing fresh local talent, though you'll hear from new bands just about any time on Radio 1.

The live music scene tends to orbit around the mothership of the **Akropolis** club (*see p217*) in the wild and woolly Žižkov district, where bands are deliberately nurtured. Tuesday evening shows, with an entrance fee of a nominal 40 Kč are an invitation to perform for new groups and are always spontaneous. Free Mondays nights at the **Roxy** (*see p219*) are also showcases for new talent, though they're generally DJs.

Surprisingly enough, the **Bontonland Megastore** (*see p179*) on Wenceslas Square is a good source of new musical talent – CDs are so cheap to record and publicise in the Czech Republic that even the hungriest indie band has one and they're generally stocked here.

Good local labels to watch out for are **Rachot** (www.rachot.cz) for world music, **East Authentic** for drum 'n' bass, **Wax** (www.wax.cz) for more varied dance material, and **Indies** for everything else. Recent discoveries typify the unique mix of elements that make up the Prague sound: elements of Slavic folk, Renaissance madrigals and a major infusion of early Velvet Underground, who were worshipped during the crackdowns of '68. A few are: **Floex** (www.floex.cz), **Jelizaveta bam** (www.jelizavetabam.cz), **The B Movie Heroes** (www.bmovieheroes.com), **Hermakouti** and **Squall**.

Henry Rollins rocks the **Akropolis**.
See p217.

Reduta
*Národní třída 20, Nové Město, Prague 1 (2493
3487/www.redutajazzclub.cz). Metro Národní třída/
6, 9, 18, 22, 51, 54, 57, 58 tram.* **Open** *Club*
9pm-midnight daily. *Concerts* start 10.30pm.
Box office 3-7.30pm Mon-Fri. **Admission** 200 Kč.
No credit cards. Map p308 H5.
That Bill Clinton once played sax here to entertain
Václav Havel hardly makes up for the steep cover,
frankly quite bland repertoire and dreary interior.
Even so, some of the best musicians in town often sit
in with the evening's band, and the club, unusually,
has a good sound system.

Tendr
*Pařížská 6, Staré Město, Prague 1 (2481 3605).
Metro Staroměstská/17, 18 tram.* **Open** 6pm-5am
daily. *Concerts* 9pm. **Admission** 100-200 Kč.
No credit cards. Map p308 H3.
Blissfully cheesy basement salsa bar where hot local
bands such as Grupo Caribe transport crowds back
to the Havana of the 1950s. Packs of Czechs turn out

to practise their steps and classes are offered weekly with Juan or Ruben. Huge, loud fun, especially
with a rum *Mojito* in hand.

U Malého Glena
*Karmelitská 23, Malá Strana, Prague 1 (5753 1717/
www.malyglen.cz). Metro Malostranská/12, 22, 57
tram.* **Open** 10am-2am daily. **Admission** 100-150
Kč. **No credit cards. Map** p307 D4.
Intimate jazz trios somehow sound wonderful in
the closet-sized basement beneath the rowdy main
floor café (*see p148*), despite a terrible sound system, about six knee-bashing tables, rock-hard seats
and noise from above. Veteran Czech players such
as guitarist Petr Zelenka, along with rising stars
and visiting talents, meld impressive grooves at U
Malého Glena with a minimal levels of pretension.
Sunday jams, led by Pavel Obermajer and Taras
the bass legend, are a blast.

U staré paní
*Michalská 9, Staré Město, Prague 1 (2422 8090/
www.ustarepani.cz). Metro Můstek/3, 9, 14, 24 tram.*
Open 7pm-1am Wed-Sat. *Concerts* 9pm-midnight.
Admission 160 Kč. **Credit** AmEx, MC, V.
Map p307 H4.
Doubling as a decent restaurant, this Old Town
hotel is a late-night favourite with top local players.
After performing for the tourists, they come here
for informal all-night jams on Saturdays. Though
the high cover charge alienates most locals, this
remains a top spot for serious jazz.

Ungelt Jazz & Blues Club
*Týn 2 (enter from Týnská ulička), Staré Město,
Prague 1 (2489 5748). Metro Můstek/3, 9, 14, 24
tram.* **Open** noon-midnight daily. **Admission**
100-150 Kč; 50-100 Kč concessions.
No credit cards. Map p308 J3.
Prague's newest jazz club is a bit too close to Old
Town Square to get very near the musical edge, but
Ungelt Jazz & Blues Club is nonetheless an appeal-
ingly relaxed cellar in which to catch a session
and a Pilsener or two.

Folk/country & western

Folk and Country & Western connect with
the Czech rural heritage. The 'trampers' – avid
hikers and campers – romanticise the American
cowboy lifestyle. Those consigned to block
housing and jobs five days a week come alive
on Friday night to act out their Marlboro Man
fantasies, singing American country without
speaking a word of English.

První Prag Country Saloon Amerika
*Korunní 101, Vinohrady, Prague 2 (2425 6131).
Metro Náměstí Míru/16 tram.* **Open** 11am-11pm
Mon; 11am-midnight Tue-Fri; 5pm-midnight Sat;
6pm-midnight Sun. **Admission** 20 Kč. **No credit
cards. Map** p313 B3.
The place for an all-Czech cowboy fiddle jam.

Nightlife

Eats to the beats, pop disco along the river, electronica in derelict buildings, plus dice and vice. Could be a long night.

Prague's been one of the key party cities in Europe ever since the days of dotty Emperor Rudolph II, so it's a good bet that wherever you land, folks will not be holding back. There are a number of venues where you'll come up against some cut-throat competition for the hippest wardrobe prize and places where no one would really notice if you arrived in your underwear. In between lies a new generation of classy little dance spaces attached to successful restaurants and bars in their own right. Two typical examples are **Kolkovna** and **Mecca** (for both, *see p226*), both usually packed.

Other places doubling as eateries are **Duplex** (*see p225*), **Zvonařka** (*see p229*), **Ultramarin** (*see p228*), **Solidní nejistota** (*see p228*) and **Radost FX** (*see p227*) but generally, you'll find beer is the only source of protein to be had while out late (with the exception, of course, of the late-night eats options listed herein; *see p229*).

DJ culture reigns supreme in Prague, but it's dominated by techno, as seen at Roxy and Mecca, and the only alternatives are usually places that favour top 40 pop, such as **Klub Lávka** (*see p226*) or **Double Trouble** (*see p224*). Clubs for danceable funk, soul or R&B are virtually non-existent. Good thing **Radost FX** comes through with at least one night a week that's not just for early twentysomethings.

Closures and openings are constant, as in the clubbing world anywhere, only even more so (*see p230* **The Roxy holds out**) in Prague as clubs tend to share buildings with residential spaces and Czechs are early risers. The other unique aspect of clubbing in Prague is a feeling of anarchy that could only be achieved in a place with virtually no safety regulations or PC culture. Bar-top stripping, crumbling walls and rampant use of stimulants can all be found within blocks of each other in Old Town on any Friday night.

Just remember that if you're caught with drugs, you're on your own. Police arrest anyone with what they deem 'more than a little' of a controlled substance and the jails are full of people still not convicted of a thing. Gambling, however, is completely legal and high rollers

Youth, bpms and crumbling walls at the **Roxy**. *See p228.*

Arts & Entertainment

Nové Město clubbing: oh so glam.

will find the city has no shortage of casinos, though none as classy as the **Palais Savarin** or **Millennium** (for both, *see p229*). Would-be Charles Bukowskis, on the other hand, will find a plenitude of material in Prague's ubiquitous *herna* bars and smoky dives lined with electronic one-armed bandits.

Note that any tram with a number in the 50s is a night tram.

Clubs

Amiveo

Karlovo náměstí 24, Nové Město, Prague 2, (2223 2382). Metro Karlovo náměstí/3, 6, 7, 14, 18, 22, 23, 51, 52, 53, 54, 55, 56, 57 tram. **Open** noon-1am Mon-Thur; noon-3am Fri; 6pm-3am Sat. **Main courses** 250 Kč. **Credit** MC, V. **Map** p310 J7.
This Mediterranean eaterie and dance club, a combination that's rare in Prague, is primarily about glam DJs working the sound system. The menu's offerings of *gigantes*, *ouzo mezedes* and *pastitsio* make for interesting club food, but be warned that the place can be dead midweek.

Batalion Rock Club

28 října 3, Staré Město, Prague 1 (2010 8148/ www.batalion.cz). Metro Můstek/3, 6, 9, 14, 18, 22, 51, 52, 54, 55, 56, 57, 58 tram. **Open** 24 hrs daily. **No credit cards. Map** p308 J5.
Grubby, throbbing with generic hip-hop tracks, packed with teenage skate punks and offering an intriguing decor of tree limbs and beat-up vinyl sofas, this is just the place to relive your yoof.

CZ Beat

Balbínova 26, Vinohrady, Prague 2 (2225 2504/ www.beat.cz). Metro Muzeum/11, 51, 57 tram. **Open** 7pm-2am Mon-Sat; 7pm-midnight Sun. **Shows** 9pm Mon-Sat. **Admission** free-120 Kč. **No credit cards. Map** p311 M7
The city's newest club hosts digital mixology with renowned local DJs. Its smallish, cyber-flavoured interior also attracts the city's most fashionable club kids, though not those who like to splash out without good reason. Thus CZ Beat is generally approachable, cheap and high quality.

Double Trouble

Melatrichova 17, Staré Město, Prague 1 (2163 2414/ www.doubletrouble.cz). Metro Můstek/3, 9, 14, 24, 51, 52, 54, 55, 56, 57, 58 tram. **Open** 5pm-3am daily. **No credit cards. Map** p308 H4.
Packed with backpackers, happily overpaying for drinks, admission and crap pop tracks. The stony cellar walls are the most appealing thing about this touristy, ear-bending disco.

Delta

Vlastina 887, Liboc, Prague 6 (3331 2443/www. noise.cz/delta). Tram 20, 26, 51/night bus 501. **Open** 7pm-2am Mon, Tue, Thur-Sun. **Admission** 60-120 Kč. **No credit cards.**
This fringe rock refuge in the midst of suburban apartments on the city's north-western border attracts a local crowd that's young, bored and aching to break out. A steady supply of uncommercial, once banned live bands such as Filip Topol, the MCH band and Echt! perform but shows are irregular. Mid-week movie nights add to the fun.

Clubs

For breakbeats
Bidlo for NY-influenced beats; **Bolond** for the Prague Sound.

For pure techno
Chris Sadler, an inveterate veteran at Mecca (*see p226*); **Agent**, hard house stylist; **Kaiser Soze**, new-generation technoista; **Krejdl**, popular club fox; **La Di Da**, glammy techno diva; **Nika 77**, a Radost FX (*see p227*) speciality; **Tráva**, a versatile character.

For house
James delivers Brit-style atmospheric; **Airto** for home-grown; **Petter Moskito**, rising Wax agency star; **Lumiere**, Radost FX hero; **Formi**, student club circuit star.

For drum 'n' bass
IM Cyber, club queen; **Jan 2** and **Jan 5**, stars in the hot band Ohm Square; **Koogi** does the Prague 3 'hood.

For trip hop
Babe LN, seasoned diva; **Blue** a rising star.

For trance
Elektromajk, rarely in Prague; **Skipworker**, young and fresh.

For jungle
Katcha, respected pro scratcher.

Duplex
Václavské náměstí 21, Nové Město, Prague 1 (2449 0440/www.duplexduplex.cz). Metro Můstek/ 3, 9, 14, 24, 51, 52, 54, 55, 56, 57, 58 tram. **Open** *Restaurant* noon-midnight daily. *Café* 10am-midnight daily. *Club* 10.30pm-4am daily. **Credit** AmEx, DC, MC, V. **Map** p308 J5.
If you have to experience a Wenceslas Square disco, this one's as good a candidate as any. Penthouse views, overpriced drinks and hustlers go with the house music sounds. In April the Italian students who walk all over Old Town in formation land here. Still, the programming has improved lately and the cuisine, while inconsistent, has won raves. Plus, there is a remarkable chill-out space on the terrace, where meals are also served.

Futurum
Zborovská 7, Smíchov, Prague 5 (5732 8571/ www.musicbar.cz). Metro Anděl/6, 9, 12, 58 tram. **Open** 8pm-3am daily. **Shows** 9pm Mon-Sat. **Admission** 80-300 Kč. **No credit cards.**

The state of house and techno in Bohemia today. The basement of an old communist 'community house' has been gloriously packed with banks of monitors, a tilework bar that looks like part of a swimming pool, and little cocktail tables lit from within. The city's biggest and brightest digital music shows come here for the sound and light systems. And the connoisseurs follow.

Guru
Rokycanova 29, Žižkov, Prague 3 (no phone/ www.techno.cz). Metro Jiřího z Poděbrad/11, 55, 58 tram. **Open** 6pm-5am daily. **Admission** 60-80 Kč. **No credit cards.**
A very Žižkov sort of club, meaning it can be brilliant or dead, depending entirely on who's booked. The space itself is a strange, worn-out, subterranean collection of split-level dance space, balconies and bar-tending zombies. They ask for a deposit on glass beer mugs, which gives you an idea of how rowdy the crowds get.

Jo's Bar & Garáž
Malostranské náměstí 7, Malá Strana, Prague 1 (0602 971478 mobile/www.josbarprague.com). Metro Malostranská/12, 22, 23, 57 tram. **Open** 11am-2am daily. **Credit** MC, V. **Map** p305 E3.
The Gothic cellar adjunct to the backpacker's first-stop, Jo's Bar (*see p147*). This rock and funk cave plays predictable DJ rock tracks, which are eagerly lapped up by budget party-goers from all over Europe and the States. That said, it's cheap, infectious and packed with booty-shaking and shouted monosyllabic conversation. When that fails, suggestive gestures are generally understood, particularly by the frequent bar-top dancers.

Industry 55
Vinohradská 40, Vinohrady, Prague 2 (0608 754 051/www.industry55.cz). Metro Jiřího z Poděbrad/11, 53 tram. **Open** 10pm-6am Mon-Thur, Sun; 10pm-noon Fri, Sat. **Admission** 50 Kč Mon-Thur, Sun; 150 Kč Fri, Sat. **No credit cards. Map** p313 A3.
The newest underground house club in town, this labyrinth of big sounds and little rooms attracts a hip, youthful crowd. Very Czech, plugged-in, and decked out patrons hit this hideout under the old Radio Palace movie hall. There are no flaming cocktails, no Spanish bar food, no smoke-free chill-out chambers but up-and-coming DJs get booked here.

Karlovy Lázně
Novotného lávka 1, Staré Město, Prague 1 (2222 0502/www.karlovylazne.cz). Metro Staroměstská/ 17, 18, 53 tram. **Open** *Club* 9pm-5am daily. *MCM Café* 10am-5am daily. **Admission** 40-100 Kč. **No credit cards. Map** p308 G4.
Prague's megaclub is in a former bathhouse next door to the Charles Bridge. The four levels of Karlovy Lázně cover every base. Paradogs does synth techno on the fourth floor, Kaleidoskop does retro hits on the third, Discotheque does radio pop and the MCM café, the only part of the club open by day books hip jazz and funk combos. Huge with teens.

Radost FX: a new angle on go-go. *See p227.*

Kolkovna

V kolkovně 8, Staré Město, Prague 1 (2481 9701).
Metro Staroměstská/17, 18, 53 tram. **Open** *Bar*
1pm-2am daily. *Restaurant* 11am-midnight daily.
Credit AmEx, MC, V. **Map** p308 J2.

Czech dining as it hasn't been practised since before
the war – with true style and class. Kolkovna is leading a revival of classic Bohemian eating, drinking
and socialising with interiors that could be in an art
nouveau coffee-table book. Dumplings stuffed with
smoked pork and sauerkraut, hearty Pilsner beer
and friendly, foxy servers show off what a grand
time going out in Prague once was, and is now
becoming again. The city's famously rude waiters
look to be finally losing ground to more modern
ideas. Booking is a must at this hotspot.

La Fabrique

Uhelný trh 2, Staré Město, Prague 1 (2423 3131).
Metro Můstek/3, 9, 14, 24, 52, 53, 55, 56, 57, 58
tram. **Admission** 80 Kč. **No credit cards.**
Map p308 H5.

Old Town's chief purveyor of pop, with nightmarish DJs who love to announce things over the songs.
At least in this case, nothing's lost by that obnox-
ious habit. Done up throughout in factory decor,
with massive gears and rusting water mains all
about, it's a subterranean maze of rooms with a narrow entrance just off the Havelská fruit market.
Revellers pack into a sweaty throng inside, hoping
to get lucky. Style-conscious Czechs and foreigners
shake it to calypso, reggae and roots. Mixed drinks,
though a house speciality, are a bit iffy – sticking to
the Czech beer on tap might be wiser.

Klub Lávka

Novotného lávka 1, Staré Město, Prague 1 (2222
2156/2108 2278/www.lavka.cz). **Metro**
Staroměstská/17, 18, 53 tram. **Open** *Bar* 24hrs
daily. *Disco* 9pm-5am Mon-Thur, Sun; 9pm-6am Fri,
Sat. **Admission** 50 Kč. **Credit** AmEx, MC, V.
Map p308 G4.

An old standby for brainless fun within spitting distance of Charles Bridge. No challenging digital
music here, just disco, go-go dancers, black light and
a lovely riverside terrace.

Mánes

Masarykovo nábřeží 250, Nové Město, Prague 1
(2493 1112). Metro Karlovo náměstí/17, 18, 53, 57,
58 tram. **Open** 11am-11pm daily. **Shows** 9pm-4am
Fri. **Admission** 50 Kč. **No credit cards.**
Map p310 G7.

This classy 1930s functionalist gallery space is more
than living art history. It's also an increasingly popular riverside dance venue, with – remarkably for
Prague – an international flavour. The current rage,
'Tropicana' nights on Friday and Saturday, brings
out some of the city's hottest mambo kings. Stick to
the edge of the dancefloor unless you know your
stuff. The attached terrace café is good for cooling
off, though it closes around 11pm.

Mecca

U průhonu 3, Holešovice, Prague 7 (8387 0522/8387
1520/www.mecca.cz). Metro Vltavská/1, 3, 12, 25,
54 tram. **Open** *Club* 9pm-4am Thur-Sat. *Restaurant*
11am-10pm Mon-Thur, Sun; 11am-midnight Fri;
6am-midnight Sat. **Admission** 100-300 Kč.
No credit cards. Map p312 E2.

A great example of what's possible on the former Eastern bloc party scene: a disused factory made over into a welcoming, big-scale dance palace with respectable restaurant service until the party starts, then shakin' till dawn with theme parties and a line-up of the city's top DJs. The C Lounge downstairs offers chill-out space and the most mellow of the three glossy bars contained within. A bit inconvenient but certainly worth the trek to Holešovice, especially for shows with DJs Loutka or Braun.

Music Club Demínka

Škrétova & Anglická streets, Nové Město, Prague 2 (0603 185 699 mobile). Metro IP Pavlova/4, 6, 11, 16, 22, 23, 34, 51, 56, 57 tram. **Open** 8pm-4am daily. **No credit cards. Map** p311 L7.

This historic First Republic restaurant for the elite has reopened after years of closed doors. Its new face is that of a slick music club, with nightly house DJs to go alongside the traditional menu of classic Czech grub. Partying and *Becherovka* shots (a minty herbal liqueur from West Bohemia) continue into the wee hours. Demínka's location just a stone's throw from Radost FX (*see below*), Prague's best-known club, provides some much-needed competition to keep the jaded Prague clubbing world on its toes.

Music Park

Francouzská 4, Vinohrady, Prague 2 (2251 5825). Metro Náměstí Míru/4, 22, 34, 51, 56, 57 tram. **Open** 9pm-5am Tue-Thur; 9pm-6am Fri, Sat. **Admission** 50 Kč. **No credit cards. Map** p313 A3.

The undisputed centre of Euro-trash disco culture in Prague. Music Park is a great place to show off your new leather jacket that says something stupid

in big letters on the back, have cheery conversations with the po-faced bouncers and pick up a German girl in a denim mini-skirt.

Punto Azul

Kroftova 1, Smíchov, Prague 5 (no phone). Tram 6, 9, 12, 57. **Open** 8pm-2am daily. **Admission** 40 Kč. **No credit cards.**

There's nothing Spanish about this place apart from the name. This little student drinking dive is on every wirehead's map despite the techno dance space that's not much bigger than a circuit board. But a consistent groove is achieved with a line-up of the city's more avant-garde house DJs.

Radost FX

Bělehradská 120, Nové Město, Prague 2 (2425 4776/ www.radostfx.cz). Metro IP Pavlova/4, 6, 11, 16, 22, 34, 51, 56, 57 tram. **Open** 11am-4am Mon-Sat; 10.30am-4am Sun. *Club* 10pm-6am Mon-Sat. **No credit cards. Map** p311 L8.

A survivor from Prague's pioneer club days, Radost still offers the best all-night mix in the city: a creative veggie café, a spaced-out backroom lounge and art gallery, a small but slick downstairs club featuring absurdly glam theme parties, endless fashion shows, local stars of house and techno, and one of the best Sunday brunches in town (*see p140*).

Rock Café

Národní třída 20, Nové Město, Prague 1 (2491 4416/www.rockcafe.cz). Metro Národní třída/ 6, 9, 18, 22, 51, 54, 57, 58 tram. **Open** 10pm-2.30am Mon-Fri; 7pm-2.30am Sat, Sun. **Admission** 80-300 Kč. **No credit cards. Map** p306 H5.

Serious debates transpire at **Zoo Bar.** *See p229*

This was once a fairly respected rock 'n' roll joint. These days it's been bequeathed to tourists and out-of-touch Czechs, but the interior is still worth a look. It tends to attract the countless Czech 'revival' bands who cover everyone from Abba to the Velvet Underground. For some reason, there are endless screenings of rock documentaries by day.

Roxy

Dlouhá 33, Staré Město, Prague 1 (2482 6296). Metro Náměstí Republiky or Staroměstská/5, 14, 17, 18, 26, 51, 54 tram. **Open** 9pm-1am daily. *Party nights* 9pm-5am. **Admission** *DJs* 80-250 Kč. *Live acts* 150-350 Kč. **No credit cards. Map** p306 J3.

The crumbled Roxy is, along with Futurum (*see p225*), one of Prague's two crucial destinations for house, dub and jungle. An increasingly rare stream of live acts from Mad Professor to local rockers also make appearances, while the cyber Galerie NoD (*see p203*) fills the venue with multiple floors of edgy, non-commercial culture and fringe art. Poupelka (girls free) and Climax parties with local DJs such as Loutka or Chris Sadler pack the place with kids.

Sedm vlků

Vlkova 7, Žižkov, Prague 3 (2271 1725/ ww.sedmvlku.cz). Metro Jiřího z Poděbrad/ 11, 51 tram. **Open** *Upstairs* 6pm-1am daily. *Downstairs* 7.30pm-3am daily. **Admission** free. **No credit cards. Map** p313 B2.

The Seven Wolves is the hippest bar-cum-club space to open in the party mecca that is Prague's Žižkov district. Having fitted out an old workers' pub with modern decor and a crisp sound system, Sedm vlků has set about slowly stealing thunder from the more established clubs around, such as the neighbouring Akropolis and the respected bar Hapu (for both *see p157*). Meanwhile, fringe DJs and vocalists team up here for fresh sounds going out to a young, plugged-in crowd of revellers.

Solidní nejistota

Pštrossova 21, Nové Město, Prague 1 (2493 3086). Metro Národní třída/6, 9, 17, 18, 22, 23, 51, 52, 53, 54, 55, 56, 57, 58 tram. **Open** noon-6am Mon-Fri; 6pm-6am Sat, Sun. **No credit cards. Map** p308 G7.

A shameless meat market spot in Prague, Solid Uncertainty at least plays danceable tracks and serves up grill food late into the night. Beefy doormen will tell you there's no space, at least at first, but while standing on the sidewalk you're encouraged to gawk through the windows at hunks and babes in skin-tight party clothes who, in turn, are gawking at you.

U Buldoka

Preslova 1, Smíchov, Prague 5 (4202 5732/9154/ www.ubuldoka.cz). Metro Anděl/6, 9, 57 tram. **Open** 11am-midnight daily. **Main courses** 100 Kč. **No credit cards.**

The Bulldog is one of those Prague rarities: a classic cheap Czech pub with well-tapped Staropramen beer and excellent trad grub, but also an international sensibility and gracious service. All-day lunch

specials such as *stropačka*, a kind of Slavic gnocchi with bacon, and *guláš* soup are on the menu, while light and dark beer, plus an impressive collection of Czech herbal liqueurs, are at the bar. Dark-wood panelling and furnishings are complemented by framed antique advertisements for alcohol, and big-screen football coverage is there for those who want it, but it never drowns out conversation.

Újezd

Újezd 18, Malá Strana, Prague 1 (no phone). Metro Malostranská/9, 12, 22, 57 tram. **Open** 6pm-4am daily. **Admission** free. **No credit cards. Map** p307 E5.

In its earlier days as Borát, this three-storey madhouse was an important alternative music club. Today it's home to some loud, badly amplified Czech rock tracks, battered wooden chairs in the café upstairs and shouted conversation in the bar below. And not an iota less popular for it. The street-level bar is rocking and packed with dreadlocked teens.

Ultramarin

Ostrovní 32, Nové Město, Prague 2 (2493 2249/www.ultramarin.cz). Metro Národní třída/ 9, 17, 18, 22, 23, 51, 52, 53, 54, 55, 56, 57, 58 tram. **Open** 11am-4am daily. **Credit** AmEx, MC, V. **Map** p308 H6.

This self-proclaimed lifestyle bar is a hit, with atmospheric retro jazz on the sound system, Sante Fe chicken salads on the menu and blond wood and mottled green walls throughout. At street level Prague's bright young things sip terrible local wine and excellent imported coffee for hours at a time. Downstairs is the real appeal, though, with credible house music blasting away in a small Gothic cellar space until 4am nightly. And, get this: the promise of friendly waiting staff is plastered on a placard out front. Is this Prague?

U zlatého stromu

Karlova 6, Staré Město, Prague 1 (2222 0441/ www.zlatystrom.cz). Metro Staroměstská/17, 18, 53 tram. **Open** *Club* 8pm-6am daily. *Restaurant* 24hrs daily. *Shows* 9pm-5am daily. **Admission** 80 Kč. **Credit** AmEx, DC, MC, V. **Map** p308 G4.

One of the strangest combinations in the Old Town area: a non-stop disco, striptease, bar, restaurant and hotel a few metres from Charles Bridge. Descend into the stone cellar labyrinth of bad pop and strippers, and you could end up in a peaceful outdoor garden or a nook for conversing. The upstairs café has a full menu plus coffee and drinks. It's 100% tourist and the staff are often unwelcoming.

Wakata

Malířská 14, Holešovice, Prague 7 (3337 0518/ www.wakata.cz). Metro Vltavská/1, 8, 25, 26, 51, 56 tram. **Open** 5pm-3am Mon-Thur, Sun; 5pm-5am Fri, Sat. **Admission** free. **No credit cards. Map** p311 L8.

Essentially a bar, but one with such a strong tradition of all-night parties that it qualifies as a club. The international crew that runs Wakata make it a sort of work in progress in which to test out its drinks and welding experiments: while the breakbeat DJ is warming up, you could try an *ořechovka* (walnut liqueur) while perched on a motorcycle-seat barstool.

XT3
Pod plynojemem 5, Libeň, Prague 8 (8482 5826/ www.xt3.cz). Metro Palmovka/3, 6, 25, 52, 55. **Open** 5pm-3am daily. **Admission** 70 Kč. **No credit cards.**
Hard and heavy house in a venue foreigners won't stumble upon. Don't forget your skateboard and bring Czech teen friends if you want to blend in with the oh-so-serious crowd of vinyl fanatics.

Zoo Bar
Jilská 18, Staré Město Prague 1 (0602 190 089). Metro Staroměstská/17, 18, 51, 52, 53, 54, 55, 56, 58 tram. **Open** 5pm-2am Mon-Sun; 5pm-5am Sat. **No credit cards. Map** p308 H4.
More for drinking than dancing, this Old Town cellar is nevertheless a part of any clubbing agenda in the district. It's the place to make a plan and compare notes with the mates while catching one of the irregular DJ nights here – and downing Herold Beer, of course.

Zvonařka
Šafaříkova 1, Vinohrady, Prague 2 (2425 1990). Metro Náměstí Míru/11, 36, 56 tram. **Open** 11am-2am Mon-Sat; 11am-midnight Sun. **Main courses** 300-400 Kč. **Credit** MC, V.
This happening disco was transformed from a popular Czech pub with a terrace that overlooks Prague's southern suburbs. Now it looks like a sci-fi movie set, with a circular bar and blue and silver motifs. There's a good energy when the place is busy but the programme can be uneven. When the DJs aren't up to much the food's good, at least.

Gambling

Gambling is big business in Prague – and one that seems to get bigger every year. First came the hernas ('gambling halls' – essentially, bars full of one-armed bandits). Then came the bigger casinos that now line Wenceslas Square. Regulation is questionable so if you want to roll the dice, stick with the respectable international chains, which are geared towards tourists, encourage small-time betting and have fairly relaxed atmospheres. The hernas cater mostly to locals, pay a maximum of 300 Kč for a 2 Kč wager, and operate on a legally fixed ratio of 60 to 80 odds.

Casinos

Millennium
V celnici 10, Nové Město, Prague 1 (2103 3401). Metro Náměstí Republiky/5, 8, 14, 52, 53, 56 tram. **Open** 3pm-4am daily. **Credit** AmEx, MC, V. **Map** p309 L3.

Dressy and palatial, this James Bond-esque casino is part of a spick and span hotel and retail complex just east of Old Town. Free drinks for players add to the fun if you can keep your head.

Palais Savarin
Na příkopě 10, Nové Město, Prague 1 (2422 1636/ www.czechcasinos.cz). Metro Můstek/5, 14, 26, 51, 54 tram. **Open** 1pm-4am daily. **Credit** MC, V. **Map** p309 K4.
The classiest operation in town with candelabras and baroque frescoes, it's a world apart from most of the betting rooms on Wenceslas Square. Just about worth a look even if you don't gamble – but if you do, drinks are on the house. American roulette and stud poker are offered along with all the traditional games of chance. Bets from 20 Kč to 5,000 Kč.

Herna bars

Herna Můstek
Inside Můstek metro station, Nové Město, Prague 1 (no phone). Metro Můstek/3, 9, 14, 24, 51, 52, 53, 54, 55, 56, 58 tram. **Open** 9am-11pm daily. **No credit cards. Map** p309 K5.
Most herna bars are pretty seedy, but this one, inside Prague's main metro station, is not too threatening.

Reno
Vodičkova 39, Nové Město, Prague 1 (2494 9133). Metro Můstek/3, 9, 14, 24, 51, 52, 53, 54, 55, 56, 58 tram. **Open** 11am-4am daily. **No credit cards. Map** p310 J6.
Patronised by nervous-looking types. Light, highly suspect food is served.

Late-night eating

For less desperate options see also chapter **Restaurants** and **Radost FX** (*p140*).

Bistro Flip
Havlíčkova 2, Nové Město, Prague 1 (no phone). Metro Náměstí Republiky/5, 14, 24, 26, 51, 52, 51, 54, 56 tram. **Open** 9am-11pm daily. **Map** p309 L3.
Desperate hunger has been known to drive folks to to this train station buffet for fried cheese.

U Havrana
Hálkova 6, Nové Město, Prague 2 (9620 0020). Metro IP Pavlova/4, 6, 16, 22, 34, 51, 56, 57 tram. **Open** 9am-6am daily. **No credit cards. Map** p311 K7.
Near Radost FX, Music Park (for both, *see p227*) and AghaRTA (*see p220*), this all-night pub is clean and friendly – that is, if you get the right waitress.

Late-night shops

Agip
Olbrachtova 1, Budějovice, Prague 4 (4144 2386). Metro Budějovická/504, 505 bus. **Open** 24 hrs daily. **Credit** AmEx, MC, V.

The Roxy holds out

Ask any local clubber worthy of their dancing shoes to name the best overall club in the city, and they'll answer you with one word: Roxy. A mainstay on the scene since 1993, when electronic music was still in its infancy in the post-communist world, the Roxy consistently brings some of the best DJs in Europe to Prague. It's not the biggest club in the city (that's four-storey meat market **Karlovy Lázně**; *see p225*) nor the trendiest (the '80s flashback **Mecca**; *see p226*). But the Roxy has proven itself to be the best place in town to lose your mind, and has earned a place in the hearts of the hundreds of pretty young things that pack the joint nightly.

The neighbours, on the other hand, curse the day the Roxy opened its doors. The club stands on one of Old Town's residential streets and neighbours say the noise from the Roxy makes a good night's sleep impossible. For years they've complained to police and city officials, trying to get the club shut down. In Miami or Berlin, they might not get far, but in Prague...

Memories in Central Europe are long, and many still recall the days before 1989, when clubs like the Roxy were unheard of and all grooving was done to Abba albums at the monthly Communist Youth dance party. Bars closed at 10pm sharp and thereafter the city streets were silent and dark. And there's clearly a faction at City Hall that longs for those bygone days. Led by a particularly school-marmish deputy mayor, they cooked up a 500,000 Kč excessive noise fine for the Roxy in late 2001 – by far the largest ever levied here. Members of the Linhart Foundation, the non-profit-making organisation that owns the Roxy, say if they're forced to pay they'll have to shut down.

The foundation has done everything it can to reduce noise from the club, including a 2-million Kč soundproofing operation, complete with decibel tests to prove noise wasn't leaking into the apartments in its building. It also banned patrons from leaving the club and then re-entering to cut noise on the pavement outside. But the 60 neighbours who signed a petition against the club still weren't impressed, apparently (although sources inside City Hall say the deputy mayor personally collected the signatures).

The Roxy isn't just a club, it's also the financial engine for all kinds of alternative

cultural projects. With money from the club, the foundation sponsors modern dance performances, live music, experimental theatre, short films, a computer lab and two permanent gallery spaces for up-and-coming artists (*see p203 and p228*).

Now the Roxy has become a political football in the cut-throat world of city politics. The law-and-order types are eager to show that they're cracking down on ne'er-do-well kids and defending residents' rights.

Worried technoheads have organised fundraisers and public awareness campaigns (www.roxy.cz/news.html), adopting the symbol of a red elephant as a way of remembering the foundation and by collecting 3,100 signatures of their own. The club also has a powerful ally in the Prague Jewish community, which owns the building. Hitler nearly vanquished the city's Jewish population, but those who remain are proud and unafraid of standing up to the authorities, and wield powerful international connections. Don't count the Roxy out just yet.

Adult entertaiment ain't so bashful.

A 24-hour petrol station with an assortment of gourmet snack foods like caviar and imported beers.

Potraviny-Lahůdky

Spálena 37, Nové Město, Prague 1 (no phone). Metro Národní třída/6, 9, 18, 22, 23, 51, 54, 57, 58 tram. **Open** 6am-midnight Mon-Fri; 8am-midnight Sat, Sun. **No credit cards. Map** p308 H5.
Last-chance groceries for the ride home, near the night tram terminus on Lazarská.

Samoobsluha

Uhelný trh 2, Staré Město, Prague 1 (2421 0548). Metro Můstek or Národní třída/6, 9, 18, 22, 23, 53, 57, 58 tram. **Open** 6.30am-11pm Mon-Fri; 8am-11pm Sat; 9am-11pm Sun. **No credit cards. Map** p308 H5.
Potraviny near Old Town Square with a decent food selection for Prague and unusually convenient hours. Probably not the best place to find rocket salad and baby carrots, however.

Adult clubs

Prostitution is illegal in the Czech Republic but is practised openly (Hanka Servis even advertises on the sides of trams). Bordellos usually operate officially as strip clubs and don't pressure visitors to go any further than bar. Sufficient funds are usually squeezed out of customers by then already, with ruinous drink prices and strippers encouraged to drink with the gullible customers.

Cabaret Atlas

Ve Smečkách 31, Nové Město, Prague 1 (9632 6069). Metro Muzeum/4, 6, 16, 22, 34, 51, 52, 54, 55, 56, 58 tram. **Open** 7pm-7am daily.
Admission 200 Kč. **Credit** MC, V. **Map** p311 K6.

Striptease for the price of a drink and whirlpools at a mere 3,500 Kč an hour and that's just for starters.

Captain Nemo

Ovocný trh 13, Staré Město, Prague 1 (2421 1868). Metro Náměstí Republiky/5, 14, 24, 26, 51, 54 tram. **Admission** 200 Kč. **Credit** DC, MC, V.
Open 7pm-5am daily. **Map** p309 L3.
The newest Old Town club goes for a nautical theme but it's not clear if anyone's noticed yet.

Goldfingers

Václavské náměstí 5, Nové Město, Prague 1 (2419 3856). Metro Můstek/3, 9, 14, 24, 51, 52, 54, 55, 56, 58 tram. **Open** 9pm-4am daily. **Admission** 450 Kč.
Credit AmEx, MC, V. **Map** p308 J5.
Viva Prague's Vegas, with drinks named for James Bond foils, a theatrical setting and dizzy dancers.

Hanka Servis

Bulharská 10, Vršovice, Prague 10 (7172 0102). Bus 135, 139, 213. **Open** 8pm-8am daily.
Admission 200 Kč. **Credit** AmEx, MC, V.
Sin of choice for the average Prague Tomáš cat and booming business but not much on atmosphere.

Lotos

Kupeckého 832, Háje, Prague 4 (7291 6825/www.lotos.cz). Metro Háje. **Open** 24hrs.
Admission 200 Kč (500 Kč with taxi).
Credit AmEx, MC, V.
Prime practitioners, known here and abroad, but not for the bargain-hunter.

Satanela

Vilová 9, Strašnice, Prague 10 (7481 6618). Metro Strašnická/7, 19, 26, 51, 55 tram. **Open** 10pm-4am Mon-Sat; 10pm-2am Sun. **Admission** varies.
No credit cards.
Whips and chains, lab coats and fetish. Who knew?

Arts & Entertainment

Black Light Theatre
IMAGE

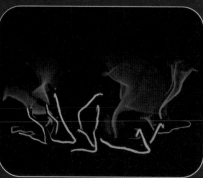

BLACK THEATRE
PANTOMIME
MODERN DANCE

Performance daily

Pařížská 4, Praha 1

Tel.: (+420) 222 314 448, 222 329 191

Fax: (+420) 224 811 167

http://www.imagetheatre.cz

e-mail: image@imagetheatre.cz

Theatre & Dance

With a playwright for president and enough dance and theatre companies for a city twice its size, Prague has no shortage of on-stage action.

Prague has a remarkably thriving and sophisticated stage scene for a city of 1.2 million people. Though classical music is still its main claim to fame, theatre and dance are strong and getting stronger. Thanks to the city's habit of absorbing the culture of whoever is in power at the time, there has always been a diverse selection of high-quality avant-garde work as well as traditional theatre and dance on offer.

Though the language barrier means most visitors can't enjoy Prague theatre, the Czech capital fortunately supports a national company of opera and ballet as well, all based in three main venues – the **National Theatre**, **Estates Theatre** (for both, *see p234*) and **Kolowrat Theatre**. There are hundreds of other smaller theatres in the city, the majority in elegant 18th-, 19th- and early 20th-century buildings that make amazing settings for theatre. A whole crop of new performance spaces aimed at wider audiences have also sprouted in buildings not designed for theatre.

Prague's best theatre and dance offerings tend to be avant-garde. The mainstream band of the companies of the National Theatre are only just beginning to shake off the constraints of the former communist regime. The National, however, has recently appointed new directors and dramaturges, still a major aspect of theatre-making in the Czech Republic. Meanwhile, formerly 'underground' creatives, although sometimes lacking technique, contribute great drive to the theatre and dance scene. Prague is also strong on alternative theatre and cross-media performance, with both local and international contributors. This is reflected in the dozens of festivals – new ones are continuously springing up dedicated to alternative theatre and dance (*see p237*). Increasingly, international top names bring ultra-modern work to Prague, usually in intimate and interesting venues such as the **Archa Theatre** (*see p234*). Another space to watch is the Meet Factory (www.meetfactory.cz), due to open in the Holešovice district in early 2003. This former ham factory owned by artist David Černý (*see also p199*) is set to be a cutting-edge performance, exhibition and meeting space for the arts.

Other venues for the radical and impractical are the art **Galerie NoD** (*see p235*) and **Alfred ve Dvoře Theatre** (*see p234*). And,

interestingly, the health and safety laws that limit so much theatre in the West are much less evident here – sometimes that's worrying and sometimes it's refreshing. Work tends to be less slick than Westerners are used to but it is invigorating, driven and consequential.

Local folk traditions also fuel today's scene. Puppet theatre is brought off with impressive flair at a handful of theatres (*see p237*).

ORIGINS

Prague theatre was at the heart of the development of the modern Czech nation. The construction of the **National Theatre** in 1868, funded entirely by patriotic donations collected over 38 years, ushered in a golden age of theatre, as did independence in 1918. After World War II, Czech theatre was largely shunted offstage in favour of the communist preference for pan-Slavic conceptions that embraced Russian brotherhood. But native theatre persisted. A new generation of actors, directors and playwrights, including Václav Havel, has struggled through, but since 1989 freedom has largely failed to produce much. Most of the new, risk-taking productions are now mounted in the city's small English-language theatre scene. Of the several troupes to come and go in this micro-community, the current survivor is the have-a-go **Prague Ensemble Theatre** directed by Cathy Meils. For information, or to volunteer, contact Ponny Conomos on 0604 461 761.

Misery Loves Company, a veteran international company, can be seen at the **Summer Shakespeare Festival**, performing at **Globe Výstaviště** (*see p234*). For info, call 2400 5229 or 9614 1179 (voicemail).

Tickets & information

Many box offices have at least a rudimentary command of English, but you're better off buying tickets through one of the central agencies listed below (though they are likely to charge a commission). They accept credit cards, unlike most venues. You can also book via their websites or by telephone in English, and there are numerous outlets throughout the city. Ticket touts tend to cluster at the **National Theatre**, **Estates Theatre** and **State Opera** (*see p234*, *p234 and p214*), so you can often get into sold out (*vyprodáno*) performances, at a price. You should wait until the last bell to get the best deal.

Bohemia Ticket International

Malé náměstí 13, Staré Město, Prague 1 (2422 7832/fax 2161 2126/www.ticketsbti.cz). Metro Můstek or Náměstí Republiky/3, 9, 14, 24 tram. **Open** 9am-5pm Mon-Fri; 9am-noon Sat, Sun. **No credit cards. Map** p309 K4.

The best agency for making advance credit card bookings from abroad for opera and concerts at the National Theatre, Estates Theatre and State Opera, though, inexplicably, you can't use a credit card if you turn up at its office.

Branch: Na příkopě 16, Nové Město, Prague 1 (2421 5031).

Ticketpro

Old Town Hall, Staroměstské náměstí, Staré Město, Prague 1 (2448 2018/www.ticketpro.cz). Metro Staroměstská/17, 18 tram. **Open** 8am-6pm daily. **Credit** AmEx, MC, V. **Map** p308 H3/J3.

Advance booking for major concerts and many smaller events. The automated toll-free number above works for all branches, found at Prague Information Service offices and hotels citywide.

Branches: Rytířská 31, Staré Město, Prague 1 (2161 0162); Salvátorská 10, Staré Město, Prague 1 (2481 4020).

Czech theatres

Committed theatre buffs who are determined to see a Czech performance should take heart – many Prague productions are adaptations of familiar works. Otherwise, try one of the performances from the thriving non-verbal or alternative theatre scenes.

Adria Theatre

Palác Adria
Jungmannova 31, Nové Město, Prague 1 (2494 6436/www.bezzabradli.cz). Metro Národní třída or Můstek/3, 6, 9, 14, 18, 22, 23 tram. **Open** *Box office* Sept-June 10am-1pm, 1.45-6pm Mon-Fri. **Tickets** 250-350 Kč. **No credit cards. Map** p310 J6.

In summer the Adria Theatre is sometimes rented out to other companies, who usually present tourist-friendly fare.

Alfred ve Dvoře Theatre

Divadlo Alfred ve Dvoře
Františka Křížka 36, Holešovice, Prague 7 (3337 6985/www.divadlo.cz/alfredvedvore). Metro Vltavská/1, 5, 8, 12, 17, 25, 26 tram. **Open** *Box office* 1hr before performance or buy tickets from Celetná Theatre box office. **Tickets** 120 Kč; 80 Kč students. **No credit cards. Map** p312 D3.

A small, curious and appealing modern building constructed inside a residential courtyard. Physical, visual, non-verbal and experimental theatre as well as some dance and mime artists.

Archa Theatre

Divadlo Archa
Na Poříčí 26, Nové Město, Prague 1 (2171 6333/www.archatheatre.cz). Metro Náměstí Republiky or Florenc/3, 24 tram. **Open** *Box office* 10am-6pm daily. **Tickets** 100-300 Kč. **Credit** AmEx, MC, V. **Map** p309 M2.

Prague's hippest and most daring theatre brings international avant-garde luminaries of dance, theatre and music to its versatile and well-equipped space. Features the cream of the Czech avant-garde crop – such as Filip Topol, Petr Nikl and Agon orchestr – as well as international acts such as Min Tanaka, Ultima Vez and Einstürzende Neubauten.

Estates Theatre

Stavovské divadlo
Ovocný trh 1, Staré Město, Prague 1 (2421 5001). Metro Můstek/3, 9, 14, 24 tram. **Open** *Box office* 10am-6pm Mon-Fri; 10am-12.30pm, 3-6pm Sat, Sun; and 30mins before performances. **Tickets** 240-1,200 Kč. **Credit** MC, V (for advance sales only). **Map** p308 J4.

Opened in 1783, this baroque wedding cake of a building is a venue of the National Theatre company (along with the National Theatre itself and Kolowrat Theatre). The theatre, which hosted the première of Mozart's *Don Giovanni* (conducted by the composer), also produces ballet and modern dance and opera. Caution: there is pre-recorded orchestration at times.

Globe Výstaviště

Výstaviště, Holešovice, Prague 7 (2271 1515/www.divadlo-globe.cz). Metro Holešovice/5, 12, 17, 25 tram. **Open** *May-Sept* varies. *Box office* 1hr before performance or Ticketpro. **Tickets** 100-390 Kč. **No credit cards.**

This replica of Shakespeare's Globe Theatre is Prague's most evocative summer venue, where Czech and English-language theatre companies perform the Bard's plays in something approximating their original setting. The carnival lights and smells of Výstaviště, the city's main exhibition ground and summer funfair in Holešovice, makes the vibe somehow even more authentic.

National Theatre

Národní divadlo
Národní 2, Nové Město, Prague 1 (2491 3437/2493 3782/www.narodni-divadlo.cz). Metro Národní třída/6, 9, 17, 18, 22 tram. **Open** *Box office* Sept-June 10am-6pm Mon-Fri; 10am-12.30pm, 3-6pm Sat, Sun. **Tickets** 60-750 Kč. **Credit** MC, V. **Map** p310 G6.

This architectural ode to Slavic myth, first completed in 1881, reopened following a fire in 1883 to the strains of Smetana's opera *Libuše*, commissioned for the occasion and based on the tale of the prophet who envisioned Prague. Productions include drama, ballet and operas in their original language, with a Czech translation projected above the stage. Guest artists have included JA Pitínský, Robert Wilson and David Pountney. Note that tickets can be

Chinese opera is among the daring fare at the **Archa Theatre**. *See p234.*

reserved through the theatre's website up to three months before a performance, but, annoyingly, must still be bought at the box office – with a 20% surcharge for reserving on the internet if you book more than 30 days before curtain. Many visitors are drawn to see the playhouse itself. Tours are available daily. On weekdays, call the National Theatre on 2491 4153; on weekends, you need to call the Prague Information Service on 544 444.

Preslova Space

Prostor Preslova
*Preslova 9, Prague 5 (2480 9125/
www.ctyridny.cz/preslova). Metro Anděl/6, 9, 12
tram.* **Open** *Box office* 10am-6pm performance
days. **Tickets** 50-100 Kč. **No credit cards**.
This modest production house for theatre, dance,
music and new media was recently established to
nurture young, local movement artists. Managed by
the Four Days Association (*see p237* Four Days in
Motion), it hosts a range of interesting avant-garde
performances in its basic and informal space.

Spiral Theatre

Divadlo Spirála
*Výstaviště, Holešovice, Prague 7 (2010 3468). Metro
Nádraží Holešovice/5, 14 tram.* **Open** *Box office*
3-7pm Tue-Fri; noon-7pm Sat, Sun. **Tickets** 200-500
Kč. **No credit cards**. **Map** p312 C1/D1.
Located in Prague's exhibition grounds, this venue
takes its name from the conical arena that allows
plenty of seating for popular shows, such as *The
Beatles' Story* or *Romeo and Juliet the Musical* in
Czech. Shows tend to be overproduced.

Divadlo Na zábradlí

Theatre on the Balustrade
*Anenské náměstí 5, Staré Město, Prague 1 (2222
2026). Metro Staroměstská/17, 18 tram.* **Open**
Box office 2-4pm, 4.30-7pm Mon-Fri; 2hrs before
performance Sat, Sun. **Tickets** 90-250 Kč.
No credit cards. **Map** p308 G4.
Founded in 1958, this theatre lay the groundwork
for Czech Theatre of the Absurd. It was the focus of
much secret police attention prior to 1989, when it
harboured such dissidents as Václav Havel and New
Wave filmmaker Jiří Menzel. Havel's celebrated play
The Garden Party premièred here, and his works are
still part of the repertoire.

Galerie NoD

*1st Floor, Dlouhá 33, Prague 1 (2482 6330/
www.roxy.cz). Metro Staroměstská or Náměstí
Republiky/3, 17, 24 tram.* **Open** 1pm-midnight
Mon-Sat. **Tickets** 60-80 Kč. **No credit cards**.
Map p308 K2.
Best described as 'very Prague', this artists' hangout
decked out in surrealist decor stages very irregular
theatre events and comedy nights. More predictable
are its art gallery events and hip café-bar. Supported
by the Linhart Foundation, a major Czech alternative
culture funder (*see p230* **The roxy holds out**), it
offers radical, though hit-and-miss, work.

Black Light theatre

The puppetry tradition in which performers
dress in black velvet to be invisible against a
black background has been all the rage here

Bust a move

Though classical ballet prevails in Prague, modern dance is catching up fast. The quarterly magazine *Dance Zone*, published in Czech and English, covers events in depth. Bohemian and Moravian folk dancing (www.folklor.cz), meanwhile, combine live music, high-energy dance and elaborate costumes. For the best, head for the folk festivals held throughout Bohemia and Moravia during summer.

Dance venues

Duncan Centre
Branická 41, Radlice, Prague 4 (4446 1810/www.osf.cz/dc). Tram 3, 16, 17, 21. **Open** varies. **Tickets** 200-1,200 Kč. **No credit cards**.
Named after the famous Isadora, this small public theatre plays host to both an array of touring foreign artists and some exciting student productions.

Ponec
Husitská 24A, Žižkov, Prague 3 (2481 7886/ 3899/www.divadloponec.cz). Metro Florenc, then 133 bus. **Open** Box office 4-8pm on performance days. **Tickets** 120-200 Kč. **No credit cards. Map** p313 B1.
This new centre for contemporary dance, which is run by Tanec Praha (*see below*), has

become the foremost stage for contemporary dance in Prague and hosts Czech and international productions on Monday and Tuesday nights year round.

Dance festivals

Konfronta(n)ce
Celetná 17, Staré Město, Prague 1 (2232 6843/www.divadlo.cz/konfrontace). Metro Náměstí Republiky/5, 14, 26 tram. **Open** Box office 9am-7.30pm Mon-Fri; noon-7.30pm Sat, Sun. **Tickets** 150-200 Kč. **No credit cards. Map** p308 J3. **Date** Oct.
Prague's annual cutting-edge dance festival (formerly the 'Progressive Central European Dance Festival') shows truly contemporary and idiosyncratic international new dance and performance art of high quality. Performances are often accompanied by workshops or seminars given by the artists.

Tanec Praha
Ponec, Husitská 24A, Žižkov, Prague 3 (2481 7886/3899/www.divadloponec.cz). Metro Florenc, then 133 bus. **Date** June.
'Dance Prague', as it translates into English, stages the modern dance event of the year, with Czech hoofers featuring alongside international stars such as the Martha Graham Dance Company.

since Czech performers blew the audience away at the World Expo '58 in Brussels. Modern practitioners with fluorescent paint, black lights, dance, pantomime and a large dose of kitsch aim at tourists. 'Black Light' is sometimes referred to as 'Magic Lantern' theatre after the venue that helped popularise it (*see below*).

Black Light Theatre of Jiří Srnec
Černé divadlo Jiřiho Srnce
Reduta, Národní 20, Prague 1 (5792 3397). Metro Národní třída/6, 9, 18, 21, 22, 23 tram. **Open** Box office 9am-7.30pm daily. **Tickets** 450-490 Kč. **No credit cards. Map** p308 H5.
Founding father of Czech Black Light theatre and co-author of *Laterna Magika's Kouzelný Cirkus*, Jiří Srnec has been putting on work for 40 years. His show moves from theatre to theatre, but as we went to press was just setting up camp at Reduta.

Image Theatre
Divadlo Image
Pařížská 4, Prague 1 (2231 4448/2232 9191/ www.imagetheatre.cz). Metro Staroměstská/

17, 18 tram. **Open** Box office 9am-8pm daily. **Tickets** 400 Kč. **No credit cards. Map** p308 H3.
With more dancing, modern jazz and pantomime than some Black Light theatres, this epitomises the modern style. There are three to four productions per month and clips from all shows are medleyed in a 'Best of Image' production each month.

Magic Lantern
Laterna Magika
Nová Scéna, Národní třída 4, Nové Město, Prague 1 (2222 2041/www.laterna.cz). Metro Národní třída/ 6, 9, 18, 22, 23 tram. **Open** Box office 10am-8pm Mon-Sat. **Tickets** 600 Kč. **No credit cards. Map** p310 G6.
Famous for pioneering the Magic Lantern style, this company's glossy, high-tech multimedia productions are professional, though no longer at the cutting edge. More slick and sentimental modern dance than traditional Black Light theatre but still with emphasis on visual tricks. The company's home is the Nová Scéna, the brutalist and impressive glass addition to the National Theatre designed by Karel Prager in 1983 (*see p234*).

Arts & Entertainment

Puppet theatre

Puppetry is not just for children in the Bohemian lands – it formed an intrinsic part of the Czech National Revival in the 1800s. Though much puppet theatre is aimed at tourists, high-quality Czech puppeteers and productions appear frequently and continue to develop the medium. The **Dragon Theatre** (Divadlo Drak) and **Buns & Puppets** (Buchty a Loutky) troupes put on inspired and entertaining shows that should not be missed. The theatres listed below regularly present puppet performances.

National Marionette Theatre

Národní divadlo marionet
Žatecká 1, Staré Město, Prague 1 (2481 9324/ www.mozart.cz). Metro Staroměstská/17, 18 tram. **Open** *Box office* 10am-8pm daily on performance days; otherwise 10am-5pm. **Tickets** 490 Kč. **No credit cards. Map** p308 H3.
This touristy company presents long and artistically inferior productions of *Don Giovanni* and *Yellow Submarine* set to recorded music. The puppets and set designs can be mildly interesting.

Spejbl & Hurvínek Theatre

Divadlo Spejbla a Hurvínka
Dejvická 38, Dejvice, Prague 6 (2431 6784/ www.volny.cz/spejblhurvinek.cz). Metro Hradčanská/ 2, 20, 25, 26 tram. **Open** *Box office* 10am-2pm, 3-6pm Tue-Fri; 1-5pm Sat, Sun. **Tickets** 50 Kč. **No credit cards.**
Spejbl and Hurvínek, a father and son duo, are among Bohemia's most famous puppet characters and all productions in this theatre are about them and their friends. Productions in foreign languages can be arranged for larger groups.

Theatre Minor

Divadlo Minor
Vodičkova 6, Prague 1 (2223 1351/www.minor.cz). Karlovo náměstí/3, 9, 14, 24 tram. **Open** *Box office* 9am-noon, 12.30-8pm Mon-Fri; 11am-8pm Sat, Sun. **No credit cards. Tickets** 50-240 Kč. **No credit cards. Map** p310 J6.
A lively and progressive Czech puppet theatre for both children and young adults. All directors and designers are contemporary guest artists invited from the worlds of opera and film as well as puppet theatre. Clown performances and productions designed for deaf and dumb children are without words and therefore good for foreigners. Shows take place every morning, weekend afternoons and usually four evenings a week.

Festivals

Mezi ploty Festival

Areál PL Bohnice, Ústavní 91, Bohnice, Prague 8 (8401 6111/www.meziploty.cz). Metro Nádraží Holešovice, then 152, 200 bus. **Date** late May, Oct.
This biannual two-day theatre, music and art festival is staged on the grounds of the Bohnice mental hospital on the outskirts of Prague. It features performances by top Czech theatre companies and bands, plus productions by Bohnice's patients.

Four Days in Motion

Festival Čtyři dny v pohybu
Info from Four Days Association (www.ctyridny.cz). Various venues. **Date** Oct. **Tickets** 100-200 Kč. **No credit cards.**
An excellent annual festival of dance and visual theatre that brings prominent practitioners of experimental international movement theatre and multimedia performance to an assortment of non-theatre spaces around Prague for four (or more often, in fact, eight) intriguing days. Recent festivals have been located creatively all over a former sewerage plant, a brewery and an ancient sports complex.

Prague Fringe Festival

Various venues (0602 549 008/ www.praguefringe.com). **Date** June.
The city's newest theatre festival combines the best of Czech and international companies in a host of unusual venues such as the catacombs of Castle Vyšehrad. In its first year, 2002, a dozen companies performed English-language productions. As in the other 36 fringe festivals worldwide, any company is welcome to join in so the result is an unpredictable cocktail – anything from cabaret to multimedia.

Faustian torments at the **Prague Fringe Festival.**

Sport & Fitness

Czech sport faces an uncertain descent from the twin peaks of sporting success it scaled in the 1990s.

The national ice hockey team failed to repeat 1998's exhilarating gold medal-winning performance at the Winter Olympics, only reaching the quarter-final in the 2002 Salt Lake City games. National team coach Josef Augusta has pledged to rebuild, and try to find replacements for ageing legends such as goaltender Dominik Hašek.

The national football team, meanwhile, is one of the notable absentees from the 2002 World Cup. Having also failed to reach France '98, it seems that stars such as Pavel Nedvěd, Karel Poborský, Patrik Berger and the other members of the talented generation that took the Czechs to the final of 1996's European championships are unlikely ever to appear on football's greatest stage.

Both sports must look to the future, and when athletes do so they surely hope to avoid the kind of fall from grace that has afflicted Czech tennis, the country's other great sporting passion. Recently the national tennis set-up has struggled to adapt to the harsh social and economic realities of post-communist life, and thus it has, so far, been unable to continue the line of tennis greats – such as Ivan Lendl, Martina Navrátilová and Petr Korda – that once graced the world's courts.

Will the football, ice hockey and tennis players of tomorrow be able to rival those once groomed under the communist regime? The future is uncertain, but only a fool would bet against the Czechs achieving further sporting success.

At this point, the Czechs' biggest asset remains the emphasis placed on active participation rather than on fandom and idol worship. Crowds at spectator sports events are often surprisingly sparse, but this apparent apathy actually disguises the country's real passion for sport. But it is a passion for playing sports, rather than simply watching others play. Many Czechs are members of amateur teams, and even recreational games are a deadly serious business here, and that seems unlikely to change.

As an increasingly affluent society builds sporting facilities to match its newfound wealth, watch out for Czech stars emerging in unlikely fields, such as acrobatic skier Aleš Valenta, a gold medallist at Salt Lake.

Spectator sports

Football

AC Sparta Praha
Stadion Sparta, Milady Horákové 98, Holešovice, Prague 7 (2057 0323/www.sparta.cz). Metro Hradčanská/8, 25, 26 tram. **Admission** *European games* 650-950 Kč. *League games* 50-150 Kč. **No credit cards.**
The dominant force in Czech football, Sparta entered the new millennium in fine form, even by its own high standards. The team benefits from a lucrative positive feedback loop: success in the Czech league guarantees entry into the Champions League, which in turn brings wealth that allows the team to buy up its domestic opponents' top players, making further league success almost certain. Sparta's 'Letná' stadium also hosts big Czech national team games.

FC Bohemians Praha
Stadion TJ Bohemians Praha, Vršovická 31, Vršovice, Prague 10 (7172 1459/www.cu-bohemians.cz). Tram 4, 6, 7, 22, 23, 24. **Admission** 90-120 Kč. **No credit cards.**
The 'Kangaroos' have traditionally been Prague's third club, lagging behind Sparta and Slavia in terms of both success and popularity, but the passion of Bohemians' fans frequently surpasses the big two's more casual support. New stadium regulations seem set to temporarily force the team to move out of its compact 'Doliček' home – and probably up to Strahov – while the old ground is expected to be completely rebuilt, depriving fans of one of the city's most atmospheric stadiums.

FK Viktoria Žižkov
Stadion FK Viktoria Žižkov, Seifertova 130, Žižkov, Prague 3 (2271 2503/www.fkviktoriazizkov.cz). Tram 5, 9, 26. **Admission** 50-70 Kč. **No credit cards.**
You'd never tell it from the humble facilities but 'Viktorka' is currently riding high in the domestic league. The fashionably grimy Žižkov district helps to give the club its unique flavour, while an unusual fanbase that contains a disproportionate number of charming old men in picturesque flat caps and a peculiar tradition of playing at 10.15 on Sunday mornings also tend to lend home games an oddly sedate atmosphere.

SK Slavia Praha
Stadion Evžena Rošického, Strahov, Prague 6 (3308 1751/www.slavia.cz). Tram 22. **Admission** 30-120 Kč. **No credit cards.**

Historically Sparta's closest competitors, Slavia are currently struggling to keep pace with their great rivals. A slow but steady slump into mediocrity since 1996's glorious league championship win has been hastened by exile to Strahov's soulless Evžen Rošický stadium, across the city from the club's Vršovice heartland. The club's spiritual home, 'Eden', is currently being rebuilt, and the temporary home is unpopular with fans.

Horse racing

It's not Epsom Downs, but the Chuchle racetrack on the outskirts of Prague offers regular chances to spend a day at the races. For an unusual treat, hold out for the Velká Pardubice steeplechase, the longest race in the world, held at Dostihový spolek in late October – the ambience is more car-boot sale than high society but the race is one of the highlights of the Czech sporting calendar.

The facilities are basic, with outdoor seating and indoor monitors for watching the action, plus a handy selection of dilapidated bars and restaurants. Betting works in a similar way to the British system, with two agents accepting minimum bets, of 20 Kč and 50 Kč, respectively. You can bet to win (*vítěz*) or place (*místo*), or you can bet on the order (*pořadí*).

Chuchle
Radotínská 69, Radotín, Prague 5 (5794 1171/9000 1703). Metro Smíchovské nádraží, then 129, 172, 241, 244 bus. **Admission** 30 Kč; 10 Kč concessions. **No credit cards.**
Races start at 2pm Sundays.

Dostihový spolek
Pražská 607, Pardubice, 110km (68 miles) east of Prague (040 633 5300/www.pardubice-racecourse.cz). Metro Florenc, then ČSAD bus to Pardubice. **Race meets** *May-Oct Sat.* **Admission** 60 Kč. **No credit cards.**
The Velká Pardubická Steeplechase is held here on the second Sunday in October.

Ice hockey

Despite Olympic success in Nagano in 1998 and World Championship triumphs in 1999, 2000 and 2001, a golden age of Czech ice hockey seems slowly to be coming to an end. Many of the country's brightest stars now choose to play abroad – primarily in North America's NHL. Still, the standards in the domestic 'Extraliga' remain high and the nation is gripped by playoff fever each spring.

The Czech Republic will host the World Championships in 2004, if a new arena is built in time in Prague.

HC Slavia Praha
Stadion SK Slavia Praha, Vršovice, Prague 10 (6731 1415). Tram 4, 7, 22, 24. **Admission** 50-80 Kč. **No credit cards.**
HC Slavia lags further behind rivals Sparta (*see p240*) than its footballing equivalents in terms of both facilities and achievements, but for basic sound and fury, a night at the minuscule 'Eden' arena is hard to beat. Don't expect comfort, however: the arena is unheated and there's usually standing room only, but downing a few cans of beer with fellow hockey fans usually helps to ease the pain.

It's a Czech thing: ice hockey is king in Prague.

HC Sparta Praha

Paegas Arena, Za elektárnou 419, Holešovice,
Prague 7 (ticket office 6672 7443/www.hcsparta.cz).
Tram 5, 12, 17. **Admission** 50-130 Kč.
No credit cards.
Sparta's home icerink, like Wembley Arena, was
state-of-the-art when it was built, but today it's
showing signs of wear and tear. The team itself,
though, is well financed and seems set to dominate
domestic ice hockey for some time. It's also the only
major sports team in Prague to sell tickets online
(www.ticketpro.cz). The large arena doesn't really
come alive until the playoffs; regular season games
are frequently poorly attended.

Active sports

Bungee jumping

They string you up. You jump. You don't hit
the ground. In theory, at least.

KI Bungee Jump

Hvězdova 2, Pankrác, Prague 4 (4140 1637/0602
250 125 mobile/www.bungee.cz). Metro Pankrác/
134, 188, 193 bus. **Open** Jumps *May-June, Sept*
11am-5pm Sat, Sun; *July, Aug* 11am-5pm Wed, Sun;
Oct-Apr closed. Office 9am-3pm Mon-Fri.
Cost 700-800 Kč. **No credit cards.**
Regular jumps are made from Zvikovské podhradí,
a bridge high over the Vltava.

Canoeing

Central European Adventures

Jáchymova 4, Staré Mûsto, Prague 1 (tel/fax 2232
8879/1051). Metro Staroměstská/17, 18 tram.
Tours *May-Sept* Sat, Sun (depending on weather).
Cost 810 Kč. **No credit cards. Map** p308 H3.
Canoeing trips on the shallow yet tricky rivers of
Bohemia are normally run at weekends, but if you
book in advance via fax they can be arranged mid-
week. For trips, participants are generally asked to
show up in front of the Astronomical Clock on Old
Town Square at 8.30am on Saturday or Sunday.

Climbing

Boulder Bar

V jámě 6, Nové Mĕsto, Prague 1 (2223 1244). Metro
Mûstek/3, 9, 14, 24 tram. **Open** 8am-10pm Mon-Fri;
12 noon-10pm Sat; 10am-10pm Sun. **Rates** 50 Kč/hr.
No credit cards.
Tackle the climbing wall, then sink a few beers
(rather than the other way round) at this curiously
Czech combination of sports facility and hip bar.

Cycling & mountain biking

Beware of biking in Prague – if the fumes don't
kill you, the cars will do their best. Bike rentals
are rare, but if you make it outside the city

It's best if you climb first then drink at the **Boulder Bar.**

limits, you'll find a network of reasonably maintained bike trails. Bike maps are available at most bookstores.

Bike Ranch

Palackého náměstí 2, Nové Město, Prague 2 (2492 2070/www.bikeranch.cz). Metro Karlovo náměstí/ 3, 4, 7, 16, 17, 34 tram. **Open** *May-Sept* 10am-6pm Mon; 9am-7pm Tue-Thur; 9am-6pm Fri; 9am-noon Sat. *Oct-Apr* 10am-6pm Mon, Wed, Fri; 10am-7pm Tue, Thur. **No credit cards**.
Just bicycle sales and repairs, but good work, done fast. Some of the staff speak English.

Central European Adventures

Jáchymova 4, Staré Město, Prague 1 (tel/fax 2232 8879/1051/www.members.tripod.com/cea51). Metro Staroměstská/17, 18 tram. **Tours** *May-Sept* Tue-Sun (depending on weather). **Cost** 680 Kč. **No credit cards. Map** p308 H3.
Cycling tours of the gorgeous wooded area and caves of Koněpruské jeskyně, just outside Prague. Cost includes renting a bike and entrance fee to this excellent natural preserve.

City Bike

Králodvorská 5, Staré Město, Prague 1 (0776 180 284 mobile/ www.citybike.cz). Metro Náměstí Repupliky/5, 8, 14 tram. **Open** *Apr-Oct* 9am-7pm daily. **No credit cards. Map** p309 K3.
Cycle tours of the city, three times a day: 10am, 2pm and sunset. Reasonable rental fees.

Fishing

River fishing is allowed from mid June to mid August. The Czech Fishing Association makes it extremely tough for foreigners to procure even temporary licences, but if you are serious and persistent, it will eventually give you the necessary paperwork and advice.

Czech Fishing Association

Nad Olšínami 31, Strašnice, Prague 10 (74811 7513). Tram 22, 26. **Open** 7am-2pm Mon-Fri. **Licence** *With trout* 1,000 Kč/day; 1.500 Kč/2 days; 2,500 Kč/7 days. *Without trout* 500 Kč/day; 750 Kč/2 days; 1,500 Kč/7 days. **No credit cards**.

Fitness

As the city grows increasingly body-conscious, fitness centres are sprouting up to meet the demand. There are also facilities at **Erpet Golf Centrum** (*see below*).

Body Island

Uruguayská 6, Vinohrady, Prague 2 (2251 7955/ http://web.quick.cz/bodyisland). Metro Náměstí Míru/ 4, 22, 34 tram. **Open** 8am-10pm Mon, Wed; 7am-10pm Tue, Thur; 8am-9pm Fri; 9.30am-7.15pm Sat; 5-9pm Sun. **Admission** *Classes* 70 Kč. *Sauna* 200 Kč/hr; 330 Kč/2 hrs. **Membership** 810 Kč /12 visits; 2,800 Kč/48 visits. **No credit cards**.

The Nautilus machines here are nothing to write home about, but this workout complex does manage to meet most bodily needs.

Crowne Plaza Prague

Koulova 15, Dejvice, Prague 6 (2439 3838/ www.posilovny.cz/holidayinn). Metro Dejvická/20, 25 tram. **Open** 6am-11pm Mon-Fri; 8am-10pm Sat, Sun. **Admission** *Gym* 70 Kč/90mins (80 Kč after 3pm). *Sauna* 70 Kč/hr (call ahead). *Solarium* 5 Kč/1min. **No credit cards**.
The machines at this fitness centre show how far things have come at what was formerly the Hotel International, once the pride of communist-era Prague. Happily for those who make it here, the bench presses and exercise bicycles are relatively underused due to the remote location. All the better for those who make the trip. Good value too.

Fitness Club Inter-Continental

Náměstí Curieových 43, Staré Město, Prague 1 (9633 1525/www.prague.interconti.com). Metro Staroměstská/17 tram. **Open** 6am-11pm Mon-Fri; 8am-11pm Sat, Sun. **Admission** *Gym* 180 Kč/hr. *Pool, sauna & Jacuzzi* 300 Kč/2 hrs. *Solarium* 180 Kč/10mins.* **Credit** AmEx, MC, V.
Popular among the rich and moderately famous, this posh workout palace features good cardio machines and an eager staff of trainers.

HIT Fitness Flora

Chrudimská 2, Flora, Prague 3 (6731 1447/ www.hitfitness.net). Metro Flora/5, 10, 11, 16 tram. **Open** 7am-11pm Mon-Fri; 8am-11pm Sat, Sun. **Admission** *Gym* 80 Kč. *Solarium* 7 Kč/1 min. *Squash* 200-380 Kč. **No credit cards**.
This is a well-equipped, modern and reasonably priced gym not far from the centre of town.

Stratos Health & Fitness

Corinthia Towers Hotel, Kongresová 1, Vyšehrad, Prague 4 (6119 1326). Metro Vyšehrad. **Open** 7am-10.30pm Mon-Fri; 9am-10.30pm Sat, Sun. **Admission** *Gym* 150 Kč/hr. *Gym, swimming & sauna* 250 Kč/hr; 3,000 Kč/10 visits. **Credit** DC, MC, V.
This 25th-floor fitness centre with panoramic views has squash courts, aerobics and a small but useful assortment of training equipment. US citizens should note, however, that because the Corinthia group is partly Libyan-owned, they are technically legally prohibited from spending money at the hotel. Which is a shame as it's very nice.

Golf

Though not exactly world-renowned for its golfing facilities, the Czech Republic has 13 courses. Only four are 18-hole, however.

Erpet Golf Centrum

Strakonická 510, Smíchov, Prague 5 (5732 1177/ www.erpet.cz). Metro Smíchovské nádraží/12 tram. **Open** 7am-11pm Mon-Fri; 8am-11pm Sat, Sun. **Rates** 150-200 Kč/hr. **Membership** 15,900 Kč/year. **Credit** AmEx, DC, MC, V.

This is the only 18-hole course in Prague, and it is restricted to members only.

Golf Club Praha
Plzeňská 215, Smíchov, Prague 5 (5721 6584/ www.gcp.cz). Metro Anděl, then 4, 7, 9 tram. **Open** 8am-4.30pm daily. **Rates** 230 Kč/round. **Credit** AmEx, DC, MC, V.
A nine-hole course and driving range on a hilltop. The course can get very dry in the summer.

Ice skating

Though you can no longer skate on the Vltava, the reservoirs at Hostivař and Divoká Šárka come alive in December with colourful skaters and grog vendors. Most indoor facilities operate from October to April. Be aware that skating in Prague – particularly ice hockey – is a serious business, and public skating plays second fiddle to organised activity. Also, it's generally assumed that you have your own equipment – don't expect to rent skates at the rink.

USK Praha Hotel Hasa Zimní stadion
Sámova 1, Vršovice, Prague 10 (7174 7128/ www.praguesite.cz/com/usk). Tram 6, 7, 24. **Open** *Sept-June* 9-10.50am Mon, Tue, Thur; 8.30am-10.50am Wed, Fri; 10am-11.45am occasional weekends. **Admission** 20 Kč. **No credit cards**.
Big and institutional, this old hall attracts serious figure skating and ice hockey teams when it's not given over for public skating.

The Krkonoše Mountains. *See p243.*

Zimní stadion HC Hvězda Praha
Za lány 1, Dejvice, Prague 6 (3535 2759). *Metro Dejvická, then 20, 26 tram.* **Open** *Sept-Mar* 3.30-5.30pm Sat, Sun. **Admission** 30 Kč. **No credit cards**.
This suburban rink attracts locals and hordes of expat kids from the nearby International School of Prague. It has irregular opening hours.

Zimní stadion Štvanice
Ostrov Štvanice 1125, Holešovice, Prague 7 (3337 8327/www.stvanice.cz). Metro Florenc or Vltavská/ 3, 8, 26 tram. **Open** *Autumn-spring* 10.30am-noon, 4-5.30pm Mon; 10.30am-noon, 4-5.30pm, 9-10.30pm Tue; 5-6.30pm, 8.30-10pm Wed; 10.30am-noon, 4.30-6pm, 8.30-10pm Thur; 10.30am-noon, 4.30-6pm, 8-9.15am Fri; 8-9.15am, 3-4.30pm, 8-9.30pm Sat; 9-10.30am, 2.30-4pm, 8-9.30pm Sun. **Admission** 40 Kč. **No credit cards**.
This rickety-looking structure on an island in the Vltava has relatively generous opening hours and a convenient location. The rink has been the subject of potential redevelopment schemes in recent years, so enjoy it while it lasts.

Jogging

Prague's infamous pollution makes jogging, even in the parks of the central part of the city, a relatively serious health hazard. But if you must run, try one of the following areas, which are far enough from the worst of the pollution to make the endeavour somewhat less than harmful. No park is safe, however, from the menacing Czech dogs which snap at your heels.

Divoká Šárka
Nebušice, Prague 7. Metro Dejvická, then 20, 26 tram or 119, 218 bus.
Challenging, hilly trails for joggers, with bulbous rock formations and thick forests. Šárka is most easily accessible from Evropská, towards the airport.

Michelský les
Krč, Prague 4. Metro Roztyly.
Avert your gaze from the hideous tower block at the base of the hill and head for the green hills behind.

Stromovka
Holešovice, Prague 7. Metro Nádraží Holešovice, then 5, 12, 17 tram.
The most central of Prague's large parks. After the initial sprint to avoid the Výstaviště crowds, you can have the woods to yourself.

Pool

Královská Šatlava
Saská 2, Mala strana, Prague 1 (5753 3199). Metro Malostranská, then 12, 22 , 23 tram. **Open** 2pm-2am daily. **Rates** 60 Kč/hr. **No credit cards**.
A modest pool hall, with reasonably priced beer, hidden away close by the Charles Bridge.

Arts & Entertainment

Czech skiers have taken gold.

Skateboarding

To get a glimpse of local talent, check out the concrete pavilion next to the **National Theatre** ticket office, the area around the giant metronome in Letná Park or the marbled section of Vítězné náměstí square, outside Video to Go's Dejvice branch. There's also a small skate park hidden away directly under Most Legie bridge, on Střelecký ostrov, an island in the Vltava.

Bugaboo
Všehrdova 27, Újezd, Prague 1 (5731 7172). Metro Malostranská, then 12, 22, 23 tram. **Open** 10am-12.30pm, 1pm-7pm Mon-Fri. **No credit cards**.

Mystic Skates
Štěpánská 31, Nové Město, Prague 1 (2223 2027). Metro Muzeum/3, 9, 14, 24 tram. **Open** 10am-7pm Mon-Fri; 10am-3pm Sat. **Credit** MC, V.

Skiing & snowboarding

Serious ski buffs head for the Tatra mountain range in Slovakia. If you don't want to cross the border, the Krkonoše mountains are your best bet for downhill skiing (*see p267* **Hit the slopes**). Stock up in Prague at one of the places listed below before heading for the hills.

Happy Sport
Národní obrany 16, Dejvice, Prague 1 (9001 0624/ www.happysport.cz). Metro Dejvická/1, 18, 25, 26 tram. **Open** *Rentals* Nov-Mar 9am-9pm daily. *Shop* Sept-Mar 9am-8pm Mon-Fri; 9am-1pm Sat, Sun. **No credit cards**.
Small chain of shops advertising 'the cheapest prices in Prague'. Snowboards can be rented for 130 Kč per day while ski rentals start at 40 Kč.

Branches: Beranových 125, Letňany, Prague 9 (shop 9001 0038/rental 9001 0042); Na Pankráci 1598, Pankrác, Prague 4 (shop 4140 3943/rental 4140 1465).

Snowboardel
Husitská 29, Žižkov, Prague 3 (2254 1271/ www.snowboardel.cz). Metro Florenc, then 133, 207 bus. **Open** 10am-6pm Mon-Fri; 9am-2pm Sat; 10am-2pm Sun. **Credit** MC, V.
A huge selection of new and used snowboards, sold by goatee-wearing aficionados. Good selection of stylish snowboardwear. No rental boards, alas.

Sport Slivka
Újezd 40, Malá Strana, Prague 1 (5700 7231). Tram 12, 22, 23. **Open** 10am-6pm Mon-Fri; 10am-2pm Sat. **Credit** MC, V.
Good, reasonable rentals for skiers – a complete package costs 160 Kč per day.

Squash

Finding a free squash court in Prague was once a Herculean task, but an increasing number of new facilities has gone a long way towards sating demand. The courts listed below rent out playing space and equipment by the hour. *See also* **Stratos Health & Fitness**, **HIT Fitness Flora** and **Erpet Golf Centrum** (*see p241 for all*).

Esquo Squash centrum Strahov
Strahov 1230, Malá Strana, Prague 6 (5721 0032/ www.squashstrahov.cz). Metro Dejvická, then 132, 143, 149, 219 bus. **Open** 7am-11pm Mon-Fri; 8am-11pm Sat, Sun. **Rates** 170-370 Kč/hr; 120 Kč/hr students. **No credit cards**.
One of the city's oldest squash centres, on two sites, both on Strahov Hill. Often mobbed with students.

Squashové centrum Václavské náměstí
Václavské náměstí 15, Nové Město, Prague 1 (2423 2752). Metro Můstek/3, 9, 14, 24 tram. **Open** 7am-11pm Mon-Fri; 8am-11pm Sat, Sun. **Rates** 140-420 Kč/hr. **No credit cards**.
Three courts and a central location draw Prague's business community to this underground facility.

Swimming

As the winter is long and the summer fickle, an indoor pool is your most reliable bet. But choose with care: many of Prague's pools are thick with chlorine, hysterical children or amorous teenagers who pointedly ignore the designated areas for lap-swimmers. If you prefer open-air swimming, dam reservoirs are usually murky as soup but wildly popular among the locals. Other options are area hotels that have fitness centres complete with pools. Some let you pay a fee to use the facilities. *See* **Fitness** (*p241*) for more details.

Arts & Entertainment

Areál Strahov Stadion

Olympijská, Malá Strana, Prague 6 (3301 4113).
Tram 22/132, 143, 149, 217 bus/funicular
from Újezd to top of Petřín Hill, then 5min walk.
Open *Sept-June* 6-8am, 8-10pm Mon; 6-7am, noon-
4pm, 8.30-10pm Tue; 6-7am, 8-9am, 10am-3pm,
7-10pm Wed; 6-8am, 3-4pm, 8.30-10pm Thur; 6-7am,
6-10pm Fri; 8am-6pm Sat. **Admission** 50 Kč/hr.
No credit cards.
This facility features a large indoor pool that also
regularly serves as a primary training site for competitive Czech swimmers.

Divoká Šárka

Nebušice, Prague 6 (no phone). Tram 20, 26,
then 5min walk. **Open** *May-mid Sept* 9am-7pm
daily. **Admission** 20 Kč; 10 Kč children.
No credit cards.
If the large, murky pond is not to your taste, follow
the striped trail further up the valley to find an outdoor pool in an idyllic setting with a sweet lawned
area on which to lounge.

Džbán Reservoir

vodní nádrž Džbán
Vokovice, Prague 6 (2056 2368). Tram 26.
Open *May-Sept* 9am-7pm daily. *Oct-Apr* closed.
Admission 20 Kč; 10 Kč children. **No credit cards.**
This is a large and popular reservoir and relatively
attractive naturist beach, close to the tram stop with
volleyball and table tennis.

Hostivař Reservoir

vodní nádrž Hostivař
Hostivař, Prague 10 (no phone). Metro Skalka, then
147, 154 bus/22, 26 tram; or Metro Háje, then 165,
170, 212, 213 bus/22, 26 tram, then 10min walk
through woods. **Open** *May-Sept* 10am-7pm daily.
Admission 20 Kč. **No credit cards.**
This reservoir is larger and deeper than Džbán, and
it also offers more activities, including rowing, wind-
surfing and tennis.

Hotel Axa

Na Poříčí 40, Nové Město, Prague 1 (232 3967).
Metro Florenc or Náměstí Republiky/3, 5, 14, 24,
26 tram. **Open** 6-9am, noon-1pm, 5-10pm Mon-Fri;
9am-9pm Sat, Sun. **Admission** 1 Kč/min (100 Kč
deposit). **No credit cards.**
The pool in this hotel is a good length and stays free
of shrieking children in the morning. Decent sauna
facilities too (100 Kč per hour; 200 Kč deposit).

SK Slavia

Stadion SK Slavia Praha, Vladivostocká 2, Vršovice,
Prague 10 (6731 0924). Tram 6, 7, 19, 22, 23, 24.
Open *Indoor* Sept-Apr 6-8am, 6-8pm Mon-Fri;
9am-7pm Sat, Sun. *Outdoor* May-Sept 6am-8pm
daily. *Sauna* 10am-10pm Mon-Fri; 10am-6pm
Sat, Sun. **Admission** *Indoor* 50 Kč/hr; 20 Kč
under-12s. *Outdoor* 60 Kč/day; 40 Kč children.
Sauna 150 Kč/2 hrs. **No credit cards.**
The Slavia complex has indoor and outdoor pools.
On hot days the outdoor pool gets far too crowded
for real swimming, however.

YMCA

Na Poříčí 12, Nové Město, Prague 1 (2487 2220/
www.scymca.cz). Metro Náměstí Republiky/5, 8,
14 tram. **Open** 6.30-9am, 1-4pm, 7-10pm Mon,
Tue; 6.30-9am, 1-2.30pm, 7-10pm Wed; 6.30-9am,
noon-3.30pm, 7-10pm Thur; 6.30-9am, 1-10pm Fri;
10am-11.30am, 12.30-5.30pm, 6.30-9pm Sat, Sun.
Rates 1.10 Kč/min. **No credit cards.**
Yes, it's true: there are YMCAs everywhere. Though
the tiny Nautilus rooms can get claustrophobic, the
pool is more spacious, and is frequented by some
reasonably serious swimmers.

Tennis

The Czech Republic has long been renowned
for its tennis stars – notably Ivan Lendl and
Martina Navrátilová. Although both defected
to the West, they're still national heroes here.
   Czech success at the 1996 Olympics and
Jana Novotná's Wimbledon triumph in 1998
were recent high points but the game has
generally struggled to come to terms with
post-communist economics. Still, the country is
fanatical about the sport, and there are quite a
few places in and around Prague to get in a
game or two while you're here.

1. ČLTK

Ostrov Štvanice 38, Holešovice, Prague 7 (2481
0238/www.cltk.cz). Metro Florenc or Vltavská.
Open 7am-midnight daily. **Rates** 250-550 Kč/hr.
No credit cards.
Six outdoor floodlit courts, at the home of the Czech
Tennis Association. Booking essential.

Tenisový klub Slavia Praha

Letenské sady 32, Holešovice, Prague 7 (3337 4033).
Tram 1, 8, 25, 26. **Open** *Apr-Oct* 7am-9pm daily.
Nov-Mar (indoor) 7am-10pm daily. **Rates** *Indoor*
600 Kč/hr. *Outdoor* 200-250 Kč/hr. **No credit cards.**
Eight floodlit outdoor clay courts on Letná Hill. The
courts are in good condition and the outdoor café is
convivial, but facilities are otherwise shoddy.

Yoga

Aruna Singhvi

Týnská 19, Staré Město, Prague 1 (2093 0073).
Metro Náměstí Republiky/5, 8, 14 tram. **Rates** 200
Kč/2hrs (individual session). **No credit cards.**
Dr Singhvi offers Classical and Ashtanga hatha
yoga tuition for all levels, in English, Czech and
German, and organises weekend retreats. Classes
are also held at the French International School,
Drtinova 7, Smíchov, Prague 5.

Jógacentrum Blanická

Blanická 17, Vinohrady, Prague 2 (2425
3702/www.joga.cz/praha). Metro Muzeum, then
11 tram. **Rates** 145-160 Kč. **No credit cards.**
The Blanická centre offers a drop-in class in English,
for beginners, at 7.15pm every Tuesday.

Trips Out of Town

Getting Started

Sleepy Renaissance towns, dramatic promontories, fortresses, ski slopes and art colonies – the Czech Republic is a rich trove for the road rambler.

While the Czech capital never comes up short on attractions, it's a world apart from the country that surrounds it. The grassroots Bohemia is the setting for countless fairytales for a reason. It's an easily accessible land of rolling hills, ruins and impossibly picturesque towns that specialise in time travel. So leave behind the noise, exhaust fumes and stresses of Prague, if only for a short break, and hit the highways of greater Bohemia and Moravia.

The trains of the former Eastern bloc are an excellent resource: a survivor of communist times, they may be somewhat shabby and overheated, but they're also cheap, efficient, scenic and go just about everywhere. Cars can be rented for around 500 Kč a day if you shop around (see **Directory: Getting Around**) and buses, also very cheap, go everywhere that the trains don't. Any of these modes of transport will immerse you in the heartlands of Central Europe and expose you to people and places that are far removed from the capital. You're likely to learn far more about modern Czech life by joining the locals, hiking through the countryside or pottering around a small town for an afternoon than you ever could from Old Town tours, relentless Mozart concerts and kitschy beerhalls.

Our suggested excursions are divided into the following categories: **Day trips** are places that are perfectly feasible to get to even if you had one too many beers the night before and don't make it out of bed until mid morning (there's also a look at green space on the outskirts of Prague; see p251 **Lights, Camera, Šarka Park**). As well as some stunning towns, we've included a selection of classic Central Bohemian castles (see p253). **Overnighters** are places worth spending a bit more time on – both bearing in mind the journey time, and how much there is to see and do when you get there. We've subdivided these longer trips into **Overnighters: Towns & Villages** (see p257) and **Overnighters: Country** (see p264). All destinations listed have been included with ease of access by public transport in mind. We've also suggested some ski options for midwinter visits (see p267 **Hit the slopes**).

If you want to get out of town with minimal effort, try one of the trips to Terezín, Karlštejn, or Karlovy Vary available through the travel

agents **Čedok** (see **Directory: Resources A-Z**). Rafting and cycling trips are also a breeze when the logistics are left to an agency like **Central European Adventures** (see p240).

If you're thinking of staying overnight at any of these destinations, the tourist offices listed in the following chapters should be able to help you book accommodation. Private houses all over the country also offer rooms, and this can be a good way to taste something of authentic Czech life.

A TOUR OF THE COUNTRY

Divided into the provinces of Bohemia in the north-west and Moravia in the south-east, the terrain of the Czech Republic is surprisingly diverse. Riddled with wooded hills and little valleys, Moravia is prettiest in autumn, where a leisurely week could be spent vineyard-hopping, combing through the region's caves, and getting your music and culture fix in Brno, the Czech Republic's second city.

Northern Bohemia, though it features a sad legacy of pollution from heavy industry, also offers the beautiful **Český ráj** (Czech Paradise; see p264), a playground for hikers and clean-air addicts. Here striking sandstone cliffs line the banks of the Labe (Elbe) river.

Southern Bohemia, with its carp ponds and dense woods, is heavily trafficked in the summer, both by tourists basking in the medieval charm of **Český Krumlov** (see p259) and by Czechs chilling out at the family *chata*. In western Bohemia, the landscape around the famed spa towns is dramatically verdant, with rolling hills and spruce forests.

Getting out of town

By bus

Many intercity bus services depart from **Florenc coach station** (see **Directory: Getting Around**). Bus services are more frequent in the morning. It's worth checking the return times before you leave, as the last bus back may depart disappointingly early (often before 6pm). The bus information line (in Czech) is on 0900 149 044 and operates non-stop every day but costs 14 Kč per minute. A few buses also leave from **Nádraží Holešovice** station. The state bus company ČSAD covers most

Picture-pretty **Karlovy Vary**. *See p248*.

destinations, although a number of private services now offer competitive prices and times. One of the largest of these is Čebus on Sokolovská street (2481 7776).

By car

There are just a few motorways in the Czech Republic, although more are planned, so drivers are often confined to A roads. Petrol stations (some marked by a big sign saying *benzína*) are ubiquitous these days and now come fully stocked with microwavable junk food and coffee machines. Petrol comes in two grades, super and special; the latter is recommended for most West European cars. Unleaded is called *natural* and diesel is *nafta*. The speed limit is 60kph (37mph) in built-up areas, 110kph (68mph) on motorways, and 90kph (56mph) everywhere else. If you have an accident, call the Emergency Road Service on 154. Prices for car hire vary widely depending on whether you're renting from an international or local company (*see* **Directory: Getting Around**).

By train

Trains often follow more scenic routes than buses, but cover less ground and usually take longer. There are four main railway stations (*see* **Directory: Getting Around**) in Prague but no real fixed pattern as to which destinations or even part of the country they serve. Hlavní nádraží is the most central station and one of two principal departure points for international services, as well as some domestic services. Timetables can be obtained at the state railways (ČSD) information office at the station, and there are English-speaking operators on its info line (2422 4200/2461 4030). **Nádraží Holešovice** is also principally used for international services. **Masarykovo nádraží** (Metro Náměstí Republiky) serves most destinations in northern and eastern Bohemia. Domestic routes to the south and west leave from **Smíchovské nádraží**. Travel is priced by the kilometre and, despite recent enormous price hikes, is still a resounding bargain by West European or American standards.

Hitch-hiking

The usual rules of courtesy and common sense apply to hitch-hiking within the Czech Republic. It's a time-honoured method of transport, particularly among students and soldiers. As with hitching a ride in any country, position yourself just outside the city limits and brandish a sign bearing your destination of choice. You should offer to help with petrol money, though your money will most likely be waved away.

Trips Out of Town

Day Trips

Spa towns, medieval silver mines, a concentration camp, a Habsburg's digs and a host of castles – Bohemia has seen it all. Now it's your turn.

Karlovy Vary

Though it's classic postcard material, and thus inevitably gets a bit cloying, the West Bohemian spa town of Karlovy Vary is surely the grandest and most venerated of the nation's collection. The usual crowd of Germans hoping to alleviate their creaky joints gets spiced up considerably during the midsummer **Karlovy Vary Film Festival** (*see p188 and p198*). It's then that this colonnaded assortement of boulevards and thermal fountains becomes the Hollywood Boulevard of Central Europe with endless screenings and celebrity-spotting making this the best time to visit. Summer is also a good time to catch one of the town's classical music festivals.

Local lore has it that Karlovy Vary began its ascent to steamy fame and fortune in 1358 when one of Charles IV's hunting hounds leaped off a steep crag in hot pursuit of a more nimble stag. The unfortunate dog fell to the ground and injured its paw, then made a miraculous recovery as it limped through a pool of hot, bubbling water. (Everyone say 'ahhh'.) Experts were summoned to test the restorative waters and declared them beneficial for all kinds of ills. From that moment, Karlovy Vary's future was ensured.

The River Ohře runs through the centre of town and disappears beneath the hulking Hotel Thermal – which stands as a fascinating symbol of the communist notion of luxury, especially when contrasted with the gracious elegance of the **Grand Hotel Pupp**. As for the town itself, the garish boutiques and inescapable wafer shops may not be your idea of relaxation – but you can always retreat to the parks, which are adorned with busts of some of the spa's more famous guests, or self-medicate with a few Becherovkas – the famous local herbal liqueur that works magic with its base of the region's pure spring water. To try a spa yourself without having to fork out for what the hotels offer, try the **Vojenský State Baths**.

Vojenský State Baths

Mlýnské nábřeží 7 (017 311 9111). **Open** 7am-3.30pm Mon-Fri Mon-Fri. **Admission** 90 Kč. **No credit cards**.

Where to stay & eat

Grand Hotel Pupp

Mírové náměstí 2 (017 310 9111). **Open** 7-10am, noon-3pm, 6-10pm daily. **Main courses** 250-550 Kč. **Credit** AmEx, DC, MC, V.
If you splurge on this lavish hotel – said to be the finest in the country – ask for a room that has not yet been refurbished; several have been unsympathetically 'modernised'. The elegant restaurant is worth a visit if you're feeling flush.

Promenáda

Tržiště 31 (017 322 5648). **Open** noon-11pm daily. **Main courses** 150-300 Kč. **Credit** AmEx, V.
Karlovy Vary is notorious for its lack of quality restaurants – odd for a place that looks so spectacular. If you can't afford the Pupp's dining room, try this – a cut above the usual goulash-and-dumplings places – with reasonably quick service, freshwater trout and steaks.

Getting there

By bus

Buses run at least every hour from Prague's Florenc station, starting at 5.30am. The journey takes about two and a half hours.

By car

130km (81 miles) west of Prague on E48.

By train

Trains leave Prague's Hlavní nádraží three times a day. The journey takes about four hours.

Tourist information

Tur-Info

Vřídelní kolonáda (017 322 9312/4097). **Open** 7am-5pm Mon-Fri; 8am-3pm Sat, Sun.
Tur-Info is situated in the big glass complex that's built around the main spring. Staff here are helpful and multi-lingual. Karlovy Vary hosts a number of arts festivals, including the annual international film festival which is held in July and several classical music festivals; you can pick up programmes and other information here.

Čedok

Dr Davida Bechera 21 (017 322 2994). **Open** 9am-5pm daily. **No credit cards**.
Information and tickets for festivals and concerts.

Hot springwater for two at **Karlovy Vary**. *See p248.*

Kutná Hora

Dramatically rising up from the wheat country
all around, Kutná Hora is an ancient gem that's
served as a movie set more than once. Its fame
and status were secured in the late 13th century
with the discovery of silver. A Gothic boom town
was born, and for 250 years Kutná Hora was
regionally second in importance only to Prague.

Don't be put off by the blighted concrete
tower blocks when you get off the train in
Sedlec. The UNESCO-designated old centre is
only a couple of kilometres to the south-west.
But first you might want to stop at Sedlec's
incredible bone chapel, where 40,000 skeletons
have been used as decoration. The Cistercian
abbey, founded in 1142 and now housing a
tobacco factory, established the ossuary a few
hundred metres north of the church on Zámecká.

It's a long walk or a short bus ride through
Sedlec to Kutná Hora's centrepiece, the
Cathedral of St Barbara. Designed in Peter
Parler's workshop, it is a magnificent 1388
building with an exterior outclassing Parler's St
Vitus's Cathedral in Prague. St Barbara was the
patron saint of silver miners and their guild
emblems decorate the ceiling. For an idea of life
in a medieval mine, head to the Hrádek ('Little
Castle') on Barborská. Here, the **Czech Silver
Museum** kits you out in protective suits and
hard hats for a trip into the tunnels.

Cathedral of St Barbara

Kostel sv. Barbory
Open *May-Sept* 9am-5.30pm daily. *Nov-Mar*
9-11.30am, 2-3.30pm Tue-Sun. *Apr-Oct* 9-11.30am,
1-4pm daily. **Admission** 30 Kč; 15 Kč children.
No credit cards.

Czech Silver Museum & Medieval Mine

Muzeum a středověké důlní dílo
Barborská 28 (0327 512 159). **Open** *May,
June, Sept* 9am-6pm Tue-Sun. *July, Aug* 10am-6pm
Tue-Sun. *Apr-Oct* 9am-5pm Tue-Sun. Last entry
90mins before closing time. **Admission** 100 Kč; 50
Kč children. **No credit cards**.
If you want to see the mine, a guided tour is
compulsory. Booking is advisable.

The Ossuary

Kostnice
Zámecká (0327 561 143). **Open** *Apr-Sept* 8am-6pm
daily. *Oct* 8am-noon, 1-5pm daily. *Nov-Mar* 9am-
noon, 1-4pm daily. **Admission** 30 Kč; 15 Kč
children. **No credit cards**.
If the Ossuary is closed, the key may be collected
from the vegetable shop at Zámecká 127.

Where to eat

Harmonia

Husova 105 (0327 512 275). **Open**
11am-11pm daily. **Main courses** 170 Kč-
190 Kč. **No credit cards**.
Beautiful terrace overlooking a picturesque lane.

Getting there

By bus

Buses leave five times a day from outside Želivského metro, and once a day from Florenc station. The journey takes about 75 minutes.

By car

70km (44 miles) from Prague. Head out through Žižkov and follow signs to Kolín to get on to Route 12; then change to road 38 to Kutná Hora. A scenic alternative is Route 333 via Říčany, further south.

By train

Trains run from Hlavní nádraží or Masarykovo nádraží, and take 50 minutes. The main Kutná Hora station is actually located in Sedlec. Local trains meet express trains coming from Prague and take visitors into Kutná Hora proper.

Tourist information

Tourist Information Kutná Hora

Palackého náměstí 377 (0327 515 556). **Open** *Apr-Oct* 9am-6.30pm Mon-Fri; 9am-5pm Sat, Sun. *Oct-Mar* 9am-5pm Mon-Fri.
Staff can book accommodation in private houses.

Mělník

A good example of Bohemia's hundreds of quiet little hamlets, half of which seem to feature some kind of castle or palace and all of which have an alcohol speciality. Mělník is just 33 kilometres (20 miles) north of Prague and has a fine castle that's been restituted to the Lobkowicz family – old Czech nobility – and a bizarre ossuary to go with its spectacular country views. The castle vineyards produce Ludmila wine, the tipple Mozart supposedly drank while composing *Don Giovanni*.

The main sights are concentrated near the lovely castle, now more château than stronghold. It occupies a prime position on a steep escarpment overlooking the confluence of the Vltava and Labe rivers, the inspiration for Smetana's anthem to Bohemia, *Ma Vlast*.

Although a settlement has existed here since the tenth century, it was Charles IV who introduced vines to the region from his lands in Burgundy. He also established a palace for the Bohemian queens, who would come here to escape Prague until the end of the 15th century.

The castle was rebuilt during the 16th and 17th centuries. Recent restitution laws have returned it to the Lobkowicz family, some of the most powerful magnates in Bohemia before they were driven into exile by the communists.

You can take a tour around the castle's interior a[...] [...]en better, another one round the

Kutná Hora: St Barbara's buttresses loom.

splendidly gloomy wine cellars. Here a lesson in viticulture is followed by tastings and a chance to walk over a bizarre arrangement of tens of thousands of upturned bottles.

Opposite the castle is the **Church of Sts Peter & Paul** (sv. Petr a Pavel), a late Gothic structure. The ossuary in the crypt consists of skulls and bones piled to the ceiling. Two speakers precariously balanced on top of a stack of femurs broadcast a breathless English commentary delivered in Hammer horror style, accompanied by liberal doses of Bach organ music. The site was established as a burial place for plague victims in the 16th century and sealed off for the next few hundred years. However, in 1914 a professor from Charles University cracked open the vault and brought in his students to arrange the 15,000 skeletons he found within. The end result includes the Latin for 'Behold death!' spelled out in skulls, and a cage displaying the remains of people with spectacular physical deformities.

The main square below the castle, **Náměstí Míru**, is lined with typically Bohemian baroque and Renaissance buildings. The fountain dates from considerably later.

The Castle

Svatováclavská 19 (0206 622 127). **Open** *Mar-Oct* 10am-5pm daily. *Nov-Feb* 11am-4pm Mon-Fri. **Admission** *Castle tour* 50 Kč; 40 Kč children. *Wine-tasting tour* 110 Kč. **No credit cards**.

The Ossuary

Kostnice
Church of Sts Peter & Paul (0206 621 2337). **Tours** (in English) 10.30am, 1pm, 3pm, 5pm daily. **Admission** 30 Kč; 15 Kč children. **No credit cards**.

Trips Out of Town

Where to eat

Castle vinárna

Svatováclavská 19 (0206 622 121). **Open**
11am-6pm Wed-Sun. **Main courses** 250 Kč.
No credit cards.
There are two restaurants inside the castle, and at
press time two more were due to open. The Castle
vinaria is the swankiest of them: the crockery is
embossed with the Lobkowicz insignia, the vaulted
walls are painted a delicate peach colour and it's
one of the best places in Bohemia to splash out
on an expensive meal.

Restaurace Stará škola

Na vyhlídce 159 (no phone). **Open** 11am-11pm daily.
Main courses 190 Kč. **No credit cards.**
This basic restaurant, close to the Church of Sts
Peter & Paul, does a decent plate of steak and chips
with a more than decent backdrop: the terrace has a
stunning view over the surrounding countryside and
the Vltava/Labe confluence.

Getting there

By bus

There are roughly ten departures a day from
Prague's Florenc station. The trip takes around 50
minutes.

By car

33km (21 miles). Head north out of Prague on Route
608; follow signs to Zdiby, then Mělník on Route 9.

Tourist information

Náměstí Míru 30 (0206 627 503). **Open** *May-Sept*
9am-5pm daily. *Oct-Apr* 9am-5pm Mon-Fri.

Terezín

Terezín, originally known as Theresienstadt,
was built as a fortress town in 1780 on the
orders of Emperor Joseph II, to protect his
empire from Prussian invaders.

Its infamy dates from 1941, when the entire
town became a holding camp for Jews en route
to death camps further east. Of 140,000 men,
women and children who passed through
Terezín, 87,000 were sent east, most of them
to Auschwitz. Only 3,000 were to return alive.
Another 34,000 people died within the ghetto
of Terezín itself.

The town's atmosphere is still distinctly
eerie, with lifeless, grid-pattern streets. The
Nazis expelled the native population, few of
whom chose to return after the war.

The **Ghetto Museum** screens documentary
films of wartime life here in several languages.
Possibly the most chilling contains clips from
the Nazi propaganda film *The Führer Gives a
Town to the Jews*, part of the sophisticated
strategy to hoodwink the world. Red Cross
officials visited the camp twice and saw a
completely staged self-governing Jewish
community with a flourishing cultural life.

The harrowing ground-floor exhibition of
artwork produced by the children of Terezín
has been removed to Prague's Pinkas
Synagogue. Upstairs is a well
laid-out exhibition on the Nazi occupation of
Czechoslovakia. Decrees of discriminating
measures against Jews are detailed – including
the certificate that a customer in a pet shop
intending to buy a canary was required to

Lights, camera, Šarka Park

An unlikely respite from the noise and traffic
of modern Prague, Divoká Šarka is a rambling
collection of woods, creeks and rocks for
scaling. There's even a popular, murky
swimming hole. Named after a figure in an
old Czech myth who led a savage all-female
army against the men, this park on the north-
western end of Prague (and accessible by
public transport) can easily be pictured as
the setting for one of the battles.

Nobles once hunted exclusively here,
but now visitors with dogs and kids have
the run of it year-round. The only concessions
to modern times are the mountain bikes seen
along the park's trail system and, in summer,
the pool and beer garden area (found about
half a kilometre downstream from the

swimming lake, or *Džbán*, which lies just
north of the McDonald's on the park's
Evropska street side). This is the more
civilised of the two swimming areas. The
larger *Džbán* is where swimmers share
facilities with ducks and nudists.

If the need to break free of the city comes
upon you suddenly, and there's no time in the
schedule for a trip to a rural castle, Šarka's
got your number.

Divoká Šarka

*Nebušice, Prague 7. Metro Dejvicka,
then 20, 26 tram or 119, 216, 218 bus.*
Open *(swimming area) May-mid Sept* 9am-
7pm daily. **Admission** 20Kč; 10 Kč children.
No credit cards.

sign, which promised that the pet would not be exposed to any Jewish people.

A 15-minute walk back down the Prague road brings you to the **Small Fortress**, built at the same time as the larger town fortress. The Gestapo established a prison here in 1940, through which 32,000 political prisoners passed. Some 2,500 died within its walls.

The approach to the Small Fortress passes through a cemetery containing 10,000 graves of Nazi victims, most marked simply with numbers. In the middle stands a giant wooden cross – an insensitive memorial considering the tiny percentage of non-Jews buried here.

The whole fortress is now a museum, and a free map (available from the ticket office) assists exploration of the Gestapo's execution ground and of courtyards and cells, some of which held more than 250 inmates at a time. The former SS commander's house is now a museum with displays detailing the appalling physical condition of the inmates.

Ghetto Museum

Komenského 411, Terezín (0416 782 577). **Open** *May-Sept* 9am-5.30pm daily. *Oct-Apr* 9am-6pm daily. **Admission** 130 Kč; 100 Kč children, students. Joint ticket for museum and Small Fortress 150 Kč; 110 Kč children, students. **No credit cards**.

Small Fortress

Malá pevnost
Malá pevnost, Terezín (0416 782 577). **Open** *May-Sept* 8am-6pm daily. *Oct-Apr* 8am-4.30pm daily. **Admission** 130 Kč; 100 Kč children, students. Joint ticket for fortress and Ghetto Museum 150 Kč; 110 Kč children, students. **No credit cards**. Guided tours for groups of ten or more.

Where to eat

Light meals and snacks can be had in the former guards' canteen just inside the entrance to the Small Fortress.

Hotel Salva Guarda

Mírové náměstí 12, Litoměřice (0416 732 506). **Open** 8am-10pm daily. **Main courses** 150 Kč. **Credit** AmEx, DC, MC, V.
The best hotel and restaurant in the area.

Restaurace u Hojtašů

Komenského 152, Terezín (0416 782 203). **Open** 10am-10pm daily. **Main courses** 150 Kč. **No credit cards**.
The best bet for a bite within Terezin town.

Getting there

By bus

Buses leave Florenc station about once every two hours. The journey takes 60-75 minutes.

By car

50km (31 miles) from Prague. Join Route 8 or the E55 at Holešovice, via Veltrusy.

Tourist information

Náměstí ČS armády 85, Terezín (0416 782 369). **Open** *Apr-Sept* 9am-4pm Mon-Fri, Sun.

A gateway at **Terezín**, marked with the Nazi slogan 'work makes you free'.

Karlštejn: rooms (and rooms and rooms) with a view.

Castles

Karlštejn

Fantastically spindly and well-situated, Charles IV's summer palace is perched over a lush bend of the Berounka river. But it's said by some that Karlštejn looks better from without than from within. Indeed, it was largely rebuilt in neo-Gothic style in the 19th century, presenting a prettier face than it had for ages, but its interiors are sadly neglected. It's also the Czech Republic's most trafficked castle, so it invariably comes with some jostling. The approach is an obstacle course of overpriced snack bars and hawkers of postcards, crystal and lace. This 14th-century stronghold, former home to the royal jewels, at least offers spectacular views to reward visitors for the short but strenuous hike up to the castle entrance from the train station. And one rewarding feature inside is the Holy Rood Chapel. Its walls are adorned with semi-precious stones and painted wooden panels by Master Theodoric, Charles IV's court portrait artist, plus an altar with a diptych by Tomaso da Modena. The remaining rooms can't match this splendour. Karlštejn is an easy and convenient trip, but be prepared for throngs of tourists.

The Castle

0311 681 617. **Open** *Mar* 9am-noon, 1-3pm daily. *Apr, Oct* 9am-noon, 1-4pm daily. *May, June, Sept* 9am-noon, 1-5pm daily. *July, Aug* 9am-noon, 1-6pm Tue-Sun. Last tour 1hr before closing. **Admission** *First tour* 200 Kč; 100 Kč children, students. *Second tour* 600 Kč; 200 Kč children, students. **No credit cards.**
Tours are available in English, but are thoroughly tedious in any language. The second, more expensive tour includes the chapel.

Where to eat

U Janů

Karlštejn 90 (0311 681 210). **Open** 11am-10pm Tue-Sun. **Main courses** 160 Kč-180 Kč. **No credit cards.**

Trips Out of Town

Guns and roses at **Konopiště**.

A cosy old-fashioned place with antlers hanging from the ceiling, a pleasant terrace garden and assorted schnitzels and goulash.

Koruna

Karlštejn 13 (0311 681 465). **Open** 10am-10pm Tue-Sun. **Main courses** 190 Kč.
Credit AmEx, MC, V.
A local favourite populated by village beer drinkers.

Getting there

By car

30km (19 miles) south-west of Prague. Take the E50-D5 or Route 5 towards Plzeň, then leave the motorway at exit 10 and follow signs for Karlštejn.

By train

Trains leave Prague's Smíchovské nádraží or Hlavní nádraží for Karlštejn about every hour. The trip takes about 40 minutes. It's a ten-minute walk from the station up to the village, and a further 15 minutes from there up to the castle.

Konopiště

An exceptional castle in a land of hundreds, Konopiště was built with seven French-style tower fortifications defending a rectangular bailey. Its contents are more stirring than most, as well, particularly the fantastic collection of weapons – and gruesomely extensive display of hunting trophies. This castle, which dates back to the 14th century, was refurbished by the Habsburgs as a hunting lodge to satisfy the passions of its most famous occupant, Archduke Francis Ferdinand. He resided here with his Czech wife Sophie, who was shot along with him at Sarajevo in 1914. The assassination triggered World War I and Ferdinand never acceded to the throne to which he was heir. As you meander through his decadent digs it will become apparent that he did enough damage, even so. Ferdinand slaughtered nearly every kind of fauna imaginable from the surrounding Sazava river woods and the countless trophies here represent only one per cent of the total collection. He supposedly felled an average of 20 animals a day, every day for 40 years.

The tour takes in sedate rooms featuring collections of wooden Italian cabinets and Meissen porcelain. A second tour of the castle, requiring a separate ticket, takes you through the Archduke's private chambers, the chapel and a Habsburg-era version of a gentlemen's club.

The castle has large grounds in which the peacocks and pheasants aren't affixed to a wall. Bears pace incessantly in the dry moat, oblivious to their unluckier brethren within.

Konopiště's popularity is second only to that of Karlštejn, so expect lots of coach parties.

The Castle

0301 721 366. **Open** *Apr, Oct* 9am-noon, 1-3pm Tue-Fri; 9am-noon, 1-4pm Sat, Sun. *May-Aug* 9am-noon, 1-5pm daily. *Sept* 9am-noon, 1-4pm daily. *Nov* 9am-noon, 1-3pm Sat, Sun. **Admission** 120 Kč; 70 Kč concessions. **Credit** DC, MC, V.

Getting there

By bus

Buses leave from Florenc station nearly every 45 minutes; the trip lasts a little over an hour.

By car

35km (22 miles) from Prague. Go south on the D1 and exit near Benešov, following the signs for Konopiště.

By train

Hourly trains to Benešov from Hlavní nádraží take about one hour. The castle is a 2-kilometre (1.25-mile) walk from the station, or you can catch one of the infrequent buses.

Křivoklát

This Gothic fortress, founded in 1109, is the perfect counterpoint to overtrafficked Karlštejn. Just inconvenient enough to remain peaceful, Křivoklát features one of the finest interiors in the country featuring a magnificent knights' hall and royal hall plastered in late Gothic paintings and sculptures.

The drive there is lovely, too, following the course of the Berounka river, past fields, meadows and a forested hill, before the castle dramatically appears before you, standing atop a lofty promontory.

Křivoklát was originally a Přemyslid hunting lodge, later converted into a defensible castle at the beginning of the 12th century by King Vladislav I. Fires followed, along with a spate of rebuilding by the Polish King Vladislav II Jagiellon, whose trademark 'W' can be seen throughout the castle. A fine altarpiece in the chapel portrays Christ surrounded by sweet-looking angels holding medieval instruments of torture. A more varied selection awaits in the dungeon: a fully operational rack, a thumbscrew, the Rosary of Shame (a necklace made of lead weights) and the Iron Maiden. The castle's enormous Round Tower dates from 1280. English alchemist Edward Kelley was locked up here after Rudolf II tired of waiting for him to succeed at turning base metals into gold.

The Castle

0313 558 120. **Open** *June-Aug* 9am-noon, 1-5pm daily. *May, Sept* 9am-noon, 1-4pm daily. *Mar, Apr, Oct* 9am-noon, 1-3pm Tue-Sun. **Admission** *Long tour* 120 Kč; 60 Kč concessions. *Short tour* (tower only) 70 Kč; 40 Kč concessions. **No credit cards.**

Two English-language tours set off every half hour up to one hour before closing time. There have to be a minimum of five English-speakers willing to take part for them to run (or a smaller number willing to pay for five tickets).

Where to eat

Hotel u Dvořáků

Roztoky 225, Křivoklát (0313 558 355). **Main courses** 150 Kč. **No credit cards.**
This is the only real place to eat near the castle, and serves a decent menu of the usual Czech fare.

Getting there

By car
45km (28 miles) from Prague. Take the E50-D5 in the direction of Beroun. Turn off at junction 14 and follow the Berounka valley west, as if going to Rakovník.

By train
Direct trains to Křivoklát are infrequent, so take one to Beroun, which leave from Smíchovské nádraží or Hlavní nádraží about every half hour (journey time around 45 minutes), and change at Beroun for Křivoklát (a further 40 minutes).

Splendour and thumbscrews at **Křivoklát**. *See p255.*

Overnighters: Town & Village

Brno impresses as the Czech Republic's second city, while Tábor, Telč and Český Krumlov offer beauty and fortifications straight out of a fairytale.

Brno

Spiked by medieval spires and surrounded by flat wine country, Brno is a kind of cultural and visual oasis in placid Moravia, the Czech Republic's sunnier eastern half. And fortunately, with a population of 400,000, almost half that of Prague, the republic's second city, a two-hour drive from Prague, has a lot more going for it than cathedrals, crypts and cobbled streets. Summer rock festivals, a seminal theatre scene and nightlife nearly as varied as Prague's add up to just as much to do but without the capital's pretensions.

Having originated as a ford across the Svratka river (the city's name is charmingly derived from the old Slavonic word for mud – and not a little onomatopoeic) in around 1100, Brno prospered from its location on important trade routes and swiftly became the capital of the Great Moravian Empire before being annexed by Bohemia.

The transfer thoroughly catholicised the city and its greatest treasures today reflect the fact. Rising above the old centre of town is the vertiginous **Petrov** cathedral. Though a bit of a disappointment inside, it balances atop a suitably dramatic hill in defiance of the heretics. Its noon bells sound at 11am, a tradition that originated during the Swedish siege of Brno, when the town was supposedly saved by an ingenious monk who knew that the attackers had decided to fight only until noon, and then up sticks and move on.

The **Capuchin Crypt**, just below Petrov and adjoining the former coal market, Zelný trh, features a sobering confrontation with the hereafter. Through the action of constant draughts, several nobles and monks buried here have mummified and are now on display, many still in their original garb. If you haven't exceeded your squeamishness quota, further lugubrious sights await in the 13th-century fortress of **Špilberk**, on a hill even higher than Petrov's, across Husova from the old centre. Here you can visit the labyrinth of dungeons, the *kasematy*, where Emperor Joseph II had prisoners suspended on the dank walls. They, at least, are no longer on display.

Back in the fresh air, Brno's streets revive you with engaging walking possibilities (and only the one encounter with the afterlife, and that of animal origin). Centuries-old pubs such as **Pegas**, the produce market on Zelný trh and half a dozen impressively ornate baroque cathedrals within strolling distance of the main square, náměstí Svobody. A sight that almost every tourist sees is the Dragon of Brno – actually an overstuffed crocodile – hanging outside the tourist information bureau. It is said to be the gift of a Turkish sultan who rather exaggerated its status – hence the name.

Červený drak, or Red Dragon, is now a popular Moravian beer which is becoming gradually more available in clubs throughout the republic. The club scene in Brno is thriving and the influence of local talents is typified by Iva Bittová, an avant-garde singer/violinist. You might even run into a local rocker or performance artist at **Spolek**, the city's newest bookstore café. This is a prime spot to try Moravia's best claim to fame and distinction from Bohemia: delectable white wines. Spolek's owners also operate a popular pool hall pub, Mýdlo, which is just around the corner.

Capuchin Crypt

Kapucínská krypta
Kapucínské náměstí (05 4221 3232). **Open** 9am-noon, 2-4.30pm Mon-Sat; 11-11.45am, 2-4.30pm Sun. **Admission** 40 Kč; 20 Kč concessions. **No credit cards.**

Castle Špilberk

Špilberk 1 (05 4221 4145). **Open** *May, June, Sept* 9am-5.15pm Tue-Sun. *July, Aug* 9am-5.15pm daily. *Oct-Apr* 9am-4.15pm Tue-Sun. **Admission** *Castle & dungeon* 60 Kč; 30 Kč concessions. *Dungeon only* 20 Kč; 10 Kč concessions. **No credit cards.**

Petrov

Biskupská and Petrská streets (05 4323 5030). **Open** 9am-6pm daily. **Admission** 30 Kč; 15 Kč concessions. **No credit cards.**

Brno's **Petrov** cathedral chimes in first. *See p257.*

Nightlife

Charlie's Hat

Kobližná 12 (05 4221 0557). **Open** *Bars*
5pm-4am Mon-Thur; 5pm-5am Fri; 6pm-5am
Sat; 6pm-4am Sun. *Garden* 11am-11pm Mon-Thur;
11am-midnight Fri; noon-midnight Sat; 3-11pm
Sun. **No credit cards**.
Handy labyrinth of bars and a patio with DJ action
and local bands.

Where to eat

Restaurant Pegas

Jakubská 4 (05 4221 0104). **Open** 9am-midnight
daily. **Main courses** 150 Kč. **Credit** DC, MC, V.
A classic, grand-scale beerhall with its own brew,
served in wheat and cinnamon varieties.

Šermířský klub LAC

Kopečná 50 (05 4323 7068). **Open** 11am-midnight
Mon-Fri; 5pm-midnight Sat, Sun. **Main courses** 150
Kč. **No credit cards**.
Ye olde Moravian inn, with waiters in medieval
tunics serving massive stuffed potato pancakes. It
is also the headquarters of the local historic sword-
fighting club.

Spolek

Orlí 22 (05 4221 9002). **Open** 10am-10pm daily. **No
credit cards**.
A short walk from the bus station, this bookstore
café is a hip but unpretentious hangout.

Where to stay

Hotel Amphone

*Třída kapitána Jaroše 29 (05 4521 1783/
fax 05 4521 1575/amphone@brn.czn.cz).* **Rates**

(incl breakfast) 950 Kč single; double 1,390 Kč.
Credit AmEx, MC, V.
The most convenient and friendly accommodation
in Brno, although it is not situated in a particularly
enchanting building.

Hotel Royal Ricc

*Starobrněnská 10 (05 4221 9262/fax 05 4221
9265/www.romantichotels.cz).* **Rates** (incl
breakfast) 2,500-3,000 Kč single; 2,800-3,200 Kč
double; 4,500 Kč suite. **Credit** AmEx, MC, V.
Guests staying at the Royal Ricc can enjoy luxurious Renaissance-era quarters with timbered ceilings,
stained-glass windows and pampering staff. For all
the historic trappings, there are modern amenities too.

Getting there

By bus

Buses leave Prague for Brno every two hours on
weekdays, less frequently on weekends, from
Florenc station, platform 10. Trip takes around
two and a half hours.

By car

110km (177km) from Prague. Take the E50/E65
motorway directly to Brno.

By train

Trains leave from Hlavní nádraži 11 times a day and
take about three and a half hours.

Tourist information

Tourist Information Brno

*Radnická 8 Brno (4221 1090/0758/www.
kultura-brno.cz).* **Open** 8am-6pm Mon-Fri;
9am-5pm Sat, Sun.
Staff can book rooms at hotels and pensions.

Český Krumlov

By far the most favoured mild weather escape from Prague, Český Krumlov actually deserves the term 'gem' that's usually tossed so loosely about. With its enormous and well-cared-for castle complex that seems to grow straight out of a rocky escarpment, the town's charm is further enhanced by its mountain foothill setting and by pubs overflowing with fine dark Eggenberg and Budvar, the local brews. In 1992 the tiny town so impressed UNESCO with its beauty that it was declared second in importance only to Venice on the World Heritage list. Krumlov's fantastic pink Renaissance tower rises high above the town, idyllically positioned on a double loop of the Vltava river on the eastern edge of the unspoiled, forested Šumava region. The streets below are a labyrinth of tiny cobbled alleyways filled with ancient architecture, craft shops and homely pubs.

The castle is one of the most extensive complexes in Central Europe, with 40 buildings in five courtyards. Founded before 1250, the fortress was adopted by the Rožmberk clan in 1302. As their wealth and influence increased, it was transformed into the palace you see today.

Cross the dry moat to enter, noting the bored bears that roam below. The tower was redone as a whimsical pink and yellow Renaissance affair in 1591, topped with marble busts and gold trimmings. The five-tiered Plášťový Bridge is equally spectacular, linking sections of the palace perched on two steep escarpments. For the best view descend to the Stag Gardens (Jelení zahrada) and look upwards. The extensive formal gardens host a **summer music festival** featuring everything from costumed period performances to Roma music.

The highlights of the castle tour include a gilded carriage built in 1638 to convey presents to the Pope, and the Mirror and Masquerade Halls, both of which are triumphs of the arts of stucco and trompe l'oeil.

On the opposite side of the Vltava from the Castle district (Latrán) is Nové město (New Town), laid out a mere seven centuries ago. On Horní street, you'll notice the impressive Church of St Vitus, circa 1439, the long slender tower of which is visible from all parts of town.

It's not just a tourist town. Residents work in graphite mining, at the Eggenberg Brewery or at the nearby paper mills. Before World War II, Český Krumlov was part of the predominantly German-speaking Sudetenland, so was annexed by Hitler in 1938. The majority of the region's German-speaking inhabitants were then expelled in 1945 and the town's centuries-old bicultural life came to an end.

Český Krumlov's **castle**. Yes, all of it.

Trips Out of Town

Even the statues groove in **Olomouc**. *See p261.*

The Castle

0337 711 687/465. **Open** *Apr, Oct* 9am-noon, 1-3pm daily. *May, Sept* 9am-noon, 1-4pm daily. *June-Aug* 9am-noon, 1-5pm Tue-Sun. **Admission** 130 Kč; 65 Kč children. **No credit cards**.
The only way to see the castle is to take an hour-long tour. Last entry is one hour before closing time.

Český Krumlov International Music Festival

Various venues (Auviex 6126 3700/www.auviex.cz). **Date** Aug. **Admission** varies according to venue.

Where to eat & stay

Hospoda Na louži

Kajovská 66 (0337 711 280). **Open** 10am-11pm daily. **Main courses** 200 Kč. **No credit cards**.
A good place to sample some Southern Bohemian cuisine, Na louži is an old-fashioned and central pub with traditional food and walls covered in tin signs.

Hotel Růže

Horní 154 (337 711 141/fax 337 711 128/ hotelruze@ck.ipex.cz). **Rates** 1,820-3,800 Kč single; 2,580-4,780 Kč double; 3,260-7,290 Kč suite. **Main courses** 350-700 Kč. **Credit** AmEx, MC, V.
A restoration of this towering Renaissance pile, a former Jesuit college, has helped to create one of the country's most luxurious hotels. The carved wood furnishings, ceiling beams, cellar wine bar and amazing views fit the town perfectly. The modern attractions feel almost out of place: a sleek fitness

centre and pool, business amenities, top-notch service and a disco. Three restaurants keep you fed.

Hotýlek a Hospoda u Malého Vítka

Radniční 27 (0337 711 925/www.krumlos.cz). **Rates** (incl breakfast) 460-600 Kč single; 700-1,380 Kč double; 1,400-2,300 Kč suite. **Credit** MC, V.
A gallery of a restored Renaissance inn just off the main square of the city's Vnitřní město district, filled throughout with handmade wooden fittings. Ingratiating service; kids and pets welcome.

Pension Ve věži

Pivovarská 28 (0337 711 742). **Rates** (incl breakfast) 1,000 Kč double. **No credit cards**.
Call well ahead to reserve one of the four rooms inside this fortress tower with metre-thick walls.

Getting there

By bus

Two buses a day leave from Roztyly station in the afternoon. The trip takes about four hours.

By car

85 miles (136km) from Prague. Either leave on the Brno motorway (D1-E50) and then take the E55 at Mirošovice past Tábor and České Budějovice, then the 159 road; or go via Pisek leaving Prague on Route 4, towards Strakonice.

By train

The trip from Hlavní nádraží takes five hours and includes a change at České Budějovice.

Otherwise, the town is a quiet, friendly escape from Prague or a good stopoff on the way to Poland, the Jeseniky mountains or the impressive nearby Bouzov Castle. Dating back at least to 1017, Olomouc was a prize city in the Czech Přemyslid land grab that ended the Great Moravian Empire. During the Hussite wars, Olomouc, like much of Moravia, sided with the Catholics, saw Hussite rebels executed on its squares, and was rewarded with a dozen handsome churches.

The Old Town is defined by a bend of the Morava river and is criss-crossed by tiny lanes that twist up to **St Wenceslas Cathedral**. No doubt it was the last thing Václav III saw before he was murdered in the chapter house in 1306. It later inspired an 11-year-old Mozart to compose his Sixth Symphony. The next door **Přemyslid Palace**, with foundations dating back to 1204, is an evocative pile with Romanesque windows but no other pulse-quickening contents.

Be sure not to miss the socialist realist make-over of the Town Hall Astronomical Clock Tower on Horní náměstí, which includes a mosaic of a scientist discovering better living for all through chemistry.

Tourist information

Tourist Information Český Krumlov

Náměstí Svornosti 1 (0337 711 183). **Open** *July, Aug* 9am-8pm daily. *Sept-June* 9am-6pm daily. **No credit cards**.
Staff can book canoe and boat tours down the Vltava. Trips range from a one-hour jaunt to an eight-hour expedition.

Vltava Travel Agency

Kájovská 62 (0337 711 978/www.ckvltava.cz). **Open** *Apr-Dec* 9am-noon, 12.30-5pm daily. *Jan-Mar* 9am-noon, 12.30-5pm Mon-Sat. **Credit** MC, V.
Can book rooms, horseback rides, canoe trips, fishing parties, bike rides and balloon flights around the area.

Olomouc

Tucked away in the heart of Moravia, Olomouc is a dazzling little town added to the UNESCO World Heritage list in 2000. Unlike other pretty old Czech hamlets, however, this one features a major university, with all the requisite clubbing, pubbing and music venues to support it. Strolling through the main squares (the town has three, cascading downhill from Václavské náměstí, through Horní náměstí to Dolní náměstí) of an evening, you'll see parties headed for the currently happening bar or dance place. Just follow along.

St Wenceslas Cathedral

Václavské náměstí (068 522 4236). **Open** 9am-6pm daily. **Admission** free.
The 100m (328ft) spire of this neo-Gothic wonder beckons from all over town, more than justifying the hike to the city's uppermost square.

Nightlife

Barumba

Mlýnská 4 (0608 081 267/www.barumba.cz). **Open** noon-midnight Mon-Thur; noon-2am Fri, Sat. **No credit cards**.
Combination internet café, split-level student bar and dance club, with name DJs and live acts from Prague often on the programme. Major scene at weekends.

Where to stay, eat & drink

Arigone

Universitní 20 (068 523 2351/www.arigone. web.worldonline.cz). **Rates** (incl breakfast) 1,600 Kč single; 1,950 Kč double. **No credit cards**.
Restored townhouse with raftered ceilings, warm service and a popular attached restaurant and bar.

Restaurace U Kapucínů

Dolní náměstí 23 (068 522 2700). **Open** 10am-10pm daily. **No credit cards**.
Well-done regional cuisine and frothy pints on tap. Restaurace U Kapucínů supplies just the basics on atmosphere, but it's good and cosy.

Trips Out of Town

Getting there

By bus

Two or three buses depart Prague's Florenc station for Olomouc daily. The trip takes around three hours.

By car

Olomouc lies 280km (51 miles) east of Prague. Take the E50/E65 south-east towards Jihlava and Brno, merging on to E462 south of Brno and on to Olomouc.

By train

The trip from Hlavní nádraží takes about three hours and trains leave hourly.

Tourist information

Town Hall

Horní náměstí (068 551 3385/www.olomoucko.cz). **Open** 9am-7pm daily. **No credit cards.**
Can book rooms, arrange tours to Bouzov Castle just outside town, and has full listings of concerts, clubs and food and drink in the area.

Tábor

The knotted little medieval lanes have been rather quiet for the last 600 years but things started with a bang around here. A band of religious radicals founded Tábor in 1420 following Jan Hus's execution (*see p8*). Led by the one-eyed general Jan Žižka, 15,000 Taborites battled the Catholic forces for nearly 15 years. Their policies of equal rights for men and women and common ownership of property did not endear them to the ruling classes and the Taborites were eventually crushed by moderate Hussite forces under George of Poděbrady. A statue of Žižka sits astride a hill overlooking Prague; Tábor honours him with a more modest sculpture in its main square.

Bone up on more details of Hussite history at the town's **Hussite Museum**. A highlight is Žižka's unusual military innovation, a crude sort of tank consisting of cannons balanced on a wagon. The museum also runs tours of a section of the underground passages, which were used as stores and refuges and snake under much of the centre. Most of the town's other bona fide points of interest are also on the main square, Žižkovo náměstí, from where the city's many labyrinthine streets and alleys radiate. Their confusing layout is not, as it might appear, due to ad hoc medieval building, but was in fact a deliberate ploy to confuse the town's enemies. The square is also adorned with a fountain statue of a Hussite, and two stone tablets that are believed to have been used for religious services.

Hussite Museum

Žižkovo náměstí 1 (0361 254 286). **Open** Apr-Oct 8.30am-5pm daily. *Nov-Mar* 8.30am-5pm Mon-Fri. **Admission** 40 Kč; 20 Kč concessions. *Tunnel tours* 40 Kč; 20Kč concessions. **No credit cards.**

Where to stay, eat & drink

Beseda

Žižkovo náměstí (no phone). **Open** 10am-10pm daily. **No credit cards.**
Beerhall within the town hall on the main square.

Černý leknín

Příběnická 695 (0361 256 405). **Rates** (incl breakfast) 1,290 Kč single; 1,550 Kč double. **No credit cards.**
A cosy Gothic villa. The best accommodation in Tábor.

Getting there

By bus

Two or three buses depart Prague's Florenc station for Tábor daily. The trip takes around two hours.

By car

82km (51 miles) south of Prague. Take the D1 south-east towards Jihlava and Brno, exiting at junction 21 to highway 3 south.

By train

Trains to Vienna from Prague stop in Tábor. The journey lasts just under two and a half hours.

Tourist information

Infocentrum

Žižkovo náměstí 2 (0361 486 230). **Open** May-Sept 8.30am-7pm Mon-Fri; 9am-1pm Sat; 1-5pm Sun. *Oct-Apr* 9am-4pm Mon-Fri.

Telč

Gorgeous but quiet to a fault, Telč is surely worth the trip if you're passing through the region on the way to Krumlov or Tábor. With a main square chock-full of immaculately preserved Renaissance buildings, still partly enclosed by medieval fortifications and surrounded by lakes, Telč undoubtedly deserves its place on UNESCO's World Heritage list. The centrepiece of the town is a large rhomboid central square dating back to the 14th century, with a delicate colonnade running along three of its sides. This colonnade and the photogenic gabled houses were added in the 16th century by Zacharía of Hradec. A trip to Genoa and a fortuitous marriage to Katerina of Wallenstein gave this Renaissance man the inspiration and means to rebuild the town following a devastating fire in 1530. Each of the pastel-hued buildings has a different façade adorned with frescoes, sgraffito or later baroque and rococo sculptures.

The narrow end of the square is dominated by the onion-domed bell towers of the 17th-century Jesuit church on one side and the Renaissance castle on the other. In 1552 Zacharía decided to turn this 14th-century family seat into his principal residence. At his invitation Italian architect Baldassare Maggi arrived with a troupe of master masons and stuccodores and set to work transforming the Gothic fort into the Italianate palace you see today. The coffered ceilings of the Golden Hall and the Blue Hall, and the monochrome trompe l'oeil decorations that cover every inch of plaster in the Treasury are among the finest Renaissance interior decorations in Central Europe. The Marble Hall exhibits fantastic armour, while the African Hall contains a collection of hunting trophies.

The castle also houses a small municipal museum whose exhibits include an unusual 19th-century mechanical nativity crib. Also on display is a permanent exhibition of works by the Moravian surrealist Jan Zrzavý (1890-1977). After you've exhausted the interior possibilities, relax in the peaceful gardens that stretch down to the lake.

The Castle

Náměstí Zachariáše z Hradce (066 724 3943). **Open** *Apr, Sept-Oct* 9-11.30am, 1-4pm (last tour 3.30pm) daily. *May-Aug* 9-11.30am, 1-5pm (last tour 4.15pm) Tue-Sun. **Admission** *Castle* 120 Kč; 60 Kč children. *Gallery* 20 Kč; 10 Kč children. **No credit cards**.
Tours are conducted in Czech but you can pick up a detailed English text at the ticket counter.

Where to eat & stay

Hotel Celerin

Náměstí Zachariáše z Hradce 43 (066 724 3477). **Rates** 350-1,100 Kč single; 1,150-1,350 Kč double. **Credit** AmEx, MC, V.
Romantic and friendly restored hotel of 12 rooms on the town's main square.

Pension Privát Nika

Náměstí Zachariáše z Hradce 45 (066 724 3104). **Rates** 350 Kč single; 700 Kč double. **No credit cards**.
Comfortable and good value.

Šenk pod věží

Palackého 116 (066 724 3889). **Open** 11am-10pm daily. **Main courses** 150 Kč. **No credit cards**.
Of the various restaurants in Telč, this is the most charming. It serves good Czech fare and has friendly staff and a terrace.

Telč: tranquility made manifest.

Getting there

By bus

Buses leave five times daily from Florenc bus station and once every afternoon from Roztyly. The journey takes just under four hours.

By car

150km (93 miles) south-east of Prague. Head out of Prague in the direction of Brno on the E50/D1 motorway. At Pávov follow signs to Jihlava; at Třešť follow signs to Telč.

Tourist information

Tourist Information Telč

Náměstí Zachariáše z Hradce 10 (066 724 3145). **Open** *July, Aug* 8am-6pm Mon-Fri; 9am-6pm Sat, Sun. *Sept-June* 8am-5pm Mon-Fri; 9am-5pm Sat, Sun. **No credit cards**.
Staff can book accommodation, plus fishing, horse riding and hunting expeditions.

Trips Out of Town

Overnighters: Country

Rock climb in the Český ráj to the north or duck your head in Moravian caves to the east. Whichever way you go, romantic Czech landscapes await.

Praguers are religious about visiting 'the nature', as they call it, swearing by the benefits of fresh air, wild mushrooms and, well, pubbing. Aside from the following destinations, all within easy reach of Prague, one option is hiking in the densely forested mountains of the **Šumava**, near **Český Krumlov** (*see p259*). It's a favourite getaway, though renting a cottage is advisable (*see below*) as camping out in the wild is not allowed. The Czech-language *Šumava* by Miloslav Martan is a handy, fairly decipherable guide that contains trail maps along with pictures of regional flora and fauna.

To help plan your escape, a new agency, **Česká Pohoda**, can arrange stays at rustic country cottages at rates significantly lower than those that even small town inns charge. So if your head needs clearing, take the cure and hit the backroads.

Česká Pohoda

V Jámě 1, Prague 1 (2416 2581/www.ceska pohoda.cz). Metro Můstek/3, 14, 24 tram. **Rates** 1,000-2,500 Kč per person per wk. **No credit cards**. Cabins in some of the prettiest corners of Bohemia, complete with woods, streams and meadows. Most involve roughing it, but in some lovely surroundings worth the sacrifice.

Český Ráj

'Czech Paradise', as it translates into English, is not helped by its name, at least not in summer when every family in Bohemia seems to flock to its lake, castles, woods and rock formations. But as Central European wildernesses go, this picturesque region – a protected national park – is nonetheless worthy of the name, especially when you compare it to the industrial pollution of the surrounding country. Though the area is accessible by road, the best way to explore it is on foot; even reluctant amateurs can cross the region in two days.

The neighbouring towns of Jičín and Turnov provide a good base from which to begin your exploration, as signposted trails can be followed almost from the centres of the towns. A great way to see Český ráj is to get the train to one town and hike over to the other for the return train journey.

The greatest concentration of protruding rocks is to be found around Hrubá skála: follow any of the marked footpaths from the village and you'll soon find yourself surrounded by these pockmarked giants. The Hotel Zámek and Hotel Štekl make the best bases for exploring the region. The most useful map is the Český ráj Poděbradsko, available at any decent Prague bookshop.

Supreme among ruined castles in the area is **Trosky** (the name means 'ruins'). Its two towers, built on dauntingly inaccessible basalt outcrops, form the most prominent silhouette in the region. The taller, thinner rock goes by the name of Panna (the Virgin), while the smaller one is Bába (Grandmother) – feminine appellations that are somewhat misleading given Trosky's hulking muscular mass. In the 14th century Čeněk of Vartemberk undertook a monumental feat of medieval engineering by building a tower on top of each of the two promontories, and constructing interconnecting ramparts between them.

The towers remained virtually impregnable, as they could only be reached by an ingenious wooden structure that could be dismantled in times of siege, leaving invaders with the choice of scaling the impossibly steep rocks or, more likely, beating a hasty retreat. In the 19th century Trosky Castle became a favourite haunt of Romantic poets, painters and patriots. Now you too can climb to the base of the tower for outstanding views of the countryside.

From 1 April until 31 October climbers can scale the sandstone pinnacles in the region. Simply pay the 40 Kč entry fee at any park attendant's booth.

Trosky Castle

Troskovice-Rovensko (0436 313 925). **Open** *May-Aug* 8am-5pm Tue-Sun. *Sept* 9am-5pm Tue-Sun. *Oct-Apr* 9am-4pm Sat, Sun, public hols. **Admission** 20 Kč; 10 Kč children. **No credit cards**.

Where to eat & stay

Places close to every main tourist sight offer filling, if uninspiring, Czech fare. If you want to sleep out, there are several campsites, but most people just seem to pitch their tent on any appealing plot of land.

Šumava:
southern idyll.

Hotel Štekl
Hrubá skála (0436 391 684). **Rates** (incl breakfast) 490 Kč single; 750 Kč double. **Open** *Restaurant* 10am-8pm daily. **Main courses** 150 Kč. **Credit** MC, V.
A decent dining room resembling an Alpine resthouse and with views over the surrounding valleys.

Hotel Zámek
Hrubá skála castle (0436 391681). **Rates** 850 Kč single; 1,120 Kč double. **Open** *Restaurant* 11am-7.30pm Wed-Sun. **Main courses** 250 Kč. **Credit** AmEx, MC, V.
Fabulous location, good prices and fantastic views from the ivy-covered turret rooms.

Getting there

By bus
Four buses a day go to Malá skála from Holešovice station. A private bus line leaves each morning from Palmovka for Jičín. Call 6631 1040 for information. It's roughly a two-hour ride.

By car
About 90km (56 miles) north-east of Prague. Follow signs to Mladá Boleslav and join the E65 or Route 10 to Turnov. Jičín is 23km (14 miles) south-west of Turnov. Hrubá skála and Trosky are both just off Route 35, which is the Turnov–Jičín road.

By train
Eight trains a day leave Hlavní nádraží for Turnov. There are local connections from Turnov to Hrubá skála and Malá skála. A local train plies the line between Jičín and Turnov.

Moravian Caves

The stars of the Czech Republic's many cave systems (*jeskyně*) are the ones north of the Moravian capital of Brno. Busloads of children and even pensioners (the rarefied air is touted as a cure for allergies and asthma) go on the guided tours through the chilly limestone caves – a welcome respite in the summer, but bring a jumper. As this is a phenomenally popular summer attraction, long queues are inevitable.

The Moravský kras ('Moravian karst'), comprising a series of 400 holes, is by far the most concentrated and accessible network of caves in the Czech Republic. Best visited as a day trip from Brno (*see p257*), these are limestone caves, created over 350 million years by the erosive action of acidic rainwater and underground streams. The Kateřinská, Sloupsko-Šošůvské and Balcarka caves are all within easy striking distance of Brno.

If you're looking to do all your caving in one go, your best bet is the **Punkevní jeskyně**, which is the largest cave in the country. Some three kilometres (two miles) of the caves' 12-kilometre (7.5-mile) length are open to the public. Passages of stalactites give way to the colossal Macocha Abyss: 140 metres (459 feet) deep, it was formed in part by the collapse of the ceiling of a cave further below. The tour then sends you down the narrow tunnels by boat. Visiting is a distinctly up-close experience: the passages are

Trosky Castle: often admired, never taken. *See p264.*

Hit the slopes

Most Czechs learn to ski in secondary school, when they can add practical feats to their already ingrained mythical knowledge of the mountains. Every Czech kid knows the legend of Krakonoš, the spirit of the northern Krkonoše mountains (*pictured*) who protected the humble peasants living there.

The least crowded slopes accessible from Prague, though they still feature relatively long lift queues for the length of the runs, are on the **Krkonoše** and **Jizerské** mountains. The trade-off for less-than-Olympic runs are costs a fraction of those in the Alps and ease of access. The next best alternative for the price, the Tatras in Slovakia, are an overnight train-ride away.

Harachov attracts masses but a better spot is **Špindlerův mlýn** (www.spindl.info/). Several inns dot the pristine mountain country near the Polish border but it's essential to book ahead in winter, especially at weekends.

There's no need to schlep skis here from Prague as they are available for rent on the slopes. A favourite ritual is to stop at a mountain *chata* – there are several near the slopes serving up restorative hot soups, *klobasa* sausages and grog.

The gentle Czech slopes are as good a spot as any for beginners, and if you want lessons, one comfortable hotel in Špindlerův mlýn, Hotel Barbora, has a ski school.

Hotel Barbora

Špindlerův mlýn www.ctg.cz/hotels/barbora. **Rates** (incl breakfast) 915-2,715 Kč single; 715-2,115 Kč double/triple; 415-975Kč extra bed. **Credit** MC, V.
Ski lessons are offered at this well-located but hardly luxurious hotel. Adult rates for lessons are 1,090 Kč for two hours. Hotel services include sauna, table tennis, pool, massage and satellite TV.

Trips Out of Town

All quiet on the eastern front: the Napoleonic war monument at **Austerlitz**.

barely wide enough for the boats, and you'd likely be impaled by a stalactite if you stood up.

Arrive early in peak season as tours can sell out by mid morning. It's even better to reserve a place by phone, as queues can be long.

There are other attractions within easy reach by car. The most popular is the spectacular Gothic castle of **Pernštejn**; others include the Napoleonic battlefield of **Austerlitz** (Slavkov) and the **Alfons Mucha Museum** housed in the Renaissance château of Moravský Krumlov.

Moravský kras

Skalní mlýn (0506 413 575). **Open** *Punkevní jeskyně* Apr-Aug 8.20am-3.50pm daily. Closed Sept-March. *Other caves* Apr-Aug 8.30am-3.30pm daily. Closed Sept-March. **Admission** *Punkevní jeskyně* 75 Kč adults; 30 Kč concessions, including chairlift to entrance and boat ride. *Other caves* 40 Kč adults; 20 Kč students; free under-6s. **No credit cards**.

Where to eat & stay

Hotel Skalní Mlýn

Skalní Mlýn (0506 418 113). **Rates** 690 Kč single; 940 Kč double. **Open** *Restaurant* 9am-11pm. **Main courses** 150 Kč. **Credit** AmEx, MC, V.
A popular place and the best base for the caves – plus there's a reasonable restaurant.

Getting there

By bus

Buses run roughly every hour between Brno and Prague. Journey time is two and a half hours.

By car

202km (126 miles) south-east of Prague. The D1 motorway runs all the way to Brno. The caves are 22km (14 miles) north-east of Brno.

By train

Trains to Brno from Prague run hourly and take between three and four hours. A dozen trains a day leave Brno for the nearby town of Blansko. Local buses then take you onwards to the caves. A tourist train travels between the Punkevní caves and the centre of Skalní Mlýn, from which the other three caves are accessible.

Tourist information

Tourist Information Brno

Old Town Hall, Radnická 8, Brno (05 4221 1090). **Open** 8am-6pm Mon-Fri; 9am-5pm Sat, Sun. **No credit cards**.
The staff here can book rooms in and around the town and can also supply you with maps, brochures and other information.

Directory

Directory

Getting Around

By air

Prague's only airport, the expanded and modernised Ruzyně, is located about 20 kilometres (12.5 miles) north-west of the centre, and is not directly accessible by metro or tram. Some of the more expensive hotels provide a pick-up service from the airport if you book ahead and there is a regular public bus service back and forth.

For information in English on arrivals and departures call 2011 3314; for other airport information call 2011 3321.

CONNECTIONS TO THE CITY

Airport taxis are regulated but still often charge illegally high prices. The ride, which should take about 20 to 25 minutes, should cost around 370 Kč to the centre. Check at the airport information kiosk for the going rate to your destination. For a more honest taxi driver you could try taking your luggage to the customs depot (where people accept air-freighted shipments from abroad) and phone one of the reputable taxi services to fetch you (see p272). They will not pick you up at the regular arrivals/departures area, though.

EXPRESS AIRPORT BUS

Two express buses run every half hour from the airport into town, first stopping in Prague 6 at Dejvická metro – the end station on the green Line A – and then at Revoluční in Prague 1. The express bus service is quick and cheap at 15 Kč for the 20-minute ride to

Dejvická and 30 Kč for the 35-minute ride to Revoluční. After hours, night bus 510 goes from the airport to Divoká Šárka, from where you can catch night tram 51 to the centre. A private bus service, CEDAZ, provides transport between the airport, Dejvická metro and Náměstí Republiky for 90 Kč from 8am to 8pm daily (2011 4296). A friendly, English-speaking commercial service, Prague Airport Shuttle (0602 395 421/www.prague-airport-shuttle.com) provides door-to-door transport – as well as transport around town and throughout the Czech Republic.

LOCAL BUS

Three local buses run from the airport to metro stations about every 20 minutes from 5am to midnight. Bus 119 runs from the airport to Dejvická metro (green Line A), bus 108 goes to Hradčanská metro (green Line A) and bus 179 goes to Nové Butovice metro (yellow Line B). This is the cheapest, slowest and most crowded alternative. If you have a lot of luggage, you will need to buy extra tickets for your bags. The buses depart from the stands in front of the arrivals hall. There you'll find orange public transport ticket machines (you'll need 12 Kč in change). There are also ticket machines and an information office in the airport lobby. For ticket details, see page 271.

By rail

International trains arrive at the Main Station (Hlavní nádraží, sometimes called Wilson Station or Wilsonovo nádraží) and Holešovice

Station (Nádraží Holešovice) – both on the red Line C of the metro. Caution: it's easy to get off at Holešovice thinking that it is the main station. If your train stops at both, wait for the last stop.

The centrally located Main Station is a beautiful art nouveau building with communist-period lower halls. It has several food stalls and a PIS (Prague Information Service) office in the main hall and public showers and a 24-hour left luggage area below in the lower hall.

It's never a good idea to hang around in the small park near the station – locals have nicknamed it Sherwood Forest because so much illegal redistribution of wealth goes on here. Enough said.

24-hour rail infoline

2422 4200/2461 4030.
National and international timetable information. English is spoken. For ticket prices, call 2461 5249 (8am-7pm daily).

Hlavní nádraží

Main Station
Wilsonova, Nové Město, Prague 2 (2422 4200/2461 4030). Metro Hlavní Nádraží/5, 9, 11, 26 tram. **Map** p309 M5.

Masarykovo nádraží

Masaryk Station
Hybernská, Nové Město, Prague 1 (2461 4030/2422 4200). Metro Náměstí Republiky/3, 5, 14, 24, 26 tram. **International ticket office open** 7.30am-6pm. **Map** p309 L3.

Nádraží Holešovice

Holešovice Station
Vrbenského, Prague 7 (2461 5865). Metro Nádraží Holešovice/12, 25 tram. **Map** p312 E1.

Smíchovské nádraží

Smíchov Station
Nádražní, Prague 5 (2461 7686). Metro Smíchovské nádraží/12 tram.

By coach

Florenc coach station may be the least pleasant place in Prague. Perhaps its best feature is that it's on two metro lines (yellow Line B and red Line C) so you can make a quick getaway. Late arrivals can take the night tram or a taxi or stay in one of the hotels on Na Poříčí, the main street in front of the metro station.

Getting around Prague

Walking is the best way to see the relatively compact centre of Prague. Every twist of the city's ancient streets reveals some new curiosity.

But if you're going further afield the city has an excellent, inexpensive and pretty much 24-hour integrated public transport system that will get you just about anywhere you want to go.

Driving in Prague takes some getting used to and it really isn't worth the bother on a short visit. Taxis are ubiquitous but unreliable – pretty cheap if you find an honest driver; ruinous if you let one rip you off.

Because the communists dammed the Vltava so thoroughly, there isn't any real freight or passenger traffic on the river – just pleasure cruises. An assortment of eccentric conveyances – including horse-drawn carriages, bike-taxis and a Disney-esque electric train that takes tourists up to the Castle and back – can all be found in Old Town Square.

Public transport

There are bus and/or tram connections and usually taxi stands at every metro station, and all of Prague's railway stations are connected to the metro network.

Public transport runs around the clock. Day service is from about 5am to midnight daily. Peak times are 5am to 8pm Monday to Friday. From about midnight to 5am, night buses and trams take over.

Metro, tram and bus lines are indicated on most city maps. Timetables can be found at every tram and bus stop. The times posted apply to the stop where you are – which is highlighted on the schedule. If your destination is listed below the highlighted stop, you are in the right place.

Prague Public Transit Company (DP) Information Offices

Ruzyně Airport (2011 5404). **Open** 7am-10pm daily.
Muzeum metro station, Nové Město (2262 3777). **Open** 7am-9pm daily. **Map** p311 L6.
Můstek metro station, Jungmannovo náměstí, Nové Město (2264 6350). **Open** 7am-9pm daily. **Map** p306 J4 and p309 K5.
Nádraží Holešovice metro station, Holešovice (806 790). **Open** 7am-6pm Mon-Fri.
Černý Most metro station, Černý Most (2264 7450). **Open** 7am-6pm Mon-Fri.
Anděl metro station, Smíchov (2264 6055). **Open** 7am-6pm Mon-Fri. Employees usually have at least a smattering of English and German and are unusually helpful. They provide free information booklets and sell tickets, maps, night transport booklets and individual tram and bus schedules (cash only).

TICKETS

Tickets (*jízdenky*) are valid for any mode of transport (metro, bus, tram, even the funicular). Most locals have passes (*see below*), probably the easiest option for visitors too as you can't buy a ticket on board trams or buses.

Ticket machines are only found in metro stations and can dispense dozens of types of ticket. Only two need concern you. An 8 Kč ticket entitles the buyer to a single 15-minute ride on any transport above ground, or one ride of up to four stops on the metro. It is not valid for use on night

transport, the Historical Tram or the funicular. A 12 Kč ticket lasts for 60 minutes at peak times (5am-8pm Mon-Fri) and 90 minutes at slow times (8pm-5am Mon-Fri and all of Sat, Sun), allowing unlimited travel throughout Prague, including transfers between metros, buses and trams.

Babies in carriages, children under six, handicapped people, small bags and skis ride free. Children aged six to 15, large items of luggage and other sizeable items need a half-price ticket. Enormous luggage and 'items that stink or look disgusting' aren't allowed on Prague public transport.

The orange ticket machines are marvels of Czechnology. They are covered with buttons marked with prices. Press once for the ticket you want, twice if you want two tickets (and so on), and then press the 'enter' button. Insert the total amount in coins (change is given) and wait an agonisingly long time for the machine's screeching mechanism to print out each ticket individually.

If you're here for anything other than a quick visit it's worth stocking up on tickets in advance. They can be bought at most tobacconists, DP information offices (*see above*) and PIS offices (*see p289*), or anywhere displaying a red and yellow DP sticker.

Stamp your ticket (face up in the direction of the arrow) in a machine as you board a bus or enter the 'paid area' of the metro. There are no guards or gates, but plain-clothes inspectors (*revizoři*) carry out random ticket checks.

TRAVEL PASSES

Most ticket outlets also sell transit passes, which allow unlimited travel on the metro, trams and buses. The 24-hour pass (only) is also available at automatic ticket machines.

To validate a short-term pass, fill in your full name and

Directory

date of birth on the reverse and then stamp them as you would an ordinary ticket. The pass is valid from the time it was stamped. A 24-hour pass costs 70 Kč, a 72-hour pass 200 Kč, a 168-hour pass (seven days) 250 Kč and a 360-hour pass (15 days) 280 Kč.

Residents usually have long-term passes valid for a month or more, available at the DP windows and at the Karlovo náměstí metro station. You will need a recent passport photo and some ID. Long-term passes cost 420 Kč for one month, 1,150 Kč for three months and 3,800 Kč for a year and are used in conjunction with coupons rather than stamping.

THE METRO

The Prague metro network, with a total length of 43.6 kilometres (27 miles) running between 48 stations along three lines, is a scaled-down copy of the grandiose Moscow metro. The stations are well lit and clearly signposted; trains are clean and frequent. A digital clock on each platform informs you of the time elapsed since the last train came along (admittedly the due time of the next arrival would be more useful).

The Prague metro consists of three lines: the green Line A (Skalka-Dejvická); the yellow Line B (Černý most-Zličín); and the red Line C (Nádraží Holešovice-Háje). A fourth line is due to open sometime in the next decade.

Transfers (*přestup*) are possible at three stations: Muzeum (between the green Line A and the red Line C), Můstek (between the green Line A and the yellow Line B) and Florenc (between the yellow Line B and the red Line C). The metro runs from 5am to midnight daily. Trains come every two minutes at peak times, and every five to ten minutes off-peak.

For a metro map, *see p316*.

TRAMS

An electric *tramvaje* service began in Prague in 1891 and trams have been the preferred method of transport for most Praguers ever since.

Trams come every six to eight minutes at peak times and every ten to 15 minutes at other times. With the newer, boxier trams, you may find you need to press the green button to open the doors.

The best tram lines for seeing the city are the 22, which runs from the Castle to Národní třída and beyond, and the Historic Tram (the 91), which runs from the Výstaviště in Prague 7 through Malá Strana, across to the National Theatre, through Wenceslas Square, Náměstí Republiky and back to Prague 7. The Historic Tram runs on Saturdays, Sundays and holidays from Easter to the middle of November and leaves Výstaviště every hour from 2pm to 7pm. The ride takes 40 minutes, and tickets cost 20 Kč for adults and 10 Kč for children.

BUSES

Since 1925, *autobusy* in Prague have provided transport to places where no other public transport dares to go. They run from about 5am to midnight, after which ten night bus lines take over (*see below*). Buses run every five to 18 minutes during peak times, every 15 to 30 minutes at other times.

Bus infoline

1034 Czech-language only. **Open** 6am-8pm Mon-Fri; 8am-4pm Sat, Sun.

NIGHT TRAMS/BUSES

Night buses and trams run about every 40 minutes from midnight to about 4.30am. Every night tram (they all have numbers in the 50s) stops at Lazarská crossroads on Spálená. There's no central stop for night buses (501-512), but many stop at the top of Wenceslas Square (near

Muzeum metro) and around the corner from IP Pavlova metro. You can buy a guide to night transport – showing all lines, times and stations – at the DP information offices (*see above*) for about 10 Kč.

DISABLED ACCESS

There are lifts at the following metro stations: Dejvická, Skalka on the green Line A; Zličín, Stodůlky, Luka, Lužiny, Hůrka on the yellow Line B; Nádraží Holešovice, Hlavní nádraží, Florenc, IP Pavlova, Pankrác, Roztyly, Chodov, Opatov and Háje on the red Line C. At some, you'll need help to operate the lift.

There are two bus routes served only by kneeling buses. The 109B starts in Černý most and runs via Florenc, Náměstí Republiky and IP Pavlova to Jižní Město. The 118D runs from Zličín via Hradčanská, Náměstí Republiky and Nádraží Holešovice to Sídliště Ďáblice.

All of the newer, boxier trams also kneel, but there's no counting on when one is going to come along. You can find out which lines are using the newer cars at DP information offices (*see p271*).

FUNICULAR RAILWAY

The funicular (*lanovka*) runs for half a kilometre from the bottom of Petřín hill at Újezd (around the corner from the tram stop of the same name), stopping midway at Nebozizek (at the pricey restaurant of the same name) and continues to the top of Petřín hill. It runs every ten or 15 minutes between 9.15am and 8.45pm daily and costs 12 Kč for adults and 6 Kč for children. Passes are valid.

Taxis

The appalling reputation of Prague's taxi drivers has caused Prague City Hall to introduce strict guidelines.

Even so, the odds are high that you will still get ripped off. The drivers waiting at ranks in obvious tourist locations are generally crooks, so avoid them. Hail a moving cab or call one of the services listed below. Make sure that you are using an authorised taxi (it should be clearly marked, with registration numbers and fares printed on the doors and a black and white checked stripe along the side). If the driver doesn't turn on the meter, insist he does. If he won't, get out immediately or agree on a fee to your destination. Do neither, and the driver will likely demand a ruinous fare at the end of your journey – and maybe even resort to violence to collect it.

Ideally, your taxi experience should go something like this: the driver does not turn on the meter (*taxametr*) until you enter the cab. When he does, 30 or 25 Kč appears as the initial amount. While you are driving inside Prague, the rate is set at '1' and should never be more than 22 or 20 Kč per kilometre. When your ride is over, the driver gives you a receipt (*účet* or *paragon*). (If he doesn't you are theoretically not required to pay the fare.)

In reality, few drivers will provide a receipt unless you request one. Honest cabbies will then print one out on the agonisingly slow machine. Rip-off merchants will write you one out on a pad.

FARES
At the time of writing, the maximum taxi rates were 30 Kč (if you hail them) or 25 Kč (if you call them) plus 4 Kč a minute for waiting (because of a passenger request or traffic) and no more than 22Kč (if you stop them on the street) or 20 Kč (if you call them) per kilometre for normal rides. However, they were scheduled for a slight increase. There is no charge for extra passengers.

AAA
14014

ProfiTaxi
14035

Taxi complaints
Živnostenský úřad
Staroměstské náměstí 4, Staré Město, Prague 1 (2447 2149). Metro Staroměstská/17, 18 tram. **Map** p308 H3.

Taxi Trojická
Trojická 24, Prague 2 (2491 6666).

On foot

It is generally safe to walk anywhere in Prague at any time – using common sense and appropriate caution in the wee hours, of course. Prague does not (yet) have any 'bad' areas that you should avoid. Beware of bad drivers, though – they've only begrudgingly begun stopping for pedestrians at crossings because compelled to by a recent law.

By bicycle

Cycling in Prague is hellish. There are no bike lanes, drivers are oblivious to your presence and pedestrians yell at you if you ride on the pavement. Mountain bikes are best, as the wide wheels shouldn't get stuck in the tram tracks. Prague does, however, have acres of parkland inside and outside the centre. On public transport, bicycles are allowed in the last car of metro trains only, and your bike is expected to purchase and stamp its own 6 Kč ticket.

By boat

The Prague Steamship Company had a monopoly on river traffic way back in 1865 – and still provides most boat services on the river today. You'll find them, and other companies plying sightseeing and booze cruises, and rowing boats for hire, along the right bank of the Vltava.

Prague Steamship Company
Pražská paroplavební služba
Rašinovo nábřeží, Nové Město, Prague 2 (2493 0017/www.paro plavba.cz). Metro Karlovo náměstí/3, 16, 17 tram. **Map** p310 G9.

Driving

The worst driving days are Friday and Sunday, when people who don't know the difference between the clutch and the brake pack their families into old Škodas for a weekend trip to their summer cottage. Czechs tend to stop in the middle of junctions on a red light and traffic has become horrendous in the city centre as incomes and car ownership have risen steeply.

RULES OF THE ROAD
Unless you have a Czech residence permit you'll need an international driving licence (ask a motoring organisation in your home country, such as the AA or AAA, how to apply).

Traffic regulations in the Czech Republic are similar to those in most European countries. There is zero tolerance for drinking and driving, though – drivers are not allowed to drink any alcohol at all; ditto for drugs. Use of seat belts is required in the front and – if the car is equipped with them – the back seat (though most Czechs will laugh at your faintheartedness if you buckle up). Children under 12 may not ride in the seat next to the driver and small children must be in approved safety seats. Trams, which follow different traffic lights to cars, always have the right of way. You must stop behind trams when passengers are getting on and off at a stop where there is no island, and you should avoid driving on tram tracks unless the road offers no alternative.

The speed limits for cars and buses are 90 kph (56 miles per hour) on roads, 130kph (81,25 miles per hour) on motorways and 50kph (31,25 miles per hour) in villages and towns.

Motorcyclists and their passengers must wear helmets and eyegear, and the speed limit for motorcycles is 90 kilometres (56 miles) per hour on roads and motorways and 50 kilometres (31.25 miles) per hour in villages and towns.

You are required to notify the police of any accident involving casualties or serious damage to a car. If you are driving your own car, you will need to have international proof of insurance (known as a Green Card; contact your motoring organisation) and pay an annual toll for using the Czech roads. If you rent a car, insurance and toll should be taken care of for you. Otherwise the toll sticker – which should be displayed on the windscreen – is 100 Kč for 10 days, 200 Kč for a month or 800 Kč for a year for cars. It can be bought at post offices, most border crossing points and petrol stations.

PETROL AND SERVICE

Leaded fuel (octane 90) is called Special, leaded fuel (octane 96) is known as Super and unleaded fuel (95D) is called Natural. Super Plus 98 and diesel fuel are also widely available. A booklet listing all the petrol and service stations (and some car parks) in Prague is available from PIS offices (see p289). Many service stations open 24 hours a day.

PARKING

Parking can be a nightmare. Watch out for special zones reserved for area residents and businesses. If you park illegally, your car can be towed away (call 158 to get it back) or clamped and cost you around 1,000 Kč to retrieve, more if there's a delay. If you're new in town, the best option is to use a car park, ideally one that has 24-hour security.

PARKING METERS

Parking meters dispense tickets for coins. Place them face up on the dashboard, visible through the windscreen.

Streets in Prague 1 are separated into three types of parking. Blue zones are reserved for local residents and companies. Orange zones are for stops of up to two hours and cost a minimum of 10 Kč for 15 minutes and 40 Kč for one hour; and green zones are for stays of up to six hours and cost cost 15 Kč for 30 minutes, 30 Kč for an hour and 120 Kč for six hours. Ignore the restrictions at your peril.

CAR HIRE

Renting a car can be pretty expensive in Prague, with many Western firms charging higher rates than they would back home. It is definitely worth shopping around, as many small local firms charge far less than the big boys. When renting a car, be sure to bring your international driving licence, passport and credit card with you. The agency should provide you with a green insurance card that you will be asked for if you are stopped by police or drive across the border. Arrange your rental a few days in advance to be sure that you get the car you want.

In addition to the places listed below, American Express (see p284) and Čedok (see p289) arrange car rental.

A Rent Car

Washingtonova 9, Nové Město, Prague 1 (4173 1793). Metro Muzeum/11 tram. **Open** 7am-7pm daily. **Rates** 2,360 Kč-4,400 Kč per day. **Credit** AmEx, DC, MC, V. **Map** p309 L5.
Branches: Ruzyně Airport, Prague 6 (2011 4370/2428 1053); Milevská 2, Prague 4 (4173 1618).

Avis

Klimentská 46, Staré Město, Prague 1 (2185 1225-6/fax 2185 1229). Metro Florenc/3, 8 tram. **Open** 7am-7pm Mon-Fri; 8am-12.30pm, 1pm-4.30pm Sat, Sun. **Rates** from 1,630

Kč per day. **Credit** AmEx, DC, MC, V. **Map** p309 M1.
Branch: Ruzyně Airport, Prague 6 (2011 4270/3536 2420).

Budget

Čistovická 100, Řepy, Prague 6 (302 5713/3530 1152/www. budget.cz). Tram 8, 22. **Open** 8am-4.30pm Mon-Fri. **Rates** from 900 Kč per day. **Credit** AmEx, DC, MC, V. **Map** p308 H1.
Branches: Ruzyně Airport, Prague 6 (2011 3253); Hotel Intercontinental, Staré Město, Prague 1 (231 9595).

European Inter Rent/ National Car Rental

Pařížská 28, Staré Město, Prague 1 (2481 0515/2481 1290). Metro Staroměstská/17, 18 tram. **Open** 8am-8pm daily. **Rates** from 2,700 Kč per day. **Credit** AmEx, DC, MC, V. Map p308 H2.
Branches in most of the major cities in the Czech Republic.

Hertz

Karlovo náměstí 28, Nové Město, Prague 2 (2223 1010/www. hertz.cz). Metro Karlovo náměstí/3, 4, 6, 14, 16, 18, 22, 24, 34 tram. **Open** 8am-8pm daily. **Rates** from 2,300 Kč per day; 4,200 Kč for 2 days. **Credit** AmEx, DC, MC, V. **Map** p310 H7.
Branches: Ruzyně Airport, Prague 6 (2011 4340); Hotel Diplomat, Evropská 15, Prague 6 (2439 4174).

Ren Auto

Černá růže Na příkopě 12, Staré Město, Prague 1 (2101 4630/0602 339 902). Metro Můstek/3, 9, 14, 24 tram. **Open** 8am-8pm daily. **Rates** from 1,500 Kč per day. **Credit** AmEx, DC, MC, V. **Map** p309 K4.
The best option for a cheap and reliable Škoda.

Czech motoring clubs

Central Automobile Club Prague

Ústřední automotoklub
Na strži 9, Michle, Prague 4 (6110 4111). **Open** 8am-4pm Mon-Fri. **No credit cards.**
Call 1230 or 6122 0220 (Renault Assistance) for the 'Yellow Angel' 24-hour emergency road service.

Autoklub Bohemia Assistance

Autoklub České republiky
Opletalova 29, Nové Město, Prague 1 (2423 0506/2224 1257). **Open** 8am-6pm Mon-Fri; 8am-noon Sat. **No credit cards.**
Call 1240 or 6619 3247 for 'ABA' 24-hour, seven-day-a-week emergency road service.

Resources A-Z

Addresses

Czech buildings have two numbers posted on them, one in red, which is used in city records only, and one in blue, which denotes the address used for letters and callers (and is the one used in this guide). The street name comes first, followed by the street number, then, on a new line, a district code and district number, followed by the country, thus:

Jan Novak
Kaprova 10
11 000 Praha 1
Czech Republic

Age restrictions

The legal age for driving in the Czech republic is 18, as it is for drinking and smoking, though it's virtually unheard of for clubs, bars and shops to ask for proof of age. The age of sexual consent for both straights and gays is 15.

Attitude & etiquette

Praguers sometimes seem stand-offish at first, as people do in many cities, especially in the service sector. But Czechs will quickly warm to you if you attempt to speak even a word or two of their language. Generally speaking there's a culture of shyness and a tradition of avoiding confrontation at all costs, and Czechs are understated to say the least about expressing happiness. To fling a few more generalisations into the mix, they tend to melt at the sight of children and dogs, are sexually liberal, deeply reverent about Czech beer and the country itself and fiscally and gastronomically conservative.

Business services

Resources & organisations

British Embassy Commercial Section
Na příkopě 21, Nové Město, Prague 1 (2224 0021/fax 2224 3622/www.britain.cz). Metro Můstek/3, 9, 14, 24 tram. **Open** 9am-noon, 2pm-5pm Mon-Fri. **Map** p309 K4.

Czechinvest
Štěpánská 15, Nové Město, Prague 2 (9634 2500/fax 9634 2502). Metro Můstek/3, 9, 14, 24 tram. **Open** 8am-4.30pm Mon-Fri. **Map** p309 L5. This Czech government agency encourages large-scale direct foreign investment and assists in joint ventures. Staff can research Czech contacts in fields of interest.

Economic Chamber of the Czech Republic
Hospodářská komora ČR Seifertova 22, Žižkov, Prague 3 (2409 6111/fax 2409 6221/info@komora.cz/ www.komora.cz). Metro Hlavní nádraží, then 5, 9, 26 tram. **Open** 8am-4pm Mon-Fri. **Map** p313 B1. Provides background information on Czech industrial sectors, companies and economic trends and establishes trade contacts.

Enterprise Ireland
Tržiště 13, Malá Strana, Prague 1 (5753 1617/fax 5753 2224). Metro Malostranská/12, 22 tram. **Open** 9am-1pm, 2-5pm Mon-Fri. **Map** p307 D3.

Prague Stock Exchange (PX)
Rybná 14, Staré Město, Prague 1 (2183 1111/www.pse.cz). Metro Náměstí Republiky/5, 8, 14 tram. **Open** 8am-4.30pm Mon-Fri. **Map** p309 K3. PX trades about 50 companies in its top-tier category. The big banks are among several dozen brokerages that can place orders. Liquidity is good, though insider trading has been a problem in the past.

US Embassy Foreign Commercial Service
Tržiště 15, Malá Strana, Prague 1 (5753 1162/fax 5753 1165). Metro Malostranská/12, 22 tram. **Open** 8am-4.30pm Mon-Fri. **Map** p307 D3.

Banking

Anyone can open a bank account in the Czech Republic, although some banks will require you to pay in a minimum deposit. Corporate bank accounts require special paperwork. Banks generally charge high fees and current accounts do not pay interest. Most banks have some English-speaking staff. Service is improving, but still expect long queues, short opening hours and lots of burdensome paperwork – even on relatively simple transactions. Czech banks usually cater to individual account holders, while international banks are largely geared to corporate accounts, but usually offer at least some traditional banking services. The five main Czech banks are Česká spořitelna (ČS), Československá obchodní banka (ČSOB), Komerční banka (KB), HVB Bank and Živnostenská banka, all of which provide a similar range of services.

Česká spořitelna
Rytířská 29, Staré Město, Prague 1, (2410 1111). Metro Můstek/3, 9, 14, 24 tram. **Open** 9am-5pm Mon-Thur; 9am-4pm Fri. **Map** p308 J4. Geared toward domestic savings accounts. Operates a large cashpoint (ATM) network throughout the city. **Branch:** Václavské náměstí 16, Prague 1 (2440 1111).

Bank Austria
Revoluční 15, Staré Město, Prague 1, (2285 4114). Metro Náměstí Republiky. **Open** 8.30am-noon, 1-4.30pm Mon-Thur; 8.30am-2pm Fri. **Map** p309 K2.

Citibank
Evropská 178, Dejvice, Prague 6 (2430 4111/www.citibank.cz). Tram 20, 26. **Open** 8.30am-5pm Mon-Fri.

Hypobank
Štěpánská 27, Nové Město, Prague 1 (2209 1911). Metro Můstek/3, 9, 14, 24 tram. **Open** 9am-noon, 1-4pm Mon-Thur; 9am-12.30pm Fri. **Map** p311 K6.

Directory

Hypobank offers a full range of banking services in a growing number of branches in Prague and around the country.

Accounting firms

The 'Big Six' international accounting firms are well established in Prague and can offer a full range of services. There are also hundreds of local companies which offer basic book-keeping and payroll services.

PriceWaterhouse Coopers

Kateřinská 40, Prague 2 (5115 1111/www.pwcglobal.com). Metro I.P.Pavlova/6, 10, 11, 22, 23 tram. **Open** 9am-5pm Mon-Fri. **Map** p311 K8.
Accounting specialists whose auditors have a good reputation both internationally and in Prague.

Deloitte & Touche

Týn 4, Staré Město, Prague 1 (2489 5500). Metro Náměstí Republiky/5, 8, 14 tram. **Open** 9am-5pm Mon-Fri. **Map** p308 J3.

KPMG

Jana Masaryka 12, Vinohrady, Prague 2 (2212 3111). Metro Náměstí Míru/4, 16, 22, 23, 34 tram. **Open** 9am-5pm Mon-Fri. **Map** p311 M10.
Smaller and more personal than the other agencies, KPMG is known particularly for its financial planning and technical expertise.

Computer rental & leasing

For repairs/supplies, *see p167.*

APS

Opletalova 33, Nové Město, Prague 1 (2421 5147/www.aps.cz). Metro Hlavní nádraží/5, 9, 11, 26 tram. **Open** 9am-1.30pm, 2-5pm Mon-Fri. **Credit** MC, V. **Map** p309 L4.
Flexible PC leasing options.

MacSource/ CompuSource

Bělehradská 68, Nové Město, Prague 2 (2251 5455/fax 2251 5456). Metro I P Pavlova/6, 11 tram. **Open** 9am-5pm Mon-Fri. **Credit** AmEx, MC, V. **Map** p311 L10.
Both PC and Macintosh equipment are available for leasing and rental, both short and long term.

Couriers/messengers

DHL

Aviatická 1048/12, Ruzyně Airport, Prague 6 (0800 103 000 toll-free/2030 0111/www.dhl.cz). **Telephone bookings** 24 hrs daily. **Credit** AmEx, MC, V.
Offers a daily pick-up service until 6pm on weekdays, 3pm on Saturdays.

Messenger Service

Patočkova 3, Dejvice, Prague 6 (2040 0000). Tram 2, 18. **Telephone bookings** 24 hrs daily. **No credit cards.**
Cycle couriers. One-hour collection and two-hour delivery on local jobs. Also delivers outside Prague.

FedEx

Olbrachtova 1, Prague 4 (4400 2200/www.fedex.com). Metro Budějovická. **Telephone bookings** 8am-7.30pm Mon-Fri; 8am-1pm Sat. **Credit** AmEx, MC, V.

Estate agents

Finding reasonably priced and adequate office space can be challenging. Estate agents tend to push expensive properties to maximise their commission. Make sure that any space has adequate (ie modern) phone lines and isn't due for noisy or disruptive repairs. If parking is important, choose a space out of the centre.

Apollo

Záhřebská 33, Vinohrady, Prague 2 (2151 1100). Metro Náměstí Míru/4, 16, 22, 23, 34 tram. **Open** 9am-5.30pm Mon-Fri. **Map** p311 M9.
Lease and sale of commercial and private real estate. Provides financial and development consulting.

Nexus

Belgická 36, Vinohrady, Prague 2 (2251 3419). Metro Náměstí Míru/4, 16, 22, 23, 34 tram. **Open** 9am-5.30pm Mon-Fri. **Map** p311 M9.
Serves small and medium-sized businesses.

Interpreting & translating

Prague has dozens of translation companies, with most offering services in all the major European languages

along with many non-European languages. Translation rates are usually determined by the page (there are reckoned to be 30 lines per page at 60 characters per line).

A-Z Lingua

Politických vězňů 14, Nové Město, Prague 1 (2423 4893). Metro Můstek/3, 9, 11, 14, 24 tram. **Map** p309 L5.
Translations in many languages.

Interlingua

Spálená 17, Nové Město, Prague 1 (2490 9250/www.interlingua.cz). Metro Národní třída/6, 9, 17, 18, 22, 23 tram. **Map** p310 H6.
Specialises in legal and financial documents.

Law firms

There are dozens of local and international law firms that can help establish a company and provide the standard range of legal services. Local firms tend to have a better grasp of the more arcane elements of Czech law, while international firms offer better linguistic skills and more polish (at a much higher price). For a referral to a local lawyer, contact the Czech Chamber of Commercial Lawyers.

Czech Chamber of Commercial Lawyers

Senovážné náměstí 23, Nové Město, Prague 1 (2414 2457). Metro Náměstí Republiky/5, 8, 14 tram. **Open** 8am-4pm Mon-Thur; 8am-3pm Fri. **Map** p309 L4.

Altheimer & Gray

Platnéřská 4, Staré Město, Prague 1 (2481 2782). Metro Staroměstská/17, 18 tram. **Open** 8am-7pm Mon-Fri. **Map** p308 H3.
Offers advice on privatisation, acquisitions and foreign investment.

Cameron McKenna

Karolíny Světlé 25, Prague 1 (9679 8111/fax 2109 8000). Metro Národní třída or Můstek/6, 9, 17, 18, 22, 23 tram. **Open** 9.30am-6pm Mon-Fri. **Map** p308 G5.
Cameron McKenna claims to have the largest network of law offices in Central Europe.

Čermák, Hořejš & Myslil

Národní třída 32, Nové Město, Prague 1 (9616 7401). Metro Národní třída/6, 9, 17, 18, 22, 23 tram. **Open** *9am-5pm Mon-Fri.* **Map** *p308 H5.*
Local firm specialising in patent and other types of corporate law.

Office hire

Business Centrum Chronos

Václavské náměstí 66 (entrance at Mezibranská 23), Nové Město, Prague 1 (2221 0291/9634 8111). Metro Muzeum/11 tram. **Open** *8am-6pm Mon-Fri.* **Map** *p311 K6.*
Offers temporary office space, phone services and secretarial help.

Regus

Klimentská 46, Staré Město, Prague 1 (2185 2100). Metro Náměstí Republiky/5, 8, 14 tram. **Open** *9am-6pm Mon-Fri.* **Map** *p309 L1.*
Can provide short-term offices and conference rooms, as well as access to the internet and email.

Photocopying

See p179.

Recruitment agencies

AYS

Krakovská 7, Nové Město, Prague 1 (2221 0013/fax 2221 0039/www.ays.cz). Metro Muzeum/11 tram. **Open** *8.30am-5pm Mon-Fri.* **Map** *p311 J7.*
Specialises in secretarial and administrative support.

Helmut Neumann International

Národní třída 10, Nové Město, Prague 1 (2495 1530/www.neumann-inter.com). Metro Národní třída/6, 9, 17, 18, 22, 23 tram. **Open** *8am-6pm Mon-Thur; 8am-4pm Fri.* **Map** *p308 H5.*
One of several international head-hunting agencies. Fills positions in all sectors of the economy.

Consumer

There is a Czech Office of Consumer Protection, but it doesn't have English-speaking services or a hotline and has been largely ineffective in any case, so it's best to adopt a philosophy of Buyer Beware.

Shops may allow you to exchange faulty goods in exchange but are not generally willing to refund money.

Customs

There are no restrictions on the import and export of Czech currency, but if you're carrying more than 350,000 Kč out of the country, you must declare it at customs. The allowances for importing goods are:
● 200 cigarettes or 100 cigars at max. 3g each or 250g of tobacco;
● 1 litre of liquor or spirits and 2 litres of wine;
● Medicine in any amount for your own needs.
    If you want to export an antique, you must have a certificate stating that it is not important to Czech cultural heritage: ask when you purchase. Every once in a while, and usually without warning or much reason, EC countries limit the import of some Czech foodstuffs – even for personal consumption.

Customs Office

Celní ředitelství pro Prahu a Středočeský kraj Washingtonova 11, Nové Město, Prague 1 (6133 4201/www.cs.mfcr.cz). Metro Muzeum/11 tram. **Open** *7am-5pm Mon-Wed; 7am-3pm Tue, Thur, Fri.* **Map** *p311 L6.*
Branch: Ruzyně Airport, Prague 6 (2011 4380).

Disabled access

According to the law, all buildings constructed after 1994 must be wheelchair-friendly. Reconstructed buildings, however, need not provide wheelchair access, though many do voluntarily. Even so, it is no picnic to be in Prague in a wheelchair. There are few ramps. Most hotels provide no wheelchair access and only five railway stations in the entire country are wheelchair-friendly. The guidebook *Accessible Prague*

(Přístupná Praha), available from the Prague Wheelchair Association (*see below*), contains maps of hotels, toilets, restaurants, galleries and theatres that are wheelchair-friendly. For travel information for the disabled, *see p272.*

Prague Wheelchair Association

Pražská organizace vozíčkářů Centre for Independent Living (Centrum samostatného života), Benediktská 6, Staré Město, Prague 1 (2482 7210/ www.pov.cz). Metro Náměstí Republiky/5, 8, 14 tram. **Open** *9am-4pm Mon-Fri.* **Map** *p309 K2.*
This organisation is run by the disabled for the disabled. In addition to its *Accessible Prague* guidebook, it provides helpers and operates a taxi service and an airport pick-up service for the disabled. Service is limited and should be ordered as far in advance as possible. It can also rent wheelchairs if people have any problem with their own.

Electricity

Electricity is 220 volts with two-pin plugs almost everywhere. Bring continental adaptors or converters with you, as they are expensive here when they are available at all.

Embassies

All embassies and consulates are closed on Czech holidays (*see p290*) as well as their own national holidays. For other embassies, you will need to consult the *Zlaté stránky* (Yellow Pages) under 'Zastupitelské úřady'.

American Embassy

Tržiště 15, Malá Strana, Prague 1 (5753 0663/emergency number 5753 2716/www.usembassy.cz). Metro Malostranská/12, 22 tram. **Open** *8am-noon Mon-Fri.* **Map** *p307 D3.*

Australian Trade Commission & Consulate

Klimentská 10, Nové Město, Prague 1 (51018350). Metro Náměstí Republiky/5, 8, 14 tram. **Open** *8.30am-1pm, 2-5pm Mon-Fri.* **Map** *p309 M1.*

British Embassy

Thunovská 14, Malá Strana, Prague 1 (5753 0278/duty officer 0602 217 700). Metro Malostranská/12, 22 tram. **Open** 8.30am-noon Mon-Fri; telephone enquiries 2-5pm Mon-Fri. **Map** p307 D3.

Canadian Embassy

Mickiewiczova 6, Dejvice, Prague 6 (7210 1800/fax 7210 1890). Metro Hradčanská/18, 22 tram. **Open** 8.30am-12.30pm Mon-Fri; 8.30-10.30am Mon-Thur to apply for a visa to Canada; 2.30-4pm Mon-Thur to obtain a visa to Canada. **Map** p312 A3.

Emergencies

All numbers are toll-free.

First aid	155
Czech police	158
Fire	150

Health

Prague isn't a very healthy place to live. The Czech diet is fatty, pork-laden and low on fresh vegetables. The Czechs top world beer-consumption charts and are unrepentant smokers. The city also has serious smog problems and an archaic public sanitation system to contend with.

All of which makes Prague a great place for hypochondriacs. The damp climate creates a haven for various moulds that can be hell for anyone with allergies. Salmonella thrives in the Czech's favourite lunch item, mayonnaise meat salads that sit out for hours.

But if you do get ill, the chronically underfunded socialised healthcare system will undoubtedly soon have you feeling worse. If you have health insurance, the doctors will try to rack up points for the care they give – sometimes overdoing it – which they redeem for money from the health insurance companies. In general, if you pay cash however (which is universally accepted), you'll get far better treatment than the locals who must rely on the state system.

GENERAL HEALTHCARE

Medical facilities are usually open from 7.15am to 6pm on weekdays only. It's usually best for expats to find a GP (*rodinný* or *praktický lékař*), dentist (*zubní lékař*) and pediatrician (*dětský lékař*) close to their home or workplace. Many Czech doctors will speak English or German, especially at larger facilities like hospitals (*nemocnice*) and medical centres (*poliklinika*).

Emergency

First Medical Clinic of Prague

Tylovo náměstí 3/15, Nové Město, Prague 2 (2425 1319/emergency 0603 555 006/ppz-fmc@mbox. vol.cz). Metro IP Pavlova/4, 6, 22, 34 tram. **Credit** AmEx, MC, V. **Open** 7am-7pm Mon-Fri; 9-11am Sat. **Map** p311 L8.
Highly recommended, with professional international staff, First Medical honours Central Health Insurance Office temporary insurance (*see p278*).

Motol Hospital

Fakultní nemocnice v Motole *V úvalu 84, Smíchov, Prague 5 (2443 3681/2443 1111/emergency 2443 1007-8/155 toll-free). Metro Hradčanská, then 108, 174 bus.* **Open** 24 hours daily. **Credit** AmEx, MC, V.
Emergency treatment, plus a hospital department dedicated to care of foreigners.

Na Homolce Hospital

Nemocnice Na Homolce *Roentgenova 2, Smíchov, Prague 5 (5727 1111, emergencies 5727 2191/ paediatrics 5727 2025/emergencies 5727 2043/www. homolka.cz). Tram 4, 7, 9/167 bus.* **Open** *Emergency* 24 hours daily. *Pediatric department* 8am-4pm daily. **Credit** AmEx, MC, V.
Provides English-speaking doctors and 24-hour emergency service. Care can be excellent but given the state of the Czech public healthcare system, a private clinic is more advisable. Home visits are possible if needed.

Helplines & crisis centres

Helplines generally run around the clock, but you have a better chance of catching an English-speaker if you call during regular office hours. For AIDS crisis helplines, *see p207*.

Alcoholics Anonymous (AA)

Na Poříčí 16, Nové Město, Prague 1 (2481 8247). Metro Florenc or Náměstí Republiky/ 5, 8, 14 tram. **Sessions** at 5.30pm daily. **Map** p309 M2.
Twelve-step programmes. Anyone with alcohol problems is welcome to call or attend. English spoken.

Crisis Intervention Centre

Centrum krizové intervence – Psychiatrická léčebna Bohnice. *Ústavní 91, Prague 8 (8401 6666). Metro Nádraží Holešovice, then 102, 177, 200 bus.* **Open** 24 hours daily.
The biggest and best-equipped mental health facility in Prague. Runs lots of outreach programmes.

Drop In

Karolíny Světlé 18, Staré Město, Prague 1 (tel/fax 2222 1431/ dropin@ecn.cz). Metro Národní třída/6, 9, 17, 18, 22, 23 tram. **Open** 9am-5.30pm Mon-Thur; 9am-4pm Fri. **Map** p308 G5.
Focusing on problems related to drug addiction, including HIV testing and counselling, this is an informal clinic. Call or just drop in 24 hours a day.

Non-emergency clinics

First Medical Clinic of Prague

Tylovo náměstí, 3/15 Nové Město, Prague 2 (2425 1319/emergency 0603 555 006/ppz-fmc@ mbox.vol.cz). Metro IP Pavlova/4, 6, 16, 22, 34 tram. **Open** 7am-7pm Mon-Fri; 9-11am Sat. **Credit** AmEx, MC, V. **Map** p311 L8.

Motol Hospital

Fakultní nemocnice v Motole *V úvalu 84, Motol, Prague 5 (general information 2443 1111/ foreigners' department 2443 3681-2/emergency 2443 1007-8/155 toll-free). Metro Hradčanská, then 108, 174 bus.* **Open** 24 hours daily. **Credit** AmEx, MC, V.

Pharmacies

Many central pharmacies (*lékárna* or *apothéka*) have been doing business in exactly the same place for centuries and have gorgeous period interiors that are worth seeking out even if you're bursting with health.

Over-the-counter medicines are only available from pharmacies, which are usually open from 7.30am to 6pm on weekdays, though some operate extended hours. All pharmacies are supposed to post directions to the nearest 24-hour pharmacy in their window, though this information will be in Czech. Ring the bell for after-hours service, for which there will usually be a surcharge of approximately 30 Kč added to your bill.

24-hour pharmacies
Belgická 37, Vinohrady, Prague 2 (2251 9731). Metro Náměstí Míru/4, 16, 22, 23, 34 tram. **Map** p311 M9.
Štefánikova 6, Smíchov, Prague 5 (5732 0918). Metro Anděl/6, 7, 12, 14 tram.

Women's health

Dr Kateřina Bittmanová
Mánesova 64, Vinohrady, Prague 2 (office 2272 4592/0603 551 393/home 7293 6895). Metro Jiřího z Poděbrad/11 tram. **Open** on 24 hr call. **Map** p313 B3.
Dr Bittmanová speaks fluent English. She runs a friendly private practice and is on call 24 hours a day. Her fee for a general examination is 900 Kč; a smear test costs an additional 450 Kč.

Bulovka Hospital
Budínova 2, Libeň, Prague 8 (6608 3239/6608 3240). Tram 12, 14. **Open** 24-hours daily.
Housed within a huge state hospital complex, the privately run MEDA Clinic here is favoured by British and American women. Prices are reasonable, the gynaecologists speak English along with some other languages and the facilities are clean and professional. Contraception and HIV testing are available.

Podolí Hospital
Podolské nábřeží 157, Podolí, Prague 4 (4143 0349 ext 315). Tram 3, 16, 17. **Open** 24-hours daily.
The Podolí Hospital has obstetricians and gynaecologists who speak English. With modern facilities and neo-natal care, it handles most births to expats.

RMA Centrum
Dukelských hrdinů 17, Holešovice, Prague 7 (3337 8809). Tram 4, 12, 14, 17, 26. **Open** 7am-5pm daily. **Map** p312 D2.
An alternative medicine centre offering homeopathy, acupuncture and acupressure, traditional Chinese medicine and massage as well as gynaecology and mammography. There's a sauna and beauty salon.

ID

Spot checks of foreigners' documents are rare but not unheard of. A photocopy of your passport is usually sufficient. Bars and clubs virtually never ask for ID but you may be asked to show a passport if changing money.

Insurance

Foreigners are technically required to present documentary evidence of health insurance to enter the Czech Republic, though in practice it is rarely asked for. Nationals of a country with which the Republic has a reciprocal emergency healthcare agreement are exempt. These countries are the United Kingdom, Greece and most of the republic's former allies in the ex-Warsaw Pact countries. Visitors requiring a visa will have to provide proof of insurance with their application, however. The relevant bodies will issue visas to foreigners only for as long as they have valid health insurance.

Všeobecná zdravotní pojišťovna (Central Health Insurance), the main health insurance provider in the Czech Republic (*see below*), provides affordable policies to foreigners for urgent care coverage for up to a year.

Most state clinics and hospitals, and a few private ones, accept VZP.

If you have your own travel insurance, make sure that it covers Central and Eastern European countries.

Central Health Insurance Office (VZP)
Všeobecná zdravotní pojišťovna, Tyršova 7, Nové Město, Prague 2 (2197 2111/www.vzp.cz). Metro IP Pavlova/4, 16, 22 tram. **Open** 8am-6pm Mon-Thur; 8am-4pm Fri. **Map** p311 L9.
Known as the VZP, this is the main provider of health insurance in the Czech Republic, offering reasonable rates for short-term coverage, issued in terms of 30-day periods.
Branches: Na Perštýně 6, Staré Město, Prague 1 (2166 8111); Orlická 4, Žižkov, Prague 3 (2175 2121/fax 2175 2177).

Property insurance

Insuring personal belongings is always wise and should be arranged before leaving home.

Internet

Most of the upper end hotels provide dataports these days, and there are Internet cafés all over Prague. Try Jáma (*see p135*) or the Globe Bookstore & Coffeehouse (*p141*).

If you have access to a modem line and a laptop, ask your ISP whether it has a Prague dial-in or a reciprocal arrangement with a local provider. Alternatively, if you are a frequent traveller or plan on a long stay, you could set up an account with a local ISP. The number of companies offering internet access here is growing and services are improving al the time. The standard rate for individual accounts, usually including unlimited browsing time and email but not call charges, starts at about 500 Kč a month. Corporate and leased lines are also available and rates rise according to the connection speed and number of accounts.

The main ISPs in Prague are listed below. Alternatively, a list of Czech providers is held at the Czech-language search engine Seznam (dir.seznam.cz/Sluzby/Pocitacove_a_sitove/Poskytovatele_Internetu).

Directory

Telenor/Nextra

*V Celnici 10, Nové Město, Prague 1
(9615 9411/www.nextra.com/
hotline 0800 138 417 toll-free).
Metro Náměstí Republiky/5, 8, 14
tram.* **Open** 8am-5am Mon-Fri.
No credit cards. Map p309 L3.
Born as the humble Terminal Bar,
long since closed, the ISP side of the
business was bought up and went
corporate and is now Prague's
leading service provider. It offers
dial-up services, web hosting
and design. Standard rates and
generally friendly and reliable (but
occasionally rather flaky) service.

Language

The Czech language was exiled
from officialdom and literature
in favour of German for much
of the history of Bohemia until
the national revival in the
19th century. Today Czech is
spoken throughout Prague,
though most places of
business, at least in the centre,
should have some English-
speaking staff. German may
help you in speaking to older
Czechs, and many younger
ones speak Russian, which was
taught compulsorily in schools
before the Velvet Revolution.

Czech is a difficult but
rewarding language to learn in
that it helps penetrate the wall
put up by rather shy Czechs.
They invariably light up upon
hearing even an attempt at
their mother tongue by a
foreigner. For essential
vocabulary, *see p291*.

Left luggage

There are left luggage offices/
lockers at Hlavní nádraží and
Nádraží Holešovice stations
and Florenc bus station (for
all, *see pp246-7*).

Libraries

For a full list of Prague's
libraries, ask at the National
Library or look in the *Zlaté
stránky* (Yellow Pages) under
'knihovny'. Admission rules
vary – generally, you don't
need to register to use reading
rooms, but you do to borrow

books, and for this you'll need
your passport and sometimes a
document stating that you are
a student, teacher, researcher
or a resident of Prague. Most
libraries have restricted
opening hours or close during
July and August.

British Council

*Národní třída 10, Nové Město,
Prague 1 (2199 1111). Metro
Národní třída.* **Open** 9am-5pm
Mon-Fri. **Map** p308 H5.
The reading room is stocked with all
the major British newspapers and
magazines but the huge library of
English-language books has been
moved to the Městská knihovna, or
City Library. For flipping through
glossies, though, the light and airy
reading room is a boon, and there
are free Internet terminals. The
downstairs library is packed with
materials and aids for TEFL and
TESL teachers, but virtually no
literature. The video selection is
eclectic, and the free screenings
can be excellent.

City Library

*Městská knihovna v Praze
Mariánské náměstí 1 (2211 3338/
232 8208). Metro Staroměstská/17,
18 tram.* **Open** *July, Aug* 9am-7pm
Tue-Fri. *Sept-June* 9am-8pm Tue-Fri;
10am-5pm Sat. Closed mid-July-mid-
Aug. **Map** p308 H3.
The freshly renovated main branch
of the City Library is now spacious,
calm and state of the art. You'll
find an excellent English-language
literature section bolstered by a
new donation of 8,000 books and
magazines from the British Council.
An impressive music and audio
collections also awaits, along with
plenty of comfortable spaces for
studying, scribbling and flipping
through tomes. To borrow books
(if you are staying in the Czech
Republic less than 6 months) you
will need your passport and 1,000 Kč
for a cash deposit.

National Library

*Národní knihovna v Praze
Klementinum, Křižovnické
náměstí 4, Staré Město, Prague 1
(2166 3331/fax 2166 3261/www.
nkp.cz). Metro Staroměstská/17,
18 tram.* **Open** 9am-7pm Mon-Sat.
Map p308 G4.
A comprehensive collection of just
about everything ever published in
Czech and a reasonable international
selection, housed in a confusing
warren of occasionally gorgeous
halls. Hours vary depending on
which reading room you want to use.
You can take books out if you show
your passport and residence permit.

Lost property

Most railway stations have
a lost property office (*Ztráty
a nálezy*). If you lose your
passport, contact your
embassy (*see p277*).

Central Lost Property Office

*Karolíny Světlé 5, Staré Město,
Prague 1 (2423 5085). Metro
Národní třída/6, 9, 17, 18, 22
tram.* **Open** 8am-5.30pm Mon,
Wed; 8am-4pm Tue, Thur; 8am-2pm
Fri. **Map** p308 G5.

Media

Business/news publications (English)

Business Central Europe

A monthly economics and
business magazine from the
Economist. Covers the whole of
Central Europe and the former
Soviet Union with regular
stories on the Czech Republic.

Central European Business Weekly

Prague-based business weekly
with full coverage of Central
and Eastern Europe.

Central European Economic Review

A monthly regional overview
published by the *Wall Street
Journal* that tends to focus its
coverage on finance, banking
and capital markets.

The Fleet Sheet

A daily one-page digest of the
Czech press offering good
coverage of major political and
financial events. Sent out as a
fax each morning.

Newsline Radio Free Europe
www.rferl.org

Dry but highly informative
daily overview of events in
Eastern Europe and the former
Soviet Union. Produced in co-
operation with Prague-based
radio Free Europe/Radio

Liberty, Newsline's information is available as an email service or from RFE's comprehensive website.

Prague Business Journal
www.pbj.cz

Weekly business newspaper that focuses on Prague and the Czech Republic. Highly informative.

The Prague Tribune

Glossy, bilingual Czech-English monthly mag with an emphasis on business, social issues and features.

Radio Prague E-News
www.radio.cz

Czech state radio offers free email copy of daily news bulletins in English, Czech and other languages. Informative website with links to other internet-based info sources.

General interest (English)

New Presence

This is the English-language version of *Nová přítomnost*, a journal dating back to inter-war Bohemia that offers a liberal and stimulating selection of opinion writing, some translated from their original Czech, by both local and international writers. It's not easy to find, but still worth seeking out for an in-depth look at the Czech Republic. Try The Globe Bookstore & Coffeehouse (*see p167*) or Big Ben Bookshop (*see p165*).

Prague Insider
www.pragueinsider.com

The Insider is a free, witty and irreverent city magazine with a funky ethos, and excellent food, drink and nightlife coverage. Columns and reviews by local characters add further zing. Pick it up at free postcard racks in any expat bar or café. Published by the *Prague Business Journal*.

The Prague Pill
www.pill.cz

A free bi-weekly that provides good counterculture balance to the *Prague Post's* more traditional style, plus a refreshingly provocative and sassy attitude. Well-informed listings recommendations on nightlife, plus an English-language translation of the lead article in *Respekt*, the most aggresively critical Czech newspaper around. Pick one up at one of the expat bars and cafés like the Globe Bookstore & Coffeehouse (*see p141*) or Radost FX (*see p140*).

The Prague Post
www.praguepost.com

The principle English-language weekly in the Czech Republic has come a long way in recent years with in-depth features and intelligent cultural coverage that betters that of many papers in larger cities of the former eastern bloc. Useful events calendar, business and entertainment features, plus a lively opinions section. Editor-in-chief Alan Levy's self-promoting 'Prague Profile' column is loved by many and hated by many.

Transitions online
www.tol.cz

A fascinating internet-only magazine covering current events in Central and Eastern Europe, the Balkans, and the former Soviet Union. A Czech nonprofit magazine dedicated to strengthening independent journalism, Transitions Online is based in Prague and uses a network of locally based correspondents to provide unique, cross-regional analysis.

Czech newspapers

Blesk

The extremely popular *Blesk* ('Lightning') is a daily tabloid packed full of sensationalised news, celebrity scandals, UFO sightings and a smattering of busty page-three girls.

Hospodářské noviny

The Czech equivalent of the *Financial Times*, this respected daily covers capital markets, exchange rates and business deals. Required reading for Czech movers and shakers.

Lidové noviny

An underground dissident paper in the communist days, *Lidové noviny's* finest hour came in the the early 1990s. Today, the paper is still respected in some right-wing and intellectual circles, but commercialism has taken a toll.

Mladá fronta Dnes

A former communist paper, *Dnes* has been the country's leading serious newspaper for several years. It now offers fairly balanced domestic and international news, and a reasonable level of independent opinion. The reporting and editing, however, can be poor.

Právo

The former Communist Party newspaper (the name means 'Justice'; it used to be *Rudé Právo* – 'Red Justice') has become a respectable, left-leaning daily with an equally respectable circulation.

Respekt

A scrappy weekly paper, *Respekt* takes a close look at the good, the bad and the ugly effects of the Czech Republic's transformation to a market economy. Not only does it ask the questions other newspapers don't but it also has some cutting-edge cartoons.

Sport

Daily sports paper, and you don't need to speak Czech to figure out the results it publishes from home and abroad. Predictably heavy on European football, ice hockey and tennis; it also gives results from the NBA and NFL.

Directory

Czech periodicals

Cosmopolitan/Elle

Cosmopolitan fails to stand up against its Western counterparts, but Czech Elle successfully appeals to both teens and middle-aged women, with flashy fashion spreads and interviews.

Reflex

Reflex is a popular, low-rent style weekly with glossy format, some interesting editorial and some very boring design.

Živel

A cool cyberpunk mag with an interesting design and a sub-cultural editorial slant – like a cross between the *Face* and *Wired*. Hip, small circulation and more likely to be found in bookshops than at newsagents. Was quarterly but now only publishes irregularly.

Listings

Annonce

A classified ad sheet into which bargain-hunting Czechs delve to find good deals on second-hand washing machines, TVs, cars, etc. *Annonce* is also a good flat-hunting tool. Place your ad for free, then simply wait by the phone – it works.

Culture in Prague

An exhaustive monthly calendar of all categories of events held throughout Prague and the republic. Published mainly in Czech, it's also available in English at Wenceslas Square bookshops. Considerably easier to decode than *Kulturní přehled* (*see below*). Notoriously unreliable movie listings.

Do města

'Downtown' is a tall-format entertainment freesheet in Czech with English translations. It's good for weekly listings of galleries, cinemas, theatres and clubs. It comes out every Thursday, and you'll find it lying around in bars, cafés and clubs pretty much all around town.

Kulturní přehled

A thorough monthly listing of cultural events in Prague. It's in Czech only but it's not too hard to understand and gives schedules for the main cultural venues, including theatres, operas, museums, clubs and exhibitions.

Týdeník

A weekly guide to what's on TV. If you're looking for the occasional English-language movie with Czech subtitles, better to check the listings in the *Prague Post* (*see p281*).

Literary magazines

Though many have folded over the past few years, a whole pile of literary magazines is still published in Prague, in both Czech and English. You should be able to track down most of them at the Globe Bookstore & Coffeehouse (*see p167*) or Big Ben Bookshop (*see p165*). The Czech-language *Revolver Review*, supposedly published quarterly (but distinctly irregular), is a hefty periodical with *samizdat* (underground culture) roots. The RR presents new works by well-known authors along with lesser-known pieces by pet favourites such as Kafka. *Labyrint Revue*, a monthly magazine, and *Literární noviny*, a weekly, are the other two main Czech publications offering original writing and reviews of new work. *Labyrint* also has music and art reviews.

English publications tend to come and go. The best and most widely known is *Trafika*, a 'quarterly' – tending to lapse to an 'occasionally' – showcase for international writers. Although it has recently been out of action, *Trafika*'s editors now look to be reviving this early and respected pioneer.

The *Prague Review*, formerly the *Jáma Review*, is a slim quarterly of plays, prose and poetry from Czechs and Czech-based expats. Its editors – who have included such Czech literary heavyweights as Bohumil Hrabal, Ivan Klíma and Miroslav Holub – generously subtitle the volume 'Bohemia's journal of international literature'.

Optimism

A more-or-less monthly literary mag that's a forum for Prague's English-speaking expatriate community; its content ranges from the intriguing to hopelessly trite but it is genuinely open to young, unproven writers.

Foreign press

Foreign newspapers are available at various stalls on and around Wenceslas Square and at major hotels. The *International Guardian*, *International Herald Tribune* and the international *USA Today* are available on the day of publication. Most other papers arrive 24 hours later.

Television

ČT1/ČT2

There are two national public channels. ČT1 tries to compete with TV Nova, but is out of its depth financially. ČT2 serves up serious music (including lots on jazz greats), theatre and documentaries to the small percentage of the population that tunes in. ČT2 sometimes broadcasts English-language movies with Czech subtitles – Woody Allen flicks are popular, as are Monty Python classics. It also airs *Euronews*, an English-language pan-European programme, on weekdays at 8am and on weekends at 7am.

Prima TV

A Prague-based regional broadcaster that has been lamely following the lead of TV Nova but is slowly being revamped by new foreign partners from the West. The last resting place of (dubbed) US action serials.

TV Nova

One of the first private television stations in Eastern Europe. Initially funded by Ronald Lauder, son of Estée, Nova TV looks like US television with lots of old Hollywood movies and recycled sitcoms dubbed into Czech. Appallingly successful.

Radio

BBC World Service (101.1 FM)

English-language news on the hour plus regular BBC programming, with the occasional Czech and Slovak news broadcast. For 30 minutes a day at around teatime it transmits local Czech news in English, courtesy of Radio Prague.

Radio Free Europe

Prague is now the world headquarters for RFE. It still beams the same old faintly propagandist stuff to Romania, Ukraine and other former Soviet republics from its HQ at the former Czechoslovak Federal Assembly building, next to the National Museum.

Radio Kiss (98.0 FM); Radio Bonton (99.7 FM); Evropa 2 (88.2 FM)

Pop music, pop music and more pop music.

Radio 1 (91.9)

Excellent alternative music station that plays everything from Jimi Hendrix to techno. Evening calendar listings have everything the hip partygoer needs to know.

Radio Prague (92.6 FM & 102.7 FM)

Daily news in English, plus interviews, weather and traffic. Nothing too inspired, but this is a well-established station with some history behind it.

Money

CURRENCY

The currency of the Czech Republic is the *koruna českáor* or Czech crown (abbreviated as Kč). One crown equals 100 hellers (*haléřů*). Hellers come as small, light coins in denominations of 10, 20 and 50. There are also 1, 2, 5, 10, 20 and 50 Kč coins in circulation. Notes come in denominations of 20, 50, 100, 200, 500, 1,000, 2,000, and 5,000 Kč. At the time of going to press, the exchange rate was running at approximately 49.3 Kč to the pound, or around 34.3 Kč to the US dollar. It's obviously impossible to predict exchange rates, but recently they have been fluctuating, largely upwards, so it's probably wise only to convert only as much as you need in the short-term.

The crown was the first fully convertible currency in the former eastern bloc. A bizarre indicator of its viability is the number of convincing counterfeit Czech banknotes in circulation. If someone stops you in the street asking if you want to change money, it's a fair bet he'll be trying to offload dodgy notes – and a sure thing he's scamming.

CASH ECONOMY

The Czech Republic has long been a cash economy, and such conveniences as cash machines (ATMs), credit cards and cheques (travellers' cheques included) are not nearly as ubiquitous here as they are in EC countries or the US. However, the situation is changing fairly rapidly and, particularly in Prague, it's not difficult to find ATMs that will pay out cash on the major credit and charge card networks such as Maestro, Cirrus and Delta. Looks for the symbol that matches the one on your card and use your usual PIN number. Many classier shops, and restaurants, especially around Wenceslas Square and the Old Town, take credit cards and travellers' cheques in a major currency such as dollars or euros.

LOSS/THEFT

Komerční banka (*see p284*) is a local agent for MasterCard, Visa; call the numbers given in case of loss or theft. For lost/stolen AmEx cards, the number is 2280 0222, Diners Club 6731 4485 and to report missing travellers' cheques, it's 2280 0237 for American Express and 2110 5371 for Thomas Cook.

Banks & currency exchange

Exchange rates are usually the same all over, but banks take a lower commission (usually one to two per cent). Unfortunately, they are only open during business hours (usually 8am-5pm Monday to Friday).

Bureaux de change usually charge a higher commission for changing cash or travellers' cheques, although some (such as those at the Charles Bridge end of Karlova street) may only take one per cent.

Bear in mind that this means little if you're getting a poor exchange rate.

OPENING AN ACCOUNT

At some banks, such as ČSOB, there is no minimum requirement to open an account and foreign currency accounts are available without the high fees once charged.

MONEY TRANSFER

To get money fast, try the American Express office or, in the case of a serious

Directory

emergency, your embassy. The Na příkopě branch of ČSOB processes transfers faster than other Czech banks.

American Express
Václavské náměstí 56, Nové Město, Prague 1 (2421 9992). Metro Můstek or Muzeum/3, 9, 11, 14, 24 tram. **Open** 9am-7pm daily. **Map** p311 L6.
Cardholders can receive their mail and faxes here and have personal cheques cashed, but can't cash third-party cheques.

Československá obchodní banka (ČSOB)
Na příkopě 14, Nové Město, Prague 1 (2411 1111). Metro Můstek or Náměstí Republiky/3, 5, 9, 14, 24 tram. **Open** 8am-5pm Mon-Fri. **Map** p309 K4.
Specialises in international currency transactions and offers exceptionally professional service, if long waits for transfers from abroad.

Komerční banka
Na příkopě 33, Nové Město, Prague 1 (2243 2111/2424 8110). Metro Můstek or Náměstí Republiky/3, 5, 9, 14, 24 tram. **Open** 8am-5pm Mon-Fri. **Map** p309 K4.
The country's largest full-service bank, with a large network of branches throughout the country. The ATM network accepts international credit cards and is a MasterCard (Eurocard) and Visa agent. Its card emergency number is 2424 8110.

Živnostenská banka
Na příkopě 20, Nové Město, Prague 1 (2412 1111). Metro Můstek/3, 5, 9, 14, 24 tram. **Open** 8.30am-5pm Mon-Fri. **Map** p309 K4.
This old trading bank, which is housed in one of the most beautiful buildings in Prague, has long experience in working with foreign clients, and most staff speak a reasonable level of English.

Numbers

Dates are written in the British order, not the American: day, month, year.

When writing figures, Czechs put commas where Americans and Britons would put decimal points and vice versa, thus ten thousand Czech crowns is written as 10.000 Kč.

Opening hours

Standard opening hours for most shops and banks are from 8am or 9am to 5pm or 6pm Monday to Friday. Many shops are open a bit longer and from 9am to noon or 1pm on Saturday. Shops with extended hours are called *večerka* (open until 10pm or midnight) and 'non-stop' (open 24 hours daily). Outside the centre, most shops are closed on Sundays and holidays. Shops frequently close for a day or two for no apparent reason; some shops close for an hour or two at lunch; and some shops and many theatres close for a month's holiday in August. Most places have shorter opening hours in winter (starting September or October) and extended hours in summer (starting April or May). Castles and some other attractions are only open in summer.

Police & security

Police in the Czech Republic are not regarded as serious crimefighters or protectors of the public and are just barely considered keepers of law and order. Their past as pawns for the regime, combined with a present reputation for corruption, racism and incompetence, has prevented them from gaining much in the way of respect. If you are the victim of crime while in Prague, then don't expect much help – or even concern – from the local constabulary.

For emergencies, call 158. The main police station, at Na Perštýně and Bartolomějská, is open 24 hours daily. In theory, an English-speaking person should be on call to assist crime victims with making a report, but in practice any encounter with the Czech police is likely to be slow, unpleasant and ineffective.

LEGALITIES

You are expected to carry your passport or residence card at all times. If you have to deal with police, they are supposed to provide an interpreter for you. Buying or selling street drugs is illegal, and a controversial Czech drug law outlaws the possession of even small quantities. The legal drinking age is 18, but nobody here seems to pay any attention to this.

Prague's pickpockets concentrate in tourist areas like Wenceslas Square, Old Town Square and the Charles Bridge and are particularly fond of the Slavia and tram 22 from Malostranské náměstí to Prague Castle. Keep an eye on your handbag or wallet, especially in crowds and on public tranport. Seedier parts of Prague include some of Žižkov, parts of Smíchov, the park in front of Hlavní nádraží (the main train station), and the lower end of Wenceslas Square and upper end of Národní třída.

Post

Stamps are available from post offices, newsagents, tobacconists and most places where postcards are sold. Postcards as well as regular letters (up to 20 grams) cost 9 Kč within Europe and 14 Kč for airmail outside Europe. Packages should be wrapped in plain white or brown paper. Always use black or blue ink – never red, or, horrors, green – or a snippy clerk will refuse to accept your mail. Even oddly shaped postcards are known to have been refused by the rule-obsessed Czech Post.

Post offices are scattered all over Prague. Though they are being thoroughly modernised, many have different opening hours and offer varying degrees of service and all are confusing. Indeed, the system designating what's on offer at

Expatriate games

Prague's ever-flourishing expat scene, as it has been portrayed in countless magazines and documentaries, is something of a phenomenom, although the city's popularity may reflect more about the desire of foreign reporters to visit a mythologised Bohemia than it does about a slightly less sexy reality. Then again, there's clearly *something* that makes otherwise hardworking, responsible young foreigners miss their flights home so often. And there must be more to it than cheap beer, cheap sex, cheap rent and an impossibly beautiful Old European atmosphere. How long could that hold anyone's interest, after all...?

In the early 1990s media reports threw around estimates of some 30,000 expats living in Prague – though their sources for that statistic were a bit fuzzy. Only a fraction of that number ever registered with their home country's embassy in Prague, but even if the more likely 10,000 is correct, it represents a far higher proportion than any other former eastern bloc capital, and not a few Western ones.

Groups of beer-chugging artisans, scribblers and entrepreneurs have often been accorded the status of a social movement. Henry David Thoreau and his Bohemian crowd ensconsed themselves at B-Farm in the 1820s and struggled to create a Utopia as a stand against the tidal wave of industrialisation and conurbation of the day. Today's refugees from the Fast Food Nations started out with much the same agenda. The difference was that communism's failure at providing an egalitarian model society had already rendered Czechs, along with everyone else in the former Soviet sphere, deeply distrustful of Utopias.

So many expats turned quickly to making a buck instead. 'Queue jumping' has been put forward as one reason for all the foreigners living in Prague. Someone who works as a video shop clerk in, say, San Francisco, might, with a little opportunism, become manager of a film production company here (then leapfrog into the higher echelons of the industry back home). And then there's the confidence thing. Czechs are not known for their assertiveness, which sometimes means significant opportunities for Westerners with far fewer qualifications. Add to this the professional standards of an emerging market.... yes, the Wild East is truly a land of opportunity. That is, as long as you don't get caught up for long in trying to sort out a better society.

---

which window is perplexing, even for some Czechs.

The Main Post Office on Jindřišská in Nové Město, Prague 1, offers the most services, some available 24 hours a day. Fax, telegram and international phone services are in the annex around the corner at Politických vězňů 4. Some services, such as poste restante (general delivery) and EMS express mail are theoretically available at all post offices, but are much easier to use at the main office on Jindřišská.

You can buy special edition stamps and send mail overnight within the Czech Republic and within a few days to Europe and the rest of the world via EMS – a cheaper but less reliable service than commercial couriers.

PACKAGES

To send or collect restricted packages or items subject to tax or duty, you must go to the Customs Post Office (*see p286*). Bring your passport, residence permit and any other ID. For incoming packages, you will also need to pay duty and tax. The biggest queues at the Customs Post Office form between 11am and 1.30pm.

Outgoing packages should be wrapped in plain white or brown paper. If they weigh more than two kilogrammes (4.4 pounds), are valued upwards of 30,000 Kč or contain 'unusual contents' such as medicine or clothing, they must officially be cleared through the Customs Post Office, but in practice this is not usually necessary.

Uninsured packages of up to two kilos don't need to be declared and can be sent from any post office – they're treated as letters (250 Kč to the UK; 593 Kč to the US), and you don't need your passport. Up to four kilos and the consignment is treated as a package, but if you don't want to insure it, it doesn't usually need to be declared and can be sent from a post office (457 Kč-505 Kč to the UK; 715 Kč-881 Kč to the US). If the package is heavier or you would like to insure it, take it to the Customs Post Office and declare it. Take your passport.

USEFUL POSTAL VOCABULARY

letters: *příjem – výdej listovin.*
packages: *příjem – výdej balíčků* or *balíků*

money transactions: *platby*
stamps: *známky* – usually
at the window marked *Kolky
a ceniny*
special issue stamps:
filatelistický servis
registered mail: *doporučeně*

Main Post Office
Hlavní pošta
*Jindřišská 14, Nové Město, Prague 1
(2113 1445/2113 1111). Metro
Můstek/3, 9, 14, 24 tram.* **Open**
7am-8pm daily. **No credit cards.**
Map p309 K5.

Non-Stop Post Office
Masarykovo nádraží
*Hybernská 15, Nové Město, Prague 1
(2224 0271). Metro Náměstí
Republiky/5, 8, 14 tram.* **Open** 1am-
midnight daily. **Map** p309 L3.

Customs Post Office
Celní Pošta
*Plzeňská 139, Smíchov, Prague
5, (5701 9105). Metro Anděl, then
4, 7, 9 tram.* **Open** 7am-3pm Mon,
Tue, Thur, Fri; 7am-6pm Wed.
No credit cards.

Religion

Services in English are held at
only these churches:

Anglican Church of Prague
*Klimentská, Nové Město, Prague 1
(2231 0094). Metro Náměstí
Republiky/5, 8, 14 tram.* **Services**
11am Sun. **Map** p309 L4.

Church of St Thomas
*Josefská, Malá Strana, Prague 1.
Metro Náměstí Republiky.* **Services**
11am Sun (in English). **Map** p309 K3.
Catholic services.

International Baptist Church of Prague
*Vinohradská 68, Žižkov, Prague 3
(2425 4646). Metro Jiřího z
Poděbrad/11 tram.* **Service** 11am
Sun. **Map** p313 B3.

International Church of Prague
*Peroutkova 57, Smíchov, Prague 5
(www.volny.cz/jx-studio). Metro
Anděl, then bus 137 or 508.*
Services 10.30am Sun.

Prague Christian Fellowship
*Ječná 19 (entry at back of house),
Nové Město, Prague 2 (5753 0020/
2431 5613). Metro Karlovo Náměstí.*
Services 2pm Sun. **Map** p310 J8.

Smoking

Smoking is not allowed on
public transport in Prague but
that's about the only place
people don't light up. One or
two restaurants now have non-
smoking areas but by and
large people around you will
freely light up, even if they are
sharing the table with you at a
pub and you are eating a meal.

Study

Charles University

Founded in 1348 by King
Charles IV, Charles University
(Universita Karlova) is the
oldest university in Central
Europe, and the hub of
Prague's student activity.
Its heart is the Carolinum, a
Gothic building on Ovocný trh
near the Estates Theatre, home
to the administration offices.
Other university buildings are
scattered all over the city.

Several cash-hungry
faculties now run special
courses for foreigners.
Contact the relevant dean or
the International Relations
Office during the university
year (October to May) for
information on courses and
admissions procedures. It is
best to enquire in person at the
university as the staff can be
difficult to reach by phone.

Below is a selection of
popular offerings. For courses
outside Prague, contact the
British Council (*see p280*).

Charles University
*International Relations Office,
Universita Karlova, Rektorát,
Ovocný trh 3-5, Staré Město,
Prague 1 (2449 1310/fax
2422 9487/www.cuni.cz).
Metro Staroměstská or Můstek/3, 9,
14, 17, 18, 24 tram.* **Open** 9am-5pm
Mon-Fri. **Map** p308 J4.

FAMU
*Smetanovo nábřeží 2, Staré Město,
Prague 1 (2422 0955/fax 2423
0285). Metro Staroměstská or
Národní třída/6, 9, 17, 18, 22, 23
tram.* **Open** 9am-3pm Mon-Fri.
No credit cards. Map p308 G4.

Famous for turning out such Oscar-
winning directors as Miloš Forman,
Prague's foremost school of film, TV
and photography runs several
English courses under its Film
For Foreigners (3F) programme and
Cinema Studies, including summer
workshops (in cooperation with NY
University, Washington, Miami and
Boston), six-month and one-year
courses in aspects of film and TV
production and a BA in photography.

The Institute of Language & Professional Training
Ústav jazykové a odborné přípravy
*Universita Karlova, Vratislavova
10, Nové Město, Prague 2 (2499
0420/fax 2499 0440/www.
cuni.cz/cuni/ujop). Metro Karlovo
náměstí/3, 16, 17, 21 tram.*
Fees one-year course of training
for future study at universities
120,000 Kč; one-year course of
Czech 94,300 Kč; 6-week session
15,000 Kč; intensive semester
46,000 Kč; individual lesson 530 Kč
for 45 minutes. **Open** *Oct-Dec* Tue-
Thur 10am-2pm. *Feb-May* Tue-Thur
10am-2pm. **No credit cards.**
Aimed at preparing foreign nationals
who want to embark on degree
courses at Czech universities, this
branch of Charles University offers
Czech-language training in the form
of a one-year course (ie 10 months) or
intensive Czech language courses for
a semester, or individual classes.

School of Czech Studies
*Filosofická fakulta, Universita
Karlova, náměstí Jana Palacha 2,
Staré Město, Prague 1 (2161
9280/www.ff.cuni.cz). Metro
Staroměstská/17, 18 tram.*
Open 9am-11am, 1-3pm Mon-Wed;
11am-3pm Thur; 9-11am, noon-2pm
Fri. **Fees** 68,000 Kč per two-semester
year for Czech Studies programme;
Czech language courses start at
28, 000 Kč. **No credit cards.**
Map p308 G3.
Runs year-long courses during
the school year, offering a mix of
language instruction and lectures in
Czech history and culture (Czech
Studies programme). Czech language
classes are available for beginner,
intermediate and advanced speakers.

Summer School of Slavonic Studies
*Filosofická fakulta, Universita
Karlova, náměstí Jana Palacha 2,
Staré Město, Prague 1 (2161 9111/
2161 9262/www.ff.cuni.cz/
http://ubs.ff.cuni.cz/f-school.html).
Metro Staroměstská/17, 18 tram.*
Open by appointment only. **Fees**
15,000 Kč (course fee and trips only);

33,000 Kč (includes dorm accommodation & meals). **No credit cards. Map** p308 G3. This one-month summer course, held yearly in August, is designed for professors and advanced students in Slavonic studies. It's best to apply by post.

Other courses

Prague Center for Further Education
Šeříkova 10, Malá Strana, Prague 1 (5731 1664/www.prague-center.cz). Metro Malostranská, then 6, 9, 12, 22, 23 tram. **Open** 9am-6pm Mon-Fri. **Fees** 1,500-4,000 Kč per course. **No credit cards. Map** p307 E5.
Provides Prague's international community access to English-language learning. Dynamic and interactive courses in everything from Czech film history to wine tasting, plus sundry other Prague-related subjects.

Anglo-American College
Lázeňská 4, Malá Strana, Prague 1 (5753 0202/www.aac.edu). Metro Malostranská/12, 18, 22, 23 tram. **Open** 9am-5pm Mon-Fri. **Fees** 33,000 Kč per five-course semester; 9,000 Kč per one-course semester. **No credit cards. Map** p307 E3/4.
A western-accredited private college offering Western-style degree courses in business, economics, the humanities and law. While the entire syllabus and all classes are in English, the student body is a mix of Czechs, Slovaks and foreign nationals. Limited course offerings during the summer session.

Language courses

Many schools offer Czech-language instruction. If you prefer a more informal approach, place a notice on one of the boards at the Charles University Faculty, the Globe Bookstore (*see p167*), Radost FX (*see p140*) or anywhere else where young Czechs and foreigners meet. Many students and other young people are happy to offer Czech conversation in exchange for English conversation. But since Czech grammar is difficult most serious learners need some systematic, professional instruction to master the basics.

Accent International House Prague
Bítovská 3, Kačerov, Prague 4 (6126 1638 /fax 6126 1688/www. akcent.cz). Metro Budějovická. **Fees** intensive 12,000 Kč; individual lesson about 500 Kč 45mins. **No credit cards.**
A co-op run and owned by the senior teachers, both Czech and foreign, this school has a good reputation for standard and quality. Choose a five-week intensive course (100 hours instruction) or a more relaxed five-month (one semester) course (two hours weekly). All classes have a maximum size of six. A bit out of the way, but worth the travel.

Angličtina Expres Office
Korunní 2, Nové Město, Prague 2 (2251 3040). Metro Náměstí Míru/4, 16, 22, 23, 34 tram. **Fees** 30-hour course 4,500 Kč (including books and tapes). **Open** 8am-8pm Mon-Thur; 8am-4pm Fri. **Credit** MC, V. **Map** p313 A3.
A well-established Czech-run school set up to teach the locals English but now with years of experience in teaching rudimentary Czech to expats. Instructors use materials developed in-house. The 30-hour course runs every weekday for four weeks in classes of eight or fewer.

Berlitz
Karlovo náměstí, Nové Město, Prague 1 (2212 5555-6/fax 2212 5558/www. berlitz.cz/infoline 0800 221 221 toll-free). Metro Karlovo náměstí/3, 6, 14, 18, 22, 24 tram. **Open** 8am-8pm Mon-Fri. **Fees** 40-minute lesson 600 Kč. **Credit** AmEx, DC, MC, V. **Map** p310 H7.
The staggering cost of lessons is testament, supposedly, to the efficiency of the Berlitz method, which emphasises speaking drills and discourages systematic grammar teaching and note-taking. With an internationally standardised method of teaching and branches all over the world (several in Prague alone), Berlitz is the McDonald's of language schools, but it gets results.
Branch: Boztěchova 2, Zlatý Anděl (5731 8898).

Lingua Viva
Spálená 57 & 21, Nové Město, Prague 1 (2492 0675/fax 2492 1142/www.linguaviva.cz). Metro Národní třída/6, 9, 18, 21, 22, 23 tram. **Open** 9am-7pm Mon-Thur; 9am-noon Fri. **Fees** 72-hour course (5 months) 5,650 Kč; intensive 64-hour course (1 month, summer only) 4,650 Kč; individual lesson 405-472 Kč 45mins, 540-630 Kč 60mins. **No credit cards. Map** p310 H6.

This small independent school is an upstart, with better rates and more informal instruction than most.

State Language School
Státní jazyková Škola
Školská 15, Nové Město, Prague 1 (Slavonic languages & Czech for foreigners 2223 2238/fax 2223 2236/summer courses 297 114/ www.sjs.cz). Metro Můstek/3, 6, 9, 14, 17, 18, 22, 23, 24 tram. **Open** 12.30-3.30pm Tue; 12.30-6.30pm Wed; 12.30-3.30pm Thur, Fri. **Fees** intensive 14,760 Kč; standard 4,065 Kč; summer 7,000 Kč. **No credit cards. Map** p310 J6.
The largest and cheapest language school in Prague is state run and teaches just about every language under the sun. The Czech for Foreigners department offers both intensive courses (16 hours weekly for five months) and standard courses (four hours weekly for five months) during the normal school year, as well as shorter intensive summer courses (20 hours weekly for one month). Classes tend to start very large, but many students drop out over the course of the term, leaving a smaller, more dedicated, but still dead cheap class.

Student travel

CKM
Mánesova 77, Vinohrady, Prague 2 (2272 1595/fax 2272 6370). Metro Jiřího z Poděbrad/11 tram. **Open** 10am-6pm Mon-Thur; 10am-4pm Fri. **No credit cards. Map** p309 K5.
Specialises in cheap flights, and can issue Euro 26 cards to under-27s to qualify them for discounts.

GTS
Ve Smečkách 33, Nové Město, Prague 1 (2221 1204/9615 7777/www.gtsint.cz). Metro Muzeum/3, 9, 14, 24 tram. **Open** 8am-7pm Mon-Fri; 11am-3pm Sat. **No credit cards. Map** p311 K6.
The best place for ISIC card-holders to find cheap student fares. Especially good international flight bargains, as well as occasional deals on bus and train travel. GTS also offers travel insurance and issues ISIC cards – though, annoyingly, only to applicants who have ID from local institutions.
Branch: Lodecká 3, Nové Město, Prague 1 (2481 2770).

Student Agency
Ječná 37, Prague 2, (2499 9666/ fax 2499 9660). Metro I.P.Pavlova/ 4, 6, 11, 16, 22, 23, 34 tram. **Open** 8am-6pm Mon-Fri. **Credit** MC, V. **Map** p310 K8.

Cheap flights, buses and trains outside the Czech Republic, especially for ISIC holders. Also offers Allianz travel insurance and issues ISIC cards, visas, working permits for programmes abroad, and international phone cards.

Telephones

Virtually all of the public coin telephones that still take 2 Kč coins are perpetually broken; the rest run on telephone cards, which come in denominations of 50 to 150 units and can be bought at newsstands, post offices and anywhere you see the blue and yellow *Český Telecom* sticker. Local calls cost 3,20 Kč for one unit (lasting two minutes from 7am-7pm weekdays, and four and a half minutes from 7pm-7am weekdays, all day weekends and public holidays and Sundays). International calls, which are horrendously expensive, can be made from any phone box or more easily at a private booth at the Main Post Office (*see p286*).

The international dialling code to the Czech Republic is 420 and the city code for Prague is 2 (02 within the republic). To call abroad from Prague, dial the prefix 00, the country and the area codes (for UK area codes omit the 0) and then the number. The prefix for the United Kingdom is 44, for America and Canada it's 1 and for Australia it's 61. On local numbers, eight digits indicate that the number is on a digital switchboard while a four-, five-, six- or seven-digit number indicates an analogue board. Czech Telecom is rapidly digitalising the entire system. Note that as this guidebook went to press a major wave of digitising was underway so that most 7-digit numbers in the city centre, such as 111 1111, were being changed to 1211 1111. If a number in this guide fails to go through, it may work to insert a 2 where indicated.

The phone system is still erratic, and it's noticeably worse when it's raining and the underground lines get wet. It often takes several attempts to get through, and you may get a disconnected tone even when a number is in service.

Český Telecom – Czech Telecom

Olšanská 3, Žižkov, Prague 3 (infocentre 0800 123 456 toll-free/ www.telecom.cz). Metro Želivského/5, 9, 16, 19 tram. **Open** 8am-4pm Mon-Fri. **Map** p313 D2.

Think Smart Cards

Pre-paid long distance calling cards marketed by this expat magazine are on sale at the Globe Bookstore & Coffeehouse (*see p141*). A 500 Kč card will get you about two hours of international talk time over internet lines with a good signal quality. Access the lines from any public or private phone via a code number.

Faxes

You can send faxes from the Main Post Office (*see p286*) from 7am to 8 pm daily (counter No.2, look for *post fax*). To Great Britain you pay 78 Kč for the first page plus 48 Kč for each additional page; to the US you pay 100 Kč for the first page plus 68 Kč for each additional page.

You can receive a fax marked clearly with your name at the Main Post Office (fax 2113 1402). You are charged 16 Kč for a maximum of 5 pages, 2 Kč for each additional page.

Mobile phones

Competition has led to improved services and lower rates in the Czech Republic but it sometimes seems that more energy goes into marketing mobile phones than providing good service and coverage. The three main companies are listed below – they offer different payment schemes and

coverage areas, so it's best to get details before deciding. They are also the only companies in town who rent out phones short-term – for exorbitant sums.

All three companies use both the 1,800 MHz and 900 MHz wavebands, which means that owners of all standard UK mobiles can use them as long as they have a roaming facility (which may need to be pre-arranged). Newer model US cell phones that are on the dual system will now function in the Czech Republic as in the rest of Europe.

EuroTel

Sokolovská 885/225, Vysočany, Prague 9 (24h service 0800 330 011 toll-free/6701 6711/www.eurotel.cz). Metro Českomoravská/8 tram. **Open** 8am-6pm Mon-Fri; 9am-1pm Sat. **No credit cards.**
The leading provider of mobile phone services and a subsidiary of telephone monopoly Český Telecom.

Radiomobil

Evropská 178, Dejvice, Prague 6 (24h service 0603 603 603/ 0603 604 604/www.paegas.cz). Metro Dejvická/1, 18, 25, 26 tram. **Open** 8am-6pm Mon-Fri. **No credit cards.**
Providers of T-Mobil, the main rival to Eurotel. English-language help and loads of different service packages are available at T-Mobil shops all over the city.

Český Mobil

Vinohradská 167, Prague 10 (0800 777 777 toll-free/www.oskarmobil.cz). Metro Strašnická/17, 18 tram. **Open** 9am-8pm Mon-Fri; 9am-2pm Sat. **No credit cards.**
Providers of the newest mobile phone service – Oskar, Český Mobil has cheaper rates under some packages but spotty coverage, especially outside Prague.

Time

The Czech Republic is on Central European Time (CET), one hour ahead of the UK, six ahead of New York and nine ahead of Los Angeles, and uses the 24-hour clock. The Czechs are prompt, and you should never be more than 15 minutes late for a meeting.

Tipping & VAT

Czechs tend to round up restaurant bills, often only by a few crowns, but foreigners are more usually expected to leave a ten per cent tip. If service is bad, however, don't feel obliged to leave anything. Service is often added on automatically for large groups. Taxi drivers expect you to round the fare up, but, if you've just been ripped off, don't give a heller.

A value-added tax of 22 per cent has been slapped on to retail purchases for years in the Czech Republic but only as recently as 2000 was a system set up to reimburse non-resident foreigners' VAT payments. You can claim a refund at the border or at the Ruzyně airport in the departure hall at the Customs desk on the left. You'll need your shop receipt, passport and a VAT refund form, which staff can supply. Purchases of over 1,000 Kč are eligible if taken out of the country within 30 days of sale.

Toilets

Usually called a 'WC' (pronounce it 'veh-tseh'), the word for toilet is *záchod* and there is sometimes a charge for using one of about 5 Kč. Calls of nature can be answered in all metro stations from at least 8am to 8pm, and at many fast-food joints and department stores. 'Ladies' is *Dámy* or *Ženy*, 'Gents' *Páni* or *Muži*.

Tourist information

The English-language weekly the *Prague Post* carries entertainment sections along with survival hints. Monthly entertainment listings mags are the small-format *Prague Insider*, *Kulturní přehled* (in Czech), *Kultura v Praze* and its shorter English equivalent *Culture in Prague*. (*See also*

p280 **Media**.) The Prague Information Service (PIS) also publishes a free monthly entertainment listings programme in English.

The use of the international blue and white 'i' information sign is not regulated, so the places carrying it are not necessarily official.

The best map for public transport or driving is the widely available *Kartografie Praha Plán města* (a book with a yellow cover), costing about 100 Kč, though for central areas the co-ordinates are sometimes far too vague. Check you've got the latest edition. For central areas the free map from Prague Information Service (*see below*) is very useful.

Čedok
Na příkopě 18, Nové Město, Prague 1 (2419 7642/2419 7615/262 904). Metro Můstek/ 3, 5, 8, 9, 14, 24 tram. **Open** 9am-7pm Mon-Fri; 9.30am-2.30pm Sat, Sun. **Map** p309 K4.
The former state travel agency is still the biggest in the Czech Republic. A handy place to obtain train, bus and air tickets and accommodation information.

PIS (Prague Information Service)
Pražská informační služba Na příkopě 20, Nové Město, Prague 1 (general info 12444/ www.prague-info.cz/www.pis.cz). Metro Můstek/3, 4, 8, 9,14, 24 tram. **Open** *Apr-Oct* 9am-7pm Mon-Fri; 9am-5pm Sat, Sun. *Nov-March* 9am-6pm Mon-Fri; 9am-3pm Sat. **Map** p309 K4.
PIS provides free information, maps and help with a smile.
Branches: Hlavní nádraží (hall of the Main Railway Station), Wilsonova, Nové Město, Prague 1 (2423 9258); Old Town Hall, Staroměstské náměstí, Staré Město, Prague 1 (2448 2202/2448 2018); Charles Bridge – Malá Strana-side Tower (summer only; 5753 1591).

Visas

Requirements can change frequently, but at press time citizens of the US, UK and other EU members and most other European countries did not need a visa to enter the Czech Republic for stays

of up to 90 days – just a valid passport with at least six months to run by the end of their visit. Under a recent law aimed at preventing illegal residence by foreigners, however, border crossings can get complicated if you don't prepare. Foreigners who do require a visa to enter the Czech Republic, including at press time Canadians, Australians, New Zealanders and South Africans, can no longer get theirs at the border but must apply at a Czech embassy outside the Czech Republic (but not necessarily in their home country). The process may take weeks, so early planning is critical.

Even visitors who don't require a visa may now be asked for proof that they have sufficient finances, pre-arranged accommodation and international health insurance.

Automated, extremely confusing visa information is available in English at the Foreigner's Police in Prague (*see below*) or at the Ministry of Foreign Affairs (2418 2125/www.mzv.cz). You are technically required to register at the local police station within 30 days of arriving (if you are staying at a hotel this will be done for you). If you are from one of the countries whose residents are allowed only 30 days in the Czech Republic, you must obtain an extended visa (confusingly called an exit visa, or *výjezdní vízum*) from the Foreigners Police office to allow you up to 90 days in total.

LONGER STAYS
The other option if you want to stay longer is a residence permit (*občanský průkaz; see p290*), which isn't easy to get and must be obtained from a Czech embassy abroad.

The Czech police conduct periodic crackdowns on illegal aliens. They're usually aimed at Romanians, Ukrainians,

Vietnamese and other nationals considered undesirable, though a few Brits and US citizens get caught. Even so, many expats reside here illegally. Some avoid dealing with the above requirements by leaving and re-entering the country. Border police are getting wise to the trick, however, and it can't be relied on. If you try it, be sure to get the required stamp in your passport as you leave and re-enter by saying *razítko prosím* (stamp please).

Foreigners Police

Cizinecká policie
Sdružení 1, Praha 4 (info 6144 1476) Metro Pankrác. **Open** 7.30am-11.30am, 12.15-3pm Mon, Tue, Thur; 8am-12.15pm, 1-5pm Wed; 7.30am-11.30pm Fri.
Branch: Olšanská 2, Žižkov, Prague 3 (6144 1366).

Weights & measures

Czechs use the metric system, even selling eggs in batches of five or ten. Things are usually measured out in decagrams or 'deka' (10 grams) or deciliters or 'deci' (10 centilitres). So a regular glass of wine is usually two deci (abbreviated dcl), and ham enough for a few sandwiches is 20 deka (dkg).

When to go

SPRING

The best season in Prague, and surely the most awaited, as the city comes out of hibernation from a long, cold, cloudy winter. While it is not unheard of for there to be snow lingering on as late as early May, temperatures are often perfect for strolling.

Averages

March 0-7°C (32-45°F), five hours' sun a day, 65mm of rain the month.
April 3-12 °C (37-54°F), six hours' sun, 78mm rain.
May 8-17°C (46-63°F), 8 hours' sun, 63mm rain.

SUMMER

Prague citizens usually leave for their country cottages (*chatas*) and abandon the city to the tourist hordes. Summers are pleasant, warm (rarely hot) and prone to thundery showers. The days are long, and it stays light until 10pm.

Averages

June 12-21°C (54-70°F), nine hours' sun a day, 50mm rain the month.
July 13-23°C (55-73°F), nine hours' sun/25mm rain.
August 14-22°C (57-72°F), eight hours' sun, 50mm rain.

AUTUMN

This can be the prettiest time of year, with crisp cool air and sharp blue skies, but can also be the wettest. September is a good month to visit the city. The streets are once again jammed with cars, the parks full of children, and the restaurants busy. The days grow shorter alarmingly quickly. By the end of October, the sun sets at around 5.30pm.

Averages

September 10-17°C (50-63°F), six hours' sun a day, 55mm rain the month.
October 5-14°C (41-57°F), four hours' sun, 100mm rain.
November 1-5°C (34-41°F), two hours' sun, 110mm rain).

WINTER

Street-side carp sellers and Christmas markets help break the monotony of the long, cold, grey winter, and when it snows, Prague is so beautiful that you forget the winter-long gloom that blankets the city. Sadly, bright, white snow is rarely accompanied by a clear blue sky. Many Prague residents burn coal for heating, and by midwinter the smog is so bad, you can't see across the river.

Averages

December 0-2°C (32-36°F), one hour's sun a day, 76mm rain the month).

January 0-5°C (32-41°F), two hours' sun, 62mm rain).
February 1-4°C (34-40°F), (three hours' sun, 73mm rain).

Public holidays

New Year's Day, 1 Jan; **Easter Monday**; **Labour Day**, 1 May; **Liberation Day**, 8 May; **Cyril & Methodius Day**, 5 July; **Jan Hus Day**, 6 July; **Statehood Day**, 28 Sept; **Czech Founding Day**, 28 Oct; **Struggle for Freedom Day**, 17 Nov; **Christmas holidays**, 24-26 Dec

Women

Traditional gender roles are entrenched in the Czech Republic and feminism is still not taken very seriously, but women's organisations do exist. Most emphasise women's rights as an integral part of human rights, rather than enter any debate about that tricky word 'feminism'.

Ženské Centrum in Prague 2 (Gorazdova 20; 2491 7224) consists of two organizations: proFem and the Centre for Gender Studies, as well as the Gender Studies Library (2491 5666), which has some materials in English.

Working in Prague

To work legally, you need a work permit and the necessary residency permit (confusingly termed a 'Temporary Visa for over 90 Days'). Unless you already have the residency permit, only available from Czech embassies and consulates outside the republic, usually after a long wait, there's little hope of finding legal work.

If you do have the residency permit, and are to be employed by a Czech company, the company needs to obtain a work permit for you. You'll need to give evidence of qualifications and in some cases proof of relevant work experience, all accompanied by official notarised translations.

Vocabulary

For food and drink and vocabulary, *see p143*.

Pronunciation

a	as in gap
á	as in father
e	as in let
é	as in air
i, y	as in lit
í, ý	as in seed
o	as in lot
ó	as in lore
u	as in book
ú,ů	as in loom
c	as in its
č	as in chin
ch	as in loch
ď	as in duty
ň	as in onion
ř	as a standard r, but flatten the tip of the tongue making a short forceful buzz like ž
š	as in shin
ť	as in stew
ž	as in pleasure
dž	as in George

The basics

Czech words are always stressed on the first syllable.

hello/good day	dobrý den
good evening	dobrý večer
good nigh	dobrou noc
goodbye	nashledanou
yes	ano (often abbreviated to no or just jo)
no	ne
please	prosím
thank you	děkuji
excuse me	promiňte
sorry	pardon
help!	pomoc!
attention!	pozor!
I don't speak Czech	nemluvím česky
I don't understand	nerozumím
Do you speak English?	Mluvíte anglicky?
sir	pán
madam	paní
open	otevřeno
closed	zavřeno
I would like...	Chtěl bych...
how much is it?	kolik to stojí?
may I have a receipt, please?	účet, prosím
can we pay, please?	zaplatíme, prosím
where is...	e je...
go left	doleva
go right	doprava

straight	rovně
far	daleko
near	blizko
good	dobrý
bad	špatný
big	velký
small	malý
no problem	to je v pořádku
who are you rooting for?	máš rád(a)?
cool shades!	máš dobře vychytaný brejle!
It's a rip-off	to je zlodějina
I'm absolutely knackered	jsem úplně na dně
the lift is stuck	výtah zůstal viset
could I speak to Václav?	mohl bych mluvit s Václavem?

Street names, etc

In conversation, as in this guide, most Prague streets are referred to by their name only, leaving off ulice, třída and so on.

avenue	třída
bridge	most
church	kostel
embankment	nábřeží or nábř.
gardens	sady or zahrada
island	ostrov
lane	ulička
monastery, convent	klášter
park	park
square	náměstí or nám.
station	nádraží or nádr.
steps	schody
street	ulice or ul.
tunnel	tunel

Numbers

0	nula
1	jeden
2	dva
3	tři
4	čtyři
5	pět
6	šest
7	sedm
8	osm
9	devět
10	deset
11	jedenáct
12	dvanáct
13	třináct
14	čtrnáct
15	patnáct
16	šestnáct
17	sedmnáct
18	osmnáct
19	devatenáct
20	dvacet
30	třicet
40	čtyřicet
50	padesát
60	šedesát
70	sedmdesát
80	osmdesát
90	devadesát
100	sto
1,000	tisíc

Days & months

Monday	pondělí
Tuesday	úterý
Wednesday	středa
Thursday	čtvrtek
Friday	pátek
Saturday	sobota
Sunday	neděle

January	leden
February	únor
March	březen
April	duben
May	květen
June	červen
July	červenec
August	srpen
September	září
October	říjen
November	listopad
December	prosinec

Spring	jaro
Summer	léto
Autumn	podzim
Winter	zima

Pick-up lines

What a babe!
To je kost!
What a stud!
Dobrej frajer!
I lost the keys to my flat. Isn't there any room for me at your place?
Ztratily se mi klíče od bytu. Nemáš u sebe místečko pro mě?
Do you want to try my goulash?
Chceš ochutnat můj guláš?
I love you Miluju Tě
Another drink? Ještě jedno?

Put-down lines

What are you staring at?
Na co čumíš?
Give me a break!
Dej mi pokoj!
Kiss my arse!
Polib mi prdel!
Shit your eye out!
Vyser si oko!
That pisses me off!
To mě sere!
You jerk! Ty vole!
You bitch! Ty děvko!

Directory

Further Reference

Books

Literature & fiction

Brierley, David
On Leaving z Prague Win·'ow
Readable but dated thriller set in post-communist Prague.

Buchler, Alexander (ed)
This Side of Reality
Absorbing anthology of modern Czech writing.

Chatwin, Bruce
Utz
Luminous tale of a Josefov porcelain collector.

Hašek, Jaroslav
The Good Soldier Švejk
Rambling, picaresque comic masterpiece set in World War I, by Bohemia's most bohemian writer.

Havel, Václav
The Memorandum; Three Vaněk Plays; Temptation
The President's work as playwright. *The Memorandum* is his ground-breaking absurdist work.

Hrabal, Bohumil
I Served The King of England; Total Fears
The living legend's most Prague-ish novel, *I Served the King of England*, tracks its anti-hero through a decade of fascism, war and communism. *Total Fears* is a lush new translation by the respected Twisted Spoon Press.

Klíma, Ivan
Love and Garbage
Reflections on the lives of intellectuals as street-sweepers.

Klíma, Ladislav
The Sufferings of Prince Sternenhoch
The virtually unknown Czech master of Gothic, Klíma's tale reads 'like a book that Edgar Allan Poe might have written if he'd read Nietzsche'.

Kundera, Milan
The Joke; The Book of Laughter and Forgetting; The Unbearable Lightness of Being
Called smug by some and disliked by many Czechs, though internationally revered, Milan Kundera's tragi-comic romances are still the runaway bestselling sketches of Prague.

Leppin, Paul
Others' Paradise/Severin's Journey into the Dark
Recently translated work from pre-War Prague German writer, both in beautiful editions.

Meyrink, Gustav
The Golem
The classic version of the tale of Rabbi Loew's monster, set in Prague's Jewish Quarter.

Neruda, Jan
Prague Tales
Wry and bitter-sweet stories of life in 19th-century Malá Strana, from Prague's answer to Dickens.

Škvorecký, Josef
The Engineer of Human Souls
The magnum opus of the chronicler of Czech jazz and skirtchasers.

Švankmajerová, Eva
Baradla Cave
A novel about Prague and caves through the eyes of a leading contemporary surrealist; illustrated by Jan Švankmajer.

Topol, Jáchym
Sister City Silver
A long-awaited translation of three noir novellas by one of the city's leading young writers, set in corrupt contemporary Prague.

Wilson, Paul (ed)
Prague: A Traveller's Literary Companion
Excellent collection, from Meyrink to Škvorecký, organised to evoke Prague's sense of place.

Ungar, Hermann
The Maimed
Thomas Mann called this rare novel 'a sexual hell, full of filth, crime and the deepest melancholy... the digression of an inwardly pure artistry.'

Kafka

Kafka, Franz
The Castle; The Transformation & Other Stories; The Trial
These Kafka classics are well worth re-reading, if only to note how postmodern Prague has completely lost all sense of Kafkaesque menace.

Kafka, Franz
Contemplation
Observations, vignettes and reflections in a beautiful illustrated edition from Twisted Spoon Press.

Anderson, Mark M
Kafka's Clothes
Erudite, subtle and unconventional book encompassing Kafka, dandyism and the Habsburg culture of ornament.

Brod, Max
Franz Kafka: A Biography
The only biography by anyone who actually knew the man.

Hayman, Ronald
K: A Biography of Kafka
Widely available, dependable, but a bit boring.

Hockaday, Mary
Kafka, Love and Courage: The Life of Milena Jesenská
Best biography of Kafka's lover, and excellent on Prague.

Karl, Frederick
Franz Kafka: Representative Man
Hefty for a holiday read, but a thorough and thoughtful account of the man, his work, and the Prague he inhabited.

History, memoir & travel

Brook, Stephen
The Double Eagle: Vienna, Budapest & Prague
Fussy but entertainingly detailed travelogue of the Habsburg capitals in the early 1980s.

Demetz, Peter
Prague in Black and Gold
Thoughtful exploration of prehistoric to First Republic life in the Czech lands.

Fermor, Patrick Leigh
A Time of Gifts
Evocative 1930s travelogue, culminating in inter-war Prague.

Garton Ash, Timothy
The Magic Lantern: The Revolution of 1989 Witnessed in Warsaw, Budapest, Berlin and Prague; History of the Present
The Oxford academic's on-the-spot 1989 history, and his look back a decade later, painfully explore the morality of the Velvet Revolution.

Pynsent, Robert B
Questions of Identity: Czech and Slovak Ideas of Nationality and Personality
Witty, erudite and incisive look at Czech self-perception.

Directory

Rimmer, Dave

Once Upon a Time in the East
Communism seen stoned and from ground level.

Ripellino, Angelo Maria

Magic Prague
Mad masterpiece of literary and cultural history, mixing fact and fiction as it celebrates the city's sorcerous soul.

Sayer, Derek

Coasts of Bohemia
Phenomenally well-researched and witty account of the millennium-long Czech search for identity.

Shawcross, William

Dubček
Biography of the Prague Spring figurehead, updated to assess his role in the 1989 Velvet Revolution.

Essays & argument

Čapek, Karel

Towards the Radical Centre
Selected essays from the man who coined the word 'robot'.

Klíma, Ivan

The Spirit of Prague
Thought-provoking essays, of which the title piece is the highlight.

Havel, Václav

Living in Truth/Letters to Olga/ Disturbing the Peace
His most important political writing, his prison letters to his wife, and his autobiographical reflections.

Miscellaneous

Holub, Miroslav

Supposed to Fly
This collecion of poetry by this former dissident was inspired by his youth in war-torn Plzeň.

Iggers, Wilma A

Women of Prague
Fascinating – the lives of 12 women, across 200 years.

Sís, Petr

Three Golden Keys
Children's tale set in Prague, with wonderful drawings.

Novak, Ladislav

The Transformations of Mr Hadliz
Ladislav Novak, a pioneer in phonetic and visual poetry, is seen here through twelve colour pictures that form the book's central motif. The volume also includes poems from Novak's alter ego, Mr Hadliz.

Putz, Harry

Do You Want to Speak Czech?
If the answer is yes, this is the book (and the cassette).

Various eds

Prague: 11 Centuries of Architecture
Solid, substantial and not too stodgy.

Film

Many of the following can be viewed on video at, or rented from, Virus Video (*see page 183*) or found periodically at film festivals or video stores.

Ecstasy (Extáze)

Gustav Machatý (1932)
Known primarily for its groundbreaking nude scene with the nubile actress who would later be known as Hedy Lamarr, this imagistic film depicts a girl frustrated with her relationship with an older man, and the strange triangle of desire that emerges.

The Long Journey (Daleká cesta)

Alfred Radok (1949)
Banned by the Communists for 20 years, this film uses innovative lighting and camera techniques to depict the deportation of Jews to concentration camps.

The Fabulous World of Jules Verne (Vynález zkázy)

Karel Zeman (1958)
A unique film, also called 'The Invention of Destruction', that tries to capture the look of the original engravings used to illustrate Verne's books. Animated flying machines and submarines are joined to live action scenes in this story of a mad inventor.

The Great Solitude (Velká samota)

Ladislav Helge (1959)
One of the few pre-new wave movies that goes deeper than farm-tool worship, this film focuses on how tough it is to be a rural party official.

Ikarie XB 1 (Voyage to the End of the Universe)

Jindřich Polák (1963)
Even in the badly re-edited and dubbed English-language version, this spaced-out thriller set on a lost rocket ship in the 25th century shows flashes of brilliance. The secret mission known only to the ship's computer pre-dates Kubrick's 2001.

The Shop on Main Street (Obchod na korze)

Ján Kadár & Elmar Klos (1964)
Set during World War II in the Nazi puppet state of Slovakia, it's about an honest carpenter who must act as the person 'Aryanising' a button shop run by an old Jewish woman. Winner of the 1966 Oscar for Best Foreign Film.

Intimate Lighting (Intimní osvětlení)

Ivan Passer (1965)
Possibly the most delightful film of the Czech New Wave, *Intimate Lightning* tells of the reunion of two old friends after many years of living very different lives, only to discover the musical ensemble in which they used to play is as tuneless as it ever was.

Larks on a String (Skřivánci na niti)

Jiří Menzel (1969)
This tale of forced labour in the steel mills of industrial Kladno deals with politics a bit, but love – and libido – somehow always triumph. Banned soon after its release, the film was not shown again until 1989 when it won the Berlin Film Festival's Golden Bear.

The Ear (Ucho)

Karel Kachyňa (written by Jan Procházka) (1970)
The full force of surveillance terror and paranoia is exposed in this chilling film, whose origins go further back than the communists to Kafka. Banned instantly, of course.

Buttoners (Knoflíkáři)

Petr Zelenka (1997)
Sardonic, schizophrenic flick that shuffles the lives of several disparate characters who are all vaguely connected through the bombing of Hiroshima. Sassy and clean-paced enough to have nabbed a few international awards.

Pelíšky (Cosy Dens)

Jan Hřebejk (1999)
A bittersweet look at the lives of neighbouring families from Christmas 1967 to 21 August 1968, the day that Russian tanks rolled in. One family supports the communist regime, one doesn't and their kids are embarrassed by it all.

Otesánek

Jan Švankmajer (2000)
Employing his usual alchemy of stop-motion animation and live action, Švankmajer updates a classic Czech myth about a childless couple who adopt an insatiable baby made from tree roots.

Directory

Musíme si pomáhat (Divided We Fall)

Jan Hřebejk (2001)
The Oscar-nominated tale of a small Czech village in wartime and its residents' confrontations with moral decisions.

Tmavomodrý svět (Dark Blue World)

Jan Svěrák (2001)
A sentimental but evocative tale of Czech RAF pilots during WWII and the misery they endured at home after the war. By the director of the Oscar-winning *Kolja*, and co-written by his father, the beloved comic Zdeněk Svěrák.

Music

Rok Ďábla (Sony Music/Bonton)

This soundtrack from the hit film of the same name presents the songs of beloved Czech folk balladeer Jarek Nohavica in a completely new light with fantasy rock versions.

Zuzana Navarová: Barvy všecky (Indies)

All Colours shows why the Prague-based singer's tender, Latin-influenced ballads pack clubs around the Czech capital but are easy on the mind.

Černý Petr (Indies)

This longtime underground jazzman, something of a legend in the Czech Republic, is definitively recorded on this album of easygoing, rather cerebral sessions.

Iva Bittová: Bílé Inferno (Indies)

One of the most listened-to double albums on the post-1989 scene, the *White Inferno* showcases the best of the Brno sound.

Yow/Citrax (Beeswax)

Yow's 'Feel For You' and Citrax's '2 FUKT 2 FUNK (Neo Carnival Vision Part I)', presented by the master Prague DJ Chris Sadler, shows off quintessential dance scene sounds from the city's premiere clubbing label and party organiser, Wax (www.wax.cz).

Hypnotix: New World Order (EMI)

The dub stars of Prague, led by the polemical Bourama Badji, mix up language and fat beats to formulate Prague's idea of a Jamaican session.

Ecstasy of St Theresa: In Dust 3 (EMI)

Jan P Muchow creates a textured digital background for the provocative vocals of Kateřina Winterová on the album most cherished as a lifestyle choice by clubby Praguers, circa 2000.

Various: Future Sound of Prague (Intellygent)

This anthology of house and trip hop presents the best of Significant Other, Southpaw, Garden Zitty and other acts on the Bohemian club circuit at the turn of the millennium.

Richard Müller (B&M Music)

The Slovak classic rocker sits in with an improbably wide range of singers, from the avant-garde Iva Bittová to the vintage chanteuse Hana Hegerová. Funky keyboards and bass underscore this poppy all-Czech top seller.

Homegrown classics

Pavel Šporcl

Pavel Šporcl (Supraphon)
This unorthodox Czech violin virtuoso has won over audiences with his deft treatment of Smetana, Dvořák, Janáček and Martinů. On this debut his star fully rises .

Czech Serenade

Antonín Dvořák, Josef Suk, Vítězslav Novák, Zdeněk Fibich, Leoš Janáček (Supraphon)
The pantheon of great Czech composers, in performances by a range of artists including the Czech Philharmonic and a gallery of top-class chamber players, mostly digitally recorded. The works incorporate old Czech and Moravian folk influences.

Zdeněk Fibich: Symphony No 1 in F major, Symphony No 2 in E flat major, Symphony No 3 in E minor

This set of symphonies by the little-known romantic Czech composer now receiving a well-deserved rivival. Performed by the Czech Philharmonic Orchestra under Karel Šejna, and including two excellent shorter works.

Martinu, Bohuslav: Double Concerto

Orchestre National de France (Teldec/Erato)

This lyrical composition, performed with sensitivity by soloist s Jean-François Heisser and Jean Camosi, and conducted by James Conlon, provides a toothsome taste of the rarely heard modernist Czech composer at his best.

Eva Urbanová: Slavné České duety

Eva Urbanová (Supraphon)
The star soprano has stirred up crowds at the State Opera and National Theatre in Prague for years. Here she's recorded a fine collection of classic Czech duets.

Jan Ladislav Dusík: Piano Concerto, Sonatas

Jan Novotný, Prague Chamber Philharmonic, conducted by Leoš Svárovský (Panton)
The Prague Chamber Philharmonic delivers the energy and spontaneity that has set it apart from the city's larger orchestras in these excellent recordings of Dusík's Concert Concerto for Piano and Orchestra in E flat major, Op 70 and two of his more lyrical sonatas, the F Sharp minor, Op 61 and the A flat major, Op 64. Novotný's playing is particularly expressive.

Chopin: The Piano Concertos, No 1&2

E Leonskaja, Czech Philharmonic, conducted by Vladimír Ashkenazy (Teldec)
A prize recording of the Czech Philharmonic, which works very well with the renowned Russian pianist, trading off with her in the execution of powerful passages, but also giving her the space to caress an emotive softer stanza when needed. Leonskaja shows an incredible range in her interpretation on this double CD.

Krzystof Penderecki: Works for Clarinet (Sharon Kam Meets Krzystof Penderecki)

Sharon Kam, Krzysztof Penderecki, Czech Philharmonic, conducted by Vladimír Ashkenazy (Teldec)
One of the Czech Philharmonic's proudest recordings is this magnificent duo. Original, rarely heard works from the modern avant-garde composer Penderecki are a rewarding, surprising treat.

Messiaen, Pärt, Dvořák, Saint-Saéns: Reflections

Jiří Bárta (Supraphon)
Arguably the Czech Republic's top cellist, Bárta performs works ranging

Czech rock: how to lose your shirt

The world of a Czech music mogul has never been an easy one. To be sure, music and Prague are inseparable and underground music is what brought down the communist regime – just ask any fan of Plastic People of the Universe. The arrest of the group's members during the 'Normalisation' period following the Prague Spring of 1968 was one of the key events that galvanised the public to act against the state's efforts to protect them from Western decadence.

The circle has now turned from fear of supression and arrest to fear of mere penury. To promote, record and release tomorrow's national heroes, you'd have to be either very rich or seriously nuts. Fortunately many in Prague are. The latter, that is.

Which is precisely why CD hunting is one of the most rewarding pursuits in the Czech capital for fans of the weird. Some excellent little labels to watch for when shopping for

Czech contemporary music are **Rachot** and **Indies** (*see p220* **Czech rock 101**). Based in a run-down office in the Žižkov district, the two-man operation that is Rachot has been teetering on the verge of bankruptcy for years, promoting such expat bands as Deep Sweden and such Prague divas such as Iva Bittová. The latter once released a record of free interpretations of Bartok pieces, recorded with the 'Romany lounge' singer Ida Kellerová. Wrapped in a red velvet package with a scarlet feather attached, it cost the tiny label so much that it could only afford to press a few hundred copies, which were swiftly snapped up, despite selling for an unheard of 600 Kč to Czechs more accustomed to paying 250 Kč for local music.

Ironically, if Rachot still had discs left, it could probably sell them for a mint. Then perhaps it just might survive the release of its next recording.

---

from plaintive to glowing in his usual intense and rich style. Among the big-name composers whose short works have inspired Bárta is the virtually unknown Zemek-Novák Sonata No 2 and *Cantus Rogans* by Kopelent, neither recorded before.

Websites

Central Europe Online
www.centraleurope.com
A flashy and popular website offering news, business and special reports on the Czech Republic and other Central European countries. Crisply designed, but somewhat dry.

Charles University
www.cuni.cz
The official site of Charles University, much of it in English, with links to a university-run news service (available via email), the university library, departments and courses for foreigners.

Czech-English Dictionary
www.foreignword.com
Thousands of words translated from Czech and dozens of other languages into English or back.

Czech Info Centre
www.muselik.com/czech/index.html
Bulletin board for meeting Czechs looking for work or travel deals.

Czech Railways and bus connections
www.idos.cz
Searchable online train and bus timetables for every city and town in the Czech Republic with a rail or bus connection.

Czech Techno
www.techno.cz
All the party and club news in the Czech Republic with links to techno-favouring clubs and promoters and the bands that rock them.

Expats.cz
www.expats.cz
Online bulletin board with handy classifieds, tips on residency, apartment hunting and job, plus forums on everything from Butoh dancing to relationships.

About.com
http://goeasteurope.about.com/cs/cityprague
Bill Biega's comprehensive overview of Eastern Europe includes excellent up-to-date Prague content – reviews, history, culture and sights. There's a tempting section on spas, too.

Prague TV
prague.tv
Tune in for archived articles from *The Prague Pill* (*see p281*), food and drink tips, links to maps and currency converters, and free-form forums.

The Prague Post
www.praguepost.cz
Prague's main English-language weekly features newly redesigned web pages with useful tourist information pages.

Prague Information Service
www.prague-info.cz /www.pis.cz
Comprehensive source for city addresses with well-organised pages of general tourist information.

Atlas
mapy.atlas.cz
A complete online map of Prague.

Radio Free Europe/Radio Liberty
www.rferl.org/newsline/
News, maps, facts and figures and lots on Czech society.

SMS.cz
www.sms.cz
Send text messages to any mobile phone in the Czech Republic.

Seznam
www.seznam.cz
A fast Czech-language search engine with data on all things Czech.

Time Out Prague Guide
www.timeout.com
Shameless self-promotion it may be, but here's where you'll the best of what's on each week in Prague.

Directory

Index

Note: Page numbers in **bold** indicate key information on a topic; page numbers in *italics* indicate photographs.

Advertisers' Index

Please refer to the relevant pages for addresses and telephone numbers.

Place of Interest and/or Entertainment	▢
Railway Stations	■
Metro Stations	Ⓜ
Parks	▢
Pedestrian Zones	▢
Churches	✚
Steps	▬
Area Name .... JOSEFOV	
Tram Routes	▬

Maps

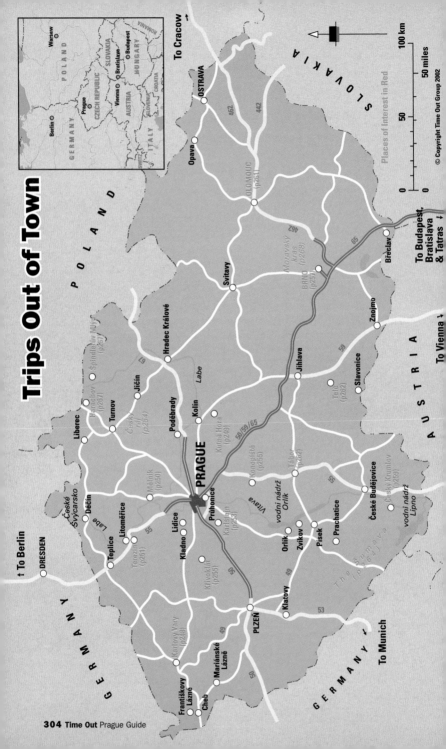

Trips Out of Town

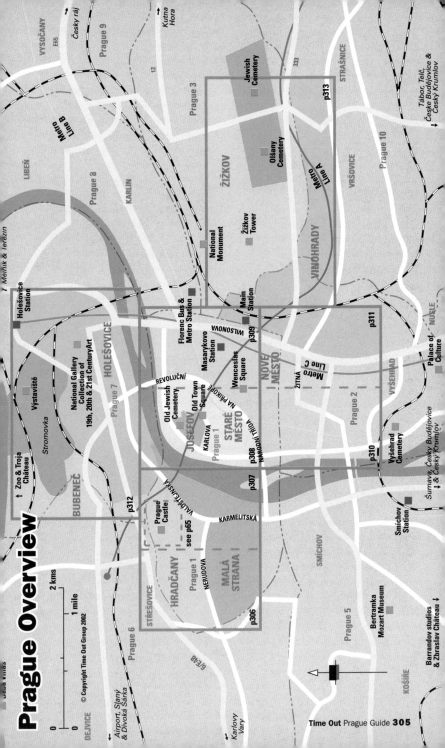

Prague Overview

0   2 kms

0   1 mile

© Copyright Time Out Group 2002

VYSOČANY

Český ráj

E65

Prague 9

Kutná Hora

Prague 3

Jewish Cemetery

STRAŠNICE

p313

Tábor, Telč, České Budějovice & Český Krumlov

Metro Line B

LIBEŇ

Prague 8

KARLÍN

ŽIŽKOV

Olšany Cemetery

Metro Line A

VRŠOVICE

Prague 10

12

333

National Monument

Žižkov Tower

VINOHRADY

NUSLE

T Mělník & Teřčzin

Holešovice Station

HOLEŠOVICE

Florenc Bus & Metro Station

WILSONOVA

Main Station

p311

Palace of Culture

National Gallery Collection of 19th, 20th & 21st CenturyArt

Prague 7

Masarykovo Station

Metro Line C

NOVÉ MĚSTO

Vystaviště

REVOLUČNÍ

Old Jewish Cemetery

Wenceslas Square

Stromovka

JOSEFOV

Old Town Square

STARÉ MĚSTO

ŽITNÁ

Prague 2

VYŠEHRAD

KARLOVA

Zoo & Troja Château

Prague 1

NA PŘÍKOPĚ

p309

BUBENEČ

p312

p308

NÁRODNÍ TŘÍDA

p310

Vyšehrad Cemetery

p307

VALDŠTEJNSKÁ

Prague Castle

KARMELITSKÁ

Smíchov Station

see p65

HRADČANY

Prague 1

NERUDOVA

MALÁ STRANA

SMÍCHOV

STŘEŠOVICE

p306

Prague 5

Bertramka Mozart Museum

DEJVICE

Prague 6

6/E48

Barrandov studios & Zbraslav Château

Airport, Slaný & Divoká Šárka

Karlovy Vary

KOŠÍŘE

Šumava, České Budějovice & Český Krumlov

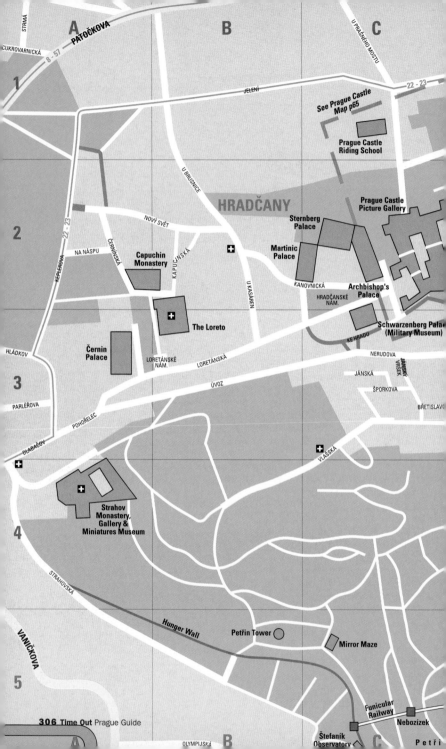

STRMÁ

PATOČKOVA

CUKROVARNICKÁ

8 - 57

JELENÍ

22 - 23

See Prague Castle
Map p65

**Prague Castle
Riding School**

U PRAŠNÉHO MOSTU

U BRUSNICE

HRADČANY

NOVÝ SVĚT

KEPLEROVA

22 - 23

NA NÁSPU

ČERNÍNSKÁ

**Capuchin
Monastery**

KAPUCÍNSKÁ

**Prague Castle
Picture Gallery**

**Sternberg
Palace**

**Martinic
Palace**

KANOVNICKÁ

HRADČANSKÉ
NÁM.

**Archbishop's
Palace**

U KASÁREN

The Loreto

**Černín
Palace**

LORETÁNSKÉ
NÁM.

LORETÁNSKÁ

HLÁDKOV

KE HRADU

**Schwarzenberg Pala
(Military Museum)**

NERUDOVA

JÁNSKÝ
VRŠEK

JÁNSKÁ

ŠPORKOVA

ÚVOZ

PARLÉŘOVA

POHOŘELEC

BŘETISLAVO

DLABAČOV

VLAŠSKÁ

**Strahov
Monastery,
Gallery &
Miniatures Museum**

STRAHOVSKÁ

VANIČKOVA

Hunger Wall

Petřín Tower

Mirror Maze

**Funicular
Railway**

Nebozízek

A   B   C

OLYMPIJSKÁ

**Štefaník
Observatory**

Petři

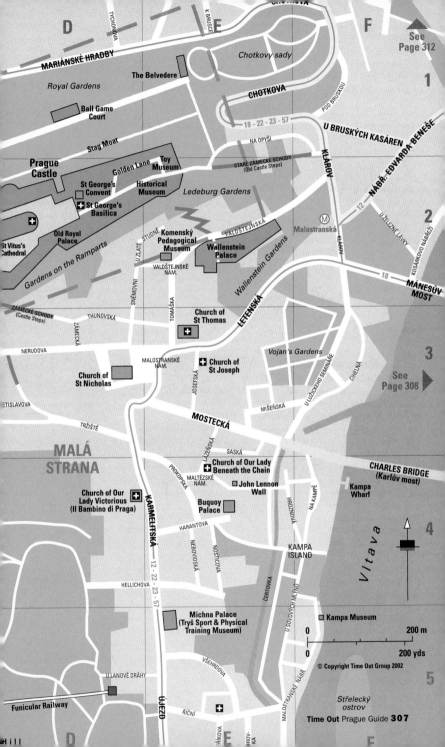

Metronome

Letná Park

1

Hanavský
Pavilion

NÁBŘ. EDVARDA BENEŠE

Vltava →

See
Page 312

ČECHŮV
WHARF

NA FRANTIŠKU

12 - 17 - 53

KOZÍ

St Agnes's
Convent

U PLOVÁRNY

NÁM.
CURIEOVYCH

DUŠNÍ

U MILOSRDNÝCH

HAŠTALSKÉ
NÁM.

U OBECNÍHO DVORA

2

KOŠÁRKOVO NÁBŘEŽÍ

DVOŘÁKOVO NÁBŘ.

BŘEHOVA

PAŘÍŽSKÁ

EL. KRÁSNOHORSKÉ

BILKOVA

JOSEFOV

HAŠTALSKÁ

RÁMOVÁ

DLOUHÁ

17 - 53

Old Jewish
Cemetery

Old-New
Synagogue

U STARÉ
ŠKOLY

Spanish
Synagogue

VĚZEŇSKÁ

KOZÍ

Rudolfinum

Klausen
Synagogue

V KOLKOVNĚ

MASNÁ

ŠTUPARTSKÁ

MÁNESŮV
MOST

18

Museum of
Decorative
Arts

ŠIROKÁ

Pinkas
Synagogue

ŠIROKÁ

KOSTEČNÁ

SALVÁTORSKÁ

DUŠNÍ

MASNÁ

MALÁ ŠTUPARTSKÁ

NÁM.
J. PALACHA

KAPROVA

MAISELOVA

JÁCHYMOVA

PAŘÍŽSKÁ

DLOUHÁ

Kinský
Palace

Church
St Jame

ALŠOVO NÁBŘ.

3

See
Page 307

Staroměstská Ⓜ

VALENTINSKÁ

ŽATECKÁ

Church of
St Nicholas

Jan Hus
Monument

House of the
Stone Bell

TÝNSKÁ

Týn
(Ungelt)

ŠTUPARTSK

KŘIŽOVNICKÁ

VELESLAVÍNOVA

MIKULÁŠSKÁ

OLD TOWN SQUARE

House of the
Gold Ring

PLATNÉŘSKÁ

MARIÁNSKÉ
NÁM.

LINHARTSKÁ

U RADNICE

Old Town
Hall

Church of Our
Lady before Týn

CELETNÁ

Church of
St Francis

PLATNÉŘSKÁ

HUSOVA

SEMINÁŘSKÁ

Clam-Gallas
Palace

Astronomical
Clock

MALÉ
NÁM.

ŽELEZNÁ

Carolinum

OVOCNÝ
TRH

CHARLES
BRIDGE

KŘIŽOVNICKÉ
NÁM.

Clementinum

KARLOVA

KARLOVA

St Michael's
Mystery

KOŽNÁ

MELANT.

Estates Thea

NOVOTNÉHO
LÁVKA

4

11 - 18 - 53

NA ZÁBRADLÍ

ANENSKÉ
NÁM.

ANENSKÁ

House of the Lords of
Kunštát & Poděbrady

ŘETĚZOVÁ

LILIOVÁ

JALOVCOVÁ

JILSKÁ

VEJVODOVA

MICHALSKÁ

**STARÉ
MĚSTO**

RICHTOVA

V KOTCÍCH

HAVELSKÁ

RYTÍŘSKÁ

NA MŮSTKU

Church of
St Gall

HAVÍŘSKÁ

PROVAZNICKÁ

Museum of
Communism

SMETANOVO NÁBŘ.

KAROLINY

BORŠOV

Bethlehem
Chapel

BETLÉMSKÉ
NÁM.

HUSOVA

Wax Museum
Prague

Ⓜ Můste

NÁPRSTKOVA

BETLÉMSKÁ

Náprstek
Museum

28. ŘÍJNA

WENCESLAS SQU

DIVADELNÍ

KONVIKTSKÁ

SKOŘEPKA

UHELNÝ
TRH

PERLOVÁ

5

0   200 m

0   200 yds

Rotunda of
the Holy Cross

SVĚTLÉ

MARTINSKÁ

NA PERŠTÝNĚ

Church of Our
Lady of the Snows

JUNGMANNOVO
NÁM.

Franciscan
Gardens

© Copyright Time Out Group 2002

KROCÍNOVA

See
Page 310

NÁRODNÍ TŘÍDA

JUNGMANNOVA

9 - 18 - 23 - 53 - 57 - 58

Národní

CHARVÁTOVA

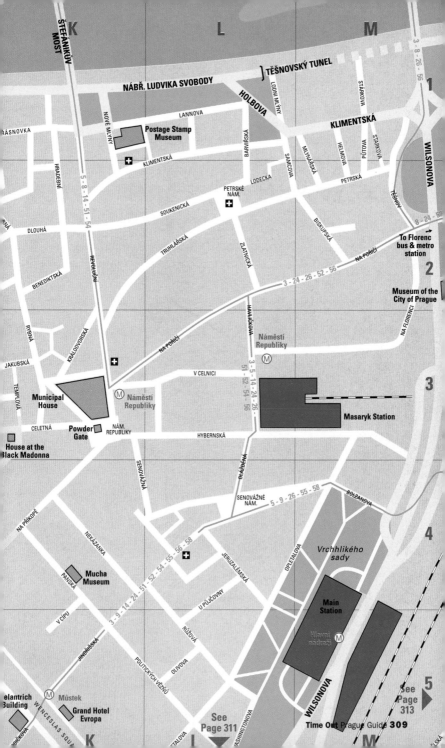

ŠTEFÁNIKŮV MOST

TĚŠNOVSKÝ TUNEL

NÁBŘ. LUDVIKA SVOBODY

HOLBOVA

LANNOVA

KLIMENTSKÁ

NOVÉ MLÝNY

STÁRKOVA

WILSONOVA

3 - 8 - 26 - 56

1

Postage Stamp
Museum

HRADEBNÍ

5 - 8 - 14 - 51 - 54

KLIMENTSKÁ

BARVÍŘSKÁ

LODNÍ MLÝNY

SAMCOVA

MLYNÁŘSKÁ

HELMOVA

PŮTOVA

STÁRKOVA

PETRSKÉ
NÁM.

PETRSKÁ

RÁSNOVKA

SOUKENICKÁ

LODECKA

TĚŠNOV

8 - 24 - 58

To Florenc
bus & metro
station

DLOUHÁ

TRUHLÁŘSKÁ

ZLATNICKÁ

BISKUPSKÁ

NA POŘÍČÍ

2

BENEDIKTSKÁ

REVOLUČNÍ

KRÁLODVORSKÁ

NA POŘÍČÍ

3 - 24 - 26 - 52 - 56

NA FLORENCI

Museum of the
City of Prague

RYBNÁ

HAVLÍČKOVA

Náměstí
Republiky
Ⓜ

JAKUBSKÁ

V CELNICI

51 - 5 - 14 - 24 - 26 -
52 - 54 - 56

TEMPLOVÁ

Municipal
House

Ⓜ Náměstí
Republiky

Masaryk Station

3

Powder
Gate

CELETNÁ

NÁM.
REPUBLIKY

HYBERNSKÁ

House at the
Black Madonna

SENOVÁŽNÁ

OPLETALOVA

SENOVÁŽNÉ
NÁM.

5 - 9 - 26 - 55 - 58

BOLZANOVA

NA PŘÍKOPĚ

NEKÁZANKA

3 - 9 - 14 - 24 - 51 - 52 - 54 - 55 - 56 - 58

Vrchhlikého
sady

4

PANSKÁ

Mucha
Museum

JERUZALÉMSKÁ

U PŮJČOVNY

Main
Station

V CÍPU

RŮŽOVÁ

Hlavní
nádraží
Ⓜ

JINDŘIŠSKÁ

POLITICKÝCH VĚZŇŮ

OLIVOVA

WILSONOVA

5

elantrich
Building

Ⓜ Můstek

WENCESLAS SQU

Grand Hotel
Evropa

See
Page 311

See
Page 313

WASHINGTONOVA

Time Out Prague Guide **309**

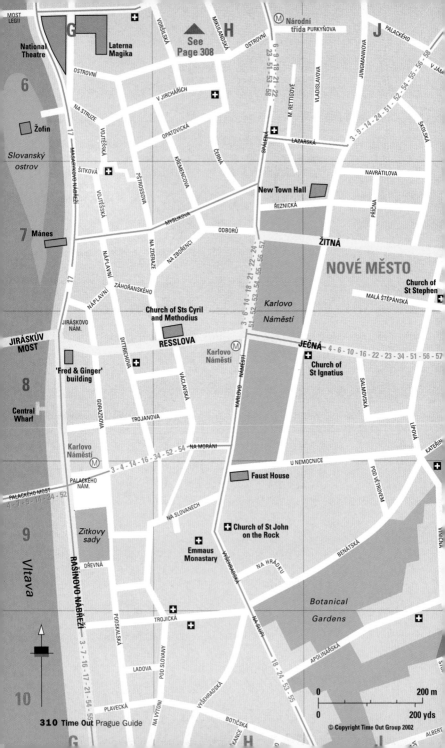

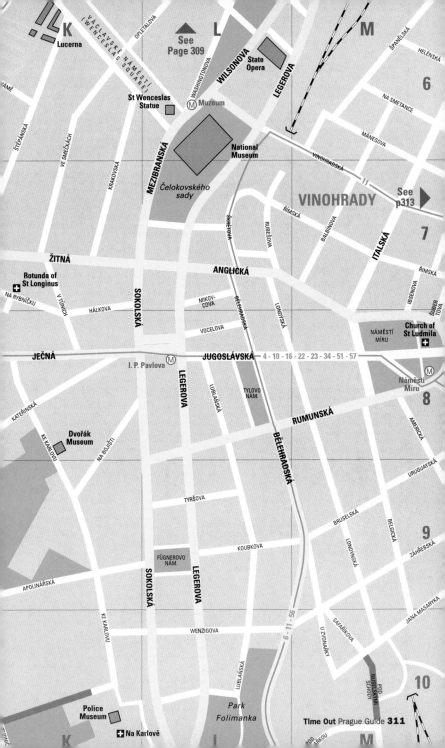

K

Lucerna

L

See
Page 309

State
Opera

M

ŠPANĚLSKÁ

HELÉNSKÁ

6

VÁCLAVSKÉ NÁMĚSTÍ (WENCESLAS SQUARE)

OPLETALOVA

WASHINGTONOVA

WILSONOVA

LEGEROVA

NA SMETANCE

MÁNESOVA

St Wenceslas
Statue

Ⓜ Muzeum

National
Museum

VINOHRADSKÁ

11

See
p313

VINOHRADY

7

ŠTĚPÁNSKÁ

ZÁMÉ

VE SMEČKÁCH

KRAKOVSKÁ

MEZIBRANSKÁ

Čelokovského
sady

ŠKRÉTOVA

RUBEŠOVA

ŘÍMSKÁ

BALBÍNOVA

ITALSKÁ

ŘÍMSKÁ

IBSENOVA

ŽITNÁ

Rotunda of
St Longinus

NA RYBNÍČKU

V TŮNÍCH

HÁLKOVA

SOKOLSKÁ

ANGLICKÁ

MIKOV-
COVA

BĚLEHRADSKÁ

LONDÝNSKÁ

ŠUBER
TOVA

VOCELOVA

NÁMĚSTÍ
MÍRU

Church of
St Ludmila

JEČNÁ

I. P. Pavlova

Ⓜ

JUGOSLÁVSKÁ ← 4 - 10 - 16 - 22 - 23 - 34 - 51 - 57

Náměstí
Míru

Ⓜ

8

KATEŘINSKÁ

KE KARLOVU

Dvořák
Museum

NA BOJIŠTI

LEGEROVA

LUBLAŇSKÁ

TYLOVO
NÁM.

BĚLEHRADSKÁ

RUMUNSKÁ

AMERICKÁ

URUGUAYSKÁ

TYRŠOVA

BRUSELSKÁ

LONDÝNSKÁ

BELGICKÁ

ZÁHŘEBSKÁ

9

APOLINÁŘSKÁ

FÜGNEROVO
NÁM.

SOKOLSKÁ

LEGEROVA

KOUBKOVA

JANA MASARYKA

6 - 11 - 56

WENZIGOVA

KE KARLOVU

ŠAFAŘÍKOVA

U ZVONAŘKY

LUBLAŇSKÁ

POD
NUSELSKÝMI
SCHODY

10

Police
Museum

✚ Na Karlově

K

I

*Park
Folimanka*

M

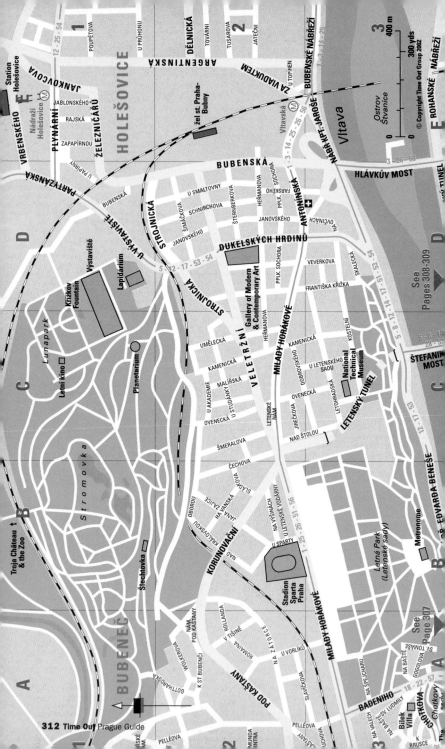

A B C D E

1 2 3

HOLEŠOVICE

BUBENEČ

Station Holešovice

Nádraží Holešovice

JANKOVCOVA
VRBENSKÉHO
PLYNÁRNÍ
ŽELEZNIČÁŘŮ
PARTYZÁNSKÁ
12 - 25 - 54
POUPĚTOVA
U PRŮHONU
JABLONSKÉHO
RAJSKÁ
ZAPAPÍRNOU
U PAPÍRNY

DĚLNICKÁ
ARGENTINSKÁ
TOVÁRNÍ
TUSAROVÁ
JATEČNÍ
ZA VIADUKTEM
U TOPÍREN
BUBENSKÉ NÁBŘEŽÍ
3 - 15 - 26

žel. st. Praha-Bubny

Vltavská
3 - 14 - 25 - 26 - 56
NÁBŘ. KPT. JAROŠE
Vltava
Ostrov Štvanice
0
HLÁVKŮV MOST
3 - 26 - 59
ROHANSKÉ NÁBŘEŽÍ

BUBENSKÁ
BUBENSKÁ
STROJNICKÁ
U VÝSTAVIŠTĚ
5 - 12 - 17 - 53 - 54
U SMALTOVNY
ŠIMÁČKOVA
SCHNIRCHOVA
ŠTERNBERKOVA
HEŘMANOVA
PPLK. SOCHORA
JANOVSKÉHO
FARSKÉHO
ANTONÍNSKÁ
U VODÁRNY

DUKELSKÝCH HRDINŮ

Gallery of Modern & Contemporary Art

VEVERKOVA
PPLK. SOCHORA
SKALECKÁ
FRANTIŠKA KŘÍŽKA

Výstaviště
Křížkov Fountain
Lapidárium
Luna park
Letní kino
Planetarium

Stromovka

UMĚLECKÁ
KAMENICKÁ
MALÍŘSKÁ
U AKADEMIE
U STUDÁNKY
OVENECKÁ
ŠMERALOVA
ČECHOVA
SLÁDKOVA
KAMENICKÁ
HEŘMANOVA
DOBROVSKÉHO
OVENECKÁ
JIREČKOVA
NAD ŠTOLOU
KOSTELNÍ
LETOHRADSKÁ
MILADY HORÁKOVÉ
U LETENSKÉHO SADU
VELETRŽNÍ
LETENSKÉ NÁM.
National Technical Museum
LETENSKÝ TUNEL
12 - 17 - 53
5 - 8 - 12 - 14 - 17 - 51 - 53 - 54
See Pages 308-309
ŠTEFÁNIKŮV MOST

Troja Château & the Zoo

Šlechtovka

KORUNOVAČNÍ
1 - 25 - 26 - 51 - 56
KRÁLOVSKOU
OBOROU
JANA VANIŠKA
NAD
JANA ZAJÍCE
NA VÝŠINÁCH
U LETENSKÉ VODÁRNY
U SPARTY
Stadion Sparta Praha
Letná Park (Letenské sady)
Metronome
EDVARDA BENEŠE

NÁM. POD KAŠTANY
WOLKEROVA
GOTTHARDSKÁ
K ST BUBENČI
NA ZÁTORCE
V TIŠINĚ
ROMAINA ROLLANDA
U VORLÍKŮ
POD KAŠTANY
MILADY HORÁKOVÉ
SLAVÍČKOVA
KAŠTANY
BADENIHO
CHOTKOVA
18 - 22 - 57
Bílek Villa
SV TOMÁŠE
NA BAŠTĚ
GOGOLOVA
NA VALECH
NA BAŠTĚ SV LUDMILY
NA BAŠTĚ SV JIŘÍ
U BRUSNICE
See Page 307
ŠPEJCHARU
PELLÉOVA
U KRÁLOVSKÉ LM.

N 0 400 m
0 300 yds
© Copyright Time Out Group 2002

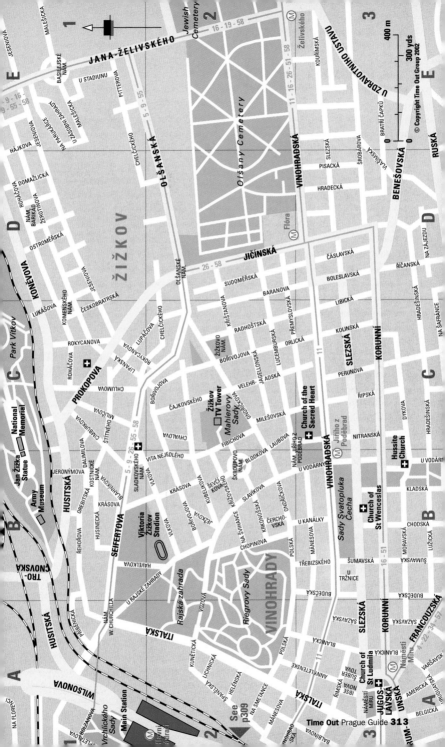

Street Index

Prague Metro

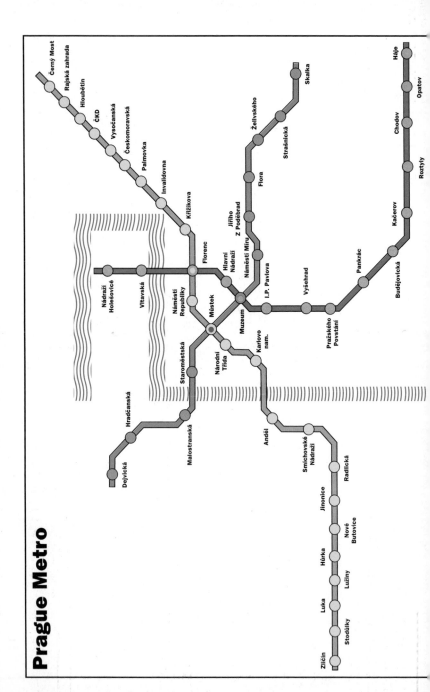

Černý Most
Rajská zahrada
Hloubětín
ČKD
Vysočanská
Českomoravská
Palmovka
Invalidovna
Křižíkova
Florenc
Nádraží Holešovice
Vltavská
Náměstí Republiky
Staroměstská
Hradčanská
Dejvická
Malostranská
Národní Třída
Můstek
Karlovo nám.
Anděl
Smíchovské Nádraží
Radlická
Jinonice
Nové Butovice
Hůrka
Lužiny
Luka
Stodůlky
Zličín
Hlavní Nádraží
Náměstí Míru
Jiřího Z Poděbrad
Flora
Želivského
Strašnická
Skalka
I.P. Pavlova
Muzeum
Vyšehrad
Pražského Povstání
Pankrác
Budějovická
Kačerov
Roztyly
Chodov
Opatov
Háje